BLUE RIBBON
·•· RECIPES ·•·

693 AWARD-WINNERS
FROM AMERICA'S
STATE AND COUNTY FAIRS

EDITED BY

BARBARA GREENMAN

ILLUSTRATED BY IRENA ROMAN

BLACK DOG
& LEVENTHAL
PUBLISHERS
NEW YORK

Published by

Black Dog & Leventhal Publishers, Inc.

151 West 19th Street

New York, New York 10011

Distributed by

Workman Publishing Company

225 Varick Street

New York, NY 10014

Designed by Susi Oberhelman

Manufactured in China

ISBN-10: 1- 57912-698-7

ISBN-13: 978-1-57912-698-8

Library of Congress Cataloging-in-Publication Data is available on file at
Black Dog & Leventhal Publishers, Inc.

g f e d c b a

CONTENTS

INTRODUCTION

Our State Fair is a great State Fair,
Don't miss it, don't even be late.
It's dollars to doughnuts
That our State Fair
is the best State Fair in our state!

From *Our State Fair*, lyrics by Oscar Hammerstein II

Every year our state, county, and regional fairs—some 3,000 of them across the United States—attract more than 150 million visitors. They offer the quintessentially American experience: food, music, rides, contests, and fun for people of all ages. Four generations of my family have attended one of these fairs, the Guilford Fair in Connecticut, and it perfectly mirrors the evolution of fairs big and small across the country. The Guilford Fair began on the Guilford Green in 1859 as an agricultural market day with just a few farm families and their cattle. Today it's a three-day extravaganza on thirty acres with food concessions, competitive exhibits, a farm museum, stage entertainment, and a carnival midway.

But some things don't change. For two hundred years, food has been a big draw at every fair. Visitors should arrive hungry, and not just for the spun sugar and candied apples. The real food events are the annual cooking competitions for the outstanding recipes in every food category imaginable. Whether awarded "first place" or "blue ribbon," "second prize" or "red ribbon," "rosette," "grand champion," "sweepstakes," or "best in show" (depending on local custom), all are winners. And who—except the winner's family and friends—has ever been able to get the award-winning recipe?

So to share with you the best of the best, we asked fairs from Maine to Hawaii to submit their most recent winners, focusing especially on recipes using regional ingredients. More than 85 fairs from all 50 states responded with hundreds of entries and introduced us to individual winners and young 4-H-ers who sent in hundreds more. Because all the recipes are prizewinners, we included as many as we possibly could. At times a recipe had to be eliminated if it was too similar to another

⚜ FATHER OF THE FAIRS ⚜

In 1807, Elkanah Watson, a New England patriot and farmer, earned the title "Father of U.S. Agricultural Fairs," by producing the first small exhibit of sheep under an elm tree in Pittsfield, Massachusetts.

entry, or if the recipe instructions or credits could not be verified. We also avoided using brand names wherever possible to ensure that a recipe could be made properly whether you lived in California or Delaware.

Why, then, do we offer 10 salsa recipes? Because we hope you can find one with your favorite salsa ingredient, whether it's mango, pear, mint, cranberry, bean, corn, or even cactus! Is apple pie a favorite? Try one with butterscotch, or tapioca, or pecans, or cranberries, or sweet potato, or a dash of bourbon. Chocolate, of course, gets top billing. It stars in many of the pies, cakes, brownies, bars, cookies, and candy recipes. Abundance, i.e., "something for everyone," rather than selectivity, seemed the right approach for creating a cookbook in the same democratic spirit of the fairs themselves.

⤻ FAIR FACTS ⤺

✕ There are 3,000 state, county, and regional fairs in the United States.

✕ One hundred fifty million people attend state and county fairs each year.

✕ The first state fair was the New York State Fair in 1841, in the village of Syracuse, New York.

✕ The first regional fair was held in Pittsfield, Massachusetts, in 1807.

✕ The largest state fair is the State Fair of Texas in Dallas.

The big surprise was the range of recipes we had to choose from. At the beginning of this process, we thought the book might be limited to baked goods and preserves, which are often the traditional cooking contest categories. But recipes for award-winning breakfast dishes, appetizers and soups, meat dishes, and vegetable casserole entries arrived as well. A request for regional dishes brought us Interior Alaska Salmon Pie from Fairbanks, Crawfish Casserole from Louisiana, Piña Colada Cream Pie from Hawaii, Blueberry Bran Muffins from Maine, Saucy Cranberry Meatballs from Wisconsin, and even a recipe for goat cheese from Washington state!

To my friends at the fairs and 4-H offices who patiently took my calls and e-mails, introduced me to their food experts, telephoned winners, then e-mailed, faxed, scanned, and mailed recipes on time: I hope I have remembered you all in the list of contributors. The energy you bring to organizing the cooking events and your pride in the winners are contagious. Many of you said, "Thanks, this is fun!" It *has* been fun, and it's your book, too, and I thank you.

And to Judy Pray, my editor, thank you for your enthusiastic support right from the beginning and for your excellent feedback and suggestions over many months. It was a pleasure to work with you and with your team: Irena Roman, illustrator, Candie Frankel, copyeditor, and Susi Oberhelman, designer.

BARBARA GREENMAN, Editor

CONTRIBUTORS

Fuchia Allen

Mary Ellen Arbaugh

Lora Arledge

Martha Barber

Carolyn Best

Kim Billiard

Georgia Bishop

Shari L. Black

Marilyn M. Block

Ann Marie Bosshemer

Ruth Cahill

Judy Carrico

Brandy Cavanagh

Lori Chappell

Penny Chronister

Patti Clifford

Janice Corones

Joyce Covington

Judy Darsey

Alice Diefenthaler

Carolyn Dooley

Lois Duffey

Priscilla Gerrard

Janet Golden

Ellen Gordon

Yvonne Green

Beth Greiner

Barbara Grimm

Sue Hitz

Kristy Horn

Connie Howell

Janita James

Lynville Jarvis

Hattie Johnson

Pam Johnson

Rochelle Johnson

Cindy Kaufman

Emily Kearns

Jeanne Keaton

Durinda Kirby

Linda Konopaske

Donna Lange

Rebecca Levesque

Mary Ann Lienhart-Cross

Rhonda Livingstone

Dona Martin

Janel Maurer

Jeannie Mayhan

Donna McDade

Pamella Meekin

Russell D. Melton

Harry Moos

Frances Monroe

Patrick Morgan

Carla Morrical-Frederking

Carol Mortensen

Hale Moss

Marilyn Muir

Candie Oesterle

Joy Pautler

Crystal Peek

Katie Phillips

Catherine Poluzzi

Wendy Pressnall

Lisa Prince

Pat Ralph

Liz Reinhiller

Milly Rice

Diane Richard

Carolynn Richardson

Yvonne Robertson

Joanne Robinson

Reagan Rodgers

Vicki Rupert

Helen Schmaling

Val Shacklett

Kent Shelhamer

Sharon Simington

Lorie Simmers

Patsy Smith

Kristine Snyder

Norita Solt

Vanessa Spencer

Debbie Stephens

Beverly Stockstill

Jamie Tate

Susan Taylor

Renee Tull

Melissa Turner

Patty Turner

Marlys Volzke

Helen Vose

Marsha Weaver

Louise Wells

Kathi Wheeler

Marylan Whitaker

Gwen Wilkerson

Gayle Williford

Imogene Woodside

Kathryn Wyatt

CHAPTER 1

BREAKFAST

FRENCH TOAST, PANCAKES, EGGS,
GRITS, COFFEE CAKES, AND MUFFINS

APPLE CIDER PANCAKES

2 cups Bisquick baking mix
1½ cups milk
4 eggs, separated
1 teaspoon apple pie spice

¾ cup freshly grated apples
Oil for frying
Apple Cider Syrup (recipe follows)
Sour cream

1. In a large mixing bowl, beat baking mix, milk, egg yolks, and apple pie spice. Stir in apples.

2. In a small mixing bowl, whip egg whites until soft peaks form. Fold into batter.

3. Heat oil in a skillet over medium-high heat. Ladle batter onto skillet and fry, turning once, until golden brown. Serve with Apple Cider Syrup and a dollop of sour cream. Makes 2 to 4 servings.

APPLE CIDER SYRUP

1 cup sugar
2 tablespoons cornstarch
1 teaspoon apple pie spice

2 cups apple cider
2 tablespoons lemon juice
¼ cup butter

1. Combine sugar, cornstarch, and apple pie spice in a medium saucepan. Stir in apple cider and lemon juice.

2. Bring to a boil and cook, stirring constantly, until mixture thickens, about 1 minute. Remove from heat. Add butter and stir until melted. Makes 2½ cups.

※ **ROOSEVELT BED AND BREAKFAST**, Coeur d'Alene, Idaho
First Place Public Favorite, Christmas Morning, Western Montana Fair, Missoula, Montana, 2005

THE FRENCHY'EST OF TOAST

¼ cup melted butter
½ cup brown sugar
2 tablespoons molasses
½ cup orange juice
8 slices of home-style bread
5 eggs

1½ cups milk
1½ teaspoons vanilla
2 teaspoons Grand Marnier or rum
Sour cream
1 cup fresh or frozen berries
½ cup walnut pieces

1. The evening before serving, mix melted butter, brown sugar, molasses, and orange juice in a 2-cup measuring cup. Pour into a 13 x 9 x 2-inch pan. Tilt to coat bottom of pan. Layer bread slices in pan, double-decking to fit if needed.

2. Combine eggs, milk, vanilla, and Grand Marnier in a blender. Pour mixture over bread. Refrigerate overnight.

3. In the morning, preheat oven to 350°F. Bake French toast for 45 minutes, or until nicely puffed and golden. Cut into servings and flip over onto plate. Top with sour cream, berries, and walnuts. Makes 4 to 6 servings.

※ **CAROLYNN RICHARDSON**, Huson, Montana
First Place Public Favorite, Christmas Morning, Western Montana Fair, Missoula, Montana, 2001

BLUEBERRY SURPRISE FRENCH TOAST CASSEROLE

Butter, for baking dish
12 slices dry white bread, cut into
 ½-inch cubes (about 8 cups), divided
2 packages (8 oz. each) cream cheese,
 cut into ¾-inch cubes

1½ cups fresh blueberries
12 eggs
2 cups milk
½ cup maple syrup
Blueberry syrup

1. One day ahead, butter a 13 x 9 x 2-inch baking dish (or two 8 x 8 x 2-inch square baking dishes). Place 4 cups of the bread cubes over the bottom of baking dish. Layer on cream cheese cubes, blueberries, and remaining 4 cups bread cubes.

2. Beat eggs in a large mixing bowl with a rotary beater. Beat in milk and maple syrup. Pour egg mixture over the casserole layers. Cover and chill in the refrigerator for 2 to 24 hours.

3. In the morning, preheat oven to 375°F. Bake casserole, covered, for 25 minutes. Uncover and bake 25 minutes more, or until topping is puffed and golden brown and a knife inserted near the center comes out clean. Let stand for 10 minutes before serving. Serve warm with blueberry syrup. Makes 8 servings.

※ **CHERYL BAKER,** Middlebury, Indiana
Second Place, Bursting with Blueberries Contest, Elkhart County 4-H Fair, Goshen, Indiana, 2005

WINNER'S CIRCLE TIP | To dry bread slices for recipes, arrange the slices in a single layer on a wire rack. Cover loosely with paper towels and let stand overnight. If you need dried bread cubes in a hurry, cut the bread and spread the cubes in a large baking pan. Bake uncovered in a 300°F oven, stirring twice, until dry, 10 to 15 minutes. Cool.

MAMANITA BREAKFAST

1 lb. beef sausage
1 lb. pork sausage
5 eggs, beaten
1 teaspoon dry mustard
3 tablespoons dry minced onion

1 can (10.5 oz.) cream of mushroom
 condensed soup
6 slices of bread, cubed
6 oz. grated cheddar cheese

1. The evening before serving, brown sausage in a skillet and drain on paper towels. Combine eggs, mustard, onion, soup, bread cubes, and cheese in a large bowl. Add sausage and mix well to combine. Transfer mixture to a 13 x 9 x 2-inch baking dish. Cover and refrigerate overnight.

2. In the morning, preheat oven to 300°F. Bake casserole, covered, for 30 minutes. Uncover and bake an additional 15 minutes, or until a knife inserted comes out clean. Let sit for 5 minutes before cutting into squares. Makes 12 large servings.

※ **WOMEN OF THE CATHOLIC RETREAT DE COLORES,** Missoula, Montana
First Place Public Favorite, Christmas Morning, Western Montana Fair, Missoula, Montana, 2005

French Apple Breakfast Casserole

4 tablespoons butter

3 large Gala apples, peeled, cored and sliced

½ cup raisins

⅔ cup brown sugar

1 teaspoon cinnamon

¼ teaspoon nutmeg

8 to 10 1-inch-thick slices of French bread, trimmed of crusts

4 large eggs

1¼ cups milk

2 teaspoons vanilla

1. The evening before serving, melt butter in a large skillet or frying pan over medium heat. Add apples and sauté for 5 minutes.

2. Add raisins, brown sugar, cinnamon, and nutmeg to skillet. Continue cooking, stirring frequently, until apples are tender, 10 minutes.

3. Spread apple mixture evenly over the bottom of a 13 x 9 x 2-inch baking dish. Layer bread slices over apples until completely covered.

4. In a medium mixing bowl, beat eggs until foamy. Beat in milk and vanilla. Pour egg mixture over the bread slices. Cover and refrigerate overnight.

5. In the morning, preheat oven to 375°F. Remove casserole from refrigerator, uncover, and bring to room temperature. Bake uncovered for 35 minutes, or until bread is golden and firm. Let sit for 10 minutes before serving. Makes 6 to 8 servings.

※ **STACY MONAHAN**, Durham, North Carolina
Second Place, N.C. Egg Association's Eggs and Apples Recipe Contest, North Carolina State Fair, Raleigh, North Carolina, 2005

Bayou Breakfast Casserole

½ lb. French bread, cubed

1 tablespoon melted butter

1 lb. shredded Colby-Jack cheese

¼ lb. salami, sliced

10 large eggs

1½ cups milk

⅓ cup white wine

3 green onions, chopped

2 teaspoons brown mustard

½ teaspoon black pepper

¼ teaspoon red pepper flakes

1 cup sour cream

½ cup freshly grated Parmesan

1. The evening before serving, grease a 13 x 9 x 2-inch baking dish. Spread bread cubes in bottom of pan and drizzle with melted butter. Top with cheese and salami.

2. In a medium bowl, beat together eggs, milk, wine, green onions, mustard, black pepper, and red pepper flakes. Pour into baking dish. Cover with aluminum foil and refrigerate overnight.

3. In the morning, preheat oven to 325°F. Remove baking dish from refrigerator 30 minutes before baking. Bake, covered, for 1 hour. Remove foil, spread sour cream over top, and sprinkle with Parmesan. Bake for 10 minutes more, or until lightly browned. Makes 10 servings.

※ **MARTHA BUEHRING**, Norman, Oklahoma
Fourth Place, Prepared Egg Contest, Oklahoma State Fair, Oklahoma City, Oklahoma, 2005

Breakfast Eggs

8 frozen hash browns
8 eggs
¼ cup milk

1½ cups cubed ham
1 cup grated cheese, any kind

1. Preheat oven to 350°F.

2. Line a 13 x 9 x 2-inch baking dish with hash browns.

3. Beat eggs in a medium bowl. Stir in milk and ham. Pour egg mixture over hash browns. Top with grated cheese. Bake for 30 minutes. Makes 4 to 6 servings.

✕ **Betsy Brugman,** Royal, Iowa
Purple Ribbon, Pride of Iowa Competition, Clay County Fair 4-H, Spencer, Iowa, 2000

Egg and Potato Bake with Mushrooms

6 cups frozen hash browns, thawed
½ cup diced white onion
½ cup melted butter or margarine,
    room temperature
1 can (10.5 oz.) cream of mushroom
    condensed soup
1 jar (4.5 oz.) sliced mushrooms, drained
¼ teaspoon dried pesto seasoning
1 container (8 oz.) sour cream, divided

2 cups shredded cheddar cheese, divided
1 package (12 oz.) bacon
12 eggs
½ teaspoon salt
¼ teaspoon pepper
1 tablespoon butter or margarine,
    room temperature, plus more for dish
1 cup French fried onions

1. Preheat oven to 350°F. Butter a 13 x 9 x 2-inch baking pan.

2. In a large bowl, combine hash browns, onion, melted butter, soup, mushrooms, pesto seasoning, ½ cup of the sour cream, and 1 cup of the shredded cheese. Pour into pan and bake for 50 minutes. Remove pan from oven, but leave oven on.

3. Meanwhile, cook bacon in a large skillet. Drain on paper towels and crumble.

4. In a medium bowl, whisk together eggs, salt, pepper, and remaining ½ cup sour cream until well blended, 2 to 3 minutes.

5. Melt butter in a skillet over medium heat. Add egg mixture and cook without stirring until eggs start to set on the bottom and around the edge of pan. Lift and fold eggs with a spatula to allow uncooked egg to flow to bottom of skillet. Continue cooking until eggs are set but still shiny and moist. Do not overcook.

6. Spread crumbled bacon over top of baked hash browns. Spread scrambled eggs over top of bacon. Top with remaining cup of shredded cheese and French fried onions. Return to oven and bake 10 to 15 minutes more, or until cheese is melted. Let stand for 10 minutes before serving. Makes 12 servings.

✕ **Carolyn Wallace,** Yukon, Oklahoma
First Place, Prepared Egg Contest, Oklahoma State Fair, Oklahoma City, Oklahoma, 2005

Eggs Benedict, Creole-Style

8 eggs

4 English muffins, split lengthwise
   and toasted

8 slices of Canadian bacon, cooked

Creole Hollandaise Sauce (recipe follows)

8 asparagus spears, blanched

Salt and pepper

1. Fill a large 4-inch deep sauté pan with 3 inches of water and bring to a simmer over medium heat. Crack open an egg and gently place in water. Cook four eggs at a time, working in two batches. Simmer for 3 to 5 minutes until yolk reaches desired hardness. Remove with a slotted spoon and blot on a dry kitchen towel to drain off as much water as possible.

2. For each serving, arrange two muffin halves, split side up, on plate. Top each muffin half with one slice of Canadian bacon and one poached egg. Spoon Creole Hollandaise Sauce over eggs and top with two asparagus spears. Season with salt and pepper to taste. Makes 4 servings.

Creole Hollandaise Sauce

4 cups plus 1 tablespoon butter, divided

2 cups margarine, room temperature

8 large eggs

4 large egg yolks

1 tablespoon lemon juice

½ tablespoon red wine

½ tablespoon cayenne pepper

1 tablespoon chicken base

½ cup chopped chives

6 oz. crawfish tail meat

1. Melt 4 cups of the butter and margarine in a large saucepan over low heat, stirring occasionally.

2. Combine eggs, egg yolks, lemon juice, red wine, cayenne pepper, and chicken base in a blender. With blender running, slowly pour in melted butter-margarine mixture. Transfer sauce to the top half of a double boiler set over slightly simmering water.

3. Melt remaining tablespoon butter in a skillet over medium heat. Add chives and crawfish and sauté. Stir crawfish mixture into hollandaise sauce. Serve within 30 minutes.

⌗ **KELLY HAGEN,** Macon, Georgia
Second Place, I Love Eggs, Sweets & Treats Breakfast Contest, Georgia National Fair, Perry, Georgia, 2005

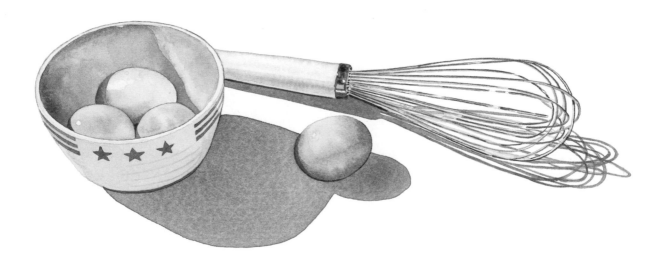

STUFFED OMELET EGGS IN BASKETS

BASKETS
12 sheets phyllo, thawed according
   to package directions
½ cup melted butter

STUFFED EGGS
6 large hard-boiled eggs
Salt and pepper

1 small Roma tomato, chopped
1 small green bell pepper, chopped
4 green onions, sliced
⅔ cup shredded cheese, any kind
4 slices cooked bacon, crumbled
½ cup sour cream
¼ cup picante sauce

1. To make baskets: Preheat oven to 375°F. Grease a 12-cup muffin tin. Cut one phyllo sheet into 6 squares. Brush each square with melted butter and layer in a single muffin cup. Repeat with remaining phyllo to make 12 baskets. Bake for 5 minutes, or until golden brown. Remove from oven. Cool.

2. To make stuffed eggs: Peel eggs and cut in half lengthwise. Scoop out yolks into a small bowl, reserving whites. Mash yolks with a fork. Season with salt and pepper.

3. Place tomato, bell pepper, and green onions in a medium bowl. Add cheese and cooked bacon and toss gently to combine.

4. Combine sour cream and picante sauce in a small bowl.

5. Add mashed yolks and sour cream mixture to tossed ingredients and mix until well blended. Spoon mixture into egg whites.

6. Place two baskets on each plate. Set one stuffed egg in each basket and serve. Makes 6 servings.

※ **ALLISON SMOLA,** Piedmont, Oklahoma
Fifth Place, Prepared Egg Contest, Oklahoma State Fair, Oklahoma City, Oklahoma, 2005

VEGETARIAN THREE-EGG OMELET

1 tablespoon vegan rice protein powder
3 tablespoons very warm water
1 tablespoon almond milk
½ teaspoon vegetable seasoning salt

¼ teaspoon liquid aminos seasoning
¼ teaspoon garlic powder
3 eggs
1 tablespoon extra virgin coconut oil

1. Combine rice protein powder, warm water, and almond milk in a small bowl. Stir until smooth. Stir in vegetable salt, liquid aminos, and garlic powder.

2. Whisk eggs in medium bowl. Add almond milk mixture to eggs and whisk to combine.

3. Heat oil in skillet over medium-high heat. Add egg mixture and cook to desired texture. Fold omelet in half and slide onto a plate to serve. Makes 1 omelet.

※ **MELBA WHITFORD,** Jones, Oklahoma
Second Place, Omelet Contest, Oklahoma State Fair, Oklahoma City, Oklahoma, 2005

Green Veggie Frittata

2 tablespoons butter, plus more for pan

1 jar (5 oz.) marinated artichokes,
    chopped, with oil reserved

1 bunch green onions, sliced

⅓ cup chopped green chiles

1 medium zucchini, sliced

¾ cup mushrooms, sliced

½ cup fresh spinach, chopped

9 eggs

2 cups grated cheddar cheese

¼ cup chopped fresh parsley

Pinch of dried thyme

Pinch of dried oregano

Salt and pepper

1. Preheat oven to 350°F. Lightly butter a quiche pan.

2. Heat butter and artichoke oil in a skillet over medium heat. Add artichokes, onions, chiles, zucchini, mushrooms, and spinach. Sauté until onions begin to soften and spinach is wilted. Drain in a colander or strainer.

3. Whisk eggs in a large bowl. Stir in cheese, parsley, thyme, and oregano. Sprinkle with salt and pepper. Fold in cooked vegetables.

4. Pour mixture into pan. Bake for 45 minutes. Makes 4 to 6 servings.

✄ **JUDY DARSEY,** Albuquerque, New Mexico
First Place, New Mexico State Fair, Albuquerque, New Mexico, 2004

Grits Over Easy Casserole

Single-crust pastry

2 cups stone-ground grits,
    cooked and slightly cooled

¼ cup unsalted butter, room temperature

¼ cup heavy cream

¾ cup shredded Colby-Jack, divided

½ lb. maple-flavor bulk sausage

½ cup chopped sweet onion

1 garlic clove, minced

⅓ cup peach preserves

4 eggs

¼ teaspoon ground peppercorn medley

1 tablespoon bacon bits

1. Preheat oven to 350°F.

2. Line bottom and sides of a 1-quart casserole dish with piecrust pastry; cut off extra and set aside.

3. Mix together grits, butter, heavy cream, and ½ cup of the Colby-Jack.

4. Cook sausage, onion, and garlic in a skillet over medium-high heat until sausage is no longer pink. Stir in peach preserves. Spoon mixture into bottom of crust. Top with grits.

5. Crack eggs one at a time over grits. Sprinkle with pepper. Make cutouts with leftover dough if desired and place on top of eggs. Bake for 20 minutes, or until eggs reach desired doneness. Garnish with remaining ¼ cup Colby-Jack and bacon bits. Makes 4 servings.

✄ **DEBRA BROOKS,** Byron, Georgia
First Place, Grits Anytime, Georgia National Fair, Perry, Georgia, 2005

BLUEBERRY STREUSEL

PASTRY

1¾ cups lard or shortening

1 tablespoon sugar

1 tablespoon vinegar

3 teaspoons salt

1 egg, beaten

½ cup water

4 cups all-purpose flour

FILLING

1 pint fresh blueberries

½ to ¾ cup sugar (according to fruit tartness)

1 tablespoon cornstarch

¼ teaspoon cinnamon

GLAZE

5 tablespoons confectioners' sugar

1 teaspoon hot water

1. Preheat oven to 350°F. Set aside a 12 x 18 x 1-inch jelly roll pan; do not grease.

2. To make pastry: In a large mixing bowl, combine lard or shortening, sugar, vinegar, salt, egg, water, and flour. Mix to make a soft dough. Roll dough into a ball, wrap in plastic wrap, and chill for 15 minutes.

3. To make filling: Combine blueberries, sugar, cornstarch, and cinnamon in a bowl until well mixed.

4. Turn out dough onto a lightly floured surface. Divide dough in half. Roll out half the dough into a large rectangle and line jelly roll pan. Spoon filling over surface. Roll out other half of dough, cut into strips, and arrange on top of filling for lattice crust. Bake for 30 to 35 minutes. Cool.

5. To make glaze: Combine confectioners' sugar and hot water. Drizzle from a tablespoon over streusel. Makes 1 streusel.

✕ **PAT MAST,** Goshen, Indiana
Third Place, Bursting with Blueberries Contest, Elkhart County 4-H Fair, Goshen, Indiana, 2005

EGG, HAM, AND CHEESE OMELET

Cooking spray

3 eggs

Salt and pepper

½ cup diced ham

¼ cup shredded cheese, any kind

¼ cup chopped red bell pepper

¼ cup chopped green bell pepper

1. Warm a nonstick pan over medium heat. Spray with cooking spray.

2. Whisk eggs in a bowl. Sprinkle with salt and pepper and beat well. Pour into pan and cook, pushing cooked portions to center with a spatula and tilting pan so that uncooked egg flows onto pan surface.

3. When top of eggs is thickened, spoon ham, cheese, red pepper, and green pepper onto half of omelet. Use spatula to fold omelet in half. Cook 30 seconds more and serve. Makes 1 omelet.

✕ **ANASTASIA RIVERS**, age 10, Ridgeville, South Carolina
First Place Cloverleaf Division, 4-H Eggonomics Contest, Coastal Carolina Fair, Ladson, South Carolina, 2005

BLUEBERRY STREUSEL COFFEE CAKE

CAKE BATTER

2⅓ cups all-purpose flour, plus
    more for baking dish
1 cup sugar
1 teaspoon salt
¾ cup unsalted butter,
    room temperature
2 teaspoons baking powder
¾ cup milk
2 eggs
1 teaspoon vanilla
1 cup fresh or frozen blueberries

CHEESE FILLING

1 cup ricotta
1 egg
2 tablespoons sugar
1 tablespoon grated lemon zest

TOPPING

1 cup reserved crumb mixture (see step 2)
½ cup finely chopped walnuts
⅓ cup brown sugar
1 teaspoon cinnamon

1. Preheat oven to 350°F. Grease and flour a 9 x 13 x 2-inch baking dish.

2. To make cake batter: Combine flour, sugar, and salt in a mixing bowl. Cut in butter until crumbly. Measure and set aside 1 cup of crumb mixture for topping. To remaining crumb mixture, add baking powder, milk, eggs and vanilla. Beat on medium speed for 2 minutes. Pour batter into pan and sprinkle blueberries over top.

3. To make cheese filling: Combine ricotta, egg, sugar, and lemon zest in a mixing bowl. Beat until smooth. Spoon evenly over blueberries.

4. To make topping: Place reserved crumb mixture, walnuts, brown sugar, and cinnamon in a bowl. Toss to combine. Sprinkle over cheese layer.

5. Bake for 45 to 60 minutes, or until a toothpick inserted in center comes out clean. Makes 1 coffee cake.

⚹ **DORIS LASKA,** Winona, Minnesota
Blue Ribbon, Winona County Agricultural & Industrial Fair, Saint Charles, Minnesota, 1995

CRUNCHY COUNTRY BITES

1 lb. hot sausage
2 cups cooked grits
1 cup Bisquick baking mix
½ cup shredded cheese, any kind

2 tablespoons chopped green onion
½ cup maple syrup
½ cup pecans, chopped

1. Preheat oven to 400°F.

2. Brown the sausage in a skillet over medium heat, crumbling into small pieces. Drain on paper towels.

3. Combine sausage, grits, baking mix, cheese, and green onions in a large bowl. Form into balls and place in a baking pan. Bake for 20 minutes. Cool.

4. Mix syrup and pecans in a small bowl. Brush mixture over cooled "bites." Makes 4 to 6 servings.

⚹ **GINGER BUTTS,** Cochran, Georgia
Second Place, Grits Anytime, Georgia National Fair, Perry, Georgia, 2005

Apple and Egg Casserole

3 cups all-purpose flour

2 teaspoons baking soda

1 teaspoon salt

2½ teaspoons cinnamon

1 teaspoon nutmeg

1¼ cups butter, room temperature,
   plus more for baking dish

3 cups sugar

4 eggs

¾ cup chopped pecans

4 cups hard juicy apples, diced

¾ cup golden raisins

1. Preheat oven to 350°F. Butter a 13 x 9 x 2-inch baking dish.

2. Sift together flour, baking soda, salt, cinnamon, and nutmeg.

3. In a large mixing bowl, beat butter, sugar, and eggs. Add sifted dry ingredients and mix until well combined. Fold in pecans, apples, and raisins. Pour batter into baking dish. Bake for 45 minutes. Makes 18 servings.

BARBARA CREASMAN, Asheville, North Carolina
First Place, North Carolina Egg Association Eggs & Apples Recipe Contest, North Carolina Mountain State Fair, Fletcher, North Carolina, 2005

Kaaz Kuchen (German Coffee Cake)

1 envelope (2.4 oz.) active dry yeast

¼ cup warm water

¼ cup milk

2 tablespoons unsalted butter,
   room temperature

¼ cup sugar

½ teaspoon salt

1 egg, beaten

1½ cups all-purpose flour

FILLING

1½ cups cottage cheese

2 eggs, beaten

¼ cup heavy cream

½ cup sugar

¼ teaspoon salt

2 bananas, sliced

1 teaspoon cinnamon

For an alternate topping, cover the cheese with thin apple slices and cooked, crumbled bacon.

1. Dissolve yeast in warm water. Grease a 9-inch pie plate.

2. Scald milk in a small saucepan over medium-high heat. Remove from heat. Stir in butter, sugar, and salt. Cool.

3. In a large bowl, combine yeast mixture, milk mixture, egg, and flour. Mix well to make a dough. Press dough into bottom and up sides of a pie plate.

4. To make filling: In a medium bowl, combine cottage cheese, eggs, cream, sugar, and salt. Mix well. Spread filling in center of pastry shell. Top with sliced bananas and cinnamon. Let rise for 1 hour. Bake in a preheated 350°F oven for 25 to 30 minutes. Makes 1 coffee cake.

ELIZABETH SLOAN, St. Ignatious, Montana
First Place, America—The Melting Pot, Western Montana Fair, Missoula, Montana, 1987

Divine Summer Tomato Grits

2 cups water

1¼ cups milk

1 teaspoon salt

1 cup grits

½ cup plus 1 tablespoon unsalted butter, divided, plus more for casserole dish

½ cup sliced green onions

2½ cups shredded cheddar cheese, divided

1 cup diced canned tomatoes

2 eggs, beaten

1. Preheat oven to 350°F. Butter a casserole dish.

2. Combine water and milk in a saucepan over medium-high heat. Bring to a boil and add salt. Slowly add grits, return to a boil, stirring, for 1 minute. Reduce heat and continue stirring another 3 minutes. Cover and cook for 3 minutes, or until grits are thick and creamy. Add ½ cup of the butter and stir until melted. Remove from heat.

3. Melt remaining tablespoon butter in a skillet. Add green onion and sauté. Add onion and 1½ cups of the cheddar cheese to the grits. Stir until cheese is melted.

4. Add tomatoes to grits and mix well. Stir in beaten eggs. Pour grits into casserole. Bake for 40 minutes. Makes 4 to 6 servings.

※ **Virginia Martin,** Oglethorpe, Georgia
Third Place, Grits Anytime, Georgia National Fair, Perry, Georgia, 2005

Cream Cheese Coffee Cakes

ICEBOX ROLL DOUGH

1 cup shortening

¾ cup sugar

1½ teaspoons salt

1 cup boiling water

2 envelopes (2.4 oz. each) active dry yeast

½ cup warm water (105° to 115°F)

3 eggs, lightly beaten

6 to 7½ cups all-purpose flour

1 cup cold water

CREAM CHEESE FILLING

1 package (8 oz.) cream cheese, room temperature

1 egg

1 tablespoon lemon juice

1 teaspoon grated lemon zest

¾ cup all-purpose flour

2½ cups confectioners' sugar

¼ cup sour cream

½ cup pecans, chopped

CONFECTIONERS' SUGAR ICING

2 cups confectioners' sugar

½ teaspoon vanilla

3 tablespoons milk

1. To make icebox roll dough: In a small bowl, combine shortening, sugar, and salt. Beat with a wooden spoon until smooth and creamy. Add boiling water and stir until smooth. Cool until lukewarm.

2. In a large bowl, sprinkle yeast over warm water and stir until dissolved. Add shortening mixture and eggs and mix well. Add flour alternately with cold water, beating until smooth. Grease top of dough. Cover bowl tightly with foil and refrigerate overnight.

3. To make cream cheese filling: In a small mixing bowl, combine cream cheese, egg, lemon juice, lemon zest, flour, confectioners' sugar, sour cream, and pecans. Beat until well mixed.

4. Divide dough in half. Roll out each half on a floured surface to make a rectangle. Spread with half of the cream cheese filling. Fold in thirds, so that long edges overlap. Place seam side down on a greased baking sheet. Cut slits in the top. Cover and let rise until double in size, 1 hour. Bake in a preheated 375°F oven for 25 minutes. Cool on a wire rack.

5. To make confectioners' sugar icing: In a small bowl, combine confectioners' sugar, vanilla, and milk until smooth. Drizzle over coffee cakes. Garnish with pecans or Maraschino cherries, if desired. Makes 2 coffee cakes.

※ **CAROLYN BROOKS,** Abilene, Texas
Best of Show, West Texas Fair & Rodeo, Abilene, Texas, 2004

STRAWBERRY OMELET

3½ oz. fresh strawberries, sliced, plus more for topping

1 tablespoon strawberry preserves

1 teaspoon brown sugar

1 tablespoon butter

3 large eggs

1 teaspoon coconut rum

Crushed almonds

Shredded coconut

Confectioners' sugar

1. Toss sliced strawberries with preserves and brown sugar until well coated.

2. Heat an 8-inch skillet over medium heat. Add butter and wait until it is bubbling, then whisk eggs and pour into skillet. Cook until eggs are set on bottom but still moist. Lift edges gently with a silicone spatula, tilting pan to let uncooked eggs run under.

3. Spoon strawberry mixture over half of the eggs. Cook just until eggs fluff. Remove from heat and sprinkle with coconut rum. Fold omelet in half to enclose filling and slide onto a serving plate. Top with remaining strawberries, crushed almonds, and shredded coconut. Sprinkle with confectioners' sugar. Makes 1 omelet.

※ **MARTHA BUEHRING,**
Norman, Oklahoma
First Place, Omelet Contest,
Oklahoma State Fair, Oklahoma
City, Oklahoma, 2005

CHICKEN AND SUMMER VEGETABLES OMELET

3 tablespoons olive oil, divided

¼ cup sliced zucchini

¼ cup sliced yellow squash

¼ cup chopped yellow onion

¼ cup chopped red and green bell pepper

1 teaspoon salt

1 teaspoon pepper

1 teaspoon ground cumin

1 teaspoon coriander

½ cup chopped cooked chicken

3 eggs

½ cup shredded Colby and Monterey Jack

1. Heat 2 tablespoons of the olive oil in a skillet over medium-high heat. Add zucchini, yellow squash, onion, bell pepper, salt, pepper, cumin, and coriander. Sauté until almost tender, 4 minutes. Add chicken and cook for another 2 minutes. Transfer to a bowl and set aside.

2. Heat remaining tablespoon olive oil in same skillet. Whisk eggs together until light and fluffy, pour into skillet, cover, and cook for 1 minute.

3. Place chicken mixture on half of omelet. Cook until egg is set, 2 to 3 minutes. Sprinkle shredded cheese over chicken, then use a spatula to fold omelet in half. Let sit 1 minute before serving. Makes 1 omelet.

※ **BILLY MABRAY,** Yukon, Oklahoma
Third Place, Omelet Contest, Oklahoma State Fair, Oklahoma City, Oklahoma, 2005

CREAMY PEACH COFFEE CAKE

2¼ cups all-purpose flour

¾ cup sugar

¼ cup unsalted butter, chilled

½ cup sour cream

½ tablespoon baking powder

½ teaspoon baking soda

1 egg

1 teaspoon almond extract

FILLING

1 package (8 oz.) cream cheese,
   room temperature

¼ cup sugar

1 egg

TOPPING

¾ cup peach preserves

1 cup crumb mixture (see step 2)

½ cup sliced almonds

1. Preheat oven to 350°F. Grease a 9 x 3-inch springform pan.

2. Combine flour and sugar in a mixing bowl. Cut in cold butter until mixture resembles coarse crumbs. Set aside 1 cup of crumb mixture for topping.

3. To the remaining crumb mixture, add sour cream, baking powder, baking soda, egg, and almond extract. Beat until well blended. Press mixture onto bottom and sides of pan.

4. To make filling: Beat cream cheese, sugar, and egg until well blended.

5. Spoon filling into the crust. Top with preserves, reserved crumb mixture, and almonds. Bake for 45 to 50 minutes. Set pan on a wire rack and run a knife around edge of pan to loosen cake. Cool completely before removing ring. Makes 1 coffee cake.

※ **LINDA GASS,** Mango, Florida
First Place, Adult Division, Florida State Fair, Tampa, Florida, 2005

CINNAMON COFFEE CAKE

1 cup unsalted butter, room temperature
1½ cups sugar
2 eggs
1 cup sour cream
2 cups all-purpose flour, plus more for pan
½ teaspoon baking soda
1½ teaspoons baking powder
1 teaspoon vanilla

TOPPING
¾ to 1 cup finely chopped walnuts
2 teaspoons cinnamon
4 tablespoons sugar

1. Grease and flour a 9-inch tube pan. Do not heat oven.
2. In a large mixing bowl, beat butter, sugar, and eggs until light and fluffy. Blend in sour cream.
3. Sift flour, baking soda, and baking powder into the creamed mixture. Add vanilla and mix well. Batter will be very thick.
4. To make topping: Combine walnuts, cinnamon, and sugar in a small bowl.
5. Spread half of batter in pan. Sprinkle with half of topping. Layer remaining batter in pan. Add remaining topping. Place pan in a cold oven. Heat oven to 350°F and bake about 55 minutes. Serve warm or cold. Makes 1 coffee cake.

❋ **CYNTHIA TEEM,** Interlachen, Florida
Best of Show, Youth Division, Florida State Fair, Tampa, Florida, 2005

BREAKFAST CASSEROLE ITALIANO

Cooking Spray
8 slices of Italian bread, trimmed of
　crusts and buttered
½ lb. Italian sausage, removed from
　casing and browned
2 tablespoons chopped basil,
　plus sprigs for garnish
1 tablespoon minced sweet red pepper

1 cup grated mozzarella
6 large eggs
1¾ cups milk
Salt and pepper
¼ teaspoon garlic powder
¼ teaspoon onion powder
¼ cup grated Parmesan

1. The evening before serving, lightly coat a 2- to 3-quart casserole with cooking spray. Place 4 pieces of the bread, buttered side down, in the bottom of dish. Cover with sausage, sprinkle with basil and peppers, and top with mozzarella. Place remaining bread slices, buttered side up, on top of cheese.
2. Whisk together eggs, milk, salt, pepper, garlic, and onion powder. Gently pour over bread. Cover and refrigerate overnight.
3. In the morning, preheat oven to 350°F. Remove casserole from refrigerator, uncover, and bring to room temperature. Bake uncovered for 45 minutes. Sprinkle Parmesan over the top and bake 15 minutes longer. Garnish with basil sprigs. Makes 4 to 6 servings.

❋ **KIMBERLY STIPE**, Bethany, Oklahoma
Second Place, Prepared Egg Contest, Oklahoma State Fair, Oklahoma City, Oklahoma, 2005

Corn Scones with Cilantro-Lime Butter

2 cups fresh local sweet corn, divided
½ cup buttermilk
2 eggs
¼ cup unsalted butter, melted
2 fresh jalapeños, minced
2 tablespoons grated onion
¼ cup finely diced red bell pepper
½ cup yellow cornmeal
½ cup all-purpose flour

1 teaspoon baking powder
½ teaspoon salt
¼ teaspoon cayenne pepper
½ teaspoon ground cumin
1 tablespoon sugar
2 tablespoons chopped fresh cilantro
Cilantro-Lime Butter (recipe follows)
Honey

1. Preheat oven to 400°F. Grease a mini scone pan.

2. Puree 1 cup of the corn kernels in a blender. Place corn purée in a large bowl. Stir in buttermilk, eggs, melted butter, jalapeños, onion, and bell pepper.

3. Combine cornmeal, flour, baking powder, salt, cayenne pepper, cumin, sugar, and cilantro. Stir into wet mixture. Fold in remaining cup of corn kernels.

4. Spoon batter into pan. Bake for 15 to 20 minutes, or until lightly browned. Serve warm with Cilantro-Lime Butter and a drizzle of honey. Makes 12 scones.

Cilantro-Lime Butter

½ cup unsalted butter, room temperature
Zest of 2 limes

Dash of hot pepper sauce
¼ cup finely chopped fresh cilantro

Mix butter, lime zest, hot pepper sauce, and cilantro until well combined. Form into a log and wrap with plastic wrap or waxed paper. Chill in refrigerator or freezer just until set. Slice off rounds to serve with scones.

※ **Cheryl Rogers,** Ames, Iowa
First Place, Creative Cooking with Fresh Corn, Iowa State Fair, Des Moines, Iowa, 2005

Apricot Coffee Cake

2 cups all-purpose flour, plus more for pan
1 teaspoon baking powder
1 cup unsalted butter, room temperature,
    plus more for pan
3 eggs

1 teaspoon vanilla
2 cups sugar
1 cup sour cream
¾ cup slivered almonds, divided
1 jar (10 to 12 oz.) apricot preserves, divided

1. Preheat oven to 350°F. Grease and flour a 10-cup Bundt pan.

2. Sift together flour and baking powder.

3. In a large mixing bowl, combine butter, eggs, vanilla, sugar, and sour cream. Beat until light and fluffy. Gradually add flour mixture, beating until well blended.

4. Spread half of batter in Bundt pan. Sprinkle half of almonds over batter. Add half of preserves, but do not spread to edge of pan. Add remaining batter to pan. Spoon remaining preserves over top. Scatter remaining almonds on top. Bake for 1 hour or until a tester inserted near center comes out clean. Makes 1 Bundt cake.

❊ **MARIE SPITZER,** Saint Charles, Minnesota
Blue Ribbon, Winona County Agricultural & Industrial Fair, Saint Charles, Minnesota, 2002

DATE-FILLED COFFEE CAKE

½ cup chopped dates
½ cup water
1½ cups sugar, divided
⅓ cup shortening
3 eggs

1 teaspoon vanilla
1½ cups all-purpose flour
1½ teaspoons salt
¾ cup milk
1 package (3.4 oz.) butterscotch instant pudding

1. Preheat oven to 350°F. Grease a 10 x 4-inch tube pan.
2. Combine dates, water, and ½ cup of the sugar in a saucepan over medium-high heat. Bring to a boil and cook, stirring constantly, for 2 minutes. Remove from heat, cool, and mix well.
3. In a large mixing bowl, combine shortening, eggs, and vanilla and beat well. With mixer running, add flour, remaining cup sugar, salt, milk, and instant pudding. Beat for 2 minutes.
4. Pour half of batter into tube pan. Add date filling on top of batter, making sure it does not touch sides of pan. Top with remaining batter. Bake for 1 hour. Invert pan on a wire rack to cool. Makes 1 coffee cake.

❊ **MAUREEN FENDANDES,** San Jacinto, California
First Place, Cakes, Riverside County Fair and National Date Festival, Indio, California, 2003–2004

BANANA WHEAT MUFFINS

1⅓ cups all-purpose flour
⅔ cup whole wheat flour
1 teaspoon baking soda
½ teaspoon salt

1 cup mayonnaise
¾ cup sugar
1 cup mashed ripe bananas

1. Preheat oven to 350°F. Grease a 12-cup muffin pan.
2. In a large bowl, whisk together flour, wheat flour, baking soda, and salt.
3. In another bowl, combine mayonnaise, sugar, and bananas.
4. Add banana mixture to flour mixture and stir just until moistened. Fill muffin cups two-thirds full. Bake for 20 to 25 minutes. Cool. Makes 12 muffins.

❊ **JANET PISTULKA,** Aberdeen, South Dakota
Best of Class, Brown County Fair & 4-H Show, Aberdeen, South Dakota, 2001

Banana-Poppy Seed Muffins

2 cups all-purpose flour
1½ tablespoons poppy seeds
2 teaspoons baking powder
½ teaspoon salt
2 ripe bananas, pureed in blender (1 cup)
1 egg
¾ cup sugar
¼ cup oil
2 teaspoons grated orange zest

CITRUS GLAZE
1¼ cups confectioners' sugar
¼ cup orange juice
1 teaspoon grated orange zest
1 teaspoon vanilla

1. Preheat oven to 375°F. Grease a 12-cup muffin pan.
2. In a large bowl, combine flour, poppy seeds, baking powder, and salt.
3. In a medium bowl, mix bananas, egg, sugar, oil, and orange zest until well blended.
4. Stir banana mixture into flour mixture until evenly moistened. Spoon batter into muffin cups. Bake for 20 minutes, or until a toothpick inserted in center comes out clean. Remove muffins from pan and set on a wire rack.
5. To make glaze: Combine confectioners' sugar, orange juice, orange zest, and vanilla until smooth. Spoon or drizzle over muffins while still warm. Makes 12 muffins.

✄ **DEBRA MONHOLLAND**, Tahlequah, Oklahoma
Sweepstakes, Tulsa State Fair, Tulsa, Oklahoma, 2003

Blackberry Corn Muffins

Cooking Spray
1 cup all-purpose flour
1 cup cornmeal
½ cup sugar
1 teaspoon baking powder
1 teaspoon baking soda

¼ teaspoon salt
2 eggs, lightly beaten
2 containers (6 oz. each) fat-free yogurt
2 tablespoons unsalted butter, melted
1 cup fresh or frozen blackberries

1. Preheat oven to 375°F. Coat a 12-cup muffin pan with cooking spray.
2. In a large bowl, combine flour, cornmeal, sugar, baking powder, baking soda, and salt.
3. In a small bowl, combine eggs, yogurt, and melted butter until smooth.
4. Stir egg mixture into flour mixture just until moistened. Fold in blackberries. Fill muffin cups three-quarters full. Bake for 18 to 22 minutes, or until a toothpick inserted in center comes out clean. Cool in pan for 5 minutes and then place muffins on a wire rack. Makes 12 muffins.

✄ **SHARON GRENARD,** La Junta, Colorado
Reserve Champion, Open Foods Category, Muffins, Arkansas Valley Fair, Rocky Ford, Colorado, 2005

BLUEBERRY BRAN MUFFINS

¾ cup natural wheat bran

½ cup vanilla yogurt

½ cup maple syrup

1 egg, beaten

¼ cup canola oil

1 cup unbleached white flour

¼ cup wheat germ

3 teaspoons baking powder

½ teaspoon salt

⅓ cup chopped almonds

1½ cups fresh blueberries

GLAZE

1 tablespoon unsalted butter,
    room temperature

½ cup confectioners' sugar

1 tablespoon maple syrup

1. Preheat oven to 400°F.

2. In a large bowl, combine bran, yogurt, and maple syrup. Add egg and oil and mix well.

3. Whisk together flour, wheat germ, baking powder, and salt.

4. Add flour mixture to bran mixture, stirring just until moistened. Fold in almonds and blueberries. Pour batter evenly into muffin cups. Bake for 18 to 20 minutes. Set on a wire rack to cool.

5. To make glaze: Combine butter, confectioners' sugar, and maple syrup in a small bowl. Spread on warm muffins. Makes 12 muffins.

✄ **PEGGY BERRY,** East Machias, Maine
First Prize, Wild Blueberry Festival Cooking Competition, Machias, Maine, 2002

BLUEBERRY-PEACH MUFFINS

Cooking spray

2 cups all-purpose flour

⅔ cup sugar

½ teaspoon baking soda

¼ teaspoon salt

1 container (6 oz.) peach yogurt

¼ cup water

1 large egg

2 large egg whites

¼ cup unsalted butter, melted

½ pint fresh blueberries

½ cup lowfat granola, lightly crushed

1. Preheat oven to 350°F. Coat a 12-cup muffin pan with cooking spray.

2. Sift together flour, sugar, baking soda, and salt.

3. In a large bowl, whisk together yogurt, water, egg, egg whites, and melted butter.

4. Add flour mixture to yogurt mixture and stir just until moistened. Gently fold in blueberries. Divide batter evenly among muffin cups, about a heaping ¼ cup batter for each. Sprinkle crushed granola over muffin tops. Bake for 20 minutes, or until crowned and golden around the edges. Cool in pan for 5 minutes. Makes 12 muffins.

✄ **BETSY BRUGMAN,** Royal, Iowa
Blue Ribbon, Open Class, Clay County Fair, Spencer, Iowa, 2005

Sweet Potato Scones with Mock Devonshire Cream

2½ cups all-purpose flour
½ cup sugar
6 teaspoons baking powder
1 teaspoon salt
¼ teaspoon cream of tartar
1 teaspoon cinnamon

½ cup unsalted butter, chilled
½ cup coarsely chopped cranberries
1¼ cups cooked mashed sweet potatoes
Up to ⅓ cup milk
Mock Devonshire Cream (recipe follows)

1. Preheat oven to 375°F. Grease a baking sheet.
2. In a large bowl, sift together flour, sugar, baking powder, salt, cream of tartar, and cinnamon. Cut in butter until crumbly.
3. In a separate bowl, combine cranberries and sweet potatoes. Add milk, a little at a time, to make a soft mash. Stir sweet potato mixture into flour mixture. Add more milk if needed to make a workable dough.
4. Turn out dough onto a lightly floured surface. Knead once or twice. Divide dough in half and pat into two disks. Place disks on baking sheet and cut into wedges. Bake for 12 to 15 minutes. Serve warm with Mock Devonshire Cream. Makes 8 to 12 scones.

Mock Devonshire Cream

½ cup heavy cream
2 tablespoons confectioners' sugar
½ teaspoon vanilla

½ teaspoon almond extract
½ cup sour cream

Beat heavy cream until soft peaks form. Add confectioners' sugar, vanilla, and almond extract and continue beating until stiff peaks form. Fold in sour cream. Chill.

✕ **Lisa Gentry,** Elko, Georgia
Fourth Place, Yammy Good Sweet Potatoes—Sweet Class, Georgia National Fair, Perry, Georgia, 2005

⚜ Butter Sculpture ⚜

The true gastronomic event at the Minnesota State Fair is the amazing gallery of butter sculpture. It's a spectacle that became the fair's highlight over a hundred years ago. Recent motifs have included public buildings, herds of cows, and busts of the reigning Dairy Princess—Princess Kay of the Milky Way—carved from 90 pounds of edible, blue-ribbon, farm-fresh butter.

Pumpkin Maple Cream Cheese Muffins

2 cups all-purpose flour
2 teaspoons baking powder
½ teaspoon baking soda
¼ teaspoon salt
¾ cup brown sugar
1 teaspoon cinnamon
½ cup chopped walnuts
2 eggs
1 cup canned pumpkin
¾ cup evaporated milk
¼ cup unsalted butter, melted
2 teaspoons maple flavoring

CREAM CHEESE FILLING

4 oz. cream cheese, room temperature
2 tablespoons brown sugar
1½ teaspoons maple flavoring

NUT TOPPING

2 teaspoons brown sugar
¼ cup chopped walnuts

1. Preheat oven to 400°F. Grease a 12-cup muffin pan or insert paper liners.

2. In a large bowl, combine flour, baking powder, baking soda, salt, brown sugar, cinnamon, and walnuts.

3. In a separate bowl, combine eggs, pumpkin, evaporated milk, butter, and maple flavoring. Add to flour mixture, mixing just until blended. Spoon batter into muffin cups.

4. To make cream cheese filling: Combine cream cheese, brown sugar, and maple flavoring in small bowl until blended. Drop a heaping teaspoon of filling into the center of each cup and press partway into batter.

5. To make nut topping: Combine brown sugar and walnuts. Sprinkle topping into each muffin cup. Bake for 20 to 25 minutes. Makes 12 muffins.

✄ **CHRISTIE PITTMAN,** Menomonie, Wisconsin
First Prize, Muffins, Dunn County HCE, Dunn County Fair, Menomonie, Wisconsin, 2004

Cheddar Dill Muffins

3½ cups all-purpose flour
1 cup (4 oz.) shredded cheddar cheese
3 tablespoons sugar
2 tablespoons baking powder
2 teaspoons chopped fresh dill
1 teaspoon salt
1¾ cups milk
2 eggs, lightly beaten
¼ cup unsalted butter, melted

1. Preheat oven to 400°F. Grease a 12-cup muffin pan or insert paper liners.
2. In a large bowl, combine flour, cheese, sugar, baking powder, dill, and salt.
3. In a small bowl, combine milk, eggs, and melted butter.
4. Add milk mixture to flour mixture and stir just until moistened. Pour batter into muffin cups until two-thirds full. Bake for 25 to 30 minutes. Cool for 10 minutes in pan and transfer to a wire rack. Serve with butter and cream cheese. Makes 12 muffins.

Lucille Schumacher, Elk Mound, Wisconsin
Fourth Prize, Muffins, Dunn County HCE, Dunn County Fair, Menomonie, Wisconsin, 2004

Cottage Cheese Muffins

1 package (12 oz.) dry cottage cheese
3 tablespoons sugar
2 eggs, slightly beaten
½ cup unsalted butter or margarine, melted
1 cup all-purpose flour
2 teaspoons baking powder
Pinch of salt

1. Preheat oven to 400°F. Grease a 12-cup muffin tin.
2. Combine cottage cheese, sugar, eggs, and melted butter or margarine. Mix well.
3. In a large bowl, combine flour, baking powder, and salt.
4. Add cottage cheese mixture to flour mixture and stir just until moistened. Spoon batter into muffin cups, filling about three-fourths full. Bake for 20 to 25 minutes, or until lightly browned. Cool. Makes 12 muffins.

Hope Foxworth, age 12, Ladson, South Carolina
First Place Cloverleaf Division, 4-H Muffin Mania Competition, Coastal Carolina Fair, Ladson, South Carolina, 2005

Hearty Oatmeal-Raisin Muffins

½ cup all-purpose flour
1 tablespoon baking powder
¼ teaspoon salt
1 teaspoon cinnamon
1 cup rolled oats
½ cup brown sugar
¼ cup raisins
1 egg
1 cup milk
¼ cup vegetable oil

1. Preheat oven to 400°F. Grease a 12-cup muffin pan.
2. In a large bowl, combine flour, baking powder, salt, cinnamon, oats, brown sugar, and raisins.
3. Whisk together egg, milk, and oil. Pour over flour mixture and stir just until moistened. Spoon batter into muffin cups until two-thirds full. Bake for 15 to 18 minutes, or until golden. Makes 12 muffins.

※ **LAUREN KARNEY,** age 11, La Junta, Colorado
Champion, On the Road to Fun & Fitness; Grand Champion, Foods and Nutrition, Arkansas Valley Fair & Expo, Rocky Ford, Colorado, 2005

Zucchini-Oatmeal Muffins

2½ cups all-purpose flour
1 tablespoon baking powder
1 teaspoon salt
1½ cups sugar
1 teaspoon cinnamon
½ cup quick-cooking rolled oats
4 eggs
¾ cup oil
¾ cup peeled, grated zucchini
1 cup chopped pecans

1. Preheat oven to 400°F. Grease a 12-cup muffin pan or insert paper liners.
2. In a large mixing bowl, combine flour, baking powder, salt, sugar, cinnamon, and oats.
3. In a separate bowl, beat eggs and oil until well blended. Fold in zucchini. Pour egg mixture over flour mixture and stir just until moistened. Stir in pecans. Spoon batter into muffin cups until three-fourths full. Bake for 20 to 25 minutes, or until a toothpick inserted in center comes out clean. Makes 12 muffins.

※ **NICOLE IHRKE,** Saint Charles, Minnesota
Champion, Winona County Agricultural & Industrial Fair, Saint Charles, Minnesota, 1999

Orange Breakfast Muffins

1 egg
½ cup milk
¼ cup oil
1½ cups self-rising flour
1 cup sugar
Brown sugar

GLAZE
1 cup confectioners' sugar
5 to 6 teaspoons orange juice
½ teaspoon grated orange zest

1. Preheat oven to 350°F. Grease a 12-cup muffin pan.
2. Whisk egg in a medium bowl. Whisk in milk and oil just until blended.
3. Sift flour and sugar into egg mixture. Stir just until moistened. Add batter to muffin cups until two-thirds full. Sprinkle with brown sugar. Bake for 20 to 30 minutes, or until a toothpick inserted in center comes out clean.
4. To make glaze: Mix together confectioners' sugar, and orange juice and zest in a small bowl. Spread glaze over hot muffins. Makes 12 muffins.

※ **BETTY HALL,** Chelsea, Oklahoma
Sweepstakes Winner, Tulsa State Fair, Tulsa, Oklahoma, 2001

J's Raisin Bran Muffins

Cooking spray
2 cups bran cereal
1¼ cups milk
1 egg
¼ cup vegetable oil

1¼ cups all-purpose flour
½ cup sugar
1 tablespoon baking powder
¼ teaspoon salt
1 cup raisins

1. Preheat oven to 400°F. Lightly coat a 6-cup muffin pan (2½-inch cups) with cooking spray.

2. In a large mixing bowl, combine bran cereal and milk. Let stand until cereal softens, 5 minutes. Add egg and oil and beat well.

3. Whisk together flour, sugar, baking powder, and salt. Add flour mixture and raisins to cereal mixture and stir just until combined. Divide batter evenly among 6 muffin cups. Bake for 20 minutes, or until lightly browned. Makes 6 muffins.

✂ **JANNINE FISK,** Malden, Massachusetts
First Place, Muffins, Topsfield Fair, Topsfield, Massachusetts, 2002

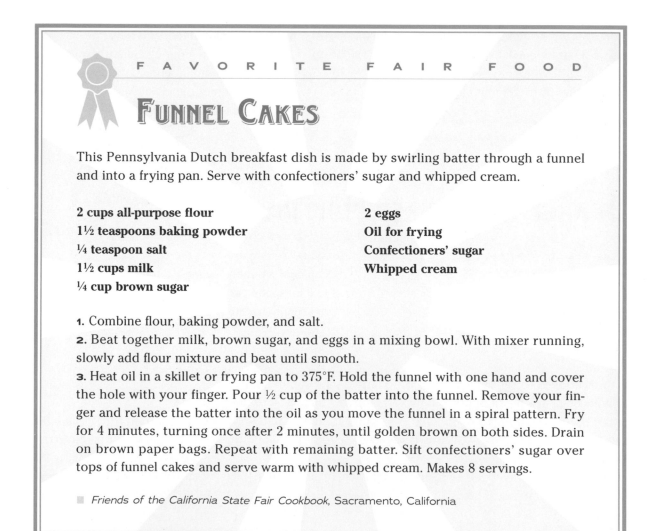

F A V O R I T E F A I R F O O D

Funnel Cakes

This Pennsylvania Dutch breakfast dish is made by swirling batter through a funnel and into a frying pan. Serve with confectioners' sugar and whipped cream.

2 cups all-purpose flour
1½ teaspoons baking powder
¼ teaspoon salt
1½ cups milk
¼ cup brown sugar

2 eggs
Oil for frying
Confectioners' sugar
Whipped cream

1. Combine flour, baking powder, and salt.

2. Beat together milk, brown sugar, and eggs in a mixing bowl. With mixer running, slowly add flour mixture and beat until smooth.

3. Heat oil in a skillet or frying pan to 375°F. Hold the funnel with one hand and cover the hole with your finger. Pour ½ cup of the batter into the funnel. Remove your finger and release the batter into the oil as you move the funnel in a spiral pattern. Fry for 4 minutes, turning once after 2 minutes, until golden brown on both sides. Drain on brown paper bags. Repeat with remaining batter. Sift confectioners' sugar over tops of funnel cakes and serve warm with whipped cream. Makes 8 servings.

■ *Friends of the California State Fair Cookbook*, Sacramento, California

HONEY-ORANGE-ALMOND MUFFINS WITH ALMOND TOPPING

⅓ cup honey

½ cup fresh orange juice

½ cup orange marmalade

4 tablespoons unsalted butter, melted

1 large egg

2 cups all-purpose flour

2 teaspoons baking powder

½ teaspoon baking soda

½ teaspoon salt

1 package (7 oz.) almond paste, grated

ALMOND TOPPING

¾ cup crushed vanilla wafers

⅓ cup all-purpose flour

½ cup sliced almonds

¼ cup unsalted butter, chilled

1. Preheat oven to 375°F. Line a 12-cup muffin pan with foil liners.

2. Combine honey, orange juice, marmalade, melted butter, and egg in a bowl.

3. In a large bowl, combine flour, baking powder, baking soda, and salt. Add almond paste and mix until all pieces are coated.

4. Pour orange juice mixture over flour mixture and beat quickly with a spoon just until combined.

5. To make almond topping: Combine vanilla wafers, flour, and almonds in a bowl. Cut in butter until mixture resembles coarse crumbs.

6. Spoon batter into muffin pan. Add almond topping to each cup. Bake for 18 to 20 minutes, or until a toothpick inserted in center comes out clean. Makes 12 muffins.

⚜ **JUANITA PERRET,** Wickenburg, Arizona
First Place, Honey Cooking, Muffins Made with Honey, Arizona State Fair, Phoenix, Arizona, 2005

 WINNER'S CIRCLE TIP | These muffins are delicious served warm with honey butter. Blend together equal parts of honey and butter.

CHOCOLATE-COVERED STRAWBERRY MUFFINS

1¾ cups all-purpose flour
½ cup sugar
2 teaspoons baking powder
¼ teaspoon salt
1 egg, beaten

¾ cup milk
¼ cup applesauce
⅓ cup dehydrated strawberries
⅓ cup semisweet chocolate chips

1. Preheat oven to 400°F. Lightly grease a 12-cup muffin pan.

2. In a large bowl, whisk together flour, sugar, baking powder, and salt.

3. In a separate bowl, combine egg, milk, and applesauce.

4. Make a well in the center of the flour mixture and pour in applesauce mixture. Stir until moistened but still lumpy. Add strawberries and chocolate chips. Spoon batter into muffin cups until two-thirds full. Bake for 20 minutes, or until golden brown. Makes 12 muffins.

✕ **KENNY HYLTON,** Second Creek, West Virginia
First Place, Applesauce Muffin Contest, State Fair of West Virginia, Lewisburg, West Virginia, 2005

MINI ZUCCHINI MUFFINS

2 cups all-purpose flour
1 cup whole wheat flour
1 teaspoon baking powder
1 teaspoon baking soda
1 teaspoon salt
1 teaspoon cinnamon
1 teaspoon nutmeg

3 eggs, lightly beaten
2 cups sugar
1 cup liquid shortening
2 teaspoons vanilla
3 cups grated zucchini
72 pecan halves

1. Preheat oven to 325°F. Grease one or more 12-cup mini muffin pans.

2. In a large bowl, combine flour, whole wheat flour, baking powder, baking soda, salt, cinnamon, and nutmeg.

3. Add eggs, sugar, liquid shortening, vanilla, and zucchini to flour mixture. Mix well. Pour batter into muffin pans. Top each muffin with a pecan half. Bake for 12 minutes. Gently turn out onto wire racks. Makes 6 dozen muffins.

✕ **PHYLLIS BOWDISH,** Weybridge, Vermont
Rosette, Muffins, Addison County Fair & Field Days, New Haven, Vermont, 2005

CHAPTER 2

APPETIZERS

SNACKS, SALSAS, DIPS,
AND SPREADS

JUST TAKE A BITE!!

5 large jalapeños
3 eggs, beaten
½ cup cornmeal
1 qt. oil for frying

1 boneless chicken breast, cooked
1 small mushroom, grilled and chopped
⅓ cup salsa
4 slices of cheddar cheese, cut into julienne

1. Slice jalapeños lengthwise down the middle. Remove seeds and white membrane.

2. Dip jalapeños in eggs and then in cornmeal to coat. Cook jalapeños in a deep fryer, following manufacturer's instructions. Drain on paper towels.

3. Shred chicken into a bowl, add mushroom, and mix well.

4. Stuff jalapeños with chicken mixture. Top with salsa and cheese. Just before serving, heat in microwave until warm and cheese is melted. Serve with sour cream, if desired. Makes 5 servings.

BRYAN CHACON, Albuquerque, New Mexico
First Place, New Mexico State Fair, Albuquerque, New Mexico, 2005

CRAB CHEESECAKE DIP

CRUST
1 cup crushed buttery round crackers
½ cup Parmesan
¼ cup margarine, melted
½ teaspoon Old Bay seasoning

DIP
2 teaspoons Old Bay seasoning
3 packages (8 oz. each) cream cheese,
½ cup sour cream
4 eggs
1¼ cups shredded cheddar cheese
¼ teaspoon lemon juice
½ teaspoon Worcestershire sauce
¼ green bell pepper, chopped very fine
1 lb. lump crabmeat, picked through
     and shell pieces removed

1. Preheat oven to 350°F.

2. To make crust: Mix together crushed crackers, Parmesan, melted margarine, and seasoning. Press mixture into bottom of a 9-inch ungreased springform pan.

3. To make dip: Beat cream cheese until soft and fluffy. Slowly beat in sour cream. Beat in eggs one at a time. Stir in cheddar cheese, Old Bay seasoning, lemon juice, Worcestershire sauce, and green pepper. Gently fold in crabmeat. Pour mixture into pan. Bake for 50 to 55 minutes, or until set.

4. Remove dip from oven and let set 15 minutes. Carefully loosen and remove springform. Set warm dip on a serving plate accompanied by assorted crackers and a cheese knife for spreading. Garnish with cherry tomatoes and parsley, if desired. Makes 8 to 12 appetizer servings.

BONNIE ROBINSON, Seaford, Delaware
First Place, Holiday Appetizer Competition, Delaware State Fair, Harrington, Delaware, 2005

Soft Molded Cheese

2 quarts pasteurized milk
⅓ cup quality buttermilk
⅛ teaspoon liquid rennet (available from
   New England Cheesemaking Supply)

¼ cup cool water
Salt

1. Heat milk in a saucepan over medium heat to 86°F, using a cheesemaking thermometer to verify the temperature. Add buttermilk as a starter and allow to ripen for 30 minutes at 86°F.

2. Combine liquid rennet and cool water. Add to warm milk and mix well. Allow to set until curd is quite firm.

3. Scoop thin slices of curd from the solid mass and layer into perforated molds for draining. If curd runs through the holes, it is still too soft. Wait 10 minutes and try again.

4. Allow molds to drain on a mat or board set in a pan until less than one-third of the original volume is left. The amount of time needed will depend on the room temperature and bacterial activity. Occasionally run a clean table knife around the inside of the mold to loosen the curd. If desired, sprinkle surface lightly with salt.

5. Loosen curd with a knife, invert molds onto a plate or board to drain, and tap bottom of mold until curd drops onto the plate. To retain a smooth cylinder shape, leave the inverted mold in place for 12 to 24 hours. Store in the refrigerator. Serve at room temperature covered with cracked or ground black pepper or minced herbs, if desired.

✂ **Clark County Dairy Goat Association**
Master Recipe, Celebrating 10 years of Goat Cheese at the Clark County Fair, Ridgefield, Washington, 1996–2006

WINNER'S CIRCLE TIP | Rennet is available from New England Cheesemaking Supply, P.O. Box 85, Ashfield, MA 01330; tel: (413) 628-3808. For a delicious treat, layer soft molded cheese in a jar with herbs and olive oil. Cheese stored this way should be used within a couple of weeks or so.

Party Cheese Ball

1 package (8 oz.) cream cheese,
   room temperature
8 oz. medium grated cheese
½ medium onion, minced

2 tablespoons dried chives
2 tablespoons mayonnaise
1 bunch parsley, chopped
1 cup roasted pecans, well chopped

1. In a bowl, combine cream cheese, grated cheese, onion, chives, mayonnaise, and parsley.

2. Roll cheese mixture into a ball. Roll ball in chopped pecans until well coated. Chill until ready to serve. Serve with crackers. Makes 1 cheese ball.

✂ **Ben Byrd,** Raleigh, North Carolina
Third Place, N.C. Pecan Association's Pecan Recipe Competition, North Carolina State Fair, Raleigh, North Carolina, 2005

MARINATED CHEESE

2 packages (8 oz. each) cream cheese
½ cup olive oil
⅜ cup red wine vinegar
⅛ cup balsamic vinegar
3 tablespoons minced fresh parsley

3 tablespoons chopped green onion
3 garlic cloves, minced
1 teaspoon dried basil
¼ teaspoon salt
¼ teaspoon pepper

1. Cut cream cheese into ½-inch cubes and place in a bowl.

2. Whisk together olive oil, red wine vinegar, balsamic vinegar, parsley, onion, garlic, basil, salt, and pepper until well blended.

3. Pour marinade over cubes of cheese. Let stand at room temperature for 90 minutes. Store in refrigerator, removing 30 minutes before serving. Serve with your favorite cracker. Makes about 3 cups.

❊ **KIM WALTON,** Farmington, Minnesota
First Prize, Dairy Cooking Contest, Dakota County Fair, Farmington, Minnesota, 2005

TRIPLE-CHEESE CRAB PUFFS

1 cup water
½ cup unsalted butter or margarine,
   room temperature
1 cup all-purpose flour
4 large eggs
1 cup shredded sharp
   cheddar cheese
¼ cup grated Parmesan
1 teaspoon salt

½ teaspoon dry mustard
½ teaspoon cayenne pepper

FILLING

1 package (6 oz.) minced crabmeat
1 package (8 oz.) cream cheese
½ cup sour cream
⅓ cup chopped green onion
¼ teaspoon minced garlic

1. Preheat oven to 450°F. Line 2 large baking sheets with parchment paper.

2. Heat water and butter in a medium-size heavy saucepan until boiling. Remove from heat. Add flour and beat vigorously with a wooden spoon until mixture forms a ball and pulls away from the sides of the pan.

3. Set pan on a damp cloth. Add eggs one at a time, beating after each addition until smooth. Add cheddar cheese, Parmesan, salt, mustard, and cayenne pepper. Mix until combined.

4. Spoon dough into a pastry bag fitted with a large plain tip or star tip. Pipe dough onto baking sheets in 1-inch mounds spaced 2 inches apart. Bake for 15 minutes. Reduce oven to 375°F and bake 12 to 15 minutes longer, or until puffs are golden brown and firm to the touch. Using the tip of a small knife, pierce the sides of puffs to let steam escape. Turn off heat and let cool in oven for 10 minutes. Transfer pans to wire racks and cool completely.

5. To make filling: Mix together crabmeat, cream cheese, sour cream, green onion, and garlic until well combined. Slice the tops from puffs. Remove any uncooked dough inside. Fill each puff with 1 teaspoon filling and replace top. Serve immediately or refrigerate and serve within 2 to 3 hours. Makes 24 appetizer servings.

✕ **DEANNE FELL,** Ionia, Michigan
First Place, Appetizers and Dips, Dairy Delight Contest, Ionia Free Fair, Ionia, Michigan, 2005

WINNER'S CIRCLE TIP | Choux pastry is not difficult to make. Cool the flour paste slightly before adding the eggs, to avoid cooking the eggs prematurely. Don't let the paste cool too much though, or the eggs will not blend in smoothly. The final flour and egg paste should be shiny, smooth, and very thick, but not stiff.

PARMESAN CRACKERS

2 cups all-purpose flour
8 tablespoons unsalted butter or
　margarine, chilled
1½ cups grated Parmesan

1 egg yolk
1 to 4 tablespoons water
Garlic salt

1. Preheat oven to 350°F. Set aside 2 or 3 baking sheets; do not grease.

2. Place flour in a large bowl. Cut in butter or margarine until the mixture resembles coarse meal. Add cheese and egg yolk and mix well. Add water 1 tablespoon at a time and stir, just until dough holds together in a ball. The texture will be somewhat crumbly, but the dough will hold together when pressed.

3. Divide dough in half. Roll out each portion on a lightly floured surface to a ¼-inch thickness. Cut out individual crackers with a biscuit cutter or a sharp knife and arrange them on baking sheets. Prick each cracker 2 or 3 times with a fork. Sprinkle with garlic salt. Bake for 10 minutes. Turn over and bake for another 5 to 10 minutes, or until medium brown. Cool on a wire rack. Makes 40 to 50 crackers.

✕ **BARB BROWN,** Elkhart, Indiana
First Place, Elkhart County 4-H Fair, Goshen, Indiana, 2005

BBQ Deviled Eggs

8 hard-boiled eggs
1 tablespoon chopped fresh dill
½ teaspoon garlic salt

2 tablespoons mayonnaise
3 tablespoons barbecue sauce
½ teaspoon white pepper

1. Peel eggs and cut in half lengthwise. Remove egg yolks with a spoon and place in a bowl. Mash egg yolks with a fork.
2. Add dill, garlic salt, mayonnaise, barbecue sauce, and white pepper to egg yolks. Mix until well combined.
3. Fill egg whites with yolk mixture. Arrange on a plate and serve. Makes 16 servings.

✕ **MICHAEL MIKOLAJCIK,** Oklahoma City, Oklahoma
Third Place, Prepared Egg Contest, Oklahoma State Fair, Oklahoma City, Oklahoma, 2005

Stuffed Green-Chile Shrimp

1 package (6 oz.) stuffing mix
2 celery stalks, chopped
½ onion, diced

½ cup chopped green chiles
2 lbs. peeled and deveined large shrimp
1 tablespoon unsalted butter, melted

1. Preheat oven to 350°F.
2. Combine stuffing mix, celery, and onion, following instructions on package to prepare stuffing. Add green chiles and mix until well combined. Roll stuffing into walnut-sized balls.
3. Slice each shrimp down the middle and add stuffing. Place stuffed shrimp on baking sheet and drizzle with melted butter. Bake for 8 to 10 minutes. Serve warm. Makes 6 to 8 servings.

✕ **NATALIE MONTOYA GALLEGOS,** Albuquerque, New Mexico
Second Place, New Mexico State Fair, Albuquerque, New Mexico, 2005

Florentine Spinach Roll-Up

1 package (16 oz.) lasagna noodles
1 package (10 oz.) frozen chopped spinach,
   cooked and drained
1 container (4 oz.) Feta
Dash of nutmeg
1 egg
Olive oil
1 garlic clove, crushed

1 small onion, chopped
¼ cup chopped fresh parsley
¼ cup chopped fresh basil
1 can (8 oz.) tomato sauce
½ cup red wine
Salt and pepper
1 container (4 oz.) ricotta

1. Preheat oven to 345°F.
2. Boil lasagna noodles, following package directions for al dente. Drain and set aside.
3. Combine spinach, Feta, nutmeg, and egg.

4. Heat olive oil in a large skillet over medium high heat. Sauté garlic and onion until well browned. Add parsley and basil and cook for 1 minute. Add tomato sauce and wine. Simmer until liquid is reduced, about 10 minutes. Season with salt and pepper.

5. Pour ⅓ cup of sauce on bottom of baking dish. Spread 1 tablespoon of spinach mixture on each lasagna noodle and roll up tightly. Stand roll-ups on end in baking dish. Top with remaining sauce and ricotta. Cover with foil and bake until warmed through and cheese is melted, about 15 minutes. Makes 6 to 8 servings.

✗ **MARY TELL,** San Diego, California
First Place, Lotsa Pasta Contest—Appetizers, San Diego County Fair, Del Mar, California, 2004

SPAGHETTI PANCAKE

4 large eggs
1 garlic clove, crushed
1 teaspoon extra virgin olive oil
2 tablespoons milk
½ cup (20 count) Kalamata olives
½ cup chopped red bell pepper

4 cups cooked spaghetti or fresine pasta
½ cup freshly grated Parmesan
Salt and freshly ground black pepper
1 teaspoon unsalted butter,
    room temperature
Cooking spray

1. In a large bowl, whisk together eggs, garlic, oil, and milk. Stir in olives and red bell pepper.

2. Add pasta and toss to coat. Add Parmesan, sprinkle with salt and pepper, and toss again.

3. Heat butter in a nonstick skillet until melted. Pour pasta mixture into skillet all at once. Cook over medium heat until the bottom of pancake is golden brown, 10 minutes. Cut pancake in half or in quarters, carefully flip each piece, and continue browning. Remove from pan, cool slightly, and serve. Makes 2 or 4 servings.

✗ **MARY TABAR,** San Diego, California
Second Place, Lotsa Pasta Contest—Appetizers, San Diego County Fair, Del Mar, California, 2004

FAVORITE FAIR FOOD

SUGAR CORN OR "KETTLE CORN"

½ cup popcorn
3 tablespoons white sugar
Oil for popping

Heat oil in medium saucepan until hot. Add popcorn and sprinkle all of the sugar over it. Cover and shake continuously until popped. Salt to taste.

✗ *Friends of the California State Fair Cookbook,* Sacramento, California

Spicy Prawn Poke

1½ lbs. prawns, cooked and peeled
¼ cup ketchup
¼ cup lime juice
1 tablespoon soy sauce
2 to 3 teaspoons hot pepper sauce
¼ teaspoon red pepper flakes

½ cup chopped tomato
½ cup chopped Maui onion
¼ cup chopped fresh cilantro
1 firm ripe avocado
¼ cup peeled, seeded and
   chopped cucumber

1. Cut prawns into 1½-inch pieces.

2. In a large bowl, combine ketchup, lime juice, soy sauce, hot pepper sauce, and red pepper flakes.

3. Add prawns, tomato, onion, and cilantro. Toss until well coated. Cover bowl and set in refrigerator to marinate, 1 to 4 hours.

4. Just before serving, peel, seed, and chop avocado. Add avocado and cucumber to prawn mixture, toss gently to combine, and serve. Makes 4 to 6 servings.

✕ **KRISTINE SNYDER,** Kihei, Hawaii
Second Prize, Local Grinds Festival, Maui, Hawaii, 1999

WINNER'S CIRCLE TIP | In the Hawaiian language, *poke* (PO-keh) literally means "to cut." The traditional poke is made of raw ahi tuna marinated in a soy sauce mixture, but now the markets carry wide varieties of poke.

Mexican Chicken Bites with Cilantro-Lime Salsa

Cooking spray
1 teaspoon ground cumin
1 teaspoon chili powder
¼ teaspoon salt
⅛ teaspoon cayenne pepper
1 lb. boneless, skinless chicken breast,
   cut into 1-inch cubes

5 12-inch flour tortillas,
   cut into 1-inch strips
Wooden skewers, one for each bite
Oil for frying
Cilantro-Lime Salsa (recipe follows)

1. Preheat broiler. Coat broiler pan with cooking spray.

2. Combine cumin, chili powder, salt, and cayenne in a medium bowl with a tight-fitting lid. Add chicken cubes, place lid on bowl, and shake to coat.

3. Spread chicken on broiler pan in a single layer. Coat generously with cooking spray. Broil 6 inches from heat for 4 minutes, or until chicken is cooked through. Let cool.

4. Wrap 1 chicken cube with a tortilla strip, tearing off excess tortilla after ends overlap. Wrap exposed sides of cube with another strip of tortilla, again tearing off excess after ends overlap. Insert a wooden skewer through overlapped ends of tortilla, through cube, and out the other side, stopping after point of skewer penetrates outer layer of tortilla.

5. Pour oil 1 inch deep in a small frying pan. Heat over medium-high heat until a small bit of tortilla sizzles when dropped into oil. Holding long ends of several skewers, fry wrapped chicken cubes until lightly browned, turning as needed to cook evenly. Drain on paper towels. Serve with Cilantro-Lime Salsa. Makes 38 to 44 chicken bites.

Cilantro-Lime Salsa

¾ cup cilantro sprigs

3 tablespoons parsley sprigs

¼ cup blanched slivered almonds

1 garlic clove

1 serrano, seeded

⅛ teaspoon salt

3 tablespoons fresh lime juice

2 tablespoons extra virgin olive oil

1 tablespoon water

1. Chop cilantro, parsley, almonds, garlic, and serrano in a food processor. Sprinkle in salt.

2. With processor running, slowly pour in lime juice and olive oil. Continue blending, occasionally stopping and scraping down sides of container, until salsa is smooth.

3. Pour salsa into bowl, add water, and stir. Cover and chill until ready to serve.

✄ **Terri Foster,** Orlando, Florida
Second Place, Meal on a Stick Contest, Central Florida Fair, Orlando, Florida, 2005

Maui Onion Wheels

1 tablespoon unsalted butter or olive oil

2 Maui onions, chopped

2 garlic cloves, minced

1 egg

1 tablespoon water

1 sheet frozen puff pastry, thawed

⅓ cup grated Swiss cheese

¼ cup grated Parmesan

2 tablespoons chopped fresh basil,
    plus more for garnish

1. Heat butter or olive oil in a small skillet over medium heat. Add onions and garlic and sauté until softened, 10 to 15 minutes. Drain in a bowl lined with paper towels. Cool to room temperature and chill.

2. Whisk egg with water in a small bowl. Unfold pastry onto a lightly floured surface and brush with half of egg mixture. Spread onion mixture over the pastry. Sprinkle Swiss cheese, Parmesan, and basil over the onions.

3. Roll up pastry jelly roll–style. Brush outside with remaining egg mixture. Refrigerate for 30 minutes or up to 8 hours.

4. Preheat oven to 425°F. Coat a baking sheet with cooking spray. Slice the roll into ½-inch thick slices and place 2 inches apart on baking sheet. Bake for 20 minutes. Serve immediately, garnished with chopped basil if desired. Makes about 20 wheels.

✄ **Kristine Snyder,** Kihei, Hawaii
First Prize and Grand Prize, Appetizers/Sides, Maui Onion Festival, Maui, Hawaii, 1998

CRANBERRY CHUTNEY

16 oz. fresh or frozen cranberries
1 cup sugar
½ cup brown sugar
½ cup golden raisins
2 teaspoons cinnamon
1½ teaspoons ginger

½ teaspoon ground cloves
¼ teaspoon ground allspice
1 cup water
1 cup chopped onion
½ cup chopped celery
1 large baking apple, peeled, cored, and chopped

1. Combine cranberries, sugar, brown sugar, raisins, cinnamon, ginger, cloves, allspice, and water in a 2-quart saucepan. Simmer over medium heat, stirring frequently, until cranberries burst and release their juices, 15 minutes.

2. Reduce heat and stir in onion, celery, and apple. Simmer, uncovered, until thick, 15 minutes. Cover and refrigerate up to 2 weeks. Makes 1 quart.

※ **BEVERLY BODINE,** Onalaska, Wisconsin
First Place, Fresh Cranberry, Warrens Cranberry Festival, Warrens, Wisconsin, 2005

PEAR SALSA WITH CINNAMON CHIPS

PEAR SALSA
Juice and zest of 2 limes
2 Bartlett pears, peeled, cored, and diced
2 red pears, peeled, cored, and diced
2 small Walla Walla onions, diced
2 shallots, diced
1½ teaspoons chopped fresh cilantro
2 tablespoons chopped fresh
    lemon mint leaves
1½ teaspoons salt

2 tablespoons clover honey
1 cup diced jicama
3 jalapeños, seeded, and finely diced
2 red bell peppers, seeded, and diced

CINNAMON CHIPS
Unsalted butter, room temperature
4 flour tortillas
    ½ teaspoon cinnamon
1½ tablespoons sugar substitute

1. To make salsa: Toss lime juice and zest and pears in a medium bowl.

2. Add onions, shallots, cilantro, lemon mint, salt, honey, jicama, jalapeños, and peppers. Mix well to combine. Chill for 2 to 4 hours.

3. To make cinnamon chips: Heat oven to 300°F. Lightly butter both sides of each flour tortilla. Stack the tortillas on a breadboard and cut into wedges.

4. Combine cinnamon and sugar substitute in a large zip-close bag. Working in batches, place the tortilla wedges in the bag, seal closed, and shake to coat. Arrange wedges on a rack set on a baking sheet. Bake until dry and crisp, 5 to 10 minutes.

Drop the pears into lime juice as soon as you dice them to prevent browning.

※ **KARL MAGNUSSON,** Salem, Oregon
First Place, Hood River Grower/Shipper Pear Dessert Contest, Oregon State Fair, Salem, Oregon, 2005

Mango Madness

4 large tomatoes
1 large onion
2 Anaheim bell peppers
3 jalapeños, seeded
½ cup chopped celery
¼ cup oil

2 tablespoons vinegar
1 teaspoon coriander, crushed
1 teaspoon mustard seed
1 teaspoon salt
1 mango, peeled and diced

1. Finely chop tomatoes, onion, bell peppers, jalapeños, and celery by hand or in a food processor; if using a food processor, chop each item separately.
2. In a large bowl, whisk together oil, vinegar, coriander, mustard seed, and salt. Add chopped vegetables and mango. Toss until well combined. Serve chilled. Makes 4 to 6 servings.

✕ **Kim Shimota,** Lakeville, Minnesota
Second Place, Salsa Contest, Dakota County Fair, Farmington, Minnesota, 2005

Mint Salsa

4 Roma tomatoes, seeded and chopped
¼ cup chopped green onions
⅓ cup chopped fresh mint leaves
1½ tablespoons fresh lime juice
1 jalapeño, seeded and chopped

¼ teaspoon salt
¼ teaspoon freshly ground pepper
1 small garlic clove, minced
1 teaspoon sugar

Combine all ingredients in a small bowl. Let stand at room temperature for 4 hours, to allow flavors to blend. Makes approximately 1 cup.

✕ **B. L. Ashworth,** Edmond, Oklahoma
Second Place, Salsa Contest, Oklahoma State Fair, Oklahoma City, Oklahoma, 2005

HIKE-AWAY-THE-BLUES TRAIL MIX

4 cups dry granola cereal
⅓ cup sunflower seeds
⅔ cup chocolate chips

⅓ cup mixed nuts
⅓ cup dried fruit bits
⅔ cup wild chews (dried wild blueberries)

1. Place granola cereal, sunflower seeds, chocolate chips, mixed nuts, fruit bits, and wild chews in a large bowl. Toss until well combined.
2. Divide mixture in half. Store in two 1-quart zip-close bags. Makes 6⅓ cups.

✄ **MATTHEW PLAISTED,** Jonesboro, Maine
First Prize, Wild Blueberry Festival Cooking Competition, Machias, Maine, 2002

PEMMICAN

Extra dry pieces of dried beef or
     buffalo jerky
Lard (do not use a substitute)
Berries

Honey
Crushed dried fruit
Chopped pine nuts

1. Cut jerky into small chunks. Chop in a food processor or pass through a meat grinder to make a fine powder.
2. Combine powdered meat, lard, berries, and honey in the proportions you desire.
3. Shape into balls. Roll balls in dried fruit or pine nuts to coat.

✄ **MARY OLD HORN OF THE CHEYENNE,** Red Lodge, Montana
First Place Public Favorite, Native American Cooking, Western Montana Fair, Missoula, Montana, 1982–1991

SALSA REYNOLDS

8 tomatoes
1 red onion
5 garlic cloves
1 yellow bell pepper, seeded
1 jalapeño, seeded
1 can (20 oz.) chopped pineapple

1 bunch cilantro, finely chopped
Juice of 1 lime
Salt
Cinnamon
Ground cumin
1 avocado

1. Finely chop tomatoes, onion, garlic, bell pepper, and jalapeño. Place in a medium bowl.
2. Add pineapple, cilantro, and lime juice. Toss until well combined. Season with salt, cinnamon, and cumin and toss again. Cover and refrigerate.
3. Just before serving, peel and dice avocado and add to salsa. Makes 3 to 3½ cups.

✄ **ROB AND BECKY REYNOLDS,** Sandy, Utah
First Place, Fresh Made Salsa Competition, Utah State Fair, Salt Lake City, Utah, 2005

Spicy Chunky Salsa

2 tablespoons olive oil

2 tablespoons fresh lemon juice

¼ cup sugar

2 garlic cloves, minced

3 medium tomatoes, diced

¼ cup diced onion

¼ cup chopped green bell peppers

2 hot chili peppers, diced

2 poblanos, diced

2 serranos, diced

2 habaneros, diced

3 jalapeños, diced (or to taste)

3 tomatillos, diced

2 Anaheim peppers, diced

2 yellow chiles, diced

2 teaspoons chopped fresh basil

2 teaspoons chopped fresh cilantro

1 medium ripe avocado

1. In a large bowl, whisk together olive oil, lemon juice, and sugar.
2. Add garlic, tomatoes, onion, bell peppers, chili peppers, poblanos, serranos, habaneros, jalapeños, tomatillos, Anaheim peppers, yellow chiles, basil, and cilantro. Toss to coat. Cover and refrigerate.
3. Just before serving, peel, seed, and dice avocado and add to salsa. Serve with chips. Makes 3½ cups.

✳ **Martha Buehring,** Norman, Oklahoma
First Place, Salsa Contest, Oklahoma State Fair, Oklahoma City, Oklahoma, 2005

Wear rubber gloves when handling hot peppers.

Salsa

5 lbs. ripe tomatoes

1 or 2 bell peppers

Jalapeños, seeded, white membrane removed (optional)

2 white Walla Walla onions

1 teaspoon salt

1 tablespoon ground cumin

2 cups tomato juice

2 tablespoons white vinegar

2 cups chili sauce

1 tablespoon Tabasco sauce

¼ teaspoon cayenne pepper

1 teaspoon lemon juice

1. Finely chop tomatoes, bell peppers, jalapeños, and onions by hand or in a food processor; if using a food processor, roughly chop each item separately before processing.
2. Place chopped vegetables in a large bowl. Add salt, cumin, tomato juice, vinegar, chili sauce, Tabasco sauce, cayenne, and lemon juice. Stir until well combined. Taste salsa and adjust seasonings. Makes 6 to 7 cups.

✳ **Leslie Marshall,** Sandpoint, Idaho
Blue Ribbon, Bonner County Fair, Sandpoint, Idaho, 2005

WINNER'S CIRCLE TIP | Vary the ratio of bell peppers and jalapeños, depending on how hot you like the salsa. If you double or triple a salsa recipe, do not increase the tomato juice by that amount. Just check the moisture of the salsa and add juice to achieve the consistency you prefer.

Sizzlin' Chipotle Salsa

6 cups seeded and diced tomatoes

2 cups diced onion

6 garlic cloves, minced

2 jalapeños, seeded and minced

½ teaspoon paprika

2 tablespoons cider vinegar

⅛ teaspoon cayenne pepper

1 tablespoon dried cilantro

1 tablespoon dried parsley flakes

2 to 3 tablespoons chipotle chiles in adobo sauce, minced

Salt

1. Combine tomatoes, onion, garlic, and jalapeños in large saucepan. Cook over medium-high heat, stirring often, for 10 minutes.

2. Stir in paprika, vinegar, cayenne, cilantro, parsley, and chipotle chiles. Cook another 10 minutes. Cool in pan. Transfer to clean jars, add a pinch of salt to each, and cover. Store in refrigerator. Makes 8 cups.

✕ **HOMER MYERS,** Lewisburg, West Virginia
First Place, Salsa Contest, State Fair of West Virginia, Lewisburg, West Virginia, 2005

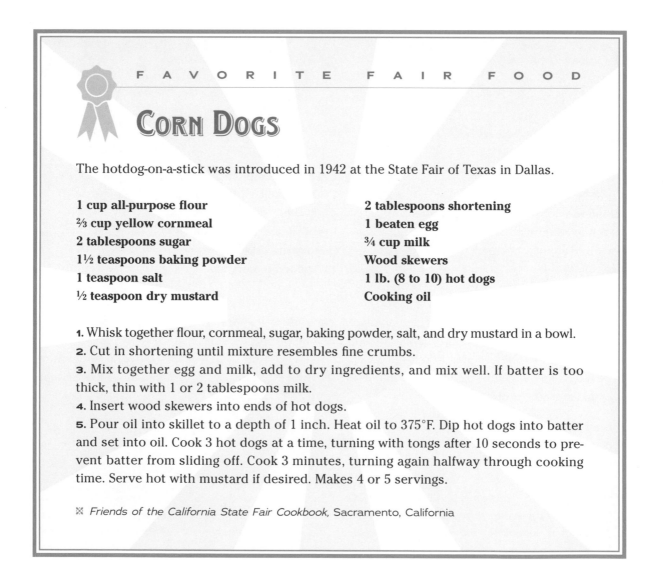

FAVORITE FAIR FOOD

Corn Dogs

The hotdog-on-a-stick was introduced in 1942 at the State Fair of Texas in Dallas.

1 cup all-purpose flour

⅔ cup yellow cornmeal

2 tablespoons sugar

1½ teaspoons baking powder

1 teaspoon salt

½ teaspoon dry mustard

2 tablespoons shortening

1 beaten egg

¾ cup milk

Wood skewers

1 lb. (8 to 10) hot dogs

Cooking oil

1. Whisk together flour, cornmeal, sugar, baking powder, salt, and dry mustard in a bowl.

2. Cut in shortening until mixture resembles fine crumbs.

3. Mix together egg and milk, add to dry ingredients, and mix well. If batter is too thick, thin with 1 or 2 tablespoons milk.

4. Insert wood skewers into ends of hot dogs.

5. Pour oil into skillet to a depth of 1 inch. Heat oil to 375°F. Dip hot dogs into batter and set into oil. Cook 3 hot dogs at a time, turning with tongs after 10 seconds to prevent batter from sliding off. Cook 3 minutes, turning again halfway through cooking time. Serve hot with mustard if desired. Makes 4 or 5 servings.

✕ *Friends of the California State Fair Cookbook*, Sacramento, California

Ol' John's Flame-Cooked Jalapeño-Cactus Salsa

⅓ cup safflower oil or vegetable oil

½ cup finely chopped jalapeños

1 lb. diced cactus

3 heaping tablespoons minced garlic

⅓ cup finely chopped carrot

½ cup finely chopped onion

½ cup finely chopped celery

¼ cup finely chopped cilantro (for that Mexican taste)

3 heaping teaspoons dried red chiles (for hotter taste)

2 cups diced tomatoes

¼ cup rice vinegar

4 cups tomato sauce

1. Combine oil, jalapeños, cactus, garlic, and carrot in a large pot. Simmer over a low flame until carrots are tender.

2. Add onion, celery, cilantro, and chiles. Simmer until onion is clear.

3. Add tomatoes, rice vinegar, and tomato sauce. Simmer until sauce thickens. Makes 8 to 10 cups.

✕ **JOHN J. ELLIS, JR.,** Rowland Heights, California
First Place, Hot Salsa, L.A. County Fair, Pomona, California, 2003

Bean and Corn Salsa

1 cup corn kernels

1 can (15.5 oz.) black beans,
  drained and rinsed

1 cup seeded, chopped tomatoes

½ cup chopped green onions

2 or 3 serranos, minced

2 tablespoons chopped fresh cilantro

3 tablespoons oil

2 tablespoons lemon juice

1 teaspoon ground cumin

½ teaspoon salt

½ teaspoon pepper

Splash of triple sec (optional)

1. Combine corn, black beans, tomatoes, onion, serranos, and cilantro in a medium bowl.

2. Place oil, lemon juice, cumin, salt, pepper, and triple sec in a glass jar. Cover tightly and shake to combine.

3. Pour dressing over salsa and toss until well combined. Cover and refrigerate overnight, to allow flavors to blend. Serve with chips, on toasted pita bread, or as a dip with fresh vegetables. Makes 4 to 6 servings.

✕ **ANN TURLEY,** Walnut, California
First Place, Vegetable Salsa, L.A. County Fair, Pomona, California, 2003

This recipe can be easily doubled to make a good side dish for barbecued chicken.

CRANBERRY SALSA

1 can (14 oz.) whole cranberries
1 can (8 oz.) crushed pineapple, drained
½ cup finely chopped green bell pepper
2 tablespoons finely chopped onion

2 jalapeños, seeded and chopped
¼ teaspoon salt
¼ cup chopped fresh cilantro
¼ teaspoon cinnamon

1. In a large bowl, toss cranberries, pineapple, green bell pepper, onion, jalapeños, salt, cilantro, and cinnamon until well combined.
2. Cover and chill for 2 hours to let flavors blend. Serve with chips or your favorite meat. Makes about 3 cups.

✂ **DANA PALMER,** Warr Acres, Oklahoma
Third Place, Salsa Contest, Oklahoma State Fair, Oklahoma City, Oklahoma, 2005

WINNER'S CIRCLE TIP | When cranberries are in season, substitute 12 oz. fresh cranberries for the canned. Chop the cranberries and add ⅔ cup sugar.

JALAPEÑO-CILANTRO HUMMUS

2 cans (15.5 oz. each) garbanzo beans
¼ cup sesame tahini
¼ cup fresh lemon juice
1 tablespoon tamari (aged soy sauce)
2 teaspoons ground cumin

1 teaspoon coriander
4 garlic cloves
2 or 3 jalapeños
½ bunch cilantro

1. Drain garbanzo beans, reserving ¾ cup of the liquid.
2. Place beans, reserved liquid, tahini, lemon juice, tamari, cumin, coriander, and garlic in a food processor. Combine until smooth.
3. Add jalapeños and cilantro and combine just until evenly distributed. Chill before serving. Serve with chips, crackers, pita bread, or vegetables. Makes about 2½ cups.

✂ **TARA WELLS,** Santee, California
First Place, Healthy Eating Contest—Ethnic Dishes, San Diego County Fair, Del Mar, California, 2004

DILLED SMOKED SALMON SPREAD

YOGURT CHEESE
2 cups nonfat plain yogurt

SPREAD
1 cup yogurt cheese
2 tablespoons minced fresh dill

1 teaspoon fresh minced chives
2 garlic cloves, crushed through a press
1 teaspoon fresh lemon juice
2 oz. smoked salmon, flaked
⅛ teaspoon seasoned salt
⅛ teaspoon white pepper

1. To make yogurt cheese: Line a large sieve with a double thickness of cheesecloth. Set the sieve over a large bowl. Spoon yogurt into the sieve, cover with plastic wrap, and place in refrigerator. Allow to drain at least 8 hours, but preferably overnight.

2. The next day, discard the liquid whey. Scrape the yogurt cheese, which will be very thick, from the sieve into a bowl. Cover and refrigerate until ready use, up to 2 weeks.

3. To make the spread: In a medium bowl, combine yogurt cheese, dill, chives, garlic, lemon juice, salmon, salt, and pepper. Mix well, cover, and refrigerate at least 2 hours to allow flavors to mellow. Serve as a spread or a dip with bagel chips, crackers, or vegetables. Makes 6 to 8 appetizer servings.

※ **BARBARA WHEELER,** Royal Oak, Michigan
First Place, Healthy Cooking Contest, Michigan State Fair, Detroit, Michigan, 2001

FAVORITE FAIR FOOD

SOFT PRETZELS

1½ teaspoons active dry yeast
½ teaspoon brown sugar
Dash of salt
1½ cups warm water, 110°F
4 cups bread flour

1 teaspoon baking soda
4 teaspoons warm water
1 cup unsalted butter, melted
Toppings (recipes follow)

1. In a large bowl, combine yeast, brown sugar, salt, and warm water. Let sit for 5 minutes.

2. Add flour to yeast mixture and stir. Turn out dough onto a lightly floured work surface and knead for 5 minutes. Place dough in a lightly greased bowl and turn once to coat. Cover with a damp towel and allow to rise in a warm place, 1 hour.

3. Divide dough into 8 to 12 equal-size pieces. Roll each piece into a rope. Shape each rope into a pretzel.

4. Stir baking soda into warm water. Submerge pretzels into mixture, one by one, and place on a lightly greased baking sheet. Bake in a preheated 550°F oven for 8 minutes, or until golden brown. Brush melted butter onto hot pretzels.

※ *Friends of the California State Fair Cookbook,* Sacramento, California

WINNER'S CIRCLE TIPS

To make Salted Pretzels, sprinkle coarse salt or kosher salt onto pretzels before baking.
To make Cinnamon-Sugar Pretzels, stir 2 tablespoons honey into melted butter and brush onto pretzels. Sprinkle pretzels with a mixture of ½ cup sugar and 1 teaspoon ground cinnamon.
To make Parmesan Pretzels, sprinkle pretzels with a mixture of ¼ cup grated Parmesan and 1 teaspoon garlic salt. Serve with marinara sauce.

Tzadziki (Cucumber Yogurt Dip)

16 oz. nonfat plain yogurt

1 large cucumber

2 garlic cloves, minced

1 tablespoon olive oil

1 tablespoon white wine vinegar

½ teaspoon chopped fresh dill

1. Line a strainer with cheesecloth or a coffee filter. Set the strainer over a bowl. Spoon yogurt into the strainer, cover with waxed paper, and allow to drain for 2 hours.

2. Peel, seed, and grate cucumber. Drain on paper towels.

3. Combine yogurt, cucumber, garlic, olive oil, white wine vinegar, and dill until well blended. Chill at least 1 hour before serving. Serve with veggies, pita bread, or as a sauce for meat. Makes 2½ cups.

✄ **LENI TIGNOR,** Escondido, California

First Place, Healthy Eating Contest—Snacks, San Diego County Fair, Del Mar, California, 2004

Chopped Liver

1 lb. chicken livers

¼ cup rendered chicken fat

3 medium onions, sliced

1 teaspoon salt

1 teaspoon pepper

1 teaspoon garlic powder

6 to 8 hard-boiled eggs, chopped

1. Rinse chicken livers and drain.

2. Heat chicken fat in a sauté pan over medium-high heat. Add onions and cook until lightly browned. Remove onions and set aside.

3. Add chicken livers to pan and sauté, tossing lightly until they lose their red color. Reduce heat and continue cooking for 10 minutes. Do not overcook. Remove from heat. Stir in salt, pepper, and garlic powder.

4. Stir together livers, onions, and eggs. Pass mixture through a food grinder fitted with a fine blade. Transfer to a storage container and refrigerate until ready to serve. Serve on a lettuce leaf as an appetizer or as a spread on crackers or rye bread. Makes 2 cups.

✄ **RUTH CANTY AND PHOEBE GOLD,** Butte, Montana

First Place Public Favorite, Jewish Holiday, Western Montana Fair, Missoula, Montana, 2004

CHAPTER 3

※

SOUPS
AND
SANDWICHES

BERRY SOUP

2 cups fresh or frozen blueberries
   or huckleberries
Water

2 tablespoons cornstarch
¼ cup honey or sugar

1. Place berries in a 4-cup measuring cup. Add water until berries plus liquid measures 4 cups.

2. Transfer berries and liquid to a saucepan. Bring to a boil and then reduce to a simmer.

3. Combine cornstarch and honey or sugar in a small bowl. Ladle some of the hot berry liquid into the bowl and stir to form a smooth paste.

4. Slowly add the paste to the simmering berry mixture and stir to combine. Continue simmering another 5 to 6 minutes. Serve hot with fry bread. Makes 4 1-cup servings.

✄ **SALISH KOOTENAI COLLEGE STUDENTS,** Pablo, Montana
First Place, Public Favorite, Native American Cooking

CAROL'S POSOLE

5 quarts chicken broth
32 oz. posole (uncooked hominy)
1½ lbs. lean pork, cut into bite-size cubes
1½ lbs. lean beef, cut into bite-size cubes
2 cups diced onion

4 garlic cloves
1 package (7 oz.) frozen chopped
   mild green chiles
1 tablespoon oregano

1. Place chicken broth, posole, pork, and beef in a 12-quart stockpot. Bring to a boil, reduce heat to a simmer, and simmer 1 hour.

2. Add onion, garlic, chiles, and oregano. Simmer until posole is tender, up to 2 hours more. Add water if mixture becomes too thick. Serve with flour tortillas, if desired.

✄ **CAROL SCHILLING,** Albuquerque, New Mexico
First Place, New Mexico State Fair, Albuquerque, New Mexico, 2005

✦ POSOLE ✦

For centuries New Mexicans have enjoyed posole, a spicy soup or stew indigenous to the Native American southwest. It is a staple winter dish among the Pueblo people. Eating posole is traditional around Thanksgiving and Christmas time, and it is often served on New Year's Eve or Day for good luck.

Potato Soup (Pat's Style)

8 slices bacon, cut into small pieces

2 cups diced yellow onion

1 cup chopped green bell pepper

3 garlic cloves, crushed

½ cup unsalted butter, room temperature

Salt and pepper

1 cup mild picante sauce

6 to 8 cups cubed potatoes

5 or 6 cans (9 oz. each) chicken broth

1 lb. yellow processed cheese, cubed

1. Cook bacon in the bottom of a stockpot until crisp. Add onion, green pepper, garlic, and butter. Sauté until onion is soft and golden, 5 to 6 minutes. Sprinkle with salt and pepper.

2. Add picante sauce, potatoes, and chicken broth. Stir to combine. Cook over medium heat until potatoes are soft, 35 to 45 minutes.

3. Add cheese cubes, stirring until cheese is melted and blended in. Makes 4 to 5 quarts.

✳ **PAT PATTERSON,** Tulsa, Oklahoma
Honorable Mention, Tulsa State Fair, Tulsa, Oklahoma, 1998

Green Chile Whiskey Stew

2 to 3 lbs. stewing beef

4 fresh roasted green chiles, divided

Honey

Jack Daniels whiskey

1 beef stew cube

3 cups boiling water

Pinch of dried cilantro

½ teaspoon ground ginger

1 cup baby carrots

2 red potatoes

2 white potatoes

½ cup red pearl onions, peeled

½ cup white pearl onions, peeled

1 can (14.5 oz.) green beans

2 yams

½ cup mushrooms

1. Two days before serving, place stewing beef and 2 of the chiles in the ceramic liner of an electric slow cooker liner. (If your slow cooker doesn't have a lift-out ceramic liner, use a large glass or stainless steel bowl for the marinating steps.) Drizzle with honey and pour in enough Jack Daniels whiskey to cover. Cover with plastic wrap, place in the refrigerator, and allow to marinate overnight.

2. The next morning, dissolve stew cube in boiling water and let cool. Add stew broth, cilantro, ginger, baby carrots, red potatoes, and white potatoes to ceramic liner. Add a splash of Jack Daniels. Cover with plastic wrap and return to the refrigerator.

3. In the evening, add red pearl onions, white pearl onions, green beans, yams, and remaining 2 chiles. Drizzle generously with honey. Place liner in electric crock pot, cover, and slow-cook overnight on low setting.

4. The next morning, lift cover and add mushrooms. Replace cover and continue cooking. The stew should be ready by lunchtime. Store leftover stew in the refrigerator. Makes 8 to 12 servings.

✳ **JONATHAN MAPLE,** Albuquerque, New Mexico
Third Place, New Mexico State Fair, Albuquerque, New Mexico, 2005

PAUL'S THICK CREAM CHILE SOUP

1 whole cooked rotisserie chicken
   (from the supermarket)
3 cups water
1 package (8 oz.) cream cheese

1 pint half-and-half
1 package (14 oz.) frozen green chiles, thawed
Salt and pepper

1. Remove all meat from chicken and shred or cut into bite-size pieces.

2. Combine water, cream cheese, half-and-half, and green chiles in a large saucepan. Cook over low heat, stirring continuously until mixture is smooth and creamy. Take care that liquid does not scald or burn.

3. Stir in chicken and simmer, stirring often, until flavors are combined and chicken is warmed through, 15 to 20 minutes. Season with salt and pepper to taste. Makes 4 to 6 servings.

✂ **PAUL WEILER,** Sandia Park, New Mexico
Second Place, New Mexico State Fair, Albuquerque, New Mexico, 2005

OLD-FASHIONED CREAM OF TOMATO SOUP

2 cans (32 oz. each) diced tomatoes
1 can (9 oz.) chicken broth
2 tablespoons unsalted butter
2 tablespoons chopped onion

Pinch of baking soda
2 tablespoons sugar
2 cups heavy cream

1. Combine tomatoes, chicken broth, butter, onion, baking soda, and sugar in a large saucepan over medium-high heat. Heat just until bubbling, then reduce heat and simmer for 1 hour.

2. Heat the heavy cream in the top half of a double boiler until warm. Add cream to hot tomato mixture and stir to combine. Makes about 2 quarts.

✂ **4-B's RESTAURANT,** Missoula, Montana
First Place, One Dish Meals, Western Montana Fair, Missoula, Montana, 1998

Tomato Florentine Soup

1 tablespoon olive oil

1 cup chopped onion

5 garlic cloves, chopped

5 cups vegetable stock, divided

1½ teaspoons oregano

1½ teaspoons dried tarragon

1½ teaspoons dried basil

½ teaspoon black pepper

¼ cup red wine

1 can (28 oz.) chopped tomatoes, drained

1 can (6 oz.) tomato paste

2 packages (9 oz. each) frozen spinach (do not thaw)

1 tablespoon balsamic vinegar

2 tablespoons Parmesan

1. Heat olive oil in the bottom of a stockpot over medium heat. Add onion and garlic and sauté until onion is soft and golden.

2. Add ½ cup of the stock. Stir in oregano, tarragon, basil, pepper, and red wine and bring to a simmer.

3. Add remaining 4½ cups stock, tomatoes, tomato paste, and spinach. Bring to a boil and then reduce to a simmer. Simmer until spinach is cooked through and flavors are blended, 25 to 30 minutes.

4. Stir in balsamic vinegar. Serve hot, garnished with Parmesan. Makes 2½ to 3 quarts.

✄ **JESSIE MARTIN,** Jamaica Plain, Massachusetts
Second Place, Hot Soups, Topsfield Fair, Topsfield, Massachusetts, 2002

Fiesta Mexican Soup

1 lb. lean ground beef

1 large onion, chopped

1 can (11¼ oz.) chili beef with beans soup

1 can (10¾ oz.) cheddar cheese
   condensed soup

2 cans (14.5 oz. each) diced tomatoes,
   not drained

2 cans (10 oz. each) diced tomatoes
   and chiles

1 can (16 oz.) refried beans

1 can (16 oz.) kidney beans, drained

1 can (15.5 oz.) yellow hominy, drained

2 cans (11.5 oz. each) tomato juice

2 tablespoons chipotle pepper sauce

1. Brown ground beef and onion in a skillet. Drain off fat.

2. Transfer cooked beef and onion to a Dutch oven over medium-high heat. Add beef with beans soup, cheddar cheese condensed soup, diced tomatoes and chiles, refried beans, kidney beans, hominy, tomato juice, and chipotle pepper sauce. Stir to combine.

3. When mixture begins to boil, reduce heat and simmer, stirring occasionally, 1 hour. Reduce heat or add water if necessary to prevent scorching. If soup becomes too thick, add water to acheive the desired consistency. If desired, serve garnished with grated cheese, sour cream, or chopped green onions and accompanied with cornbread. Makes 8 to 10 servings.

✄ **CAROLYN WALLACE,** Yukon, Oklahoma
Sixth Place, Mexican Contest, Oklahoma State Fair, Oklahoma City, Oklahoma, 2005

The San Diego County Fair

Tall tales and fantastic stories have been associated with the San Diego County Fair in Del Mar, California, since the first fair was held in 1936. More than just a little rain fell during that 1936 fair; on the second day it rained for five hours and people actually arrived in rowboats. So the frequency of rainy days at the fall fair was a consideration when the decision was made to move the fair dates to June and July of each year.

One year at the fair in San Diego, a Hollywood stunt man was hired to ride a motorcycle through a 40-foot-long burning building twice daily. On the fifth day of the fair, he caught fire and promptly quit.

Light and Healthy Ratatouille Soup

3 tablespoons extra virgin olive oil, divided
1 eggplant, peeled and chopped
1 large onion, coarsely chopped
1 large red bell pepper, chopped
1 medium zucchini, chopped
3 large garlic cloves, minced
1 can (14.5 oz.) diced tomatoes, drained
2 teaspoons dried thyme
¾ cup low-sodium chicken broth
¼ cup lowfat plain yogurt, plus more for garnish
Freshly ground black pepper
Chopped chives, for garnish

1. Heat 2 tablespoons of the olive oil in a large, heavy, deep skillet over medium heat. Add eggplant, onion, bell pepper, zucchini, and garlic. Cook, stirring occasionally, until vegetables begin to soften, 15 minutes.
2. Add remaining tablespoon olive oil, tomatoes, and thyme. Reduce heat to medium-low. Cover and cook, stirring occasionally, until vegetables are very tender, 20 minutes.
3. Working in batches, puree the vegetable mixture with chicken broth in a blender. Transfer to a tureen. Stir in yogurt. Add pepper to taste. To serve, ladle soup into bowls and top with yogurt and chives. Makes 4 servings.

Mike Schaude, Escondido, California
Fourth Place, Healthy Eating Contest—Ethnic Dishes, San Diego County Fair, Del Mar, California, 2004

BBQ Chicken Club Wrap

1 boneless chicken breast
Barbecue sauce
4 slices bacon, cooked
Shredded Monterey Jack
4 plain tortillas
Ranch dressing
Shredded lettuce
Diced tomatoes

1. Grill the chicken breast, basting with barbecue sauce, until browned and tender.
2. Slice the chicken breast into 4 pieces. Arrange the slices on a plate, spread barbecue sauce over the top, and top each with bacon and cheese. Microwave 1 minute on high, or until cheese is melted.

3. To assemble wraps: Place each tortilla on a plate, spread with ranch dressing, and add a slice of the chicken. Top with shredded lettuce and diced tomato. Fold in the sides of the wrap to make a roll. Makes 4 sandwich wraps.

⚹ **CAROLINE LAPRISE,** age 9, Saunderstown, Rhode Island
Blue Ribbon, 4-H Favorite Foods Fair, West Greenwich, Rhode Island, 2005

SALMON SALAD SANDWICH WITH AÏOLI

AÏOLI
¼ cup mayonnaise
3 garlic cloves
2 tablespoons chopped fresh dill
2 teaspoons onion powder

1 cup cooked, flaked salmon
2 tablespoons chopped green bell pepper
Romaine leaves
1 tomato, sliced
Sandwich bun

1. To make aïoli: Combine mayonnaise, garlic, dill, and onion powder in a food processor until smooth.
2. Pour aïoli into a bowl, add salmon and green pepper, and mix to combine.
3. To assemble sandwich: Layer lettuce and tomato on bottom half of sandwich bun. Spoon on the salmon salad. Top with the other half of the bun and serve. Makes 1 sandwich.

⚹ **SALLY SIBTHORPE,** Rochester Hills, Michigan
Third Place, Winners Cook-Off Challenge "Sandwich," Michigan State Fair, Detroit, Michigan, 2000

ANNIE'S SUMMER CHICKEN SALAD SANDWICH

CHICKEN SALAD
2 cups diced poached chicken breast
2 teaspoons white wine
4 teaspoons diced celery hearts
2 teaspoons sliced watercress
2 teaspoons fresh rosemary leaves
4 teaspoons diced water chestnuts
1 teaspoon lemon juice

1 cup mayonnaise
Salt and pepper

FOR SANDWICH
Sandwich bread
Shredded lettuce
Chopped chives
Chopped rosemary

1. Place chicken in a glass bowl, sprinkle with white wine, and toss to combine. Let marinate 5 minutes.
2. Add celery hearts, watercress, rosemary, and water chestnuts to chicken. Toss to combine.
3. Stir lemon juice into mayonnaise. Season with salt and pepper. Pour dressing over chicken mixture and toss to combine. Store in refrigerator until ready to serve.
4. To make sandwiches, put desired amount of salad on bread. Garnish with lettuce, chives, and rosemary. Makes 4 to 6 sandwiches.

⚹ **CINDY REDLAWSKI,** Grosse Pointe, Michigan
Second Place, Winners Cook-Off Challenge "Sandwich," Michigan State Fair, Detroit, Michigan, 2000

GAMEDAY SANDWICH ROUND

1 1-lb. round loaf white bread

½ cup mayonnaise or salad dressing

2½ teaspoons dried Italian seasoning

1 teaspoon black pepper

2 tablespoons olive oil

1 large onion, thinly sliced

2 medium green or sweet peppers, cut into strips

1 lb. thinly sliced cooked ham

1½ cups cheddar/pepperjack cheese blend,
   shredded

1. Slice off the top third of bread loaf and set it aside. Hollow out the bottom section with your fingers, leaving a ½-inch shell. Crumbs can be reserved for another use.

2. Combine mayonnaise, Italian seasoning, and pepper. Brush inside of bread shell with half of mixture. Set shell and remaining mixture aside.

3. Heat olive oil in a large skillet over medium-high heat. Add onion and peppers and cook, stirring often, until tender.

4. Arrange half of ham slices in bread shell. Top half of vegetable mixture and sprinkle with half of cheese. Spread remaining mayonnaise mixture over cheese. Add remaining vegetable mixture, ham slices, and cheese. Replace top of bread. If desired, paint a school emblem or school logo on the top of the sandwich using a mixture of egg yolk and food coloring.

5. Wrap sandwich in heavy-duty aluminum foil. Bake at 400°F until heated through, about 30 minutes. Cut into wedges to serve. Makes 6 to 8 wedges.

GAIL FULLER, Raleigh, North Carolina
First Place, N.C. The National Pork Board, We Want Wow Now Pork Recipe Rally, North Carolina State Fair, Raleigh, North Carolina, 2005

GRILLED PORK SANDWICHES WITH SAUTÉED ONIONS

1 large white onion

2 tablespoons olive oil

1 tablespoon Worcestershire sauce

2 garlic cloves, minced

8 slices of French bread

4 slices provolone

1 lb. barbecue pork loin, cooked and shredded

⅓ cup mayonnaise

3 tablespoons unsalted butter,
   room temperature

1. Cut onion into very thin slices and separate into rings.

2. Heat olive oil and Worcestershire sauce in a large skillet over medium heat. Add onion and garlic and sauté until tender, 5 minutes. Remove from heat.

3. To assemble sandwiches: Lay out 8 bread slices. On each of 4 slices, layer 1 slice of provolone cheese, one-fourth of the shredded pork loin, and one-fourth of the onions. Spread mayonnaise on the other four bread slices and close the sandwiches.

4. Lightly butter both sides of each sandwich. Grill each sandwich until golden brown, 4 to 5 minutes. Cut sandwiches in half, if desired, and serve with a side of slaw and a pickle spear. Makes 4 sandwiches.

SHARON GATES, Leicester, North Carolina
Third Place, Tarheel Pork Challenge, North Carolina Mountain State Fair, Fletcher, North Carolina, 2005

CHAPTER 4

✦

SALADS, DRESSINGS, AND SAUCES

Quick and Easy "Maque Choux" Salad

1 cup homemade or purchased corn relish
⅓ cup mayonnaise
1 tablespoon minced fresh flat-leaf parsley
¼ cup diced orange and green bell pepper

¼ cup diced onion
¼ cup sliced celery
¼ cup diced tomato
Romaine leaves

1. Combine corn relish, mayonnaise, and parsley in a medium bowl.
2. Add bell pepper, onion, celery, and tomato to corn mixture. Toss gently to combine.
3. Serve arranged on lettuce leaves. Garnish with parsley, if desired. Makes 2 to 4 servings.

✂ **NORITA SOLT,** Bettendorf, Iowa
First Place, Corn Salad Contest, Second Place, Cooking with Fresh Corn, Iowa State Fair, Des Moines, Iowa, 2005

Garlic, Basil, and Rosemary Vinegar

3 quarts red wine vinegar
3 cups whole fresh basil stalks

10 garlic cloves
2 stalks fresh rosemary

1. Place red wine vinegar in a stockpot. Cook over high heat until bubbles begin to form around the edges.
2. Wash basil and place in a 1-gallon crock. Add garlic and pour in vinegar. Wash rosemary stalks and stand upright in crock and seal the lid. Set crock aside, out of direct sunlight, and cure for 1 month.
3. Pour cured vinegar through a strainer to remove basil, garlic, and rosemary. Transfer to sterilized bottles. Makes about 3½ quarts.

✂ **PAT MINNICH,** El Cajon, California
First Place, San Diego County Fair, Del Mar, California, 2004

Cooked Cranberry Sauce

2 pounds cranberries, fresh or frozen
2 fresh pears, cored and diced
2 fresh apples, cored and diced
2 cups sugar

1 cup orange juice
2 teaspoons cinnamon
⅓ teaspoon nutmeg
⅓ cup brandy or wine (optional)

Combine cranberries, pears, apples, sugar, orange juice, cinnamon, and nutmeg in a large saucepan over medium-high heat. Bring to a boil, reduce heat, and simmer until cranberries pop and pears and apples soften, 12 minutes. Add brandy or wine, if using. Makes 4 to 5 cups.

✂ **MARIAN S. WERTH,** Madison, Wisconsin
Honorable Mention, Fresh Division, Warrens Cranberry Festival, Warrens, Wisconsin, 1999

☙ THE IOWA STATE FAIR ❧

The internationally acclaimed Iowa State Fair in Des Moines, Iowa, is the single largest event in the state of Iowa and one of the oldest and largest agricultural and industrial expositions in the country. The inspiration for the original novel *State Fair* by Iowan Phil Stong, three motion pictures, and Rodgers and Hammerstein's Broadway musical, it is billed as "America's Classic State Fair" because it features all of the traditional events expected of a state fair, from farm machinery and food exhibits to grandstand shows and competitive events. Approximately 85,000 ribbons (including 30,000 blue ribbons), rosettes, and banners are awarded annually to winners.

More than twenty types of food can be purchased "on-a-stick" at the Iowa State Fair. The list includes pork chops, dill pickles, corn dogs, cheese, Cajun chicken, caramel apples, chili dogs, beef, cotton candy, veggie corn dogs, turkey drumsticks, nutty bars, chocolate cheesecake, hot bologna, chocolate-covered bananas, taffy, fried pickles, honey, wonder bars, deep-fried Twinkies, meatballs, Ho-Hos, and fudge puppies (waffles drenched in chocolate sauce).

GREEK SALAD DRESSING

½ cup salad oil

2 tablespoons vinegar

1 egg

1 oz. anchovy fillets, drained

1 celery stalk, chopped

¼ small onion, chopped

1 medium carrot, chopped

3 radishes, chopped

1 teaspoon capers, drained

1 small garlic clove, crushed

1½ tablespoons sugar

½ teaspoon dried oregano

½ teaspoon paprika

¼ teaspoon salt

Dash of black pepper

1. Combine all ingredients in a blender container.

2. Cover and blend on low until smooth, about 2 minutes. Makes 1 to 1½ cups.

✄ **MARIA CARKULIS,** Missoula, Montana
First Place, America—The Melting Pot, Western Montana Fair, Missoula, Montana, 2004

WINNER'S CIRCLE TIP | Serve Greek Salad Dressing over a tossed salad of lettuce greens, crumbled feta, cauliflower florets, tomato wedges, Kalamata olives, and anchovy fillets.

Roasted Chicken Salad with Honey Pecan-Balsamic Dressing

8 oz. roasted chicken

1 bag (16 oz.) mixed salad greens
(iceberg lettuce, romaine,
carrots, red cabbage)

2 Granny Smith apples

Honey Pecan Balsamic Dressing
(recipe follows)

Glazed Pecans (recipe follows)

1. Remove skin from chicken. Tear chicken meat into bite-size pieces.

2. Divide chicken and salad greens into equal portions and place on individual plates.

3. Slice apples into small wedges and arrange on top of each salad.

4. Drizzle Honey Pecan Balsamic Dressing on salads and garnish with Glazed Pecans. Makes 3 or 4 servings.

Honey Pecan-Balsamic Dressing

¼ cup chopped pecans

4 teaspoons balsamic vinegar

½ cup olive oil

½ cup honey

½ teaspoon garlic powder

½ teaspoon onion powder

1 teaspoon maple syrup

½ teaspoon Dijon mustard

1. Spread pecans on a toaster oven tray. Bake at 300°F until lightly toasted, 10 minutes.

2. Place balsamic vinegar, olive oil, and honey in a small bowl and whisk to combine. Add garlic powder, onion powder, maple syrup, and mustard one at a time, whisking well after each addition. Whisk in toasted pecans. Makes 1¼ cups.

Glazed Pecans

¾ cup confectioners' sugar

2 tablespoons water

⅛ teaspoon maple syrup

1 cup pecans

1. Preheat oven to 300°F.

2. Combine confectioners' sugar, water, and maple syrup in a small bowl. Add pecans, tossing to coat.

3. Spread pecans on a baking sheet. Bake in oven until lightly toasted, 10 minutes. Allow pecans to cool on baking sheet to set the glaze. Makes 1 cup.

DENISE WALKER, Cary, North Carolina
First Place, N.C. Pecan Association's Pecan Recipe Competition, North Carolina State Fair, Raleigh, North Carolina, 2005

PINEAPPLE CHICKEN SALAD

½ cup mayonnaise or salad dressing

2 teaspoons mustard

2 cups shredded cooked chicken

½ cup thinly sliced celery

1 tablespoon finely chopped onion

½ cup sliced fresh mushrooms

¼ cup chopped green bell pepper

¼ cup sliced ripe olives

Lettuce leaves

1 can (20 oz.) pineapple chunks or tidbits, drained

1 can (11 oz.) mandarin orange sections, drained

Croutons

1. Combine mayonnaise and mustard in a medium bowl. Stir in chicken, celery, onion, mushrooms, green pepper, and olives. Cover and refrigerate for several hours.

2. To serve, arrange lettuce leaves on plates. Add pineapple and mandarin orange pieces to chicken salad and toss gently to combine. Spoon salad onto lettuce and top with croutons. Makes 6 servings.

✕ **FAYE SPAFFORD,** Tulsa Oklahoma
Honorable Mention, Tulsa State Fair, Tulsa, Oklahoma, 1998

WINNER'S CIRCLE TIP | For a well-chilled salad, drain the canned fruit pieces one day ahead and refrigerate them overnight.

PEPPERY CHICKEN PASTA SALAD

3 cups bow-tie pasta

2 cups green beans, cut into 1-inch pieces

2 cups skinless, boneless breast meat
    from a rotisserie-cooked chicken

⅔ cup celery, cut diagonally into
    ½-inch-thick slices

1 red bell pepper, seeded and chopped

½ small red onion, thinly sliced

DRESSING

2 tablespoons water

3 tablespoons light mayonnaise

4 teaspoons fresh lemon juice

4 teaspoons commercial pesto

½ teaspoon black pepper

¼ teaspoon salt

1. Cook pasta in boiling water, following package directions for al dente, about 11 minutes. Add green beans during final 5 minutes of cooking. Drain and rinse under cold running water.

2. Place pasta and beans, chicken, celery, pepper, and onion in a large bowl. Toss gently to combine.

3. To make dressing: Combine water, light mayonnaise, lemon juice, pesto, pepper, and salt in a small bowl. Stir with a fork to combine. Drizzle dressing over pasta salad and toss gently to coat. Makes 6 servings.

✕ **TULIE TREJO,** Chula Vista, California
Sweepstakes Winner, Lotsa Pasta Contest—Salads, San Diego County Fair, Del Mar, California, 2004

MIXED GREENS SALAD

DRESSING

½ cup olive oil

¼ cup raspberry vinegar

½ cup sugar

1 teaspoon Worcestershire sauce

1 teaspoon poppy seeds

1 teaspoon sesame seeds

SALAD

16 oz. mixed salad greens, such as
red leaf, endive, and spinach

Red onion slices

1 cup sliced strawberries

½ cup walnut pieces

1. To make dressing: Mix together olive oil, raspberry vinegar, sugar, Worcestershire sauce, poppy seeds, and sesame seeds.

2. Wash and prepare salad greens. Toss with red onion slices.

3. Divide salad greens evenly among serving plates. Pour dressing over salad. Sprinkle strawberries and walnuts over salad. Makes 4 to 6 servings.

✂ **PAULINE RYE,** Titus, Alabama
Prize Winner, Alabama National Fair, Montgomery, Alabama, 1998–2000

BASIC RED CHILE SAUCE

10 dried red chile pods,
seeds and stems removed

2 cups warm water

½ teaspoon sea salt

1 teaspoon mesquite honey

1. Soak chile pods in warm water for 1 hour.

2. Remove 3 pods from water with tongs. Toast over an open flame until slightly charred. Return pods to soaking water.

3. Pour soaking water and chiles into a blender. Puree for 1 to 2 minutes. Pour purée into a saucepan. Cook over low heat to desired consistency, thinning with water if necessary. Stir in sea salt and honey. Makes 2 cups.

✂ **ANDREA FEUCHT,** Cedar Crest, New Mexico
First Place, New Mexico State Fair,
Albuquerque, New Mexico, 2005

CORN BREAD SALAD

DRESSING

½ cup mayonnaise
½ cup hot 'n' spicy mayonnaise
1 cup sour cream
1 envelope (1 oz.) ranch dressing mix

LAYERS

8-inch pan of baked corn bread, crumbled
2 cans (11 oz. each) corn, drained
2 cans (15 oz. each) black beans, rinsed and drained
1 green bell pepper, seeded and diced
2 cups fresh tomatoes, seeded and chopped
8 oz. shredded Mexican-flavored cheese
⅔ cup crumbled cooked bacon
6 green onions, white and green parts, chopped

1. To make the dressing: Stir together plain mayonnaise, hot 'n' spicy mayonnaise, sour cream, and ranch dressing mix until well combined.

2. To assemble the layers: Layer one-third of the crumbled corn bread in the bottom of a large bowl. Add one-third each of the corn, black beans, green bell pepper, tomatoes, dressing, cheese, bacon, and green onion. Repeat the layering process two more times, until all the ingredients are used. Makes 8 to 10 servings.

✕ **CHERYL ROGERS,** Ames, Iowa
First Place, Perfect Potluck Pleasures, Iowa State Fair, Des Moines, Iowa, 2005

WALDORF CHICKEN PASTA SALAD

DRESSING

1 container (8 oz.) lemon yogurt
2 teaspoons honey
1 cup fat-free sour cream
1 teaspoon lemon zest
Salt and pepper

SALAD

1 lb. rotini
1 cup chopped celery
2 tablespoons chopped parsley
3 cups chopped red and yellow apples
4 cooked boneless chicken breasts,
    cut into bite-size pieces
¼ cup sliced green onion
⅓ cup toasted walnuts

1. To make dressing: Combine yogurt, honey, sour cream, and lemon zest. Add salt and pepper to taste. Chill until ready to use.

2. Cook rotini in boiling water, following package directions. Drain, rinse, and cool.

3. Place rotini, celery, parsley, apples, chicken, green onion, and walnuts in a large bowl. Pour dressing over top and toss to combine. Chill for 1 hour before serving. Makes 6 servings.

✕ **SHELIA DILL,** Utica, Michigan
Second Place, Healthy Cooking Contest, Michigan State Fair, Detroit, Michigan, 2001

Chicken Salad with Horseradish Dressing

1 lb. chicken

1 tablespoon olive oil, optional

2 cups diced red onion

3 tablespoons finely chopped fresh parsley

2 green onions, sliced

Horseradish Dressing (recipe follows)

4 cups mixed salad greens

⅔ cup grated pepperjack

2 tablespoons chopped fresh chives

1. Cook chicken on a grill or in a ridged grill skillet brushed with 1 tablespoon olive oil.

2. Cut or tear chicken into bite-size pieces, removing any skin and bones. Combine chicken pieces, red onion, parsley, and green onions.

3. Pour Horseradish Dressing into a large salad bowl. Add salad greens and toss to combine. To serve, mound salad greens onto center of each plate. Arrange the chicken mixture around the greens. Garnish with pepperjack and chives. Makes 4 to 6 servings.

Horseradish Dressing

1 cup mayonnaise

1 tablespoon minced garlic

½ cup horseradish

Juice from 1 lemon

1 teaspoon Dijon mustard

½ teaspoon Tabasco sauce

Salt and pepper to taste

Whisk together mayonnaise, garlic, horseradish, lemon juice, mustard, and Tabasco sauce. Season with salt and pepper. Cover and chill for 1 hour. Makes 1½ cups.

✕ **Martha Buehring,** Norman, Oklahoma
Second Place, Meat Salad Contest, Oklahoma State Fair, Oklahoma City, Oklahoma, 2005

Blueberry Chicken Salad

2 cups fresh blueberries,
   plus more for garnish

2 cups cubed cooked chicken

¾ cup chopped or diced celery

½ cup diced sweet red bell pepper

½ cup thinly sliced onion

1 carton (6 oz.) lemon yogurt

3 tablespoons mayonnaise

½ teaspoon salt

Bibb lettuce leaves, optional

1. Place blueberries, chicken, celery, red pepper, and onion in a large bowl. Toss gently to combine.

2. Stir together yogurt, mayonnaise, and salt. Drizzle over chicken mixture and toss gently to coat. Cover and refrigerate for at least 30 minutes. Serve on lettuce-lined platter or on individual plates, garnished with extra blueberries. Makes 4 to 6 servings.

✕ **Flo Helbling,** Goshen, Indiana
First Place, Bursting with Blueberries Contest, Elkhart County 4-H Fair, Goshen, Indiana, 2005

Sensationally Easy 'n' Lite Caesar Chicken-Pasta Salad

6 oz. penne (3 cups after cooking)

3 cups skinned, shredded deli-style
    roasted chicken breast

2 cups thinly sliced romaine

1½ cups grape tomatoes

½ cup thinly sliced fresh basil

½ cup chopped green onions

⅓ cup fat-free Caesar dressing

1 package (4 oz.) crumbled Feta

1 garlic clove, minced

1. Cook penne in boiling water, following package directions. Drain, rinse, and cool.

2. Combine penne, chicken, lettuce, tomatoes, basil, green onions, Caesar dressing, feta, and garlic in a large bowl. Toss well until all pieces are coated with dressing. Refrigerate until ready to serve. Makes 6 to 8 servings.

✂ **CARLA GARNTO,** Warner Robins, Georgia
First Place, Cluckin' Good Chicken Lite Contest, Georgia National Fair, Perry, Georgia, 2005

WINNER'S CIRCLE TIP | This hearty yet light one-dish meal is easy to make. While the penne is cooking, you can prepare and assemble the other ingredients.

Fresh Corn Salad

8 ears fresh corn, husked

½ cup vegetable oil

¼ cup cider vinegar

1½ teaspoons lemon juice

¼ cup minced fresh parsley

2 teaspoons sugar

1 teaspoon salt

½ teaspoon dried basil

⅛ teaspoon cayenne pepper

2 large tomatoes, seeded and chopped

½ cup chopped onion

⅓ cup chopped green bell pepper

⅓ cup chopped sweet red bell pepper

1. Place corn in a stockpot or large saucepan, cover with water, and bring to a boil. Cook until tender, 5 to 7 minutes. Drain and set aside to cool.

2. Place oil, vinegar, lemon juice, parsley, sugar, salt, basil, and cayenne pepper in a large bowl. Mix to combine.

3. Cut cooled corn off the cob. The yield should be about 4 cups.

4. Add corn, tomatoes, onion, green pepper, and red pepper to the oil mixture. Mix well. Cover and chill for several hours or overnight before serving. Makes 6 to 8 servings.

✂ **PAT STAHLY,** Goshen, Indiana
First Place, Home and Family Arts Open Class—Special Contest, Elkhart County 4-H Fair, Goshen, Indiana, 2002

CUCUMBER SALAD

1 medium cucumber,
   quartered and sliced
1 medium tomato, chopped
½ cup chopped green bell pepper
½ cup chopped sweet onion

2 tablespoons lime juice
2 tablespoons red wine vinegar
¾ teaspoon chopped fresh dill
½ teaspoon salt
¼ teaspoon pepper

1. Combine cucumber, tomato, green bell pepper and onion in a large bowl.
2. In a small bowl, whisk together lime juice, vinegar, dill, salt, and pepper.
3. Pour lime juice mixture over cucumber mixture and toss to coat. Cover and refrigerate for 15 minutes. Makes 4 servings.

✖ **MARTHA BUEHRING,** Norman, Oklahoma
Fourth Place, Vegetable Salad Contest, Oklahoma State Fair, Oklahoma City, Oklahoma, 2005

CARROT-DATE SALAD

1 package (1 lb.) carrots
½ cup chopped dates

Mayonnaise
¼ cup sugar

1. Peel and shred the carrots.
2. Combine carrots and dates in a large bowl. Mix in just enough mayonnaise to bind and moisten the ingredients.
3. One hour before serving, add sugar and mix well. Makes 4 to 6 servings.

✖ **MAUREEN FERNANDES,** San Jacinto, California
First Place, Salads, Riverside County Fair and National Date Festival, Indio, California, 2003–2004

Smoked Mozzarella and Tomato Ensalada

6 oz. smoked mozzarella, cut into small cubes
2 packages (10 oz. each) grape tomatoes
⅔ cup freshly grated Parmesan
1 garlic clove, minced
1 tablespoon plus 1 teaspoon Italian seasoning
⅓ cup extra-virgin light olive oil
Salt and pepper
1 bag (16 oz.) mixed salad greens
⅓ cup balsamic vinegar

1. Combine mozzarella cubes, tomatoes, Parmesan, garlic, Italian seasoning, and olive oil in a bowl. Season with salt and pepper.
2. Arrange salad greens on a platter or on individual salad plates. Spoon cheese-tomato mixture on top and drizzle with balsamic vinegar. Makes 4 to 6 servings.

⁜ **Michelle Mitchell Robertson,** Norman, Oklahoma
Third Place, Vegetable Salad Contest, Oklahoma State Fair, Oklahoma City, Oklahoma, 2005

Dilly Bean-Potato Salad

4 lbs. red potatoes
1 lb. fresh green beans
1 medium red onion, thinly sliced
1 medium Vidalia onion, thinly sliced
1 cup chopped celery
8 dill pickles, sliced
2 tablespoons chopped fresh dill
2 tablespoons minced fresh parsley
4 garlic cloves, minced
Vinaigrette

1. Place potatoes in a large saucepan, cover with water, and bring to a boil. Reduce heat, cover, and cook until tender, 15 to 20 minutes. Drain and cool.
2. Place beans in a large skillet, add 1 inch of water, and bring to boil. Reduce heat, cover, and simmer for 10 minutes. Drain and set aside.
3. Cut potatoes into ¼-inch-thick slices and place in a large bowl. Add red onion, Vidalia onion, celery, pickles, dill, parsley, and garlic. Drizzle vinaigrette over the top. Add beans and toss gently to combine. Makes 8 to 10 servings.

⁜ **Pauline Rye,** Titus, Alabama
Prize Winner, Alabama National Fair, Montgomery, Alabama, 1998–2002

FAVORITE BBQ SAUCE

1 tablespoon oil
1 cup chopped onion
1 can (15 oz.) tomato sauce
1 teaspoon ground allspice
¼ teaspoon nutmeg

¾ cup brown sugar
⅓ cup red hot pepper sauce
¼ cup Worcestershire sauce
3 teaspoons brown mustard

1. Heat oil in a large skillet over medium heat. Add onion and sauté until soft and golden.

2. Add tomato sauce, allspice, nutmeg, brown sugar, red hot pepper sauce, Worcestershire sauce, and brown mustard, stirring to combine. Simmer until thickened. Store in refrigerator. Makes 2 to 3 cups.

✂ **SUE SILKWORTH,** Poughkeepsie, New York
Best of Canning, Best of Culinary, Dutchess County Fair, Rhinebeck, New York, 2002

PEANUT SPINACH SALAD

¼ cup bottled raspberry-walnut vinaigrette
1 cup shelled boiled peanuts
3 oz. fresh spinach leaves, washed and dried
½ cup chopped ham
½ cup croutons, plus more for garnish
1 small apple, cut into bite-size pieces
⅓ cup peach slices

⅓ cup chopped onion
⅓ cup chopped celery
⅓ cup chopped bell pepper
¼ cup diced cucumber
1 medium tomato, diced
Salt

1. Combine raspberry-walnut vinaigrette and peanuts in a small saucepan over medium heat. Cook for 7 minutes.

2. Place spinach, ham, croutons, apple, peaches, onion, celery, bell pepper, cucumber, and tomato in large salad bowl. Add peanut mixture and toss to combine. Season with salt. Serve topped with croutons, if desired. Makes 4 to 6 servings.

✂ **ALBERTA ALLISON,** Kathleen, Georgia
Second Place, Georgia Peanut Recipe—Unsweet, Georgia National Fair, Perry, Georgia, 2005

CRANBERRY-ORANGE VINEGAR

1 quart white vinegar
2 cups fresh or frozen cranberries
Peel of 1 orange

Fresh cranberries, for garnish
Fresh orange peel, cut with scissors,
   for garnish

1. Heat vinegar in a medium saucepan to a simmer.

2. Place cranberries and orange peel in a 1½-quart glass jar. Add the warm vinegar, cover the jar, and set in a cool, dark place. Cure for 2 weeks.

3. Set a large strainer over a 1½-quart bowl. Pour vinegar through strainer to remove cranberries and orange peel.

4. Place fresh cranberries and fresh orange peel into decorative bottles. Decant vinegar into bottles using a funnel. Cap or cork the bottles. Makes approximately 1 quart.

✳ **WENDY NICKEL,** Kiester, Minnesota
Third Place, Fresh Cranberry, Warrens Cranberry Festival, Warrens, Wisconsin, 2005

TAPIAPPLE FRUIT SALAD

1 tablespoon all-purpose flour
½ cup sugar
2 tablespoons quick-cooking tapioca
2 tablespoons cider vinegar
1 can (8 oz.) crushed pineapple,
   drained with juice reserved

1 package (3 oz.) tapioca pudding mix
1 container (16 oz.) frozen whipped
   topping, thawed
2 Granny Smith apples, cored and chopped
2 red Delicious apples, cored and chopped
2 cups unsalted peanuts

1. Combine flour, sugar, tapioca, vinegar, and reserved pineapple juice in a 1-quart saucepan. Cook over medium heat, stirring constantly, until thick. Remove from heat and chill.

2. Mix dry tapioca pudding mix and whipped topping in a medium bowl until well blended.

3. Combine pineapple, apples, peanuts, and chilled tapioca mixture in a large bowl. Fold in the whipped topping. Chill for at least 1 hour before serving. Makes 8 servings.

✳ **ANNETTE SHARP,** Oklahoma City, Oklahoma
First Place, Fruit Salad Contest, Oklahoma State Fair, Oklahoma City, Oklahoma, 2005

SHRIMP-BASIL PASTA SALAD

1 lb. orzo pasta
½ lb. shrimp, cooked, peeled, and deveined
1½ cups diced seeded tomato
1 cup diced red onion
½ cup toasted pine nuts
1 teaspoon salt
¼ teaspoon freshly ground black pepper

½ teaspoon red pepper flakes
Zest of 1 lemon

DRESSING
1 bunch (approximately 1¼ cups)
   fresh basil leaves
½ cup olive oil flavored with lemon

1. Cook orzo in boiling water, following package directions for al dente. Drain well. Cool.

2. Combine shrimp, tomato, onion, pine nuts, salt, pepper, red pepper flakes, and lemon zest in a large bowl. Add orzo and toss gently to combine.

3. To make dressing: Combine basil and olive oil in a food processor until finely chopped. Pour dressing over salad and mix well. Cover and store in refrigerator at least 1 hour until ready to serve. Makes 8 to 10 servings.

✳ **PATTY KNIGHTON,** San Diego, California
Second Place, Lotsa Pasta Contest—Salads, San Diego County Fair, Del Mar, California, 2004

WONDERFUL FRUIT SALAD

1 can (11 oz.) mandarin oranges

1 teaspoon sugar

2 green apples, chopped

1 cup green grapes

½ cup red grapes

3 kiwifruit, peeled and chopped

1 can (20 oz.) pineapple chunks, drained

½ cup vanilla yogurt

1 large firm banana

1. Combine oranges and sugar in a large bowl. Let stand for 10 minutes.

2. Add apples, red and green grapes, kiwifruit, pineapple, and yogurt. Toss gently to combine. Cover and refrigerate for 30 minutes. Slice banana and add just before serving. Makes 8 to 10 servings.

✕ **MARTHA BUEHRING,** Norman, Oklahoma
Third Place, Fruit Salad Contest, Oklahoma State Fair, Oklahoma City, Oklahoma, 2005

STRAWBERRY SPINACH SALAD

16 oz. spinach leaves

2 carrots, peeled and shredded

2 cups sliced strawberries

2 cups sliced mushrooms

⅓ cup slivered almonds

RASPBERRY DRESSING

1 packet Homemade Gourmet Raspberry
   Velvet Fruit Dip

¼ cup raspberry preserves

⅔ cup vegetable oil

¼ cup water

1. Place spinach, carrots, strawberries, mushrooms, and almonds in a large bowl. Toss to combine.

2. To make raspberry dressing: Whisk together Raspberry Velvet Fruit Dip, raspberry preserves, vegetable oil, and water. Pour half of dressing over salad and toss to coat. Add more dressing to taste. Makes 8 to 10 servings.

✕ **JENNIFER CROY,** Yukon, Oklahoma
Fourth Place, Fruit Salad Contest,
Oklahoma State Fair,
Oklahoma City, Oklahoma, 2005

Sweet/Sour Orange and Green Salad

4 cups romaine, washed, dried,
  and torn apart

1½ cups raw broccoli florets,
  cut into small pieces

½ cup crushed Ramen noodles,
  chicken flavor (use only the noodles)

1 can (14 oz.) mandarin oranges, drained

¼ cup red wine vinegar

½ cup olive oil

2 tablespoons sugar

1. Toss lettuce, broccoli florets, Ramen noodles, and mandarin oranges in a large bowl.

2. Whisk together vinegar, olive oil, and sugar. Pour over salad and toss to coat. Makes 4 to 6 servings.

✳ **Jinny Caldwell,** Oklahoma City, Oklahoma
Second Place, Vegetable Salad Contest, Oklahoma State Fair, Oklahoma City, Oklahoma, 2005

✦ THE OKLAHOMA STATE FAIR ✦ BY THE NUMBERS

The Oklahoma State Fair is the largest single entertainment event in Oklahoma. Close to a million people visit every year, consuming more than 60,000 gallons of liquid beverages, 6 miles of hot dogs, 44,246 tacos, 45,000 cinnamon rolls, and 12 tons of turkey legs. In 2005, the Oklahoma State Fair was chosen as one of the locations of the GoldenPalace.com World Championship Grilled Cheese Eating Competition.

Orange- and Ginger-Flavored Fruit Salad

1 cup water

½ cup sugar

5 pieces crystallized ginger

4 tablespoons orange liqueur

2 cups fresh or frozen peach slices

1 cup sliced fresh or frozen strawberries

1 cup green grapes

1 cup sliced fresh banana

1. Combine water, sugar, ginger, and orange liqueur in a small saucepan. Bring to a boil, remove from heat, and let cool. Remove and discard ginger.

2. Place peach slices, strawberries, grapes, and banana in a large bowl. Pour syrup over top and mix well to coat. Makes 4 to 6 servings.

✳ **Jinny Caldwell,** Oklahoma City, Oklahoma
Second Place, Fruit Salad Contest, Oklahoma State Fair, Oklahoma City, Oklahoma, 2005

Refreshing Shrimp and Pasta Salad

½ lb. bow-tie pasta

2 lemons, thinly sliced

1 medium yellow onion, halved and
  thinly sliced

1 red bell pepper, julienned

3 teaspoons capers, drained

1 lb. large shrimp, boiled, peeled,
  and deveined

¼ cup apple cider vinegar

¼ cup olive oil

1 teaspoon prepared horseradish

1 package (.6 oz.) dried Italian dressing mix

1. Cook pasta in boiling water, following package directions for al dente, about 11 minutes. Drain and rinse under cold running water.

2. Combine pasta, lemon, onion, bell pepper, capers, and shrimp in a large bowl.

3. Whisk together vinegar, olive oil, horseradish, and Italian dressing mix in a small bowl. Pour over pasta mixture and mix well. Cover and refrigerate until well chilled, 12 hours. Makes 6 servings.

✕ **Kelly Hagen,** Macon, Georgia
First Place, World of Pastabilities, Cooking Lite, Georgia National Fair, Perry, Georgia, 2005

Summer Seafood Salad

3 lbs. shrimp, cooked, peeled,
  and deveined

6 hard-boiled eggs, chopped

Juice of 2 lemons

Juice of 1 lime

1 cup chopped celery

½ cup chopped green onion

1 tablespoon chopped fresh dill

1 cup chopped toasted pecans

1 cup mayonnaise

½ cup sour cream

2 teaspoons Creole seasoning

Salt and pepper

Boston lettuce

1. Combine shrimp, eggs, lemon juice, lime juice, celery, onion, dill, and pecans in a large bowl.

2. Stir together mayonnaise, sour cream, and Creole seasoning. Season with salt and pepper. Pour dressing over salad and mix well. Cover and refrigerate. Serve chilled on a platter or on individual salad plates lined with Boston lettuce. Makes 6 to 8 servings.

✕ **Annette Sharp,** Oklahoma City, Oklahoma
First Place, Meat Salad Contest, Oklahoma State Fair, Oklahoma City, Oklahoma, 2005

CHAPTER 5

MAIN DISHES

POULTRY, BEEF, PORK, LAMB,
SEAFOOD, AND PASTA

Apricot-Glazed Chicken with Dried Plums and Sage

1 roasting chicken, cut into pieces,
  or 3 lbs. chicken pieces
6 oz. apricot preserves
8 to 10 pitted dried plums
2½ tablespoons olive oil

½ tablespoon white vinegar
¼ teaspoon salt
¼ teaspoon black pepper
5 garlic cloves, peeled
10 fresh sage leaves

1. Preheat oven to 400°F.

2. Trim fat from chicken pieces.

3. Combine apricot preserves, dried plums, olive oil, vinegar, salt, pepper, garlic, and sage in a large bowl and mix well. Add chicken pieces and toss until evenly coated.

4. Arrange chicken pieces skin side up in roasting pan. Roast until tops of chicken are browned and juices run clear, 40 to 45 minutes. Makes 4 to 6 servings.

✄ **Mary Beth Pederson,** Morton, Illinois
First Place, Main Dish Using Chicken, Illinois State Fair, Springfield, Illinois, 2005

Down-on-the-Farm Chicken Casserole

HASH BROWNS LAYER

1 package (30 oz.) frozen hash browns,
  thawed
1 can (10.5 oz.) cream of celery
  condensed soup
1 cup light sour cream
½ cup grated onion
2 tablespoons diced pimento
1 cup shredded cheddar cheese

CHICKEN LAYER

3 cups of cooked skinless, boneless bite-size
  chicken pieces
1 can (10.5 oz.) cream of chicken condensed soup
1 can (10.5 oz.) cream of mushroom condensed soup
1 cup light sour cream
1 package (8 oz.) buttery round crackers, crushed

CRUMB LAYER

1 tablespoon poppy seeds
½ cup unsalted butter, melted

1. Preheat oven to 375°F. Lightly grease a 13 x 9 x 2-inch baking dish.

2. To assemble hash browns layer: Combine hash browns, cream of celery soup, light sour cream, onion, pimento, and cheddar cheese in a medium bowl. Mix well. Spread mixture the bottom of baking dish.

3. To assemble chicken layer: Combine chicken pieces, cream of chicken soup, cream of mushroom soup, and sour cream in a large bowl. Stir until well blended. Pour mixture over hash browns layer.

4. To make crumb layer: Whisk together crushed crackers and poppy seeds. Stir in melted butter. Spread crumb mixture evenly over chicken layer. Bake until heated through and lightly browned on top, 30 to 45 minutes. Makes 10 to 12 servings.

✄ **Wendi DeFore,** Warner Robins, Georgia
First Place, Cluckin' Good Favorite Chicken, Georgia National Fair, Perry, Georgia, 2005

TUTTI-FRUTTI CHICKEN KABOBS

BARBECUE MARINADE AND SAUCE

1 cup ketchup

1 cup brown sugar

1 cup white wine

½ teaspoon red wine vinegar

½ teaspoon Worcestershire sauce

1½ tablespoons Maraschino juice

1½ tablespoons pineapple juice

½ teaspoon chopped garlic

⅛ teaspoon nutmeg

1/16 teaspoon ground cloves

Cinnamon

KABOBS

1 to 1½ lbs. boneless, skinless chicken

1½ lbs. pears

1½ lbs. apples

1½ lbs. peaches

1 can (20 oz.) pineapple chunks

1 jar (10 oz.) Maraschinos
   (use partial jar if desired)

1. To make barbecue marinade: In a large bowl, combine ketchup, brown sugar, white wine, vinegar, Worcestershire sauce, Maraschino juice, pineapple juice, garlic, nutmeg, cloves, and cinnamon. Measure and set aside 1 cup of marinade to serve as sauce with cooked kabobs.

2. Cut chicken into 1- to 1½-inch cubes. Add chicken to marinade and toss until coated. Cover and refrigerate for 1 to 2 hours and up to overnight.

3. To assemble kabobs: Cut pears, apples, and peaches into cubes. Assemble chicken, cubed fruit, pineapple chunks, and Maraschinos on skewers. Grill kabobs over medium heat, turning occasionally, until chicken is cooked through and juices run clear, 15 to 25 minutes. Serve with rice or salad. Makes 4 to 6 servings.

※ **JACQUELYN DOAN,** Clinton Township, Michigan
First Place, Cooking with Michigan Wine, Michigan State Fair, Detroit, Michigan, 2000

APPLE-AND-ARTICHOKE CHICKEN BREASTS

2 tablespoons oil

4 boneless, skinless chicken breasts

1 medium onion, sliced

1 garlic clove, minced

4 oz. fresh sliced mushrooms

1 can (14 oz.) artichoke hearts

1 can (14 oz.) lowfat chicken broth

2 apples, peeled, cored, and sliced

1 cup dry white wine

1 tablespoon cornstarch

2 tablespoons cold water

Noodles, cooked and drained

1. Heat oil in a large skillet over medium-high heat. Add chicken breasts and cook, turning once, until browned on both sides, 8 to 10 minutes.

2. Add onion, garlic, and mushrooms. Sauté until onion is soft and tender, 5 minutes.

3. Add artichoke hearts, chicken broth, apples, and wine. Simmer until apples are tender, 10 minutes.

4. Add cornstarch to cold water and mix thoroughly. Add to skillet and stir. Continue simmering until sauce thickens. Serve over noodles. Makes 4 servings.

※ **SHELIA DILL,** Utica, Michigan
Second Place, Healthy Cooking Contest, Michigan State Fair, Detroit, Michigan, 2000

Chicken Breast with Fresh Mushrooms, Red Peppers, and Great Red Wine

2 tablespoons unsalted butter,
    room temperature
2 tablespoons olive oil
4 to 5 boneless chicken breasts,
    cut in strips
1 lb. mushrooms, sliced thin
2 medium onions, diced
2 garlic cloves, mashed
1 large red pepper, coarsely chopped
1 beef bouillon cube
1 cup red wine
1 teaspoon dried parsley

1 teaspoon dried basil
1 to 2 teaspoons dried oregano
2 cans (10 oz. each) diced tomatoes
2 cans (15 oz. each) tomato sauce
2 cans (6 oz. each) tomato paste
1 whole cinnamon stick
8 whole cloves
1 teaspoon ground allspice
1 cup water
2 tablespoons honey
Pasta of your choice
Grated Parmesan, for garnish

1. Heat butter and olive oil in a large skillet over medium heat. Add chicken, mushrooms, onions, garlic, red pepper, bouillon, and red wine and cook for 5 minutes.

2. Stir in parsley, basil, and oregano. Reduce to a simmer. Add tomatoes, tomato sauce, and tomato paste and continue simmering.

3. Wrap cinnamon stick, cloves, and allspice in a piece of cheesecloth and tie with butcher's twine. Add spice bundle and water to sauce and continue simmering. Stir in honey.

4. Cook pasta in boiling water, following package directions for al dente. Drain well but do not rinse. Transfer pasta to serving platter or individual plates. Pour sauce over pasta and top with freshly grated Parmesan. Makes 6 to 8 servings.

※ **Barbara Conti,** Waterford, Michigan
Second Place, Cooking with Michigan Wine, Michigan State Fair, Detroit, Michigan, 2001

Cold Chicken and Wild Rice

1 cup wild rice
2 cups water
1½ cups chicken broth
1 garlic clove, peeled
3 tablespoons unsalted butter,
    room temperature
1 bunch scallions, white part and
    some of green, chopped
½ lb. chopped mushrooms

3 strips of lean bacon, fried and diced
½ cup chopped green or black olives
⅓ cup olive oil
3 tablespoons tarragon wine vinegar
½ teaspoon dried marjoram
½ cup sliced celery
2 cups diced cooked chicken
Salt and pepper

1. Soak wild rice in water overnight. Drain and rinse.

2. Combine rice, chicken broth, and garlic in a saucepan. Simmer until all liquid is absorbed and rice is dry but fluffy. Discard garlic.

3. Melt butter in a skillet, add scallions, and sauté over low heat until soft. Add mushrooms and continue sautéing until mushrooms are slightly room temperature. Remove from heat.

4. Combine rice, scallion-mushroom mixture, bacon, olives, olive oil, vinegar, marjoram, celery, and chicken in a large bowl. Toss until well mixed. Season with salt and pepper. Cover and refrigerate overnight. Serve chilled. Makes 4 to 6 servings.

※ **JULIE MIEDINGER,** St. Ignatious, Montana
First Place, One Dish Meals, Western Montana Fair, Missoula, Montana, 2005

WINNER'S CIRCLE TIP | Cold Chicken and Wild Rice is the perfect dish for a hot summer day. Serve it with garden-fresh tomato slices on the side.

DATE CHUTNEY-STUFFED CHICKEN BREAST

SOUR CREAM MARINADE
¾ cup lowfat sour cream
½ cup light salad dressing
   (such as Miracle Whip)
1 tablespoon lemon juice
1 teaspoon onion powder
½ teaspoon coriander
¼ teaspoon salt
¼ teaspoon white pepper

4 skinless, boneless split chicken breasts
1 lb. fresh mozzarella
Crushed cornflakes
½ cup finely chopped walnuts

DATE CHUTNEY
½ cup walnuts
2 tablespoons balsamic vinegar
2 tablespoons water
2 tablespoons unsalted butter
1 onion, chopped
¼ teaspoon salt
¼ teaspoon white pepper
1 tablespoon dried chopped rosemary
1 tablespoon sugar
½ cup dates
1 apple, cored and chopped
1 pear, cored and chopped
1 tablespoon vinegar

1. To make sour cream marinade: Combine sour cream, salad dressing, lemon juice, onion powder, coriander, salt, and white pepper in a small bowl. Spread mixture on both sides of chicken breasts, reserving remainder of mixture for garnish. Place chicken in refrigerator and allow to marinate 4 hours or overnight. (Also refrigerate reserved marinade.)

2. To make date chutney: Place walnuts, balsamic vinegar, water, butter, and onion in a deep skillet. Cook until onions are lightly browned. Add salt, pepper, rosemary, sugar, dates, apple, pear, and vinegar. Cook on low heat until thickened, 10 minutes.

3. Preheat oven to 350°F. Cut mozzarella into 8 pieces, each 2½-inches by ½-inches. Place a slice of mozzarella at the small end of each breast half and rollup, tucking in the sides of the breast. Set breasts side by side in a baking pan. Sprinkle cornflakes and walnuts over the top. Bake 35 minutes. Serve with reserved marinade and date chutney. Makes 8 servings.

※ **PAULINE SPEER,** Indio, California
First Place, Riverside County Fair & National Date Festival, Indio, California, 2003–2004

CURRIED CHICKEN PENNE WITH FRESH MANGO CHUTNEY

CHUTNEY

2 cups diced mango

1 cup finely chopped onion

½ cup water

2 tablespoons brown sugar

1 tablespoon curry powder

1 tablespoon fresh lime juice

½ teaspoon black pepper

½ teaspoon chopped peeled fresh ginger

¼ teaspoon salt

CHICKEN PENNE

2 cups penne (about 4 cups cooked)

1 teaspoon olive oil

2 garlic cloves, minced

1 lb. skinless, boneless chicken breasts,
    cut into 1-inch pieces

1 cup light coconut milk

2 tablespoons sugar

1 teaspoon salt

1½ teaspoons red curry paste

1½ teaspoons Thai fish sauce

2 cups broccoli florets

2 cups cauliflower florets

2 tablespoons chopped green onion

Grated Parmesan

1. To make chutney: Combine mango, onion, water, brown sugar, curry powder, lime juice, black pepper, ginger, and salt in a large saucepan. Bring to a boil, reduce heat, and simmer, stirring occasionally, until most of the liquid evaporates and mixture thickens, about 15 minutes.

2. Cook penne in boiling water, following package directions for al dente, about 11 minutes. Drain and rinse.

3. Heat olive oil in a large nonstick skillet over medium-high heat. Add garlic and chicken and sauté for 5 minutes.

4. Whisk together coconut milk, sugar, salt, red curry paste, and fish sauce. Add mixture to skillet and bring to a simmer.

5. Add broccoli and cauliflower florets to skillet. Cover and cook, stirring occasionally, until vegetables are crisp-tender, 7 minutes.

6. Add chutney and penne to skillet. Toss well to combine. Serve sprinkled with green onion and Parmesan. Makes 6 servings.

✂ **TULIE TREJO,** Chula Vista, California
First Place, Lotsa Pasta Contest-Entrees,
San Diego County Fair,
Del Mar, California, 2004

FIESTA CHICKEN

2 or 3 chicken breasts, cut in 1-inch pieces
Salt and pepper
Paprika
2 tablespoons unsalted butter
¼ lb. pork sausage
1 cup broccoli florets

¾ cup sliced green onions with tops
3 cups cooked rice
1 can (12 oz.) whole kernel corn
   with peppers, drained
2 teaspoons lemon juice

1. Preheat oven to 350°F.

2. Sprinkle chicken breasts with salt, pepper, and paprika. Melt butter in a large skillet over medium-high heat. Add chicken and cook, turning once, until well browned on both sides. Drain on paper towels.

3. Cook sausage, broccoli, and onions in same skillet, stirring frequently, until vegetables are crisp-tender. Add rice, corn, and lemon juice and mix well. Cook for 2 minutes more.

4. Transfer vegetable-rice mixture to a shallow baking dish. Arrange chicken breasts on top, pressing slightly into rice, and cover with foil. Bake until heated through, 20 to 30 minutes. Makes 6 servings.

※ **BETH WALLACE,** Greenbrier, Arkansas
Honorable Mention, Special Entries, Arkansas State Fair, Little Rock, Arkansas, 2005

CHICKEN-PECAN QUICHE

CRUST
1 cup all-purpose flour
1 cup (4 oz.) shredded sharp
   cheddar cheese
1 cup chopped pecans
½ teaspoon salt
¼ teaspoon paprika
⅓ cup vegetable oil

QUICHE FILLING
3 eggs, beaten
1 container (8 oz.) sour cream
¼ cup mayonnaise or salad dressing
½ cup chicken broth
2 cups chopped chicken
½ cup (2 oz.) shredded sharp cheddar cheese
¼ cup minced onion
¼ teaspoon dried dill weed
3 drops hot sauce
¼ cup pecan halves

1. To make crust: Preheat oven to 350°F. Combine flour, cheddar cheese, pecans, salt, and paprika in a large bowl. Stir in oil. Set aside one-fourth of the mixture. Press remainder of mixture in bottom and up sides of a 9-inch quiche dish. Bake for 10 minutes.

2. To make filling: Reduce oven temperature to 325°F. Combine eggs, sour cream, mayonnaise, and chicken broth in medium bowl and stir well. Stir in chicken, cheese, onion, dill weed, and hot sauce.

3. Pour egg mixture into prepared crust. Sprinkle reserved crumb mixture over filling and top with pecans. Bake for 45 to 55 minutes. Makes 6 to 8 servings.

※ **GAIL FULLER,** Raleigh, North Carolina
Second Place, N.C. Pecan Association's Pecan Recipe Competition, North Carolina State Fair, Raleigh, North Carolina, 2005

Orange Chicken with Rice Pilaf

4 skinless chicken leg quarters (3½ lbs.)

1 teaspoon salt

⅛ to ¼ teaspoon black pepper

1¾ cups water

1 cup shredded carrot

1 cup chopped celery

¾ cup uncooked long-grain rice

3 tablespoons chopped fresh parsley

¼ cup minced onion

2 tablespoons unsalted butter or margarine, melted

1 tablespoon chicken bouillon granules

3 tablespoons orange juice concentrate

1 tablespoon honey

1 teaspoon prepared mustard

1. Preheat oven to 375°F. Grease a 13 x 9 x 2-inch baking pan. Arrange chicken in pan. Sprinkle with salt and pepper. Bake uncovered for 25 minutes.

2. Combine water, carrot, celery, rice, parsley, onion, butter, and bouillon granules in an ungreased 13 x 9 x 2-inch baking pan. Cover with foil and bake for 25 minutes.

3. Combine orange juice concentrate, honey, and mustard in a small bowl.

4. Remove both pans from oven. Remove foil and stir rice in its baking dish. Transfer chicken pieces to top of rice and brush orange juice mixture onto chicken. Return baking dish to oven for 15 minutes. Baste once more with orange juice mixture and bake until rice is tender and meat juices run clear, 15 minutes more. Makes 4 servings.

✂ **Bonnie Stahlman,** Gordonville, Missouri
Second Place, Food & Poultry Recipe Contest, Southeast Missouri District Fair, Cape Girardeau, Missouri, 2003

Quick and Easy Chicken Alfredo

2 tablespoons olive oil

1 tablespoon crushed garlic

8 oz. fresh sliced mushrooms

⅓ cup white wine

1 jar (16 oz.) Alfredo sauce

½ cup milk

½ cup grated Parmesan,
   plus more for garnish

½ cup goat cheese,
   plus more for garnish

⅛ teaspoon cayenne pepper

1 teaspoon Old Bay seasoning

Salt and pepper

2 cups rotisserie chicken, deboned, skinned,
   and broken up into bite-size pieces

1 box (16 oz). fettuccine, cooked, and drained

1. Heat olive oil in a deep skillet over medium heat. Add garlic and sauté just until it sizzles. Add mushrooms and wine and cook until most of the liquid is evaporated.

2. Stir in Alfredo sauce, milk, Parmesan, goat cheese, cayenne pepper, and Old Bay seasoning. Season with salt and pepper. Add chicken and simmer for 20 minutes.

3. Cook fettucine in boiling water, following package directions for al dente. Drain well. Add cooked pasta to skillet and toss until well coated. Serve topped with extra cheeses. Makes 6 to 8 servings.

✂ **Rhonda Hitch,** Kathleen, Georgia
Third Place, Cluckin' Good Favorite Chicken, Georgia National Fair, Perry, Georgia, 2005

Tea'd Off Kickin' Chicken Wraps

7 cups water

7 peach-flavored black tea bags

1½ lbs. skinless, boneless chicken breasts

½ cup olive oil

2 tablespoons finely diced jalapeño

¾ cup diced yellow bell pepper

1½ tablespoons dried chopped basil

1 teaspoon minced garlic

¾ cup skinned and diced fresh peaches

20 cherry tomatoes, quartered

3 large rectangular tomato- or spinach-flavored bread wraps

¾ cup shredded smoked sharp cheddar cheese

Ranch dressing, for dipping

1. Place water and tea bags in a 3-quart pot over high heat. Bring to a boil and add chicken breasts. Return to a boil and then reduce to a simmer. Continue simmering until chicken is "tea'd off" (thoroughly cooked), 30 minutes.

2. Remove cooked chicken from tea and set on a clean plate. Cool for 5 minutes. Pull chicken apart into bite-size shreds with your fingers.

3. Place olive oil, jalapeño, bell pepper, basil, garlic, peaches, and tomatoes in a large zip-close bag. Add chicken to zip-close bag, squeeze out extra air, and seal shut. Gently swish the bag until chicken is fully coated. Set bag in refrigerator and marinate at least 1 hour.

4. About 15 minutes before serving, warm a skillet on medium-high heat, add the marinated chicken, and sauté until thoroughly heated, 10 minutes.

5. Lay the wraps on a clean counter and sprinkle with cheese. Spoon one-third of the chicken onto each wrap. Roll up from the longer edge. Cut each rolled wrap in half and wrap three-quarters of surface with foil or parchment paper to catch drippings and maintain the warmth of the chicken. Serve with a small bowl of ranch dressing for dipping. Makes 6 servings.

Enjoy these chicken wraps with freshly brewed iced tea.

※ **Diana Wara,** Washington, Illinois
Second Place, Main Dish Using Chicken, Illinois State Fair, Springfield, Illinois, 2005

Ranch Cheddar Chicken

½ cup ranch dressing

1 tablespoon flour

4 skinless boneless chicken breasts

¼ cup shredded sharp cheddar cheese

¼ cup grated Parmesan

1. Preheat oven to 375°F.

2. Mix together dressing and flour. Dip each chicken breast into mixture and arrange on a baking sheet.

3. Combine cheddar cheese and Parmesan in a small bowl. Sprinkle cheeses over chicken. Bake 25 minutes, or until done. Makes 4 servings.

※ **Morgan Johnston,** Sanbornton, New Hampshire
Second Place, Junior Division, Belknap County 4-H Food Festival, Belmont, New Hampshire, 2006

FARM HOUSE FAJITA SKILLET

3 tablespoons vegetable oil,
    plus more for cooking
1 package (6 oz.) Mexican corn bread mix
⅔ cup milk
1 egg, beaten
1 can (8¾ oz.) whole kernel corn,
    well drained

1 can (10 oz.) diced tomatoes with
    lime juice and cilantro, drained
1 package (9 oz.) precooked fajita chicken strips,
    thawed and cut into cubes
¼ cup diced green bell pepper
¼ cup diced yellow onion
1 teaspoon salt

1. Preheat oven to 400°F.

2. Heat extra oil in a 10-inch cast iron skillet over low heat.

3. Place corn bread mix in a large mixing bowl. Add milk and egg and mix well.

4. Add corn, tomatoes, chicken, bell pepper, onion, salt, and 3 tablespoons vegetable oil to batter and blend well. Pour batter into preheated skillet. Bake in oven until golden brown, 30 minutes. Serve garnished with chopped fresh cilantro, sour cream, grated cheese, or guacamole, if desired. Makes 4 to 6 servings.

✕ **BRENDA DEFORD,** Heber Springs, Arkansas
Honorable Mention, Special Entries, Arkansas State Fair, Little Rock, Arkansas, 2005

CHICKEN-PASILLA TAMALES

2½ lbs. tomatillos
2½ lbs. fresh pasilla chiles
3 to 6 jalapeños
8 large garlic cloves, roasted
1 large onion, cut in small chunks
4 or 5 teaspoons sea salt, divided

2 whole chickens, boiled and shredded
5 lbs. prepared masa
2 teaspoons baking powder
2 or 3 packages corn husks, soaked in
    hot water for 1 hour or overnight

1. Place tomatillos, pasilla chiles, and jalapeños on a foil-lined baking sheet or broiler pan. Set under broiler, turning once, until dark on both sides.

2. Transfer pasilla chiles to a zip-close plastic bag and seal closed. Let chiles steam in bag for 15 to 20 minutes. Skin and seed pasillas, cut into thick strips, and set aside.

3. Place tomatillos, jalapeños, garlic, onion, and 2 teaspoons of the sea salt in a blender. Pulse 8 to 10 times to combine. If sauce is too thick, and 1 teaspoon of water as needed. Add more salt if necessary, to taste.

4. Measure and set aside 1½ cups of the tomatillo sauce. Place remaining sauce in a large mixing bowl. Add chicken and pasilla chiles and mix well.

5. Combine masa, remaining 2 to 3 teaspoons sea salt, baking powder, and reserved tomatillo sauce in another large bowl. Stir until completely blended.

6. To assemble tamales: Drain cornhusks, remove any red corn silk, and stack. Lay 1 cornhusk flat, smooth side up. Place about 3 tablespoons of masa mixture on the bottom half of cornhusk and smooth with the back of a large soup spoon. Add 1 to 2 teaspoons of tomatillo-chicken filling in the center of the cornhusk above the masa. Fold up the wide end over the filling and then the other. Fold one side (that has no filling) to the underside, making sure that the filling is covered; fold the other side under that. Continue making tamales in this manner.

7. Add water to tamale steamer and line bottom with extra cornhusks. Set tamales in a circle inside steamer in two layers. Cover with a dish towel and more cornhusks. Place lid on steamer.

8. Place steamer on stove over medium-high heat, bring to a boil, and reduce to a simmer. Simmer until tamales are cooked through, 1 to 1½ hours; check for doneness after 1 hour. Remove cooked tamales from steamer and allow to cool and set before serving. Makes 4 dozen tamales.

※ **DAVID FERNANDES, JR.,** Glendora, California
First Place, Comidas Mexicanas Tamale Contest, L.A. County Fair, Pomona, California, 2003

PEANUT CABBAGE SLAW WITH MARINATED CHICKEN AND PEANUT BUTTER VINAIGRETTE

PEANUT BUTTER VINAIGRETTE AND MARINADE

1 cup peanut butter
½ cup rice vinegar
½ cup soy sauce
½ cup honey
¼ cup brown sugar
½ teaspoon garlic powder
½ teaspoon ginger
1½ lbs. chicken tenders
1 tablespoon peanut oil

CABBAGE SLAW

½ Chinese cabbage, chopped
1 package oriental-flavored ramen noodles, crushed, plus seasoning packet
½ cup matchstick carrots
½ cup chopped peanuts
½ cup diced red onion
¼ cup sliced green onion
½ cup cubed pineapple

1. To make peanut butter vinaigrette and marinade: In a bowl, combine peanut butter, rice vinegar, soy sauce, honey, brown sugar, garlic powder, and ginger; mix until smooth. Set aside half of mixture for vinaigrette.

2. Place chicken tenders in a large zip-close bag. Pour remaining half of mixture over chicken, seal bag, and chill to marinate, 1 hour. Drain.

3. Heat peanut oil in a skillet over medium-high heat. Sauté chicken tenders, turning once, until cooked through and browned on both sides.

4. To make cabbage slaw: In a large bowl, combine Chinese cabbage, crushed noodles, carrots, peanuts, red onion, green onion, and pineapple. Sprinkle contents of seasoning packet over the top. Add half of the vinaigrette and toss to combine. Add chicken and toss to coat. Place on a serving platter and garnish with peanuts and green onions, if desired. Serve remaining vinaigrette on the side. Makes 6 to 8 servings.

※ **RACHEL BROOKS,** Byron, Georgia
First Place, Georgia Peanut Recipe—Unsweet, Georgia National Fair, Perry, Georgia, 2005

MEXICAN CASSEROLE

2 tablespoons water

12 corn tortillas, cut into 1-inch strips

2½ to 3 cups cooked shredded turkey breast

1 can (10.5 oz.) cream of mushroom
  condensed soup

1 can (10.5 oz.) cream of chicken
  condensed soup

1 cup picante sauce (in desired hotness)

10 oz. grated Monterey Jack

½ cup chopped onion (optional)

1. Preheat oven to 350°F.

2. Place water in a 13 x 9 x 2-inch baking dish. Line bottom of dish with one-third of tortilla strips. Layer one-third of shredded turkey over tortilla strips.

3. Combine mushroom soup, chicken soup, and picante sauce in a bowl. Pour one-third of this mixture over turkey in dish.

4. Layer another one-third each of tortilla strips, turkey, and sauce into pan. Repeat once more. Top with cheese and onion, if using. Bake uncovered for 45 minutes. Serves 6 to 8.

Mexican Casserole also tastes delicious when made with chicken or pork.

✄ **TRACY L. HORD,** Weaverville, North Carolina
First Place, Carolina Turkey Breast Recipe Contest, North Carolina Mountain State Fair, Fletcher, North Carolina, 2005

QUICK AND ZESTY GROUND SIRLOIN WRAPS

½ teaspoon salt

1 lb. ground sirloin

½ red onion, chopped

½ yellow bell pepper, chopped

2 garlic cloves, chopped

1½ teaspoons fennel seed, crushed

1½ teaspoons dried oregano

⅓ cup chili sauce

Zest of 2 large oranges

¼ cup fresh orange juice

6 tortillas (any flavor)

½ cup grated Parmesan

8 oz. sharp cheddar cheese,
  sliced and cut into triangles

Paprika

1. Heat a large skillet over medium-high heat. Sprinkle salt into bottom of skillet, add ground sirloin, and cook, stirring occasionally, until lightly browned, 1 to 2 minutes.

2. Add red onion, yellow bell pepper, garlic, and fennel seed to skillet. Continue cooking until meat is no longer pink in the middle, 6 minutes. Spoon mixture into a strainer and drain out fat. Return mixture to pan, but remove from heat. Stir in oregano, chili sauce, and orange zest and juice until well combined.

3. Spread out tortillas on a clean countertop. Spoon meat mixture, evenly divided, onto middle of tortillas. Sprinkle with Parmesan. Fold in opposite edges of tortilla over middle, then fold in ends. (When wrapped, tortillas look like stuffed envelopes.)

4. Arrange tortillas in a microwave-safe glass baking dish. Top each with a triangle of cheese. Cover baking dish with plastic wrap. Microwave on high until cheese is melted, about 2 minutes. Sprinkle with paprika. Makes 6 servings.

✄ **DIANNA WARA,** Washington, Illinois
Second Place, Main Dish Using Beef, Illinois State Fair, Springfield, Illinois, 2005

BOURSIN CHEESE-STEAK PIZZA

1 envelope (2.4 oz.) active dry yeast
½ teaspoon brown sugar
1½ cups warm water (110°F)
1 teaspoon salt
2 tablespoons olive oil, plus more for bowl
3½ cups all-purpose flour, divided

Boursin Cheese Sauce (recipe follows)
Peppers and Onions (recipe follows)
Crispy Steak-ums (recipe follows)
½ cup mild banana pepper rings
1 cup grated Fontina

1. In a large bowl, dissolve yeast and brown sugar in water. Let sit for 10 minutes.

2. Stir salt and olive oil into yeast solution. Mix in 2½ cups of the flour.

3. Turn out dough onto a well-floured surface. Knead in more flour, up to 1 cup, until dough is no longer sticky. Gather dough into a ball. Place in a well-oiled bowl and turn once to coat. Cover and let rise until double in size, 1 hour.

4. Preheat oven to 425°F. Punch down dough. Roll into a tight ball. Allow dough to relax for 1 minute. Press out onto a lightly greased pizza stone. Spread Boursin Cheese Sauce on the crust. Top with Crispy Steak-ums and Peppers and Onions. Add banana pepper rings and sprinkle with Fontina. Bake until cheese and crust are golden brown, 15 to 20 minutes. Makes 6 to 8 servings.

BOURSIN CHEESE SAUCE

1 cup heavy cream
1 package (5.2 oz.) Boursin cheese, broken apart

Heat heavy cream in a saucepan over medium heat. Add Boursin cheese. Simmer, stirring constantly with a wire whisk, until cheese is melted and mixture is hot. Cool slightly. Makes 1¼ cups.

PEPPERS AND ONIONS

½ red bell pepper, seeded
  and cut into strips
½ green bell pepper, seeded
  and cut into strips

½ yellow bell pepper, seeded
  and cut into strips
½ Vidalia onion, chopped
1 teaspoon minced garlic

Coat a nonstick skillet with canola oil spray. Add red, green, and yellow pepper strips, Vidalia onion, and minced garlic. Sauté until onion is transparent.

CRISPY STEAK-UMS

6 Steak-ums
1 tablespoon steak sauce

Cut Steak-ums into strips. Cook in a skillet over medium heat, breaking into small pieces as strips become crunchy. Remove from heat. Splash with steak sauce.

※ **ALLI CURRY,** Lewisburg, West Virginia
First Place, Pizza Contest, State Fair of West Virginia, Lewisburg, West Virginia, 2005

QUICK AND EASY BEEF DISH

4 red potatoes

3 lbs. skirt steak

¼ cup olive oil, divided,
    plus more for coating steak

Salt and peper

Garlic powder

¼ cup unsalted butter

2 tablespoons minced garlic

1 onion, chopped

1 red bell pepper, cut into 1-inch strips

1 green bell pepper, cut into 1-inch strips

1 yellow bell pepper, cut into 1-inch strips

1. Place potatoes in a saucepan, add cold water to cover, and set over medium-high heat. Bring to a boil and cook until tender, 10 minutes. Cool slightly. Cut into quarters.

2. Brush skirt steak with olive oil; sprinkle with salt, pepper, and garlic powder. Heat 2 tablespoons of the olive oil in a skillet over medium-high heat. Add steak and cook, turning once, until seared on both sides. Remove steak from skillet, but leave behind juices.

3. Melt butter in the same skillet over medium heat. Add potatoes, garlic, onion, and bell peppers. Sauté until peppers are tender and onion is transparent. Remove from heat and set aside.

4. Grill skirt steak over medium heat for 5 minutes. Slice into 1-inch strips. Arrange steak strips on individual serving plates and surround with potatoes, onion, and peppers. Makes 4 to 6 servings.

❊ **JAMES DEXTER, JR.,** Lewisburg, West Virginia
First Place, Quick and Easy Beef Competition, State Fair of West Virginia, Lewisburg, West Virginia, 2005

TURKEY LASAGNA

12 lasagna noodles

2 lbs. ground turkey

2 cans (6 oz. each) tomato paste

2 cans (15 oz. each) tomato sauce

Garlic salt

Pizza seasoning

2 containers (16 oz. each) cottage cheese

1 cup grated Parmesan, divided

1 egg

16 oz. mozzarella, sliced

1. Preheat oven to 350°F. Set aside a 13 x 9 x 2-inch baking pan; do not grease.

2. Cook lasagna noodles according to package directions. Drain, rinse in cold water to cool, and drain again.

3. Brown ground turkey in a large sauté pan over medium heat. Add tomato paste, tomato sauce, 6 shakes of garlic salt, and 9 shakes of pizza seasoning. Simmer until ready to layer lasagna.

4. In a large bowl, combine cottage cheese, ¼ cup of the Parmesan, egg, and 9 shakes of pizza seasoning. Stir until well blended.

5. Layer 6 lasagna noodles in bottom of pan. Top with half of the meat sauce, spread evenly, half of the cheese mixture, and 5 slices mozzarella. Add remaining noodles, meat sauce, cheese mixture, and mozzarella in layers. Bake uncovered for 20 minutes, or until bubbly. Makes 6 to 8 servings.

❊ **DEBBIE SORRELLS,** Fargo, North Dakota
Grand Champion, Red River Valley Fair, West Fargo, North Dakota, 2005

Easy Cheesy-Chili Bean Tamales

1 lb. stewing beef

3 cans (15.5 oz. each) Great Northern
white beans

1 can (15.5 oz.) whole pinto beans

1 can (14 oz.) Mexican-stewed tomatoes

2 packets (1.25 oz. each) chili mix
(i.e., Lawry's)

3 dozen dried cornhusks

3 lbs. prepared masa

Monterey Jack or mild cheddar cheese, sliced

1. Cut beef into bite-size pieces. Place in a skillet over medium-high heat, turning to brown all sides. Do this in batches to avoid crowding in skillet.

2. Rinse and drain white beans and pinto beans. Place beans in a stockpot. Add beef, tomatoes, and chili mix. Add water to cover. Simmer until meat is tender and chili is slightly thickened.

3. Soak cornhusks in warm water until softened. Remove from water and pat dry. Place cornhusks on a baking sheet. Cover with a warm damp towel.

4. Place masa in a mixing bowl. Beat in about ½ cup of the chili broth for color. Mix until blended.

5. Spread ½ cup of masa on wide end of cornhusk (smooth side) to about halfway down husk. Place 1 tablespoon of chili in center of cornhusk. Place 1 slice of cheese over chili. Fold in wide end to cover filling. Fold in sides then fold narrow end over to make a packet. Set filled tamales in a casserole dish.

6. To cook tamales, add water to a stockpot to a depth of about 1 inch. Set a cake pan turned upside down in the bottom of the pot and set a round wire rack on top of it, to raise tamales above water level. Stack tamales in pot, making sure no water touches them. Top with remaining cornhusks and a wet towel. Cover pot with lid, bring to a boil over high heat, then reduce to a simmer. Cook until masa easily pulls away from husks, about 1½ hours. Makes 16 to 20 servings.

❋ **Laura Palomino,** Chino, California
First Place, Comidas Mexicanas Tamale Contest, L.A. County Fair, Pomona, California, 2003

CHICKEN-CHILE QUICHE

1 unbaked 9-inch pastry shell
1 cup chopped cooked chicken
½ cup shredded Monterey Jack
½ cup shredded longhorn cheese
½ cup chopped green chiles
¼ cup finely chopped onion
2 eggs, beaten

¾ cup mayonnaise
¾ cup milk
½ teaspoon dried oregano
⅛ teaspoon pepper
¼ teaspoon minced garlic
Minced fresh parsley, for garnish
Paprika

1. Preheat oven to 375°F. Pierce pastry shell all over with fork. Bake for 10 minutes and remove from oven.
2. Reduce oven temperature to 350°F. Toss chicken, Monterey Jack, longhorn cheese, chiles, and onion in a large bowl until well combined. Spoon mixture into pastry shell.
3. Stir together eggs, mayonnaise, milk, oregano, pepper, garlic in small bowl until smooth. Pour over chicken mixture. Sprinkle parsley and paprika over top. Bake until golden and knife inserted in center comes out clean, 40 minutes. Makes 4 to 6 servings.

✻ **ANN HILLMEYER,** Sandia Park, New Mexico
First Place, New Mexico State Fair, Albuquerque, New Mexico, 1984

RUBBED TURKEY

Whole fresh turkey

INJECTION LIQUID
Garlic juice
Butter flavoring
Onion powder
Kosher salt
White wine
Honey

BRAISING LIQUID
2 cups white wine
4 tablespoons white wine vinegar
4 tablespoons white Worcestershire sauce
2 tablespoons honey
4 garlic cloves, chopped

DRY RUB
8 parts light brown sugar
3 parts kosher salt
1 part chili powder
1 part spice mix (equal parts round black pepper, cayenne pepper, ground mustard,
Old Bay Seasoning, rubbed thyme, onion powder, adobo powder)

1. Rinse turkey and pat dry.
2. To make injection liquid: At least 3 hours before cooking, combine garlic juice, butter flavoring, onion powder, kosher salt, white wine, and honey in a saucepan. Cook over low heat until honey melts. Cool. Using a meat injector, insert liquid into turkey breast, thighs, and drumsticks. Let rest in refrigerator.

3. To make dry rub: At least 2 hours prior to cooking, combine light brown sugar, kosher salt, chili powder, and spice mix. Working in one area at a time, lift turkey skin, being careful not to tear it, and rub mixture directly onto flesh with your fingers. Let rest in refrigerator.

4. To make braising liquid: Combine white wine, white wine vinegar, white Worchestershire sauce, honey, and garlic in a saucepan over low heat, stirring until honey is melted. Pour mixture into Camp Chef Ultimate Turkey Pot. Add the turkey and cook until done, 5 to 6 minutes per pound. Check braising liquid periodically and add wine or water if it appears to be running dry.

✕ **BRETT ANJEWIERDEN,** West Valley City, Utah
First Place, Camp Chef Ultimate Turkey Challenge Cook-off, Utah State Fair, Salt Lake City, Utah, 2005

TURKEY OR CHICKEN PIE

1 package (10 oz.) frozen peas and carrots
⅓ cup margarine or unsalted butter
⅓ cup Bisquick baking mix
½ teaspoon onion powder
½ teaspoon pepper
1 can (10¾ oz.) cream of chicken
    condensed soup
1 cup milk
1¾ cups cooked turkey or chicken,
    torn into bite-size pieces

PASTRY
2⅓ cups Bisquick baking mix
⅓ cup unsalted butter or margarine,
    room temperature
¼ cup boiling water

1. Preheat oven to 425°F. Set aside a large, deep-dish pie plate.

2. Rinse frozen peas and carrots and drain.

3. Melt margarine or butter in a saucepan over low heat. Add baking mix, onion powder, and pepper. Cook, stirring constantly, until mixture is smooth and bubbly. Remove from heat. Stir in condensed soup and milk. Return to heat, bring to a boil, and cook, stirring constantly, for 1 minute. Stir in chicken or turkey and peas and carrots.

4. To make pastry: Combine baking mix and butter or margarine in a bowl. Add boiling water; stir until a soft dough forms. Divide dough in half. Roll each half into a ball, flatten into a patty, and roll out to ¼-inch thickness between sheets of waxed paper dusted with baking mix.

5. Ease one pastry into pie plate. Spoon in cooked filling. Lay second pastry on top. Trim, seal, and crimp the edges. Cover the edge with 3-inch strips of aluminum foil to prevent excessive browning. Pierce vent holes in top crust. Bake for 25 minutes, or until crust is brown. Let stand for 15 minutes before serving. Makes 6 servings.

✕ **PRISCILLA GERRARD,** Danvers, Massachusetts
First Place, Mrs. Essex County Contest, Topsfield Fair, Topsfield, Massachusetts, 1997

WINNER'S CIRCLE TIP | For a leaner version of this recipe, substitute lowfat or nonfat soup and dairy products. Any frozen vegetable can be used in place of the peas and carrots.

TACO TARTS

1 lb. ground chuck

2 tablespoons taco seasoning mix

2 tablespoons ice water

1 cup sour cream

2 tablespoons taco sauce

2 oz. black olives, chopped

1 cup tortilla chips, crushed

½ cup shredded cheddar cheese

1. Preheat oven to 350°F.

2. Combine ground chuck, taco seasoning, and water in a bowl and mix well. Press mixture into bottom and sides of the cups in a tart pan.

3. Combine sour cream, taco sauce, olives, and ¾ cup of the tortilla chips. Spoon filling into each shell, mounding slightly.

4. Combine remaining ¼ cup tortilla chips and cheese. Sprinkle over each tart. Bake for 10 minutes. Serve with taco sauce. Makes 32 small tarts.

✄ **JEANNE MAY,** Kearney, Nebraska
First Place, What's for Dinner Beef Cook-Off, River City Roundup Rodeo, Omaha, Nebraska, 2005

COUNTRY FLORENTINE BURGERS WITH BABY PORTABELLA SAUCE

FILLING

1 package (10 oz.) frozen, chopped spinach, thawed and well-drained

1½ tablespoons grated Parmesan

⅛ teaspoon garlic salt

4 oz. marbled Monterey Jack/cheddar cheese

SAUCE

3 tablespoons unsalted butter

1 package (8 oz.) baby portabella mushrooms, cleaned and sliced

⅛ teaspoon garlic salt

1 tablespoon Worcestershire sauce

1 tablespoon flour

¼ cup water

PATTIES

2 lbs. ground chuck

1 teaspoon salt

¼ teaspoon coarsely ground black pepper, plus more for bacon

2 tablespoons Worcestershire sauce

6 large onion buns, split

12 slices bacon, cooked

1. To prepare filling: Combine spinach, Parmesan, and garlic salt in a medium bowl. Slice the cheese into 6 equal portions.

2. To make sauce: Melt butter in a medium saucepan over medium heat. Add mushrooms, garlic salt, and Worcestershire sauce. Simmer until most of the liquid has evaporated, 5 to 8 minutes. Sprinkle flour over the mixture and stir to combine. Add water and stir. Reduce heat to medium-low and continue simmering until sauce thickens.

3. To prepare patties: Combine ground chuck, salt, black pepper, and Worcestershire sauce in a large bowl. Mix just to combine, handling meat as little as possible. Divide into 12 equal portions and form into patties. Spoon spinach filling onto 6 patties to within ½ inch of the edge. Top each with a slice of cheese. Place remaining patties on top and seal the edges.

4. To cook patties: Heat a grill pan over medium-high heat or preheat a gas grill. When hot, add patties and cook, turning once, until medium-well, 5 to 7 minutes per side. During the final minutes of grilling, place onion buns, cut side down, on grill pan or grill to lightly toast.

5. Place bacon on a microwave-safe tray. Sprinkle with pepper. Microwave on high until crisp, 30 to 45 seconds.

6. To serve, place bottom halves of buns on individual serving plates. Set a patty on each bun, spoon on some sauce, and top each with 2 slices of bacon. Add the top halves of buns. Makes 6 servings.

✖ **CARLA STAGEMEYER,** Page, Nebraska
Second Place, What's for Dinner Beef Cook-Off, River City Roundup Rodeo, Omaha, Nebraska, 2005

MOUSSAKA (GREEK CASSEROLE)

3 medium to large eggplants
½ cup olive oil, divided
3 medium onions, finely chopped
2 lbs. ground beef, browned
1 can (15 oz.) tomato sauce
1 can (8 oz.) tomato sauce
4 garlic cloves, minced
2 teaspoons dried oregano
½ to 1 teaspoon salt
¼ teaspoon black pepper

CHEESE SAUCE

6 tablespoons margarine or unsalted butter
6 tablespoons flour
3 cups lowfat milk
½ to 1 teaspoon salt
⅛ to ¼ teaspoon pepper
3 eggs
1 cup grated Parmesan

1. Peel eggplants and cut in half crosswise. Stand upright on cut ends and cut down to make ¼-inch-thick slices. Brush both sides of each slice lightly with olive oil. Place under broiler or cook on a griddle, turning once, until browned on both sides.

2. Layer half of the eggplant in the bottom of a 13 x 9 x 2-inch baking pan, overlapping if necessary.

3. Heat 2 tablespoons of the olive oil in a large skillet over medium-high heat. Add onions and sauté until tender. Add browned ground beef, both cans of tomato sauce, garlic, oregano, salt, and pepper. Cook until warmed through, 5 to 6 minutes. Taste and adjust seasonings if necessary.

4. Pour meat sauce over eggplant, spreading evenly. Layer remaining eggplant slices on top.

5. To make cheese sauce: Melt margarine or butter in large saucepan over medium heat. Add flour and stir until well combined; do not brown. Gradually add milk, stirring continuously, until thick and bubbly, 8 to 10 minutes. Sprinkle with salt and pepper. Taste and adjust seasonings if necessary.

6. In a small bowl, beat eggs. Stir in some of the hot white sauce, then add egg mixture to saucepan and stir to blend. Stir in cheese until melted. Pour cheese sauce over eggplant in baking dish. Bake in oven at 350°F for 45 minutes. Makes 8 to 10 servings.

✖ **LILLIAN CALLOWAY,** Deatsville, Alabama
Prize Winner, Alabama National Fair, Montgomery, Alabama, 1998–2002

Hawaiian Burgers

1 lb. ground beef
1 tablespoon Cookie's All-Purpose Seasoning
¼ teaspoon cinnamon
¼ teaspoon paprika
¼ teaspoon curry powder
⅛ teaspoon ground ginger

⅛ teaspoon nutmeg
¼ cup soy sauce
1 can (20 oz.) pineapple rings
4 hamburger buns, split
4 slices bacon, cooked

1. Place beef in a bowl. In a second bowl, stir together Cookie's seasoning, cinnamon, paprika, curry powder, ginger, and nutmeg in a small bowl. Sprinkle seasoning over beef and mix to combine. Divide into 4 equal portions and shape into patties.

2. Grill patties, basting with soy sauce and turning once, until done. Toward end of grilling time, add 4 pineapple rings to grill; grill until lightly browned.

3. To serve, place bottom halves of buns on individual serving plates. Set burgers on buns, top each with a pineapple ring and a slice of bacon, and add top halves of buns. Makes 4 servings.

⌘ **RICK BURGER,** Goshen, Indiana
First Place, Beef: Ground, Elkhart County 4-H Fair, Goshen, Indiana, 2005

Gorgonzola- and Mushroom-Stuffed Beef Tenderloin with Merlot Sauce

One beef tenderloin, about 2½-lbs.
1 tablespoon unsalted butter
1 cup sliced fresh mushrooms
1 cup soft bread crumbs
½ cup crumbled Gorgonzola

¼ cup chopped fresh parsley
1 tablespoon olive oil
¼ teaspoon salt
Merlot Sauce (recipe follows)

1. Preheat oven to 425°F. So that tenderloin can be filled and rolled, use a sharp boning knife to cut horizontally down length of beef, about ½ inch from top of beef and stopping ½ inch from opposite side. Open flat. Turn beef over and repeat, cutting from inside edge. Open flat.

2. Melt butter in a 10-inch skillet over medium-high heat. Add mushrooms and cook until tender and liquid has evaporated. Cool 5 minutes. Add bread crumbs, cheese, and parsley; toss to combine.

3. Sprinkle bread crumb mixture over beef to within 1 inch of edges. Beginning with a long edge, roll up beef tightly; turn under narrow end about 6 inches so entire roll cooks evenly. Tie rolled beef with butcher's string at 1½-inch intervals.

4. Place rolled tenderloin seam side down on a rack set in a shallow roasting pan. Brush with oil. Sprinkle with salt. Insert a meat thermometer so tip is in center of thickest part of beef. Bake uncovered until internal temperature of meat registers 140°F on thermometer, 30 to 40 minutes. Remove from oven, cover loosely with foil, and let stand until thermometer reads 145°F, about 15 minutes.

5. To serve, remove string from tenderloin and carve into slices. Serve Merlot Sauce on the side. Makes 8 to 10 servings.

MERLOT SAUCE

½ cup currant jelly

½ cup Merlot

¼ cup beef broth

1 tablespoon unsalted butter

Combine currant jelly, Merlot, beef broth, and butter in a 1-quart saucepan over medium-high heat. Bring to a boil, stirring occasionally. Reduce heat and simmer, uncovered, stirring occasionally, until slightly reduced and syrupy, 35 to 40 minutes.

✳ **MARY BETH PEDERSON,** Morton, Illinois
First Place, Main Dish Using Beef, and Reserve Grand Champion, Blue Ribbon Culinary Contest, Illinois State Fair, Springfield, Illinois, 2005

For a lighter flavor, try Zinfandel or a nonalcoholic red wine in place of Merlot.

CHICKEN SATAY WITH PEANUT SAUCE

20 bamboo skewers, soaked in
    water for 1 hour

4 chicken breast halves,
    each cut into 5 strips

½ cup soy sauce

¼ cup olive oil

3 tablespoons curry powder

3 tablespoons turmeric

1 tablespoon ground cumin

1 tablespoon coriander

½ cup brown sugar

⅓ cup coconut milk

PEANUT SAUCE

2 tablespoons olive oil

4 garlic cloves, minced

2 tablespoons red curry paste

5 oz. unsweetened coconut milk

½ cup crushed pineapple with juice

2 tablespoons brown sugar

1 cup crunchy peanut butter

3 tablespoons lime juice

3 tablespoons fresh cilantro, chopped

2 tablespoons sweetened coconut

Cilantro sprigs, for garnish

1. Thread chicken strips onto soaked skewers. Layer chicken in a 13 x 9 x 2-inch glass baking dish.

2. Combine soy sauce, oil, curry powder, turmeric, cumin, coriander, sugar, and coconut milk in a small bowl. Spread marinade over chicken and let stand at least 1 hour. Remove chicken from marinade and let drain.

3. To make peanut sauce: Combine olive oil, garlic, curry paste, coconut milk, pineapple, brown sugar, peanut butter, lime juice, and cilantro in a medium bowl. Whisk until blended. Consistency should be liquid, but not runny; thin with coconut milk, if necessary.

4. Cook chicken strips over hot grill or under a broiler until lightly browned and well done. Line serving platter with lettuce, if desired. Place bowl of peanut sauce in middle of platter and arrange chicken skewers around it, spoke fashion. Sprinkle shredded coconut over chicken and garnish with cilantro. Makes 4 servings.

✳ **BETTIE SECHRIST,** Montgomery, Alabama
Prize Winner, Alabama National Fair, Montgomery, Alabama, 1998–2002

SAUCY CRANBERRY MEATBALLS

2 lbs. ground turkey
2 eggs, beaten
1 cup fine dry bread crumbs
1 envelope (1 oz.) dry onion soup mix
1 can (16 oz.) whole-berry cranberry sauce

1 cup ketchup
1 cup brown sugar
1 can (16 oz.) sauerkraut, rinsed and drained
1 cup water

1. Preheat oven to 350°F.

2. Combine ground turkey, eggs, bread crumbs, and soup mix in a large bowl. Form into meatballs, using approximately 2 tablespoons of mixture for each meatball. Arrange meatballs in a single layer in a 13 x 9 x 2-inch baking dish.

3. Combine cranberry sauce, ketchup, brown sugar, sauerkraut, and water in a medium bowl. Mix well. Pour sauce over meatballs. Bake until bubbling, about 1 hour. Makes 6 to 8 servings.

✳ **DELORES F. RASMUSSEN,** Portage, Wisconsin
First Place, Processed Cranberry, Warrens Cranberry Festival, Warrens, Wisconsin, 2005

PPP (3 PEPPERS AND PEPPERONI) PIZZA

One 12" prebaked pizza crust
½ cup Italian-flavored tomato sauce
2 cups sliced pepperoni
2½ cups shredded mozzarella, divided

1 medium red bell pepper, sliced
1 medium green bell pepper, sliced
1 medium yellow bell pepper, sliced

1. Preheat oven to 400°F.

2. Place pizza crust on pan. Spread tomato sauce evenly over crust.

3. Arrange pepperoni slices over sauce. Top with 1¼ cups of the mozzarella. Arrange sliced bell peppers over cheese. Top with remaining 1¼ cups mozzarella. Bake for 35 to 40 minutes. Makes 4 to 6 servings.

✳ **EVAN WILLIAMS,** age 12, Summerville, South Carolina
First Place, Junior Division, 4-H Pizza Pizazz Competition, Coastal Carolina Fair, Ladson, South Carolina, 2005

RED-EYE RIBEYES

Six 1-inch-thick ribeye steaks
Coffee Barbecue Rub (recipe follows)
Espresso Barbecue Sauce (recipe follows)

One day in advance, rub Coffee Barbecue Rub generously onto all surfaces of steaks. Refrigerate for 24 hours. The next day, grill steaks over medium heat, turning once, until the internal temperature reaches 145°F to 155°F, 6 to 8 minutes per side. Let rest for 5 minutes. Serve with Espresso Barbecue Sauce. Makes 6 servings.

COFFEE BARBECUE RUB

2 tablespoons ground espresso or coffee

2 tablespoons sweet paprika

2 tablespoons dark brown sugar

2 tablespoons coarse salt

2 tablespoons ground black pepper

2 teaspoons garlic powder

Whisk together all ingredients until well combined. Makes ¾ cup.

ESPRESSO BARBECUE SAUCE

¾ cup espresso or strong coffee

¾ cup ketchup

7 tablespoons heavy cream

½ cup honey

⅓ cup Dijon mustard

¼ cup dark brown sugar

3 tablespoons apple cider vinegar

3 tablespoons hot sauce

3 tablespoons water

Salt and pepper

Combine espresso or coffee, ketchup, heavy cream, honey, mustard, dark brown sugar, vinegar, hot sauce, and water in a medium saucepan over medium-high heat. Sprinkle with salt and pepper. Bring to a boil, reduce heat to medium, and simmer for 6 to 10 minutes. Taste and adjust seasonings; add more brown sugar, vinegar, or hot sauce according to taste. Makes about 3 cups.

⌗ **MARSHALL KING,** Goshen, Indiana
First Place, Beef: Cut, Elkhart County 4-H Fair, Goshen, Indiana, 2005

HAMBURGER CASSEROLE

2 lbs. ground beef or ground chuck

1 small onion, chopped

½ medium green bell pepper, chopped

1 can (14.5 oz.) sliced stewed
   tomatoes, chopped

2 cans (14.5 oz. each) whole kernel
   yellow corn, drained

1 package (12 oz.) egg noodles

2 packages (8 oz. each) sharp grated cheddar

1. Preheat oven to 300°F. Brown ground beef or ground chuck in a large skillet over medium-high heat. Remove from skillet and drain off fat.

2. In the same skillet, sauté onion and bell pepper. Drain off excess liquid.

3. Combine stewed tomatoes and corn in a saucepan over low heat. Simmer until warmed through, 20 minutes.

4. Cook egg noodles according to package directions. Rinse and drain well.

5. Combine ground beef or ground chuck, onion and bell pepper, tomato-corn mixture, and noodles in a large bowl. Sprinkle 1 package of grated cheese over the top. Toss until well combined. Spoon into a casserole dish. Top with remaining cheese. Bake just until top cheese melts. Makes 8 to 10 servings.

⌗ **KYASHON REESE,** age 14, Hazlehurst, Mississippi
Second Place, Casseroles, Copiah County Fair, Gallman, Mississippi

LEG OF LAMB SUPREME

One leg of lamb, about 4 lbs., boned,
trimmed of excess fat, and tied as a roast
1 lemon, cut in half
1 jar (10 oz.) mint jelly or mint-apple jelly
1 tablespoon ground ginger

1 teaspoon paprika
1 teaspoon salt
1 teaspoon pepper
½ teaspoon garlic powder
1 can (14.5 oz.) consommé

1. The day before, rinse lamb well and dry with paper towels. Gash with the tip of knife several times so that sauce will be absorbed. Rub surface with lemon, squeezing out a little juice as you rub.

2. Combine jelly, ginger, paprika, salt, pepper, and garlic powder. Spread over lamb until completely covered. Let stand in refrigerator overnight to marinate.

3. The next day, preheat oven to 300°F. Roast lamb until the outside is a rich, dark-brown color, 30 to 35 minutes per pound. The marinade and drippings with be dark brown and the consistency of taffy. Drain off fat and mix consommé with drippings to make a pan gravy. Makes 8 to 10 servings.

✕ **ZELMA MEYER,** Butte, Montana
First Grand Place; Meat Recipe Contest, Jewish Holiday, Western Montana Fair, Missoula, Montana, 2001

GARDEN BURRITOS

2 cups cooked cubed chicken breast
¼ cup teriyaki sauce
3 medium tomatoes, peeled and diced
1 large red or green bell pepper, diced
1 medium onion, diced

Dash of salt
10 flour tortillas
8 oz. shredded cheddar cheese
8 oz. shredded mozzarella
½ cup pecans, chopped

1. Preheat oven to 350°F.

2. Combine chicken and teriyaki sauce in a nonstick pan. Add tomatoes, peppers, onion, and salt. Cook over medium heat until vegetables begin to soften.

3. Spoon mixture into center of tortilla shells. Top with shredded cheddar and mozzarella and pecans.

4. Fold each tortilla shell burrito-style and place on a baking sheet seam side down. Bake 15 minutes and serve. Makes 10 burritos.

✕ **JILL BODENSTEIN,** Gordonville, Missouri
Second Place, Food & Poultry Recipe Contest, Southeast Missouri District Fair, Cape Girardeau, Missouri, 2004

WINNER'S CIRCLE TIP | Garden Burritos can be assembled up to one day ahead and refrigerated. To serve, warm the burritos in the microwave and then bake for 20 minutes.

THAT'S AMORE! STUFFED BURGERS

1½ lbs. ground chuck

1 package (4 to 5 oz.) savory herb and
    garlic seasoning mix

4 oz. Genoa salami, chopped

Salt and pepper

12 small sundried tomatoes, chopped

2 oz. Feta with green peppers and
    roasted garlic, crumbled

3 tablespoons dry minced onions, reconstituted
    according to package instructions

4 hamburger buns

3 tablespoons unsalted butter,
    room temperature

¼ cup shredded Parmesan,
    romano, and Asiago cheese mix

4 slices (1 oz. each) Provolone

1 cup mild peppers in sauce

1. Combine ground chuck, savory herb and garlic seasoning mix, and salami in a bowl. Sprinkle with salt and pepper. Divide into 8 equal portions and shape into thin patties.

2. Mix sundried tomatoes and Feta cheese in a bowl. Divide into 4 equal portions and spoon on top of 4 patties. Place remaining 4 patties on top and lightly press edges together to seal. Press reconstituted minced onions onto tops and bottoms of patties. Cook burgers on a countertop grill, turning once, until well done.

3. Preheat broiler. Open and separate hamburger buns and place on a baking sheet. Butter each half. Sprinkle cheese mix on bottom buns. Place a slice of Provolone on top buns. Set under broiler until cheeses melt.

4. Place peppers in sauce in a microwave-safe bowl. Microwave on high for 2 minutes until hot.

5. To serve, place bottom halves of buns on individual serving plates. Set a burger on each bun, spoon on some peppers and sauce, and add top halves of buns. Makes 4 servings.

✕ **AMBER DAVIS,** Lincoln, Nebraska
Third Place, What's for Dinner Beef Cook-Off, River City Roundup Rodeo, Omaha, Nebraska, 2005

PEACHY CABBAGE-N-MEATBALLS

8 oz. ground beef
1 teaspoon coriander
Salt
1 package (16 oz.) frozen peaches
⅓ cup chopped green cabbage
⅓ cup chopped bell pepper

1 jalapeño pepper, chopped (optional)
⅓ cup chopped onion
⅓ cup chopped celery
1 tablespoon onion soup mix
½ cup water

1. Place ground beef in a bowl, sprinkle with coriander and salt, and mix loosely to combine. Form into bite-size meatballs.

2. Heat a large skillet over medium heat, add meatballs, and cook, rolling occasionally, until evenly browned. Drain on paper towels.

3. Wipe out skillet. Add peaches, cabbage, bell pepper, jalapeño, if using, onion, celery, soup mix, and water to skillet. Cook over medium-low heat until cabbage is tender.

4. Stir meatballs into cabbage mixture. Simmer for 15 minutes. Serve hot. Makes 4 servings.

※ **ALBERTA ALLISON,** Kathleen, Georgia
First Place, Just Peachy Contest, Georgia National Fair, Perry, Georgia, 2005

CROWN ROYAL ROAST RIB OF BEEF AU JUS AND HORSERADISH CREAM

One beef rib roast, 6 to 7 lbs.
2 tablespoons minced onions
2 tablespoons whole peppercorns
2 tablespoons gourmet coarse sea salt
2 tablespoons dried sage
2 tablespoons granulated garlic
1 tablespoon paprika

1 tablespoon dried thyme
1 tablespoon dried marjoram
Rib bones
1 large onion, sliced
1 cup of Crown Royal whiskey or beef broth
2 tablespoons flour
Horseradish Cream (recipe follows)

1. Trim excess fat from rib roast. In a small food mill, grind minced onions, peppercorns, sea salt, sage, garlic, paprika, thyme, and marjoram to make a dry rub. Rub mixture into rib roast until entire surface is coated; prepare more rub if needed.

2. Preheat a Dutch oven to 350°F over medium heat for 10 minutes. Place 2 or 3 rib bones on the bottom of Dutch oven. Set roast on rib bones. Top with sliced onions. Pour in whiskey or beef broth. Roast for 2½ to 3 hours, or until internal temperature reaches 140°F; change coals every 45 minutes. Remove roast from oven and let it stand for 15 to 20 minutes before slicing.

3. To make gravy, add flour to pan drippings and mix well. Bring to a boil, reduce heat, and simmer until thickened. Strain through a coarse sieve. Slice the roast and place on a serving platter. Serve with gravy and Horseradish Cream. Makes 8 to 10 servings.

HORSERADISH CREAM

¾ cup heavy cream

½ cup mayonnaise

¼ cup prepared horseradish

1 tablespoon Dijon mustard

Pinch of sugar

Salt and freshly ground black pepper

1. In a small mixing bowl, whip heavy cream until soft peaks form.

2. In a separate bowl, combine mayonnaise, horseradish, and mustard. Fold in whipped cream with a rubber spatula. Stir in sugar. Season with salt and pepper. Makes 1½ cups.

✕ **ROSA AND MARISELA SANCHEZ,** Clearfield, Utah

First Place, Utah Farm Bureau Great American Dutch Oven Cook-Off, Utah State Fair, Salt Lake City, Utah, 2005

WINNER'S CIRCLE TIP | The heavy cast iron Dutch oven nestles into the hot coals or sits right on the grill. Use tongs to place more hot coals around the lid rim for uniform heating above and below. A slightly raised edge on the rim prevents the coals from rolling off the lid.

MEAT LOAF

2 tablespoons unsalted butter

½ cup finely chopped onion

⅓ cup chopped celery

⅓ cup chopped green pepper

2 lbs. ground beef

½ lb. ground pork

½ cup rolled oats

2 eggs

¾ cup chili sauce

¼ cup tomato juice

2 teaspoons salt

¼ teaspoon black pepper

5 tablespoons Worcestershire sauce, divided

¼ teaspoon Tabasco sauce

1 cup grated sharp cheddar cheese

½ cup catsup

½ cup brown sugar

1 tablespoon dry mustard

1. Preheat oven to 300°F. Set aside a 13 x 9 x 2-inch baking or roasting pan.

2. Melt butter in a skillet over medium heat. Add onion, celery, and green pepper. Sauté until onion is soft and golden.

3. In a large bowl, combine ground beef, ground pork, oats, eggs, chili sauce, tomato juice, salt, black pepper, 3 tablespoons of the Worcestershire sauce, Tabasco sauce, and cheddar cheese. Add sautéed onion mixture and mix well.

4. Shape mixture into two loaves. Place side by side in pan. Bake for 1 hour. Drain off excess grease.

5. Combine catsup, brown sugar, dry mustard, and remaining 2 tablespoons Worcestershire sauce in a small saucepan over medium heat. Bring to a boil and pour over meat loaves. Return pan to oven and bake for another 30 minutes. Makes 8 to 10 servings.

✕ **DALE BERKENBOSCH,** Prairie City, Iowa

First Place, My Favorite Meat Loaf, Iowa State Fair, Des Moines, Iowa, 2005

CHILI CHILI, BANG BANG!

1 to 2 tablespoons olive oil

3 lbs. tender beef chuck, cubed

6 to 8 garlic cloves, minced

2 cans (14½ oz. each) beef broth

1 or 2 cans (14½ oz. each) tomato purée

4 dashes of Tabasco sauce

1½ tablespoons onion powder

¾ teaspoon cayenne pepper

2 teaspoons beef bouillon granules

1 teaspoon chicken bouillon granules

¾ teaspoon garlic powder

1½ tablespoons ground cumin

¾ teaspoon white pepper

6 tablespoons chili powder

Salt

1. Heat olive oil in a skillet over medium heat. Add beef and garlic; cook, turning occasionally, until beef is browned on all sides.

2. Add beef broth to skillet to cover beef. Stir in half of the tomato purée. Add Tabasco sauce, onion powder, cayenne pepper, and beef and chicken bouillon granules. Cook at a low boil until meat is tender. Add water or more tomato purée if more liquid is needed.

3. About 30 minutes before serving, stir in garlic powder, cumin, white pepper, and chili powder. Simmer to a smooth consistency. Season with salt to taste. Makes 8 to 10 servings.

✄ **BEN AND KIM WATSON,** West Jordan, Utah
First Place, Budweiser Chili Cook-Off, Utah State Fair, Salt Lake City, Utah, 2005

SCANDINAVIAN FESTIVAL SWEDISH MEAT BALLS

2 lbs. lean ground beef

4 slices bread, dampened in water

2 medium onions, grated

1 teaspoon dry mustard

2 teaspoons salt

½ to 1 teaspoon pepper

Mayonnaise, for cooking meatballs

1 can (10.5 oz.) cream of mushroom condensed soup

1 can (10.5 oz.) cream of chicken condensed soup

2 cans (12 oz. each) evaporated milk

1. Preheat oven to 325°F.

2. Combine ground beef, bread, onions, dry mustard, salt, and pepper in a large bowl. Mix with your hands until well combined. Form into 42 to 45 small meatballs.

3. Melt mayonnaise in a skillet over medium-high heat. Add meatballs in batches and cook until evenly browned. Drain on paper towels.

4. Transfer meatballs to a large baking dish. Whisk together mushroom soup, chicken soup, and evaporated milk. Pour over meatballs. Bake for 1 to 1½ hours. Makes 42 to 45 small meatballs.

✄ **KIM ONDOV,** Missoula, Montana, and **CAROLYNN RICHARDSON,** Huson, Montana
First Place, Public Favorite, Scandinavian, Western Montana Fair, Missoula, Montana, 1997

WINNER'S CIRCLE TIP │ Salad dressing (such as Miracle Whip) is no substitute for mayonnaise in this recipe. Use the real thing!

THE OTHER WHITE MEAT CHILI

2 tablespoons oil
1 teaspoon garlic salt
½ teaspoon pepper
1 lb. pork loin, roast or chops, trimmed
 of fat and cut into ¾-inch cubes
1 medium onion, finely chopped
2 garlic cloves, finely chopped
1 or 2 jalapeños, finely chopped
1 can (4 oz.) chopped green chiles, drained

1 cup salsa
1 can (15½ oz.) white beans, drained
1 can (14½ oz.) chicken broth
½ teaspoon ground cumin
½ teaspoon cayenne pepper
1 cup sour cream
2 cups grated Monterey Jack cheese, divided
¼ cup chopped cilantro

1. Heat oil in a Dutch oven or stew pot over medium heat. Sprinkle garlic salt and pepper over pork and toss to coat all pieces. Add pork to pan and cook, stirring occasionally, until lightly browned on all sides.
2. Add onion, garlic, and jalapeño to pot. Continue cooking until onion and jalapeños are soft, about 5 minutes. Increase heat to medium high. Stir in chiles, salsa, white beans, chicken broth, cumin, and cayenne until well combined. Bring to a boil, reduce heat to low, and simmer for 20 minutes.
3. Stir in sour cream and 1½ cups of the Monterey Jack. Heat just until mixture returns to a simmer. Remove from heat. Garnish with remaining ½ cup Monterey Jack and cilantro. Makes 4 servings.

Got leftover cooked pork? Cube it and add into the pot, along with the onions and garlic.

※ **CONNIE PEGG,** Asheville, North Carolina
First Place, Tarheel Pork Challenge, North Carolina Mountain State Fair, Fletcher, North Carolina, 2005

PORK STACKS

10 pork loin chops
4 tablespoons apple brandy, divided
Salt and pepper
2 tablespoons lemon juice
4 tablespoons maple syrup

1 Granny Smith apple, grated,
 plus more slices for garnish
1 sprig fresh sage, chopped,
 plus more leaves for garnish
1 tablespoon olive oil

1. Brush pork loin chops with 2 tablespoons of the apple brandy. Sprinkle with salt and pepper. Cook on a grill to desired doneness.
2. In a medium bowl, combine remaining 2 tablespoons apple brandy, lemon juice, maple syrup, apple, sage, and olive oil to make slaw.
3. To assemble, stack grilled chops, spooning a bit of slaw in between. Push 1 or 2 bamboo skewers through entire stack to hold in place. Garnish with apple slices and sage leaves. Makes 10 servings.

※ **KAREN HARSHBARGER,** Mediapolis, Iowa
First Place, The National Pork Board, We Want Wow Now Pork Recipe Rally, Iowa State Fair, Des Moines, Iowa, 2005

Honey Mustard Pork Burgers

2 lbs. ground pork
40 saltine crackers, crushed
½ cup Dijon mustard

¼ cup honey
2 tablespoons lemon juice

1. Combine ground pork, crushed crackers, mustard, honey, and lemon juice in a large bowl. Form into 8 patties.
2. Grill on medium heat, turning once, until juices run clear, about 12 minutes. Makes 8 burgers.

Kevin Eyer, Goshen, Indiana
First Place, Pork: Ground, Elkhart County 4-H Fair, Goshen, Indiana, 2005

Blueberry-Rhubarb Pork Chops

4 pork chops
¼ cup all-purpose flour
Salt and pepper
Cooking spray
2 cups chopped rhubarb

2 cups blueberries
2 tablespoons honey
2 tablespoons brown sugar
⅛ teaspoon cinnamon

1. Dredge chops in flour; sprinkle with salt and pepper. Coat skillet with cooking spray. Set skillet over medium-high heat, add chops, and cook until browned.
2. Combine rhubarb, blueberries, honey, brown sugar, and cinnamon. Spoon over chops in skillet. Cook over medium-low heat for 20 to 30 minutes. Makes 4 servings.

Suzanne Plaisted, Jonesboro, Maine
Overall Winner, Wild Blueberry Festival Cooking Competition, Machias, Maine, 2003

CAROLINA RIESLING PORK CHOPS

8 boneless ½-inch-thick pork chops

2 teaspoons salt

1 teaspoon coarsely ground black pepper

¼ cup olive oil

2 tablespoons minced fresh garlic

8 oz. sliced fresh mushrooms

3 tablespoons fresh lemon juice

2 cups Riesling

½ cup heavy cream

1. Sprinkle pork chops with salt and pepper. Heat olive oil in a heavy sauté pan. Add pork chops and brown on both sides. Remove chops from pan and set aside.

2. Reduce heat, add garlic to pan, and cook, stirring, for 2 minutes. Add mushrooms and cook until simmering, 5 minutes. Add lemon juice and Riesling.

3. Return chops to pan, cover, and simmer on low heat until chops are tender, 30 to 40 minutes. Remove chops and set aside.

4. Add heavy cream to pan juices and continue cooking on low until slightly thickened, 5 to 10 minutes. Serve with pasta or baked sweet potatoes and fresh asparagus. Makes 8 servings.

Seasoning the pork chops ahead of time, even earlier in the day, enhances the flavor.

✕ **PAULETTE GRAHAM,** Raleigh, North Carolina
First Place, The National Pork Board We Want Wow Now Pork Recipe Rally, North Carolina State Fair, Raleigh, North Carolina, 2005

BLACK WELL BAR-B-QUE SAUCE AND PORK ROAST

1 container (10 oz.) orange juice
   concentrate, thawed

2 tablespoons lemon juice concentrate

15 oz. water

15 oz. white vinegar

½ tablespoon cayenne pepper

1 tablespoon lemon pepper

1 teaspoon garlic salt

2 teaspoons prepared dry mustard or
   ¼ cup yellow salad mustard

Pecans, unshelled

4 lb. pork shoulder

1. Combine orange juice concentrate, lemon juice concentrate, water, white vinegar, cayenne, lemon pepper, garlic salt, and mustard in a 2-quart jar. Shake well to combine.

2. Prepare a charcoal grill for slow roasting by pushing hot coals to one side of grill bed. To flavor the smoke, place unshelled pecans directly on the coals. Set grill rack in place.

3. Put pork shoulder on opposite side of grill rack, away from direct heat. Cover the grill and crack open the top and bottom vents to less than ¼ inch. Slow-roast the pork to an internal temperature of 170°F, 5 to 7 hours. Rebuild the fire as needed and baste pork occasionally with sauce. Serve with remaining sauce on the side. Makes 6 to 8 servings.

✕ **JEFF WALTON,** Farmington, Minnesota
First Prize, BBQ Contest, Dakota County Fair, Farmington, Minnesota, 2005

TAILGATING PORK STIR FRY

3 tablespoons cooking oil, divided
¼ cup onion, chopped
¼ cup chopped sweet bell pepper
1½ lbs. boneless pork chops, cut into strips
Dash of salt

1 cup sweet-and-sour sauce
1 can (15.5 oz.) snap beans, cut and drained
1 can (20 oz.) pineapple tidbits, drained
Cooked rice or noodles
2 teaspoons peanuts

1. Heat 1 tablespoon of the oil in a skillet over medium-high heat. Add onion and fry until soft and golden. Stir in peppers and cook 4 minutes. Remove peppers and onions and drain on paper towels.
2. Add remaining 2 tablespoons oil to pan. Place pork strips in pan, add a dash of salt, and sauté, turning once, until browned on both sides.
3. Add sweet-and-sour sauce to pan. Stir in peppers and onions, beans, and pineapple. Cook until heated through. Serve over rice or noodles. Sprinkle peanuts on top. Makes 6 to 8 servings.

✕ **DONNA BAREFOOT,** Benson, North Carolina
Second Place, The National Pork Board, We Want Wow Now Pork Recipe Rally, North Carolina State Fair, Raleigh, North Carolina, 2005

KJØTTBOLLER (NORWEGIAN MEATBALLS)

2 lbs. ground chuck
½ lb. ground pork
2 tablespoons flour
1 teaspoon pepper
¼ teaspoon nutmeg
¼ teaspoon ground ginger
1 small onion, finely chopped
2 eggs
2 cups half-and-half

1½ quarts beef stock
Unsalted butter, for frying

BROWN SAUCE
2 tablespoons unsalted butter,
   at room temperature
3 tablespoons flour
2 cups reserved beef stock (see step 4)
Salt and pepper to taste

1. Place ground chuck and ground pork in a large bowl. In a small bowl, whisk together flour, pepper, nutmeg, ginger, and onion. Work mixture into meat with your hands. Mix in eggs one at a time. Gradually add half-and-half, mixing until spongy and light.
2. Shape mixture into small meatballs using a teaspoon dipped in ice water.
3. Heat beef stock in a large pot until boiling. Drop meatballs into boiling stock and cook for 5 minutes.
4. Melt butter in a skillet over medium-high heat. Lift meatballs from stock with a slotted spoon, transfer to skillet, and cook, stirring occasionally, until evenly browned. Drain on paper towels. Measure and set aside 2 cups of beef stock for brown sauce.
5. To make brown sauce: Melt butter in a large saucepan over medium-low heat. Add flour, stirring continuously until smooth. Slowly whisk in reserved beef stock. Season with salt and pepper. Cook at a gentle boil until thick and rich. Add meatballs to brown sauce and stir gently until heated through. Makes 72 small meatballs.

✕ **VALBORG TOLLEFSON,** Missoula, Montana
First Place, Meat Dish, What Mother Would Have Done, Western Montana Fair, Missoula, Montana, 1999

Pork Piccadillo

1½ lbs. ground or diced pork (¼-inch dice)
1 envelope (1.3 oz.) sloppy joe mix
1 cup water
1 can (6 oz.) tomato paste

⅓ cup apple cider vinegar
¼ cup molasses
½ cup seedless raisins

1. Brown pork in nonstick skillet over medium heat, stirring to crumble, about 5 minutes.

2. Sprinkle sloppy joe mix over pork. Add water and tomato paste, mixing to combine. Reduce heat and simmer for 2 minutes.

3. Add cider vinegar, molasses, and raisins; mix well. Simmer for another 10 minutes. Serve over rice (the traditional Cuban way), wrap in a tortilla, or spoon into a taco shell, if desired. Makes 6 to 8 servings.

❊ **JANE BLANCO,** Raleigh, North Carolina
Second Place, The National Pork Board, We Want Wow Now Pork Recipe Rally, North Carolina State Fair, Raleigh, North Carolina, 2005

WINNER'S CIRCLE TIP | Piccadillo, is traditionally made with beef. This recipe was developed using Boston pork butt or boneless country ribs as a tasty and healthy alternative.

Carol's Carne Adovada

2 tablespoons olive oil
3 lbs. pork roast
½ teaspoon garlic powder
½ teaspoon onion powder
1 teaspoon Herbs de Provence

CHILI SAUCE
2 tablespoons canola oil
3 tablespoons flour

3 tablespoons mild chili powder
2½ cups warm water
1 teaspoon beef bouillon granules
1 teaspoon onion powder
3 garlic cloves, crushed
1½ teaspoons oregano
½ teaspoon ground cumin
1 tablespoon salt

1. Preheat oven to 350°F. Massage olive oil into pork roast. In a small bowl, combine garlic powder, onion powder, and Herbs de Provence; rub over surface of pork roast. Set pork on a rack in roasting pan. Roast for 1½ hours.

2. To make chili sauce: While roast is cooking, heat canola oil in a saucepan over low heat. Add flour, stirring constantly with a whisk, until golden. Blend in chili powder. Add warm water a few table-spoons at a time, stirring after each addition, until thickened. Add bouillon, onion powder, garlic, oregano, cumin, and salt. Simmer for 20 minutes.

3. Slice pork roast into thin pieces while still hot. Layer slices in an electric slow cooker. Pour chili sauce over pork and stir to coat all pieces. Cover and cook on low setting until meat can be easily shredded with a fork, about 6 hours. Makes 8 to 10 servings.

❊ **CAROL SCHILLING,** Albuquerque, New Mexico
First Place, New Mexico State Fair, Albuquerque, New Mexico, 2005

Pork Rib Salad Wraps

1½ lbs. boneless pork ribs

3 cups 100% grape juice

⅓ cup bacon, cooked and crumbled

⅓ cup pecans, chopped

1 cup mayonnaise

1 container (8 oz.) sour cream

2 tablespoons fresh basil, chopped

½ teaspoon dried onion, minced

½ teaspoon garlic powder

1 tablespoon prepared yellow mustard

¼ teaspoon black pepper

¼ teaspoon salt

½ cup Romano, shredded

30 red seedless grapes, quartered

4 slices of flatbread

Lettuce leaves

1. Combine pork ribs and grape juice in a Dutch oven; add water to cover. Bring to a boil over high heat. Reduce heat, cover, and simmer until ribs are fully cooked and meat is falling off bones, 1 hour.

2. Set ribs in a colander over a bowl and drain off fat, 10 minutes. Place ribs on a clean cutting board and use two forks to flake the meat into bite-size pieces.

3. In a large bowl, combine bacon, pecans, mayonnaise, sour cream, basil, onion, garlic powder, mustard, pepper, salt, and cheese until well blended. Add pork meat and grapes; mix well. Refrigerate until ready to serve.

4. To serve, evenly divide rib salad among four pieces of flatbread. Spread the salad from end to end. Lay lettuce leaves on top of the rib salad. Roll up tightly from the short end. Cut each roll in half and serve. Makes 4 large or 8 small servings.

Flat breads to use for this recipe include Middle Eastern wraps, pita, and tortillas.

✕ **Diana Wara,** Washington, Illinois
First Place, Main Dish Using Pork, Illinois State Fair, Springfield, Illinois, 2005

Plump Pork-Stuffed Tofu Dumplings

SAUCE

⅓ cup soy sauce

¼ cup unseasoned rice vinegar

2 teaspoons Chinese chili-bean paste

2 large scallions, white part only, thinly sliced

DUMPLINGS

2¼ lbs. tofu, cut into thirty-six 1½-inch cubes

1 lb. ground pork

¼ cup soy flakes

4 large scallions, green part only, thinly sliced

3 tablespoons soy sauce

1 tablespoon Chinese chili-bean paste

1 tablespoon cornstarch

1 garlic clove, minced

1 large egg, beaten

½ teaspoon kosher salt

¼ teaspoon freshly ground pepper

1. To make the sauce: Combine soy sauce, rice vinegar, chili-bean paste, and scallions.

2. To make dumplings: With a small melon baller, hollow out tofu cubes, reserving both the balls and the shells.

3. In a large bowl, combine tofu balls, ground pork, soy flakes, scallions, soy sauce, chili-bean paste, cornstarch, garlic, egg, kosher salt, and pepper. Mix thoroughly with your hands.

4. Carefully stuff each tofu shell with 1 level tablespoon of filling, mounding it over the opening.

5. Fill a large skillet or wok with 2 inches of water and bring to a boil. In a large steamer basket or flat mesh pan, arrange dumplings in a single layer with space between. Set over boiling water. Cover and steam until filling is firm and cooked through, about 10 minutes. Serve dumplings with the sauce. Makes 36.

✳ **SULLEN CALHOUN,** Des Moines, Iowa
Second Place, It's Soy Amazing, Iowa State Fair, Des Moines, Iowa, 2005

WHEN PIGS FLY

1 lb. pork shoulder steaks	½ teaspoon salt
2 teaspoons unsalted butter, room temperature	Dash of pepper
¼ cup onions, chopped	PORT WINE SAUCE
½ cup Granny Smith apple, diced	1 cup Port
⅓ cup prunes, diced	4 prunes, quartered
2 cups fresh bread crumbs	1 cup chicken stock
1 teaspoon sage	1 tablespoon pan drippings
¼ teaspoon nutmeg	1 tablespoon flour

1. Preheat oven to 350°F. Divide pork shoulder steaks into four portions. Trim off excess fat. Pound thin with a meat mallet.

2. Melt butter in a heavy skillet over medium heat. Add onions and apples. Sauté just until onions are translucent and apples are crisp-tender; do not brown. Remove from heat. Stir in prunes, bread crumbs, sage, nutmeg, salt, and pepper until well combined.

3. Spoon bread crumb mixture on top of pork pieces. Roll up each pork piece into a compact "bird" shape and tie with butcher's twine. Place the "birds" in an ovenproof skillet over medium heat, turning to brown all sides, 4 to 6 minutes. Place skillet in oven and cook until meat is no longer pink, 30 minutes. Transfer pork to a plate and cover with foil. Reserve pan drippings.

4. To make Port wine sauce: Begin the sauce while the pork is roasting. Combine Port and prunes in a heavy saucepan over medium heat. Simmer until reduced by half. Strain mixture into chicken stock, pressing with the back of a spoon to extract juice from the prunes.

5. Pour pork pan drippings into a heavy saucepan; set over low heat. Add flour and whisk continuously to make a roux. Slowly add chicken stock mixture, whisking continuously and raising heat if necessary, until slightly thickened. To serve, arrange pork "birds" on a plate and spoon sauce over the top. Serve with the remaining sauce. Makes 4 servings.

If you don't have a good meat mallet and a strong arm, ask the butcher to pound the meat for you.

✳ **PAT BARKER,** Orlando, Florida
First Place, Pork Cook-Off, Central Florida Fair, Orlando, Florida, 2005

FAMILY RECIPE TAMALES

½ lb. pasilla chiles
7 lbs. boneless pork loin or shoulder
2 tablespoons salt
1 whole yellow or white onion
5 whole garlic cloves
1 bay leaf
10 cups cold water
8 oz. corn husks

2 oz. New Mexico chiles
1 tablespoon Mexican allspice
½ teaspoon ground cumin
8 tomatillos, cooked
10 lbs. prepared masa
Black olives
All-purpose deli paper, for steaming

1. Roast pasilla chiles on a griddle until soft. Remove and discard stems and seeds. Place chiles in a separate soup pot. Add enough broth from pork pot to cover. Soak for 4 hours.

2. Place pork, salt, onion, garlic, and bay leaf in a large soup pot. Add cold water to cover. Bring to a boil over high heat. Reduce to a simmer and cook until pork is tender, 2 hours. Remove pork from pot, reserving the broth. When pork is cool enough to handle, shred it with your fingers.

3. Place cornhusks in water to soak.

4. Place soaked chiles, New Mexico chiles, allspice, and cumin in a blender; blend until smooth. Add tomatillos and enough broth from the pork pot to make mixture smooth.

5. Pour chili mixture into a soup pot. Cook over low heat for 10 minutes. Allow to cool. Add pork to chili mixture.

6. To assemble tamales: Spread ½ cup masa evenly over cornhusk. Spoon ¼ cup pork mixture over masa. Fold up cornhusk around filling and top with a black olive. Wrap the tamales in all-purpose deli wrap papers. Place in a steamer or pressure cooker; steam for about 2 hours. Makes 7 to 8 dozen.

✕ **VICTORIA RAMOS,** Pomona, California
First Place, Comidas Mexicanas Tamale Contest, L.A. County Fair, Pomona, California, 2003

JUST IN THYME PORK ROAST

3 tablespoons oil
One pork roast, about 3 lbs.
2 onions, sliced
½ cup barbecue sauce with brown sugar

¼ cup apple juice
2 tablespoons dried thyme
6 apples, cored and sliced

1. Preheat oven to 350°F.

2. Heat oil in a large ovenproof pot over medium-high heat. Add pork roast and onions and cook, turning occasionally, until roast is browned on all sides.

3. Combine barbecue sauce, apple juice, and thyme; pour over pork roast and onions. Cover pot and simmer for 10 minutes.

4. Place pot in oven. Bake for 2 hours. Add apple slices, return pot to oven, and bake until apples are tender and pork is cooked through, 30 minutes more. Makes 8 to 10 servings.

✕ **BARBARA PENNEY,** Roland, Arkansas
Honorable Mention, Special Entries, Arkansas State Fair, Little Rock, Arkansas, 2005

Pork Spare Ribs

4 lbs. pork spare ribs

4 garlic cloves, minced

1 medium onion, chopped

2 cups barbecue sauce

1 cup plum or grape jelly

1. Place spare ribs, garlic, and onion in an electric slow cooker. Cook on low setting for 8 hours.

2. Drain off juices. Add barbecue sauce and jelly. Cook on high setting until warmed through, 30 minutes. Makes 4 to 6 servings.

※ **Robert Davis,** Deer Creek, Illinois
First Place, Heart of Illinois Fair, Peoria, Illinois, 2003

Sweet-and-Sassy Barbecue Ribs

4 lbs. baby back ribs

2 tablespoons salt

2 tablespoons celery salt

1 tablespoon onion powder

¾ cup A.1. steak sauce

½ cup ketchup

¾ cup apricot preserves

1 teaspoon hot pepper sauce

2 tablespoons orange marmalade

1. Rub baby rack ribs with salt, celery salt, and onion powder. Set in a Dutch oven. Add water to cover. Cover and cook over medium heat until tender, 1 to 1½ hours.

2. Combine steak sauce, ketchup, apricot preserves, hot pepper sauce, and marmalade in a saucepan. Cook over medium heat until warmed through.

3. Baste ribs with sauce and brown on a barbecue grill. Serve remaining sauce separately for dipping. Makes 4 to 6 servings.

※ **Bonnie Robinson,** Seaford, Delaware
First Place, Tail Gate Party Entree Competition, Delaware State Fair, Harrington, Delaware, 2005

Pigseye Hickory Ribs

½ cup brown sugar

½ cup dry barbecue seasoning

3 slabs of pork ribs

Barbecue sauce, for serving

1. The day before, combine brown sugar and barbecue seasoning. Apply rub to 3 slabs of ribs. Set in refrigerator overnight to marinate.

2. The next day, set up grill with hickory charcoal. Grill rib slabs for 3 hours. Cut apart and serve with barbecue sauce. Makes 6 to 8 servings.

※ **Greg Casura,** Inver Grove Heights, Minnesota
Second Prize, BBQ Contest, Dakota County Fair, Farmington, Minnesota, 2005

4-H Clubs

The 4-H Club is a community of more than seven million young people across America who turn to the 4-H to learn leadership, citizenship, and life skills. All 50 states and more than 80 countries worldwide have 4-H programs. 4-H has as its goal the four-fold development of youth: head, heart, hands and health. This pledge sums up the 4-H mission:

> **"I Pledge my Head to clearer thinking,**
> **my Heart to greater loyalty,**
> **my Hands to larger service,**
> **and my Health to better living,**
> **for my club, my community, my country,**
> **and my world."**

Spice Supreme Rub and BBQ Sauce for Pork Roast

Spice Supreme Rub

½ cup seasoning salt (such as Lawry's)
¼ cup steak seasoning (such as KC Masterpiece)
1 teaspoon black pepper
1 teaspoon garlic powder

Combine all ingredients; mix well. Makes about ¾ cup.

BBQ Sauce

1 jar (8 oz.) grape jam
1 bottle (18 oz.) barbecue sauce (such as Open Pit)
1 bottle (18 oz.) ketchup
1 can (15 oz.) tomato sauce
¾ cup brown sugar

Combine all ingredients in a medium saucepan over high heat. Bring to a boil, reduce heat, and simmer, stirring occasionally, 15 to 20 minutes. Makes about 60 oz.

Use this combination of rub and BBQ sauce when grilling a 3- to 4-lb. pork roast. Apply the rub before grilling. Cook roast on a covered charcoal grill until internal temperature reaches 180 to 200°F, about 3 hours. Baste with BBQ sauce during final 30 minutes of cooking.

John Silveus, Granger, Indiana
First Place, Fresh Cut Pork, Elkhart County 4-H Fair, Goshen, Indiana, 2005

Pork Ribs Sauce Duo

Basting Sauce

2 cups ginger vinegar

1 cup white vinegar

1 teaspoon crushed black pepper

1 teaspoon crushed red pepper

1 tablespoon salt

2 cups apple juice

1 tablespoon molasses

Combine all ingredients in a large saucepan over medium-high heat. Bring to a boil, reduce heat, and simmer for 30 minutes. Makes 4 to 5 cups.

BBQ Sauce

6 Roma tomatoes, chopped

2 medium onions, chopped

1 green bell pepper, chopped

3 garlic cloves, chopped

1 jalapeño, chopped

1 cup brown sugar

1 tablespoon onion powder

1 tablespoon salt

1 tablespoon black pepper

2 bottles (18 oz. each) barbecue sauce
   (such as Open Pit)

Combine tomatoes, onions, pepper, garlic, and jalapeño in a large skillet over medium-high heat. Cook until vegetables are soft. Add sugar, onion powder, salt, pepper, and barbecue sauce. Bring to a boil, reduce heat, and simmer for 30 minutes. Makes 6 to 7 cups.

To use the sauce duo: Marinate 4 to 6 lbs. of ribs in basting sauce overnight. Cook on a covered grill over indirect heat, basting every 30 to 45 minutes, until cooked through, 4 to 5 hours. During the final 30 minutes of cooking, place ribs over direct heat and baste with BBQ sauce, turning often.

✖ **Gerald Straw,** Goshen, Indiana, and **Chico Ubanu,** Detroit, Michigan
First Place, Best of Michiana Ribs, Elkhart County 4-H Fair, Goshen, Indiana, 2005

SUPER SWEET SPARERIBS

Cooking spray
3 to 4 lbs. country-style spare ribs
1 can (15½ oz.) crushed pineapple
½ cup brown sugar
2 tablespoons soy sauce

½ cup ketchup
1 teaspoon ranch dressing
⅔ cup water
½ teaspoon salt
Pinch of black pepper

1. Preheat oven to 450°F. Coat a deep baking pan with cooking spray. Arrange ribs in pan and bake for 30 minutes. Drain off fat.

2. In a blender or food processor, puree pineapple, brown sugar, soy sauce, ketchup, ranch dressing, water, salt, and pepper. Transfer purée to a large saucepan and cook over medium heat until warmed through, 5 to 10 minutes.

3. Reduce oven temperature to 350°F. Pour sauce over ribs in pan. Return pan to oven and bake, basting every 15 minutes, for 30 to 45 minutes. Makes 6 to 8 servings.

✄ **CAROL NELSON,** Spokane, Washington
Second Prize, The National Pork Board, We Want Wow Now Pork Recipe Rally, Spokane County Interstate Fair, Spokane, Washington, 2005

PORK WITH BROCCOLI-MUSHROOM STIR-FRY

One pork tenderloin, 1½- to 2-lbs.
1 bottle (12 oz.) garlic and lime marinade
   (such as Lawry's Havana)
4 tablespoons cornstarch, divided
1 teaspoon sugar
½ teaspoon red pepper flakes
½ teaspoon salt
⅔ cup canned low-sodium chicken broth,
   undiluted, divided
¼ cup rice vinegar
½ cup low-sodium soy sauce
2 teaspoons dark sesame oil

3 teaspoons prepared chopped ginger, divided
3 teaspoons prepared minced garlic, divided
Vegetable cooking spray
4 cups fresh broccoli flowerets
2 cans (8 oz. each) sliced water chestnuts, drained
3 cups fresh mushrooms, sliced
1 tablespoon sesame seeds
1½ cups fresh green onions, sliced
6 cups cooked rice
Mandarin orange slices
Mint leaves

1. Trim fat from pork tenderloin and cut in half lengthwise. Cut each half crosswise into thin slices.

2. In a medium bowl, combine marinade and 2 tablespoons of the cornstarch. Add pork slices and toss to combine. Cover with plastic wrap and refrigerate 4 hours or overnight.

3. Combine remaining 2 tablespoons cornstarch, sugar, red pepper, salt, chicken broth, rice vinegar, soy sauce, dark sesame oil, 2 teaspoons of the ginger, and 2 teaspoons of the garlic. Stir well.

4. Coat a large nonstick skillet with cooking spray. Place over medium-high heat until hot. Drain excess marinade from pork and set aside. Add pork slices to skillet; stir-fry until browned, 4 minutes. Remove pork from skillet.

5. In the same skillet, add some reserved marinade to moisten pan. Add remaining teaspoon ginger and remaining teaspoon garlic; stir-fry for 30 seconds. Add broccoli and water chestnuts; stir-fry for 2 minutes. Add mushrooms and sesame seeds; stir-fry for 2 minutes.

6. Return pork to skillet. Add green onions and chicken broth mixture; bring to a boil. Cook, stirring constantly, until thickened, 1 minute. Serve over rice. Garnish with mandarin orange slices and mint leaves. Makes 6 servings.

※ **KRISTY LEWIS,** Solana Beach, California
First Place, Healthy Eating Contest—Main Dishes, San Diego County Fair, Del Mar, California, 2004

For added flavor, use chicken broth instead of water to prepare cooked rice.

SIZZLING SHRIMP ETOUFFÉE

2 tablespoons olive oil
2 garlic cloves, crushed
¼ cup scallions, thinly sliced on a diagonal
2 red bell peppers, thinly sliced
1 cup onions, thinly sliced
1 lb. medium raw shrimp, peeled and deveined

1 to 2 teaspoons Cajun seasoning
1 can (10.5 oz.) cream of shrimp condensed soup
1 tablespoon flour
10.5 oz. white wine (measure with empty soup can)
4 cups hot cooked rice

1. Heat olive oil in a large skillet over medium-high heat. When oil sizzles, add garlic, scallions, red peppers, and onion. Sauté, stirring frequently, until vegetables soften, 4 minutes.
2. Add shrimp and Cajun seasoning. Cook until shrimp barely turn pink. Reduce heat to low.
3. In a bowl, whisk together condensed soup and flour. Gently whisk in wine. Add mixture to skillet. Cook until the sauce thickens a bit, 3 minutes. Spoon over hot rice and serve. Makes 4 servings.

※ **MARY DEAN CAMPSIE,** Pleasant Ridge, Michigan
Third Place, Cooking with Michigan Wine, Michigan State Fair, Detroit, Michigan, 2001

SAUSAGE-STUFFED MUSHROOMS

36 medium size mushrooms
½ lb. sausage
3 green onions, chopped

1 cup herb stuffing mix
Mayonnaise or salad dressing

1. Clean mushrooms and remove stems.
2. Chop mushroom stems. Combine with sausage and onions in a skillet. Cook over medium heat until sausage is browned. Drain off fat.
3. In a large bowl, combine cooked sausage mixture and stuffing mix. Add just enough mayonnaise or salad dressing to moisten stuffing and hold mixture together.
4. Place mushroom caps in a baking dish. Fill with sausage mixture. Cover and chill. To serve, bake mushrooms in a 450°F oven until heated through, 10 to 15 minutes. Makes 36.

※ **STACEY EVANS,** Little Rock, Arkansas
Honorable Mention, Special Entries, Arkansas State Fair, Little Rock, Arkansas, 2005

"HOLY MOLE" STUFFED PORK LOIN

One 3- to 5-lb. boneless pork loin
1 jar (8.25 oz.) mole sauce

1 cup honey
Taco seasoning

1. With a sharp boning knife, cut lengthwise through the center of the pork loin, stopping about ½ inch from the opposite edge. Make two more cuts from the same side, ½ inch from and parallel to the first cut. Make two cuts from opposite side, interleaving the first three cuts. Spread out loin and flatten; it will be uneven.
2. Combine mole and honey, adding a little hot water if needed to make it easier to stir. Spread mixture over loin.
3. Roll the loin lengthwise and tie with butcher's twine at even spaces along roll. Rub liberally with taco seasoning.
4. Grill loin until the internal temperature reaches 160°F. Remove from grill, wrap in foil, and allow to rest for 15 minutes. Slice and serve. Makes 6 to 8 servings.

※ **RUSSELL VAN CAMP,** Spokane, Washington
First Prize, Wow Now Pork Recipe Rally, Spokane County Interstate Fair, Spokane, Washington, 2005

GROUND LAMB-K-BOBS

Grape tomatoes
Bell peppers
Onion
Lemon
Black olives
Squash
1 lb. ground lamb
½ teaspoon salt
½ teaspoon pepper

1 egg yolk
Pinch of minced fresh thyme
¼ teaspoon garlic powder

GLAZE
1 cup crushed pineapple with juice
1 teaspoon garlic
½ cup brown sugar
½ teaspoon rosemary leaves

1. Cut grape tomatoes, bell peppers, onion, lemon, black olives, and squash into wedges, slices, or random shapes, or leave whole.
2. In a large bowl, combine ground lamb, salt, pepper, egg yolk, thyme, and garlic powder. Roll into 1-inch meatballs. Place on waxed paper.
3. To assemble k-bobs: Place vegetables and meatballs on skewers in following order, or as desired: black olive, onion, tomato, lamb, lemon, lamb, squash, lamb, pepper, lamb. The size of the k-bob is up to you.
4. To make glaze: Combine pineapple, garlic, brown sugar, and rosemary.
5. Wrap k-bobs in foil and grill for 10 minutes. Remove foil, brush with glaze, and grill until lamb is nicely browned and vegetables are charred. Makes 6 to 8 servings.

※ **MARIANN HOLLOPETER,** Syracuse, Indiana
First Place, Lamb: Ground, Elkhart County 4-H Fair, Goshen, Indiana, 2005

BAKED HAM WITH DATE SAUCE

One 3- to 5-lb. canned ham
Whole cloves

DATE SAUCE
2 cups apple cider
⅓ cup light corn syrup

½ cup sugar
2 tablespoons fresh lemon juice
2 tablespoons margarine, at room temperature
2 tablespoons cornstarch
⅛ teaspoon cinnamon
1 cup chopped dates

1. Preheat oven to 350°F. Set aside a 13 x 9 x 2-inch baking pan. Dot top of ham with cloves.

2. To make date sauce: Combine apple cider, light corn syrup, sugar, and lemon juice in a medium saucepan over medium-high heat. Bring to a boil and cook until reduced to 1⅓ cups, 15 minutes. Reduce heat to low. Stir margarine, cornstarch, and cinnamon in a cup until smooth. Whisk into cider mixture and simmer until slightly thickened, 1 minute. Add dates and stir.

3. Reserve 1 cup of sauce. Pour remaining sauce over ham, wrap tightly in foil, and bake for 1 hour. Slice and serve with the remaining sauce.

※ **TWILA BOOTH,** San Jacinto, California
Second Place, Entree, Riverside County Fair and National Date Festival, Indio, California, 2003–2004

QUEPUEDAH

1 round winter squash
Unsalted butter or olive oil
¼ cup brown sugar
2 cups cooked meat (pork roast,
   sausage, or chicken)

4 large apples, cored and cut
   in large chunks
1 sliced onion
½ teaspoon sage
Salt and pepper

1. Preheat oven to 325°F. Set aside a deep baking dish large enough to hold squash.

2. Cut out top of squash, as for a jack-o-lantern. Scoop out and discard seeds and stringy pulp. Rub inside of squash with butter or olive oil and brown sugar.

3. In a bowl, toss together meat, apples, onion, and sage. Sprinkle with salt and pepper. Place meat mixture inside squash. Replace the squash lid.

4. Set squash in baking dish. Add water to a 2-inch level. Bake until a fork easily pierces through squash skin, 1 to 1½ hours. Check water level periodically during baking and replenish if necessary. Using the squash as a serving bowl, spoon meat-apple mixture and squash onto individual plates at the table. Makes 4 to 6 servings.

Choose a large winter squash with a pumpkin shape to make Quepuedah.

※ **KATE SOON TO FOLLOW,** Browning, Montana
First Place Public Favorite, Native American Cooking, Western Montana Fair, Missoula, Montana, 1997

SUMMER SAVORY LAMB STIR FRY

1 lb. spinach noodles

1 tablespoon rosemary

3 tablespoons oregano leaves

Small bunch basil, coarsely chopped

2 teaspoons finely chopped chives

3 teaspoons vegetable oil
   or olive oil, divided

1 lb. lamb, sliced into ½-inch strips

1 teaspoon minced garlic

6 oz. fresh sliced mushrooms

6 oz. young snow peas

1 medium red or green sweet bell pepper, sliced

3 small yellow summer squash,
   sliced ¼-inch thick

3 small zucchini, sliced ¼-inch thick

3 to 4 firm plum tomatoes, sliced ¼-inch thick

5 to 6 green onions, chopped

1 tablespoon unsalted butter, room temperature

¼ cup grated Parmesan

1 cup sour cream

¼ cup sliced black olives

Salt and pepper

1. Cook spinach noodles in a large pot of boiling water, according to package directions. Drain.

2. Combine rosemary, oregano, basil, and chives.

3. Heat 1½ teaspoons of the oil in an electric wok to 350°F. Add lamb, garlic, and half of the herb mixture. Sauté briefly; remove lamb while it is still pink.

4. Add remaining 1½ teaspoons oil to wok and heat to 350°F. Add mushrooms, snow peas, bell pepper, yellow squash, zucchini, tomatoes, green onions, and remaining herb mixture. Stir-fry until crisp and tender. Lower the heat, stir in the lamb, and cook until lamb is no longer pink.

5. Drain spinach noodles and toss with butter and Parmesan. Place noodles in a warmed serving dish. Spoon stir-fry mixture over the noodles. Garnish with sour cream and black olives. Sprinkle with salt and pepper. Makes 6 servings.

✳ **NATALIE WILLIAMS,** Howell, Michigan
First Place, Lamb Dish Contest, Michigan State Fair, Detroit, Michigan, 2000

PINEAPPLE GINGER LAMB KABOBS

MARINADE

1 2-inch piece fresh ginger, peeled
   and coarsely chopped

3 garlic cloves, coarsely chopped

3 scallions, chopped

1 jalapeño, seeded and coarsely chopped

¼ cup cilantro, chopped

¼ cup pineapple, chopped

1½ cups pineapple juice

Sage (optional)

⅓ cup soy sauce

¼ cup dark sesame oil

2 strips (1½ inches by ½ inch) lemon zest,
   white pith removed

2 tablespoons fresh lemon juice

½ teaspoon freshly ground black pepper

KABOBS

3 lbs. lamb shoulder, cut in
   1-inch chunks

2 small ripe pineapples, cut in 1-inch chunks

Sage or cilantro, chopped

1. To make marinade: Combine ginger, garlic, scallions, jalapeño, cilantro, pineapple, pineapple juice, sage, if using, soy sauce, sesame oil, lemon zest, lemon juice, and black pepper in a blender; puree until smooth.

2. Pour marinade into a large bowl. Add lamb and toss to combine. Place in refrigerator to marinate, 3 to 4 hours. Place bamboo skewers in water to soak during final 30 minutes of marinating.

3. Remove lamb from marinade with a slotted spoon and set aside. Strain marinade into a large saucepan. Bring to a boil over high heat, stirring frequently, until thick, 10 minutes.

4. Thread lamb and pineapple on skewers, alternating between meat and fruit. Brush with marinade. Lay kabobs on an oiled grill grate over medium-hot charcoal. Grill, turning to brown all sides and until internal temperature of lamb is 145°F, 8 to 12 minutes. Serve sprinkled with sage or cilantro. Serve remaining marinade on the side as a dipping sauce. Makes 6 to 8 servings.

✕ **MARSHALL KING,** Goshen, Indiana
First Place, Lamb: Cut, Elkhart County 4-H Fair, Goshen, Indiana, 2005

PERSIAN LAMB PATTIES WITH HUMMUS MAYONNAISE

HUMMUS MAYONNAISE

¼ cup hummus

¼ cup mayonnaise

2 tablespoons plain yogurt

2 tablespoons Feta, finely crumbled

2 tablespoons roasted
red pepper, minced

2 tablespoons parsley, finely chopped

PATTIES

1¼ cups eggplant, peeled and shredded

1½ lbs. ground lamb

2 garlic cloves, crushed

¼ cup onion, grated

1 tablespoon tomato paste

2 teaspoons salt

½ teaspoon pepper

4 tablespoons red wine

½ teaspoon lemon zest, grated

4 crusty sandwich rolls, split

4 to 8 small romaine lettuce leaves

8 small tomato slices

1. To make hummus mayonnaise: In a small mixing bowl, whisk together hummus, mayonnaise, and yogurt. Stir in feta cheese, roasted red peppers, and parsley. Cover and chill.

2. To make patties: Combine eggplant, lamb, garlic, onion, tomato paste, salt, pepper, red wine, and lemon zest, handling meat as little as possible. Gently pat into four oval patties.

3. Preheat an electric grill. Place lamb patties on grill and cook until browned, about 6 minutes. Line bottom of rolls with a few small romaine lettuce leaves and tomato slices. Place grilled lamb patties on tomato slices. Spread hummus mayonnaise over patties. Add tops of rolls. Makes 4 servings.

✕ **SALLY SIBTHORPE,** Rochester Hills, Michigan
Second Place, Lamb Dish Contest, Michigan State Fair, Detroit, Michigan, 2001

CRAWFISH ETOUFFÉE

2 teaspoons salt
2 teaspoons cayenne pepper
1 teaspoon white pepper
1 teaspoon dried sweet basil
½ teaspoon dried thyme
¼ cup chopped onion
¼ cup chopped celery
¼ cup chopped green bell pepper

7 tablespoons vegetable oil
¾ cup all-purpose flour
3 cups clam juice, divided
1 cup unsalted butter, divided
2 lbs. peeled crawfish tails
1 cup very finely chopped green onions
4 cups hot cooked rice

1. In a small bowl, combine salt, cayenne pepper, white pepper, basil, and thyme for seasoning mix.
2. In a separate bowl, combine onion, celery, and bell pepper.
3. Heat oil in a large cast-iron skillet over medium-high heat until it begins to smoke, about 4 minutes. Gradually whisk in flour until smooth. Continue cooking, whisking continuously, until roux is a dark red-brown color, 3 to 5 minutes.
4. Remove skillet from heat. Immediately add onion mixture and 1 tablespoon of the seasoning mix, stirring continuously with a wooden spoon until cooled, about 5 minutes.
5. Place 2 cups of the clam juice in a 2-quart saucepan; bring to a boil over medium-high heat. Add gradually to roux mixture, whisking constantly until thoroughly dissolved. Reduce heat to low and cook, whisking constantly so that bottom of pan does scorch, until flour taste is gone, 2 minutes. Remove clam sauce from heat.
6. Melt ½ cup of the butter in a 4-quart saucepan over medium heat. Stir in crawfish tails and green onions and sauté, stirring constantly, for 1 minute. Add remaining ½ cup butter, clam sauce, and remaining cup clam juice. Cook, constantly shaking pan from side to side (do not stir) until butter melts and is mixed into the sauce, 4 to 6 minutes. If sauce starts to separate, add 2 tablespoons of clam juice or water and shake pan until it combines. Stir in remaining seasoning mix. Remove from heat. Serve immediately over rice. Make 6 to 8 servings.

※ **KELLY HAGEN,** Prattville, Alabama
Prize Winner, Alabama National Fair, Montgomery, Alabama, 1998–2002

VEGETARIAN FETTUCCINE

8 oz. fettuccine
⅓ cup unsalted butter, melted,
    plus more for skillet
1 zucchini, grated
2 carrots, grated

1 small onion, minced
1 to 2 cups chopped broccoli
Cherry tomatoes
¾ cup heavy cream
¾ cup grated Parmesan

1. Cook fettuccine according to package directions. Drain well and rinse.
2. While fettuccine is cooking, heat butter in a large skillet over medium heat. Add zucchini, carrots, onion, broccoli, and cherry tomatoes. Sauté until soft and cooked through.
3. Toss hot pasta with melted butter, cream, and Parmesan. Add sautéed vegetables. Makes 4 servings.

※ **SUSAN SORVAAG,** Argusville, North Dakota
Grand Champion, Red River Valley Fair, West Fargo, North Dakota, 2004

Lamb Chops with Mango Salsa and Sticky Rice

1 cup pineapple juice
1 tablespoon soy sauce
1 teaspoon Worcestershire sauce
¾ teaspoon ground cumin
8 lamb loin chops

MANGO SALSA
1 cup chopped mango
½ cup chopped nectarine
1 tablespoon tropical mango jam
¼ teaspoon cumin

STICKY RICE
1 cup Arborio rice
2 cups chicken broth
1 cup frozen peas
½ cup portabella mushrooms

1. Combine pineapple juice, soy sauce, Worcestershire sauce, and cumin in a large bowl. Add lamb chops and marinate in refrigerator, 3 to 4 hours.
2. To make mango salsa: Combine mango, nectarine, mango jam, and cumin in a small bowl. Cover and chill.
3. To make sticky rice: Cook rice in chicken broth, following package instructions. Stir in peas during final 5 minutes of cooking.
4. Remove lamb chops from marinade. Grill lamb chops over hot coals, turning once until browned on both sides, 15 to 20 minutes. Place on a hot platter and cover. Grill mushrooms and stir into sticky rice. Serve lamb chops and sticky rice with mango salsa. Makes 4 servings.

✕ **DIANE TITE,** Chesterfield, Michigan
First Place, Lamb Dish Contest, Michigan State Fair, Detroit, Michigan, 2001

Lamb with Pine-Nut Butter

Garlic-flavored cooking spray
8 lamb chops
1 teaspoon salt
½ teaspoon black pepper
½ cup green onions, sliced
¼ cup chopped fresh parsley

¼ cup chopped fresh chives
½ cup pine nuts, plus more for pan
6 garlic cloves, crushed
¼ cup lemon
2 tablespoons brandy
½ cup unsalted butter, melted

1. Preheat oven to 350°F. Coat a 13 x 9 x 2-inch baking pan with garlic-flavored cooking spray.
2. Sprinkle lamb chops with salt and pepper.
3. Place green onions, parsley, chives, pine nuts, and garlic in a food processor. Add lemon juice and brandy. Combine to make a paste.
4. Spread paste over both sides of lamb chops. Set chops in pan. Scatter additional pine nuts over the top and drizzle with melted butter. Bake until meat is cooked through, 40 minutes. Makes 4 servings.

✕ **SALLY SIBTHORPE,** Rochester Hills, Michigan
Second Place, Lamb Dish Contest, Michigan State Fair, Detroit, Michigan, 2000

Egg Foo Yong

6 eggs, slightly beaten
1 cup cubed pork, cooked
½ cup celery, sliced fine
½ cup sliced green onion,
    plus more for topping
1 teaspoon sugar
1 tablespoon soy sauce
1 tablespoon cornstarch
Cooking spray

SAUCE

2 tablespoons soy sauce
3 teaspoons cornstarch
1 cup water
Water

1. Combine eggs, pork, celery, green onion, sugar, soy sauce, and cornstarch in a bowl.

2. Lightly coat a skillet or coat with cooking spray. Heat pan over medium-high heat. Add egg mixture, ¼ cup at a time, and fry like small pancakes. Brown slightly on both sides, until egg is cooked. Keep warm in oven while cooking remaining egg mixture.

3. To make sauce: Combine soy sauce, cornstarch, and a few spoonfuls of water in a small saucepan over medium-high heat. Cook until boiling, adding more water if needed; sauce should be smooth and slightly thick. Place egg foo yong on a serving platter, spoon sauce over top, and garnish with sliced green onions. Makes 4 servings.

✳ **TA WONG,** Missoula, Montana
First Place, America—The Melting Pot, Western Montana Fair, Missoula, Montana, 1998

Crustless "Nearly Crab" Quiche

2 cups zucchini, cut into chunks
1 can (6 oz.) flake tuna
1 sleeve stale saltine crackers
2 eggs
1 tablespoon Old Bay seasoning
2 tablespoons chopped onion
2 sprigs parsley
2 tablespoons minced red bell pepper
⅓ cup mayonnaise

TARTAR SAUCE

½ cup mayonnaise
1 tablespoon yellow mustard
¼ cup vinegar drained from a jar
    of homemade sweet pickles
1 tablespoon grated onion
1 tablespoon homemade zucchini relish
    or pickle relish

1. Preheat oven to 350°F. Grease a quiche dish or deep-dish pie plate.

2. Combine zucchini, tuna, crackers, eggs, Old Bay seasoning, onion, parsley, bell pepper, and mayonnaise in a food processor and pulse until totally blended. Pour into quiche dish or pie plate. Bake until set, 30 to 40 minutes.

3. To make tartar sauce: Stir together mayonnaise, mustard, pickle vinegar, onion, and relish in a small bowl.

4. To serve, slice quiche and set on serving plates. Pass tartar sauce on the side. Makes 6 to 8 servings.

✳ **NORITA SOLT,** Bettendorf, Iowa
First Place, Centsible Cooking, Iowa State Fair, Des Moines, Iowa, 2005

CRUSTY LAMB CHOPS

1 tablespoon mayonnaise
2 teaspoons spicy brown mustard
1 tablespoon sour cream
1 slice bread, torn into small pieces
½ cup ground pecans
⅛ teaspoon crushed dried rosemary leaves

Dash of ground cloves
Dash of garlic powder
Dash of onion salt
¼ teaspoon freshly ground black pepper
1 lb. lamb blade chops

1. Preheat oven to 350°F. Grease a baking pan.

2. Combine mayonnaise, mustard, and sour cream in a small bowl.

3. Place bread, pecans, rosemary, cloves, garlic powder, onion salt, and pepper in a blender. Pulse to combine. Pour into a shallow bowl.

4. Brush mustard mixture onto each lamb chop. Dip into crumb mixture to coat. Bake until cooked through, 35 to 45 minutes. Makes 4 servings.

※ **EANINE MOWER ANDERSON,** Bountiful, Utah
First Place, Woolgrowers, Utah State Fair, Salt Lake City, Utah, 2005

Main-Dish Strudel

STRUDEL

3 cups all-purpose flour, plus more
    for rolling out dough

2 teaspoons baking powder

½ teaspoon salt

3 or 4 eggs

Water or milk

Unsalted butter, room temperature

6 to 8 slices bacon, cut into pieces

2 cups diced potatoes

½ to 1 cup sauerkraut, drained
    and rinsed (optional)

Toasted bread crumbs

1. In a mixing bowl, whisk together flour, baking powder, and salt. Beat in eggs and just enough water or milk to make a soft dough.

2. Rough out dough on a lightly floured surface to a ¼-inch thickness. Spread with butter. Roll up tightly, jelly roll–style, and cut into 1-inch pieces for strudel.

3. Heat a large, heavy skillet that has a lid over medium-high heat. Add bacon and potatoes and cook until bacon is crisp and potatoes are browned. Add sauerkraut, if using. Top with rolled strudel. Cover and simmer until potatoes at bottom of pan are crispy and dry, 30 to 40 minutes. Sprinkle toasted bread crumbs over the top. Makes 4 to 6 servings.

✂ **Carla Emery,** Idaho
First Place Public Favorite, America—The Melting Pot, Western Montana Fair, Missoula, Montana, 1986

Dairy Seafood Lasagna

2 tablespoons vegetable oil

2 tablespoons plus ½ cup unsalted butter,
    divided

1 green onion, chopped

½ cup chicken broth

1 bottle (8 oz.) clam juice

1 lb. bay scallops

1 lb. small raw shrimp, peeled and deveined

1 package (8-oz.) imitation crabmeat, chopped

¼ teaspoon black pepper, divided

½ cup all-purpose flour

1½ cups milk

½ teaspoon salt

1 cup heavy cream

½ cup grated Parmesan, divided

9 lasagna noodles, cooked and drained

1. Preheat oven to 350°F. Grease a 13 x 9 x 2-inch baking dish.

2. Heat oil and 2 tablespoons butter in a large skillet over medium-high heat. When butter is melted, add green onion and sauté until tender.

3. Stir in broth and clam juice. Bring to a boil. Add scallops, shrimp, crabmeat, and ⅛ teaspoon of the pepper. Bring to a boil, reduce heat, and simmer uncovered, stirring gently, until shrimp turn pink and scallops are opaque, 4 to 5 minutes. Drain seafood mixture and set aside; reserve liquid.

4. Melt ½ cup butter in a saucepan over medium heat. Stir in flour until smooth. Combine milk and reserved cooking liquid; gradually add to the saucepan. Add salt and remaining ⅛ teaspoon pepper. Bring to a boil and cook, stirring, until thickened, 2 minutes. Remove white sauce from heat. Stir in heavy cream and ¼ cup of the Parmesan.

5. Stir ¾ cup of the white sauce into the seafood mixture. Spread ½ cup of the white sauce in pan. Top with three lasagna noodles. Layer half of the seafood mixture over the noodles. Top with 1¼ cups of white sauce. Layer 3 more noodles, remaining seafood mixture, and another 1¼ cups of white sauce. Top with remaining 3 noodles, remaining white sauce, and remaining ¼ cup Parmesan. Bake, uncovered, until golden brown, 35 to 40 minutes. Let stand for 15 minutes before cutting. Makes 6 to 8 servings.

※ **JUANITA SPRAGUE,** Saranac, Michigan
First Place and Grand Champion, Quiches and Casseroles, Dairy Delight Contest, Ionia Free Fair,
Ionia, Michigan, 2004

SOUTHWEST CRAWFISH CASSEROLE

Cooking spray
¼ cup unsalted butter
1 cup chopped onion
½ cup chopped celery
½ cup chopped green onions
2 lbs. Louisiana crawfish tail meat

1 lb. jalapeño sausage, thinly sliced
2 packages (8 oz. each) cream cheese
3 cups cooked long-grain rice
2 cans (14 oz. each) tomatoes with green chiles
½ cup chopped fresh cilantro
1½ cups grated Monterey Jack

1. Preheat oven to 350°F. Coat a 13 x 9 x 2-inch baking dish with cooking spray.

2. Melt butter in a large skillet over medium heat. Add onion, celery, and green onions; sauté until wilted. Add crawfish and sauté 5 minutes more.

3. In a separate pan, cook sausage over medium-high heat until browned. Drain off fat. Add cream cheese to sausage and stir until melted.

4. In a large bowl, toss sausage mixture, crawfish mixture, rice, tomatoes and cilantro until well combined. Pour into baking dish. Bake until bubbly, 15 to 20 minutes. Top with grated cheese and place under broiler until cheese melts. Makes 6 servings.

※ **RENEE M. TULL,** West Monroe, Louisiana
Special Entry, State Fair of Louisiana, Shreveport, Louisiana, 2005

INTERIOR ALASKA SALMON PIE

1 can (15.5 oz.) salmon, flaked or
  2 cups flaked cooked fresh salmon
1 cup cooked peas, drained (fresh or frozen)
2 tablespoons finely chopped green bell pepper

1 cup grated cheese
½ cup plus ⅓ cup milk, divided
2 tablespoons mayonnaise
1 cup Bisquick baking mix

1. Preheat oven to 450°F. Grease an 8 x 8-inch baking dish.

2. In a bowl, combine salmon, peas, and green pepper. Spread in bottom of baking dish. Mix grated cheese and ½ cup milk. Pour over salmon mixture.

3. In a small bowl, combine ⅓ cup milk, mayonnaise, and baking mix; stir with a fork until moistened. Drop by spoonfuls onto salmon. Bake until browned, 10 to 15 minutes. Makes 4 to 6 servings.

※ **SAMANTHA CASTLE KIRSTEIN,** Fairbanks, Alaska
Special Contest Winner, Tanana Valley State Fair, Fairbanks, Alaska, 2005

Tuscan Pasta Bake

1 tablespoon olive oil, plus more for pan
1 package (8 oz.) sliced white mushrooms
1 small white onion, chopped
1 garlic clove, minced
1 can (14 oz.) diced tomatoes with garlic,
    oregano, and basil

1 cup low-sodium fat-free chicken broth
2 tablespoons cornstarch
½ cup Parmesan
½ lb. frozen precooked and deveined
    large shrimp, thawed
½ box (8 oz.) whole wheat penne rigate, cooked

1. Preheat oven to 350°F. Lightly oil a baking dish or casserole.

2. Heat oil in a large skillet over medium heat. Add mushroom, onion, and garlic; sauté until onion is soft.

3. Add tomatoes, chicken broth, and cornstarch. Cook, stirring, until thickened. Stir in Parmesan until melted.

4. Combine the shrimp and cooked penne in baking dish or casserole. Pour sauce over the top and toss to combine. Bake until shrimp is pink and heated through, 20 minutes. Makes 6 servings.

※ **RACHEL BROOKS,** Byron, Georgia
Second Place, Cooking Lite the ADA Way, Georgia National Fair, Perry, Georgia, 2005

Greek Pasta Casserole

¼ cup olive oil, plus more for pan
1 lb. small pasta shells
4 large garlic cloves, minced
1 can (14 oz.) diced tomatoes with juice
1 jar (7 oz.) roasted peppers,
    well-drained and dried

¼ cup pitted and roughly chopped black olives
2 tablespoons red wine
¼ teaspoon crushed red pepper flakes
¼ cup finely chopped fresh parsley
1½ teaspoons dried oregano
1 cup (5 oz.) finely crumbled Feta

1. Preheat the oven to 375°F. Lightly oil a 13 x 9 x 2-inch glass baking dish.

2. Cook pasta shells to al dente following package directions. Drain well in a colander. Place cooked shells in a large bowl.

3. Heat olive oil in a small saucepan over medium-low heat. Add garlic, cook for 30 seconds, and remove from heat. Cool slightly. Pour oil over pasta and toss until pasta is glistening. Cool to room temperature, tossing occasionally to prevent sticking.

4. Add tomatoes, peppers, olives, red wine, red pepper flakes, parsley, oregano, and Feta to pasta; toss to combine. Put mixture into baking dish. Cover with foil. Bake until hot and bubbly, 25 minutes. Remove the foil and bake until top is lightly browned, 5 minutes more. Makes 6 to 8 servings.

※ **KRISTEN WRIGHT,** age 16, West Greenwich, Rhode Island
Grand Champion & Best of Show, 4-H Favorite Foods Fair, West Greenwich, Rhode Island, 2005

WINNER'S CIRCLE TIP | Prepare Greek Pasta Casserole up to 24 hours ahead and refrigerate. Bring to room temperature before baking.

4-Cheese Lasagna

1 lb. ground beef
1 garlic clove, minced
½ teaspoon salt
2 jars (26 oz. each) spaghetti sauce
1 can (6 oz.) tomato paste
1 package (1 lb.) lasagna noodles
2 eggs, lightly beaten
2 cups ricotta
1 cup cottage cheese
1 cup Parmesan
2 tablespoons chopped fresh parsley
Dash of black pepper
2 cups shredded mozzarella

1. Preheat oven to 350°F. Grease a 13 x 9 x 2-inch pan.
2. Brown ground beef in a large skillet over medium-high heat. Drain off fat. Add garlic and salt. Simmer for 3 to 5 minutes. Stir in spaghetti sauce and tomato paste. Simmer for 10 to 15 minutes.
3. Cook lasagna noodles to al dente according to package directions. Drain well and rinse.
4. In a large bowl, mix together eggs, ricotta, cottage cheese, Parmesan, parsley, and pepper until well blended.
5. Spoon 1 cup of meat sauce on bottom of baking pan and even out. Top with 3 or 4 strips lasagne noodles. Add a layer of cheese mixture, a layer of meat sauce, and a layer of mozzarella. Bake for 30 minutes. Let stand for 10 minutes before serving. Pass remaining meat sauce on the side. Makes 4 to 6 servings.

⁂ **Andrea Hubbell,** Shoreham, Vermont
Best Dairy Foods, Addison County Fair and Field Days, New Haven, Vermont, 2004

Aglio e Olio con Limoni and Broccoli

1 package (16 oz.) penne rigate
⅓ cup olive oil
10 to 12 garlic cloves, pressed
½ teaspoon red pepper flakes
⅓ cup lemon juice
1 tablespoon lemon pepper
⅓ cup salsa
1 cup boiling water
2 chicken bouillon cubes
4 cups broccoli
2 cups cherry tomatoes, halved

1. Cook penne rigate according to package directions. Drain well and rinse.
2. Combine olive oil, garlic, and red pepper flakes in a large skillet over medium heat. Sauté until garlic turns slightly brown. Stir in lemon juice, lemon pepper, and salsa. Reduce heat to low.
3. In a large microwave-safe container, combine boiling water, chicken bouillon cubes, and broccoli. Microwave on high for 2 minutes. Add broccoli mixture to skillet, stirring to combine. Cook until warmed through.
4. In a large serving bowl, toss pasta, broccoli, and cherry tomatoes until well combined. Serve as a meal or as a side dish with lemon-pepper chicken. Makes 6 to 8 servings.

⁂ **David Volk,** Fargo, North Dakota
Runner-Up, Red River Valley Fair, West Fargo, North Dakota, 2005

CHEESE BLINTZ CASSEROLE

1 cup all-purpose flour

1 tablespoon baking powder

Salt

1 cup unsalted butter, melted

¾ cup sugar, divided

¼ cup milk

2 large eggs, beaten

1 teaspoon vanilla

2 packages (8 oz. each) cream cheese,
  room temperature

1¾ cups small-curd cottage cheese

2 tablespoons fresh lemon juice

1. Preheat oven to 300°F. Grease a 13 x 9 x 2-inch baking dish.

2. In a medium bowl, combine flour, baking powder, and a dash of salt. Stir in melted butter, ½ cup of the sugar, milk, eggs, and vanilla until well combined.

3. Pour half of batter into baking pan.

4. In a medium mixing bowl, beat cream cheese at medium speed until creamy. Add cottage cheese, remaining ¼ cup sugar, lemon juice, and a dash of salt. Beat until blended.

5. Spread cream cheese mixture over batter in pan. Pour remaining batter over cream cheese mixture. Bake, uncovered, for 55 minutes, or until lightly browned. Serve with fresh fruit, if desired. Makes 12 servings.

✄ **KARIN JELSMA,** Lowell, Michigan
First Place, Quiches and Casseroles, Dairy Delight Contest, Ionia Free Fair, Ionia, Michigan, 2005

JOMONJI'S PASTA SAUCE

2 lbs. sweet Italian sausage

6 garlic cloves, crushed

6 tablespoons dried sweet basil

3 tablespoons dried oregano

2 tablespoons raw sugar

½ teaspoon sea salt

2 cans (6 oz. each) tomato paste

2 cans (28 oz. each) crushed tomatoes

1 cup Merlot

Cooked pasta

Freshly grated Parmesan

1. Remove sausage from casing and place in heavy stockpot. Cook over medium heat until slightly brown. Drain off fat.

2. Add garlic to pan and cook over low heat until softened. Stir in basil, oregano, sugar, and salt. Add tomato paste and crushed tomatoes, stirring to combine.

3. Add wine and simmer until thickened, 30 to 45 minutes or longer, if desired. Add water or wine if sauce becomes too thick during simmering. Serve over pasta with freshly grated Parmesan. Makes a great lasagna sauce. Makes 10 to 12 cups sauce.

✄ **MONI J. FOX,** Sparks, Nevada
Honorable Mention, Nevada State Fair, Reno, Nevada, 2005

CHAPTER 6

VEGETABLES

RICE AND BEANS WITH CREOLE SAUCE

1 cup dried red kidney beans

1½ teaspoons salt, divided

Black pepper

6 to 8 cups water

3 tablespoons margarine, divided

2 cups white rice

Creole Sauce (recipe follows)

1. Sort and rinse beans. Place beans in a large stockpot, add water to cover, and stir in ½ teaspoon of the salt and black pepper. Bring to a boil, reduce to a simmer, and simmer until beans are tender but whole, 60 to 90 minutes. Drain beans, reserving the liquid. Add water as needed to liquid to make 4 cups.

2. Melt 1 tablespoon of the margarine in a large saucepan over medium heat. Add rice and stir, cooking until grains turn milky and opaque, 1 to 2 minutes.

3. Add 4 cups of liquid from beans, remaining 1 teaspoon of salt, and a dash of black pepper. Reduce heat, add beans, and cover tightly. Simmer until rice is tender and all liquid is absorbed, about 20 minutes. Fluff the rice and beans with a fork and serve hot with Creole Sauce. Makes 4 to 6 servings.

CREOLE SAUCE

Unsalted butter or oil for cooking

1 or 2 onions, cut into very thin slices

¼ lb. lean diced bacon

2 tomatoes, peeled, seeded, and diced

2 cups watercress leaves (strip from stems)

2 cups water

Salt and pepper

1. Melt butter or oil in a large sauté pan over medium heat. Add onion, bacon, and tomato; cook until onion turns soft and golden.

2. Add watercress leaves to pan and cook until wilted.

3. Add water and salt and pepper. Simmer for 15 minutes. Makes 4 servings.

✄ **MADELYN WINSLOW,** Center Barnstead, New Hampshire
First Place, Junior Division, Belknap County 4-H Food Festival, Belmont, New Hampshire, 2006

VERMONT MAPLE BAKED BEANS

1 lb. yellow eye beans

1 teaspoon baking soda

1 cup maple syrup

1 teaspoon dry mustard

½ teaspoon ground ginger

½ cup brown sugar

¼ lb. salt pork, cubed

¼ cup chopped onion

Salt and pepper

1. Sort and rinse beans. Place beans in a large stockpot, add water to cover, and stir in baking soda. Bring to a boil and cook just until beans float to top, 2 to 3 minutes.

2. Drain beans and return them to pot. Add cold water to cover. Bring to a boil, reduce to a simmer, and simmer until tender, 1 hour.

3. Preheat oven to 325°F. Transfer beans and remaining cooking water to ovenproof bean pot. Stir in maple syrup, mustard, ginger, brown sugar, salt pork, and onion. Sprinkle with salt and pepper. Bake, adding more water if needed, until beans are soft and flavors are fully melded, 8 hours. Makes 6 to 8 servings.

✂ **HANNAH FERRELL,** Addison, Vermont
First Place, Baked Bean Bonanza, Addison County Fair & Field Days, New Haven, Vermont, 2005

ARTICHOKE AND SPINACH CASSEROLE

2 cans (14 oz. each) artichoke hearts, drained

1 box (9 oz.) frozen spinach,
  thawed and drained

1 can (4½ oz.) green chiles, drained

1 cup mayonnaise

1¼ cups shredded Parmesan

2 tablespoons diced roasted red peppers

1 tablespoon bottled jalapeños, diced

3 garlic cloves, minced

1 teaspoon ground cumin

Dash of salt

Tortilla chips, broken

1. Preheat oven to 350°F.

2. Combine artichoke hearts, spinach, chiles, mayonnaise, Parmesan, red peppers, jalapeños, garlic, cumin, and salt in a large bowl.

3. Spoon mixture into casserole dish. Bake for 30 minutes. Remove from oven, arrange broken tortilla chips around edge of casserole, and return to oven for another 10 minutes. Makes 8 servings.

✂ **REBECCA BROOKS,** Byron, Georgia
First Place, Favorite Vegetable Casserole, Perry, Georgia, 2005

MEXICAN CORN CASSEROLE

4 eggs

1 can (15¼ oz.) whole kernel corn, drained

1 can (14¾ oz.) cream-style corn

1½ cups cornmeal

1¼ cups buttermilk

1 cup unsalted butter or margarine,
  room temperature

8 oz. chopped green chiles

2 medium onions, chopped

1 teaspoon baking soda

3 cups shredded cheddar cheese, divided

Jalapeño and sweet red pepper rings,
  for garnish

1. Preheat oven to 325°F. Grease a 13 x 9 x 2-inch baking dish.

2. Beat eggs in a large bowl. Add kernel corn, cream-style corn, cornmeal, buttermilk, butter or margarine, chiles, onions, and baking soda and mix well. Stir in 2 cups of the shredded cheese.

3. Pour mixture into baking dish. Bake, uncovered, for 60 minutes. Top with remaining 1 cup cheese. Let stand 15 minutes before serving. Garnish with pepper rings. Makes 12 to 15 servings.

✂ **ROBERT DAVIS,** Deer Creek, Illinois
First Place, Heart of Illinois Fair, Peoria, Illinois, 2003

BRAISED RED CABBAGE

1 large (3 lbs.) red cabbage,
    finely shredded
Salted water (1 teaspoon salt per quart)
¼ cup bacon fat or margarine
2 teaspoons salt
½ to 1 teaspoon freshly ground
    black pepper
1 cup sweet rosé

2 green onions, white part only, sliced
2 large tart apples, unpeeled, cored, and diced
2 tablespoons brown sugar
4 whole cloves
¼ teaspoon cinnamon
¼ teaspoon nutmeg
¼ cup medium dry sherry
1 tablespoon vinegar

1. Place cabbage in a stockpot or large bowl. Add enough salted water so that cabbage is completely submerged. Soak for 5 minutes and drain well.

2. Melt bacon fat or margarine in a heavy 6-quart Dutch oven over medium heat. Add cabbage and stir until coated with fat. Add salt, pepper, and rosé. Simmer for 5 minutes.

3. Add onions, apples, brown sugar, cloves, cinnamon, nutmeg, sherry, and vinegar. Cover and simmer until cabbage is tender and flavors are mingled, about 1 hour. Makes 6 to 8 servings.

✕ **RUTH CAHILL,** Columbus, Ohio
Grand Prize, Cooking with Ohio Wine, Ohio State Fair, Columbus, Ohio, 1990

SOUTHWEST SQUASH CASSEROLE

¼ cup unsalted butter,
    room temperature
1 teaspoon minced garlic
2 lbs. yellow squash, sliced into
    ¼-inch rounds
2 cups chopped onion
¼ cup water
1 tablespoon ground cumin

1½ teaspoons chili powder, divided
Salt and pepper
2 eggs, beaten
1 cup (8 oz.) shredded pepperjack
¼ cup shredded goat cheese
1 cup crushed tortilla chips
1 tablespoon unsalted butter, melted

1. Heat butter in a large skillet over medium heat. Stir in garlic and cook until it sizzles. Add squash and onion and toss to combine. Add water, cover, and steam until vegetables are soft, 4 to 6 minutes. Remove lid and continue cooking until all the liquid is evaporated.

2. Stir in cumin and 1 teaspoon chili powder. Sprinkle with salt and pepper. Add eggs and cook, stirring gently, until eggs are cooked through.

3. Turn off heat and add pepperjack and goat cheese. Cover and let stand until cheese is melted. Stir to combine.

4. Spoon squash mixture into an ovenproof dish. Combine tortilla chip crumbs, remaining ½ teaspoon chili powder, and melted butter in a small bowl. Sprinkle over squash. Set under broiler to brown, 1 to 2 minutes. Makes 6 to 8 servings.

✕ **RHONDA HITCH,** Kathleen, Georgia
Third Place, Favorite Vegetable Casserole, Georgia National Fair, Perry, Georgia, 2005

ASPARAGUS CASSEROLE

1 cup melted butter, divided
1½ cups crumbled buttery round crackers
3 tablespoons flour
1½ cups half-and-half
6 oz. grated Colby

½ cup sharp cheddar cheese
Salt and pepper
2 cans (16 oz. each) asparagus, drained
1 can (8 oz.) sliced water chestnuts, drained
3 hard-boiled eggs, peeled and sliced

1. Preheat oven to 350°F.

2. Add ½ cup of the melted butter to the crumbled crackers and stir to combine. Press half of the crumb mixture into the bottom of a casserole dish.

3. Add remaining ½ cup melted butter to flour and mix to moisten. Slowly add half-and-half, stirring to combine. Stir in Colby cheese and sharp cheese. Sprinkle with salt and pepper.

4. Layer half of asparagus in casserole dish, followed by half of water chestnuts and half of egg slices. Repeat layering once more. Pour cheese sauce over layers and sprinkle remaining crumb mixture over the top. Bake for 45 minutes. Makes 4 servings.

※ **BOB KEATON,** Fort Pierce, Florida
Blue Rosette, Saint Lucie County Fair, Fort Pierce, Florida, 2005

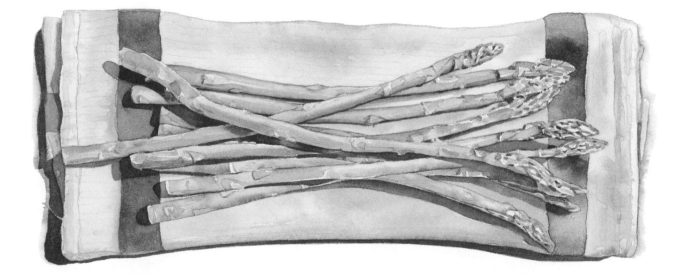

BBQ Corn

10 fresh ears of corn, unhusked
1 quart inexpensive beer

1 bag of ice
1 tablespoon Cajun seasoning

1. Place unhusked corn in an ice chest. Pour beer over the ears and set bag of ice on top. Place lid on ice chest. Let cure overnight.

2. Preheat smoker to 250°F or prepare grill. Place corn on racks and stack racks in smoker. Cook for 1 to 2 hours, turning every 20 minutes or so. If grilling, cook for 10 to 15 minutes and keep a close watch so that husks do not burn. Corn is cooked when kernels give easily under pressure. Makes 10 servings.

✄ *Friends of the California State Fair Cookbook,* Sacramento, California

CORN-JALAPEÑO FRITTERS

2 cups milk, divided
1 cup quick-cooking yellow grits
3 tablespoons unsalted butter or margarine, room temperature
1 teaspoon baking powder
1 teaspoon salt
2 large eggs, lightly beaten
¼ cup finely chopped red bell pepper

½ cup finely chopped green onions, plus more for topping
1 to 2 teaspoons seeded and minced jalapeños
2 tablespoons finely chopped fresh basil
1 cup corn, cut fresh from cob (about 2 ears)
¼ cup all-purpose flour
2 tablespoons olive oil, divided

1. Combine ½ cup of the milk and the grits in a small bowl.

2. Heat remaining 1½ cups milk in a medium saucepan over medium-high heat. Bring to a boil, whisk in grits, and cook, whisking continuously, until thickened, about 2 minutes. Remove from heat, pour into a large bowl, and cool slightly.

3. Add butter, baking powder, salt, eggs, bell pepper, onion, jalapeños, basil, corn, and flour to grits mixture. Stir until well combined.

4. Heat 1 tablespoon of the olive oil in a large nonstick skillet or griddle over medium heat until. Ladle 1 tablespoon of batter for each fritter into hot oil. Cook until tops of fritters are covered with bubbles and edges are slightly browned. Turn over and cook other side. Repeat with remaining olive oil and batter. Serve with sour cream and green onions, if desired. Makes 2 dozen fritters.

✄ **LAURA SCHAUB,** Peoria, Illinois
First Place, Heart of Illinois Fair, Peoria, Illinois, 2005

Scalloped Carrots

6 cups water
12 medium carrots, sliced (4 cups)
½ cup unsalted butter, divided
1 medium onion, finely chopped
¼ cup whole wheat flour
1 teaspoon salt

¼ teaspoon dry mustard
¼ teaspoon celery salt
Dash of black pepper
2 cups milk
2 cups shredded cheddar cheese
3 slices of whole wheat bread, cut into small pieces

1. Preheat oven to 350°F. Grease a 7 x 11 x 2-inch baking dish.

2. Place water in a large saucepan, bring to a boil, and add carrots. Cook until carrots are tender, about 5 minutes.

3. Melt ¼ cup of the butter in saucepan over medium heat. Add onion and sauté for 5 minutes. Stir in flour, salt, mustard, celery salt, and pepper until blended. Gradually add milk and stir. Bring to a boil and cook, stirring continuously, until thickened, about 2 minutes.

4. Layer half of the carrots, the cheese, and the white sauce in baking dish. Repeat the layers. Bake for 30 minutes. Melt remaining ¼ cup butter, toss with bread pieces, and sprinkle on top of casserole. Bake 5 minutes longer, until topping is lightly browned. Makes 4 to 6 servings.

✕ **LISA GENTRY,** Elko, Georgia
Second Place, Favorite Vegetable Casserole, Perry, Georgia, Georgia National Fair, 2005

Garden Vegetable Pie

Cooking spray
1 cup chopped broccoli
1 cup sliced cauliflower
½ teaspoon onion powder
1 cup grated cheddar cheese
1½ cups lowfat milk

¾ cup low-cholesterol egg product
¾ cup biscuit mix
¼ teaspoon salt
¼ teaspoon black pepper
¼ teaspoon garlic powder

1. Preheat oven to 400°F. Coat the inside of a 10-inch pie plate with cooking spray.

2. Combine broccoli, cauliflower, onion powder, and cheese in a large bowl. Spread evenly in pie plate.

3. Combine milk, egg product, biscuit mix, salt, pepper, and garlic powder in a blender. Mix on high until smooth, about 15 seconds. Pour over vegetables in pie plate. Bake until lightly browned and a knife inserted about 3 inches from the edge comes out clean, 35 to 40 minutes. Cool 5 to 10 minutes before serving. Makes 6 to 8 servings.

✕ **PRISCILLA GERRARD,** Danvers, Massachusetts
First Place, Mrs. Essex County Contest, Topsfield, Fair, Topsfield, Massachusetts, 1996

WINNER'S CIRCLE TIP | Make this recipe even "lighter" by substituting frozen vegetables or zucchini and tomatoes when they are in season.

DATE-CARROT CASSEROLE

3 carrots, peeled and thinly sliced
3 medium apples, peeled and sliced
⅓ cup orange juice or apple cider
1 teaspoon cinnamon
⅓ cup all-purpose flour

⅓ cup sugar
1 teaspoon nutmeg
2 tablespoons margarine, cold
¾ cup chopped dates

1. Preheat oven to 350°F.

2. Place carrots in a small saucepan, add water to cover, and bring to a boil. Reduce to a simmer and cook 20 minutes. Drain well.

3. Place carrots and apples in a greased 8 x 8 x 2-inch pan. Pour orange juice or cider over the top and sprinkle with cinnamon. Cover with foil. Bake until carrots are almost tender, about 35 minutes.

4. Mix together flour, sugar, and nutmeg. Cut in margarine until crumbly. Remove casserole from oven. Remove foil and sprinkle crumb mixture and chopped dates over top. Bake, uncovered, until lightly brown and carrots are tender, 10 to 15 minutes longer. Makes 6 to 8 servings.

※ **TWILA BOOTH,** San Jacinto, California
Third Place, Savory Side Dish, Riverside County Fair and National Date Festival, Indio, California, 2003–2004

CHIMAYO CORN PUDDING

1 can (12 oz.) cream-style corn
1 cup yellow cornmeal
1 cup unsalted butter, melted
¾ cup buttermilk
2 medium onions, chopped

2 eggs, beaten
½ teaspoon baking soda
2 cups grated sharp cheddar cheese, divided
⅓ cup chopped green chiles

1. Preheat oven to 350°F. Grease a 9 x 9 x 2-inch baking pan.

2. Combine corn, cornmeal, butter, buttermilk, onions, eggs, and baking soda in a medium bowl and mix well.

3. Pour half of batter into pan. Add 1 cup of the cheese, all of the chopped chiles, the remaining cup of cheese, and the remaining batter. Bake for 1 hour. Cool 15 minutes before serving. Makes 8 to 10 servings.

※ **PATRICIA KALB,** Albuquerque, New Mexico
Second Place, New Mexico State Fair, Albuquerque, New Mexico, 2005

VEGGIE CASSEROLE

1 medium eggplant
2 medium yellow squash
2 small zucchini
1 small onion

1 tablespoon olive oil
1 tablespoon unsalted butter, room temperature
1 can (28 oz.) crushed tomatoes with garlic
3 tablespoons Parmesan and/or Asiago

BLOOMIN' ONION

2 large sweet onions, unpeeled
Oil for deep-fat frying
1¼ cups all-purpose flour

1 teaspoon Cajun seasoning
1 cup milk
Dipping Sauce (recipe follows)

1. Peel away the outer skin of the onion, leaving the root end intact. Cut a small slice off the top.

2. Starting at the top of the onion and on one side, make a cut downward toward the root end, stopping ½ inch from bottom. Make additional cuts ⅛ inch from the first until there are cuts completely across the onion.

3. Turn the onion a quarter turn so the slices are horizontal to you. Repeat the cuts ⅛ inch apart from each other until there is a checkerboard pattern across the entire top of onion.

4. Heat oil in deep fryer to 350°F. Combine flour and Cajun seasoning in a 1-gallon zip-close plastic bag. Place milk in a small deep bowl. Dip each onion in flour, then in milk, and then back into flour. Submerge onions in hot fat and fry for 5 minutes, turning once.

5. Remove onions from oil and place on a serving plate. Discard the very center of the fried onion blossom. Place a few spoonfuls of Dipping Sauce into the center of each blossom and serve immediately. Makes 4 servings.

DIPPING SAUCE

½ cup mayonnaise
½ cup sour cream

1 teaspoon chili powder
1½ teaspoons Cajun seasoning

Combine all ingredients in a small bowl. Mix well and set aside.

※ *Friends of the California State Fair Cookbook,* Sacramento, California

1. Peel eggplant and cut into 1-inch cubes. Cut yellow squash, zucchini, and onion into bite-size pieces.

2. Heat olive and butter in a large skillet over medium heat. Add onion and sauté for 1 minute.

3. Add yellow squash and zucchini to skillet and sauté, stirring often, until softened, 3 to 5 minutes. Add eggplant and cook until softened, 3 to 5 minutes. Stir in tomatoes and cook 3 to 5 minutes. Add cheese, remove from heat, and stir until melted. Transfer to a large platter or individual plates and serve. Makes 4 servings.

※ **LU HESS,** Port Saint Lucie, Florida
Blue Ribbon, Saint Lucie County Fair, Fort Pierce, Florida, 2005

OVEN-ROASTED MAUI ONION TART

7 medium Maui onions, divided

3 tablespoons olive oil, divided

2 garlic cloves, minced

Salt and freshly ground black pepper, divided

3 tablespoons cream

2 teaspoons minced fresh basil

1 sheet frozen puff pastry, thawed

Flour for rolling out pastry

1 egg

1 tablespoon water

1. Preheat oven to 325°F.

2. Peel and trim onions. Slice 4 of the onions thinly. Heat 1 tablespoon of the olive oil in a large non-stick skillet over medium heat. Add sliced onions and garlic and sauté 1 minute. Reduce heat, cover, and cook, stirring occasionally, until tender, about 15 minutes.

3. Remove cover and season onions with salt and pepper. Stir in cream and cook until most of the liquid has evaporated, about 5 minutes. Stir in basil. Remove skillet from heat and allow mixture to cool. Adjust seasonings. (The recipe can be made in advance up to this point; if not continuing immediately, store onions in a covered container in the refrigerator.)

4. Cut remaining 3 onions lengthwise into 8 to 10 wedges each, keeping wedges intact. Set wedges, narrow sides up, on an oiled baking sheet. Brush lightly with remaining olive oil. Season with salt and pepper. Roast in oven until tender, about 20 minutes. Allow to cool.

5. Increase oven temperature to 425°F.

6. Lay pastry on a lightly floured surface and roll out with a rolling pin into an 11½-inch x 11½-inch square. Invert an 11-inch metal tart pan onto the dough and cut out a circle of pastry. Remove the excess dough around the edges. Re-roll to make the pastry circle ½ inch larger in diameter.

7. Mix egg and water in a small bowl. Place the pastry in the tart pan and brush bottom with egg mixture. Place tart pan on a baking sheet and refrigerate until firm, about 10 minutes.

8. Spread onion mixture evenly in pastry shell. Arrange roasted onions on top. Season with salt and pepper. Bake until golden, 20 to 25 minutes. Garnish with additional basil, if desired. Makes 6 to 8 servings.

✄ **KRISTINE SNYDER,** Kihei, Hawaii
First Prize, Main Dishes, Maui Onion Festival, Maui, Hawaii, 2000

⊹ THE MAUI ONION FESTIVAL ⊹

Onions are serious business in Maui, Hawaii. "Authentic" Maui onions are grown by only a handful of farmers on the slopes of Haleakala, a massive dormant volcano.

The Maui Onion Festival showcases these sweet onions through food vendors, entertainment, tastings, a farmers market, and a Maui onion cook-off contest. The highlight of the two-day festival is the celebrated raw Maui onion-eating contest, which includes a kids' division.

Maui onions are sold in Hawaii and in some West Coast cities but can be difficult to find otherwise. Some compare the Maui onion to its sweet cousins, the Vidalia onion from Georgia or the Walla Walla onion from Washington state.

Maui Onions Wellington

4 large Maui onions, unpeeled
1 head of garlic
Olive oil
1 medium-sized red or white potato
½ cup shredded Parmesan
Salt and pepper, divided
½ lb. portabella mushrooms

2 tablespoons unsalted butter,
    room temperature
2 tablespoons dry white wine
2 sheets frozen puff pastry, thawed
Flour for rolling out pastry
1 egg
1 tablespoon water

1. Preheat oven to 375°F.

2. Trim root ends of onions so they will stand upright. Cut 1 inch off the pointed tops. Brush onions and garlic with olive oil and set on a rimmed baking sheet. Roast until centers of onions are tender, 1 hour. Allow to cool.

3. Carefully remove the center of each onion, leaving two outer layers of peel intact. Puree the onion centers in a food processor and set in a strainer to drain.

4. Peel potato and cut into 2-inch pieces. Cook in boiling water until soft, 15 minutes. Drain well. Place warm potato pieces in a bowl and mash with a potato masher or fork. Allow to cool.

5. Cut off the top of the garlic head and squeeze flesh into a small dish. Mash garlic with a fork. Add garlic, Parmesan, and half of the onion purée to mashed potato and stir to combine. Season with salt and pepper.

6. Coarsely chop portabellas in a food processor. Melt butter in a large, nonstick skillet over medium heat. Add remaining onion purée, mushrooms, and wine to skillet. Sauté until mushrooms are dark-colored and all liquid is absorbed, 15 to 20 minutes. Season with salt and pepper. Cool completely.

7. Stuff the bottom half of each onion shell with mushroom mixture. Fill top half with potato mixture. Refrigerate stuffed onions until cold, at least 1 hour.

8. Lay 1 pastry sheet on a lightly floured surface, roll out into a 10 x 18-inch rectangle, and cut in half. Repeat with second pastry sheet. Beat egg with water. Brush pastry sheets lightly with egg mixture. Stand 1 stuffed onion on each sheet. Draw up pastry around onion and pinch together at top. Brush each onion package with egg mixture and place on a greased baking sheet. Chill 30 minutes. Bake at 425°F until crust is a rich golden color, 25 to 30 minutes. Makes 4 servings.

✕ **Kristine Snyder,** Kihei, Hawaii
First Prize and Grand Prize, Main Dishes,
Maui Onion Festival, Maui, Hawaii, 1999

Stuffed Maui Onion Gratiné

4 large Maui onions, unpeeled

2 tablespoons olive oil,
  plus more for onions

Salt and pepper

3 skinless, boneless chicken breasts

2 large garlic cloves, finely minced

1 tablespoon flour

⅓ cup heavy cream

¾ cup grated Parmesan

½ cup shredded Swiss cheese, divided

½ cup shredded mozzarella, divided

3 fresh sage leaves, minced

2 teaspoons chopped fresh rosemary

2 tablespoons chopped fresh parsley

1. Preheat oven to 350°F.

2. Trim root ends of onions so they will stand upright. Brush onions with olive oil and set on rimmed baking sheet. Roast until centers are tender, about 1 hour. Cool.

3. Cut off onion tops and remove outermost peel. Carefully remove the center of each onion, leaving two outer layers intact. Sprinkle shells with salt and pepper. Coarsely chop onion centers and set aside.

4. Cut chicken breasts into ¾-inch pieces. Heat olive oil in a large, nonstick skillet over medium heat, add chicken pieces, and sauté until no longer pink, 6 minutes. Add garlic and flour and sauté for 2 minutes. Stir in reserved chopped onion, cream, and Parmesan. Cook until mixture thickens, about 5 minutes.

5. Add ¼ cup each of the Swiss cheese and mozzarella. Remove mixture from heat. Add sage, rosemary, and parsley. Season with salt and pepper.

6. Stuff each onion shell with chicken mixture. Mix together remaining ¼ cup Swiss cheese and ¼ cup mozzarella. Divide evenly atop stuffed onions. Bake until cheese is melted and bubbly, 15 minutes. Makes 4 servings.

⌗ **Kristine Snyder,** Kihei, Hawaii
First Prize and Grand Prize, Main Dishes, Maui Onion Festival, Maui, Hawaii, 2001

Green Tomato Pie

Double-crust pie pastry

4 cups sliced green tomatoes

1⅓ cups sugar

3 tablespoons flour

¼ teaspoon salt

¾ teaspoon cinnamon

5 tablespoons lemon juice

1 teaspoon lemon flavoring

2 tablespoons unsalted butter

1. Preheat oven to 450°F. Line a 9-inch pie pan with half of pastry.

2. Combine green tomatoes, sugar, flour, salt, cinnamon, lemon juice, and lemon flavoring in a large bowl. Mix well.

3. Pour filling into pie pan, dot with butter, and cover with remaining pastry. Press and crimp the edges to seal. Bake for 10 minutes. Reduce temperature to 350°F and bake 40 minutes longer. Makes 6 to 8 servings.

⌗ **Janice Nostrom,** Humboldt, Iowa
Blue Ribbons, Clay County Fair, Spencer, Iowa, 2004, 2005

SWISS SCALLOPED POTATOES

5 to 6 medium potatoes
1 lb. ground beef
½ cup chopped onion
¼ cup margarine
¼ cup all-purpose flour
2 cups milk

½ cup sour cream
Dash of garlic powder
½ teaspoon salt
Black pepper
1 cup grated cheddar cheese, divided

1. Preheat oven to 350°F.

2. Place unpeeled potatoes in a large saucepan, add cold water to cover, and bring to a boil. Cook until soft and heated through, 15 minutes. Drain and set aside to cool.

3. Brown ground beef and onion in a skillet over medium heat. Drain off fat.

4. Heat margarine in a saucepan or large skillet until melted. Add flour and milk and stir. When mixture thickens, stir in sour cream, garlic powder, salt, and pepper.

5. Peel and slice potatoes. Layer half of potatoes in the bottom of a casserole dish. Top with cooked ground beef. Pour half of white sauce over ground beef. Add ½ cup of the cheddar cheese. Layer on remaining potatoes, white sauce, and cheese. Bake for 30 minutes. Makes 6 servings.

✕ **NATHAN BRANTLEY,** Millbrook, Alabama,
Prize Winner, Alabama National Fair, Montgomery, Alabama, 1998–2002

WINNER'S CIRCLE TIP | When you're feeding a crowd, double this recipe and bake it in a 13 x 9 x 2-inch baking dish. It freezes well, so you can make it ahead of time. Add more cheese, or mix in some Monterey Jack with the cheddar, if you like an extra cheesy taste.

EASY AND LIGHT WILD RICE CASSEROLE

1 cup long-grain wild rice
1 can (10.5 oz.) low-sodium,
   fat-free beef broth
1 can (10.5 oz.) low-sodium condensed
   French onion soup

1 can (4 oz.) sliced mushrooms
2 tablespoons butter, cut into ½-inch cubes

1. Preheat oven to 375°F.

2. Place rice in a medium-size oven-proof casserole dish. Pour in beef broth and condensed French onion soup. Do not stir. Scatter mushrooms over the top. Dot with butter.

3. Cover and bake for 1 hour. Remove dish from oven. Stir to combine ingredients. Let stand a few minutes before serving. Serves 4.

✕ **CARLA GARNTO,** Warner Robins, Georgia
First Place, Cooking Lite with Grains, Georgia National Fair, Perry, Georgia, 2005

Veggies Italiana

1 loaf round bread
Margarine for cooking
3 small garlic cloves (from center of head)
1 medium onion, chopped
1 medium zucchini, cut in half lengthwise
  and sliced crosswise
½ green bell pepper, seeded and
  finely chopped
¾ red bell pepper, seeded and finely chopped

¾ yellow bell pepper, seeded and finely chopped
18 asparagus tips
½ red tomato, chopped
½ yellow tomato, chopped
1½ teaspoons dried Italian seasoning
1 teaspoon fresh orange juice
1 teaspoon sun-dried tomato pesto
Salt and pepper

1. Slice off the top third of bread loaf. Hollow out the bottom section with your fingers, leaving a ½-inch shell. Top and crumbs can be reserved for another use.

2. Heat margarine in a large skillet. Add garlic and sauté for 1 to 2 minutes. Remove garlic. Add onion and sauté just until it begins to soften, 3 to 4 minutes. Push onion to side of pan.

3. Add zucchini to skillet, sauté to soften, and push to one side. Sauté green, red, and yellow peppers together and push to side of pan. Repeat for asparagus tips and red and yellow tomatoes.

4. Add Italian seasoning and stir to combine all ingredients. Sprinkle orange juice over the top. Stir in pesto. Season with salt and pepper. Spoon hot vegetables into hollowed-out bread bowl. Makes 6 servings.

Warm the bread bowl in the oven before filling, if you prefer.

※ **MARY DEAN CAMPSIE,** Pleasant Ridge, Michigan
First Place, Vegetarian Main Dish Contest, Michigan State Fair, Detroit, Michigan, 2001

Barley and Whole Wheat Pilaf

½ cup unsalted butter
1 large onion, chopped
3 carrots, sliced
1½ cups mushrooms, quartered
1 tablespoon oil
1½ cups barley

½ cups whole wheat
2 cups beef or chicken broth
1½ cups water
Salt and pepper
¾ cup sliced scallions

1. Preheat oven to 350°F.

2. Melt butter in a large skillet over medium heat. Add onion, carrots, and mushrooms. Sauté just until barely tender. Transfer to a large casserole dish.

3. In the same skillet, combine oil, barley, and wheat. Sauté until golden, about 6 minutes. Add to casserole dish. Pour broth and water over top. Sprinkle with salt and pepper.

4. Cover and bake until grains are tender, about 45 minutes. If mixture becomes dry before cooking is complete, add a little more water. Just before serving, fluff up grains and garnish with scallions. Serves 6 to 8.

※ **SHEILA GENTRY,** Elko, Georgia
Third Place, Cooking Lite with Grains, Georgia National Fair, Perry, Georgia, 2005

CHAPTER 7

BREADS, ROLLS,
AND BISCUITS

TRADITIONAL WHITE BREAD

1 cup water
2 tablespoons unsalted butter or
    margarine, melted
3 cups bread flour

2 tablespoons nonfat dry milk
1½ teaspoons salt
1 tablespoon sugar
2 teaspoons active dry yeast

1. Add water and melted butter or margarine to the bread pan of a bread machine.

2. Whisk together flour, nonfat dry milk, salt, and sugar. Add to bread pan.

3. Use your finger or a spoon to form a shallow well in the flour. Pour the yeast into the well. (Note: The yeast must not come into contact with any liquid ingredients during this step.)

4. Close the lid of the bread machine. Choose the desired settings for baking and crust color and start the machine. Machine will knead, rise, and bake the bread, generally 3 to 4 hours. Slice bread and serve warm with butter and jam or jelly. Makes one 1½-lb. loaf.

TRACY MEATS, Rock Springs, Wyoming
First Place, Bread Machine Contest, Sweetwater County Fair, Rock Springs, Wyoming, 2003

THE GUILFORD FAIR

The Guilford Fair, established in 1859, is the second oldest agricultural fair in Connecticut. The early fairs on the Guilford Green became famous for their cattle shows. By 1903 indoor exhibitions featured Guilford merchants displaying meat, potted plants, millinery, and photographs; there were also displays of Indian arrowhead collections and quilts and needlework. The advent of the trolley car in 1910 contributed to a then-unprecedented fair crowd of nearly 10,000 people. In 1969 the Guilford Fair outgrew the confines of the 8-acre Guilford Green and relocated to the 30-acre Hunter Farm off Lover's Lane. Today the fair features many traditional agricultural programs, as well as new exhibits, activities, and fair foods to sample.

CHARLES PELUSE'S TRADITIONAL WHITE BREAD

5 to 6 cups white high-gluten bread flour,
    divided, plus more for kneading
½ cup nonfat dry milk
3 tablespoons sugar

1 tablespoon salt
2 envelopes (2.4 oz. each) active dry yeast
2¼ cups water
½ cup unsalted butter, room temperature

1. Combine 2 cups of the flour, nonfat dry milk, sugar, salt, and yeast in a large mixing bowl.

2. Heat butter and water to 120°F. Pour warm liquid into flour mixture, stirring completely to dissolve the yeast. Stir in 2 to 3 more cups flour until dough leaves the sides of the bowl cleanly.

3. Turn dough onto a lightly floured surface. Knead dough, adding flour as necessary, until smooth and elastic. Place dough in greased bowl and turn once to coat. Cover and let rise in a warm place until double in size, about 1 hour.

4. Punch down dough. Divide dough in half. Roll each half into a rectangle. Shape into two loaves and place in two 9 x 5 x 3-inch loaf pans. Cover and let rise until double in size, about 1 hour.

5. Preheat oven to 425°F. Bake 25 minutes, or until crust is deep golden brown. Remove from pans and cool. Makes 2 loaves.

✳ **CHARLES PELUSE,** Guilford, Connecticut
Blue Ribbon, White Yeast Bread; Rosette, Best Bread; Best in Show trophy, Guilford Fair, Guilford, Connecticut, 2003

PERFECT WHITE BREAD

6 cups bread flour

6 cups all-purpose flour, plus more
    for kneading

1 envelope (2.4 oz.) active dry yeast

¼ cup warm water

¼ cup sugar or honey

2 tablespoons shortening

4 teaspoons salt

2 cups milk

2 cups cold water

Melted unsalted butter (optional)

1. Whisk together bread flour and all-purpose flour.

2. Dissolve yeast in warm water.

3. In a large bowl, combine sugar or honey, shortening, and salt. Scald milk in a saucepan and pour over shortening mixture. After shortening melts, add cold water to bowl and stir to combine.

4. Add 2 cups of the combined flours to the liquid ingredients. Mix thoroughly. Add yeast and mix to combine. Add more flour, 1 or 2 cups at a time, mixing thoroughly after each addition, until dough forms.

5. Turn out dough onto a lightly floured surface. Knead until smooth and elastic, 8 to 10 minutes, dusting surface with flour as needed to prevent sticking. Shape dough into a ball, place in a lightly greased bowl, and turn once to coat. Cover with a clean towel and let rise in a warm place until double in size, 2 to 2½ hours.

6. Punch down dough, fold in sides, and turn over. Cover and let rise until double in size, about 1 hour.

7. Turn out dough onto a floured surface. Let rest 10 minutes. Cut into 4 pieces. Shape each piece into a loaf and place in a greased 9 x 5 x 3-inch loaf pan. To ensure a light texture during baking, do not overhandle the dough at this stage. Cover and let rise until double in size, about 1 hour.

8. Preheat oven to 375°F. Bake 45 minutes, or until tops of loaves are golden brown. Brush baked loaves with melted butter, if desired. Remove loaves from pans and cool on wire racks. Slice with a serrated bread knife. Serve warm or at room temperature. (Note: Room temperature bread is easier to slice.) Makes 4 loaves.

✳ **DEBBY PAYNE,** Wappingers Falls, New York
Blue Ribbon, Dutchess County Fair, Rhinebeck, New York, 1997

WINNER'S CIRCLE TIP | **This dough can also be used to make cinnamon rolls. Roll the dough flat, dot with butter, sprinkle with cinnamon sugar and raisins, and roll up. Bake the roll seam side down. Slice and serve while still warm.**

PUMPKIN-SHAPED WHITE YEAST BREAD

1 cup water
⅛ cup sugar
1 teaspoon salt
2 tablespoons unsalted butter,
    room temperature

3¼ cups all-purpose flour
2½ teaspoons active dry yeast
Yellow, red, and blue food coloring
2 tablespoons water

1. Add water, sugar, salt, butter, flour, and yeast to the bread machine. Run the machine through the dough cycle.

2. Punch down dough and form into a pumpkin shape with a small stem at the top. Set on a lightly greased baking sheet. Let rise until double in size, 1 to 2 hours.

3. Preheat oven to 375°F. Add a few drops each of yellow and red food coloring to water to make a warm orange wash. Transfer a small amount of orange wash to another container and add 1 drop of blue to make a olive green wash. Carefully brush green wash on pumpkin stem. Cut vertical slits in the pumpkin part of the dough to suggest ridge lines. Brush orange wash on the pumpkin part of the dough. Bake for 35 minutes, or until loaf sounds hollow when tapped. Cool on wire rack. Makes 1 pumpkin-shaped loaf.

✕ **ALINA CORNEJO,** DeLand, Florida
First Place, Baked Goods—Youth Senior, Volusia County Fair, DeLand, Florida, 2004

SPECIALTY BREAD

2 tablespoons shortening
2 tablespoons sugar
2 teaspoons salt
1 cup boiling water
1 cup scalded milk

1 yeast cake softened in ¼ cup
    lukewarm water
6 to 6½ cups bread flour, divided,
    plus more for kneading

1. Place shortening, sugar, and salt in a large bowl. Add boiling water and scalded milk. Cool to lukewarm.

2. Add yeast to mixture and stir. Add 3 cups of the flour and mix thoroughly. Mix in 2 more cups of the flour. Gradually add another ½ to 1 cup of flour, mixing in just enough to prevent dough from sticking to the bowl.

3. Turn out dough onto a work surface lightly dusted with flour. Cover and let rest 10 minutes, for easier handling. Knead until smooth and elastic, incorporating more flour if needed. Place in an oiled bowl and turn once to coat. Cover and let rise until double in size, 1 to 2 hours.

4. Punch down dough, shape into loaf, and set on a baking sheet. Cover and let rise until double in size, about 1 hour.

5. Preheat oven to 375°F. Bake loaf for 15 minutes. Lower oven temperature to 350°F and continue baking another 25 to 30 minutes. Loaf should make a hollow sound when plunked on the top. Makes 1 round loaf.

✕ **BARBARA CHITTUM,** Abingdon, Virginia
Specialty Bread Winner, Washington County Fair, Abingdon, Virginia, 2004

100% Whole Wheat Bread

1 tablespoon active dry yeast
2½ cups warm water, divided
2 tablespoons honey
2 tablespoons molasses

1 tablespoon coarse salt
¼ cup unsalted butter, melted
6 cups whole wheat flour, plus more
    for kneading

1. In a large bowl, dissolve yeast in ½ cup of the warm water. Stir in honey, molasses, salt, and butter.

2. Add flour to yeast mixture 1 cup at a time, mixing well after each addition, until dough becomes hard to stir.

3. Turn out dough onto a lightly floured surface. Let rest 10 minutes. Knead until smooth, elastic, and no longer tacky, 8 to 10 minutes. Place dough in a greased bowl and turn once to coat. Cover with plastic wrap. Let rise until double in size, 2 or more hours.

4. Punch down dough. Turn out dough onto a work surface. Divide dough in half and shape into two loaves. Place loaves into two greased 9 x 5 x 3-inch loaf pans. Cover lightly with a clean kitchen towel. Let dough rise until it reaches the tops of the pans, about 1 hour.

5. Preheat oven to 350°F. Bake loaves for 45 minutes. Cool on a wire rack. Makes two loaves.

✄ **JAY TRAPP,** Red Hook, New York
Blue Ribbon, Dutchess County Fair, Rhinebeck, New York, 2002

Sesame French Bread

2 envelopes (2.4 oz. each) active dry yeast
2½ cups warm water
2 tablespoons sugar
2 tablespoons vegetable oil
2 teaspoons salt

6 to 6½ cups all-purpose flour, divided
Cornmeal
1 egg white
1 tablespoon water
2 tablespoons sesame seeds

1. Dissolve yeast in warm water in the large bowl of an electric mixer. Add sugar, oil, salt, and 4 cups of the flour. Beat until smooth using the paddle attachment. Add more flour as needed to form a soft dough.

2. Turn out dough onto a lightly floured surface. Knead until smooth and elastic, 8 to 10 minutes (or knead in mixer for 10 minutes).

3. Place dough in a greased bowl and turn once to coat. Cover and let rise until double in size, 2 to 4 hours.

4. Punch down dough, cover, and let rise again, 1 to 2 hours.

5. Beat together egg white and 1 tablespoon water. Grease 2 baking sheets and sprinkle with cornmeal. Turn out dough onto lightly floured work surface. Divide in half. Roll each half into a 15 x 10-inch rectangle. Roll up from a long edge and seal well. Place on baking sheet seam side down. Brush tops of loaves with egg white mixture and sprinkle with sesame seeds. Cover and let rise until double in size, 1 hour.

6. Preheat oven to 400°F. Use a sharp knife to make 4 shallow cuts across the top of each loaf. Bake for 25 minutes, or until lightly browned. Cool on wire racks. Makes 2 loaves.

✄ **JUNE WEBER,** Dousman, Wisconsin
Grand Champion, Waukesha County Fair, Pewaukee, Wisconsin, 2001

SWEDISH RYE BREAD

1½ cups warm water
1 tablespoon sugar
⅓ cup dark molasses
1 tablespoon margarine,
    room temperature
¼ cup nonfat dry milk

¼ cup brown sugar
1 teaspoon salt
3 cups white flour
1 cup medium rye flour
1 package (2.4 oz.) quick-rising yeast
2 teaspoons caraway seed

1. Put ingredients in a bread machine in the order suggested in the instruction manual. Operate on dough setting.

2. Divide dough in half and shape into two loaves. Place into two greased 9 x 5 x 3-inch loaf pans. Cover and let rise until double in size, 1 hour.

3. Preheat oven to 350°F. Bake loaves for 40 to 45 minutes. Cool on wire racks. Makes 2 loaves.

※ **BETSY BRUGMAN,** Royal, Iowa
Blue Ribbons, Open Class and 4-H, Clay County Fair, Spencer, Iowa, 2005

IRISH SODA BREAD

3 cups all-purpose flour, plus more
    for kneading
¼ cup sugar
2 teaspoons baking powder
½ teaspoon baking soda

½ teaspoon salt
1 tablespoon caraway seeds
1 cup raisins
1½ cups buttermilk

1. Preheat oven to 350°F. Lightly grease and flour a glass or ceramic pie plate.

2. Combine flour, sugar, baking powder, baking soda, salt, caraway seeds, and raisins in a large bowl. Add buttermilk and stir just until moistened.

3. Turn out dough onto a lightly floured surface. Using floured hands, knead and form dough into a round loaf and place in pie plate. Cut a cross in top of loaf with a knife. Sprinkle flour and then water on top of loaf. Bake for 50 minutes. Turn out onto a wire rack and cool. Makes 1 loaf.

※ **BRIAN DAYTE,** Poughkeepsie, New York
Blue Ribbon, Dutchess County Fair, Rhinebeck, New York, 2004

PINWHEEL BREAD

2 envelopes (2.4 oz. each) active dry yeast
2 cups warm water
2 cups milk
½ cup sugar
½ cup shortening

2 tablespoons salt
8½ cups all-purpose flour, plus more
    for kneading
¼ cup molasses
4 to 4½ cups whole wheat flour

1. Dissolve yeast in warm water in a large bowl.

2. Heat milk, sugar, shortening, and salt in a saucepan over low heat just until warm (shortening does not need to melt). Add to yeast mixture. Stir in 4 cups of the flour and beat until smooth. Cover and let rise in a warm place for 1 hour.

3. Stir down batter. Turn about half of batter into another mixing bowl. To one bowl, add enough of remaining 4½ cups all-purpose flour to make a moderately stiff dough. Turn out dough onto a floured surface. Knead until smooth and elastic, 6 to 8 minutes. Place dough in greased bowl and turn once to coat. Cover and let rise until double in size, 45 to 60 minutes.

4. Stir molasses into remaining batter until well blended. Add enough of the whole wheat flour to make a moderately stiff dough. Turn out dough onto a floured surface. Knead for 6 to 8 minutes. Place dough in greased bowl and turn once to coat. Cover let rise until double in size, 45 to 60 minutes.

5. Punch down each dough. Let rest for 10 minutes. Divide each dough into thirds. Roll out each portion into an 8 x 12-inch rectangle. Layer a dark (whole wheat) piece on a light piece and roll up tightly, beginning at short edge. Place in a greased 9 x 5 x 3-inch loaf pan, seam side down. Repeat with remaining dough to make 3 pinwheel loaves. Cover and let rise until almost double in size, 45 to 60 minutes.

6. Preheat oven to 375°F. Bake loaves for 30 to 35 minutes, covering with foil after 20 minutes to prevent overbrowning. Remove from pans and cool on wire racks. Makes 3 loaves.

⌘ **ARLENE PAQUET,** Poughkeepsie, New York
"Best of Breads," "Best of Culinary," Dutchess County Fair, Rhinebeck, New York, 2003

ROSEMARY FOCACCIA

1 envelope (2.4 oz.) active dry yeast
½ teaspoon sugar
1 cup lukewarm water
3½ cups unbleached all-purpose flour
1 teaspoon salt

5 tablespoons olive oil, divided
½ teaspoon minced garlic
1 tablespoon finely chopped fresh rosemary
  leaves, plus sprigs for garnish
1 teaspoon coarse salt

1. Combine yeast, sugar, and water in the bowl of an electric mixer fitted with the dough hook attachment. Let stand until mixture is foamy, about 5 minutes.

2. Add flour, salt, and 3 tablespoons of the oil to the yeast mixture. Combine and knead with dough hook until soft and slightly sticky, about 2 minutes. Form dough into a ball, transfer to an oiled bowl, and turn once to coat. Cover and set in a warm place until double in size, 1½ hours.

3. Punch down dough, wrap in plastic, and refrigerate overnight.

4. Bring dough to room temperature. Lightly oil a 15½ x 10½ x 1-inch jelly roll pan. Press dough evenly into pan, cover loosely, and set in a warm place to rise until almost double in size, 1 hour.

5. Preheat oven to 400°F. Combine garlic, rosemary, and remaining 2 tablespoons oil in a small bowl. Dimple the dough by making ¼-inch deep indentations with your fingertips. Brush oil mixture over surface of dough and sprinkle with coarse salt. Bake in bottom third of oven for 35 to 45 minutes, or until golden brown. Cool in pan on a wire rack. Serve warm or at room temperature, garnished with rosemary sprigs. Makes 1 focaccia.

⌘ **CATHY POLUZZI,** Poughkeepsie, New York
Blue Ribbon, Dutchess County Fair, Rhinebeck, New York, 2000

Hoska (Bohemian Christmas Bread)

5 to 6 cups unsifted flour, divided
½ cup sugar
1½ teaspoons salt
1 teaspoon grated lemon zest
⅛ teaspoon mace
2 envelopes (2.4 oz. each) active dry yeast
1 cup milk

⅔ cup water
¼ cup margarine, room temperature
2 eggs at room temperature
½ cup slivered almonds
½ cup dark seedless raisins
Vegetable oil
½ cup confectioners' sugar frosting

1. Combine 1½ cups of the flour, sugar, salt, lemon zest, mace, and yeast in a large bowl of an electric mixer.

2. Heat milk, water, and margarine in a saucepan over low heat until very warm, 120°F to 130°F. Margarine does not need to melt. Add to dry ingredients and beat at medium speed for 2 minutes. Add eggs and ½ cup of the flour. Beat at high speed for 2 minutes. Stir in almonds, raisins, and enough additional flour to make a stiff dough.

3. Turn out dough onto lightly floured surface. Knead until smooth and elastic. Cover with plastic wrap and a towel. Let rest 20 minutes.

4. Divide dough in half. Divide one half into 4 equal pieces. Roll 3 pieces into ropes 14 inches long. Braid the ropes on a greased baking sheet and tuck in the ends. Divide the remaining piece into thirds, roll into 3 ropes 9 inches long, and braid together. Place the smaller braid on the larger bread, tucking in the ends. Braid a second loaf in same way. Cover loosely with waxed paper brushed with vegetable oil and top with plastic wrap. Refrigerate 2 to 24 hours.

5. Preheat oven to 375°F. Remove dough from refrigerator and let stand at room temperature for 10 minutes. Bake for 25 minutes. Add water, a teaspoon at a time, until the mixture reaches the consistency of a thick glaze. Remove loaves from baking sheets and cool on wire racks. Drizzle with confectioners' sugar frosting while still warm. Makes 2 loaves.

✹ **Jennifer Golden,** age 14, La Junta, Colorado
Grand Champion, Specialty Foods, Arkansas Valley Fair, Rocky Ford, Colorado, 2000; Colorado Wheat Award, 2000

Bagels

4¼ to 4¾ cups all-purpose flour, divided
2 envelopes (2.4 oz. each) active dry yeast
1½ cups warm water (110° to 115°F)
3 tablespoons sugar

1 tablespoon salt
1 gallon water
1 tablespoon sugar

1. Combine 1½ cups of the flour and yeast in the bowl of an electric mixer.

2. Combine warm water, sugar, and salt in a measuring cup. Pour over flour mixture and combine at low speed, scraping down sides of bowl, for 30 seconds. Beat at high speed for 3 minutes. Add remaining flour in increments, stirring with a wooden spoon until you can incorporate no more.

3. Turn out dough onto a lightly floured surface. Knead in enough remaining flour to make a dough that is moderately stiff, smooth, and elastic, 6 to 8 minutes. Cover and let rest for 10 minutes.

4. Divide dough into 12 portions. Shape each piece into a smooth ball. Punch a hole in the center of each ball and pull gently to enlarge hole, 1½ to 2 inches. Place bagels on greased baking sheets. Cover and let rise 20 minutes. Heat 5 inches under a broiler for 3 to 4 minutes, turning once so tops do not brown.

5. Combine water and sugar in a large stockpot. Bring to a boil and reduce to a simmer. Add bagels 4 or 5 at a time and cook, turning once, 7 minutes. Remove with tongs, drain, and place on a greased baking sheet. Bake in a preheated 375°F oven for 25 to 30 minutes. Makes 12 bagels.

✖ **RACHEL BERNARDO,** Poughkeepsie, New York
Blue Ribbon, Dutchess County Fair, Rhinebeck, New York, 2005

WINNER'S CIRCLE TIP | Just before baking, brush the tops of these bagels with beaten egg and sprinkle with poppy seeds or toasted sesame seeds.

APRICOT DAISY RING

3 to 3½ cups all-purpose flour, divided
1 envelope (2.4 oz.) active dry yeast
¾ cup milk
¼ cup unsalted butter or margarine, room temperature
2 tablespoons sugar

1 teaspoon salt
2 eggs
½ cup apricot, cherry, strawberry, or peach preserves
2 tablespoons chopped nuts
Confectioners' sugar icing

1. Combine 1½ cups of the flour and yeast in a large bowl of an electric mixer.

2. Combine milk, butter or margarine, sugar, and salt in a saucepan. Place over low heat until milk is warm, 115° to 120°F, and butter is almost melted. Add milk mixture and eggs to flour mixture. Beat at low speed for 30 seconds, scraping down sides of bowl constantly. Beat at high speed for 3 minutes. Use a spoon to stir in as much of the remaining flour as you can.

3. Turn out dough onto a lightly floured surface. Knead in enough of the remaining flour to make a moderately stiff dough. Knead until smooth and elastic, 6 to 8 minutes. Place in a greased bowl and turn once to coat. Cover and let rise in a warm place until double in size, 1¼ hours.

4. Punch down dough. Cover and let rest 10 minutes. Transfer to a greased baking sheet and shape into daisy-style coffee ring (see "To Make a Daisy Ring," below). Let rise until nearly double in size, 45 minutes. Bake in a preheated 375°F oven for 20 to 25 minutes, or until golden. Cool on a wire rack. Combine preserves and chopped nuts, spread evenly on top of ring, and drizzle with icing. Makes 1 coffee cake ring.

✖ **NANCY PEARSON,** Tulsa, Oklahoma
Sweepstakes, Tulsa State Fair, Tulsa, Oklahoma, 2002

WINNER'S CIRCLE TIP | To make a daisy ring, roll dough on a baking sheet into a 14-inch circle. Set a beverage tumbler in center (do not press down) and use a knife to make 4 evenly spaced cuts from edge of tumbler to edge of dough. Cut each section into 5 strips, for 20 strips total. Twist the strips together in pairs, making 10 twists, and pinch the ends. Remove tumbler, remove one twist completely; coil and place in center. Coil remaining twists toward center to form daisy design.

Sesame Wheat Braids

3 envelopes (2.4 oz. each) active dry yeast

2¼ cups warm water (110°F to 115°F)

⅓ cup sugar

1 tablespoon vegetable oil

1 cup whole wheat flour

2 eggs

1 tablespoon water

1 tablespoon salt

5 to 6 cups all-purpose flour, divided

2 tablespoons sesame seeds

1. In a large mixing bowl, dissolve yeast in warm water. Add sugar and oil. Mix well. Stir in whole wheat flour. Let stand until mixture bubbles, about 5 minutes.

2. Beat eggs and water in a small bowl. Measure and set aside 2 tablespoons of the egg mixture, covered, in the refrigerator. Stir the remaining egg mixture and salt into the yeast mixture.

3. Add 4 cups of the flour to the yeast mixture. Beat until smooth. Add enough of the remaining flour to form a soft dough.

4. Turn dough onto a floured surface. Knead until smooth and elastic, 6 to 8 minutes. Place in a greased bowl and turn once to coat. Cover and let rise in a warm place until double in size, about 20 minutes.

5. Punch down dough. Divide dough in half, then divide each half into thirds. Roll each piece into a rope 15 inches long. Braid three ropes on a greased baking sheet, pinching and tucking in the ends. Braid a second loaf. Brush tops with reserved egg mixture and sprinkle with sesame seeds. Let rise until double in size, 15 to 20 minutes. Bake in a preheated 350°F oven for 20 to 25 minutes. Remove from baking sheets and cool on wire racks. Makes 2 loaves.

✳ **Nancy Pearson,** Tulsa, Oklahoma
Sweepstakes Winner, Tulsa State Fair, Tulsa, Oklahoma, 2001

Apricot Braid

2½ to 3 cups all-purpose flour, divided

2 tablespoons sugar

1 teaspoon salt

1 envelope (2.4 oz.) active dry yeast

¾ cup milk

2 tablespoons unsalted butter,
   room temperature

1 egg

1 can (14 oz.) apricot filling

TOPPING

½ cup all-purpose flour

2 tablespoons sugar

2 teaspoons cinnamon

2 tablespoons unsalted butter,
   room temperature

1 egg yolk

2 tablespoons milk

1. In a large mixing bowl, combine ¾ cup of the flour, sugar, salt, and yeast.

2. Heat milk and butter in a saucepan over low heat until milk is warm and butter melts. Remove from heat. Pour gradually into flour mixture, running mixer at low speed. Beat at medium speed for 2 minutes. Add egg and another ¼ cup of the flour. Beat at high speed for 2 minutes to make a thick batter. Stir in just enough of the remaining flour to make a soft dough.

3. Turn out dough onto a lightly floured surface. Knead until smooth and elastic, 8 to 10 minutes. Place in a greased bowl and turn once to coat. Cover and let rise in a warm place until doubled in size, about 1 hour.

4. Punch down dough. Divide in half. Roll out each half into a 14 x 8-inch rectangle. Place on two greased or parchment-lined baking sheets. Spread half of apricot filling down the center of each rectangle. Slit dough at 1-inch intervals along each side and fold to center. Cover and let rise until doubled in bulk.

5. To make topping: Mix together flour, sugar, and cinnamon in a small bowl. Cut in butter until crumbly. Mix egg yolk and milk in a separate bowl. Brush egg mixture over tops of pastries and sprinkle with crumb topping. Bake in a preheated 350°F oven for 20 minutes, or light golden brown. Makes 2 pastry loaves.

✕ **ANNE MURRAY,** Poughkeepsie, New York
Best of Breads, Best of Culinary, Dutchess County Fair, Rhinebeck, New York, 2004

SAGE BREAD

1 cup warm water (120°F)	2 tablespoons cornmeal
¼ cup nonfat dry milk	4½ teaspoons dried minced onion
1½ teaspoons active dry yeast	1½ teaspoons celery seed
3⅓ cups all-purpose flour, plus more for kneading	¾ teaspoon poultry seasoning
1 tablespoon sugar	½ teaspoon dried rubbed sage
1 tablespoon brown sugar	½ teaspoon black pepper
1 teaspoon salt	2½ tablespoons margarine

1. In a large mixing bowl, combine warm water and nonfat dry milk. Add the yeast and let proof for 5 minutes.

2. In a separate bowl, combine flour, sugar, brown sugar, salt, cornmeal, minced onion, celery seed, poultry seasoning, sage, and pepper. Cut in margarine until crumbly. Add flour mixture to yeast mixture and mix together until dough forms a soft ball.

3. Turn out dough onto a lightly floured surface. Knead until smooth and elastic, 5 to 7 minutes. Place in a greased bowl and turn once to coat. Cover and let rise in a warm place until double in size, about 45 minutes.

4. Punch down dough. Divide in half. Shape dough into 2 round balls. Place on greased baking sheets and let rise until double in size, about 30 minutes. Bake in a preheated 350°F oven for 25 minutes, or until golden brown. Makes 2 loaves.

✕ **JANICE NOSTROM,** Humboldt, Iowa
Blue Ribbon, Clay County Fair, Spencer, Iowa, 2003, 2004

 WINNER'S CIRCLE TIP | Prepare the dough for this recipe in a bread machine, if you prefer. This bread is especially tasty when used for turkey and cranberry sandwiches the day after Thanksgiving.

SWEET PETALS

¼ cup lukewarm water

1 envelope (2.4 oz.) active dry yeast

¾ cup scalded milk, cooled to lukewarm

3 tablespoons shortening

¾ cup plus 2 tablespoons sugar, divided

½ teaspoon salt

2½ to 3 cups all-purpose flour

¼ cup brown sugar

2 teaspoons cinnamon

½ cup unsalted butter, melted

ICING

½ cup confectioners' sugar

1 to 2 teaspoons milk

1. Place water in a large bowl, add yeast, and stir to dissolve. Add milk, shortening, 2 tablespoons of the sugar, salt, and flour. Mix until well combined.

2. Turn out dough onto a lightly floured surface. Knead until smooth and elastic, 6 to 8 minutes. Place in a greased bowl and turn once to coat. Cover and let rise in a warm place until double in size, 1 hour.

3. Combine remaining ¾ cup of the sugar, brown sugar, and cinnamon in a small bowl. Pinch off a 1-inch ball of dough and roll into a log shape. Dip into melted butter and then into sugar mixture, turning to coat. Place log in the middle of a round pizza pan. Continue making logs, forming a radiating circle pattern on pan, until all dough is used. Let rise until light. Bake in a preheated 350°F oven for 30 minutes. Cool in pan.

4. To make icing: Combine confectioners' sugar and 1 teaspoon of the milk in a small bowl. Add more milk only if icing is too thick. Drizzle over pastry. Makes 10 to 12 servings.

✗ **DANIELLE WEBER,** Ellis Sunflower 4-H Club, Hays, Kansas
Best Bread, Ellis County Fair, Hays, Kansas, 2005

FRY BREAD

2 cups all-purpose flour

1 teaspoon salt

2 teaspoons baking powder

½ cup nonfat dry milk

1 tablespoon sugar

1 cup warm water

1. Mix together flour, salt, baking powder, nonfat dry milk, sugar, and water to make a soft dough.

2. Divide dough into four pieces. Pat each piece into a ½-inch-thick circle. Cut each circle into 6 wedges. Cut a slit in the center of each wedge.

3. Heat oil in a deep fryer to just below the smoking point. Fry each piece quickly, until nicely browned. Set on paper towels to drain. Serve with honey. Makes 24 servings.

✗ **SALISH KOOTENAI COLLEGE STUDENTS,** Pablo, Montana
First Place Public Favorite, Native American Cooking, Western Montana Fair, Missoula, Montana, 2005

WINNER'S CIRCLE TIP | Fry bread is usually made by frying a yeast bread dough that is slightly risen. In this variation, the dough is puffier and lighter.

Swedish Limpa Bread

2½ cups warm water

2 envelopes (2.4 oz. each) active dry yeast

1 tablespoon salt

¼ cup molasses

¼ cup brown sugar

¼ cup unsalted butter, room temperature

2 tablespoons grated orange zest

1 teaspoon anise seed

4 to 5 cups rye flour, unsifted

4½ cups all-purpose flour, plus more for kneading

Cornmeal

2 tablespoons melted unsalted butter

1. Place water in a large mixing bowl and sprinkle with yeast. Stir to dissolve.

2. Add salt, molasses, brown sugar, butter, oranage zest, anise seed, and rye flour to yeast mixture. Beat until smooth.

3. Add all-purpose flour in increments, mixing with your hands until dough leaves side of bowl. If more flour is needed to achieve desired consistency, add rye flour.

4. Turn out dough onto a lightly floured surface. Knead until smooth, about 10 minutes. Place dough in a lightly greased bowl and turn once to coat. Cover and let rise in a warm place until double in size, about 1½ hours.

5. Punch down dough. Divide in half. Shape into 2 loaves. Grease a baking sheet and sprinkle lightly with cornmeal. Place loaves at opposite ends of baking sheet. Let rise until double in size. Bake on middle rack of a preheated 375°F oven for 30 minutes. Brush melted butter over tops of loaves while still warm. Cool on a wire rack. Makes 2 loaves.

⌘ **HELEN DAHLBERG,** Missoula, Montana
First Place, Foreign Breads, Western Montana Fair, Missoula, Montana, 2004

Country Swirl Cinnamon Bread

2 cups all-purpose flour

1 teaspoon baking powder

½ teaspoon baking soda

½ teaspoon salt

¼ cup unsalted butter, room temperature

1⅓ cups sugar, divided

1 egg

1 cup buttermilk

1 tablespoon cinnamon

1. Preheat oven to 350°F. Grease an 8 x 4 x 2-inch loaf pan.

2. Combine flour, baking powder, baking soda, and salt.

3. In a large bowl, cream butter and 1 cup of the sugar. Add egg and blend well. Add dry ingredients alternately with buttermilk, mixing well after each addition.

4. Mix ⅓ cup remaining sugar and cinnamon in a small bowl.

5. Pour one-third of the batter into pan. Sprinkle one-third of the cinnamon sugar over batter. Repeat layering the batter and cinnamon sugar two more times. Bake for 45 to 50 minutes. Cool on a wire rack. Makes 1 loaf.

⌘ **LINDA GASS,** Mango, Florida
First Place, Adult Division, Florida State Fair, Tampa, Florida, 2005

Banana Nut Bread

2 cups all-purpose flour, plus more for pan
½ teaspoon baking soda
1½ teaspoons baking powder
¼ teaspoon salt
½ cup unsalted butter, room temperature
1 cup sugar
2 eggs, well beaten
3 large ripe bananas, well mashed
1½ tablespoons buttermilk
1 teaspoon lemon juice
1 cup pecans, coarsely chopped

1. Preheat oven to 350°F. Grease and flour a 9 x 5 x 3-inch loaf pan.
2. Sift together flour, baking soda, baking powder, and salt.
3. Cream butter and sugar in the bowl of an electric mixer fitted with a paddle attachment. Add eggs, bananas, buttermilk, and lemon juice, beating well after each addition.
4. Add pecans and sifted dry ingredients. Mix just enough to moisten. Transfer batter to pan. Bake for 1 hour. Turn out of pan and cool on a wire rack. Makes 1 loaf.

※ **Melvelene Clark,** Sweetwater, Texas
First Place, West Texas Fair & Rodeo, Abilene, Texas, 2004

Challah Bread

1 cup hot water
½ cup unsalted butter, room temperature
¼ cup sugar
1 tablespoon salt
2 envelopes (2.4 oz. each) active dry yeast
4 extra-large eggs
7 cups all-purpose flour, divided
1 egg yolk
2 tablespoons milk

1. Pour hot water into a large mixing bowl and add butter. Let stand until butter is melted and water is lukewarm. Add sugar, salt, and yeast and stir to dissolve.
2. Beat eggs slightly, add to yeast mixture, and stir until well combined. Slowly stir in 2 to 3 cups of the flour. Continue stirring until well blended. Add another 3½ to 4 cups of the flour, beating until dough comes away from the sides of bowl.
3. Turn out dough onto a lightly floured surface. Using floured hands, knead until dough is smooth and elastic, 5 "honest" minutes. Place dough in an oiled bowl and turn once to coat. Cover and let rise in a warm, draft-free place until double in size, 45 minutes to 1 hour.
4. Punch down dough. Divide in half. Divide each half into thirds. Roll each piece into a rope. Braid three ropes, tuck in ends, and place in a greased 9 x 5 x 3-inch loaf pan. Braid a second loaf. Mix egg yolk and milk in a small bowl. Brush half of the egg wash over tops of braids. Let rise in a warm place for 1 hour. Brush with egg wash again. Bake in a preheated 350°F oven for 30 minutes. Turn out of pans and cool on wire racks. Makes 2 loaves.

※ **Esther Jacks,** Missoula, Montana
Best of Show, Breads, Western Montana Fair, Missoula, Montana, 2004

TROPICAL FRUIT BREAD

2¼ cups white bread flour, plus more
   for kneading
⅞ cup unprocessed bran flakes
½ teaspoon salt
½ teaspoon ground ginger
1 envelope (2.4 oz.) active dry yeast
2 tablespoons brown sugar

2 tablespoons unsalted butter, cut into small pieces
Scant 1¼ cups tepid water
½ cup candied pineapple, finely chopped
1 oz. dried mango, finely chopped
⅓ cup plus 2 tablespoons sweetened flaked
   Coconut, plain or toasted, divided
1 egg, beaten

1. Sift flour into a large bowl. Stir in bran flakes, salt, ginger, yeast, and brown sugar. Add butter and work in with your fingertips until crumbly. Add water and mix to form dough.

2. Turn out dough onto a lightly floured surface. Knead until smooth, 5 to 8 minutes. Place in a greased bowl and turn once to coat. Cover and let rise in a warm place until double in size, 30 minutes.

3. Knead the pineapple, mango, and ⅓ cup of the coconut into the dough. Form dough into a circle and place on a greased baking sheet. Score the top with the back of a knife. Cover and let rise in a warm place, 30 minutes.

4. Brush the loaf with egg and sprinkle with remaining 2 tablespoons coconut. Bake in a preheated 425°F oven for 30 minutes, or until golden brown. Cool on a wire rack. Makes 1 loaf.

✖ **ELLEN McFARLAND,** Clearwater, Florida
Best of Show, Adult Division, Florida State Fair, Tampa, Florida, 2005

WINNER'S CIRCLE TIP | Substitute dried apricots or dates for the mango to give a different tropical twist to the flavor of this bread.

BANANA BREAD

1½ cups all-purpose flour,
   plus more for pan
1 teaspoon salt
1 teaspoon baking soda

4 ripe bananas
1 egg
1 cup sugar
¼ cup unsalted butter, room temperature

1. Preheat oven to 325°F. Lightly grease and flour a 9 x 5 x 3-inch loaf pan. Sift together flour, salt, and baking soda.

2. Place bananas in a large bowl and mash with a fork. Add egg and mix thoroughly. Stir in sugar.

3. Add dry ingredients to banana mixture. Stir until well combined. Add butter and mix until well blended. Spoon batter into pan. Bake for 50 to 60 minutes. Turn out of pan and cool on a wire rack. Makes 1 loaf.

✖ **REBECCA McCULLEY,** Pierson, Florida
First Place, Baked Goods—Adult, Volusia County Fair, DeLand, Florida, 2004

Butterscotch Quick Bread

2 cups all-purpose flour, plus more for pan

1 teaspoon baking powder

1 teaspoon baking soda

1 teaspoon salt

½ cup unsalted butter or margarine,
    room temperature

½ cup sugar

½ cup brown sugar

2 eggs, beaten

½ cup applesauce

½ cup milk

1 teaspoon butterscotch flavoring

½ cup toffee or butterscotch baking chips

1. Preheat oven to 350°F. Grease and flour two 9 x 5 x 3-inch loaf pans.

2. Sift together flour, baking powder, baking soda, and salt.

3. In a large mixing bowl, cream butter or margarine, sugar, and brown sugar. Add eggs, applesauce, milk, and butterscotch flavoring. Mix well. Mix in sifted dry ingredients. Fold in baking chips.

4. Pour batter into pans. Bake for 1 hour, or until a toothpick inserted in center comes out clean. Cool in pans for 10 minutes and then turn out onto wire racks. Makes 2 loaves.

✕ **Lorraine Conley,** Spencer, Iowa
Blue Ribbon, Clay County Fair, Spencer, Iowa, 2000

Sourdough Banana Bread

2 cups all-purpose flour, plus more for pans

2 teaspoons baking powder

1 teaspoon baking soda

1 teaspoon salt

½ cup margarine, room temperature

1 cup mashed bananas

1 cup sugar

1 cup Sourdough Starter (see below)

2 eggs

1 cup chopped nuts

1. Preheat oven to 350°F. Grease and flour two 9 x 5 x 3-inch loaf pans.

2. Sift together flour, baking powder, baking soda, and salt.

3. Cream together margarine, bananas, and sugar. Add sourdough starter and eggs. Mix well. Add sifted dry ingredients and mix until well combined. Stir in nuts. Pour batter in pans. Bake for 40 to 45 minutes. Turn out of pan and cool on a wire rack. Makes 2 loaves.

Sourdough Starter

Combine 2 cups of flour, 1 package of active dry yeast, and 2 cups of warm water in a large glass or plastic container. Let stand uncovered overnight or, for a stronger ferment, up to 48 hours. Once the starter is fermented, use it right away or store it in the refrigerator. "Feed" your starter once or twice a week with 1 cup milk, 1 cup all-purpose flour, and ¼ cup sugar.

✕ **Amy Eichelberger,** Odessa, Florida
First Place, Sweepstakes, Florida State Fair, Tampa, Florida, 2005

BANANA-CHOCOLATE QUICK BREAD

1¼ cups all-purpose flour, plus more for pan

½ cup whole grain flour

½ cup sugar

½ cup dark brown sugar

1 teaspoon baking soda

1 teaspoon salt

2 medium bananas, mashed

Juice and pulp of ½ orange

¼ teaspoon orange extract

¼ teaspoon almond extract

¼ cup unsalted butter or margarine, room temperature

2 tablespoons orange juice

1 egg

½ cup chocolate chips

1. Preheat oven to 350°F. Grease and flour a 9 x 5 x 3-inch loaf pan.

2. Combine all-purpose flour, whole grain flour, sugar, brown sugar, baking soda, and salt in the bowl of an electric mixer fitted with the paddle attachment.

3. With mixer running, add bananas, orange juice and pulp, orange extract, almond extract, butter or margarine, orange juice, and egg. Beat at medium speed for 3 minutes. Fold in chocolate chips.

4. Pour batter into pan. Bake for 50 to 60 minutes, or until a toothpick inserted in center comes out clean. Cool in pan for 10 minutes and turn out onto a wire rack. Makes 1 loaf.

✕ **JOHNNY WALLEN,** Age 11, Del Mar, California
First Place, San Diego County Fair, Del Mar, California, 2004

WINNER'S CIRCLE TIP | For rich, complex taste, combine several different types of chocolate chips—such as semisweet, milk, and double chocolate—to make up the measured amount.

BLUEBERRY-BANANA BREAD

2½ cups all-purpose flour

1 teaspoon baking soda

1 teaspoon salt

½ cup unsalted butter, room temperature

1¼ cups sugar

1½ cup ripe bananas

½ cup buttermilk

2 eggs

1 teaspoon vanilla

1 cup blueberries

1. Preheat oven to 350°F. Grease the bottom only of a 9 x 5 x 3-inch loaf pan.

2. Sift together flour, baking soda, and salt.

3. Cream together butter and sugar. Stir bananas, buttermilk, eggs, and vanilla. Mix in sifted dry ingredients. Gently fold in blueberries. Pour batter into loaf pan. Bake for 1 hour 15 minutes. Cool on a wire rack. Makes 1 loaf.

✕ **AMANDA SQUITIERI,** Brandon, Florida
First Place, Youth Division, Florida State Fair, Tampa, Florida, 2005

BLUEBERRY BREAD

2 cups all-purpose flour, plus more for pan

1 cup sugar

1½ teaspoon baking powder

½ teaspoon baking soda

1 teaspoon salt

¼ cup shortening

¾ cup orange juice

1 tablespoon grated orange zest

1 egg, well beaten

½ cup chopped nuts

1 to 2 cups blueberries

1. Preheat oven to 350°F. Grease and flour a 9 x 5 x 3-inch loaf pan.

2. Sift together flour, sugar, baking powder, baking soda, and salt. Cut in shortening until mixture resembles cornmeal.

3. Combine orange juice and zest and egg. Pour all at once into dry ingredients. Mix just enough to moisten. Fold in nuts and blueberries.

4. Spoon batter into pan, spreading corners and sides slightly higher than the center. Bake for 1 hour, or until top is golden brown and a toothpick inserted in center comes out clean. Turn out of pan and cool on a wire rack. Makes 1 loaf.

✕ **ROBBIE J. JOHNSON,** Anchorage, Alaska
First Place, Alaska State Fair, Palmer, Alaska, 2005

WINNER'S CIRCLE TIP | **Toss blueberries with a few tablespoons of confectioner's sugar before adding them to the batter.**

BLUEBERRY-ORANGE BREAD

2 cups all-purpose flour, plus more for pan

1 cup sugar

1 teaspoon baking powder

½ teaspoon baking soda

½ teaspoon salt

1 egg

½ cup orange juice

⅓ cup water

2 tablespoons unsalted butter or
   margarine, melted

2 tablespoons grated orange zest

¾ cup fresh or frozen blueberries

1. Preheat oven to 350°F. Grease and flour a 9 x 5 x 3-inch loaf pan.

2. In a large bowl, combine flour, sugar, baking powder, baking soda, and salt.

3. In a small bowl, combine egg, orange juice, water, melted butter or margarine, and orange zest. Add egg mixture to flour mixture. Stir just until combined. Fold in blueberries. Pour batter into loaf pan. Bake for 65 to 70 minutes, or until a toothpick inserted near center comes out clean. Cool for 10 minutes in pan and then turn out onto a wire rack. Makes 1 loaf.

✕ **G. JEAN SNYDER,** Oceanside, California
First Place, San Diego County Fair, Del Mar, California, 2004

BRAIDED DOUBLE CHOCOLATE BREAD

2 cups lukewarm water

2 envelopes (2.4 oz. each) active dry yeast

8 tablespoons sugar, divided

3 tablespoons unsalted butter,
    room temperature

1 large egg yolk

7 cups all-purpose flour, divided

1 tablespoon salt

2 tablespoons cocoa

1 cup chocolate chips

Confectioners' sugar

1. Place water in the large bowl of an electric mixer. Add yeast and 1 tablespoon of the sugar. Let sit until yeast dissolves, 3 to 5 minutes.

2. Add butter and egg yolk to proofed yeast. Stir using a paddle attachment.

3. Change to the dough hook attachment. Slowly add 6 cups of the flour, salt, cocoa, and remaining 7 tablespoons sugar. Knead until smooth. Knead in chocolate chips.

4. Turn out dough onto a lightly floured surface and form into a ball. Place in a greased bowl and turn once to coat. Cover and let rise in a warm place until doubled in size, 2 to 2½ hours.

5. Divide dough into 6 equal pieces. Roll each piece into a rope 12 inches long and 2 inches wide. Braid 3 ropes together, tuck in ends, and place on a baking sheet. Braid a second loaf and place on the same baking sheet. Cover both loaves with a moist towel and let rise, 1 hour.

6. Preheat oven to 375°F. Set a pan on the lower oven rack and fill with hot water. Place the baking sheet on the upper rack. Bake for 20 minutes. Lower the oven temperature to 350°F and bake an additional 20 minutes, or until the bread sounds hollow when tapped. Serve bread while still warm. Makes 2 loaves.

※ **MIKE MITCHELL,** age 13, Valley Center California
First Place, San Diego County Fair, Del Mar, California, 2004

CHEESY APPLE BREAD

2¼ cups all-purpose flour

¼ teaspoon salt

1 teaspoon baking powder

1 teaspoon baking soda

½ cup unsalted butter, room temperature

1 cup sugar

2 eggs

¼ cup sour milk

1 teaspoon vanilla

1 cup grated apples

1 cup grated sharp cheddar cheese

1. Preheat oven to 350°F. Grease a 9 x 5 x 3-inch loaf pan. Stir together flour, salt, baking powder, and baking soda.

2. In a large mixing bowl, cream butter and sugar. Add eggs one at a time, beating well after each addition.

3. Add dry ingredients, then sour milk and vanilla. Stir until well blended. Fold in apples and cheese. Pour batter into pan. Bake for 1 hour. Cool on a wire rack. Makes 1 loaf.

※ **CHUCK AUSMAN,** Menomonie, Wisconsin
First Prize, Quick Breads, Dunn County HCE, Dunn County Fair, Menomonie, Wisconsin, 2005

CHEESY BACON QUICK BREAD

3 cups all-purpose flour

3 teaspoons baking powder

1 teaspoon salt

¼ teaspoon cream of tartar

2 teaspoons sugar

½ teaspoon garlic salt

½ cup unsalted butter

¼ cup minced onion

½ cup crumbled cooked bacon

½ cup grated mild cheddar cheese

1 large egg

⅔ cup milk

1 teaspoon sesame seeds

½ teaspoon dried parsley flakes

¼ teaspoon paprika

¼ cup grated Parmesan

½ cup grated mozzarella

1. Preheat oven to 350°F. Grease a 9 x 5 x 3-inch loaf pan.

2. In a large bowl, combine flour, baking powder, salt, cream of tartar, sugar, and garlic salt. Cut in butter with a pastry blender until crumbly.

3. Add onion, bacon, cheddar cheese, egg, and milk. Mix until well moistened. Put batter into pan. Sprinkle sesame seeds, parsley flakes, paprika, Parmesan, and mozzarella over the top. Bake for 45 minutes, or until a toothpick inserted in center comes out clean. Cool on a wire rack. Makes 1 loaf.

⌘ **GAIL LIND,** Dousman, Wisconsin
Special Merit, Waukesha County Fair, Pewaukee, Wisconsin, 2001

HERB CHEESE BISCUIT LOAF

1½ cups all-purpose flour

¼ cup grated Parmesan,
   plus more for garnish

2 teaspoons yellow cornmeal

2 teaspoons baking powder

½ teaspoon salt

¼ cup unsalted butter or margarine,
   room temperature

2 eggs

½ cup heavy cream

¾ teaspoon dried basil

¾ teaspoon dried oregano

⅛ teaspoon garlic powder

1. Preheat oven to 425°F. Grease a large baking sheet.

2. In a large bowl, combine flour, Parmesan, cornmeal, baking powder, and salt. Cut in butter or margarine with a pastry blender or two knives until mixture resembles coarse crumbs.

3. Beat eggs in a medium bowl. Add cream, basil, oregano, and garlic powder and beat until well blended. Add egg mixture to flour mixture. Stir just until mixture clings together and forms a ball of soft dough.

4. Turn out dough onto a well-floured surface. Knead gently 10 to 12 times. Place dough on baking sheet. Roll or pat into a 7-inch round, about 1 inch thick. Starting at center, use the tip of a sharp knife to score top of dough into 8 wedges; do not cut completely through dough. Sprinkle with Parmesan. Bake for 20 to 25 minutes, or until a toothpick inserted in center comes out clean. Set baking sheet on a wire rack and cool 10 minutes. Serve warm. Makes 8 servings.

⌘ **KATHY FRIERSON,** DeLand, Florida
First Place, Baked Goods—Senior Adult, Volusia County Fair, DeLand, Florida, 2004

Frosted Cinnamon Loaf

2 envelopes (2.4 oz. each) active dry yeast
½ cup warm water
½ cup scalded milk
⅓ cup sugar
2 teaspoons salt
2 eggs
⅓ cup vegetable shortening
2 tablespoons unsalted butter,
  room temperature

4 cups all-purpose flour, divided, plus more
  for kneading
1 cup raisins
Cinnamon

MAPLE FROSTING
3 tablespoons unsalted butter, room temperature
½ lb. confectioners' sugar
⅓ cup maple syrup

1. In a large bowl, dissolve yeast in warm water. Let stand for 10 minutes.

2. In a separate bowl, combine scalded milk, sugar, salt, eggs, shortening, and butter. Cool.

3. Add milk mixture to proofed yeast. Beat in 2 cups of the flour. Gradually add remaining 2 cups flour. Mix until well combined.

4. Turn out dough onto a lightly floured surface. Knead 5 to 10 minutes. Place dough in a greased bowl and turn once to coat. Let rise in a warm place until double in size, 1 to 2 hours.

5. Punch down dough. Knead in 1 cup of raisins. Cover and let rise, 1 hour.

6. Roll out dough into a large rectangle. Sprinkle generously with cinnamon. Roll up jelly-roll style. Cut into 1-inch slices. Stand the slices side by side on end in a baking pan to form a loaf. Set aside to rise for 1 hour. Bake in a preheated 350°F oven for 25 to 30 minutes. Cool.

7. To make maple frosting: In a small bowl, cream together butter and confectioners' sugar. Add syrup slowly, beating until fluffy. Spread frosting over loaf while loaf is still warm. Makes 1 loaf.

⌘ **SANDI NIQUETTE,** Colchester, Vermont
Sweepstakes Winning Recipe, Champlain Valley Exposition, Essex Junction, Vermont, 2004

Soft Roll Dough

2 oz. active dry yeast
4 oz. sugar
1½ lbs. warm water
2½ lbs. bread flour

4 oz. shortening
1oz. salt
2 oz. milk solids

1. Place yeast, sugar, and water in a large mixing bowl and stir to combine. Set aside 5 minutes to proof.

2. With mixer running, add bread flour, shortening, salt, and milk solids. Mix until dough looks smooth. Place in a large bowl and let rise until double in size.

3. Shape dough into round balls, 1½ oz. each. Bake in a preheated 350°F oven for 30 minutes.

⌘ **DANIELLE TUCKER,** Interlachen, Florida
First Place, Youth Division, Florida State Fair, Tampa, Florida, 2005

For a better result, weigh the ingredients for this recipe on a kitchen scale.

CORN, A NATIVE NORTH AMERICAN CROP

The United States is the largest corn producer in the world. The Corn Belt, the major growing area, is centered in Iowa and Illinois and extends into Minnesota, South Dakota, Nebraska, Kansas, Missouri, Indiana, and Ohio. Farmers grow corn on every continent, except Antarctica. It takes 25 gallons of water to grow one ear of corn.

Sweet corn is the type of corn most likely grown in a home garden. Corn-on-the-cob, canned corn, and frozen corn all come from sweet corn. Popcorn is made from the kind of corn that is allowed to dry on the stalk. Americans consume some 16.5 billion quarts of popped popcorn annually, more than anyone else in the world. About 30 percent of that is eaten at fairs, movie theaters, ballparks, and schools,

CORN BREAD

1 egg
1 cup milk
¾ cup cornmeal, divided
½ cup all-purpose flour

1½ teaspoons baking powder
½ teaspoon baking soda
1 teaspoon salt

1. Preheat oven to 450°F. Grease two 6-mold corn-stick pans. Place pans in oven. In a small bowl, combine ½ cup cornmeal, flour, baking powder, baking soda, and salt.
2. In a bowl, combine egg and milk; stir in dry ingredients until combined. Stir in remaining cornmeal.
3. Pour batter into hot corn-stick pans. Bake for 10 to 12 minutes, or until golden brown. Makes 12 corn bread sticks.

✖ **MOZELLE WHARTON,** Merkel, Texas
First Place, West Texas Fair & Rodeo, Abilene, Texas, 2005

CORN STICKS

1¼ cups all-purpose flour
¾ cup cornmeal
¼ cup sugar, plus more for sprinkling
2 teaspoons baking powder

½ teaspoon salt
1 cup skim milk
¼ cup vegetable oil
1 beaten egg

1. Preheat oven to 400°F. Grease one or more 6-mold corn-stick pans.
2. In a large bowl, combine flour, cornmeal, sugar, baking powder, and salt. Stir together milk, oil, and egg and add to dry ingredients all at once. Stir just until dry ingredients are moistened. Do not overmix.
3. Pour batter into corn-stick molds. Sprinkle sugar over top. Bake for 10 to 15 minutes, or until golden brown. Serve warm. Makes 18 corn sticks.

✖ **JILL STRONG,** Waukesha, Wisconsin
Grand Champion, Waukesha County Fair, Pewaukee, Wisconsin, 2001

HOT-AND-SASSY CORN BREAD

1 cup stone-ground yellow cornmeal

¾ cup all-purpose flour

¼ cup whole wheat flour

1 teaspoon baking powder

½ teaspoon baking soda

¾ teaspoon salt

Dash of black pepper

1 cup canned cream-style corn

½ cup fresh or frozen corn kernels
 (thaw if frozen)

½ cup sour cream

½ cup milk

2 eggs, lightly beaten

2 tablespoons vegetable oil

1 tablespoon light brown sugar

1 jalapeño, seeded and minced

1. Preheat oven to 400°F. Butter an 8 x 8 x 2-inch baking pan.

2. In a large mixing bowl, combine cornmeal, flour, whole wheat flour, baking powder, baking soda, salt, and black pepper.

3. In a separate bowl, combine cream-style corn, corn kernels, sour cream, milk, eggs, oil, light brown sugar, and jalapeño. Add wet corn mixture to dry ingredients, stirring just until blended. Pour batter into pan. Bake for 25 minutes, or until top is golden brown and a knife inserted in the center comes out clean. Cool slightly in the pan before cutting. Makes 8 servings.

※ **MORGAN BREENE,** age 13, West Greenwich, Rhode Island
Blue Ribbon, Southern Rhode Island 4-H Fair, Richmond, Rhode Island, 2005

SOUTH-OF-THE-BORDER CORN BREAD BAKE

1 package (6.0 oz.) corn bread mix

1 can (14.5 oz.) cream-style corn, divided

1 egg, well beaten

1 tablespoon honey

½ cup milk

1 lb. ground beef

1 large onion, chopped

1 large bell pepper, chopped

2 garlic cloves, minced

1 can (14.5 oz.) diced tomatoes and
 green chiles

1 can (15.5 oz.) kidney beans, drained

1 teaspoon chili powder

½ teaspoon ground cumin

2 cups grated sharp cheddar cheese

Fresh cracked pepper

1. Preheat oven to 350°F.

2. In a mixing bowl, combine corn bread mix, half of the cream-style corn, egg, honey, and milk. Mix until well blended. Consistency should resemble cake batter.

3. Heat a heavy cast-iron skillet, 10 inches or larger, over medium-high heat. Add ground beef, onion, bell pepper, and garlic. Cook, stirring occasionally, until beef is nicely browned. Drain off fat.

4. Add the remaining cream-style corn, diced tomatoes and chiles, kidney beans, chili powder, and cumin to the skillet. Cook until vegetables are heated through, 5 minutes. Top with grated cheese. Remove from heat.

5. Pour corn bread batter over the meat and cheese filling. Sprinkle with fresh cracked pepper. Bake for 45 to 50 minutes, or until golden brown. Cool 10 minutes before serving. Makes 4 to 6 servings.

※ **PETRA MITCHELL,** Watertown, Tennessee
Honorable Mention, Wilson County Fair, Lebanon, Tennessee, 2005

Oatmeal Yeast Bread

3 envelopes (2.4 oz. each) active dry yeast
½ cup warm water
1 tablespoon sugar
3 cups water
1½ cups quick-cooking rolled oats
¾ cup vegetable oil

3 eggs
1 cup brown sugar
2¼ teaspoons salt
9 cups all-purpose flour, divided, plus
   more for kneading
Egg white, beaten

1. Place yeast in a small bowl. Pour ½ cup warm water over yeast, add sugar, and let stand.

2. Bring 3 cups of water to a boil in a large saucepan. Add oats and oil. Reduce heat and simmer for 1 minute. Transfer to a large bowl.

3. Add eggs, brown sugar, salt, yeast mixture, and 4½ cups of the flour to the oat mixture. Mix until well combined. Add enough of the remaining 4½ cups to make a soft dough.

4. Turn out dough onto a lightly floured surface. Knead until smooth, about 8 minutes. Place dough in a greased bowl and turn once to coat. Cover and let rise in warm place until double in size, about 1 hour.

5. Punch down dough. Divide into fourths. Shape each portion into a loaf and place in a 9 x 5 x 3-inch loaf pan. Brush tops with egg white. Let rise until nearly double in size. Bake in a preheated 350°F oven for 30 to 40 minutes, or until golden brown. Makes 4 loaves.

※ **Marge Rainwater,** Abilene, Texas
First Place, West Texas Fair & Rodeo, Abilene, Texas, 2005

Tropical Date Bread

1 cup crushed pineapple with juice
1 cup chopped dates
1¾ cups all-purpose flour
2 teaspoons baking powder
½ teaspoon salt
¼ teaspoon baking soda
3 tablespoons unsalted butter,
   room temperature

¾ cup brown sugar
2 eggs
Fresh pineapple chunks (optional)
Shredded or flaked coconut (optional)
2 tablespoons sugar
½ teaspoon cinnamon

1. Preheat oven to 350°F. Grease a 9 x 5 x 3-inch loaf pan.

2. Combine crushed pineapple and dates in a small bowl.

3. Sift together flour, baking powder, salt, and baking soda.

4. In a large mixing bowl, cream butter and sugar. Beat in eggs. Add half of the flour mixture and beat until well combined. Add the pineapple-date mixture and remaining flour mixture, beating well after each addition.

5. Spoon batter into pan. Add pineapple chunks and coconut to top, if using. Mix sugar and cinnamon in a small bowl and sprinkle over top of loaf. Bake for 1 hour. Cool on a wire rack. Makes 1 loaf.

※ **David and Karlene Ponte,** San Jacinto, California
First Place, Breads, Riverside County Fair and National Date Festival, Indio, California, 2003–2004

THE RIVERSIDE COUNTY FAIR & NATIONAL DATE FESTIVAL

The Riverside County Fair & National Date Festival in Indio, California, began in 1921 as a celebration of the harvest of dates. The Blessing of the Date Ceremony is an important tradition at the fair. The first date palms in the United States were planted in California's Coachella Valley in 1903. Approximately 300 pounds of fruit can be harvested from one date palm tree. An average date has 23 calories and no fat, cholesterol, or sodium.

DATE-BANANA BREAD

2½ cups all-purpose flour

1 cup sugar

2 eggs

1 teaspoon salt

1 teaspoon baking soda

¼ cup margarine, melted

1½ cups chopped dates

6 very ripe bananas, mashed

1 cup chopped walnuts

1. Preheat oven to 350°F.

2. In a large bowl, combine all ingredients. Mix until well combined.

3. Pour batter into 2 loaf pans. Bake 1 hour. Cool on wire racks. Makes 2 loaves.

✳ **TWILA BOOTH,** San Jacinto, California
Second Place, Breads, Riverside County Fair and National Date Festival,
Indio, California, 2003–2004

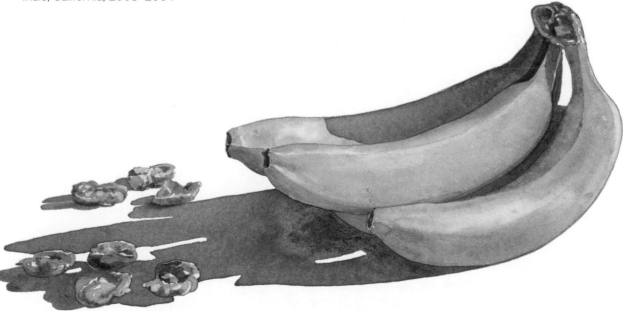

LEMON FRUIT TWIST

1 tablespoon active dry yeast

1 cup plus 1 to 2 tablespoons
   warm water, divided

¼ cup sugar

3¼ cups all-purpose flour, divided, plus
   more for kneading

1 egg

2 tablespoons margarine, room temperature

1 teaspoon salt

1 tablespoon grated lemon zest,
   plus more for topping

1 tablespoon poppy seeds

⅛ cup chopped Maraschinos, well drained

⅛ cup raisins

⅓ cup sliced almonds, plus more
   for topping

½ teaspoon vanilla

½ cup confectioners' sugar

1. Dissolve yeast in 1 cup of the warm water.

2. In a large mixing bowl, combine sugar and 1 cup of the flour. Add yeast mixture and stir until well combined. Stir in egg, then margarine. Add salt and remaining 2¼ cups all-purpose flour. Stir to make a soft dough.

3. Turn out dough onto a lightly floured work surface. Divide in half. Add zest and poppy seeds to one portion. Knead for 5 minutes. Add Maraschinos, raisins, and almonds to the other portion. Knead for 5 minutes.

4. Roll each dough portion into a rope 15 inches long. Place the ropes side by side on a greased baking sheet and twist together gently and loosely. Pinch ends to seal. Cover and let rise in a warm place until double in size, about 1 hour. Bake in a preheated 350°F oven for 15 to 30 minutes. Set on a wire rack to cool.

5. Stir vanilla into confectioners' sugar to make a thick glaze. Drizzle over pastry while still warm. Top with additional lemon zest and sliced almonds. Makes 1 twist, 6 to 8 servings.

⊠ **SANDI NIQUETTE,** Colchester, Vermont
First Prize, Champlain Valley Exposition, Essex Junction, Vermont, 2004

MAUI ONION TURTLE BREAD

1 envelope (2.4 oz.) active dry yeast

2 teaspoons honey

1 cup lukewarm water

3 tablespoons olive oil

1 teaspoon salt

3½ to 4 cups high-gluten bread flour

2 large Maui onions, thinly sliced

2 tablespoons olive oil

½ cup shredded mozzarella

¾ cup sliced Spanish olives, divided

¼ cup shredded Parmesan

1. In a large mixing bowl, combine yeast, honey, and lukewarm water. Let stand for 10 minutes.

2. Add olive oil, salt, and 3½ cups of the flour. Mix to combine. Using a dough hook attachment, knead for 3 minutes; add remaining flour if necessary to form a soft dough. Place dough in an oiled bowl and turn once to coat. Cover and let rise until double in size, about 1½ hours.

3. Punch down dough. Pinch off 5 golf ball-sized pieces. Flatten the remaining dough on a lightly oiled baking sheet, forming a large circle; pinch out one end for the turtle's tail. Shape the head and feet from the five dough pieces and attach them to the body. Brush dough lightly with olive oil. Cover and let rise until double in size, 1 hour.

4. In a large bowl, gently toss onions with olive oil. Sprinkle mozzarella and ½ cup of the olives over the turtle body. Arrange onion slices on top. Decorate with remaining olives and Parmesan. Bake in a preheated 375°F oven for 30 to 35 minutes until golden. Makes 1 large loaf.

※ **KRISTINE SNYDER,** Kihei, Hawaii
First Prize, Appetizers/Sides, Maui Onion Festival, Maui, Hawaii, 1999

MAPLE BUTTER TWISTS

1 envelope (2.4 oz.) active dry yeast
¼ cup warm water (105° to 110°F)
½ cup warm milk (105° to 110°F)
¼ cup unsalted butter or margarine,
    room temperature
3 tablespoons sugar
1½ teaspoons salt
2 eggs
3½ cups all-purpose flour, divided

FILLING
½ cup brown sugar
⅓ cup sugar
¼ cup unsalted butter or margarine,
    room temperature
¼ cup maple (or maple-flavored) syrup
¼ cup all-purpose flour
1 teaspoon cinnamon
½ teaspoon maple flavoring
½ cup chopped pecans

1. Dissolve yeast in warm water.

2. In a large bowl, combine warm milk, butter or margarine, sugar, and salt. Add yeast mixture. Stir in eggs. Add 1¾ cups of the flour; beat with a wooden spoon until smooth. Stir in enough of the remaining 1¾ cups flour to make a moderately soft dough.

3. Turn out dough onto a floured surface. Knead until smooth, 3 to 5 minutes. Place dough in a greased bowl and turn once to coat. Cover and set aside in a warm place until double in size, about 1 hour. Punch down dough. Divide in half. Cover and let rest 10 minutes.

4. To make filling: In a medium bowl, combine brown sugar, sugar, margarine, maple syrup, flour, cinnamon, and maple flavoring.

5. Roll out one portion of dough on a lightly floured surface to make an 8 x 14-inch rectangle. Spread with half of the filling. Sprinkle half of the pecans over filling. Roll up, starting with a long side. Seal ends and seam. Prepare a second roll in the same way.

6. Grease two 8 x 1½-inch round cake pans. Grease the outsides of two 6 oz. custard cups. Set a custard cup upside down in the center of each pan. Cut each roll in half lengthwise. Place two halves side by side and twist together, keeping the cut sides up. Gently stretch to 18 inches long. Form into a ring, moisten ends, and press to seal. Set ring around the custard cup in the baking pan. Cover and let rise until nearly double in size, 30 to 40 minutes.

7. Place pans on baking sheets to catch any drips while baking. Bake in a preheated 350°F oven for 22 to 25 minutes, or until golden. Cool in pans on wire racks for 5 minutes. Loosen edges and carefully remove cups. Transfer twists to wire racks. Serve warm or cool. Makes 2 round twists, 6 to 8 servings each.

※ **CINDY BOHL,** Glenarm, Illinois
First Place, Yeast Breads, Illinois State Fair, Springfield, Illinois, 2005

Blue-Ribbon Idaho Potato Bread

1 medium Idaho potato, about ½ lb.

½ cup sugar

½ cup nonfat dry milk

1 teaspoon salt

3 eggs

1 cup potato water (see step 1)

2 tablespoons rapid-rise yeast

5 to 5½ cups all-purpose flour

1. Peel and cube potato. Place potato in saucepan, add water to cover, and bring to boil. Cook until soft. Drain, reserving 1 cup of the potato water.

2. In a large mixing bowl, combine potato, sugar, nonfat dry milk, and salt. Mix until smooth. Beat in eggs. Add potato water and mix well. Add yeast and enough flour to form a soft dough. Knead with a dough hook on high for 5 minutes. Place dough in an oiled bowl and turn once to coat. Cover and let rise until double in size, about 2 hours.

3. Punch down dough. Divide in half. Shape into two loaves. Place in two 9 x 5 x 3-inch loaf pans. Let rise until double in size. Bake in a preheated 350°F oven for 40 minutes. Makes 2 loaves.

▧ **Jodee Burnham,** Pocatello, Idaho
First Place, North Bannock County Fair, Pocatello, Idaho, 2005

WINNER'S CIRCLE TIP | To mix the bread dough in a bread machine, add flour until the dough cleans the sides of the bowl. If you are not using the dough right away, knead it down and store it in the refrigerator. Properly wrapped and chilled, the dough will keep as long as a week or 10 days.

Texas Pecan Swedish Tea Ring

2 tablespoons active dry yeast

¾ cup warm water

2 cups lukewarm milk

3 tablespoons sugar

3 tablespoons shortening

1 tablespoon salt

7 to 8 cups all-purpose flour

2 tablespoons margarine, soft

½ cup brown sugar

2 teaspoons cinnamon

¾ cup pecans, chopped

GLAZE

¾ cup confectioners' sugar

1 tablespoon milk

1 teaspoon vanilla

Chopped pecans

1. In a large bowl, dissolve yeast in warm water. Stir in milk, sugar, shortening, and salt. Add 4 cups of the flour. Stir until smooth. Add enough of the remaining 3 to 4 cups flour, one cup at a time, until dough is smooth and easy to handle.

2. Turn out dough onto a lightly floured surface. Knead for 10 minutes. Place dough in an oiled bowl and turn once to coat. Cover and let rise until double in size, 2 to 4 hours.

3. Punch down dough. Divide in half. Roll out each portion into a 15 x 9-inch rectangle. In a small bowl, combine margarine, brown sugar, and cinnamon until crumbly. Sprinkle half of mixture over dough. Top with half of pecans. Roll up from a long edge and seal the edge. Place on a baking sheet

or round pizza pan and shape into ring, sealing the join. Cut into the outside edge of ring two-thirds toward the center; turn each cut section on its side. Form a second ring. Let rings rise ½ hour. Bake in a preheated 375°F oven for 25 minutes. Remove from oven and cool slightly.

4. To make glaze: In a small bowl, combine confectioners' sugar, milk, and vanilla until smooth. Spread over top of ring. Sprinkle pecans on top. Makes 2 rings.

※ **LOIS DOERSCHUK,** Baird, Texas
First Place, West Texas Fair & Rodeo, Abilene, Texas, 2005

CINNAMON OATMEAL-RAISIN BREAD

1¼ cups milk

3 cups bread flour

¾ cup quick-cooking rolled oats

2 tablespoons brown sugar

1½ teaspoons salt

3 teaspoons cinnamon

2 tablespoons margarine, cut into 4 pieces

1 envelope (2¼ teaspoons) active dry yeast

½ cup raisins

1. Pour milk into the bread pan of a bread-making machine. Add flour, oats, brown sugar, salt, and cinnamon to pan. Tap pan to settle dry ingredients, then level. Place margarine in four corners of pan. Make well in the center of dry ingredients and add yeast.

2. Place pan into oven chamber. Program the machine for a sweet bread and light color. When the alert sounds, add raisins. Makes one 1½-lb. loaf.

※ **JANICE NOSTROM,** Humboldt, Iowa
Blue Ribbon, Clay County Fair, Spencer, Iowa, 2005

WHOLE WHEAT ZUCCHINI BREAD

3 cups whole wheat flour

1 teaspoon salt (optional)

1 teaspoon baking soda

¼ teaspoon baking powder

3 teaspoons cinnamon

3 eggs

2 cups sugar or honey

1 cup oil

2 cups grated zucchini

1. Preheat oven to 350°F. Grease a 9 x 5 x 3-inch loaf pan.

2. Sift together flour, salt, baking soda, baking powder, and cinnamon.

3. In a large bowl, whisk together eggs, sugar or honey, and oil. Add zucchini and stir to combine. Add sifted dry ingredients and mix well.

4. Spread batter in pan. Bake for 50 to 60 minutes, or until a toothpick inserted near center comes out clean. Makes 1 loaf.

※ **SUZANNE KANEHL,** Columbus, Indiana
Reserve Grand Champion, Fancy Quick Breads, Bartholomew County 4-H Fair, Columbus, Indiana, 2005

BUTTERMILK LEFSA
(SCANDINAVIAN POTATO BREAD)

5 cups mashed potatoes

1 cup buttermilk

2 tablespoons sugar

1 tablespoon unsalted butter, room temperature

1 teaspoon salt

2 to 3 cups all-purpose flour

1. In a large mixing bowl, combine mashed potatoes, buttermilk, sugar, butter, and salt. Beat until smooth. Refrigerate overnight.

2. The next day, stir in 2 cups of the flour to make a stiff dough. Add up to 1 cup additional flour only if needed to stiffen dough. Divide dough into 15 to 25 portions. Work with one portion at a time and keep the remaining dough chilled in the refrigerator until ready to use.

3. Roll out dough on a floured pastry cloth until very thin. Heat a griddle to between 400° and 425°F and brush lightly with cooking oil. Cook dough on griddle until light brown spots appear, 1 minute per side. Stack cooked lefsa, interleaved with sheets of waxed paper to prevent sticking and covered with a towel to keep warm. Makes 15 to 25.

✕ **MARCELLA MELNHOFF,** Student, Missoula, Montana
First Place Public Favorite, America—The Melting Pot, Western Montana Fair, Missoula, Montana, 1990

WINNER'S CIRCLE TIP | Serve lefsa wrapped around meats and cheeses, as a rolled sandwich. For a traditional treat, spread with butter, sprinkle with sugar and cinnamon, and roll up tight.

JANET'S PUMPKIN BREAD

3½ cups all-purpose flour

2 teaspoons baking soda

2 teaspoons salt

1 teaspoon baking powder

1 teaspoon nutmeg

1 teaspoon ground allspice

1 teaspoon cinnamon

½ teaspoon cloves

3 cups sugar

1 cup oil

4 eggs, beaten

1 can (16 oz.) pumpkin

⅔ cup water

1. Preheat oven to 350°F. Grease and flour two 9 x 5 x 3-inch loaf pans.

2. Sift together flour, baking soda, salt, baking powder, nutmeg, allspice, cinnamon, and cloves.

3. In a large mixing bowl, blend sugar and oil. Add eggs and pumpkin and mix well. Add sifted dry ingredients alternately with water, mixing well after each addition. Pour batter into pans. Bake for 1½ hours, or until a tester inserted in center comes out clean. Cool 10 minutes in pans and then turn out onto wire racks. Makes 2 loaves.

✕ **JANET PISTULKA,** Aberdeen, South Dakota
Best of Class, Brown County Fair and 4-H Show, Aberdeen, South Dakota, 1998, 2000

Piña Colada Bread

5 cups all-purpose flour

¾ cup sugar

2 tablespoons baking powder

1 teaspoon cinnamon

½ teaspoon nutmeg

2 teaspoons salt

4 eggs

1 cup unsalted butter, melted

1 can (8 oz.) pineapple, undrained

1 cup cream of coconut

⅔ cup chopped walnuts

⅔ cup soft golden raisins

TOPPING

2¾ cups flaked coconut, divided

⅔ cup cream of coconut

1. Preheat oven to 350°F. Lightly coat two 9 x 5 x 3-inch loaf pans with cooking spray.

2. In a large bowl, combine flour, sugar, baking powder, cinnamon, nutmeg, and salt. Set aside 2 tablespoons of the mixture.

3. In a medium mixing bowl, beat eggs until frothy. Stir in melted butter, pineapple, and cream of coconut. Pour over flour mixture and stir just until moistened. Toss walnuts and raisins with reserved flour mixture to coat; stir into batter. Pour batter into baking pans. Bake for 30 to 45 minutes. Cool in pans for 10 minutes before turning out onto wire racks. Cool completely.

4. To make topping: Combine 1¾ cups of the coconut and cream of coconut. Spread over top of loaves. Toast remaining 1 cup of coconut until lightly browned. Sprinkle over top. Makes 2 loaves.

✖ **SHIRLEY J. MYRSIADES,** Pinella Park, Florida
First Place, Adult Division, Florida State Fair, Tampa, Florida, 2005

Robbie's Pumpkin Bread

1½ cups sugar

1 cup cooked or canned pumpkin

½ cup oil

¼ cup water

¼ cup maple syrup

2 eggs

1⅔ cup all-purpose flour

½ teaspoon baking powder

1 teaspoon baking soda

¾ teaspoon salt

1 teaspoon cinnamon

½ teaspoon nutmeg

¼ teaspoon ground cloves

½ cup chopped walnuts

½ cup raisins or currants (optional)

1. Preheat oven to 350°F. Grease a 9 x 5 x 3 inch loaf pan.

2. In a large bowl, combine sugar, pumpkin, oil, water, maple syrup, and eggs, stirring with a wooden spoon.

3. Whisk together flour, baking powder, baking soda, salt, cinnamon, nutmeg, and cloves. Add to pumpkin mixture and mix until well combined. Stir in nuts and raisins or currants, if using.

4. Pour batter into pan. Bake for 65 to 70 minutes, or until a tester inserted in center comes out clean. Cool in pan for 10 minutes before turning out onto a wire rack. Makes 1 loaf.

✖ **ROBBIE J. JOHNSON,** Anchorage, Alaska
First Place, Alaska State Fair, Palmer, Alaska, 2005

Sweet Dough Frosted Cinnamon Rolls

1 envelope (2.4 oz.) active dry yeast
1½ cups warm water (105° to 115°F)
⅓ cup nonfat dry milk
½ cup margarine, room temperature
½ cup sugar
1 teaspoon salt
½ teaspoon vanilla
1 beaten egg
4½ to 5 cups bread flour

FILLING

¼ cup margarine, melted
1½ to 2 teaspoons cinnamon
⅓ cup sugar

FROSTING

2½ cups confectioners' sugar
1 tablespoon margarine, melted
1 tablespoon vanilla
4 to 4½ tablespoons half-and-half

1. Dissolve yeast in warm water in a large mixing bowl.

2. Add nonfat dry milk, margarine, sugar, salt, vanilla, and egg to yeast mixture. Mix until well combined. Slowly mix in enough flour to make a soft dough.

3. Turn out dough onto a lightly floured surface. Knead until smooth and elastic, 8 to 10 minutes. Place in a greased bowl and turn once to coat. Cover and let rise until double in size, about 1 hour.

4. To make filling: Punch down dough. Turn out onto a lightly floured surface. Roll out into a 12 x 16-inch rectangle. Spread melted margarine over surface of dough. Combine sugar and cinnamon in a small bowl and sprinkle over dough. Roll up jelly-roll style.

5. Cut roll into 8 pieces, each 2 inches wide. Place in two generously buttered 8 x 8 x 2-inch baking pans. Cover with plastic wrap and a towel and let rise in doubled in size, 40 to 50 minutes. Bake in a preheated 350°F oven for 18 to 22 minutes. Invert rolls onto the shiny side of freezer paper or another nonstick surface. Cool for 15 minutes.

6. To make frosting: Mix together confectioners' sugar, margarine, vanilla, and half-and-half. Drizzle frosting over warm rolls or frost entire top of roll. Makes 8 rolls.

✕ **Janice Nostrom,** Humboldt, Iowa
Blue Ribbon, Clay County Fair, Spencer, Iowa, 2001, 2002

WINNER'S CIRCLE TIP | Use a strong thread held taut between your fingers to cut cinnamon rolls. It prevents the dough from compacting, so the rolls stay light and fluffy.

Jalapeño Cheese Wheat Rolls

1½ cups warm water
3 tablespoons sugar
3 teaspoons active dry yeast
1½ teaspoons salt
1 egg
3 tablespoons margarine or oil
3 cups all-purpose flour, divided

1 cup whole wheat flour
3 cups Mexican cheese
1½ cups chopped onion
6 jalapeños, chopped, plus more for topping
1 tablespoon salt-free seasoning
1 egg, beaten
Sesame seeds

1. Place warm water in a large bowl. Add sugar and stir to dissolve. Sprinkle yeast over top of water.
2. Add salt, egg, margarine or oil, and 1 cup of the flour-yeast mixture. Beat until smooth. Add remaining 2 cups all-purpose flour and whole wheat flour 1 cup at a time, beating well after each addition to make a soft dough. Cover and let rise in warm place until double in size, 2 to 4 hours.
3. Line a 12-inch Dutch oven with parchment paper. Roll out dough onto a lightly floured surface to make a large rectangle. Layer cheese, onion, and jalapeños on dough. Sprinkle with salt-free seasoning. Roll up tightly, cut into slices or triangles, and place in Dutch oven. Brush tops with beaten egg and sprinkle sesame seeds and jalapeños over top. Cover and let rise until almost double in size, 1 hour. Bake in a preheated 350°F oven for 25 to 30 minutes. Cool slightly before serving. Makes 8 servings.

✳ **Rosa and Marisela Sanchez,** Clearfield, Utah
First Place, Utah Farm Bureau Great American Dutch Oven Cook-off, Utah State Fair, Salt Lake City, Utah, 2005

Sweetest Sweet Potato Biscuits

2 or 3 medium sweet potatoes
¼ cup sugar
¼ cup light brown sugar
1 teaspoon cinnamon
¼ teaspoon nutmeg
¼ teaspoon ground ginger
2 tablespoons honey

3 cups all-purpose flour
4 teaspoons baking powder
½ teaspoon salt
½ cup butter-flavored shortening
1 egg
⅔ cup milk

1. Preheat oven to 400°F. Lightly grease a baking sheet or baking pan.
2. Microwave sweet potatoes until cooked through, following manufacturer's recommendations. Remove peels and mash the pulp. Measure 2 cups of the mashed potatoes and place in a medium bowl. Add sugar, brown sugar, cinnamon, nutmeg, ginger, and honey. Stir to combine.
3. In a large bowl, combine flour, baking powder, and salt. Cut in shortening. Mix egg and milk and add to flour mixture, stirring just until blended. Stir in sweet potato mixture. Do not overmix.
4. Turn out dough onto a floured surface. Roll out to a ⅝-inch thickness. Cut dough with a 2½-inch round biscuit cutter and place on baking sheet. Bake for 15 minutes, or until lightly browned. Makes 16 biscuits.

✳ **Shirley J. Myrsiades,** Pinella Park, Florida
First Place, Adult Division, Florida State Fair, Tampa, Florida, 2005

Sugar-free Prune, Bran, and Nut Bread

⅔ cup juice, reserved from stewed prunes

2 cups bran flakes

⅔ cup skim milk

1 tablespoon vinegar

1 tablespoon corn oil

½ cup sugar substitute

1 egg

1¼ cups all-purpose flour

¼ teaspoon salt

1½ teaspoons baking soda

⅔ cup cooked, chopped prunes

½ cup chopped nuts

1. Preheat oven to 325°F. Grease a 9 x 5 x 3-inch loaf pan.

2. In a large bowl, combine prune juice, bran flakes, milk, and vinegar.

3. In a separate bowl, combine oil and sugar substitute. Add egg and mix well. Add flour, salt, and baking soda. Mix well.

4. Add flour mixture to bran flakes mixture. Mix until well combined. Stir in prunes and nuts. Pour batter into pan. Bake for 45 to 60 minutes. Cool on a wire rack. Makes 1 loaf.

✄ **SUSAN ZIELINSKI,** Catawissa, Pennsylvania
First Place, Bloomsburg Fair, Bloomsburg, Pennsylvania, 2004

WINNER'S CIRCLE TIP | Use home-cooked prunes and their stewing juice to make this delicious, nutritious bread. Follow the directions on the prune package to stew the prunes.

Fire-Roasted Chiles Brioche

4 cups bread flour

1 tablespoon active dry yeast

1 tablespoon salt

2 tablespoons sugar

4 eggs

¼ cup milk

¼ cup water

½ cup cold unsalted butter, cut into cubes,
    plus more for pan

1 can (7 oz.) roasted chiles, chopped

1 tablespoon crushed red pepper

2 teaspoons black pepper

1. Combine flour, yeast, salt, and sugar in the bowl of an electric mixer. Whisk together eggs, milk, and water. With mixer running, add egg mixture and then butter cubes to dry ingredients. Continue mixing until dough no longer sticks to bowl. Stir in chiles, crushed red pepper, and black pepper.

2. Cover dough and set aside to rise until double in size, 2 to 4 hours.

3. Punch down dough. Shape into a round loaf and place in a buttered pan. Let rise until double in size, 45 to 60 minutes. Bake in a preheated 375°F oven for 35 minutes. Makes 1 brioche.

✄ **GENE FREELAND,** Rancho Santa Fe, California
First Place, San Diego County Fair, Del Mar, California, 2004

RICH DINNER CRESCENT ROLLS

1 cup warm milk

¼ cup sugar

1 teaspoon salt

½ cup warm water (105°F to 115°F)

2 eggs, beaten

2 envelopes (2.4 oz. each) active dry yeast

Approximately 5¼ cups all-purpose flour, divided

¼ cup unsalted butter, melted, divided

1. Whisk together milk, sugar, salt, water, and eggs.

2. Place yeast and 2 cups of the flour in the bowl of an electric mixer. With mixer running, slowly add milk mixture. Continue mixing until well combined. Add enough of the remaining flour, up to 3¼ cups, to make a soft dough.

3. Turn out dough onto a floured surface. Knead until smooth and elastic. Do not add much flour at this point. Place dough in a greased bowl and turn once to coat. Cover and let rise until double in size, 2 to 4 hours.

4. Turn out dough onto a work surface. Divide dough into thirds. Shape into three balls. Roll out each ball into a 12-inch circle. Brush melted butter over the top of each circle and cut into 12 wedges. Roll up each wedge tightly from the wide end. Place on greased baking sheets 2 inches apart with points underneath. Curve to form crescents. Cover and let rise until double in size, 1 to 2 hours.

5. Brush tops of crescents with melted butter. Bake in a preheated 400°F oven for 12 minutes, or until golden brown. Makes 36 crescent rolls.

✕ **JANETTE SWANSON STANEK,** Pocatello, Idaho
First Place, North Bannock County Fair, Pocatello, Idaho, 2005

BAKING POWDER BISCUITS

2 cups all-purpose flour

4 teaspoons baking powder

½ teaspoon salt

½ teaspoon cream of tartar

2 teaspoons sugar

½ cup shortening

⅔ cup milk

1. Preheat oven to 450°F.

2. In a large bowl, combine flour, baking powder, salt, cream of tartar, and sugar. Cut in shortening until mixture resembles coarse crumbs. Make a well in dry mixture and add milk all at once. Stir quickly with a fork just until dough follows fork around bowl.

3. Turn out dough onto a lightly floured surface. Dough should be soft. Knead gently 10 to 12 strokes and then roll or pat to ½-inch thickness. Dip a biscuit cutter into flour and press straight down into dough, without twisting, to cut biscuits. Bake on an ungreased baking sheet for 10 to 12 minutes, until lightly browned. Makes 12 biscuits.

✕ **KATHY NOVSTRUP, JO SPERRY, AND LINDA FRIEZ,** Aberdeen, South Dakota
Best of Show, and Several Purple Ribbons, Brown County Fair & 4-H Show, Aberdeen, South Dakota, 1992

BUTTERMILK BUNS

3 cups buttermilk

½ cup sugar

½ cup shortening

1 teaspoon salt

1 teaspoon baking soda

1 tablespoon active dry yeast

Warm water

Flour

1. Warm buttermilk in a large saucepan over low heat. Add sugar, shortening, salt, and baking soda. Dissolve yeast in small amount of water and add to buttermilk mixture. Remove from heat and cool slightly.

2. Transfer buttermilk mixture to a large bowl. Add flour ½ cup at a time until a stiff dough forms.

3. Turn out dough onto a lightly floured surface. Knead until satiny, 8 to 10 minutes. Place in an oiled boil and turn once to coat. Cover and set in a warm place to rise, 2 to 4 hours.

4. Punch down dough. Knead again. Place in bowl and let rise, 1 to 2 hours.

5. Shape dough into buns. Place on a baking sheet. Bake in a preheated 350°F oven for 20 minutes. Makes 24 buns.

▨ **EVELYN HUEBLEIN,** Lewiston, Minnesota
Blue Ribbon, Winona County Agricultural & Industrial Fair, Saint Charles, Minnesota, 2005

CARAMEL-NUT STICKY BUNS

6 to 7 cups all-purpose flour, divided

½ cup sugar

2 teaspoons salt

2 envelopes (2.4 oz. each) active dry yeast

1 cup water

1 cup milk

½ cup margarine or unsalted butter, room temperature

1 egg

PAN COATING

1 cup brown sugar

1 cup softened margarine or unsalted butter, room temperature

4 tablespoons light corn syrup

Chopped pecans

FILLING

4 tablespoons margarine or unsalted butter, room temperature

½ cup sugar

2 teaspoons cinnamon

1. In a large mixing bowl, combine 2 cups of the flour, sugar, salt, and yeast.

2. Heat water, milk, and margarine or butter in a small saucepan over low heat until very warm, 120° to 130°F.

3. Add warm liquid and egg to flour mixture. Blend at low speed until moistened. Beat at medium speed for 3 minutes. Gradually add 3 cups of the remaining flour and stir by hand. Continue stirring until dough pulls away cleanly from sides of bowl.

4. Turn out dough onto a floured surface. Knead in 1 to 2 cups of the remaining flour until dough is smooth and elastic, about 10 minutes. Place dough in a greased bowl and turn once to coat. Cover loosely with plastic wrap and a cloth towel. Let rise in a warm place until light and doubled in size, 45 to 60 minutes.

5. To make pan coating: Generously grease two 13 x 9 x 2-inch pans. Combine brown sugar, margarine or butter, and light corn syrup in a bowl. Drop mixture by spoonfuls into pans. Sprinkle with chopped pecans.

6. To add filling: Punch down dough to remove all air bubbles. Divide dough in half. Roll out each half into a 20 x 12-inch rectangle. Spread each rectangle with 2 tablespoons margarine or butter. Combine sugar and cinnamon in a small bowl. Sprinkle half of mixture over each rectangle.

7. Starting at a 20-inch side, roll up dough jelly-roll fashion; pinch edges firmly to seal seams. Cut into twenty 1-inch slices and place cut side down in pan. Cover and let rise in a warm place until light in color and doubled in size, 35 to 45 minutes. Bake in a preheated 375°F oven for 25 to 30 minutes, or until deep golden brown. Cool in pan for 1 minute and turn out onto a wire rack. Makes 40 rolls.

✳ **BARBARA RIALS,** Shelby, North Carolina
First Prize, Cleveland County Fair, Shelby, North Carolina, 2005

CAMMIE'S CINNAMON ROLLS

1 teaspoon active dry yeast

1 cup warm water

3 cups all-purpose flour, plus more for
for kneading

1½ teaspoons salt

4 tablespoons unsalted butter at
room temperature, divided

2 tablespoons dry milk

¼ cup plus 1 tablespoon sugar, divided

2 teaspoons cinnamon

CONFECTIONERS' SUGAR GLAZE

1 cup sifted confectioners' sugar

1 teaspoon unsalted butter, room temperature

1 tablespoon milk or water

½ teaspoon vanilla

1. Dissolve yeast in warm water in a large mixing bowl.

2. Add flour, salt, 2 tablespoons of the butter, dry milk, and ¼ tablespoon of the sugar to yeast mixture. Mix until well combined.

3. Turn out dough onto a lightly floured surface. Knead for 10 minutes. Place in a lightly greased bowl and turn once to coat. Cover and let rise until double in size, 2 to 4 hours.

4. Punch down dough. Roll out into 15 x 9-inch rectangle. Spread remaining 2 tablespoons butter over dough. Mix together remaining ¼ cup sugar and cinnamon and sprinkle over dough. Roll up, jelly roll-style, and pinch edges to seal. Stretch roll to even out diameter. Cut into 1½-inch slices. Arrange slices in two greased 9 x 9 x 2-inch baking pans. Let rise until double in size, 40 minutes. Bake in a preheated 375°F oven for 20 to 25 minutes, or until golden brown.

5. To make confectioners' sugar glaze: Combine all ingredients in a bowl, stirring until smooth. Spread over slightly warm rolls. Makes 6 rolls.

✳ **CAMMI WAGGONER,** Goshen, Indiana
First Place, Elkhart County 4-H Fair, Goshen, Indiana, 2005

CUSTARD CRESCENT ROLLS

1 envelope (2.4 oz.) active dry yeast
¼ cup warm water
1 cup scalded milk
¼ cup unsalted butter, room temperature

½ teaspoon salt
1 package (3.9 oz.) custard dessert mix
1 egg yolk
3 to 3½ cups all-purpose flour, divided

1. Dissolve yeast in warm water. Let stand for 5 minutes.

2. Combine milk, butter, and salt in a large bowl, stirring until butter melts.

3. Add custard mix and stir until mixture cools to lukewarm. Add egg yolk and yeast mixture. Mix well.

4. Add 1 cup of the flour and mix for 1 minute. Continue adding flour ½ cup at a time, until a soft dough forms. Mix for 2 minutes after each addition until well incorporated.

5. Turn out dough onto a lightly floured surface. Knead until smooth. Place dough in a lightly greased bowl and turn once to coat. Cover and let rise until double in size, 1½ hours.

6. Turn out dough onto a work surface. Divide dough into thirds. Shape into three balls. Roll out each ball into a circle and cut each circle into 12 wedges. Roll up each wedge tightly from the wide end. Place on greased baking sheets 2 inches apart with points underneath. Curve to form crescents. Cover and let rise until double in size, 1 to 2 hours. Bake in a preheated 350°F oven for 10 minutes, or until lightly browned. Makes 36 rolls.

✄ **AISLYN KARNEY,** age 14, Sand and Sage 4-H Club, La Junta, Colorado
Grand Champion, Arkansas Valley Fair & Expo, Rocky Ford, Colorado, 2005; Reserve Champion, Colorado State Fair, Pueblo, Colorado, 2005; Otero County Colorado Wheat Administrative Committee Award, 2005

WINNER'S CIRCLE TIP | Serve this recipe with your Thanksgiving or Christmas dinner. It's also a good dough for making cinnamon rolls.

DROPPED HERB BISCUITS

2 cups all-purpose flour, plus more
   for rolling out
1 tablespoon sugar
1 tablespoon baking powder

1 teaspoon salt
1 tablespoon dried dill weed
½ cup shortening
1 cup whole milk

1. Preheat oven to 450°F. Line a baking sheet with parchment paper.

2. Sift together flour, sugar, baking powder, and salt. Whisk in dill weed.

3. Cut in shortening using a pastry blender or two knives. Add milk and stir just until dough is soft and sticky.

4. Turn dough onto a lightly floured surface. Knead gently 10 times. Drop by teaspoonsful onto baking sheet. Bake for 10 minutes, or until lightly browned. Cool on a wire rack. Makes 12 biscuits.

✄ **ANGELA FLESLAND,** Poughkeepsie, New York
Blue Ribbon, Dutchess County Fair, Rhinebeck, New York, 1999

CHAPTER 8

❈

PRESERVES

JAMS AND JELLIES, FRUITS,
VEGETABLES, PICKLES, RELISHES,
SOUPS AND SAUCES

A Note on Safe Canning and Preserving

Canning is a safe method of food preservation if practiced properly. The canning process involves placing foods in canning jars and heating them to a temperature that destroys microorganisms that could contaminate the food. Air is driven from the jar during heating, and as it cools, a vacuum seal is formed.

There are two safe ways of canning: the boiling-water method and the steam-pressure method. The method chosen depends on the type of food being preserved.

The boiling water method is safe for high-acid foods, like fruits, tomatoes, pickles, jams, and jellies. You place the prepared food in sterilized canning jars, put on the lids, and heat the jars in a boiling-water canner. If you don't have a canner, you can improvise by setting a wire rack in the bottom of an 8- to 10-quart pot to keep the glass jars away from direct heat.

The steam-pressure method is the only safe way to preserve low-acid foods such as vegetables, meats, poultry, and seafood. Closed, sterilized jars of food are placed in 2 to 3 inches of water in a pressure canner, which is heated to a temperature of at least 240°F.

If you are located at an elevation higher than 1,000 feet above sea level, you must adjust the processing time when using both methods of preserving. Adjust as indicated by the altitude charts.

BOILING-WATER CANNER		STEAM-PRESSURE CANNER		
Altitude in Feet	Increase Processing Time	Altitude in Feet	Weighted Gauge	Dial Gauge
1,001–3,000	5 minutes	0–1,000	10	11
3,001–6,000	10 minutes	1,001–2,000	15	11
6,001–8,000	15 minutes	2,001–4,000	15	12
8,001–10,000	20 minutes	4,001–6,000	15	13
		6,001–8,000	15	14
		8,001–10,000	15	15

Home Canning Essentials for All Foods

⌗ Use only the best-quality ingredients. Preserve fruits and vegetables at their peak of ripeness.

⌗ Follow manufacturer's directions for sterilizing home canning jars and two-piece vacuum caps.

⌗ Fill hot, sterilized jars with the prepared recipe. Leave recommended headspace. Remove air bubbles by sliding a nonmetallic spatula between the jar and food; press gently on the food to release trapped air. Repeat around the circumference of the jar.

⌗ Wipe rim and threads with a clean, damp cloth. Center heated lid on jar. Screw band down evenly and firmly until a point of resistance is met—fingertip tight.

⌗ After processing, remove the jars from the canner and set them upright on a towel to cool. Do **not** retighten the bands or check for a seal while the jars are hot.

⌗ After 24 hours, check the lids for a seal. Sealed lids curve downward. Press the center of the lid to ensure it does not flex up or down. (Reprocess or refrigerate any unsealed jars.) Remove the bands. Wipe the jars and lids with a clean, damp cloth and dry. Wash the bands in soapy water, dry, and store.

⌗ Label and store the jars in a cool, dry, dark place. Use home-canned foods within one year.

For detailed information on safe home canning, see the USDA Complete Guide to Home Canning at www.uga.edu/nchfp/publications.

FRUIT JAM

4 cups peaches, chopped and peeled
4 cups pears, chopped and peeled
1 cup apples, chopped and peeled

¼ cup lemon juice
5 cups sugar

1. Combine peaches, pears, and apples in a large saucepan over medium-low heat. Cook slowly until tender, 15 minutes. Add lemon juice and sugar.

2. Bring to a boil, stirring frequently. Boil to the jam stage, 15 minutes. (Fruit will be very soft and almost formless.) Remove from heat. Stir and skim for 5 minutes.

3. Pour jam into hot, sterilized half-pint jars, leaving ¼-inch headspace. Remove air bubbles. Secure flat lids and rings. Process in a boiling-water canner bath for 10 minutes, or adjust time to your altitude. See "Safe Canning and Preserving," page 182, for detailed instructions. Makes 3 pints.

✄ **MARYLAN WHITAKER,** Chubbuck, Idaho
First Place, North Bannock County Fair, Pocatello, Idaho, 2004

TRIPLE-BERRY JAM

2 cups crushed strawberries
1 cup crushed raspberries
1 cup crushed blackberries

7 cups sugar
1 pouch (3 oz.) liquid fruit pectin

1. Combine strawberries, raspberries, and blackberries in a large saucepan over medium-low heat. Gradually stir in sugar.

2. Bring to a boil and quickly stir in pectin. Return to a boil for 1 minute. Skim off foam.

3. Pour jam into hot, sterilized half-pint jars, leaving ¼-inch headspace. Remove air bubbles. Secure flat lids and rings. Process in a boiling-water canner bath for 15 minutes, or adjust time to your altitude. See "Safe Canning and Preserving," page 182, for detailed instructions. Makes 3 pints.

✄ **JARED C. ZONDLER,** age 13, Carlsbad, California
First Place, San Diego County Fair, Del Mar, California, 2004

Apricot Jam

5 cups chopped unpeeled apricots
¼ cup lemon juice

7 cups sugar
1 box (1.75 oz.) powdered fruit pectin

1. Place apricots in a 6- or 8-quart saucepan. Add lemon juice. Gradually stir pectin into fruit.

2. Bring to a boil over high heat, stirring constantly. Add sugar, stirring to dissolve. Return to a full boil for 1 minute, stirring constantly. Remove from heat. Skim off foam, if necessary.

3. Ladle jam into hot, sterilized half-pint jars, leaving ¼-inch headspace. Remove air bubbles. Secure flat lids and rings. Process in a boiling-water canner bath for 10 minutes, or adjust time to your altitude. See "Safe Canning and Preserving," page 182, for detailed instructions. Remove jars and place on towel to cool, 12 to 24 hours. Makes 3 pints.

✕ **Ron Haratyk,** Del Mar, California
Best of Show, San Diego County Fair, Del Mar, California, 2004

Bitter (Seville) Orange Marmalade

2 Seville oranges
1 lemon
¾ cup water

3¼ cups sugar
1 pouch (3 oz.) liquid fruit pectin

1. Remove peels from oranges and lemon in quarter-sections. Slice off and discard about half of the white pith. Cut peels into thin slivers with sharp knife. Combine peels and water in a saucepan over medium-high heat. Bring to a boil, cover, and reduce to a simmer. Simmer for 15 minutes.

2. Cut orange and lemon pulp into sections, discarding seeds and membrane. Place pulp in a bowl and crush with a fork. Add simmering liquid with peel and stir to combine.

3. Measure 1⅔ cups of the fruit mixture, adding water if necessary, and pour into a large saucepan. Add sugar and mix to combine. Let stand for 30 minutes.

4. Bring mixture to a boil over medium-high heat, stirring constantly, 2 minutes. Remove from heat and stir in pectin.

5. Ladle marmalade into hot, sterilized half-pint jars, leaving ¼-inch headspace. Remove air bubbles. Secure flat lids and rings. Process in a boiling-water canner bath for 10 minutes, or adjust time to your altitude. See "Safe Canning and Preserving," page 182, for detailed instructions. Makes 2½ pints.

✕ **Barry Slipock,** El Cajon, California
First Place, San Diego County Fair, Del Mar, California, 2004

Wild Muscadine Grape Marmalade

4 lbs. grapes (to make 6 cups cooked
 grape pulp, any type of grape)
1 cup water

7½ cups sugar
1 box (1.75 oz.) powdered fruit pectin
1 tablespoon margarine

1. Remove and discard grape stems. Slip skins from grapes and set aside.

2. Combine grape pulp and water in small saucepan over medium heat. Cook for 5 minutes. Pass pulpy mixture through a food mill to remove seeds.

3. Chop grape skins in a blender. Combine chopped skins and seeded pulp in a large saucepan over medium heat. Add pectin and margarine. Bring to a rolling boil. Add sugar all at once. Return to a rolling boil. Boil hard for 1 minute.

4. Pour marmalade into hot, sterilized jars, leaving ¼-inch headspace. Remove air bubbles. Secure flat lids and rings. Process in a boiling-water canner bath for 10 minutes, or adjust time to your altitude. See "Safe Canning and Preserving," page 182, for detailed instructions. Makes 2½ quarts.

✄ **PHYLLIS CANIPE,** Lawndale, North Carolina
Blue Ribbon, Cleveland County Fair, Shelby, North Carolina, 2004

BLUEBERRY JAM

4 cups crushed blueberries
2 tablespoons lemon juice
1 box (1.75 oz.) powdered fruit pectin

¼ teaspoon butter
4 cups sugar

1. Combine blueberries and lemon juice in a large saucepan over medium heat. Gradually add pectin.

2. Bring to full rolling boil, stirring constantly. Add butter. Add sugar all at once; return to full rolling boil. Boil hard for 1 minute. Remove from heat and skim off foam.

3. Ladle jam into hot, sterilized jars, leaving ¼-inch headspace. Remove air bubbles. Secure flat lids and rings. Process in a boiling-water canner bath for 10 minutes, or adjust time to your altitude. See "Safe Canning and Preserving," page 182, for detailed instructions. Stand upright and cool, 12 to 24 hours. Makes 3 pints.

✄ **SCOTT JACOBSON,** age 9, San Diego, California
First Place, San Diego County Fair, Del Mar, California, 2004

RASPBERRY JAM

6 cups raspberries, crushed with a potato masher
1 box (1.75 oz.) powdered fruit pectin
8½ cups sugar

1. Combine crushed raspberries and pectin in a Dutch oven over medium-high heat. Bring to a rolling boil, stirring constantly. Stir in sugar. Return to a rolling boil; boil for 4 minutes. Skim off any foam.

2. Ladle jam into hot, sterilized jars, leaving ¼-inch headspace. Remove air bubbles. Secure flat lids and rings. Process in a boiling-water canner bath for 10 minutes, or adjust time to your altitude. See "Safe Canning and Preserving," page 182, for detailed instructions. Makes 8½ pints.

✄ **KARI HUGHES,** Pocatello, Idaho
First Place, North Bannock County Fair, Pocatello, Idaho, 2005

PEACH JAM

4 cups finely chopped peaches
2 tablespoons fresh lemon juice
1 box (1.75 oz.) powdered fruit pectin

½ teaspoon butter
5½ cups sugar

1. Combine peaches, lemon juice, pectin, and butter in a large saucepan over medium-high heat. Bring to a full rolling boil. Quickly stir in sugar. Return to a rolling boil, stirring constantly, for 1 minute. Remove from heat and skim off any foam.

2. Ladle jam into hot, sterilized jars, leaving ¼-inch headspace. Remove air bubbles. Secure flat lids and rings. Process in a boiling-water canner bath for 5 minutes, or adjust time to your altitude. See "Safe Canning and Preserving," page 182, for detailed instructions. Makes 6½ pints.

✳ **JILL STRONG,** Waukesha, Wisconsin
Grand Champion, Waukesha County Fair, Pewaukee, Wisconsin, 2000

BOYSENBERRY JAM

4 cups crushed boysenberries
1 box (1.75 oz.) powdered fruit pectin
7 cups sugar

1. Combine boysenberries and pectin in a large saucepan. Bring to a boil, stirring often. Add sugar. Return to a boil over high heat, stirring constantly. Boil for 1 minute.

2. Ladle jam into hot, sterilized jars, leaving ¼-inch headspace. Remove air bubbles. Secure flat lids and rings. Process in a boiling-water canner bath for 10 minutes, or adjust time to your altitude. See "Safe Canning and Preserving," page 182, for detailed instructions. Makes 3 pints.

✳ **FRANCINE RIPPY,** Hacienda Heights, California
First Place, Los Angeles County Fair, Pomona, California, 2003

WINNER'S CIRCLE TIP | Use fresh or frozen boysenberries for this jam. Allow frozen boysenberries to thaw in the refrigerator before mashing them.

SUGAR-FREE BLACKBERRY JAM

3 cups crushed blackberries
5 cups crushed blackberries or
   2 cups fresh blackberry juice

1 package (1.75 oz.) sugar-free pectin
7 cups sugar substitute (such as Splenda)

1. Combine crushed berries, berry juice if using, and sugar-free pectin in a large saucepan. Bring to a rolling boil, stirring continuously. Boil for 1 minute. Remove from heat.

2. Ladle jam into hot, sterilized half-pint jars, leaving ¼-inch headspace. Remove air bubbles. Secure flat lids and rings. Process in a boiling-water canner bath for 10 minutes, or adjust time to your altitude. Check seals after 24 hours; if not sealed, store in the refrigerator and use within 3 weeks. See "Safe Canning and Preserving," page 182, for detailed instructions. Makes 3 pints.

✕ **NICOLE MIDSTOKKE,** age 17, Bonsall 4-H, California
First Place, San Diego County Fair, Del Mar, California, 2004

WINNER'S CIRCLE TIP | **Use berry juice instead of crushed berries to cut down on the seeds in the jam. To make 2 cups of blackberry juice, heat 5 cups of crushed blackberries in a saucepan and then pour through a jelly bag or cheesecloth to strain off the juice.**

LEMONADE MARMALADE

7 to 9 large lemons
¼ teaspoon baking soda
1½ cups water

5 cups sugar
½ teaspoon butter
1 pouch (3 oz.) liquid fruit pectin

1. Use a zester to remove yellow zest from all lemons.

2. Cut lemons into wedges. Remove and discard all seeds and white pith. Chop the pulp.

3. Combine lemon zest, baking soda, and water in a large saucepan. Cook over medium heat, stirring constantly, until mixture comes to a boil. Add sugar and chopped lemon pulp. Return to a boil. Add butter to cut foam. Bring to a full rolling boil, stirring constantly. Boil hard for 5 minutes. Remove from heat. Stir in liquid fruit pectin. Led stand, stirring occasionally to distribute fruit, 3 to 5 minutes.

4. Ladle marmalade into hot, sterilized half-pint jars, leaving ¼-inch headspace. Remove air bubbles. Secure flat lids and rings. Process in a boiling-water canner bath for 10 minutes, or adjust time to your altitude. See "Safe Canning and Preserving," page 182, for detailed instructions. Makes 2½ pints.

✕ **SUE SATTERLEE,** Vista, California
First Place, San Diego County Fair, Del Mar, California, 2004

STRAWBERRY-ORANGE MARMALADE

2 medium blood oranges
8 cups strawberries, hulled and sliced
2 tablespoons lemon juice

1 pouch (3 oz.) liquid fruit pectin
1 box (1.75 oz.) powdered fruit pectin
7 cups sugar

1. Cut 1 orange into ¼-inch-thick slices and remove the seeds. Halve the slices. Drain on paper towels.
2. Quarter and seed the remaining orange. Finely chop or grind the orange pulp in a food processor.
3. Combine orange pulp, strawberries, lemon juice, and pectin in a large saucepan over medium-high heat. Bring to a full rolling boil, stirring constantly. Add sugar. Return to a full rolling boil. Boil hard, stirring constantly, 1 minute. Remove from heat. Skim off foam with a metal spoon.
4. Ladle marmalade into hot, sterilized jars. Using tongs, push 1 or 2 orange slices into marmalade in each jar, leaving ¼-inch headspace. Remove air bubbles. Secure flat lids and rings. Process in a boiling-water canner bath for 15 minutes, or adjust time to your altitude. See "Safe Canning and Preserving," page 182, for detailed instructions. Makes 3½ to 4 pints.

✕ **STAR SLIPOCK,** El Cajon, California
First Place, San Diego County Fair, Del Mar, California, 2004

CINNAMON-APPLE JELLY

1 quart apple juice
1 box (1.75-oz.) powdered fruit pectin

4½ cups sugar
3 tablespoons red cinnamon candies

1. Combine apple juice and pectin in a large saucepan over medium-high heat. Bring to a rolling boil. Add sugar and cinnamon candies. Cook, stirring constantly, until sugar is dissolved and candies are melted. Bring to boil and cook, stirring occasionally, for 2 minutes. Remove from heat. Let stand 1 to 2 minutes. Skim foam from top.
2. Pour jelly into hot, sterilized half-pint jars, leaving ¼-inch headspace. Remove air bubbles. Secure flat lids and rings. Process in a boiling-water canner bath for 15 minutes, or adjust time to your altitude. See "Safe Canning and Preserving," page 182, for detailed instructions. Makes 6 to 7 pints.

✕ **MARYLAN WHITAKER,** Chubbuck, Idaho
First Place, North Bannock County Fair, Pocatello, Idaho, 2004

STRAWBERRY JAM

5 cups crushed strawberries
1 box (1.75 oz.) powdered fruit pectin

1 tablespoon margarine
7 cups sugar

1. Combine crushed strawberries, fruit pectin, and margarine in a large saucepan over medium-high heat. Bring to a rolling boil. Add sugar all at once. Return to a rolling boil. Boil hard for 1 minute. Remove from heat. Skim off any foam.

2. Pour jam into hot, sterilized jars, leaving ¼-inch headspace. Remove air bubbles. Secure flat lids and rings. Process in a boiling-water canner bath for 10 minutes, or adjust time to your altitude. See "Safe Canning and Preserving," page 182, for detailed instructions. Makes 4 pints.

✄ **PHYLLIS CANIPE,** Lawndale, North Carolina
Blue Ribbon, Cleveland County Fair, Shelby, North Carolina, 2005

> It takes about 2 quarts of fresh strawberries to make 5 cups of crushed strawberries.

PEAR-LIME JAM

8 or 9 pears, peeled, cored,
  and roughly chopped
¼ cup fresh lime juice
1 tablespoon grated lime zest

1 box (1.75 oz.) powdered fruit pectin
1 tablespoon butter
5 cups sugar

1. Puree pears in a food processor until smooth.

2. Combine 4 cups pear purée, lime juice, lime zest, pectin, and butter in a large saucepan over medium-high heat. Bring to a full rolling boil, stirring constantly. Add sugar. Return to a full rolling boil, stirring constantly, for 1 minute. Remove from heat.

3. Pour jam into hot, sterilized jars, leaving ¼-inch headspace. Remove air bubbles. Secure flat lids and rings. Process in a boiling-water canner bath for 10 minutes, or adjust time to your altitude. See "Safe Canning and Preserving," page 182, for detailed instructions. Makes 3 to 3½ pints.

✄ **KATHLEEN MCNAMARA,** San Diego, California
First Place, San Diego County Fair, Del Mar, California, 2004

BLACKBERRY JELLY

2½ quarts fresh blackberries, washed
1 box (1.75 oz.) powdered fruit pectin

½ teaspoon butter
4½ cups sugar

1. Crush blackberries one cup at a time until mixture measures 3¾ cups. Add up to ½ cup water if necessary to make up exact amount. Strain mixture through cheesecloth to eliminate pulp and seeds.

2. Combine blackberry juice, pectin, and butter in a Dutch oven over medium-high heat. Bring to a full rolling boil, stirring constantly. Add sugar all at once. Return to a full rolling boil. Boil hard for 1 minute. Remove from heat. Skim off foam.

3. Pour jelly into hot, sterilized half-pint jars, leaving ¼-inch headspace. Remove air bubbles. Secure flat lids and rings. Process in a boiling-water canner bath for 10 minutes, or adjust time to your altitude. See "Safe Canning and Preserving," page 182, for detailed instructions. Makes 2 to 2½ pints.

✄ **STEPHANIE HORINE,** Beggs, Oklahoma
First Place, Tulsa State Fair, Tulsa, Oklahoma, 2003

ORANGE-WALNUT MARMALADE

4 lbs. oranges
5 cups water
1 box (1.75 oz.) powdered fruit pectin

7½ cups sugar
2 cups chopped walnuts

1. Cut off and discard top and bottom of each orange. Cut up remainder, including peels, and place in a 6- to 8-quart saucepan. Add water. Bring to a rapid boil, reduce heat, and simmer, uncovered, until peel is tender, 1 hour.

2. Transfer mixture to a food processor and chop into small pieces. Return chopped pulp to saucepan. Add pectin and stir, scraping down sides of pan all the pectin dissolves.

3. Bring mixture to a boil over medium-high heat, stirring constantly and reducing heat, if necessary, to prevent scorching. Add sugar, continue stirring, and bring to a full rolling boil. Add nuts. Boil hard, stirring constantly, for 3 minutes. Remove from heat. Skim off foam.

4. Pour marmalade into hot, sterilized half-pint jars, leaving ¼-inch headspace. Remove air bubbles. Secure flat lids and rings. Process in a boiling-water canner bath for 10 minutes, or adjust time to your altitude. See "Safe Canning and Preserving," page 182, for detailed instructions. Makes 3½ pints.

✕ **KATHY JONES,** Chubbuck, Idaho
First Place, North Bannock County Fair, Pocatello, Idaho, 2005

JALAPEÑO JELLY

¾ pound jalapeños, stems and
    seeds removed
2 cups cider vinegar, divided

6 cups sugar
2 pouches (3 oz. each) powdered fruit pectin
Green food coloring

1. Combine jalapeños and 1 cup of the cider vinegar in a food processor. Puree until smooth.

2. Combine purée, remaining 1 cup cider vinegar, and sugar in a large saucepan over medium-high heat. Bring to a boil. Boil, stirring continuously, for 10 minutes. Add pectin and stir. Return to a boil. Boil hard, stirring constantly, for 1 minute. Remove from heat. Skim off foam. Stir in food coloring.

3. Ladle jelly into hot, sterilized jars, leaving ¼-inch headspace. Remove air bubbles. Secure flat lids and rings. Process in a boiling-water canner bath for 10 minutes, or adjust time to your altitude. See "Safe Canning and Preserving," page 182, for detailed instructions. Makes 2½ pints.

Be sure to wear rubber gloves when handling hot peppers.

✕ **JANEL MAURER,** Spencer, Iowa
Blue Ribbon, Clay County Fair, Spencer, Iowa, 2005

Apple or Crab Apple Jelly

5 lbs. apples or crab apples

5 cups water

1 box (1.75 oz.) powdered fruit pectin

1 tablespoon margarine

9 cups sugar

1. Cut off and discard stem and blossom ends of apples. Cut apples into small pieces.

2. Combine apples and water in a large saucepan over medium-high heat. Bring to a boil, reduce to a simmer, and cook until apples are tender, 10 minutes. Stir and crush apples. Simmer 5 minutes longer. Drain through cheesecloth two times to extract and strain 7 cups of juice.

3. Combine apple juice, pectin, and margarine in a large saucepan over medium-high heat. Bring to a rolling boil. Add sugar all at once. Return to a rolling boil. Boil hard for 1 minute.

4. Pour jelly into hot, sterilized half-pint jars, leaving ¼-inch headspace. Remove air bubbles. Secure flat lids and rings. Process in a boiling-water canner bath for 10 minutes, or adjust time to your altitude. See "Safe Canning and Preserving," page 182, for detailed instructions. Makes 5 pints.

✂ **Phyllis Canipe,** Lawndale, North Carolina

Blue Ribbon, Cleveland County Fair, Shelby, North Carolina, 2004, 2005

Watermelon Rind Preserves

Rind of one watermelon

3½ quarts water, divided

4 tablespoons salt

4 cups sugar

¼ cup lemon juice

½ cup thinly sliced and seeded lemon (1 medium)

1. Trim the green outer peel and pink inner flesh from the thick rind of one watermelon. Cut rind into 1-inch pieces and place in a large bowl. Stir salt into 2 quarts of the water until dissolved, and pour over watermelon. Let stand for 6 hours. Drain well, rinse, and drain again.

2. Place watermelon rind in large saucepan. Add water to cover. Cook over medium heat until tender, 20 to 30 minutes. Drain.

3. In a large saucepan, combine remaining 1½ quarts water, sugar, and lemon juice. Bring to a boil and cook for 5 minutes. Add watermelon rind. Continue boiling until syrup thickens. Add lemon slices. Remove from heat. Skim off foam.

4. Ladle preserves into hot, sterilized jars, leaving ½-inch headspace. Remove air bubbles. Secure flat lids and rings. Process in a boiling-water canner bath for 20 minutes, or adjust time to your altitude. See "Safe Canning and Preserving," page 182, for detailed instructions. Makes 3½ pints.

✂ **Phyllis Canipe,** Lawndale, North Carolina

Blue Ribbon, Cleveland County Fair, Shelby, North Carolina, 2003, 2004

LEMON-LIME JELLY

⅜ cup fresh lime juice
⅜ cup fresh lemon juice
1¾ cups water

½ teaspoon baking soda
1 box (1.75 oz.) powdered fruit pectin
3½ cups sugar

1. Combine lime juice, lemon juice, water, and baking soda in a large saucepan over medium-high heat. Stir in pectin until dissolved. Bring to a boil over high heat, stirring constantly. Add sugar all at once and stir. Return to a full rolling boil. Boil hard, stirring constantly, for 1 minute. Remove from heat. Skim off foam.

2. Ladle jelly into hot, sterilized jars, leaving ¼-inch headspace. Remove air bubbles. Secure flat lids and rings. Process in a boiling-water canner bath for 5 minutes, or adjust time to your altitude. See "Safe Canning and Preserving," page 182, for detailed instructions. Makes 2 pints.

✄ **BARRY SLIPOCK,** El Cajon, California
First Place, San Diego County Fair, Del Mar, California, 2004

GREEN PEPPER JELLY

7 sweet green peppers, divided
1 hot green pepper
1½ cups vinegar, divided
1½ cups apple juice

1 box (1.75 oz.) powdered fruit pectin
½ teaspoon salt
5 cups sugar
Green food coloring

1. Remove stems and seeds from peppers. Cut into strips. Combine half of pepper strips and half of vinegar in a food processor. Chop very fine. Place in a large bowl. Chop remaining pepper strips and add to bowl. Add apple juice to mixture. Refrigerate overnight.

2. Strain pepper-apple juice mixture through cheesecloth to measure 4 cups of juice. Add more apple juice if needed to reach this measure.

3. Combine juice, pectin, and salt in a large saucepan over medium-high heat. Bring to a rolling boil. Add sugar all at once. Return to a rolling boil. Boil hard for 1 minute. Remove from heat. Skim off foam. Stir in a few drops of food coloring.

4. Pour jelly into hot, sterilized jars, leaving ¼-inch headspace. Remove air bubbles. Secure flat lids and rings. Process in a boiling-water canner bath for 10 minutes, or adjust time to your altitude. See "Safe Canning and Preserving," page 182, for detailed instructions. Makes 6½ pints.

✄ **PHYLLIS CANIPE,** Lawndale, North Carolina
Blue Ribbon, Cleveland County Fair, Shelby, North Carolina, 2005

STRAWBERRY JELLY

3 quarts strawberries
¾ cup to 1½ cups water
1 box (1.75 oz.) powdered pectin

2 tablespoons lemon juice
5 cups sugar

1. Wash strawberries and remove stems and hulls. Place strawberries and water in a large saucepan over medium heat. Crush berries slightly. Cover and cook until fruit is soft, 15 minutes. Strain mixture through a damp jelly bag or several layers of cheesecloth to extract juice. Measure 3½ cups of juice, adding water if necessary to reach this measure.

2. Combine strawberry juice, powdered pectin, and lemon juice in a large saucepan over high heat. Bring to a rolling boil. Add sugar, stirring constantly. Return to a rolling boil. Boil hard for 1 minute. Remove from heat. Skim foam if necessary.

3. Ladle jelly into hot, sterilized half-pint jars, leaving ¼-inch headspace. Remove air bubbles. Secure flat lids and rings. Process in a boiling-water canner bath for 10 minutes, or adjust time to your altitude. See "Safe Canning and Preserving," page 182, for detailed instructions. Makes 2½ pints.

✄ **LISA FINDLAY,** Chubbuck, Idaho
First Place, North Bannock County Fair, Pocatello, Idaho, 2005

SLOW-COOKED APPLE BUTTER

4 lbs. apples, peeled, cored, and quartered　　**4 cups sugar**
2 cups water　　**2 teaspoons cinnamon**

1. Combine apples and water in a large saucepan over medium-high heat. Simmer until apples are soft, 20 to 30 minutes. Puree through a food mill.

2. Combine 2 quarts of the apple purée, sugar, and cinnamon in an electric slow cooker. Cook on low, stirring occasionally, until mixture thickens, 4½ to 5 hours.

3. Ladle apple butter into hot, sterilized jars, leaving ½-inch headspace. Remove air bubbles. Secure flat lids and rings. Process in a boiling-water canner bath for 10 minutes, or adjust time to your altitude. See "Safe Canning and Preserving," page 182, for detailed instructions. Makes 3 pints.

✄ **PHYLLIS CANIPE,** Lawndale, North Carolina
Blue Ribbon, Cleveland County Fair, Shelby, North Carolina, 2005

CHERRY PRESERVES

3 lbs. pitted red cherries　　**1 tablespoon margarine**
1 box (1.75 oz.) powdered fruit pectin　　**5 cups sugar**

1. Combine cherries and powdered pectin in a large saucepan over medium-high heat. Bring to boil. Add margarine, stirring to prevent sticking. Add sugar, stirring until dissolved. Bring to a rolling boil. Boil hard for 1 minute, stirring constantly. Remove from heat. Skim off foam. Stir to distribute fruit, 3 minutes.

2. Ladle preserves into hot, sterilized jars, leaving ½-inch headspace. Remove air bubbles. Secure flat lids and rings. Process in a boiling-water canner bath for 15 minutes, or adjust time to your altitude. See "Safe Canning and Preserving," page 182, for detailed instructions. Makes 6½ pints.

✄ **PHYLLIS CANIPE,** Lawndale, North Carolina
Blue Ribbon, Cleveland County Fair, Shelby, North Carolina, 2003, 2005

Plums

2½ lbs. firm, ripe plums
2 cups sugar
4 cups water

1. Wash plums. Prick each plum in several places with a needle or large pin.

2. Combine sugar and water in a large saucepan over medium-high heat. Bring to a boil, stirring gently until sugar is dissolved.

3. Pack plums into hot, sterilized quart jars. Pour boiling syrup over plums, leaving ½-inch headspace. Remove air bubbles. Secure flat lids and rings. Process in a boiling-water canner bath for 25 minutes, or adjust time to your altitude. See "Safe Canning and Preserving," page 182, for detailed instructions. Makes 4 pints.

✄ **FRANCINE RIPPY,** Hacienda Heights, California
First Place, L.A. County Fair, Pomona, California, 2003

Peaches with Brandy and Cinnamon Stick

Water   **3 cups sugar**
6 large peaches   **Apricot brandy**
½ cup pineapple juice   **Cinnamon sticks**

1. Bring a large stockpot of water to a boil over medium-high heat. Using a large slotted spoon, quickly dip peaches in and out of boiling water to loosen skins. Cool slightly. Peel off skins. Slice peaches, discarding pits, and place in a glass bowl. Pour pineapple juice over peach slices.

2. Combine sugar and 3 cups water in a large saucepan over medium-high heat. Bring to a boil, reduce to a simmer, and cook until slightly thickened, 20 minutes.

3. Pack drained peaches into hot, sterilized jars. Add 2 tablespoons apricot brandy and a cinnamon stick to each jar. Pour in hot sugar syrup, leaving ½-inch headspace. Remove air bubbles. Secure flat lids and rings. Process in a boiling-water canner bath for 20 minutes, or adjust time to your altitude. See "Safe Canning and Preserving," page 182, for detailed instructions. Makes 2 to 3 pints.

✄ **SANDY TRIFILO,** Glenham, New York
Best of Fruit, Dutchess County Fair, Rhinebeck, New York, 2005

Slow-Cooked Peach Butter

2 quarts peach pulp

4 cups sugar

½ teaspoon cinnamon

4 to 4½ lbs. peaches

1. Combine peach pulp, sugar, and cinnamon in an electric slow cooker. Cook on low heat, stirring occasionally, until thickened, 6 to 8 hours.

2. Ladle peach butter into hot, sterilized half-pint jars, leaving ½-inch headspace. Remove air bubbles. Secure flat lids and rings. Process in a boiling-water canner bath for 10 minutes, or adjust time to your altitude. See "Safe Canning and Preserving," page 182, for detailed instructions. Makes 4 pints.

⌘ **Phyllis Canipe,** Lawndale, North Carolina
Blue Ribbon, Cleveland County Fair, Shelby, North Carolina, 2005

Rhubarb with Orange Juice

Unpeeled rhubarb, washed and cut into 1-inch lengths

½ to 1 cup sugar per quart of chopped rhubarb

½ to 1 cup orange juice per quart of chopped rhubarb

1. Place rhubarb in a large stockpot. Cover with sugar and mix well. Allow to stand for several hours.

2. Combine rhubarb and orange juice in a large saucepan over medium heat. Heat slowly to boiling.

3. Pack rhubarb into hot, sterilized pint or quart jars, leaving ½-inch headspace. Remove air bubbles. Secure flat lids and rings. Process in a boiling-water canner bath for 15 minutes, or adjust time to your altitude. See "Safe Canning and Preserving," page 182, for detailed instructions. Yield varies.

⌘ **Francine Rippy,** Hacienda Heights, California
First Place, L.A. County Fair, Pomona, California, 2003

Strawberry-Fig Preserves

3 cups mashed figs

3 cups sugar

2 packages (3 oz. each) strawberry gelatin

1. Combine figs, sugar, and gelatin in a large saucepan over medium-high heat. Bring to a boil, reduce heat slightly, and continue to boil, stirring often, 3 to 5 minutes.

2. Ladle preserves into hot, sterilized half-pint jars, leaving ½-inch headspace. Remove air bubbles. Secure flat lids and rings. Process in a boiling-water canner bath for 10 minutes, or adjust time to your altitude. See "Safe Canning and Preserving," page 182, for detailed instructions. Makes 3 pints.

⌘ **Amy Jones,** Shelby, North Carolina
First Prize, Strawberry Preserves, Cleveland County Fair, Shelby, North Carolina, 2005

Apple Preserves

6 cups sliced, peeled apples
1 cup water
1 tablespoon lemon juice

1 box (1.75 oz.) powered pectin
4 cups sugar
1 tablespoon margarine

1. Combine apples, water, and lemon juice in a large saucepan over medium heat. Cover and simmer for 10 minutes.

2. Add pectin and stir. Bring to a boil, stirring frequently. Add sugar and stir to dissolve. Bring to a rolling boil. Stir in margarine. Boil hard for 1 minute. Skim foam if necessary.

3. Ladle preserves into hot, sterilized jars, leaving ½-inch headspace. Remove air bubbles. Secure flat lids and rings. Process in a boiling-water canner bath for 10 minutes, or adjust time to your altitude. See "Safe Canning and Preserving," page 182, for detailed instructions. Makes 6½ pints.

※ **Phyllis Canipe,** Lawndale, North Carolina
Blue Ribbon, Cleveland County Fair, Shelby, North Carolina, 2003, 2004, 2005

Apple Pie Filling

6 quarts peeled, cored, and sliced apples
   (use firm crisp apples)
Cold water
5½ cups sugar
1½ cups clear gel

1 tablespoon cinnamon
1 teaspoon nutmeg (optional)
5 cups apple juice from concentrate
1¾ cup bottled lemon juice
7 drops yellow food coloring (optional)

1. Place apples in a large saucepan over medium-high heat and add water to cover. Boil for 1 minute. Drain, transfer fruit to a bowl, and cover.

2. In a large saucepan, combine sugar, clear gel, cinnamon, and nutmeg. Mix thoroughly so clear gel doesn't clump. Add 1½ cups cold water and apple juice. Stir to combine. Cook over medium-high heat until mixture thickens and begins to bubble. Add lemon juice and food coloring. Boil, stirring constantly, for 1 minute. Fold in apple slices.

3. Spoon filling into hot, sterilized jars, leaving 1-inch headspace. Remove air bubbles. Secure flat lids and rings. Process in a boiling-water canner bath for 25 minutes, or adjust time to your altitude. See "Safe Canning and Preserving," page 182, for detailed instructions. Makes 7 quarts.

※ **Jennifer Egbert,** Chubbuck, Idaho
First Place, North Bannock County Fair, Pocatello, Idaho, 2005

Apricot-Almond Conserve

3 lbs. ripe apricots
⅓ cup water
3 cups sugar

1 cup slivered almonds
2 tablespoons lemon juice
Pat of butter (optional)

1. Wash, peel, and pit apricots. Chop to make 4½ cups.

2. Combine chopped apricots and water in a large saucepan over medium heat. Bring to a boil, reduce to a simmer, and cover. Simmer, stirring frequently to prevent scorching, until apricots are tender, 5 to 10 minutes.

3. Add sugar, almonds, lemon juice, and butter, if using, stirring constantly. Bring to a full rolling boil. Continue cooking until the conserve is of desired consistency. Remove from heat.

4. Ladle conserve into hot, sterilized jars, leaving ½-inch headspace. Remove air bubbles. Secure flat lids and rings. Process in a boiling-water canner bath for 5 minutes, or adjust time to your altitude. See "Safe Canning and Preserving," page 182, for detailed instructions. Makes 3 to 4 pints.

✄ **DANIELLE MIDSTOKKE,** age 13, Bonsall 4-H, California
First Place, San Diego County Fair, Del Mar, California, 2004

CANNED PEACHES IN LIGHT JUICE

8 to 10 lbs. peaches
3 cups sugar

5 cups water
2 tablespoons lemon juice

1. Wash, peel, and pit peaches. Cut into chunks.

2. Combine peaches, sugar, water, and lemon juice in large saucepan over medium-high heat. Bring to a boil and cook, stirring occasionally, until tender, 20 minutes.

3. Pack peaches and their juices into hot, sterilized jars, leaving ½-inch headspace. Remove air bubbles. Secure flat lids and rings. Process in a boiling-water canner bath for 10 minutes, or adjust time to your altitude. See "Safe Canning and Preserving," page 182, for detailed instructions. Makes 10 to 12 pints.

✄ **RACHEL BROWN,** age 8; **DAYLEEN YANEZ,** age 9; **TORI KNETTLE,** age 12; **SHANNA JAMES,** age 10; **EMILY BROWN,** age 11; **CANDACE YANEZ,** age 12; **AMANDA HUBER,** age 8; Ramona Wranglers 4-H
First Place, San Diego County Fair, Del Mar, California, 2004

PEAR PRESERVES

5 cups sliced pears (¼-inch-thick slices)
1 lemon, sliced very thin
8 cups sugar

1. Place pear and lemon slices in a large saucepan. Pour sugar over pears. Cover and let stand in a cool place for 12 to 24 hours.

2. Place saucepan over medium-low heat. Cook until liquid turns an amber-pinkish color, 1 hour. Remove from heat.

3. Pack preserves into hot, sterilized jars, leaving ½-inch headspace. Remove air bubbles. Secure flat lids and rings. Process in a boiling-water canner bath for 20 minutes, or adjust time to your altitude. See "Safe Canning and Preserving," page 182, for detailed instructions. Makes 3½ pints.

✄ **MARILYN McSWAIN,** Kings Mountain, North Carolina
Blue Ribbon, Cleveland County Fair, Shelby, North Carolina, 2005

NIKKI'S PICKLED VEGETABLES

2 cups white wine vinegar
2 cups water
2 tablespoons pickling salt
1 medium cauliflower, broken and
  cut into pieces
½ cup seeded and diced red bell pepper

½ cup seeded and diced green bell pepper
½ cup seeded and diced yellow bell pepper
1 cup sliced carrots
2 teaspoons cumin seeds
2 teaspoons coriander seeds
2 teaspoons fennel seeds

1. Combine vinegar, water, and pickling salt in a saucepan over medium-high heat. Bring to a boil.
2. In a bowl, toss cauliflower, red bell pepper, green bell pepper, yellow bell pepper, and carrots to combine.
3. Divide cumin, coriander, and fennel evenly among 8 hot, sterilized half-pint jars. Pack vegetables firmly into jars, leaving ½-inch headspace. Remove air bubbles. Secure flat lids and rings. Process in a boiling-water canner bath for 10 minutes, or adjust time to your altitude. See "Safe Canning and Preserving," page 182, for detailed instructions. Store the cooled jars in a cool, dry, dark place for at least 3 weeks before eating. Makes 4 pints.

✂ **NICOLE MIDSTOKKE,** age 17, Bonsall 4-H, California
First Place, San Diego County Fair, Del Mar, California, 2004

REGAL TOMATO SOUP

6 onions, chopped
1 bunch celery, chopped
Water
8 quarts fresh tomatoes, stems removed

1 cup sugar
¼ cup salt
1 cup butter, room temperature
1 cup flour

1. Combine onions and celery in a stockpot. Add just enough water to keep them from burning during cooking. Simmer over medium-low heat. Add tomatoes. Continue cooking until celery and onions are tender and tomatoes are cooked through, 20 to 30 minutes.
2. Pass cooked vegetable and their juice through food mill to remove tomato skins and large chunks. Return pulp and juice to stockpot. Add sugar and salt.
3. Cream butter and flour until well blended. Stir into pulp and continue cooking until slightly thickened, 10 to 15 minutes. Remove from heat.
4. Pour soup into hot, sterilized pint jars, leaving 1-inch headspace. Secure flat lids and rings. Process in a steam-pressure canner at 5 lbs. of pressure for 10 minutes, or adjust to your altitude. See "Safe Canning and Preserving," page 182, for detailed instructions. Makes 8 to 10 pints.

✂ **BETSY BRUGMAN,** Royal, Iowa
Blue Ribbon, Clay County Fair, Spencer, Iowa, 2005

The tomato soup will thicken even more as it cools, becoming rich and creamy.

Dilled Green Beans

¼ cup canning salt

2½ cups vinegar

2½ cups water

2 lbs. green beans, washed and trimmed

4 garlic cloves, washed

4 dill heads, washed

1. Combine canning salt, vinegar, and water in a Dutch oven over medium-high heat. Bring to a boil.

2. Pack green beans into hot, sterilized pint jars. Add a garlic clove and dill head to each jar. Ladle hot brine over green beans, leaving ½-inch headspace. Remove air bubbles. Secure flat lids and rings. Process in a boiling-water canner bath for 10 minutes, or adjust time to your altitude. See "Safe Canning and Preserving," page 182, for detailed instructions. Makes 4 pints.

✕ **Kari Hughes,** Pocatello, Idaho
First Place, North Bannock County Fair,
Pocatello, Idaho, 2005

Green Tomato Mincemeat

2 quarts chopped green tomatoes
    (about 20 small)

1 tablespoon salt

Boiling water

1 orange

2½ quarts peeled, cored, and chopped
    apples (about 12 medium)

1 lb. seedless raisins

1½ cups (6 oz.) chopped suet

3½ cups brown sugar

½ cup vinegar

2 teaspoons cinnamon

1 teaspoon nutmeg

½ teaspoon ground allspice

½ teaspoon ground cloves

½ teaspoon ground ginger

1. Place tomatoes in a large bowl. Sprinkle salt over tomatoes. Let stand for 1 hour. Drain in a colander and return tomatoes to bowl. Pour boiling water over tomatoes to cover. Let stand for 5 minutes. Drain well.

2. Remove the orange zest and chop the orange pulp, picking out the seeds.

3. Combine green tomatoes, orange zest and pulp, apples, raisins, suet, brown sugar, vinegar, cinnamon, nutmeg, allspice, cloves, and ginger in a stockpot over medium-high heat. Cook until boiling hot.

4. Pour mincemeat into hot, sterilized quart jars, leaving 1-inch headspace. Secure flat lids and rings. Process in a steam-pressure canner at 10 lbs. of pressure for 25 minutes, or adjust to your altitude. See "Safe Canning and Preserving," page 182, for detailed instructions. Makes about 5 quarts.

✕ **Barbara Lamy,** Terryville, Connecticut
Blue Ribbon, First Place, Terryville Country Fair, Terryville, Connecticut, 2005

WINNER'S CIRCLE TIP | To chop green tomatoes quickly, pass them through a food grinder fitted with a coarse blade. Twelve medium green tomatoes make about 2½ quarts when chopped.

CHICKEN SOUP

4 quarts chicken stock

3 cups diced chicken

1½ cups diced celery

1½ cups peeled and sliced carrots

1 onion, diced

Salt and pepper to taste

3 chicken bouillon cubes

1. Combine chicken stock, chicken, celery, carrots, and onion in large stockpot over medium-high heat. Bring to a boil, reduce to a simmer, and simmer for 30 minutes. Season with salt and pepper. Add bouillon cubes and stir until dissolved.

2. Ladle soup into hot, sterilized pint or quart jars, leaving 1-inch headspace. Adjust lids. Process pints 1 hour and 15 minutes, quarts 1 hour and 30 minutes, at 10 lbs. pressure in pressure canner. Adjust time to your altitude. See "Safe Canning and Preserving," page 182. Makes 4 to 4½ quarts.

✕ **JANEL MAURER,** Spencer, Iowa
Blue Ribbon, Clay County Fair, Spencer, Iowa, 2005

CHUNKY GARDEN-VEGETABLE SOUP

2 cups sliced celery

4 cups whole kernel yellow corn

4 cups peeled and sliced carrots

2½ cups chopped yellow onions

2 quarts tomatoes, chopped and peeled

3 cups cut green beans

1¾ cups cubed potatoes

5 cups beef stock

Salt and pepper

1. Combine celery, corn, carrots, onions, tomatoes, green beans, potatoes, and beef stock in a large stockpot over medium-high heat. Bring to a boil. Boil for 10 minutes. Season with salt and pepper.

2. Ladle soup into hot, sterilized quart jars, leaving 1-inch headspace. Remove air bubbles. Secure flat lids and rings. Process in a steam-pressure canner at 10 lbs. of pressure for 1 hour and 15 minutes, or adjust to your altitude. See "Safe Canning and Preserving," page 182, for detailed instructions. Makes 6 to 7 quarts.

✕ **MARILYN MCSWAIN,** Kings Mountain, North Carolina
Blue Ribbon, Cleveland County Fair, Shelby, North Carolina, 2005

GRANDMA ELSIE MULLINS' CHOW CHOW

24 medium green tomatoes

½ medium head cabbage

2 large green bell peppers

6 jalapeños

2 large white onions

4 cups distilled white vinegar

5 cups sugar

6 teaspoons salt

5 teaspoons celery seed

4 teaspoons mustard seed

1. Chop tomatoes in a food processor. Drain off liquid. Place tomatoes in a large stockpot.
2. Chop cabbage, bell peppers, jalapeños, and onions in a food processor. Add to tomatoes. Add vinegar, sugar, salt, celery seed, and mustard seed. Simmer over medium-low heat for 15 minutes.
3. Ladle mixture into hot, sterilized pint jars, leaving 1-inch headspace. Remove air bubbles. Secure flat lids and rings. Process in a boiling-water canner bath for 10 minutes, or adjust time to your altitude. See "Safe Canning and Preserving," page 182, for detailed instructions. Makes 6 pints.

✄ **NANCY MULLINS,** Tulsa, Oklahoma
Sweepstakes Winner, Tulsa State Fair, Tulsa, Oklahoma, 2001

BEET PICKLES

3 quarts beets (about 24 small)   1½ teaspoons salt
2 cups sugar   3½ cups vinegar
2 cinnamon sticks   1½ cups water
1 tablespoon whole allspice

1. Place beets in a large saucepan, add water to cover, and bring to boil over medium-high heat. Boil until skins loosen, 8 minutes. Cool slightly. Peel off skins and remove tops.
2. Combine sugar, cinnamon, allspice, salt, vinegar, and water in a large saucepan over medium-high heat. Bring to a boil, reduce heat, and simmer for 15 minutes. Remove cinnamon sticks.
3. Pack beets into hot, sterilized jars, leaving ½-inch headspace. Remove air bubbles. Secure flat lids and rings. Process in a boiling-water canner bath for 30 minutes, or adjust time to your altitude. See "Safe Canning and Preserving," page 182, for detailed instructions. Makes 4 to 6 pints.

✄ **KATHY JONES,** Chubbuck, Idaho
First Place, North Bannock County Fair, Pocatello, Idaho, 2005

BABY GARLIC-DILL PICKLES

7½ cups water   6 sliced onions
5 cups vinegar   12 garlic cloves
½ cup plus 2 tablespoons canning salt 40 pickling cucumbers
6 heads dill   (2 to 3 inches long), washed

1. Combine water, vinegar, and canning salt in Dutch oven over medium-high heat. Bring to a boil.
2. Divide dill heads, sliced onions, and garlic cloves among hot, sterilized jars. Add cucumbers and cover with hot brine, leaving ½-inch headspace. Remove air bubbles. Secure flat lids and rings. Process in a boiling-water canner bath for 10 minutes, or adjust time to your altitude. See "Safe Canning and Preserving," page 182, for detailed instructions. Makes 6 quarts.

✄ **KARI HUGHES,** Pocatello, Idaho
First Place, North Bannock County Fair, Pocatello, Idaho, 2004

LIME PICKLES

8 lbs. cucumbers, seeded and sliced
    lengthwise into quarters or eighths
2 gallons water
1½ cups pickling lime

SYRUP

2 quarts white vinegar (5%)
9 cups (4½ lbs.) sugar
1 teaspoon celery seed
1 teaspoon whole cloves
1 teaspoon pickling spice
1 tablespoon pickling salt

1. Place cucumbers in a large crock. Combine water and pickling lime. Pour over cucumbers. Soak for 24 hours.

2. Drain and rinse cucumbers. Soak in fresh water for 1 hour. Drain and rinse. Repeat the fresh water soak two more times. Drain well.

3. Place cucumbers in a large stockpot. Combine white vinegar, sugar, celery seed, cloves, pickling spice, and pickling salt. Pour over cucumbers. Let stand overnight.

4. Drain cucumbers, reserving syrup. Bring syrup to a boil, reduce to a simmer, and simmer for 10 minutes.

5. Pack cucumbers into hot, sterilized jars, leaving ½-inch headspace. Remove air bubbles. Secure flat lids and rings. Process in a boiling-water canner bath for 30 minutes, or adjust time to your altitude. See "Safe Canning and Preserving," page 182, for detailed instructions. Cool in a draft-free location. Store in a cool, dry, dark place. Makes 8 pints.

✂ **CHUCK DAHL,** Jackson, Wyoming
Division Champion for Pickles and Relish, Teton County Fair, Jackson, Wyoming, 2005

JENNIE COLLIN'S GREAT DILL PICKLES

2 quarts water
1 quart white vinegar
⅔ cup pickling salt
1 tablespoon sugar
2 bay leaves
Cucumbers, washed

Garlic cloves, peeled and washed
Sliced onions
Dill seeds
Dried dill weed
Fresh dill, washed

1. Combine water, vinegar, pickling salt, sugar, and bay leaves in a large saucepan over medium-high heat. Heat until boiling.

2. Pack cucumbers into hot, sterilized jars. Add garlic cloves, sliced onions, dill seeds, dill weed, and fresh dill to each jar. Use tongs to remove bay leaves from boiling brine. Pour brine over cucumbers, leaving ½-inch headspace. Remove air bubbles. Secure flat lids and rings. Process in a boiling-water canner bath for 10 minutes, or adjust time to your altitude. See "Safe Canning and Preserving," page 182, for detailed instructions. Yield varies.

✂ **NICOLE MIDSTOKKE,** age 17; **DANIELLE MIDSTOKKE,** age 13, Bonsall 4-H, California
First Place, San Diego County Fair, Del Mar, California, 2004

WATERMELON PICKLES

Rind of 1 large watermelon
Salt
Water
4 cups vinegar
8 cups sugar

16 cinnamon sticks
8 teaspoons whole cloves
Pinch of mustard seed
Green or red food coloring

1. Remove outer green skin and pink flesh from watermelon rind. Cut into 1-inch cubes. Place in a stockpot. Add salted water to cover (4 tablespoons salt to 1 quart of water). Let stand overnight. Drain.

2. Drain off salted water. Add fresh water to cover. Cook watermelon rind over medium heat until almost tender, 20 to 30 minutes. Drain.

3. Combine vinegar and sugar in a large saucepan over medium-high heat. Tie cinnamon sticks, cloves, and mustard seed in a cheesecloth bag. Add to syrup. Heat to boiling. Remove from heat and let stand for 15 minutes.

4. Add watermelon rind to syrup, bring to a boil, and cook until syrup is clear. Stir in food coloring.

5. Pack rind and syrup into hot, sterilized jars, leaving ½-inch headspace. Remove air bubbles. Secure flat lids and rings. Process in a boiling-water canner bath for 10 minutes, or adjust time to your altitude. See "Safe Canning and Preserving," page 182, for detailed instructions. Makes 6 pints.

✄ **CASSIE PALMER,** Broken Arrow, Oklahoma
First Place, Junior Division, Tulsa State Fair, Tulsa, Oklahoma, 2003

PEACH PICKLES

3 quarts cold water
1 teaspoon powdered fruit protector
8 lbs. small- to medium-size firm, ripe
    peaches, peeled, halved, and pitted
6¾ cups sugar

1 quart white vinegar (5% acidity)
4 3-inch cinnamon sticks
2 tablespoons whole cloves
1 tablespoon fresh peeled and grated ginger

1. Combine water and fruit protector in a large container. Drop peaches into water. Let stand until ready to use.

2. Combine sugar and vinegar in a large saucepan over medium-high heat. Bring to a boil and cook for 5 minutes. Tie cinnamon sticks, cloves, and ginger in a cheesecloth bag. Add to syrup.

3. Drain peaches and add to syrup mixture. Cook, uncovered, just until peaches are tender when pierced with a fork, 3 minutes. Remove from heat. Cover and let stand at room temperature for 24 hours.

4. Bring peaches and syrup to a boil over medium-high heat. Ladle into hot, sterilized pint or quart jars, leaving ½-inch headspace. Remove air bubbles. Secure flat lids and rings. Process in a boiling-water canner bath, 15 minutes for pints, 20 minutes for quarts, or adjust time to your altitude. See "Safe Canning and Preserving," page 182, for detailed instructions. Makes 6 pints.

✄ **MARILYN McSWAIN,** Kings Mountain, North Carolina
Blue Ribbon and Ball Canning Award, Cleveland County Fair, Shelby, North Carolina, 2005

Pumpkin Pickles

8 cups cubed pumpkin
2½ cups vinegar
2½ cups sugar
1 teaspoon cinnamon

1 teaspoon pickling spice
1 teaspoon nutmeg
1 teaspoon whole cloves

1. Steam the cubed pumpkin until tender. Remove the rind.

2. Combine vinegar, sugar, cinnamon, pickling spice, nutmeg, and cloves in a large saucepan over medium-high heat. Bring to a rolling boil. Reduce heat and simmer for 10 minutes. Add pumpkin and continue simmering, 5 minutes longer.

3. Ladle pumpkin and brine into hot, sterilized pint jars, leaving ½-inch headspace. Remove air bubbles. Secure flat lids and rings. Process in a boiling-water canner bath for 10 minutes, or adjust time to your altitude. See "Safe Canning and Preserving," page 182, for detailed instructions. Makes 5 pints.

✕ **DANIELLE MIDSTOKKE,** age 13, Bonsall 4-H, California
First Place, San Diego County Fair, Del Mar, California, 2004

Squash Pickles

8 cups sliced yellow summer squash
2 cups sliced sweet onion
1 tablespoon non-iodized salt
1 cup seeded and diced green bell pepper
½ cup seeded and diced red bell pepper

2 cups cider vinegar
3½ cups sugar
1 teaspoon celery seed
1 teaspoon mustard seed

1. Combine squash and onion in a large stockpot. Sprinkle with salt. Let stand 1 hour.

2. Add green pepper, red pepper, vinegar, sugar, celery seed, and mustard seed to squash and onions. Bring to a boil.

3. Pack squash and brine into hot, sterilized jars, leaving ½-inch headspace. Remove air bubbles. Secure flat lids and rings. Process in a boiling-water canner bath for 10 minutes, or adjust time to your altitude. See "Safe Canning and Preserving," page 182, for detailed instructions. Makes 6 pints.

✕ **CLARENCE JONES,** Shelby, North Carolina
First Prize, Squash Pickles, Cleveland County Fair, Shelby, North Carolina, 2005

1st-Prize Dills

⅓ bushel pickling-size cucumbers
Ice water
1 cup canning salt
1 quart white vinegar

3 quarts water
Fresh dill heads, washed
Garlic cloves, peeled and washed

1. Wash cucumbers and put in ice water 2 hours or longer.

2. Combine canning salt, white vinegar, and water in a large saucepan over medium-high heat. Heat to boiling.

3. Put 1 dill head and 1 garlic clove in each hot, sterilized canning jar. Fill jars with cucumbers. Pour hot brine into jars, leaving ½-inch headspace. Remove air bubbles. Secure flat lids and rings. Process in a boiling-water canner bath for 10 minutes, or adjust time to your altitude. See "Safe Canning and Preserving," page 182, for detailed instructions. Makes 10 quarts.

※ **DENNIS VOLZKE,** Aberdeen, South Dakota
Best of Show, Senior Food Preservation; and **NATALIE VOLZKE,** Aberdeen, South Dakota Best of Show, Junior Food Preservation, Brown County Fair & 4-H Show, Aberdeen, South Dakota, 2005 Second Place, South Dakota State Fair, Huron, South Dakota, 2005

BREAD-AND-BUTTER PICKLES

4 lbs. 4- to 6-inch cucumbers,
    cut into ¼-inch slices
2 lbs. onions, thinly sliced (about 8 small)
Ice cubes
⅓ cup canning salt
2 cups sugar

2 tablespoons mustard seed
2 teaspoons turmeric
2 teaspoons celery seed
1 teaspoon ground ginger
3 cups vinegar

1. Layer cucumber and onion slices with salt in a large bowl. Cover with ice cubes. Let stand for 1½ hours. Drain well. Rinse. Drain again.

2. Combine sugar, mustard seed, turmeric, celery seed, ginger, and vinegar in a large stockpot over medium-high heat. Bring to a boil. Add cucumbers and onions. Return to a boil.

3. Pack pickles and liquid into hot, sterilized jars, leaving ½-inch headspace. Remove air bubbles. Secure flat lids and rings. Process in a boiling-water canner bath for 10 minutes, or adjust time to your altitude. See "Safe Canning and Preserving," page 182, for detailed instructions. Makes 7 pints.

※ **LISA FINDLAY,** Chubbuck, Idaho
First Place, North Bannock County Fair, Pocatello, Idaho, 2005

Fruit Relish

4 pears, peeled, cored, and cut into quarters

4 peaches, peeled and pit removed

4 ripe tomatoes, peeled

1 onion, peeled and cut into quarters

1 green pepper, seeded and cut
into quarters

¾ cup sugar

1½ cups vinegar

2 teaspoons salt

¼ teaspoon cayenne

⅛ teaspoon cinnamon

⅛ teaspoon ground cloves

1. Combine pears, peaches, tomatoes, onion, and green pepper in a food processor. Chop or grate into small pieces.

2. Combine chopped mixture, sugar, vinegar, salt, cayenne, cinnamon, and cloves in a large saucepan over medium-high heat. Bring to a boil, reduce to a simmer, and cook, stirring frequently, until thick.

3. Pour relish into hot, sterilized jars, leaving ½-inch headspace. Remove air bubbles. Secure flat lids and rings. Process in a boiling-water canner bath for 15 minutes, or adjust time to your altitude. See "Safe Canning and Preserving," page 182, for detailed instructions. Makes 3 pints.

✄ **FRANCINE RIPPY,** Hacienda Heights, California
First Place, Best of Division, L.A. County Fair, Pomona, California, 2003

Zucchini Relish

2½ cups finely chopped fresh zucchini
(about 4 medium zucchini)

1 finely chopped cup onion

½ cup seeded and finely chopped
sweet green bell pepper

½ cup seeded and finely chopped
sweet red bell pepper

1 cup cider vinegar

2 tablespoons salt

1¾ cups sugar

2 teaspoons celery seed

1 teaspoon mustard seed

1. Combine zucchini, onion, and green and red bell pepper in a large stockpot. Sprinkle with salt and cover with cold water. Let stand for 2 hours. Drain, rinse, and drain again thoroughly.

2. Combine vinegar, salt, sugar, celery seed, and mustard seed in a large saucepan over medium heat. Add zucchini mixture. Simmer until heated through, 10 to 15 minutes.

3. Pack relish into hot, sterilized half-pint jars, leaving ½-inch headspace. Remove air bubbles. Secure flat lids and rings. Process in a boiling-water canner bath for 10 minutes, or adjust time to your altitude. See "Safe Canning and Preserving," page 182, for detailed instructions. Makes 2 pints.

✄ **TAMMY CIAMMITTI,** Desert Hills, Arizona
First Prize, Arizona State Fair, Phoenix, Arizona, 2005

SWEET PEPPER RELISH

4 cups seeded and chopped
    sweet green bell pepper
2 cups seeded and chopped
    sweet red bell pepper
1 cup chopped onion
Boiling water

¾ cup sugar
2 teaspoons salt
1½ cups vinegar
½ tablespoon celery seed
½ tablespoon mustard seed

1. Combine green bell pepper, red bell pepper, and onion in a large bowl. Add boiling water to cover. Let stand for 5 minutes. Drain. Cover again with boiling water. Let stand for 10 minutes. Drain.
2. Combine sugar, salt, vinegar, celery seed, and mustard seed in a large saucepan over medium-low heat. Simmer for 15 minutes. Add peppers and onion and simmer 10 minutes longer.
3. Pack relish into hot, sterilized jars, leaving ½-inch headspace. Remove air bubbles. Secure flat lids and rings. Process in a boiling-water canner bath for 15 minutes, or adjust time to your altitude. See "Safe Canning and Preserving," page 182, for detailed instructions. Makes 4½ pints.

※ **PHYLLIS CANIPE,** Lawndale, North Carolina
Blue Ribbon, Cleveland County Fair, Shelby, North Carolina, 2003

DATE-PEAR RELISH

3 cups cored and diced peeled pears
1 cup cored and chopped peeled apples
½ cup diced onions
2 cups chopped dates
½ cup seeded and diced red bell peppers
½ cup seeded and diced green bell peppers
1 cup diced celery

3 cups sugar
⅓ teaspoon ground allspice
⅓ teaspoon salt
⅓ teaspoon cinnamon
1¾ cups apple cider vinegar
3 cinnamon sticks, broken in half

1. Combine pears, apple, onion, dates, red and green bell pepper, celery, sugar, allspice, salt, cinnamon, and apple cider vinegar in a stockpot. Cover and let stand overnight.
2. Place stockpot over medium-high heat. Bring to a boil. Cook for 15 minutes.
3. Pack relish and half a cinnamon stick into hot, sterilized jars, leaving ½-inch headspace. Remove air bubbles. Secure flat lids and rings. Process in a boiling-water canner bath for 20 minutes, or adjust time to your altitude. See "Safe Canning and Preserving," page 182, for detailed instructions. Makes 6 pints.

※ **TWILA BOOTH,** San Jacinto, California
First Place, Relishes, Riverside County Fair and National Date Festival, Indio, California, 2003–2004

BLACKBERRY JUICE

Blackberries
Sugar

1. Crush blackberries in a large stockpot. Place pot over low heat, add a small amount of water to prevent sticking, and simmer until blackberries are soft.

2. Strain berry mixture through several layers of cheesecloth. Measure juice, pour back into stockpot, and add 1 cup sugar per quart of juice. Cook for 5 minutes.

3. Ladle juice into hot, sterilized jars, leaving ½-inch headspace. Remove air bubbles. Secure flat lids and rings. Process in a boiling-water canner bath for 15 minutes, or adjust time to your altitude. See "Safe Canning and Preserving," page 182, for detailed instructions. Yield varies.

For clearer juice, let strained juice stand in refrigerator overnight before cooking.

✂ **PHYLLIS CANIPE,** Lawndale, North Carolina
Blue Ribbon, Cleveland County Fair, Shelby, North Carolina, 2005

APRICOT NECTAR

2 lbs. apricots, pitted and sliced (about 6 cups)
5 cups water
1 cup sugar

1. Combine apricots and water in a Dutch oven over medium heat. Cook until apricots are softened, 10 minutes.

2. Puree apricots and water in a blender. Measure 7 cups of purée. Put purée and sugar into Dutch oven over medium heat. Cook until sugar is dissolved and mixture is heated through.

3. Pour juice into hot, sterilized jars, leaving ½-inch headspace. Remove air bubbles. Secure flat lids and rings. Process in a boiling-water canner bath for 10 minutes, or adjust time to your altitude. See "Safe Canning and Preserving," page 182, for detailed instructions. Before serving, chill and shake well. Makes 4 pints.

✂ **KARI HUGHES,** Pocatello, Idaho
First Place, North Bannock County Fair,
Pocatello, Idaho, 2005

Red Pepper–Tomato Relish

½ cup olive oil

1⅔ cups chopped onion

1¾ lbs. sweet red bell peppers, blanched
    or charred, skins removed

1½ cups red wine vinegar

1½ lbs. ripe plum tomatoes, scalded
    with skins removed

1¼ cups sugar

1 tablespoon lemon juice

1 cup golden raisins

2 medium garlic cloves

¼ teaspoon ground ginger

½ teaspoon salt

¼ teaspoon ground allspice

¼ teaspoon red pepper flakes

1. Combine olive oil and onion in a large heavy saucepan over medium-low heat. Cook, stirring often, until onions are golden.

2. Core red bell peppers, cut into quarters, and slice crosswise into ¼-inch strips (about 2 cups). Add pepper to onion. Cover cook over low heat until pepper is softened, 10 minutes.

3. Add red wine vinegar to onion and peppers. Bring to a boil and cook, uncovered, until reduced by half.

4. Cut up tomatoes and puree in food processor. Pass through a sieve to remove seeds. Stir 2 cups tomato purée into peppers and onions. Add sugar, lemon juice, raisins, garlic, ginger, salt, allspice, and red pepper flakes. Bring to a simmer. Cover and cook over low heat for 1½ hours, stirring occasionally. Remove cover during last ½ hour of cooking.

5. Spoon relish into hot, sterilized jars, leaving ½-inch headspace. Remove air bubbles. Secure flat lids and rings. Process in a boiling-water canner bath for 10 minutes, or adjust time to your altitude. See "Safe Canning and Preserving," page 182, for detailed instructions. Relish will thicken as it cools. Makes 2½ pints.

※ **Cheryl Lewis,** Escondido, California
First Place, San Diego County Fair, Del Mar, California, 2004

Rhubarb Sauce

Rhubarb, washed
Sugar
Red food coloring (optional)

1. Trim off both ends of rhubarb stalks. Cut into ½-inch pieces.

2. Measure rhubarb into stockpot. Add ½ to 1 cup sugar per quart of rhubarb. Let stand, covered, at room temperature to draw out juices, 4 hours.

3. Place stockpot over medium heat and gradually bring mixture to a boil. Boil for 30 seconds. Remove from heat. Add a few drops of red food coloring if desired.

4. Pour sauce into hot, sterilized jars, leaving ½-inch headspace. Remove air bubbles. Secure flat lids and rings. Process pints and quarts in a boiling-water canner bath for 15 minutes, or adjust time to your altitude. See "Safe Canning and Preserving," page 182, for detailed instructions. Yield varies.

※ **Barbara Lamy,** Terryville, Connecticut
Blue Ribbon, First Place, Terryville Country Fair, Terryville, Connecticut, 2005

CHILI SAUCE

4½ cups distilled white vinegar
2 tablespoons whole cloves
3 cinnamon sticks, broken in half
1 tablespoon celery seed
1 tablespoon whole allspice
15 lbs. (about 45 medium) tomatoes,
    peeled and chopped, divided

3 cups sugar, divided
½ cup chopped onion
½ teaspoon cayenne
2 tablespoons salt

1. Combine white vinegar, cloves, cinnamon sticks, celery seed, and allspice in a medium saucepan over medium heat. Remove from heat and let stand.

2. Combine half of the tomatoes, 1½ cups of the sugar, onion, and cayenne in a 6- to 8-quart saucepan over medium-high heat. Bring to a boil, reduce heat, and simmer, stirring often, 40 minutes.

3. Add remaining tomatoes and remaining 1½ cups sugar. Boil, stirring often, 40 minutes longer.

4. Strain the reserved vinegar mixture and discard spices. Stir vinegar and salt into tomato mixture. Cook until mixture reaches desired consistency, 30 minutes.

5. Pour sauce into hot, sterilized jars, leaving ½-inch headspace. Remove air bubbles. Secure flat lids and rings. Process in a boiling-water canner bath for 15 minutes, or adjust time to your altitude. See "Safe Canning and Preserving," page 182, for detailed instructions. Makes 6 pints.

MARYLAN WHITAKER, Chubbuck, Idaho
First Place, North Bannock County Fair, Pocatello, Idaho, 2005

WINNER'S CIRCLE TIP | Adding the tomatoes and sugar in two batches helps preserve the red color. Avoid using pots and utensils made of zinc, iron, brass, copper, aluminum, or galvanized metal when making chili sauce as these react chemically with both the acids and the salt in the chili sauce mixture.

CHAPTER 9

FRUIT DESSERTS

PUDDINGS, PUFFS, CUSTARDS, AND DUMPLINGS

Apple Enchilada Dessert

4 oz. cream cheese, room temperature
½ cup sugar, divided
¼ teaspoon vanilla
6 8-inch flour tortillas
1 can (21 oz.) apple pie filling
Cinnamon
½ cup water
½ cup brown sugar
⅓ cup unsalted butter, room temperature

TOPPING
½ cup confectioners' sugar
⅛ teaspoon vanilla
2 teaspoons milk
Chopped pecans
Pecan halves

Garnish these dessert enchiladas with red and green apple peelings.

1. Preheat oven to 350°F. Lightly grease an 8 x 8 x 2-inch baking pan.

2. In a small mixing bowl, beat cream cheese, ¼ cup of the sugar, and vanilla until thoroughly blended.

3. Spread cream cheese mixture evenly over the six flour tortillas. Top with apple pie filling and sprinkle with cinnamon. Roll up tortillas and place seam side down in baking pan.

4. Combine water, remaining ¼ cup sugar, brown sugar, and butter in a medium saucepan. Bring to a boil, reduce heat, and simmer, stirring continuously, for 3 minutes. Pour sauce evenly over tortillas; sprinkle with cinnamon. Bake for 20 minutes. Remove from oven and cool slightly.

5. To make topping: In a small bowl, combine confectioners' sugar, vanilla, and milk. Place each tortilla on a serving plate. Drizzle glaze over top and decorate with chopped pecans and pecan halves. Makes 6 large tortillas.

⌘ **Elaine Hrdy-Straka,** Oklahoma City, Oklahoma
Second Place, Mexican Contest, Oklahoma State Fair, Oklahoma City, Oklahoma, 2005

Autumn Apple Pudding

2 cups cinnamon bread crumbs
2 cups chopped apples
½ cup raisins
½ cup sweetened dried cranberries
¾ cups sugar
2 tablespoons flour
½ teaspoon cinnamon
½ teaspoon mace
½ teaspoon nutmeg

2 large eggs, beaten
½ cup melted butter
1 teaspoon vanilla

BRANDIED NUTMEG HARD SAUCE
½ cup soft unsalted butter, room temperature
1½ cup confectioners' sugar
2 teaspoons ginger brandy
1 teaspoon nutmeg

1. Preheat oven to 325°F. Set aside a pudding mold or baking dish for the pudding. Set aside a large pan for the water bath.

2. In a large bowl, toss bread crumbs, apples, raisins, cranberries, sugar, flour, cinnamon, mace, and nutmeg until well combined.

3. Whisk together eggs, melted butter, and vanilla; pour over crumb mixture and stir until combined. Pour pudding mixture into mold or baking dish; cover tightly with aluminum foil. Set mold in large pan and pour boiling water into pan to make water bath. Bake for 2 hours, or until pudding pulls away from side of pan and is firm to the touch. Cool for 20 minutes. Unmold into a serving dish.

4. To make brandied nutmeg hard sauce: In a small mixing bowl, cream together butter, confectioners' sugar, ginger brandy, and nutmeg. Place hard sauce in a separate serving dish to accompany pudding. Makes 4 to 6 servings.

※ **SALLY SIBTHORPE,** Rochester Hills, Michigan
First Place, Michigan Apple Dessert Day Contest, Michigan State Fair, Detroit, Michigan, 2001

CREAMY LEMON SUPREME

CRUST
Cooking spray
16 lemon cream-filled sandwich cookies, finely chopped (1½ cups)
5 tablespoons butter, room temperature
1 lemon, thinly sliced

FILLING
4 teaspoons cornstarch
4 tablespoons instant lemon drink mix
½ cup sugar
2 cups water, divided

2 egg yolks
1 tablespoon butter or margarine, room temperature
¼ cup lemon juice
2 packages (8 oz. each) cream cheese, room temperature
½ cup plus 2 tablespoons confectioners' sugar, divided
1½ teaspoons grated lemon zest, divided
2 cups heavy cream
½ cup fresh raspberries, or ½ cup raspberry syrup

1. To make crust: Lightly coat a 10-inch springform pan with cooking spray. Combine cookie crumbs and butter. Press crumb mixture into bottom of pan. Arrange 6 lemon slices on top of crust. Chill.

2. To make filling: Combine cornstarch, lemon drink mix, sugar, ¼ cup of the water, and egg yolks in medium saucepan; stir until blended. Add remaining 1¾ cups water. Cook over medium heat, stirring continuously, until mixture comes to a boil. Remove from heat. Measure and set aside ½ cup of the filling. Cool remaining filling slightly and then whisk in butter and lemon juice. Cool for 15 minutes, stirring twice.

3. In a large mixing bowl, beat cream cheese and ½ cup of the confectioners' sugar until fluffy. Whisk in reserved ½ cup filling and 1 teaspoon of the lemon zest.

4. In a separate mixing bowl, whip heavy cream and remaining 2 tablespoons confectioners' sugar until stiff peaks form. Fold 2 cups of the whipped cream into the cream cheese mixture. Spread filling over crust. Stir filling in the saucepan, spoon it over cream cheese mixture, and spread evenly. Chill at least 6 hours. To serve, run a knife around the sides of pan and release and remove the collar. Top with remaining whipped cream, remaining ½ teaspoon zest, and raspberries. Garnish with lemon wedges, if desired. Makes 12 servings.

※ **MACKENZIE MERCER,** age 15, Ionia, Michigan
First Place and Grand Champion Dessert, Dairy Delight Contest, Ionia Free Fair, Ionia, Michigan, 2005

Apple Bread Pudding

½ cup unsalted butter, room temperature
2 cups milk
1 cup sugar
4 eggs, beaten
1 teaspoon vanilla
12 Hawaiian sweet dinner rolls
2 apples, finely chopped
¾ teaspoon cinnamon
¼ teaspoon nutmeg

CARAMEL SAUCE
½ cup unsalted butter, room temperature
¼ cup sugar
¼ cup brown sugar
¼ cup heavy cream
1 teaspoon vanilla

1. Preheat oven to 350°F. Lightly grease a baking dish.
2. Combine butter, milk, and sugar in a medium saucepan over low heat; cook until butter is melted. Cool. Mix in eggs and vanilla until well blended.
3. Tear dinner rolls into small pieces. Layer into baking dish.
4. Microwave chopped apples on high for 1 minute, until warm. Layer apples into baking dish. Pour custard over the apples. Combine cinnamon and nutmeg and sprinkle over the top. Bake for 20 to 30 minutes.
5. To make caramel sauce: Combine butter, sugar, and brown sugar in a small saucepan over medium heat. When butter is melted, add heavy cream. Boil for 1 minute. Remove from heat and stir in vanilla. To serve, spoon pudding into individual dishes and drizzle with caramel sauce. Makes 4 to 6 servings.

※ **DONNA HUNN,** Cary, North Carolina
Third Place, N.C. Egg Association's Eggs & Apples Recipe Contest, North Carolina State Fair, Raleigh, North Carolina, 2005

Lemon Dessert

Butter for custard cups
4 eggs, separated
1¾ cups sugar
6 tablespoons cake flour
2 cups milk

Juice of 2 lemons
Grated zest of 1 lemon
Hot water
Whipped cream

1. Preheat oven to 275°F. Butter 8 custard cups. Set cups in a large shallow pan for the water bath.
2. In a medium mixing bowl, beat egg yolks until light and lemon-colored. Add sugar, flour, milk, lemon juice, and zest; mix until well blended.
3. In a separate bowl, beat egg whites until stiff peaks form. Fold gently into lemon mixture.
4. Pour mixture into custard cups. Place water bath pan in oven. Carefully pour hot water into pan around cups. Bake for 1 hour. Cool. To serve, invert cups onto individual plates and top with whipped cream. Lemon pudding will be on top of the cake after inverting. Makes 8 servings.

※ **VI GRUNDMAYER,** Eagan, Minnesota
Third Prize, Dairy Cooking Contest, Dakota County Fair, Farmington, Minnesota, 2005

CARAMEL EGGS AND APPLE BREAD PUDDING

Cooking spray
4 large eggs
2 cups milk
½ cup sugar
1 teaspoon vanilla
1 teaspoon cinnamon

5 medium to large croissants
1 container (8 oz.) honey nut cream cheese
1 oz. raisins
1 large Granny Smith apple, peeled,
    cored and grated
½ cup caramel topping

1. Preheat oven to 350°F. Lightly coat a 2-quart casserole dish with cooking spray.

2. In a large bowl, whisk eggs until frothy. Whisk in milk, sugar, vanilla, and cinnamon until well combined.

3. Slice croissants in half and open them up. Spread one half of each croissant generously with cream cheese. Divide raisins evenly among the croissants, sprinkling them over the cream cheese. Pile apples on top of raisins. Place tops back on croissants, sandwiching the fillings in between. Place croissants in casserole dish, squeezing them together to fit. Pour egg mixture into dish; press down on croissants to help them absorb the liquid. Bake for 40 minutes, or until middle is set. Serve hot with caramel topping. Makes 4 to 6 servings.

※ **CONNIE PEGG,** Asheville, North Carolina
Second Place, North Carolina Egg Association's Eggs & Apples Recipe Contest, North Carolina Mountain State Fair, Fletcher, North Carolina, 2005

WINNER'S CIRCLE TIP | You can make this now and bake it later. Cover and refrigerate the pudding if you won't be baking it until the next day.

BLUEBERRY DESSERT PIZZA

1 package (18.2 oz.) yellow cake mix
1½ cups quick-cooking rolled oats, divided
½ cup margarine, divided
1 egg

½ cup chopped nuts
¼ cup brown sugar
½ teaspoon cinnamon
1 can (21 oz.) blueberry pie filling

1. Preheat oven to 350°F. Lightly grease a 12-inch pizza pan.

2. In a large mixing bowl, combine cake mix, 1 cup of the oats, and 6 tablespoons of the margarine until crumbly. Set aside 1 cup of the crumb mixture for the topping. To the remaining mixture, add egg and blend well. Press mixture into bottom of pizza pan. Bake for 12 minutes.

3. To make topping, combine reserved crumb mixture, remaining ½ cup oatmeal, remaining 2 tablespoons margarine, nuts, brown sugar, and cinnamon until well blended.

4. Spread blueberry pie filling over crust in pizza pan. Sprinkle topping over blueberries. Bake for 15 to 20 minutes, or until the crumbs are light golden brown. Serve warm or at room temperature. Makes 6 to 8 servings.

※ **ANDREA HOWARD,** Dickinson County, Kansas
Second Place, Central Kansas Free Fair, Abilene, Kansas, 2005

APPLE CRISP

4 cups peeled, cored, and sliced tart apples
¾ cup sugar
½ cup all-purpose flour
½ cup rolled oats

¾ teaspoon cinnamon
¾ teaspoon nutmeg
⅓ cup unsalted butter, room temperature

1. Preheat oven to 375°F. Lightly grease an 8 x 8 x 2-inch baking pan.
2. Layer apple slices in pan.
3. In a medium bowl, combine sugar, flour, oats, cinnamon, and nutmeg. Cut in butter until crumbly. Sprinkle mixture over apples. Bake until topping is golden brown and apples are tender, about 30 minutes. Makes 4 to 6 servings.

✂ **NATHAN MOORE,** Leicester, Vermont
Best Apple Baked Goods, Addison County Fair & Field Days, New Haven, Vermont, 2005

APPLE DUMPLINGS

2 apples, peeled, cored, and quartered
2 tubes (8 oz. each) refrigerated
    crescent rolls
1 cup water

1 cup sugar
¾ cup brown sugar
½ cup unsalted butter, room temperature
Cinnamon

1. Preheat oven to 350°F.
2. Wrap each apple quarter in a triangle of crescent roll dough and place in a round baking dish.
3. Combine water, sugar, brown sugar, and butter in a medium saucepan. Bring to a boil; pour over dumplings. Sprinkle cinnamon over top. Bake for 30 to 40 minutes. Serve warm with cream, if desired. Makes 8 dumplings.

✂ **DRUSILLA TROYER,** Montezuma, Georgia
First Place, Georgia Apple Recipe Contest, Georgia National Fair, Perry, Georgia, 2005

APPLE-CRANBERRY DELIGHT

4 cups peeled, cored, and chopped apples
½ cup whole fresh or frozen cranberries
½ cup light brown sugar
½ teaspoon pumpkin pie spice
⅛ teaspoon nutmeg
½ cup fresh orange juice

TOPPING
¾ cup graham cracker crumbs
½ cup rolled oats
⅓ cup flaked coconut
2 tablespoons sugar
¼ cup margarine, room temperature
½ cup chopped pecans

1. Preheat oven to 350°F.

2. In a 10-inch round glass baking dish, combine apples, cranberries, light brown sugar, pumpkin pie spice, nutmeg, and orange juice. Bake for 1 hour, or until apples are tender. Cool.

3. To make topping: In a 10-inch skillet, combine graham cracker crumbs, oats, coconut, sugar, margarine, and pecans over medium heat. Cook until lightly browned. Pour over apples. Return baking dish to a 350°F oven for 20 minutes, to warm apples. Cool slightly. Serve with whipped cream or ice cream, if desired. Makes 6 to 8 servings.

✻ **MARY HOYLMAN,** White Sulphur Springs, West Virginia
First Place, Apple Dessert Celebration, State Fair of West Virginia, Lewisburg, West Virginia, 2005

> Use Golden Delicious apples for a pretty contrast with the red cranberries.

CREAMY APPLE PUFFS

1 package (17.3 oz.) puff pastry shells
1 teaspoon grated lemon zest
¾ cup part-skim ricotta
¼ cup crumbled Gorgonzola
¼ cup whipped cream cheese spread
¼ cup honey

4 or 5 Granny Smith apples, peeled, cored, and sliced into bite-size pieces (3½ cups)
1 tablespoon unsalted butter, room temperature
2 tablespoons cinnamon sugar
Sweetened whipped cream

1. Preheat oven to 400°F. Bake pastry shells according to package directions. Remove tops and pull out centers of shells.

2. In a medium mixing bowl, combine lemon zest, ricotta, Gorgonzola, cream cheese spread, and honey. Beat until well blended. Chill.

3. Set a large sauté pan over medium heat for 2 to 3 minutes. Add butter and swirl to coat bottom of pan. Add apples and sprinkle with cinnamon sugar. Cover and cook, stirring occasionally, until tender and browned, 6 to 8 minutes. Cool.

4. Spoon cheese mixture into pastry shells. Top with apple mixture. Pipe whipped cream on top. Chill until ready to serve. Makes 6 servings.

✻ **KAREN SLAUGHTER,** Warner Robins, Georgia
Georgia National Fair, Perry, Georgia, 2005

FROZEN BANANAS

4 ripe bananas
8 ice pop sticks
2 cups chocolate chips or broken semisweet baking chocolate, divided
Chopped nuts (optional)

1. Peel bananas and cut crosswise in half. Insert an ice pop stick into each cut end for a handle.
2. Melt about ½ cup of the chocolate in a deep coffee cup. Dip bananas until well coated.
3. Roll bananas in remaining 1½ cups chocolate chips and bits and in nuts until well coated.
4. Place bananas on a tray covered with waxed paper. Freeze for at least 1 hour before serving. Makes 8 servings.

※ *Friends of the California State Fair Cookbook,* Sacramento, California

BLUEBERRY-OAT DESSERT

½ **cup sugar**
2 tablespoons cornstarch
⅓ **cup water**
1 teaspoon lemon juice
2½ **cups fresh or frozen blueberries**

1 package (8¼ oz.) yellow cake mix
1½ **cups quick-cooking rolled oats, divided**
8 tablespoons cold unsalted butter, divided
2 eggs
¼ **cup brown sugar**

1. Preheat oven to 350°F. Coat a 13 x 9 x 2-inch baking dish coated with cooking spray.
2. Combine sugar and cornstarch in a large saucepan. Gradually whisk in water and lemon juice until smooth. Bring to a boil, stirring continuously. Stir in blueberries. Cook, stirring continuously, until thickened and bubbly, 2 minutes longer. Remove from heat.
3. In a large bowl, combine cake mix and 1 cup of the oats. Cut in 6 tablespoons of the butter until crumbly. Set aside 1 cup of the crumb mixture for the topping. To the remaining mixture, add eggs and blend well. Press mixture into baking dish to within ¼ inch of edges. Pour blueberry mixture over crust.
4. To make topping, combine reserved crumb mixture, remaining ½ cup oats, and brown sugar; cut in remaining 2 tablespoons butter until crumbly. Sprinkle evenly over blueberries. Bake for 30 to 35 minutes, or until golden brown. Serve warm. Makes 18 servings.

※ **MARISSA GRENARD,** Country Kids 4-H, La Junta, Colorado
First Place, Bar Cookies, Arkansas Valley Fair, Rocky Ford, Colorado, 2005

BREAD PUDDING

1½ cups bread cubes, firmly packed
2 cups milk
3 eggs, lightly beaten
2 ripe bananas, sliced
1 apple, peeled, cored, and thinly sliced

½ cup raisins
½ cup sugar
1½ teaspoons cinnamon
Hot water
1 cup whipped cream

1. Preheat oven to 350°F. Butter a soufflé dish. Set aside a large shallow pan for the water bath.

2. Combine bread cubes and milk in a large bowl. Let stand for 10 minutes.

3. Mash the bread mixture with a fork. Stir in eggs, bananas, apple, raisins, sugar, and cinnamon. Pour mixture into soufflé dish. Set dish in large pan and pour hot water into pan for water path. Bake until a knife inserted in center comes out clean, 1 to 1½ hours. Cool and serve with whipped cream. Makes 6 to 8 servings.

⌗ **XARVELL BARKLEY,** DeLand, Florida
First Place, Baked Goods—Exceptional, Volusia County Fair, DeLand, Florida, 2004

PEACHES AND CREAM DESSERT

PASTRY
2 cups all-purpose flour
¼ teaspoon baking powder
2 tablespoons sugar
½ teaspoon salt
½ cup unsalted butter, just at
    room temperature

FILLING
8 large ripe Delaware-grown peaches, peeled
1 tablespoon grated lemon zest
½ cup sugar
¾ teaspoon cinnamon
2 egg yolks
1 cup heavy cream

1. Preheat oven to 400°F. Set aside a 9 x 9 x 2-inch glass baking dish; do not grease.

2. To make pastry: In a medium bowl, sift together flour, baking powder, sugar, and salt. Cut in butter until mixture resembles cornmeal. Press firmly onto bottom and sides of baking dish.

3. To make filling: Slice peaches in half and remove pits. Drain on paper towels. Arrange 9 peach halves on bottom of pastry. Cut the remaining 7 peach halves into 1-inch thick slices. Arrange slices over pastry to fill in the bare spaces. Sprinkle lemon zest over peaches. Combine sugar and cinnamon; sprinkle over top. Bake for 15 minutes.

4. Reduce oven temperature to 375°F. Combine egg yolks and heavy cream until well blended. Pour mixture over top of peaches, being careful not to disturb the cinnamon-sugar topping. Bake 30 minutes longer, or until custard is firm. Serve warm or chilled. Refrigerate leftovers. Makes 9 servings.

⌗ **CLARICE KWASNIESKI,** Middletown, Delaware
First Place, Fifer Orchards' Annual Peach Dessert Competition, Delaware State Fair, Harrington, Delaware, 2005

WINNER'S CIRCLE TIP | To substitute canned peaches for fresh, use 29-oz. cans of peach halves and peach slices. Drain 9 peaches halves and 24 peach slices. Save the leftover peaches and juice for another use.

Noodle Pudding with Apples

1¼ cups unsalted butter, room temperature,
   plus more for pan
1 package (16 oz.) medium egg noodles
6 oz. cream cheese at room temperature
1 cup honey
1 teaspoon vanilla

¼ to ½ teaspoon cinnamon
5 eggs
1 cup sour cream
4 crisp apples, peeled, cored, and diced
¼ cup sliced almonds

1. Preheat oven to 350°F. Butter a 13 x 9 x 2-inch baking pan.

2. Cook noodles according to package directions. Drain and rinse immediately in cold water. Let drain well. Transfer noodles to a large bowl.

3. In a medium mixing bowl, cream together butter and cream cheese. Beat in honey, vanilla, and cinnamon. Add eggs one at a time, beating well after each addition. Beat in sour cream.

4. Pour creamed mixture over noodles and mix well. Add apples and toss to coat. Transfer pudding into baking pan. Sprinkle with almonds. Bake 45 to 60 minutes, or until set and golden brown. Cut into squares and serve warm. Makes 10 to 12 servings.

✕ **FELICE BOGUS,** Raleigh, North Carolina
First Place, N.C. Egg Association's Eggs & Apples Recipe Contest, North Carolina State Fair, Raleigh, North Carolina, 2005

Blueberry-Maple Mousse

6 egg yolks
⅔ cup maple syrup, heated

1 pint heavy cream
1 pint Maine wild blueberries

1. The day before, place a 1½-quart mold in freezer overnight to chill.

2. Beat egg yolks in the top half of a double boiler until thick. Beat in hot syrup. Place over simmering water and cook, beating continuously, until slightly thickened. Cool.

3. In a small mixing bowl, beat heavy cream until stiff peaks form. Fold whipped cream into yolk mixture. Fold in half of the blueberries. Place remaining blueberries in chilled mold. Pour cream mixture over the top. Chill until ready to serve. Makes 8 servings.

✕ **GENIE HALL,** Machias, Maine
Overall Winner, Wild Blueberry Festival Cooking Competition, Machias, Maine, 1997

Easy Baked Peach Dumplings

1 package (8 oz.) crescent rolls
1 can (28 oz.) sliced peaches, drained
   with 1 cup of juice reserved
1 cup sugar

¼ cup unsalted butter, melted
½ teaspoon nutmeg
½ teaspoon cinnamon

1. Preheat oven to 350°F. Lightly coat 13 x 9 x 2-inch baking dish with cooking spray.

2. Roll out two crescent rolls together, sealing seams to form a rectangle. Cut in half to form two squares.

3. Spoon 5 or 6 peach slices in the center of each crescent square. Pinch edges and corners together to seal. Place in baking dish with pinched edges down.

4. Combine reserved juice, sugar, melted butter, nutmeg, and cinnamon in a microwave-safe dish. Microwave for 1 minute and stir. Repeat if needed until sugar is dissolved. Pour over peach dumplings. Bake for 35 to 40 minutes, or until golden. Serve warm. Makes 8 servings.

✳ **CARLA GARNTO,** Warner Robins, Georgia
Third Place, Just Peachy Contest, Georgia National Fair, Perry, Georgia, 2005

PEACHES AND DREAMS

1 box (3.4 oz.) instant vanilla pudding
1 cup cold milk
1 cup heavy cream
8 medium to large ripe peaches, peeled and
   thinly sliced, plus more slices for garnish

1 angel food cake
Fresh mint leaves
Whipped cream

1. In a blender, combine pudding, milk, and heavy cream; blend for 2 minutes.

2. Pour pudding mixture into a large bowl. Add sliced peaches. Blend with a hand-held mixer for 5 minutes.

3. Cut angel food cake into cubes. Layer cubes and peach mixture into individual glass dessert dishes, repeating the layers until the dishes are full. Chill until ready to serve. Garnish each serving with a peach slice, mint leaves, and whipped cream. Makes 8 servings.

✳ **JEROME RASKA,** Detroit, Michigan
First Place, Peach Dessert Contest, Michigan State Fair, Detroit, Michigan, 2001

RICE PUDDING

1 quart whole milk
½ cup rice
½ cup sugar

Dash of salt
2 egg yolks
½ cup heavy cream

1. The day before, combine milk, rice, sugar, and salt in a large saucepan over medium-high heat. Bring to a boil, stirring occasionally, until mixture begins to thicken.

2. Add egg yolks to mixture and transfer to the top half of a double boiler. Cook over simmering water, stirring occasionally, until thickened. Cover and chill overnight.

3. Just before serving, beat heavy cream until soft peaks form; fold into pudding. Serve chilled with fresh fruit or cookies, if desired. Makes 8 servings.

✳ **KASSA ANDREASEN,** Rosemount, Minnesota
Second Prize, Dairy Cooking Contest, Dakota County Fair, Farmington, Minnesota, 2005

BLUEBERRY-LEMON DELIGHT

1 egg
½ cup unsalted butter,
    room temperature
½ cup milk
1½ teaspoons lemon flavoring
1 teaspoon grated lemon zest
2 cups all-purpose flour
¾ cup sugar
2 teaspoons baking powder

½ teaspoon salt
1½ cups fresh blueberries
¾ cup pecans, chopped

TOPPING
½ cup sugar
⅓ cup all-purpose flour
¼ cup unsalted butter, chilled
½ cup chopped pecans

1. Preheat oven to 375°F. Grease a 9 x 9 x 2-inch baking pan.
2. In a large mixing bowl, beat egg and butter until light and fluffy. Beat in milk, lemon flavoring, and zest. With mixer running, add flour, sugar, baking powder, and salt. Gently fold in blueberries and pecans. Spread batter into baking pan.
3. To make topping: In a small bowl, whisk together sugar and flour. Cut in butter until crumbly. Stir in pecans. Sprinkle topping evenly over batter in pan. Bake for 35 minutes, or until a tester inserted in center comes out clean. Cool in pan. Makes 8 servings.

✕ **CHRISTINE McDANIEL,** Dearborn Heights, Michigan
Second Place, Michigan Blueberry Creation, Michigan State Fair, Detroit, Michigan, 2000

RØMMEGRØT (NORWEGIAN CREAM PUDDING)

1 quart heavy cream
¾ cup all-purpose flour
1 quart milk, boiled
½ teaspoon salt

¼ cup unsalted butter, melted
White or brown sugar
Cinnamon
Raisins, soaked in water and drained (optional)

1. Place heavy cream in a large saucepan over medium-high heat. Bring to a boil and cook for 15 minutes.
2. Slowly add flour, stirring continuously. Add boiled milk, stirring continuously. Reduce heat to a simmer. Continue cooking until thick. Stir in salt.
3. Pour pudding into a serving dish. Pour melted butter over top. Sprinkle with sugar and cinnamon. Dot with raisins, if using. Makes 10 to 12 servings.

✕ **CORA HALVERSON,** Lake Side, Montana
First Place, What Mother Would Have Made, Western Montana Fair, Missoula, Montana, 2004

CHAPTER 10

PIES, COBBLERS,
AND TARTS

Loraine's Apple Pie

CRUST

1 cup all-purpose flour, plus more
    for rolling out dough
½ teaspoon salt
⅓ cup shortening
Water

FILLING

3 cups chopped apples
⅓ cup all-purpose flour
1 cup sugar
½ teaspoon cinnamon
½ teaspoon nutmeg
Pinch of salt

1. Preheat oven to 375°F. Lightly grease a pie plate.

2. To make crust: Whisk together flour and salt in a bowl. Cut in shortening with your fingers. Sprinkle water over the top, mixing just until all flour is moistened and dough is soft and workable.

3. Gather up dough and divide in half. Pat into two round disks. Roll out one disk on a lightly floured surface until slightly larger than pie plate. Fold into quarters, set in pie plate, and gently unfold. Chill pie shell and remaining dough while making filling.

4. To make filling: Combine chopped apples, flour, sugar, cinnamon, nutmeg, and salt.

5. Spoon filling into pie shell. Roll out second dough disk and lay over pie filling. Trim, seal, and flute the edges. Cover the edges with strips of aluminum foil to prevent excess browning. Cut slits in top crust for steam to escape. Bake for 40 minutes. Makes 1 double-crust pie.

✂ **LORAINE HESCOCK,** Shoreham, Vermont
Best Apple Pie, Addison County Fair & Field Days, New Haven, Vermont, 2004

WINNER'S CIRCLE TIP | Use a blend of apples for more flavor and texture. Try a mix of Granny Smith, Cortland, Empire, Gala, and Red Delicious.

Whiskey Apple Pie

Double-crust pie pastry
2 tablespoons all-purpose flour, plus
    more for rolling out dough
6 or 7 Golden Delicious apples
⅓ cup sugar
½ teaspoon cinnamon

½ teaspoon nutmeg
¼ teaspoon salt
½ cup bourbon whiskey
2 tablespoons lemon juice
2 tablespoons butter, cut into small pieces
Whipped cream

1. Preheat oven to 425°F. Divide pastry in half. Roll out one half on a lightly floured surgace and fit into a 9-inch pie plate. Roll out the remaining pastry for the top crust and set it aside on a sheet of waxed paper.

2. Peel, core, and halve the apples. Cut into ¼-inch-thick slices, about 7 to 8 cups.

3. In a 4-quart saucepan, whisk together sugar, flour, cinnamon, nutmeg, and salt. Whisk in bourbon whiskey and lemon juice until evenly blended. Cook over medium-high heat, whisking frequently, until the mixture boils and thickens slightly. Add apples and stir until evenly coated. Continue cooking, stirring continuously, for 3 minutes. Set aside to cool, stirring once or twice, for 20 minutes.

4. Pour apple mixture into the pie shell, mounding apples slightly in the center. Dot with butter. Add top crust. Seal, trim, and flute the edges. With the point of a sharp knife, slash several vents in the top crust for steam to escape. Bake for 25 minutes at 425°F. Reduce temperature to 350°F and bake 45 minutes longer, or until the crust is browned, juices are bubbling, and fruit is tender when pierced with a knife inserted through one of the vents. Serve warm or at room temperature with a dollop of whipped cream. Makes 1 double-crust pie.

LINDA RAPP, Columbus, Indiana
Grand Champion, Open Class Pies, Bartholomew County 4-H Fair, Columbus, Indiana, 2005

APPLE/CRAN PIE WITH TOASTED WALNUT CRUST

FILLING

1 cup sugar
¼ teaspoon salt
3 tablespoons cornstarch
¼ cup light corn syrup
2 tablespoons water
1¼ cups frozen cranberries
5 cups sliced apples
1 tablespoon orange zest
2 tablespoons unsalted butter,
   room temperature

CRUST

3 cups all-purpose flour, plus more for
   rolling out dough
1 teaspoon salt
1 cup shortening
1½ teaspoons orange zest
1 tablespoon orange juice
Ice water
⅓ cup walnuts, chopped and toasted
1 egg
1 tablespoon water
Sugar

1. Preheat oven to 400°F. Set aside a 9-inch pie plate; do not grease.

2. To make filling: Combine sugar, salt, and cornstarch in a large saucepan over medium heat. Gradually stir in light corn syrup and water. Cook until mixture thickens slightly and comes to a boil. Add cranberries and apples; cook until cranberries burst their skins, 3 to 5 minutes. Stir in orange zest. Cool.

3. To make crust: In a large bowl, sift together flour and salt. Cut in shortening with a pastry blender. Add orange zest and juice. Add ice water 1 tablespoon at a time and stir, just until mixture forms a ball.

4. Divide dough in half. Roll half of dough in toasted walnuts. Roll out walnut dough on a lightly floured surface and line pie plate. Roll out remaining dough and cut into strips for lattice.

5. Pour filling into pie shell. Top with lattice strips. Beat together egg and water to make a wash; brush egg mixture on top of lattice strips. Sprinkle sugar over top of pie. Bake at 400°F for 10 minutes. Reduce oven temperature to 375°F and bake 25 minutes longer, or until crust is golden brown. Makes 1 lattice-crust pie.

Use Paula Red and Gala apples; they make a winning combination with cranberries.

KATHLEEN LUCIDO, Harper Woods, Michigan
First Place, Apple Pie Contest, Michigan State Fair, Detroit, Michigan, 2001

Ruth Overby's Apple Pie

6 Duchess apples, peeled, cored, and sliced

1 cup sugar

3 tablespoons tapioca

1 teaspoon cinnamon

½ teaspoon nutmeg

¼ teaspoon salt

½ cup frozen apple juice concentrate, thawed

1 teaspoon vanilla

Double-crust pie pastry

Flour

1 tablespoon unsalted butter, room temperature

Milk

1. Preheat oven to 375°F.

2. Combine apples, sugar, tapioca, cinnamon, nutmeg, and salt in a large saucepan. Pour apple juice into saucepan and stir. Cook over medium heat until apples are tender, 5 to 10 minutes. Remove from heat and stir in vanilla.

3. Roll out half of pie pastry on a lightly floured surface and line a 9-inch pie plate. Spoon filling into pie shell. Dot with butter. Brush edge of pie shell with milk. Roll out top crust and layer over filling. Trim and seal the edges. Crimp or flute as desired. Cut vents in top crust for steam to escape. Bake at 375°F for 15 minutes. Reduce heat to 350°F and bake 30 minutes longer, or until crust is light brown. Makes 1 double-crust pie.

✖ **Ruth Overby,** Mellette, South Dakota
First Place, Pie Contest, Brown County Fair & 4-H Show, Aberdeen, South Dakota, 2003

Butterscotch Crumb Apple Pie

CRUST

2 cups all-purpose flour, plus
   more for rolling out dough

¼ teaspoon salt

1 cup shortening

½ cup 7-Up

FILLING

4 cups peeled, cored, and sliced tart
   cooking apples

1½ teaspoons lemon juice

½ cup sugar

¼ cup all-purpose flour

1 teaspoon cinnamon

⅛ teaspoon salt

CRUMBLE TOPPING

1 cup butterscotch chips

¼ cup unsalted butter, room temperature

¾ cup all-purpose flour

⅛ teaspoon salt

GARNISH

Whipped cream or ice cream

1. Preheat over to 375°F.

2. To make crust: Combine flour and salt in a bowl. Cut in shortening with a pastry blender until mixture resembles coarse crumbs. Slowly add 7-Up, tossing lightly with a fork until dough forms a ball.

3. Divide dough in half. Shape into two thick patties. Let rest for 10 minutes. Roll out one patty on a lightly floured surface for bottom crust. Ease into a 9-inch pie plate. Trim off excess even with rim of pie plate. Wrap second patty in plastic wrap, place in a zip-close freezer bag, and freeze for later use.

4. To make filling: In a large bowl, toss apples with lemon juice to coat. Stir in sugar, flour, cinnamon, and salt. Mix until well combined. Spoon filling into pie shell. Cover edges with aluminum foil. Bake at 375°F for 20 minutes.

5. To make crumble topping: In a microwave-safe bowl, combine butterscotch chips and butter. Microwave on high for 1 minute; stir to blend. Add flour and salt; blend until mixture forms large crumbs. Remove foil from pie. Put crumble topping over hot apples. Reduce oven temperature to 350°F. Return pie to oven and bake 25 minutes longer. Serve warm with whipped cream or ice cream. Makes 1 pie, plus an extra single-crust pie pastry.

✂ **RUTH OVERBY,** Mellette, South Dakota
Best of Show, Pie Contest, Brown County Fair & 4-H Show, Aberdeen, South Dakota, 2004

RUTH CAHILL'S APPLE PIE

PASTRY

2 cups all-purpose flour, plus
    more for rolling out dough
¾ teaspoon salt
⅔ cup shortening
4 to 6 tablespoons cold water

FILLING

6 large tart apples, peeled, cored, and diced
¼ cup water
¼ cup unsalted butter, melted
½ cup brown sugar
½ cup chopped pecans

¼ cup sugar
¼ cup brown sugar
2 tablespoons flour
½ teaspoon cinnamon
⅛ teaspoon salt
1 tablespoon lemon juice
1 tablespoon unsalted butter,
    room temperature

1. Preheat oven to 425°F. Lightly grease a 9-inch pie plate.

2. To make pastry: Sift flour and salt into a bowl. Cut in shortening with a pastry blender. Add cold water a tablespoon at a time, stirring just until dough holds together.

3. Gather up dough and divide in half. Roll out one half on a lightly floured surface and line pie plate. Roll out other half for top crust; hold aside.

4. To make filling: Simmer apples and water in a saucepan over medium heat until tender, 5 minutes. In a small bowl, combine melted butter, brown sugar, and pecans. Spoon pecan mixture into pie shell. Add cooked apples.

5. To make topping: In a small bowl, combine sugar, brown sugar, flour, cinnamon, and salt. Sprinkle over apples. Splash with lemon juice and dot with butter.

6. Dampen edges of lower crust with cold water. Layer top crust over filling. Seal edges and crimp or flute as desired. Cut steam vents in top crust. Bake at 425°F for 15 minutes. Reduce heat to 350°F and bake 35 minutes longer. Makes 1 double-crust pie.

✂ **RUTH CAHILL,** Columbus, Ohio
First Prize, Ohio State Fair, Columbus, Ohio, 2005

Apple Butter-Yam Pie

CRUST

1 cup unsifted all-purpose flour, plus
   more for rolling out dough
½ teaspoon salt
⅓ cup shortening
3 to 4 tablespoons cold water

FILLING

1 cup hot mashed yams or sweet potatoes
   (about ¾ lb. before cooking)
½ cup margarine or unsalted butter,
   room temperature

½ cup light brown sugar
2 tablespoons flour
1 jar (15 oz.) apple butter
½ cup milk
1½ teaspoons grated orange zest
¼ teaspoon salt
3 eggs

GARNISH

Whipped cream
Nuts

1. Preheat oven to 400°F.

2. To make crust: In a medium bowl, whisk together flour and salt. Cut in shortening until crumbly. Sprinkle water, 1 tablespoon at a time, over top, mixing just until dough is moist enough to hold together.

3. Gather up dough into a ball. Place dough on a lightly floured surface and press down to form a flat circle with smooth edges. Roll out circle to a ⅛-inch thickness. Circle should be about 1½ inches larger than an inverted 9-inch pie plate. Ease dough into pie plate. Trim crust ½ inch beyond edge of pie plate, fold under the excess, and flute as desired. Chill pie shell whle making filling.

4. To make filling: In a large mixing bowl, combine yams or sweet potatoes, margarine or butter, light brown sugar, and flour. Beat until well blended. Add apple butter, milk, zest, salt, and eggs; beat well.

5. Turn filling into pie shell. Bake for 10 minutes at 400°F. Reduce oven temperature to 350°F and bake 50 minutes longer, or until a knife inserted near edge comes out clean. Cool. Serve warm or chilled, topped with whipped cream and nuts. Store leftover pie in the refrigerator. Makes 1 single-crust pie.

✄ **KATHY FRIERSON,** DeLand, Florida
First Place, Baked Goods—Senior Adult, Volusia County Fair,
DeLand, Florida, 2004

STRAWBERRY COBBLER

Butter-flavored cooking spray

FILLING

½ cup sugar

1 tablespoon cornstarch

1 cup water

3 cups sliced, frozen strawberries

2 tablespoons margarine,
   room temperature

DOUGH

1 cup all-purpose flour

¼ cup packed dark brown sugar

1½ teaspoons baking powder

½ teaspoon salt

3 tablespoons melted margarine,
   room temperature

¼ cup dark brown sugar

¾ cup half-and-half

TOPPING

¼ cup margarine, room temperature

¼ cup dark brown sugar

1. Preheat oven to 400°F. Coat a 2-quart baking dish with butter-flavored cooking spray.

2. To make filling: Combine sugar, cornstarch, water, and strawberries in a medium saucepan over medium heat. Cook, stirring continuously, until thick and hot. Pour mixture into baking dish. Dot with margarine.

3. To make dough: In a bowl, combine flour, dark brown sugar, baking powder, and salt. Blend in melted margarine. Stir in half-and-half. Mixture will be soft. Spoon dough onto strawberry filling and spread as evenly as possible; dough may sink to bottom of pan. Bake for 20 to 25 minutes, or until cobbler is almost done.

4. To make topping: In a microwave-safe bowl, combine margarine and dark brown sugar. Microwave until melted. Brush on top of cobbler. Bake for 5 to 10 minutes longer. Makes 6 servings.

※ **PEGGY LONG,** Oklahoma City, Oklahoma
Third Place, Old Fashioned Cobbler Contest, Oklahoma State Fair, Oklahoma City, Oklahoma, 2005

APRICOT PIE

Double-crust pie pastry

2 cans (17 oz. each) apricots, drained and
   sliced, with ¾ cup of juice reserved

1 cup sugar

3 tablespoons cornstarch

1 tablespoon tapioca

1½ tablespoons unsalted butter, room temperature

1 tablespoon lemon juice

1. Preheat oven to 425°F. Line an 8-inch pie plate with half of pastry. Cut remaining pastry into strips for lattice. Chill pie shell and strips while making filling.

2. Combine apricot juice, sugar, cornstarch, and tapioca in small saucepan over medium heat. Cook until thickened. Remove from heat. Stir in butter and lemon juice. Add apricots. Cool.

3. Pour filling into pie shell. Add lattice strips and flute the edges. Bake for 10 minutes at 425°F. Reduce heat to 375°F and bake 20 to 25 minutes longer, or until golden brown. Makes 1 lattice-crust pie.

※ **DACIA TOBIAS,** Edinburgh, Indiana
Grand Champion, Bartholomew County 4-H Fair, Columbus, Indiana, 1998

Fresh Blackberry Pie

CRUST

2⅔ cups all-purpose flour, plus
    more for rolling out dough
1 teaspoon salt
½ cup unsalted butter,
    room temperature
½ cup shortening
7 tablespoons cold water

FILLING

6 cups fresh blackberries
1 cup sugar
¼ cup all-purpose flour
¼ teaspoon salt
2 tablespoons unsalted butter, cut into dice

2 tablespoons milk
1 tablespoon sugar
Chopped almonds

1. Preheat oven to 425°F.

2. To make crust: In a medium bowl, whisk together flour and salt. Cut in butter and shortening until mixture resembles coarse crumbs. Sprinkle water over top, a tablespoon at a time, tossing with a fork just until dough begins to come together. Divide dough in half, shape into two disks, and wrap with plastic wrap. Chill for 20 minutes.

3. Roll out one dough disk on a lightly floured surface into a 12-inch circle. Place dough in pie plate and press gently against sides of a 9-inch pie plate. Roll out remaining dough and cut into strips for lattice top. Chill pie shell and strips until ready to use.

4. To make filling: Combine blackberries, sugar, flour, and salt. Spoon filling into pie shell. Dot with butter. Lay lattice strips over filling in a crisscross pattern. Brush milk on exposed surfaces of pastry. Sprinkle with sugar. Bake for 25 minutes at 425°F. Reduce heat to 375°F and continue baking 20 to 25 minutes longer, or until crust is golden to medium brown and filling is bubbling. Remove from oven. Cool. Sprinkle edges of pie with chopped almonds. Makes 1 lattice-crust pie.

✄ **PATTY KNIGHTON,** San Diego, California
Second Place, San Diego County Fair, Del Mar, California, 2004

Blueberry Pie XII

CRUST

¾ cup shortening
2 tablespoons heavy cream
1 teaspoon salt
½ cup boiling water
2 cups all-purpose flour, plus
    more for rolling out dough

FILLING

5 cups fresh blueberries
1¼ cups sugar
Juice of ½ lemon
2 tablespoons sifted all-purpose flour
Pinch of salt
Unsalted butter, room temperature

1. Preheat oven to 350°F.

2. To make crust: In a large mixing bowl, whip together shortening, heavy cream, and salt. Add boiling water and whip to combine. Beat in flour.

3. Divide dough in half and shape into two disks. Roll out each disk between lightly floured sheets of waxed paper. Line a 9-inch pie plate with one piece of pastry. Chill pie shell and remaining pastry while making filling.

4. To make filling: Combine blueberries, sugar, lemon juice, flour, and salt. Spoon into pie shell. Dot with 5 pats of butter.

5. Lay remaining pastry over filling. Trim, seal, and crimp or flute the edges. Cut vents in top crust for steam to escape. Bake for 45 to 55 minutes. Makes 1 double-crust pie.

※ **GABLE HIGGINBOTHAM,** Frederick, Maryland
Best Two-Crust Pie, Wild Blueberry Festival Cooking Competition, Machias, Maine, 2004

FIRST-DAY-OF-SCHOOL VERMONT APPLE PIE

CRUST

3 cups all-purpose flour, plus
   more for rolling out dough
1 tablespoon sugar
1½ teaspoons salt
1¼ cups cold unsalted butter, diced
4 to 6 tablespoons ice water

FILLING

¼ cup plus 2 tablespoons sugar, divided
⅓ cup brown sugar

2 tablespoons cornstarch
1 teaspoon cinnamon, divided
¼ teaspoon nutmeg
Pinch of salt
8 or 9 large early Vermont apples,
   such as Paula Red
1 tablespoon lemon juice
2 tablespoons cold unsalted butter,
   thinly sliced

2 tablespoons milk

1. To make crust: Place flour, sugar, and salt in a food processor; pulse to combine. Add butter and pulse just until butter is incorporated. Transfer mixture to a bowl. Sprinkle with ice water, 2 tablespoons at a time, tossing with a fork just until dough comes together.

2. Gather up dough, divide in half, and form into two balls. Flatten each ball into a disk, wrap in plastic wrap, and refrigerate.

3. To make filling: Combine ¼ cup of the sugar, brown sugar, cornstarch, ½ teaspoon cinnamon, nutmeg, and salt in a small bowl.

4. Peel, core, and slice apples. Toss apple slices with lemon juice in a large bowl. Sprinkle sugar mixture over apples and toss well.

5. Roll out one dough disk on a lightly floured surface until several inches larger than a 10-inch pie plate. Fold pastry into quarters and transfer to pie plate. Unfold carefully so that dough does not stretch.

6. Pile filling into pie shell, mounding apples slightly higher in the middle. Dot with butter.

7. Roll out second dough disk. Fold into quarters. Use a sharp knife to cut several short slits at the folded corner for steam vents. Transfer pastry to top of filling and unfold carefully. Trim edges of both crusts with a ¾-inch overhang. Fold the top crust under the edge of the bottom crust and press to seal. Crimp or flute the edge as desired.

8. Brush the top crust with milk. Gather up dough scraps into a ball, reroll, and cut out shapes with a knife or small cookie cutters. Place cutouts on the top crust and brush with milk. Mix remaining 2 tablespoons sugar and ½ teaspoon cinnamon and sprinkle evenly over top crust. Place pie on a baking sheet. Bake for 10 minutes. Reduce heat to 350°F, rotate the pie 180°, and bake for another 50 to 60 minutes, or until crust is golden brown and filling is bubbling. Cool on a wire rack. Makes 1 double-crust pie.

※ **ANNE TREADWELL,** Burlington, Vermont
First Prize, Champlain Valley Exposition, Essex Junction, Vermont, 2004

"Let's Celebrate" Blueberry Pie

CRUST

1 ¾ cups all-purpose flour, plus
   more for rolling out dough

¼ cup sugar

½ teaspoon salt

2 teaspoons grated lemon zest

½ cup butter-flavored shortening

½ teaspoon vanilla

4 tablespoons cold water

2 tablespoons almonds, finely chopped

BLUEBERRY FILLING

2 cups frozen blueberries, slightly
   thawed, divided

2 tablespoons cornstarch

2 tablespoons sugar

1 tablespoon lemon juice

1 tablespoon grated lemon zest

2 tablespoons unsalted butter,
   room temperature

2 teaspoons Chambord liqueur

ALMOND FILLING

1½ (6 oz. each) white chocolate candy bars

1 coddled egg yolk (see Winner's Circle Tip, below)

2 tablespoons water

¼ teaspoon vanilla

¼ cup sliced almonds

1 cup heavy cream

1 tablespoon confectioners' sugar

WHIPPED CREAM LAYER

1 cup heavy cream

2 tablespoons confectioners' sugar

¼ teaspoon vanilla

1. Preheat oven to 425°F. Set aside a 9-inch pie plate; do not grease.

2. To make crust: In a large bowl, combine flour, sugar, salt, lemon zest, butter-flavored shortening, vanilla, cold water, and almonds. Form dough into a ball and flatten slightly. Roll out between two sheets of lightly floured waxed paper to make a 12-inch circle. Line pie plate with pastry. Bake for 10 to 12 minutes, or until golden brown. Let cool.

3. To make blueberry filling: Combine 1 cup of the blueberries, cornstarch, sugar, lemon juice, and lemon zest in a saucepan over low heat. Cook until mixture thickens and turns clear. Add remaining 1 cup blueberries, butter, and Chambord liqueur. Cool slightly. Spoon filling into pie shell.

4. To make almond filling: Break up white chocolate candy bars into a small saucepan; set over low heat until melted. Beat egg yolk with water, add to white chocolate, and blend well. Cool. Stir in vanilla and almonds. In a small bowl, beat heavy cream, adding confectioners' sugar, until soft peaks form. Stir a few spoonfuls of whipped cream into white chocolate mixture; fold in remaining whipped cream. Spread almond filling evenly over blueberry layer.

5. To make whipped cream layer: Beat heavy cream, confectioners' sugar, and vanilla until stiff. Spread over almond filling. Makes 1 single-crust pie.

※ **KATHLEEN LUCIDO,** Harper Woods, Michigan
First Place, Michigan Blueberry Creation Contest, Michigan State Fair, Detroit, Michigan, 2000

WINNER'S CIRCLE TIP | To coddle—or partially cook—an egg yolk, cook a whole egg in boiling water for 1 minute, as if you were soft-boiling the egg. Crack the egg open and spoon out the yolk.

BOURBON CHOCOLATE PECAN PIE

CRUST

1½ cups all-purpose flour, plus
   more for rolling out dough
1 teaspoon salt
½ cup shortening
4 to 5 tablespoons ice water

FILLING

4 large or 3 extra-large eggs
1 cup light corn syrup
½ cup sugar
¼ cup brown sugar
1 tablespoon all-purpose flour
3 tablespoons bourbon
1 tablespoon vanilla
1 cup coarsely chopped pecans
1 cup semisweet chocolate morsels, melted

1. Place oven rack in lowest position. Preheat oven to 350°F.

2. To make single crust: In a medium bowl, sift together flour and salt. Cut in shortening until pieces are pea-sized. Add ice water a few tablespoons at a time, tossing lightly with a fork just until dough sticks together. Form dough into a ball and flatten into a patty. Roll out on a lightly floured surface to fit a 9-inch pie plate. Ease into pie plate. Trim and flute the edges. Chill pie shell while making filling.

3. To make filling: In a large mixing bowl, beat eggs and light corn syrup until fluffy. Whisk together sugar, brown sugar, and flour; add to eggs and beat well. Combine bourbon and vanilla and whisk into egg mixture. Stir in pecans and melted chocolate.

4. Pour filling into pie shell. Bake for 55 to 60 minutes, shielding crust with foil after it turns light brown to prevent burning. Cool on a wire rack. Makes 1 single-crust pie.

✖ **NELDA CREWS,** Winston-Salem, North Carolina
First Place, Bailey and Thomas Attorneys' Chocolate Pie Contest, Dixie Classic Fair, Winston-Salem, North Carolina, 2005

TRIPLE-LAYER MUD PIE

2 squares (1 oz. each) semisweet
   baking chocolate, melted
¼ cup sweetened condensed milk
1 prepared 9-inch (6 oz.) chocolate
   sandwich cookie crumb pie shell

¾ cup chopped pecans, toasted
2 cups cold milk
2 packages (3.9 oz. each) chocolate flavor
   instant pudding and pie filling
1 container (8 oz.) frozen whipped topping, thawed

1. Combine melted chocolate and sweetened condensed milk, stirring until smooth. Pour into pie shell. Press pecans evenly into chocolate mixture. Chill until set, 10 minutes.

2. In a large bowl, whisk milk and pudding mix until well blended, 1 minute. Spoon 1½ cups of the pudding over the pecans.

3. Stir half of the whipped topping into remaining pudding; spread over pudding in pie shell. Spread remaining whipped topping over pie. Chill for 3 hours. Refrigerate until ready to serve. Garnish as desired. Makes 8 servings.

✖ **TRACY MEATS,** Rock Springs, Wyoming
Overall Grand Champion, Refrigerated Dessert Contest, Sweetwater County Fair, Rock Springs, Wyoming, 2005

THREE-LAYER DRIED CHERRY-PECAN PIE

1 cup dried cherries

½ cup chopped pecans

1 cup sour cream

1 cup sugar

2 eggs, beaten

½ teaspoon cinnamon

¼ teaspoon ground cloves (optional)

¼ teaspoon salt

1 tablespoon unsalted butter, room temperature

1 small package (3 oz.) cream cheese, room temperature

½ cup sifted confectioners' sugar

1 cup heavy cream

1 9-inch prebaked pie shell or cookie crumb crust

1. Combine dried cherries, pecans, sour cream, sugar, eggs, cinnamon, cloves if using, and salt in a large saucepan over medium-high heat. Bring to a boil, reduce heat, and cook, stirring constantly, until thickened. Remove from heat, add butter, and stir until melted. Cool completely.

2. In a small mixing bowl, blend cream cheese and confectioners' sugar. In a separate bowl, whip the cream until soft peaks form. Fold whipped cream into cream cheese mixture.

3. Spread half of cream cheese mixture into pie shell. Add dried fruit mixture. Top with remaining cream cheese mixture. Makes 1 single-crust pie.

Try this pie using sweetened dried cranberries instead of dried cherries

✕ **JANE ADAMS,** Lake Geneva, Wisconsin
First Place, Best of Show, Dairy Delight Contest, Walworth County Fair, Elkhorn, Wisconsin, 2005

BOYSENBERRY PIE

CRUST

2½ cups sifted all-purpose flour, plus more for rolling out dough

½ teaspoon salt

1 cup shortening

5 tablespoons water

FILLING

4 cups fresh boysenberries

4 tablespoons tapioca

1½ cups sugar

1 teaspoon lemon juice

1. Preheat oven to 375°F.

2. To make crust: Combine flour and salt. Cut in shortening until mixture resembles coarse crumbs. Add water all at once and mix with a fork. Pull dough together with your fingers. Divide dough in half and roll into two balls. Flatten into disks. Chill for 30 minutes if dough appears too soft to handle.

3. Roll out one dough disk between two lightly floured sheets of waxed paper. Line an 8-inch pie plate.

4. To make filling: Combine boysenberries, tapioca, sugar, and lemon juice in a large bowl; toss until well combined. Spoon filling into pie shell. Roll out second dough disk and layer over filling. Trim, seal, and flute or crimp edges. Cut several slits in top to vent steam. Bake for 35 to 45 minutes. Makes 1 double-crust pie.

✕ **HOWARD BETTENCOURT,** Livermore, California
First Place, Alameda County Fair, Pleasanton, California, 2005

Cherry Delight Pie

CRUST

2 cups all-purpose flour, plus
   more for rolling out dough
1 teaspoon salt
2⅓ cups plus 1 tablespoon shortening
2 tablespoons sugar
4 tablespoons ice water

FILLING

1⅓ cups sugar
3 tablespoons cornstarch
4 cups fresh cherries, pitted
¼ teaspoon lemon juice
¼ teaspoon almond extract
2 tablespoons unsalted butter, room temperature

2 tablespoons unsalted butter, melted
Colored sugar
Sugar

1. Move oven rack to lowest level. Line a pizza stone with aluminum foil and place in oven. Heat oven to 400°F.

2. To make crust: In a medium bowl, whisk together flour and salt. Cut in shortening with two knives until shortening pieces are the size of small peas. Sprinkle with ice water 1 tablespoon at a time, tossing with a fork until flour is moistened and pastry leaves side of bowl.

3. Gather pastry into a ball and divide in half. On a lightly floured surface, roll out each half into an 11-inch round. Fold one round in half, place in a 9-inch pie plate, and gently unfold, pressing dough into bottom and up sides of pan. Trim off and reserve the excess dough. Chill remaining round while making filling.

4. To make filling: In a large bowl, combine sugar and cornstarch. Add cherries, lemon juice, and almond extract, tossing gently to combine. Pour mixture into pie shell. Dot with butter.

5. Layer remaining pastry round over filling. Trim, seal, and flute the edges. Cut slits for steam vents. Place pie on pizza stone and bake at 400°F for 20 minutes. While pie is baking, roll out leftover dough, cut out round cherry shapes, and sprinkle with colored sugar. Remove pie from oven. Brush crust with melted butter, add the cherry cutouts, and sprinkle with sugar. Place pie back on pizza stone and draw foil up around pie to cover loosely. Bake 15 to 20 minutes longer, or until filling bubbles. Cool on a wire rack for 2 to 3 hours. Makes 1 double-crust pie.

※ **JUDITH LUIBRAND,** Shelby Township, Michigan
First Place, Michigan's Cherry Pie Baking Contest, Michigan State Fair, Detroit, Michigan, 2001

CRANBERRY-WALNUT PIE

2 eggs
1 cup sugar
⅔ cup unsalted butter, melted
1 cup all-purpose flour
2½ cups fresh or thawed frozen cranberries

1 unbaked 9-inch pie shell
½ cup brown sugar
½ cup walnuts
2 to 3 tablespoons unsalted butter,
  room temperature

1. Preheat oven to 350°F.

2. Whisk together eggs, sugar, melted butter, and flour.

3. Arrange cranberries evenly in bottom of pie shell. Combine brown sugar, walnuts, and butter in a small bowl. Sprinkle over cranberries.

4. Spread egg mixture evenly over cranberries. Bake for 45 minutes. Makes 1 single-crust pie.

✖ **MELISSA RADDATZ,** Wausau, Wisconsin
Second Place, Fresh Cranberry, Warrens Cranberry Festival, Warrens, Wisconsin, 2005

CHERRY-BERRY PIE

Double-crust pie pastry
Flour

FILLING
1 can (20 oz.) cherries with juice
2 cups fresh blackberries
¾ cup sugar
2 tablespoons cornstarch
1 teaspoon almond extract

CRUMB TOPPING
¾ cup all-purpose flour
¾ cup brown sugar
⅓ cup unsalted butter, room temperature
½ teaspoon cinnamon

GLAZE
1 cup confectioners' sugar
½ teaspoon almond extract
Milk
Sliced toasted almonds

1. Preheat oven to 350°F.

2. Divide pastry dough in half. Roll out one half on a lightly floured surface and line the bottom of a 9-inch pie plate. Roll out other half of pastry. Using a cake pan as a template, cut one 8-inch round. From remaining pastry, cut 8 leaf shapes freehand or with a cookie cutter. Place round and leaves on a baking sheet; pierce pastry with a fork. Bake pastry round and leaves for 8 to 10 minutes, pie shell for 10 to 12 minutes, or until lightly browned. Cool round and leaves on a wire rack.

3. To make filling: Drain cherries, reserving the juice. Place cherries and blackberries in a medium bowl. Combine cherry juice, sugar, and cornstarch in a small saucepan over medium heat. Cook, stirring continuously, until thick and bubbly. Add almond extract. Carefully pour syrup over cherry-blackberry mixture; toss gently to combine.

4. To make crumb topping: Combine flour, brown sugar, butter, and cinnamon until crumbly.

5. Pour filling into pie shell. Set the 8-inch round on top of the filling. Press crumb topping around outer edges. Bake for 10 minutes. Cool slightly.

6. To make glaze: In a small bowl, mix confectioners' sugar and almond extract. Stir in just enough milk to make a drizzling consistency. Dip pastry leaves into glaze, sprinkle with sliced toasted almonds, and place on a wire rack until set. Drizzle glaze over center of pie and sprinkle with sliced almonds. Arrange leaves on pie. Makes 1 double-crust pie.

⌘ **ALBERTA DUNBAR,** San Diego, California
Second Place, San Diego County Fair, Del Mar, California, 2004

CHERRIES-IN-THE-SNOW

CRUST
1¼ cups graham cracker crumbs
¼ cup sugar
½ cup unsalted butter, melted

FILLING
1 small package (3 oz.) cream cheese, softened
½ cup sugar
1 teaspoon almond extract or vanilla
1 cup heavy cream
2 tablespoons sugar
1 can (21 oz.) cherry pie filling
¾ cup sour cream

1. Preheat oven to 400°F.
2. To make crust: Combine graham cracker crumbs, sugar, and melted butter. Press into the bottom of an 11 x 7 x 2-inch baking pan. Bake for 5 minutes. Cool.
3. To make filling: In a small mixing bowl, beat cream cheese, sugar, and almond flavoring or vanilla until well combined. In a large mixing bowl, whip heavy cream until soft peaks form. Add sugar and continue whipping until stiff. Fold cream cheese mixture into whipped cream. Pour filling over crust. Pour cherry pie filling over creamy filling. Top with sour cream. Chill thoroughly. Makes 6 to 8 servings.

⌘ **CHUCK AUSMAN,** Menomonie, Wisconsin
First Prize, Desserts, Dunn County HCE, Dunn County Fair, Menomonie, Wisconsin, 2004

CHOCOLATE-COVERED PEANUT PIE

1 refrigerated single-crust pie pastry

½ cup brown sugar

½ cup sugar

½ cup melted margarine, room temperature

2 eggs

1 cup peanuts, chopped

1 cup chocolate chips

1. Preheat oven to 350°F. Unfold piecrust and ease into a 9-inch pie plate.

2. In a medium bowl, combine brown sugar, sugar, melted margarine, eggs, peanuts, and chocolate chips until well mixed. Pour into crust. Bake for 30 minutes. Serve with vanilla ice cream, if desired. Makes 1 single-crust pie.

✕ **RACHEL BROOKS,** Byron, Georgia
First Place, Georgia Peanut Recipe—Sweet, Georgia National Fair, Perry, Georgia, 2005

CHOCOLATE-COVERED STRAWBERRY PIE

COCOA CRUST

1¼ cups all-purpose flour, plus
   more for rolling out dough

⅓ cup sugar

¼ cup sweetened cocoa

½ teaspoon salt

½ cup shortening

½ teaspoon vanilla

2 to 3 tablespoons ice water

FILLING

2 cups sliced fresh strawberries

¼ cup sugar

4½ teaspoons cornstarch

1 package (8 oz.) cream cheese

⅓ cup confectioners' sugar

1 cup white chocolate chips, melted

1 cup heavy cream, beaten to stiff peaks

TOPPING

⅓ cup heavy cream

½ cup semisweet chocolate chips

GARNISH

Melted white chocolate

Sweetened whipped cream

Chocolate-covered strawberry

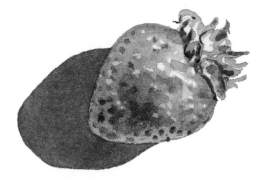

1. Preheat oven to 425°F.

2. To make cocoa crust: In a medium bowl, whisk together flour, sugar, cocoa, and salt. Cut in shortening until crumbly. Add vanilla and ice water, a tablespoon at a time, tossing with a fork just until dough holds together.

3. Gather dough into a ball and flatten into a patty. Roll out on a lightly floured surface to fit a 9-inch pie plate. Ease into pie plate. Trim and flute edges. Bake for 15 minutes. Cool on a wire rack.

4. To make filling: Combine strawberries, sugar, and cornstarch in small saucepan over medium heat. Cook, stirring constantly, until thick. Cool to room temperature. Refrigerate until cold.

5. In a medium mixing bowl, beat cream cheese and confectioners' sugar until light and fluffy. Blend in melted white chocolate chips. Add strawberry mixture and beat until well blended. Fold in whipped cream. Pour filling into piecrust. Smooth the top with a spatula.

6. To make topping: Heat heavy cream in a small saucepan over medium heat until bubbly. Stir in chocolate chips until smooth. Pour topping over pie filling, spreading close to edge of crust.

7. To garnish pie: Drizzle melted white chocolate over top of pie. Pipe sweetened whipped cream around the edge. Set a chocolate-covered strawberry in the center. Chill for 2 hours before serving. Makes 1 single-crust pie.

✄ **PATRICIA LAPIEZO,** La Mesa, California
First Place, San Diego County Fair, Del Mar, California, 2004

FUDGE CROSTATA WITH RASPBERRY SAUCE

Double-crust pie pastry
Flour

FILLING

1 cup semisweet chocolate chips
8 tablespoons unsalted butter,
    room temperature
⅔ cup sugar
1 cup ground almonds
1 egg
1 egg yolk

SAUCE

1 package (12 oz.) frozen raspberries
    without syrup, thawed
¾ cup sugar
1 teaspoon lemon juice

GARNISH

Sweetened whipped cream
Chocolate curls
Whole raspberries

1. Preheat oven to 375°F.

2. Roll out half of pastry on a lightly floured surface and fit into a 9-inch pie plate. Roll out remaining pastry and cut into ½-inch-wide strips for lattice top. Chill pie shell and lattice while making filling.

3. To make filling: Melt chocolate chips and 2 tablespoons of the butter in a small saucepan over low heat, stirring continuously until smooth. In a medium bowl, whisk remaining 6 tablespoons butter and sugar until light and fluffy. Stir in almonds, egg, egg yolk, and chocolate mixture until well blended. Spread mixture evenly in pie shell.

4. Arrange strips of pastry over filling in a lattice pattern. Trim, seal, and crimp edges. Bake for 45 to 50 minutes. During last 10 to 15 minutes of baking, cover edge of crust with strips of aluminum foil to prevent overbrowning. Cool for 1½ hours.

5. To make sauce: Place raspberries in a blender. Blend on high speed. Press berries in strainer, collecting and reserving the juice. Discard raspberry pulp and seeds. Combine raspberry juice, sugar, and lemon juice in a small saucepan over medium-high heat. Bring to a boil and cook, stirring constantly, for 3 minutes. Cool to room temperature and refrigerate. To serve, place slices of pie on individual serving plates. Drizzle sauce over the top. Garnish with sweetened whipped cream, chocolate curls, and whole raspberries. Makes 6 to 8 servings.

✄ **STACEY ROE,** Columbus, Indiana
Grand Champion, Pie Contest, Bartholomew County 4-H Fair, Columbus, Indiana, 2005

Mocha Brownie Pie

CRUST

½ cup unsalted butter, room temperature

1 cup all-purpose flour

¼ cup sugar

½ cup chopped pecans

BROWNIE FILLING

2 squares (1 oz. each) unsweetened chocolate

4 oz. semisweet chocolate

1¼ cups sugar

½ cup plus 2 tablespoons butter

3 tablespoons instant coffee crystals

3 eggs

⅔ cup all-purpose flour

½ teaspoon baking powder

½ teaspoon salt

WHIPPED GANACHE TOPPING

6 oz. semisweet chocolate chips

1 cup heavy cream

1 tablespoon instant coffee crystals

1. Preheat oven to 325°F.

2. To make crust: In a medium bowl, combine butter, flour, and sugar until crumbly. Stir in pecans. Press mixture onto bottom and up sides of a 9-inch pie plate.

3. To make brownie filling: Combine unsweetened chocolate, semisweet chocolate, and butter in a large microwave-safe bowl. Microwave on low until melted. Whisk in sugar and coffee crystals. Add eggs one at a time, beating well after each addition. Continue to mix until smooth and glossy.

4. Whisk together flour, baking powder, and salt. Stir into chocolate mixture just until incorporated. Pour batter into piecrust. Bake for 35 to 40 minutes. Cool.

5. To make whipped ganache topping: Place chocolate chips in a medium mixing bowl. Heat heavy cream in a small saucepan over low heat. When cream begins to boil, remove from heat, pour over chocolate chips, and add instant coffee. Let sit for 1 minute, or until chocolate melts and coffee dissolves. Stir gently to combine. Chill in refrigerator just until cold. Whip on high speed until soft peaks form. To serve, place slices of pie on individual serving plates and add a dollop of whipped ganache topping. Makes 6 to 8 servings.

✕ **VIRGINIA BABCOCK,** Casper, Wyoming
First Place, Coffee Contest, Wyoming State Fair, Douglas, Wyoming, 2005

Buttermilk Pie

½ cup unsalted butter, room temperature

2 cups sugar

3 tablespoons flour

3 eggs, beaten

1 cup buttermilk

1 teaspoon vanilla

¼ teaspoon nutmeg

1 9-inch deep-dish unbaked pie shell

1. Preheat oven to 350°F.

2. Cream butter and sugar in a mixing bowl. Add flour and eggs; beat until well combined. Stir in buttermilk, vanilla, and nutmeg.

3. Pour mixture into pie shell. Bake for 45 to 50 minutes. Cool on a wire rack. Makes 1 single-crust pie.

✕ **PAUNELL COURTNEY,** Abilene, Texas
First Place, West Texas Fair & Rodeo, Abilene, Texas, 2004

CRÈME BRÛLÉE PIE

3 large eggs
2 cups heavy cream, warmed in microwave
½ cup sugar

¾ teaspoon vanilla
1 prebaked pie shell (recipe follows)

1. Preheat oven to 250°F. Set a 9-inch glass pie plate in a large shallow pan for the water bath.

2. In a small mixing bowl, beat eggs until creamy. Stir in warm cream. Pass mixture through a strainer. Stir in sugar and vanilla. Pour mixture into pie plate; add water to water bath. Bake for 1 hour, or until custard is set. Cool to room temperature and then chill in refrigerator. Loosen and slide custard into prebaked pie shell. Makes 1 single-crust pie.

PREBAKED PIE SHELLS

2½ cups sifted all-purpose flour
½ teaspoon salt

1 cup shortening
5 tablespoons water

1. In a medium bowl, whisk together flour and salt. Cut in shortening until pieces are the size of peas. Add water all at once and mix with fork. Pull the dough together with your hands, divide in half, and form into two round patties. Wrap with plastic wrap. Chill for 30 minutes.

2. Roll out each patty between two sheets of waxed paper into a 12-inch round. Ease into a 9-inch pie plate. Bake in a preheated 375° oven for 8 to 10 minutes. Cool. Makes two 9-inch pie shells.

✕ **HOWARD BETTENCOURT,** Livermore, California
First Place, Alameda County Fair, Pleasanton, California, 2005

LEMON SPONGE PIE

FILLING
3 tablespoons unsalted butter,
    room temperature
1¼ cups sugar
4 eggs, separated
3 tablespoons flour

Pinch of salt
1¼ cups milk
2 tablespoons grated lemon zest
⅓ cup lemon juice

1 unbaked 9-inch pie shell

1. Preheat oven to 375°F.

2. To make filling: In a large mixing bowl, cream butter and sugar until light and fluffy. With mixer running, add egg yolks, flour, salt, milk, and lemon zest and juice. Beat until well blended.

3. In a separate mixing bowl with clean beaters, beat egg whites until fluffy but not dry. Fold egg whites into the filling.

4. Pour filling into unbaked pie shell. Bake for 15 minutes. Reduce temperature to 300°F and bake 45 minutes longer, or until top is golden and a toothpick inserted in center comes out clean. Makes 1 single-crust pie.

✕ **CONNIE FIELD,** Janesville, Wisconsin
Second Place, Dairy Delight Contest, Walworth County Fair, Elkhorn, Wisconsin, 2005

TOLL-HOUSE PIE

2 extra-large eggs
½ cup all-purpose flour
½ cup sugar
½ cup brown sugar
1 cup unsalted butter, melted

1 cup semisweet chocolate chips
1 cup coarsely chopped peanuts
1 unbaked 9-inch pie shell
Whipped cream

1. Preheat oven to 325°F.

2. In a medium mixing bowl, beat eggs until fluffy. Add flour, sugar, and brown sugar and beat until well combined. Blend in melted butter. Stir in chocolate chips and peanuts.

3. Pour filling into pie shell. Bake for 45 to 60 minutes. Serve slightly warm topped with whipped cream. Makes 1 single-crust pie.

✕ **B. L. ASHWORTH,** Edmond, Oklahoma
Second Place, Peanut Contest, Oklahoma State Fair, Oklahoma City, Oklahoma, 2005

DOUBLE-LEMON-RASPBERRY MARBLE PIE

RASPBERRY FILLING
1 box (10 oz.) frozen raspberries in
   syrup, thawed
1 tablespoon sugar
1 tablespoon cornstarch
1 cup fresh raspberries

1 prebaked 10-inch deep-dish pie shell

LEMON FILLING
1 package (8 oz.) cream cheese,
   room temperature
4 oz. white chocolate, melted and cooled
1 can (14 oz.) sweetened condensed milk
½ cup fresh lemon juice
1 cup heavy cream, stiffly beaten

LEMON CURD
4 large egg yolks
½ cup plus 2 tablespoons sugar
3 tablespoons lemon juice
¼ cup unsalted butter, room temperature
Pinch of salt
1 teaspoon finely grated lemon zest

GARNISH
Sweetened whipped cream
Fresh raspberries
White chocolate shavings

1. To make raspberry filling: Puree raspberries in a blender and strain. Set aside 1 tablespoon purée. Heat remaining purée, sugar, and cornstarch in a small saucepan over medium heat until mixture thickens and comes to a boil. Remove from heat and pour into prebaked pie shell. Top with fresh raspberries. Chill.

2. To make lemon filling: In a medium mixing bowl, beat cream cheese until smooth. Add chocolate and beat until blended. Beat in sweetened condensed milk. Stir in lemon juice. Fold in whipped cream. Pour lemon filling over raspberry layer and smooth with a spatula.

3. To make lemon curd: Beat egg yolks and sugar in a medium saucepan until well blended. Add lemon juice, butter, salt, and zest. Cook over medium-low heat, stirring constantly, until mixture thickens and resembles a thin hollandaise sauce. Do not boil. When thickened, pour at once into a strainer. Discard residue. Pour lemon curd over lemon filling to within 1 inch of edge. Drizzle reserved raspberry purée over lemon curd and swirl a knife through curd only to create a marbled effect. Chill until set. Garnish with whipped cream, raspberries, and white chocolate shavings. Makes 1 single-crust pie.

※ **PAT LAPIEZO,** La Mesa, California
First Place, San Diego County Fair, Del Mar, California, 2004

My Love-for-Peanuts Pie

PASTRY

1 cup sifted all-purpose flour, plus
    more for rolling out dough

½ cup sifted cake flour

⅜ teaspoon salt

½ cup unsalted butter, room temperature

1 egg

½ tablespoons white vinegar

2½ tablespoons ice water

¼ cup chopped cocktail peanuts

FILLING

3 fresh eggs, slightly beaten

½ cup brown sugar

½ cup light corn syrup

½ cup dark corn syrup

2 tablespoons unsalted butter, melted

1 teaspoon vanilla

1½ cups chopped peanuts

3 tablespoons liquid chocolate

3 tablespoons chopped peanuts

Peanut halves

1. Preheat oven to 350°F.

2. To make pastry: Combine all-purpose flour, cake flour, and salt. Cut in butter with a pastry blender until crumbly. Whisk together egg, vinegar, and ice water. Sprinkle on flour mixture and mix with a fork until moistened.

3. Gather dough together and press firmly into a ball. Roll out on a lightly floured surface. Ease pastry into a 9-inch pie pan. Trim pastry to within ½ inch of outer edges. Fold under extra pastry and flute the edge. Press chopped cocktail peanuts into bottom of pastry shell.

4. To make filling: Combine eggs, brown sugar, light corn syrup, dark corn syrup, melted butter, and vanilla. Fold in chopped peanuts. Pour filling into pie shell. Bake for 50 to 55 minutes, or until a knife inserted halfway between center and edge comes out clean. Cool slightly on wire rack.

5. To add topping: Drizzle liquid chocolate over warm pie. Add chopped peanuts and peanut halves. Makes 1 single-crust pie.

※ **ELAINE HRDY-STRAKA,** Oklahoma City, Oklahoma
First Place, Peanut Contest, Oklahoma State Fair, Oklahoma City, Oklahoma, 2005

WINNER'S CIRCLE TIP | Reroll any leftover pie dough and cut out small shapes with a cookie cutter. Sprinkle with sugar, place on a baking sheet, and bake in a 350°F oven until golden brown, 10 to 15 minutes. Add the cutouts to the top of the pie for decoration.

BUTTERY PEACH TOFFEE PIE

CRUST

2 cups all-purpose flour, plus
    more for rolling out dough
1 teaspoon salt
1 teaspoon sugar
⅔ cup shortening
6 to 8 teaspoons cold water

FILLING

5 cups sliced peaches
¾ cup sugar
3 tablespoons flour
2 tablespoons quick-cooking tapioca
1 teaspoon butter flavor
16 toffee candies

1. Preheat oven to 350°F.

2. To make crust: Whisk together flour, salt, and sugar. Cut in shortening. Sprinkle cold water, 2 tablespoons at a time, over top and stir just until moistened. Fluff dough with a fork. Divide dough in half. Roll out onto a lightly floured surface into two 12-inch circles. Chill dough while making filling.

3. To make filling: Combine peaches, sugar, flour, tapioca, and butter flavor. Grind candies in a food processor to make very small pieces and stir into peach mixture.

4. Line a pie plate with half of pastry and spoon in filling. Layer remaining pastry on top; seal and flute the edges. Cut vents in top crust for steam to escape. Bake for 45 minutes, or until crust is golden brown. Makes 1 double-crust pie.

✕ **EMILY SIBTHORPE-TRITTSCHLER,** Dryden, Michigan
First Place, Peach Pie Contest, Michigan State Fair, Detroit, Michigan, 2000

CLASSIC PECAN PIE

PASTRY

1 cup all-purpose flour, plus
    more for rolling out dough
¼ teaspoon salt
¼ teaspoon baking powder
⅓ cup plus 1 tablespoon shortening
2 tablespoons cold water

FILLING

3 eggs, slightly beaten
1 cup sugar
1 cup corn syrup
2 tablespoons melted margarine or
    unsalted butter, room temperature
1 teaspoon vanilla
1¼ cups pecans

1. Preheat oven to 350°F.

2. To make pastry: Whisk together flour, salt, and baking powder. Cut in half of the shortening until texture resembles cornmeal. Cut in remaining shortening. Add cold water and blend with fork.

3. Gather dough together and press firmly into a ball. Roll out onto a lightly floured surface. Fit pastry into a 9-inch pie plate. Trim pastry to within ½ inch of outer edges. Fold under extra pastry and flute edge.

4. To make filling: Combine eggs, sugar, corn syrup, melted margarine or butter, and vanilla. Fold in pecans. Pour filling into piecrust. Bake for 50 to 55 minutes, or until a knife inserted in center comes out clean. Makes 1 single-crust pie.

✕ **KATHY SARGEANT,** Leicester, Vermont
Rosette, Pies, Addison County Fair & Field Days, New Haven, Vermont, 2005

RAZZCHERRY PIE

EXTRA-FLAKY PASTRY

2 cups all-purpose flour, plus
  more for rolling out dough

1 teaspoon salt

1 tablespoon sugar

¾ cup butter-flavored shortening

¼ cup ice water

1 egg

1 tablespoon vinegar

RAZZCHERRY PIE FILLING

1 package (10 oz.) frozen raspberries,
  thawed and drained, juice reserved

2 cups pitted frozen cherries, thawed
  and drained, juice reserved

4 tablespoons cornstarch

1 cup sugar

Dash of salt

½ teaspoon almond extract

½ teaspoon ground orange zest

Dash of cinnamon

1 tablespoon unsalted butter, chilled

1. Preheat oven to 425°F.

2. To make extra-flaky pastry: Sift flour, salt, and sugar into a mixing bowl. Cut in shortening with a pastry blender. Whisk together ice water, egg, and vinegar; sprinkle egg mixture 1 tablespoon at a time onto flour mixture while fluffing with a fork. Cover and chill.

3. To make razzcherry pie filling: Place reserved juice in a 2-cup measuring cup, add water to make 1½ cups, and pour into a medium saucepan. Add cornstarch, sugar, and salt; stir to dissolve. Cook over low heat, stirring until mixture thickens and turns clear. Add raspberries, cherries, almond extract, orange zest, and cinnamon. Stir gently. Remove from heat.

4. Divide pastry in half. Roll out one half onto a lightly floured surface and line a 9-inch pie plate. Pour in pie filling and dot with butter. Roll out remaining pastry and place over top of pie. Trim, seal, and crimp the edge. Bake for 35 to 45 minutes, or until crust is golden brown. Makes 1 double-crust pie.

✕ **CAROL BARTHOLOMEW,** Holladay, Utah

First Place, Governor Huntsman Favorite Pie, Utah State Fair, Salt Lake City, Utah, 2005

WINNER'S CIRCLE TIP | For a golden piecrust, brush the surface of the dough with a mixture of 1 egg white and 1 tablespoon cold water, beaten together.

Best-Ever Lemon Meringue Pie

1½ cups sugar

1½ cups plus ⅓ cup water, divided

½ teaspoon salt, divided

½ cup cornstarch

4 eggs, separated

½ cup lemon juice

3 tablespoons unsalted butter or margarine, room temperature

1 teaspoon grated lemon zest

1 baked 9-inch pie shell

1. Preheat oven to 250°F.

2. Combine 1½ cups of the sugar, 1½ cups of the water, and ½ teaspoon of the salt in a heavy saucepan. Bring to a boil over medium-high heat. Meanwhile, mix cornstarch and remaining ⅓ cup water to make a smooth paste. Gradually stir cornstarch paste into boiling mixture. Cook, stirring constantly, until thickened and clear. Remove from heat.

3. In a small mixing bowl, beat egg yolks and lemon juice. Add to sugar mixture, return saucepan to heat and cook, stirring constantly, until mixture bubbles again. Remove from heat and stir in butter and lemon zest. Cover and cool to lukewarm.

4. In a separate mixing bowl, beat egg whites and remaining ¼ teaspoon salt until frothy. Gradually add remaining ½ cup sugar, beating to form glossy peaks. Stir 2 rounded tablespoons of meringue into lukewarm filling. Pour into pie shell. Top with remaining meringue and spread evenly. Bake for 15 minutes, or until meringue is lightly browned. Makes 1 single-crust pie.

✕ **DACIA TOBIAS,** Edinburgh, Indiana
Grand Champion, Bartholomew County 4-H Fair, Columbus, Indiana, 1996

Triple-Chocolate Parfait Pie

COCOA CRUST

1¼ cups all-purpose flour

⅓ cup sugar

¼ cup cocoa

½ teaspoon salt

½ cup shortening

½ teaspoon vanilla

2 to 3 tablespoons ice water

BOTTOM LAYER

⅓ cup heavy cream

½ cup semisweet chocolate chips

MIDDLE LAYER

8 oz. milk chocolate chips

2 tablespoons unsalted butter, room temperature

1 cup heavy cream

2 teaspoons vanilla

TOP LAYER

1 package (8 oz.) cream cheese

⅓ cup confectioners' sugar

2 tablespoons crème de cacao

1 cup white chocolate chips, melted

1 cup heavy cream, stiffly beaten

1. Preheat oven to 350°F.

2. To make cocoa crust: In a medium bowl, whisk together flour, sugar, cocoa, and salt. Cut in shortening until crumbly. Add vanilla and 2 tablespoons of the ice water and stir. If dough does not come together, stir in another tablespoon of ice water. Press mixture into bottom and up sides of a 9-inch pie plate. Bake for 10 minutes. Cool.

3. To make bottom layer: Heat heavy cream in a saucepan over medium heat until bubbly. Add chocolate chips, stirring until melted. Pour mixture into bottom of pie shell. Chill.

4. To make middle layer: Melt milk chocolate chips and butter in a small saucepan over medium heat. Cook, stirring constantly, until smooth. Cool slightly, 10 minutes. In a small bowl, beat heavy cream and vanilla until soft peaks form. Fold one-third of the whipped cream into the chocolate mixture; fold in remaining whipped cream. Spread over first layer in pie shell. Chill.

5. To make top layer: In a medium mixing bowl, beat cream cheese and confectioners' sugar until light and fluffy. Beat in crème de cacao. Blend in melted white chocolate. Fold in whipped cream. Pipe or spread mixture over middle layer in pie shell. Chill for 2 hours. Decorate with shaved chocolate or chocolate leaves, if desired. Makes 1 pie.

✳ **PATRICIA LAPIEZO,** La Mesa, California
First Place, San Diego County Fair, Del Mar, California, 2004

PEANUT BUTTER–FUDGE PIE

CRUST

1½ cups all-purpose flour, plus
    more for rolling out dough
1 teaspoon sugar
½ teaspoon salt
6 tablespoons cold unsalted butter,
    cut into small pieces
1½ tablespoons cold solid
    vegetable shortening
3 tablespoons ice water,
    plus more as needed

FILLING

4 oz. semisweet chocolate
3 tablespoons unsalted butter or
    margarine, room temperature
⅓ cup plus 3 tablespoons peanut butter, divided
1½ teaspoons vanilla
½ cup plus 2 tablespoons sugar
3 eggs
1 cup dark corn syrup
½ cup milk
⅔ cup coarsely chopped roasted unsalted peanuts
4 oz. semisweet chocolate bar,
    broken into small pieces
3 tablespoons peanut butter

1. Preheat oven to 325°F.

2. To make crust: Place flour, sugar, salt, butter, and shortening in the bowl of a food processor. Pulse until crumbly. Add ice water and pulse until mixture begins to clump together. Gather dough into a ball, sprinkling with a few more drops of water, if needed. Flatten into a disk, wrap in plastic wrap, and chill for at least 30 minutes before rolling out.

3. Using a floured rolling pin, roll out dough on a lightly floured surface to a ⅛-inch thickness. Fit dough into a 9-inch pie plate. Trim and flute edges.

4. To make filling: Melt chocolate and butter in the top of a double boiler over low heat. In a large mixing bowl, beat ⅓ cup of the peanut butter, vanilla, sugar, and eggs until fluffy. Combine corn syrup and milk; gradually beat into peanut butter mixture. Stir in melted chocolate mixture and peanuts.

5. Pour filling into pie shell. Sprinkle broken chocolate over filling. Dot with remaining 3 tablespoons peanut butter. Bake for 50 to 60 minutes, or just until filling is set. Cool on a wire rack to room temperature. Chill at least 2 hours before serving. Makes 1 single-crust pie.

✳ **CINDY BOHL,** Glenarm, Illinois
First Place, Pies, Illinois State Fair, Springfield, Illinois, 2005

ELEGANT PECAN PIE

¼ cup unsalted butter, room temperature
½ cup brown sugar
1 cup dark corn syrup
¼ teaspoon salt

3 eggs
1 cup coarsely chopped pecans
1 unbaked 9-inch pie shell
12 whole pecan halves

1. Preheat oven to 350°F.

2. Cream butter just until soft. Add sugar and cream slowly until light and fluffy. Beat in corn syrup and salt. Add eggs one at a time, beating well after each addition. Stir in pecans.

3. Pour filling into pie shell. Arrange pecan halves on the top. Bake for 50 minutes, or until knife inserted in center comes out clean. Cool. Makes 1 single-crust pie.

⌘ **MARLYS VOLZKE,** Aberdeen, South Dakota
Best of Class, Pastry, Brown County Fair & 4-H Show, Aberdeen, South Dakota, 1995, 1998

SOUR CREAM PEACH PIE

CRUST
1½ cups all-purpose flour
½ cup unsalted butter, melted
1 teaspoon salt

FILLING
4 cups canned peaches, drained
1 cup sugar, divided
1 egg
1 teaspoon vanilla
2 tablespoons flour
1 teaspoon salt
1 cup sour cream

TOPPING
¼ cup unsalted butter, room temperature
⅓ cup sugar
⅓ cup all-purpose flour
1 teaspoon cinnamon

1. Preheat oven to 400°F.

2. To make crust: Combine flour, melted butter, and salt. Press mixture into bottom and up sides of a 9-inch or 10-inch pie plate.

3. To make filling: In a large bowl, combine peaches and ¼ cup of the sugar. In a separate bowl, combine remaining ¾ cup sugar, egg, vanilla, flour, salt, and sour cream and mix well. Fold sour cream mixture into peaches.

4. To make topping: Combine butter, sugar, flour, and cinnamon until crumbly.

5. Pour filling into pie shell. Bake for 10 minutes. Reduce heat to 375°F and bake for 20 minutes. Increase heat to 400°F, sprinkle topping over pie, and bake another 10 minutes. Makes 1 single-crust pie.

⌘ **WENDY KORITNIK,** Rock Springs, Wyoming
First Place, Peach Dessert Contest, Sweetwater County Fair, Rock Springs, Wyoming, 2005

Mincemeat Pie Filling

2½ to 3 lbs. roasted beef (ground or chopped)
½ lb. suet (ground or chopped)
5 or 6 large tart apples, peeled, cored, and chopped
1 orange, peeled, seeded, and chopped
1 cup dark raisins
1 cup golden raisins
1 cup dark brown sugar
1 teaspoon ground allspice
1 teaspoon ground cinnamon
¼ teaspoon cloves
Water

1. In a large Dutch oven or heavy stockpot, combine beef, suet, apples, orange, dark raisins, golden raisins, dark brown sugar, allspice, cinnamon, and cloves.
2. Set over medium-high heat. Add just enough water to allow mixture to boil slowly for 15 minutes. Makes 1 quart of filling, or enough for one 8-inch or 9-inch pie.

Cecil Whitmire, Wauseon, Ohio
First Place, Fulton County Fair, Wauseon, Ohio, 2005

WINNER'S CIRCLE TIP | **Bake a double-crust mincemeat pie in a preheated 350°F oven for 50 to 60 minutes, or until light brown and dry. Remember to cut steam vents in the top crust.**

Traditional Pumpkin Pie

1 can (16 oz.) pumpkin
1 can (14 oz.) sweetened condensed milk
2 eggs
1 teaspoon cinnamon
½ teaspoon ground ginger
½ teaspoon nutmeg
½ teaspoon salt
1 unbaked 9-inch pie shell

SOUR CREAM TOPPING
1½ cups sour cream
2 tablespoons sugar
1 teaspoon vanilla

1. Preheat oven to 425°F.
2. Combine pumpkin, condensed milk, eggs, cinnamon, ginger, nutmeg, and salt.
3. Pour mixture into pie shell. Bake for 15 minutes. Reduce oven temperature to 350°F and bake 30 minutes longer.
4. To make sour cream topping: Combine sour cream, sugar, and vanilla until well mixed. Spread topping evenly over pie. Bake 10 minutes longer, or until knife inserted 1 inch from edge comes out clean. Cool. Makes 1 single-crust pie.

Sharon Owens, Clyde, Texas
First Place, West Texas Fair & Rodeo, Abilene, Texas, 2004

CHOCOLATE BANANA CREAM PIE

1¼ cups sugar

⅓ cup cocoa

⅓ cup cornstarch

¼ teaspoon salt

3 cups milk

3 tablespoons unsalted butter,
    room temperature

1½ squares semisweet chocolate

1½ teaspoons vanilla

1 baked 9-inch pie shell

2 bananas, sliced

Whipped cream

1. Combine sugar, cocoa, cornstarch, and salt in a large saucepan over medium heat. Gradually add milk, stirring continuously, until mixture boils. Continue boiling, stirring continuously, for 3 minutes. Remove from heat.

2. Blend in butter and chocolate, stirring until melted. Stir in vanilla. Let cool.

3. Pour some of filling into pie shell, just until bottom crust is covered. Add a single layer of banana slices. Pour remaining filling over bananas. Top with whipped cream and remaining banana slices. Serve chilled. Makes 1 single-crust pie.

✄ **BARBARA BAUMAN,** Drummond, Montana
First Place, Western Montana Fair, Missoula, Montana, 1990

PECAN PRALINE DELIGHT

CRUST

1½ cups all-purpose flour, plus
    more for rolling out dough

½ teaspoon salt

½ cup vegetable oil

¼ cup milk

TOPPING

1½ cups heavy cream

⅓ cup sifted confectioners' sugar

1 tablespoon pecan praline liqueur

¼ cup ground toasted pecans

¼ cup toffee baking bits

FILLING

1½ packages (8 oz. each) cream cheese,
    room temperature

3 tablespoons pecan praline liqueur

1 package (12 oz.) white chocolate chips, melted

¾ cup ground toasted pecans

¾ cup English toffee baking bits

1 cup heavy cream, whipped stiff

1. Preheat oven to 350°F.

2. To make crust: Combine flour, salt, vegetable oil, and milk in a small bowl. Mix well with a fork. Gather mixture into a ball and roll out between two sheets of lightly floured waxed paper. Layer into a 9-inch glass pie plate. Prick with fork. Bake for 9 to 12 minutes. Cool.

3. To make filling: In a large mixing bowl, beat cream cheese and liqueur until smooth. With mixer running, add melted chocolate chips and beat until well blended. Mix in pecans and toffee bits. Fold in whipped cream with a wooden spoon. Turn mixture into piecrust. Chill until set.

4. To make topping: In a small mixing bowl, combine heavy cream, confectioners' sugar, and liqueur. Beat until stiff. Spoon one third of topping into a pastry bag fitted with a large star tip. Spread remaining topping over pie filling. Pipe large rosettes around the outer edges and sprinkle nuts and toffee baking bits on top. Chill until ready to serve. Makes 1 single-crust pie.

✄ **ALBERTA DUNBAR,** San Diego, California
First Place, San Diego County Fair, Del Mar, California, 2004

WINNER'S CIRCLE TIP | Chocolate-dipped pecan halves are tasty on their own or as a decoration on a pie. Just dip each pecan into dipped chocolate that has been warmed in the microwave. Set pecans on waxed paper until the chocolate hardens. Chill until set.

FRESH STRAWBERRY-RHUBARB PIE

CRUST

2 cups all-purpose flour, plus
   more for rolling out dough
1 teaspoon salt
⅔ cup shortening
5 to 7 tablespoons ice water

FILLING

2 cups hulled strawberries
1 cup sugar
3 cups chopped rhubarb, or 1 package (16 oz.)
   frozen sliced rhubarb, thawed and well drained
¼ cup cornstarch

1. Preheat oven to at 400°F.

2. To make crust: Whisk together flour and salt. Cut in shortening with a pastry blender or fork until mixture resembles coarse crumbs. Sprinkle ice water, 1 tablespoon at a time, over flour while tossing and mixing lightly with fork. Continue adding water just until dough is moist enough to form a ball when lightly pressed together.

3. Divide dough in half and shape into two balls. Flatten one ball to a ½-inch thickness, rounding and smoothing the edges. Roll out on a lightly floured surface into an 11-inch circle. Gently fold pastry in half. Place pastry in a 9-inch pie plate. Unfold and gently ease pastry into bottom and sides of pan. Do not stretch. Trim pastry even with pan edge. Roll out remaining pastry; chill pastry and pie shell while making filling.

4. To make filling: Combine strawberries, sugar, rhubarb, and cornstarch. Mix lightly.

5. Spoon filling into pie shell. Layer remaining pastry on top. Trim, seal, and flute the edges. Cut several slits in top pastry. Bake for 45 to 60 minutes, or until golden brown. During final 15 minutes of baking time, set a baking sheet under pie plate to catch any oozing filling. Cool. Serve with cream and whole strawberries, if desired. Makes 1 double-crust pie.

✄ **MARJORIE WIMSATT,** Valrico, Florida
First Place, Crisco Competition, Florida State Fair, Tampa, Florida, 2005

WINNER'S CIRCLE TIP | The right amount of moisture is key when working with pie dough. Too much water causes dough to become sticky and tough. Too little moisture causes cracked edges and tearing when rolling it out.

Piña Colada Cream Pie

1 refrigerated piecrust

FILLING
⅔ cup sugar
5 teaspoons cornstarch
Dash of salt
2 cans (8 oz. each) crushed pineapple
   in juice

TOPPING
3 tablespoons cornstarch
3 tablespoons flour
½ cup sugar
½ teaspoon salt
¾ cup nonalcoholic piña colada mix, divided
2¼ cups whole milk
1 egg plus 1 egg yolk
1 teaspoon vanilla
1 tablespoon unsalted butter, room temperature
½ cup heavy cream
Toasted coconut

1. Preheat oven to 425°F.

2. Prepare piecrust according to manufacturer's directions. Bake for 5 minutes.

3. To make filling: Combine sugar, cornstarch, and salt in a medium saucepan. Stir in pineapple. Cook over medium-high heat, stirring constantly, until mixture thickens and just begins to boil, about 8 minutes. Pour filling into pie shell. Bake for 9 to 14 minutes, or until filling is set and crust is golden. Cool completely.

4. To make topping: In the same saucepan, combine cornstarch, flour, sugar, and salt. Whisk in ¼ cup of the piña colada mix until smooth. Gradually whisk in milk and remaining ½ cup piña colada mix. Cook over medium heat, stirring frequently, until mixture thickens and begins to boil, about 8 minutes.

5. Remove pan from heat. Beat egg and egg yolk in a medium bowl. Stir about 1 cup of the hot topping into beaten eggs until well blended. Gradually pour yolk mixture back into topping and cook over medium heat, stirring constantly, 1 minute. Remove from heat. Add vanilla and butter, stirring until butter is melted. Cover surface with plastic wrap and chill for 1 hour.

6. Beat heavy cream in a chilled mixing bowl until stiff peaks form. Gently fold whipped cream into topping. Spoon topping over pineapple filling. Sprinkle toasted coconut evenly over top of pie. Refrigerate at least 1 hour before serving. Makes 1 single-crust pie.

✄ **KRISTINE SNYDER,** Kihei, Hawaii
First Prize, Maui Pineapple Festival, Maui, Hawaii, 2001

GLAZED PINEAPPLE PIE

Perfect Piecrust Pastry (recipe follows)
¼ cup all-purpose flour, plus
    more for rolling out dough
¾ cup flaked coconut
1 cup sugar
¼ teaspoon salt
1 tablespoon lemon juice
1 tablespoon unsalted butter or margarine,
    room temperature
1 can (20 oz.) crushed pineapple,
    drained with liquid reserved

GLAZE

½ cup confectioners' sugar
¼ teaspoon vanilla or rum extract
About 1 tablespoon reserved pineapple juice

1. Preheat oven to 375°F.

2. Roll out one pastry disk on a lightly floured surface and line a 9-inch pie plate. Trim pastry even with edge of plate rim. Sprinkle coconut over bottom.

3. Combine sugar, ¼ cup flour, salt, lemon juice, melted butter, and pineapple. Spoon filling into pie shell over coconut. Roll out a second pastry disk to fit top of pie and layer over filling. Trim, seal, and flute the edges. Cut slits in top to let steam escape. Bake for 45 to 50 minutes, or until crust is golden brown and filling is bubbly. Set on a wire rack to cool.

4. To make glaze: Combine confectioners' sugar and vanilla or rum extract in a small bowl. Stir in just enough of the pineapple juice to make a thick glaze. Drizzle glaze over pie while still warm. Cool completely on wire rack. Makes 1 double-crust pie.

PERFECT PIECRUST PASTRY

4 cups all-purpose flour
1 tablespoon sugar
1 teaspoon salt
1½ cups lard

1 egg
½ cup ice water
1 tablespoon vinegar

1. Whisk together flour, sugar, and salt in a large bowl. Cut in lard with a pastry blender.

2. Beat egg in a small bowl. Add ice water and vinegar and beat until well combined. Add egg mixture to flour mixture and mix until texture resembles soft clay.

3. Divide dough into four equal parts. Shape each portion into a disk. Wrap in plastic and chill until ready to use. Makes pastry for 4 single-crust or 2 double-crust pies.

✕ **JANICE NOSTROM,** Humboldt, Iowa, and **CAROLYN HARTMANN,** Dakota City, Iowa
Blue Ribbon Pie Presentation, 2002; Blue Ribbon, 2005, Clay County Fair, Spencer, Iowa

KEY LIME PIE

2 cups vanilla wafers

1 cup slivered almonds

⅓ cup unsalted butter, melted

2 packages (3 oz.) cream cheese,
    room temperature

¼ cup unsalted butter, room temperature

1 can (14 oz.) sweetened condensed milk

⅓ cup key lime juice

Grated lime zest

Whipped topping

1. Preheat oven to 350°F.

2. Pulse vanilla wafers in a food processor until crumbly. Add almonds and pulse until finely ground.

3. Place crumb mixture and melted butter in a bowl and stir to combine. Press mixture on bottom and up sides of a 9-inch pie plate. Bake for 10 minutes, or until lightly browned. Cool.

3. Combine cream cheese and butter in a food processor until fluffy, scraping down sides of bowl as necessary. Add condensed milk and key lime juice. Combine until well blended, stopping to scrape bowl as necessary.

4. Pour mixture into pie plate, cover with plastic wrap, and refrigerate at least 4 hours. Garnish with lime zest and whipped topping. Makes 1 single-crust pie.

※ **KASEY MEEK,** Hawthorne, Florida
Best of Show, Youth Division, Florida State Fair, Tampa, Florida, 2005

FAVORITE OKLAHOMA PECAN PIE

CRUST

1½ cups plus 3 tablespoons flour

1½ teaspoons sugar

½ teaspoon salt

½ cup canola oil

2 tablespoons cold milk

FILLING

¾ cup dark corn syrup

¼ cup maple syrup

½ cup sugar

3 extra large eggs

1 teaspoon vanilla

2 tablespoons unsalted butter, melted

1½ cups pecan halves

½ teaspoon salt

1. Preheat oven to 350°F.

2. To make crust: Whisk together flour, sugar, and salt in a medium bowl. Place oil in a 1-cup measuring cup, add milk, and stir with a fork. Pour over flour mixture and stir until well combined. Turn out crust mixture into a 9-inch pie plate. Pat down and shape with your fingers to fill pie pan. Flute the edges.

3. To make filling: Whisk together corn syrup, maple syrup, sugar, eggs, and vanilla. Carefully stir in melted butter. Add pecans and salt.

4. Pour filling into pie shell. Bake for 45 minutes. Cool on a wire rack. Makes 1 single-crust pie.

※ **DIANE BUCHNER,** Tulsa, Oklahoma
Sweepstakes Winner, Tulsa State Fair, Tulsa, Oklahoma, 2002

SWEET POTATO PIE

FILLING

2 medium sweet potatoes

1½ cups sugar, divided

½ cup heavy cream, plus more if needed

⅜ cup evaporated milk

¼ cup melted margarine,
   room temperature

2 eggs

1 teaspoon vanilla

1 unbaked 9-inch pie shell

TOPPING

1 egg

1 cup brown sugar

1 tablespoon melted margarine,
   room temperature

1 teaspoon vanilla

¼ cup pecans (optional)

1. Preheat oven to 350°F.

2. To make filling: Peel sweet potatoes, cut into pieces, and place in a greased casserole dish. Sprinkle ½ cup of the sugar over potatoes. Pour heavy cream over potatoes. Cook uncovered until tender, 20 to 30 minutes. If potatoes appear to be drying out, add more cream or cover with a tent of aluminum foil.

3. Mash cooked potatoes.

4. Mix 2 cups of the mashed potatoes, remaining cup of sugar, evaporated milk, melted margarine, eggs, and vanilla until well combined. Pour mixture into pie shell. Bake for 25 to 35 minutes, or until center of pie is firm.

5. To make topping: Combine egg, brown sugar, melted margarine, and vanilla. Pour topping over pie and sprinkle with pecans, if using. Return to oven and bake 10 minutes longer, or until topping is browned. Makes 1 single-crust pie.

✕ **VIRGINIA MARTIN,** Oglethorpe, Georgia
First Place, Yammy Good Sweet Potatoes—Sweet Class, Georgia National Fair, Perry, Georgia, 2005

⚬ NUTS ABOUT PECANS ⚬

Pecans are the only tree nuts native to North America. The United States produces more than 80% of the world's pecan crop, and Georgia is the leading pecan-producing state. There are more than 1,000 varieties of pecans. The name "pecan" comes from the Algonquin Indian word meaning "a tough nut to crack."

Pecans are available in many forms—vacuum-packed in jars, sealed in plastic bags, or packed in cans. For the freshest and most flavorful pecans, choose whole ones in the shell. When choosing whole unshelled pecans, look for nuts that are heavy for their size and don't rattle when shaken. There shouldn't be any cracks or holes in the shells. Unshelled pecans may be stored for about three months at room temperature.

My Raisin Pie

Double-crust pie pastry
Flour
½ cup plus 2 teaspoons sugar
¼ cup brown sugar
3 tablespoons cornstarch
⅓ cup orange juice

1 teaspoon grated orange zest
1¾ cups water
3 cups raisins
1 tablespoon milk

1. Preheat oven to 375°F.

2. Roll out half of pastry on a lightly floured surface and line a 9-inch pie plate.

3. Combine sugar, brown sugar, and cornstarch in a medium-size heavy saucepan. Stir in orange juice and zest. Stir in water and raisins. Cook over medium heat until mixture bubbles and thickens. Cool to room temperature.

4. Pour filling into pie shell. Roll out remaining pastry and layer over filling. Trim, seal, and flute the edges. Cut steam vents. Sprinkle remaining 2 teaspoons sugar and milk on top of pie. Bake for 40 to 45 minutes, or until pie is golden. Makes 1 single-crust pie.

✕ **LOUISE PIPER,** Garner, Iowa
Blue Ribbon, Clay County Fair, Spencer, Iowa, 1986

Raspberry-Blueberry Cream Pie

RASPBERRY FILLING
¾ cup sugar
¼ cup cornstarch
⅛ teaspoon salt
1¾ cups water
1 package (3 oz.) raspberry gelatin
1 package (12 oz.) frozen unsweetened
   raspberries
¾ cup fresh blueberries

CREAM FILLING
4 oz. cream cheese, room temperature
⅓ cup confectioners' sugar
1 teaspoon vanilla
⅛ teaspoon salt
1½ cups frozen whipped topping, thawed,
   plus more for garnish

1 baked 9-inch pie shell, cooled

1. To make raspberry filling: Combine sugar, cornstarch, and salt in a medium saucepan. Gradually stir in water. Cook over medium heat, stirring continuously until mixture comes to a boil, thickens, and is clear. Add gelatin and stir until dissolved. Stir in raspberries and blueberries. Refrigerate until slightly thickened.

2. To make cream filling: Combine cream cheese, confectioners' sugar, vanilla, and salt in a medium mixing bowl. Beat at medium speed until smooth. Beat in 1½ cups whipped topping.

3. Spread half of cream filling on bottom of pie shell. Top with half of raspberry filling. Repeat layers. Refrigerate for 1 hour. Garnish with whipped topping. Makes 1 single-crust pie.

✕ **PHYLLIS SZYMANEK,** Apollo Beach, Florida
Best of Show, Florida State Fair, Tampa, Florida, 2005

Rum-Raisin Cream Cheese Pie

⅓ cup rum

1 cup raisins

Single-crust pie pastry

Flour

1½ packages (12 oz.) cream cheese, room temperature

⅔ cup sugar

¼ teaspoon salt

2 eggs

⅔ cup heavy cream

1 teaspoon vanilla

SOUR CREAM TOPPING

1 cup sour cream

3 tablespoons sugar

1. The day before, heat rum in a small saucepan over medium-low heat just until simmering. Add raisins, cover, and set aside overnight to plump.

2. Roll out half of pastry on a lightly floured surface and line a 9-inch glass pie plate. Trim and flute edges.

3. In a large mixing bowl, beat cream cheese until soft and smooth. Add sugar and salt and continue beating until well blended. Beat in eggs until smooth. Stir in cream and vanilla. Stir in raisins and any remaining liquid.

4. Pour filling into pie shell. Bake for 10 minutes. Reduce heat to 350°F and bake 20 to 25 minutes longer, or until filling has puffed slightly and has set around the edges. The center should remain slightly soft; it will become firm as it cools. Cool for 1 hour.

5. To make sour cream topping: Stir together sour cream and sugar until sugar dissolves. Spread topping over pie, concealing any surface cracks. Chill for 1 hour before serving. Makes 1 single-crust pie.

※ **LINDA RAPP,** Columbus, Indiana
Reserve Grand Champion, Pie Contest, Bartholomew County 4-H Fair, Columbus, Indiana, 2005

Cooked Strawberry Pie

1 container (32 oz.) sweetened frozen strawberries, thawed and drained, with juice reserved

3 tablespoons sugar

2½ tablespoons quick-cooking tapioca

1½ tablespoons cornstarch

1 teaspoon lemon juice

Double-crust pie pastry

1½ tablespoons unsalted butter, room temperature

1. Preheat oven to 400°F.

2. Combine 1⅓ cups of reserved strawberry juice, sugar, tapioca, and cornstarch in a saucepan. Cook rapidly over medium-high heat until thickened; do not boil. Cool.

3. Add strawberries and lemon juice to syrup and stir to coat.

4. Line a 9-inch pie pan with pastry. Pour filling into pie shell and dot with butter. Layer remaining pastry over filling. Trim, seal, and flute the edges. Cut vents in top crust for steam to escape. Bake for 40 minutes until nicely browned. Makes 1 double-crust pie.

※ **PAUL McDADE,** Middletown, Ohio
First Place, Butler County Fair, Hamilton, Ohio, 1994, 1995, 1996, 1997, 1998, 2000, 2001
Best of Show, Pies, Butler County Fair, Hamilton, Ohio, 1996
First Place, Ohio State Fair, Columbus, Ohio, 1997

RED RASPBERRY FRESH-FRUIT PIE

CRUST

1½ cups all-purpose flour, plus
   more for rolling out dough

¾ teaspoon salt

½ cup plus 2 tablespoons shortening

3 tablespoons ice water

FILLING

1 cup sugar

3 tablespoons cornstarch

3 tablespoons white corn syrup

½ teaspoon lemon juice

Pinch of salt

1 cup water

½ teaspoon cinnamon

1 box (3 oz.) raspberry gelatin

2 cups red raspberries

1. Preheat oven to 475°F.

2. To make crust: Combine flour and salt. Cut in shortening with a pastry blender to form pea-sized particles. Sprinkle ice water over top and mix lightly with a fork. Gather dough together and form into a ball. Roll out on a lightly floured surface. Line a 9-inch pie plate with pastry. Prick pastry all over with a fork and bake for 8 to 10 minutes. Cool.

3. To make filling: Combine sugar, cornstarch, corn syrup, lemon juice, salt, and water in a large heavy saucepan. Cook over medium heat until thick. Remove from heat and stir in cinnamon and gelatin. Cool.

4. Place raspberries in a large bowl. Pour filling mixture over top and toss gently to combine. Pour into pie shell. Cool for several hours. Serve with whipped topping or ice cream, if desired. Makes 1 single-crust pie.

This recipe can also be followed to make pies filled with strawberries, peaches, or black raspberries.

✕ **NANCY HAWKINS,** Middlebury, Indiana
First Place, Elkhart County 4-H Fair, Goshen, Indiana, 2005

PECAN-SWEET POTATO CHEESECAKE TART

CRUST

½ cup all-purpose flour

½ cup chopped pecans

2 tablespoons unsalted butter, melted

TOPPING

2 tablespoons chopped pecans

1 tablespoon brown sugar

1 tablespoon unsalted butter, room temperature

FILLING

1 package (8 oz.) light cream cheese

1 cup sweet potato, cooked and mashed

¼ cup sugar

2 eggs

1. Preheat oven to 350°F.

2. To make crust: In a small bowl, combine flour, pecans, and melted butter. Press mixture into bottom of a 9-inch tart pan. Bake for 5 minutes. Remove from oven.

3. To make filling: In a small mixing bowl, beat light cream cheese, sweet potato, sugar, and eggs until well blended. Pour mixture over pecan crust.

4. To make topping: Combine pecans, brown sugar, and butter. Sprinkle over filling. Return pan to oven and bake 30 minutes longer, or until filling is set. Serve warm or chilled with ice cream or a dollop of whipped topping, if desired. Makes 8 to 10 servings.

⌗ **CARLA GARNTO,** Warner Robins, Georgia
Second Place, Yammy Good Sweet Potatoes, Georgia National Fair, Perry, Georgia, 2005

BLUEBERRY BUCKLE III

½ **cup unsalted butter, room temperature**
1½ **cups sugar**
2 **eggs, beaten**
1 **cup milk**
4 **cups all-purpose flour**
4 **teaspoons baking powder**
1 **teaspoon salt**
1¼ **teaspoons cinnamon**
2 **cups blueberries**

TOPPING
½ **cup unsalted butter, cut into pieces**
⅔ **cup all-purpose flour**
1 **cup sugar**
½ **teaspoon mace or nutmeg**

LEMON SAUCE
1 **cup unsalted butter, room temperature**
2 **cups sugar**
2 **cups water**
2 **eggs, beaten**
Grated zest and juice of 1 large lemon

1. Preheat oven to 375°F. Grease a 13 x 9 x 2-inch baking pan.

2. In a large mixing bowl, cream butter and sugar until light and fluffy. Add eggs and milk and beat well.

3. Whisk together flour, baking powder, salt, and cinnamon. Add to butter mixture and stir to combine. Gently fold in blueberries. Pour batter into pan.

4. To make topping: Combine butter, flour, sugar, and mace or nutmeg until crumbly. Sprinkle evenly over batter. Bake for 45 minutes, or until a toothpick inserted in center comes out clean.

5. To make lemon sauce: Preheat broiler. Melt butter in a large saucepan over medium heat. Add sugar, water, and eggs. Bring to a boil. Remove from heat and stir in lemon zest and juice. Pour as much of the lemon sauce as possible over the baked cake. Broil until bubbly and golden. Cut into squares. Serve with remaining sauce. Makes 12 servings.

⌗ **LOVERN STOCKWELL,** Bangor, Maine
First Prize, Wild Blueberry Festival Cooking
Competition, Machias, Maine, 2000

CRIMSON PIE WITH SOUR CREAM CRUST

FILLING

½ small orange, unpeeled, cut in pieces,
    and seeded

4 cups frozen blueberries, thawed

12 oz. cranberries

1½ cups sugar

3 tablespoons cornstarch

2 tablespoons unsalted butter,
    cut in pieces

SOUR CREAM CRUST

¼ cup plus 2 tablespoons sour cream

2 tablespoons ice water

1 teaspoon sugar

¾ teaspoon salt

2¼ cups all-purpose flour, plus more
    for rolling out dough

¼ cup cake flour

½ cup chilled unsalted butter, room temperature

½ cup chilled vegetable shortening

Milk (do not use nonfat milk)

Sugar

1. To cook filling: Coarsely grind orange in a food processor or blender. Combine orange, blueberries, cranberries, sugar, and cornstarch in a medium saucepan over medium-high heat. Bring to a boil and cook, stirring continuously, until thick, 3 minutes. Cool completely.

2. To make crust: Combine sour cream, ice water, sugar, and salt.

3. In a large bowl, whisk together all-purpose flour and cake flour. Cut in butter and shortening with a pastry blender or your fingers until mixture resembles coarse meal. Add sour cream mixture and stir just until dough comes together.

4. Turn out dough onto a lightly floured surface. Divide in half. Form each half into a ball and flatten into a disk. Wrap each disk in plastic wrap. Chill for 1 hour.

5. Position oven rack in center of oven. Heat oven to 400°F.

6. Roll out one disk on a lightly floured surface to a ⅛-inch thickness. Roll up dough on the rolling pin and transfer to a 9-inch pie plate. Press gently into place. Trim off the excess dough, leaving a ¼-inch overhang.

7. Spoon filling into pie shell, mounding slightly in center. Dot with butter. Roll out second dough disk and layer on top of filling. Trim, seal, and crimp or flute edges. Cut several slits in top crust for steam to escape.

8. Gather up dough trimmings and roll out to a ⅛-inch thickness. Using a cookie cutter or small sharp knife, cut out 6 or 7 small leaf shapes. Brush top pastry with milk. Place leaves on top and press gently. Brush tops of leaves with milk. Sprinkle entire top pastry with sugar. Place pie plate on a rimmed baking sheet on the middle rack of a preheated 400°F oven. Bake for 50 minutes, or until golden brown. Cool on a wire rack 1 hour. Serve warm or at room temperature. Makes 1 double-crust pie.

✄ **CHRISSY THIBODEAU,** Woodbridge, Virginia
Best Pie, Wild Blueberry Festival Cooking Contest, Machias, Maine, 2000

You can prepare this pie pastry up to one month in advance and store it in the freezer.

APPLE CRISP

⅔ cup melted margarine, room temperature,
    plus more for pan
6 cups sliced apples
2 tablespoons lemon juice
1 cup chopped walnuts

⅔ cup all-purpose flour
1 cup light brown sugar
2 cups rolled oats
1 teaspoon salt
2 teaspoons cinnamon

1. Preheat oven to 375°F. Grease the bottom of a 13 x 9 x 2-inch baking pan with margarine or cooking spray.

2. Layer apples in pan. Sprinkle lemon juice over apples.

3. In a large bowl, combine walnuts, flour, light brown sugar, melted margarine, oats, salt, and cinnamon until well blended. Sprinkle over top of apples. Bake for 30 minutes. Serve warm with vanilla ice cream or whipped cream, if desired. Makes 8 to 10 servings.

✄ **JENNIFER HELMING,** Bristol, Connecticut
Blue Ribbon, Terryville Country Fair, Terryville, Connecticut, 2005

WINNER'S CIRCLE TIP | Sprinkling lemon juice over the apples keeps the apples from turning brown and also add a little tang to the recipe.

MONA'S RASPBERRY-CHERRY PIE

1½ cups sugar
3 tablespoons quick-cooking tapioca
2 cups fresh or frozen unsweetened
    raspberries
1 cup pitted tart cherries (fresh,
    frozen, or canned)

1 teaspoon lemon juice
Double-crust pie pastry
Flour
Unsalted butter, room temperature

1. Preheat oven to 350°F.

2. In a medium bowl, combine sugar and tapioca. Add raspberries, cherries, and lemon juice. Toss to coat. Let stand for 15 minutes.

3. Roll out half of pastry on a lightly floured surface and line a 9-inch pie plate. Spoon filling into pie shell. Dot with butter. Roll out top crust and layer over filling. Trim, seal, and flute the edges. Cut slits in pastry. Cover edges loosely with foil. Bake for 60 to 70 minutes, or until golden brown. Cool on a wire rack. Store in the refrigerator. Makes 1 double-crust pie.

✄ **MARCO AYALA,** South Hero, Vermont
Best Cherry Pie, Champlain Valley Exposition, Essex Junction, Vermont, 2005

Peach Cobbler

PASTRY

2 cups all-purpose flour

1 teaspoon salt

⅔ cup shortening

5 to 7 tablespoons ice water

FILLING

¾ cup sugar, plus more for topping

2 tablespoons cornstarch

½ cup water

4 cups peeled and sliced peaches, fresh or frozen

Milk

1. Preheat oven to 400°F. Set aside an 8-inch baking pan.

2. To make pastry: In a large bowl, whisk together flour and salt. Cut in shortening with a pastry blender until mixture resembles coarse meal. Add ice water and mix with a fork just until dough is moistened and gathers into a ball. Roll out dough on a floured surface. Press into bottom and up sides of an 8 x 8 x 2-inch baking pan.

3. To make filling: Combine sugar, cornstarch, cinnamon, water, and peaches in a large saucepan over medium-high heat. Bring to a boil and cook, stirring often, for 1 minute.

4. Pour peach mixture into pastry-lined pan. Brush edges of pastry with milk and sprinkle with sugar. Bake for 25 to 30 minutes, or until golden brown. Makes 6 to 8 servings.

✕ **PEGGY LONG,** Oklahoma City, Oklahoma

Fourth Place, Old Fashioned Cobbler Contest, Oklahoma State Fair, Oklahoma City, Oklahoma, 2005

Georgia Apple-Pecan Torte

2 refrigerated piecrusts

5 Georgia apples, peeled, cored, and diced

3 tablespoons unsalted butter, divided

½ teaspoon cinnamon

2 tablespoons flour

1 cup plus 3 tablespoons sugar, divided

3 egg yolks

1 cup evaporated milk

¾ cup chopped pecans

¾ cup flake coconut

Caramel sauce

1. Preheat oven to 450°F. Cut each piecrust in half, place on baking sheets, and bake for 8 minutes, or until browned.

2. In a microwave-safe bowl, combine apples, 1 tablespoon of the butter, cinnamon, flour, and 3 tablespoons of the sugar. Microwave on high for 3 minutes.

3. Combine egg yolks, remaining cup of sugar, evaporated milk, and remaining 2 tablespoons butter in a saucepan over medium-high heat. Cook until thickened. Stir in pecans and coconut.

4. Place one baked half-piecrust on a cutting board. Spread one-quarter of apple mixture on piecrust; top with one-quarter of pecan mixture. Repeat the layering three more times. Cut in wedges, place on individual serving plates, and drizzle caramel sauce over the top. Makes 4 to 6 servings.

✕ **DEBRA BROOKS,** Byron, Georgia

Second Place, Georgia Apple Recipe Contest, Georgia National Fair, Perry, Georgia, 2005

TRIPLE-BERRY PIE

1¼ cups fresh blueberries

1¼ cups fresh raspberries

1¼ cups fresh blackberries

½ teaspoon almond extract

1¼ cups sugar

¼ cup quick-cooking tapioca

¼ teaspoon nutmeg

¼ teaspoon salt

Double-crust pie pastry

Flour

1 tablespoon lemon juice

1. Preheat oven to 400°F.

2. Combine blueberries, raspberries, blackberries, and almond extract in a large bowl. Toss to coat.

3. Mix together sugar, tapioca, nutmeg and salt. Pour over fruit and stir gently to combine. Let stand for 15 minutes.

4. Roll out half of pastry on a lightly floured surface and line a 9-inch pie plate. Trim pastry even with edge of rim.

5. Stir lemon juice into fruit filling. Spoon filling into pie shell. Roll out remaining pastry, cut into strips, and arrange on top of filling for a lattice crust. Seal strips at edges and trim off excess. Flute edges if desired. Bake for 20 minutes. Reduce heat to 350°F and bake 30 minutes longer, or until the crust is golden brown and filling is bubbly. Makes 1 lattice-crust pie.

※ **LAURA SCHAUB,** Peoria, Illinois
First Place, Heart of Illinois Fair, Peoria, Illinois, 2005

To substitute frozen berries for fresh, thaw and drain the berries first.

BLACKBERRY COBBLER

FILLING

½ cup sugar

1 tablespoon cornstarch

2½ cups canned blackberries and juice

Unsalted butter, room temperature

TOPPING

1 cup all-purpose flour

1 tablespoon sugar

1½ teaspoons baking powder

½ teaspoon salt

3 tablespoons shortening

½ cup milk

1. Preheat oven to 400°.

2. To make filling: Combine sugar and cornstarch in a saucepan. Gradually stir in blackberries and juice over medium-high heat. Bring to a boil and cook, stirring constantly, for 1 minute. Remove from heat. Pour filling into 1½-quart baking dish. Dot with butter.

3. To make topping: Sift together flour, sugar, baking powder, and salt. Cut in shortening with a pastry blender until mixture resembles coarse meal. Stir in milk just until moistened. Drop by spoonfuls onto berries. Bake for 25 to 30 minutes, or until golden brown. Serve warm. Makes 6 servings.

※ **SYLVIA BAYLESS,** Midwest City, Oklahoma
First Place, Old Fashioned Cobbler Contest, Oklahoma State Fair, Oklahoma City, Oklahoma, 2005

Maple-Walnut Torte with Coconut Cream

Cooking Spray
¾ cup self-rising flour
¾ cup finely ground walnuts
¾ cup sugar substitute blend for baking
3 eggs
½ cup melted margarine, room temperature
½ cup sour cream

½ teaspoon maple flavoring
½ cup frozen unsweetened coconut, thawed

COCONUT CREAM
¼ cup sour cream
½ cup frozen unsweetened coconut, thawed
¼ cup sugar substitute blend for baking

1. Preheat oven to 325°F. Coat a 10-inch tart pan with cooking spray.

2. In a large mixing bowl, combine flour, walnuts, and sugar substitute.

3. In a small bowl, combine eggs, melted margarine, sour cream, maple flavoring, and coconut. Stir into flour mixture. Pour batter into pan. Bake for 30 minutes, or until lightly browned; do not overbake.

4. To make coconut cream: In a small bowl, combine sour cream, coconut, and sugar substitute. Let stand for 10 minutes. Spoon evenly over torte. Makes 10 servings.

※ **Debra Brooks,** Byron, Georgia
Third Place, Cooking Lite the ADA Way, Georgia National Fair, Perry, Georgia, 2005

Fresh Fruit Tart

½ cup unsalted butter, room temperature
1¼ cups plus 1 tablespoon sugar, divided
1 large egg
½ teaspoon vanilla
1 tablespoon milk
1¾ cups all-purpose flour, plus
    more for rolling out dough
1 teaspoon baking powder

¼ teaspoon salt
1 small package (3 oz.) cream cheese
1 cup sour cream
Grapes, blueberries, sliced strawberries,
    sliced kiwi, or other fresh fruit
½ cup apricot jelly
3 tablespoons water

1. In a large mixing bowl, cream butter and 1 cup of the sugar. Beat in egg, vanilla, and milk. Whisk together flour, baking powder, and salt; blend into creamed mixture. Gather dough into a ball, wrap in plastic wrap, and chill for 1 hour.

2. Preheat oven to 400°F. Roll out dough to a ¼-inch thickness. Press into bottom and up sides of an 11 x 1-inch round tart pan. Trim off excess. Prick pastry all over with a fork, and bake for 20 minutes, or until light brown.

3. In a small mixing bowl, beat cream cheese until soft and fluffy. Fold in sour cream and ¼ cup of the sugar. Spread mixture on baked crust. Sprinkle with remaining tablespoon of sugar. Arrange grapes, blueberries, strawberries, kiwi, or other fresh fruit on top.

4. Combine apricot jelly and water in a small saucepan over low heat. Cook, stirring, until jelly is dissolved. Drizzle glaze over top of fruit. Chill for 1 hour. Cut into wedges. Makes 14 to 16 servings.

※ **Eugenie Delaney,** North Ferrisburg, Vermont
Best Dairy Food, Addison County Fair & Field Days, New Haven, Vermont, 2005

CHAPTER 11

CAKES AND CHEESECAKES

COFFEE-BROWN SUGAR ANGEL FOOD CAKE

1¼ cups sifted cake flour

2 cups brown sugar, divided

2 tablespoons instant coffee dissolved in
    1 tablespoon hot water

12 large egg whites, at room temperature
    for 15 minutes

1½ teaspoons cream of tartar

1 teaspoon salt

2 teaspoons vanilla

Confectioners' sugar

1. Preheat oven to 350°F.

2. Sift together cake flour and 1 cup of the brown sugar.

3. Combine coffee mixture and egg whites in a mixing bowl. Beat until foamy. Add cream of tartar and salt and beat until soft peaks form. Add remaining 1 cup brown sugar, 2 tablespoons at a time, beating until stiff peaks form and brown sugar dissolves.

4. Sift flour mixture over egg whites ¼ cup at a time, folding in after each addition. Fold in vanilla. Spoon batter into a 10 x 4-inch tube pan. Cut through batter with a knife to break up air pockets. Bake in bottom half of oven for 40 minutes. Invert pan and cool. Loosen edges with a metal spatula and place on a cake plate. Sprinkle confectioners' sugar over top. Makes 1 angel food cake.

✕ **CORINNA LEINWEBER,** Douglas, Wyoming
Second Place, Coffee Contest, Wyoming State Fair, Douglas, Wyoming, 2005

ANGEL FOOD CAKE

1¼ cups confectioners' sugar

1 cup cake flour

1⅔ cups egg whites (12 to 14 whites),
    room temperature

1½ teaspoons cream of tartar

½ teaspoon salt

2 teaspoons vanilla

½ teaspoon almond extract

1¼ cups sugar

1. Preheat oven to 375°F.

2. Combine confectioner's sugar and cake flour.

3. In a large mixing bowl, combine egg whites, cream of tartar, and salt. Beat at high speed until soft peaks form. Beat in vanilla and almond extract.

4. With mixer running, sprinkle in sugar, 2 tablespoons at a time, beating until sugar is completely dissolved and whites stand in stiff peaks. Fold in flour mixture just until flour disappears.

5. Pour batter into an ungreased 10 x 4-inch tube pan. Bake for 30 to 35 minutes, or until cake springs back when lightly touched. Invert pan on a funnel or bottle and cool completely. Loosen edges with a metal spatula and place on cake plate. Makes 1 angel food cake.

✕ **MADDIE CONLEY,** age 11, Spencer, Iowa
Blue Ribbon, Clay County Fair, Spencer, Iowa, 2004, 2005

ALMOND POUND CAKE

2 cups sifted all-purpose flour, plus
   more for pans
1 cup unsalted butter, room temperature
1 roll (7 oz.) pure almond paste,
   chopped into small pieces

1 cup sugar
4 eggs
1 teaspoon baking powder
½ cup milk

1. Preheat oven to 325°F. Grease and flour two 8½ x 4½ x 2½-inch loaf pans.
2. Cream butter, almond paste, and sugar in a mixing bowl until fluffy. With mixer running, add eggs one at a time and mix well to combine.
3. Add flour and baking powder alternately with milk, mixing well after each addition to make a smooth batter. Pour batter into loaf pans until two-thirds full. Bake for 50 minutes, or until top is golden brown and cake springs back when touched. Makes 2 pound cakes.

To bake this batter in a Bundt pan, increase the baking time to 60 minutes.

✄ **MARJORIE WIMSATT,** Valrico, Florida
First Place, Adult Division, Florida State Fair, Tampa, Florida, 2005

APPLE SPICE CAKE TRIFLE

1 package (18¼ oz.) spice cake mix
1¼ cups applesauce
3 eggs
⅓ cup vegetable oil
1 can (21 oz.) apple pie filling
1 tablespoon unsalted butter or
   margarine, room temperature

7 teaspoons cinnamon, divided
3 cups cold milk
1 package (5.1 oz.) instant vanilla
   pudding mix
1 envelope (3.2 oz.) whipped topping mix
1 carton (12 oz.) frozen whipped topping, thawed
½ cup chopped walnuts, divided

1. Preheat oven to 350°F. Grease a 13 x 9 x 2-inch baking pan.
2. Combine cake mix, applesauce, eggs, and oil in a mixing bowl. Beat at medium speed for 2 minutes. Pour into pan and bake for 35 to 40 minutes, or until a toothpick inserted in center comes out clean. Cool on a wire rack.
3. Combine apple pie filling, butter, and 1 teaspoon of the cinnamon in a saucepan. Heat over medium-low heat until butter is melted. Stir until well blended. cool.
4. Combine milk, pudding mix, whipped topping mix, and remaining 6 teaspoons cinnamon in a mixing bowl. Beat on high speed to make a thick custard, about 5 minutes. Let stand 5 minutes.
5. To assemble trifle: Cut cake into bite-size cubes. Layer half of the cake cubes in the bottom of a 6-quart glass trifle bowl. Spread one-third of the whipped topping over the cake cubes. Top with half of the apple filling, ¼ cup of the walnuts, and half of the custard. Repeat the layers, ending with remaining topping mixture. Cover and chill for at least 2 hours. Makes 20 to 24 servings.

✄ **GENEVA PARKER,** Lewisburg, West Virginia
First Place, Apple Sauce Dessert Contest, State Fair of West Virginia, Lewisburg, West Virginia, 2005

Apple Cake

4 large tart apples, peeled, cored,
   and chopped
1 cup sugar
1 cup chopped nuts
⅔ cup unsalted butter, melted
2 eggs, beaten
2 teaspoons vanilla

2 cups all-purpose flour
2 teaspoons baking soda
2 teaspoons ground cinnamon
2 teaspoons ground allspice
1 teaspoon cardamom
½ teaspoon salt

1. Preheat oven to 350°F. Grease two 8 x 8 x 2-inch baking pans.

2. Combine apples, sugar, nuts, and melted butter in a large bowl. Stir in eggs and vanilla.

3. Sift together flour, baking soda, cinnamon, allspice, cardamom, and salt. Add flour mixture to apple mixture and stir until blended.

4. Divide batter between pans. Bake for 45 to 50 minutes. Cool on wire racks and cut into bars. Makes 16 bars.

✕ **Linda L. Shumate,** San Diego, California
First Place, San Diego County Fair, Del Mar, California, 2004

Rum-Brandy Apple Cake

Cooking spray
1 cup unbleached all-purpose flour
1 cup whole wheat flour
2 teaspoons baking soda
2 teaspoons cinnamon
½ teaspoon ground cloves
½ teaspoon nutmeg
⅓ cup dark raisins
½ cup chopped walnuts, lightly toasted
¾ cup unsweetened apple juice
   concentrate, thawed

¾ cup sugar substitute
½ cup liquid egg substitute
1½ cups canola oil
¼ cup plus ½ teaspoon rum
¼ cup brandy
1 teaspoon vanilla
4 cups apples, peeled, cored, and sliced
⅓ cup fruit-only strawberry preserves
Fresh strawberries
Fresh mint leaves

1. Preheat oven to 350°F. Generously coat 12-cup Bundt pan with cooking spray.

2. Sift together all-purpose flour, whole wheat flour, baking soda, cinnamon, cloves, and nutmeg in a medium bowl. Drop in raisins and walnuts and toss to coat.

3. In a large mixing bowl, combine apple juice concentrate, sugar substitute, egg substitute, oil, ¼ cup of the rum, brandy, and vanilla. Add flour mixture and stir just until moistened. Add apples and stir gently. Pour the batter into pan. Bake for 1 hour. Cool for 10 minutes in pan and turn out onto a wire rack.

4. Heat preserves in a saucepan over low heat until melted. Add remaining ½ teaspoon rum and stir well to combine. Drizzle sauce over warm cake and cool complete. Garnish with strawberries and mint leaves. Makes 1 Bundt cake.

✕ **Tulie Trejo,** Chula Vista, California
Sweepstakes Winner, Healthy Eating Contest—Desserts, San Diego County Fair, Del Mar, California, 2004

BLACKBERRY JAM CAKE

3 cups all-purpose flour, plus more for pans

1 teaspoon baking soda

¼ teaspoon salt

1 teaspoon ground allspice

½ teaspoon ground cloves

1 teaspoon cinnamon

1 teaspoon nutmeg

1 cup pecans, chopped

1 cup dates, chopped

1 cup unsalted butter, room temperature

1½ cups sugar

3 eggs, beaten

1 cup seedless blackberry jam

1 cup buttermilk

CREAM CHEESE FROSTING

¼ cup unsalted butter, room temperature

1 package (8 oz.) cream cheese

1 lb. confectioners' sugar

1 teaspoon vanilla

1. Preheat oven to 350°F. Grease and flour three 9 x 2-inch round cake pans.

2. Whisk together flour, baking soda, salt, allspice, cloves, cinnamon, and nutmeg to combine.

3. Place pecans and dates in a small bowl. Add a few tablespoons of the flour mixture and toss to coat.

4. Cream butter and sugar in a mixing bowl until fluffy. Beat in eggs and jam. Add flour mixture alternately with buttermilk, beating until smooth after each addition. Stir in pecans and dates. Divide batter among 3 cake pans. Bake for 20 to 30 minutes. Turn out onto wire racks and cool.

5. To make cream cheese frosting: Combine butter, cream cheese, confectioners' sugar, and vanilla in a mixing bowl. Beat until smooth. Assemble cake layers, spreading frosting between layers and on sides and top of cake. Makes 1 three-layer cake.

※ **ANGEL VELEZ,** Rotan, Texas
First Place, West Texas Fair & Rodeo, Abilene, Texas, 2005

PEACH POUND CAKE

2½ cups plus 1 tablespoon flour, divided,
  plus more for pan

2 peaches, sliced

2 tablespoons brown sugar

¾ cup margarine, room temperature

1 cup sugar

1 teaspoon baking powder

½ teaspoon baking soda

¼ teaspoon salt

1 teaspoon vanilla

1 container (8 oz.) lemon yogurt

1 egg

1 egg white

1. Preheat oven to 325°F. Grease and flour a 12-cup Bundt pan.

2. In a bowl, combine peaches, brown sugar, and 1 tablespoon of the flour until peaches are well coated. Layer peaches in Bundt pan.

3. In a mixing bowl, cream margarine and sugar. Stir in remaining 2½ cups flour, baking powder, baking soda, and salt. Add vanilla, yogurt, egg, and egg white. Beat at medium speed for 3 minutes.

4. Pour batter over peaches. Bake for 1 hour. Cool for 10 minutes in pan and turn out cake onto a wire rack. Makes 1 Bundt cake.

※ **GAIL STRONG,** Hartland, Wisconsin
Grand Champion, Waukesha County Fair, Pewaukee, Wisconsin, 1996

+ ENTERING THE CONTEST +

Farm wives in the early days were renowned for their cooking skills. A woman who provided enticing meals for the farm help was an asset to a farmer who wanted to attract the hardest-working farmhands at harvest time. Getting ready for the fair in the early part of the last century, a farm wife said, "was filled with agony and joy. Everyone pitched in. If you entered a cake, you were putting your reputation as a housewife on display. At judging time your heart was in your mouth."

From article by Jenny Nolan, courtesy of *The Detroit News*

CARROT HARVEST CAKE

2 cups all-purpose flour, plus
   more for pans
2 teaspoons baking soda
1 teaspoon salt
2 teaspoons cinnamon
⅓ cup vegetable oil
1 cup water
2 cups brown sugar
3 eggs
⅓ cup apple butter
2 cups grated carrots

MAPLE BUTTERCREAM FROSTING
4 tablespoons unsalted butter, room temperature
¼ maple syrup
3 cups confectioners' sugar

GARNISH
2 cups coarsely chopped walnuts
¼ cup semisweet chocolate chips, melted
¼ cup chopped almonds
½ cup golden raisins
2 tablespoons dark raisins
2 tablespoons chopped dried apricots
2 tablespoons dried cranberries

1. Preheat oven to 375°F. Grease and flour two 9 x 2-inch round cake pans.

2. Combine flour, baking soda, salt, and cinnamon.

3. Combine oil, water, brown sugar, eggs, apple butter, and carrots in a mixing bowl. Beat on low speed until well blended. Add flour mixture and beat for 2 minutes. Pour batter into pans. Bake for 35 to 40 minutes, or until a toothpick inserted in center comes out clean. Cool in pans for 10 minutes and turn out onto wire racks.

4. To make maple buttercream frosting: Beat butter and syrup in a small mixing bowl. With mixer running, gradually add confectioners' sugar and beat until smooth.

5. To frost and garnish cake: Place one cake layer on a serving plate and spread frosting over top. Add second cake layer. Spread remaining frosting over top and sides of cake. Press walnuts into side of cake. Pipe melted chocolate chips onto cake for tree trunk. Combine almonds, golden and dark raisins, apricots, and cranberries in a small bowl. Press most of mixture into frosting at top of trunk to look like leaves. Press remaining mixture around base of trunk to look like fallen leaves. Makes 1 two-layer cake.

⌗ **KELLY B. EVERHART,** Seffner, Florida
First Place, Adult Division, Florida State Fair, Tampa, Florida, 2005

DOUBLE-GINGER BUNDT CAKE

Cooking spray
Butter
3¼ cups all-purpose flour, plus more for pan
5 teaspoons ground ginger
2½ teaspoons baking soda
1½ teaspoons cinnamon
¼ teaspoon salt
1 cup light molasses
1 cup sugar
¼ cup sour cream
2 large eggs

2 teaspoons vanilla
1 cup boiling water
1 cup vegetable oil
¼ cup chopped crystallized ginger
1 cup chopped toasted walnuts

GLAZE
½ cup lemon curd (or 3 tablespoons lemon juice)
2 tablespoons unsalted butter, room temperature
Grated zest of 1 lemon
2 cups sifted confectioners' sugar

1. Preheat oven to 350°F. Coat a 12-cup Bundt pan with cooking spray. Grease with butter. Dust lightly with flour.

2. Sift together flour, ginger, baking soda, cinnamon, and salt.

3. Whisk molasses, sugar, sour cream, eggs, and vanilla in large bowl until well blended. Whisk in boiling water and oil, followed by flour mixture. Fold in crystallized ginger and walnuts. Pour batter into pan. Bake for 45 minutes, or until tester inserted near center comes out clean. Cool in pan on a wire rack for 20 minutes before turning out onto a plate.

4. To make glaze: Combine lemon curd (or lemon juice) and butter in a microwave-safe bowl. Microwave on high for 1 minute, or until butter is melted and curd is softened. Add zest and sugar, stirring until smooth. Drizzle glaze over cake and serve. Makes 1 Bundt cake.

✕ **PATRICIA PHELAN,** La Jolla, California
First Place, San Diego County Fair, Del Mar, California, 2004

APPLE TWEED CAKE

Butter
2 cups all-purpose flour, plus more for pan
1 cup cake flour
1½ teaspoons baking soda
½ teaspoon cinnamon
¼ teaspoon ground cloves
¼ teaspoon mace

¼ teaspoon ground ginger
½ teaspoon salt
1½ cups vegetable oil
2 cups sugar
3 eggs
3½ cups chopped, unpeeled apples
¾ cup chopped toasted walnuts

1. Preheat oven to 325°F. Butter and flour 4 individual loaf pans.

2. Sift together all-purpose flour, cake flour, baking soda, cinnamon, cloves, mace, ginger, and salt.

3. Combine oil and sugar in a mixing bowl. Beat for 3 minutes. Beat in eggs, one at a time. Gradually fold in flour mixture and combine thoroughly. Stir in apples and walnuts with a spatula. Divide batter among pans. Bake for 1 hour. Makes 4 mini loaves.

✕ **MARY BARGIEL,** Vergennes, Vermont
Best Apple Baked Goods, Addison County Fair & Field Days, New Haven, Vermont, 2004

BLUEBERRY-PUMPKIN POUND CAKE

3 cups all-purpose flour, plus more for pan

4 teaspoons baking powder

¼ teaspoon baking soda

¼ teaspoon salt

1½ teaspoons cinnamon

½ teaspoon nutmeg

½ teaspoon ground cloves

1 cup unsalted butter,
    room temperature

1 cup sugar

1 cup brown sugar

1 teaspoon vanilla

3 eggs, room temperature

1⅓ cups canned pumpkin

½ cup milk

1¼ cups blueberries, fresh or frozen

PUMPKIN GLAZE

1 cup sifted confectioners' sugar

1 tablespoon canned pumpkin

¼ teaspoon vanilla

2 to 3 teaspoons milk

1. Preheat oven to 325°F. Grease and lightly flour a 10 x 4-inch tube pan.

2. Whisk together flour, baking powder, baking soda, salt, cinnamon, nutmeg, and cloves.

3. In a large mixing bowl, cream butter at high speed for 30 seconds. Set mixer to medium speed and add sugar and brown sugar, 2 tablespoons at a time. When all sugar is added, beat at medium speed for 6 minutes. Add vanilla. Add eggs one at a time, beating on low speed for 1 minute after each addition and scraping down sides of bowl frequently.

4. With mixer on low speed, add flour mixture, pumpkin, and milk alternately until well combined. Stir in berries. Pour batter into pan. Bake for 1 hour 15 minutes. Cool in pan 15 minutes. Turn out onto a wire rack and cool completely.

5. To make pumpkin glaze: Combine confectioners' sugar, pumpkin, and vanilla in a small bowl. Add milk and stir to make a thick glaze. Pour glaze over top of cake. Makes 1 cake.

✕ **DEBBIE AYERS,** Crawford, Maine
Overall Winner, Wild Blueberry Festival Cooking Competition, Machias, Maine, 1999

FRESH-PICKED BLACKBERRY CAKE

3 cups self-rising flour, plus more for pan

1 cup unsalted butter or margarine,
   room temperature

2 cups sugar

3 eggs

1 teaspoon cinnamon

½ teaspoon nutmeg

1½ cups blackberries, with some juice

1. Preheat oven to 350°F. Grease and lightly flour a 10 x 4-inch tube pan.

2. Cream butter and sugar in a mixing bowl. Beat in eggs.

3. Add flour and mix until well combined. Stir in cinnamon and nutmeg. Fold in blackberries. Batter will be a purplish color. Spoon batter into pan. Bake for 1 hour, or until cake separates from pan and a toothpick inserted in center comes out clean. Cool on a wire rack. Makes 1 cake.

※ **YVONNE GREEN,** Ashland, Kentucky
Blue Ribbon, Boyd County Fair, Ashland, Kentucky, 2005

WINNER'S CIRCLE TIP | Don't feel obligated to glaze this cake. It can stand alone without any additional flavoring or decoration.

COCONUT POUND CAKE

2¼ cups all-purpose flour, plus more for pan

1½ teaspoons baking powder

½ teaspoon salt

2 cups sugar

1 stick (½ cup) butter-flavored shortening

5 eggs

1½ teaspoons coconut extract

1 cup buttermilk

GLAZE

½ cup sugar

¼ cup water

1½ teaspoons coconut extract

1 cup toasted coconut

1. Preheat oven to 350°F. Grease and flour a 9 x 5 x 3-inch loaf pan.

2. Combine flour, baking powder, and salt.

3. In a large mixing bowl, combine sugar and shortening. Beat on low speed until well blended. Add eggs one at a time, beating slowly after each addition. Add coconut extract.

4. With mixer running, add flour mixture and buttermilk alternately. Beat until well combined. Pour batter into a loaf pan. Bake for 50 minutes. Turn out onto a wire rack.

5. To make glaze: Heat sugar, water, and coconut extract in a saucepan over medium-high heat. Bring to a boil, remove from heat, and cool for 15 minutes. Set warm cake on a rack and slip waxed paper underneath to catch drips. Poke holes in top of cake with a skewer. Spoon glaze over top of cake and sprinkle with coconut. Makes 1 loaf cake.

※ **LINDA GASS,** Mango, Florida
First Place, Adult Division, Florida State Fair, Tampa, Florida, 2005

BANANA POUND CAKE

3 cups all-purpose flour, plus more for pan

1 teaspoon baking powder

½ teaspoon salt

3 ripe bananas, mashed

3 tablespoons milk

2 teaspoons vanilla

1 cup shortening

½ cup unsalted butter, room temperature

3 cups sugar

5 large eggs

1. Preheat oven to 350°F. Grease and flour a 10 x 4-inch tube pan.

2. Combine flour, baking powder, and salt in a small bowl.

3. Mix bananas, milk, and vanilla in a separate bowl until well blended.

4. Cream shortening and butter in a mixing bowl at medium speed for 2 minutes. Gradually add sugar and beat well, 5 to 7 minutes. Beat in eggs one at a time. With mixer running, add banana mixture and flour mixture alternately. Mix until well combined. Pour batter into pan. Bake for 1 hour 20 minutes. Invert pan and cool. Makes 1 cake.

✄ **CASEY COBURN,** Hawthorne, Florida
Best of Show, Youth Division, Florida State Fair, Tampa, Florida, 2005

CARROT CAKE

1½ cups all-purpose flour, plus more for pans

1½ cups sugar

1 teaspoon baking powder

½ teaspoon baking soda

1 teaspoon salt

½ teaspoon cinnamon

½ teaspoon ground ginger

½ teaspoon nutmeg

1 cup cooked mashed carrots

¾ cup vegetable oil

1 can (8¼ oz.) crushed pineapple

3 eggs

1 teaspoon vanilla

1 tablespoon hot water

½ cup chopped walnuts

¼ cup raisins

CREAM CHEESE FROSTING

1 package (8 oz.) cream cheese

½ cup unsalted butter, room temperature

1 lb. confectioners' sugar

1 teaspoon vanilla

1. Preheat oven to 350°F. Grease and flour two 9 x 2-inch round cake pans.

2. In a large bowl, whisk together flour, sugar, baking powder, baking soda, salt, cinnamon, ginger, and nutmeg.

3. Combine carrots, oil, pineapple, eggs, vanilla, and water. Add to flour mixture and stir until smooth. Stir in walnuts and raisins. Pour batter into pans. Bake for 35 to 40 minutes, or until cake springs back when lightly touched. Remove from pans and cool on wire racks.

4. To make cream cheese frosting: Combine cream cheese, butter, confectioners' sugar, and vanilla in a mixing bowl. Beat until smooth. Assemble cake layers, spreading frosting between layers and on sides and top of cake. Makes 1 two-layer cake.

✄ **SUE HAMMEL,** Wakarusa, Indiana
First Place, President's Baked Item, Elkhart County 4-H Fair, Goshen, Indiana, 2005

Carrot Cupcakes

2 cups all-purpose flour
1 teaspoon baking powder
1 teaspoon baking soda
¼ teaspoon salt
2 teaspoons cinnamon
¼ teaspoon nutmeg
4 eggs
2 cups sugar
1½ cups vegetable oil
2 cups grated carrots

FROSTING
½ cup unsalted butter, room temperature
3 oz. cream cheese
3¾ cups confectioners' sugar
1 teaspoon vanilla
1 tablespoon orange juice
2 to 3 tablespoons milk

1. Preheat oven to 350°F. Insert paper liners in the cups of two 12-cup muffin tins.
2. Whisk together flour, baking powder, baking soda, salt, cinnamon, and nutmeg.
3. Combine eggs, sugar, and oil in a mixing bowl. Add flour mixture and mix until well combined. Stir in carrots. Pour batter into cupcake liners. Bake for 25 to 30 minutes, or until a toothpick inserted in center comes out clean. Cool on wire racks.
4. To make frosting: Cream butter and cream cheese in a mixing bowl until smooth. Gradually beat in confectioners' sugar, vanilla, and orange juice. Add milk to achieve desired consistency. Spread frosting on tops of cupcakes. Makes 24 cupcakes.

✳ **Maggie Lucia,** Enosburg Falls, Vermont
Sweepstakes Winner Recipe, Champlain Valley Exposition, Essex Junction, Vermont, 2005

WINNER'S CIRCLE TIP | **For a whimsical touch, reserve a small amount of frosting and tint it orange and green. Decorate the top of each cupcake with a frosting carrot.**

Black Pepper Pound Cake

3 cups all-purpose flour, plus more for pan
1 cup unsalted butter, room temperature
3 cups sugar
3 teaspoons coarsely ground black pepper

2 teaspoons lemon extract
6 eggs
1 cup heavy cream

1. Preheat oven to 325°F. Grease and flour a 10 x 4-inch tube pan.
2. In a large mixing bowl, cream butter and sugar. Beat in black pepper and lemon extract. Add eggs one at a time, beating well after each addition. Add flour alternately with cream. Mix well.
3. Pour batter into pan. Bake for 70 to 75 minutes, or until a toothpick inserted near center comes out clean. Cool in pan for 10 minutes. Transfer to a wire rack and cool completely. Makes 1 cake.

✳ **Melvelene Clark,** Sweetwater, Texas
First Place, West Texas Fair & Rodeo, Abilene, Texas, 2005

Orange-Cardamom Cupcakes

4½ cups cake flour, plus more for muffin cups
3½ teaspoons ground cardamom
2¼ teaspoons baking powder
¾ teaspoon salt
2¼ cups sticks unsalted butter,
   room temperature

3¾ cups sugar
9 large eggs
1½ tablespoons grated orange zest
1 tablespoon vanilla
2 teaspoons orange-flower water
1 cup buttermilk

1. Preheat oven to 325°F. Grease and flour the cups of four 12-cup muffin pans or use paper liners.
2. Sift together flour, cardamom, baking powder, and salt.
3. In a large mixing bowl, cream butter until light and fluffy. Gradually add sugar, beating until well blended. Whisk together eggs, orange zest, vanilla, and orange-flower water. Add to creamed mixture in thirds, beating well after each addition. Add flour mixture a cup at a time, alternating with buttermilk; beat and well and scrape down sides of bowl after each addition.
4. Fill muffin cups until ¾ full. Bake for 25 minutes, or until puffy and a tester inserted in center comes out clean. Tops should not be brown. Cool on wire racks. Frost as desired. Makes 48 cupcakes.

✄ **Terry Jannuzzo,** Red Hook, New York
Blue Ribbon, Dutchess County Fair, Rhinebeck, New York, 2005

WINNER'S CIRCLE TIP | Give buttercream frosting the scent of orange blossoms. Dissolve 1 teaspoon of an instant orange drink in ⅓ cup orange flower water. Use the orange flower water and 2 tablespoons Grand Marnier to thin the icing. Flavor it further with 1 teaspoon of grated orange zest. Orange-flower water is sold in grocery stores with large spice/foreign food departments. It is also available in gourmet shops.

Strawberry Butterfly Delight Cake

Cooking spray
1½ cups shortening
1¼ cups sugar
2 eggs
1½ cups mashed strawberries
2¼ cups all-purpose flour

2½ teaspoons baking powder
½ teaspoon baking soda
½ teaspoon salt
Commercially prepared frosting
Assorted candies and decorations

1. Preheat oven to 375°F. Lightly coat two 9 x 2-inch round cake pans with cooking spray.
2. In a large mixing bowl, cream shortening and sugar. With mixer running at low speed, gradually add eggs, strawberries, flour, baking powder, baking soda, and salt. Scrape down sides of bowl frequently with a rubber spatula. When ingredients are well combined, beat at high speed for 5 minutes.
3. Pour batter into pans. Bake for 25 minutes. Cool in pans for 10 minutes and turn out onto wire racks. Cool completely. Frost with frosting of your choice and decorate as desired. Makes 1 two-layer cake.

✄ **Grace Johnson,** age 10
First Place, San Diego County Fair, Del Mar, California, 2004

LEMON-POPPY SEED POUND CAKE

3 cups sifted all-purpose flour,
plus more for pan
1 cup buttermilk
¼ cup poppy seeds
½ teaspoon baking powder
½ teaspoon baking soda

¾ teaspoon salt
1 cup unsalted butter, room temperature
2 cups sugar
4 eggs
2 teaspoons lemon extract

1. Preheat oven to 325°F. Grease and flour a 12-cup Bundt pan or tube pan.
2. Combine buttermilk and poppy seeds in a microwave-safe container. Microwave for 30 seconds. Leave in microwave.
3. Sift together flour, baking powder, baking soda, and salt.
4. In a large mixing bowl, cream butter and sugar until thoroughly blended. Add eggs one at a time, beating at medium speed for 2½ minutes after each addition. Stir in lemon extract.
5. Microwave buttermilk mixture for another 20 seconds. Add flour mixture and buttermilk mixture alternately to creamed mixture, beginning and ending with flour mixture; stir to combine. Beat for 2½ minutes at medium speed; do not overbeat or cake will fall during baking. Pour batter into pan. Bake for 1 hour, or until a toothpick inserted in center comes out clean. Cool in pan 10 minutes; turn out onto wire rack. Makes 1 Bundt cake.

⊠ **JOANNE SEARLES,** Wann, Oklahoma
Sweepstakes, Tulsa State Fair, Tulsa, Oklahoma, 2003

LIAM'S CARROT CAKE

¾ cup unsalted butter or margarine,
room temperature, plus more for pan
2 cups unbleached white flour,
plus more for pan
2 teaspoons baking soda
2 teaspoons cinnamon
½ teaspoon salt
4 eggs
2 cups brown sugar

¾ cup vegetable oil
3 cups carrots, finely grated
1 cup chopped nuts (optional)

CREAM CHEESE ICING
½ cup unsalted butter, room temperature
1 package (8 oz.) cream cheese
1 lb. confectioners' sugar
½ to 1 teaspoon vanilla

1. Preheat oven to 350°F. Butter and flour two 8 x 2-inch cake pans.
2. Sift together flour, baking soda, cinnamon, and salt.
3. Beat eggs in a large mixing bowl. With mixer running, slowly add brown sugar, butter, oil, and flour mixture until well combined. Stir in carrots and nuts, if using. Pour batter into pans. Bake for 30 minutes, or until a pick inserted in center comes out clean. Turn out onto wire racks and cool.
4. To make cream cheese icing: Combine butter, cream cheese, confectioners' sugar, and vanilla in a small mixing bowl. Beat until smooth. Assemble cake layers, with frosting. Makes 1 two-layer cake.

⊠ **LIAM DONNELLY,** Burlington, Vermont
First Prize, Champlain Valley Exposition, Essex Junction, Vermont, 2004

Autumn Cake

2 cups crushed vanilla wafers
1 cup chopped pecans
¾ cup softened unsalted butter,
    room temperature
2 cups sugar
1 can (16 oz.) pumpkin
1 cup vegetable oil
4 eggs, beaten
2½ cups all-purpose flour
2 teaspoons baking soda

1 teaspoon salt
2 teaspoons cinnamon

CARAMEL PECAN FILLING
3 cups confectioners' sugar
⅔ cup softened unsalted butter, room temperature
4 oz. cream cheese
2 teaspoons vanilla
¼ cup caramel topping
1 cup pecan halves

1. Preheat oven to 350°F. Grease and flour three 8 x 1½-inch round cake pans.

2. In a large mixing bowl, combine vanilla wafer crumbs, chopped pecans, and butter. Beat at medium speed until crumbly. Press mixture evenly in bottom of pans.

3. In a large mixing bowl, combine sugar, pumpkin, oil, and eggs. Beat at medium speed for 1 minute. Whisk together flour, baking soda, salt, and cinnamon; add to pumpkin mixture. Beat at medium speed 3 minutes. Spread batter over crumb mixture in pans. Bake for 30 to 35 minutes. Cool in pans for 10 minutes before turning out onto wire racks. Cool completely.

4. To make filling: In a small mixing bowl, combine confectioners' sugar, butter, cream cheese, and vanilla. Beat at medium speed until light and fluffy.

5. To assemble cake: Layer the cakes nut side down on a serving plate, spreading ½ cup of the filling between the layers. Frost the sides of the cake with the remaining filling. Spread caramel topping over top of cake, allowing some to drizzle down the sides. Arrange pecan halves in a ring on top of cake. Makes 1 three-layer cake.

✂ **CANDI ECHOLS,** Oceanside, California
First Place, San Diego County Fair, Del Mar, California, 2004

Lemon-Raspberry Cake

3 cups sifted cake flour, plus more for pans
1 cup unsalted butter, room temperature
2 cups sugar
4 large eggs
2½ teaspoons baking powder
½ teaspoon salt
1 cup milk
1 teaspoon lemon extract

1 teaspoon vanilla
1 jar (10 oz.) seedless raspberry preserves

LEMON BUTTERCREAM FROSTING
1¼ cups unsalted butter, room temperature
2 teaspoons grated lemon zest
3 tablespoons lemon juice
3 cups sifted confectioners' sugar

1. Preheat oven to 375°F. Grease three 9 x 2-inch round cake pans and line with waxed paper; grease and lightly flour the waxed paper.

2. In a large mixing bowl, cream butter until soft. Gradually beat in sugar. Add eggs one at a time, beating well after each addition.

3. Sift together cake flour, baking powder, and salt. With mixer running, add flour mixture and milk alternately to creamed mixture, beginning and ending with flour. Beat until well blended. Stir in lemon extract and vanilla. Pour batter into baking pans. Bake for 18 to 20 minutes, or until a toothpick inserted in center comes out clean. Cool in pans on wire racks for 10 minutes. Turn out cakes onto wire racks and cool completely.

4. Slice each cake in half horizontally to make 6 layers total. Place one layer cut side up on cake plate; spread with 3 tablespoons preserves. Repeat procedure with remaining 5 layers, omitting preserves on top of last layer.

5. To make lemon buttercream frosting: In a mixing bowl, cream butter and lemon zest and juice. Gradually beat in confectioners' sugar until frosting is of spreading consistency. Spread 1¾ cups of frosting on sides and top of cake. Put remaining 1 cup frosting in a pastry bag fitted with a star tip. Pipe decorative designs onto top of cake. Garnish as desired. Store in an airtight container in refrigerator. Makes 1 three-layer cake.

✖ **SANDRA BIRKY,** Valparaiso, Indiana
Overall Purple Ribbon, Foods, Porter County Fair, Valparaiso, Indiana, 2005

SOUR CREAM CHOCOLATE CAKE

2 cups all-purpose flour, plus more for pans

4 squares (1 oz. each) unsweetened chocolate, melted and cooled

1 cup water

¾ cup sour cream

¼ cup shortening

1 teaspoon vanilla

2 eggs, beaten

2 cups sugar

½ teaspoon baking powder

1¼ teaspoons baking soda

1 teaspoon salt

FROSTING

½ cup unsalted butter, room temperature

6 squares (1 oz. each) unsweetened chocolate, melted and cooled

6 cups confectioners' sugar

½ cup sour cream

6 tablespoons milk

2 teaspoons vanilla

⅛ teaspoon salt

This luscious layer cake gets wonderful moistness from sour cream.

1. Preheat oven to 350°F. Grease and flour two 9 x 2-inch round cake pans.

2. In a large mixing bowl, combine unsweetened chocolate, water, sour cream shortening, vanilla, and eggs. Beat until smooth.

3. Whisk together flour, sugar, baking powder, baking soda, and salt. Add gradually to chocolate mixture, beating on low speed just until moistened. Beat on high speed for 3 minutes.

4. Pour batter into pans. Bake for 30 minutes, or until a toothpick inserted near center comes out clean. Cool for 10 minutes in pans before turning out onto wire racks. Cool completely.

5. To make frosting: In a medium mixing bowl, combine butter, chocolate, confectioners' sugar, sour cream, milk, vanilla, and salt. Beat until smooth and creamy.

6. Assemble the cake layers, spreading frosting between the layers and on sides and top of cake. Store in the refrigerator. Makes 1 two-layer cake.

✖ **JEAN FIESBECK,** Columbus, Indiana
Reserve Grand Champion, Cakes, Bartholomew County 4-H Fair, Columbus, Indiana, 2005

WALDORF ASTORIA'S RED VELVET CAKE

2¼ cups cake flour, plus more for pans
½ cup shortening
1½ cups sugar
2 oz. red liquid food coloring
2 heaping tablespoons cocoa
1 cup buttermilk
2 teaspoons vanilla
2 eggs
1 teaspoon vinegar
1 teaspoon baking soda

FILLING

1 tablespoon unsalted butter, room temperature
1 tablespoon sour cream
1 cup sifted confectioners' sugar

FROSTING

5 tablespoons flour
1 cup milk
1 cup unsalted butter, room temperature
1 cup sugar
2 teaspoons vanilla

1. Preheat oven to 350°F. Grease and flour three 8 x 2-inch or 9 x 2-inch round cake pans.

2. In a large mixing bowl, cream shortening and sugar. Stir together food coloring and cocoa to make a paste. Stir into creamed mixture. Add buttermilk and cake flour alternately to creamed mixture, mixing well after each addition. Add eggs one at a time, mixing well after each addition. Stir in vanilla.

3. Place vinegar in a small cup, add baking soda, and hold over batter. As soon as the mixture has stopped fizzing and growing, pour it over the batter and blend gently. Do not beat. Pour batter into cake pans. Bake for 25 minutes. Cool on wire racks.

4. To make filling: In a small mixing bowl, beat butter, sour cream, and confectioners' sugar until smooth.

5. To make frosting: Combine flour and milk in a small saucepan. Cook over medium-high heat, stirring often, until thickened. In a mixing bowl, cream butter, sugar, and vanilla. Add flour mixture and beat until frosting is of spreading consistency.

6. Assemble cake layers, spreading filling between the layers. Add frosting to top and sides. Makes 1 three-layer cake.

✳ **CAROLYNN RICHARDSON,** Huson, Montana
First Place, It's Going To Be a Chocolate Sunday, Western Montana Fair, Missoula, Montana, 1997

WINE CAKE

3 cups all-purpose flour, plus more for pan
1 cup unsalted butter, room temperature
3 cups sugar
6 eggs
1 cup sour cream
½ cup sweet wine
¼ teaspoon rum flavoring
¼ teaspoon almond extract
1 teaspoon lemon extract
Grated zest of 1 lemon
1 teaspoon vanilla

¼ teaspoon baking soda
1 teaspoon salt

ORANGE AND CREAM CHEESE FROSTING

1 package (16 oz.) confectioners' sugar
4 oz. lowfat cream cheese
2 tablespoons fat-free sour cream
1 to 2 tablespoons orange juice
½ teaspoon vanilla
1 teaspoon lemon extract
Yellow food coloring, paste or liquid

1. Preheat oven to 325°F. Grease and flour a 12-cup tube pan or Bundt pan.

2. In a large mixing bowl, cream butter and sugar. Add eggs one at a time, beating well after each addition.

3. In a small bowl, combine sour cream, sweet wine, rum flavoring, almond extract, lemon extract, zest, and vanilla.

4. Sift together flour, baking soda, and salt. Add flour mixture and sour cream mixture alternately to creamed mixture, blending well after each addition. Pour batter into pan. Bake for 70 to 90 minutes, or until a toothpick inserted in center comes out clean. Cool in pan for 10 minutes before turning out onto a wire rack. Cool completely.

5. To make orange and cream cheese frosting: In a medium mixing bowl, combine confectioners' sugar, cream cheese, sour cream, orange juice, vanilla, lemon extract, and yellow food coloring until well blended. Spread frosting on sides and top of cake. Makes 1 cake.

✄ **KENNA-MARIE MCCULLEY,** Pierson, Florida
First Place, Baked Goods, Youth Junior, Volusia County Fair, DeLand, Florida, 2004

WINNER'S CIRCLE TIP | **If you prefer frosting you can drizzle, add an extra 1 to 2 tablespoons orange juice. It needs to be of a thinner consistency than a frosting you plan to spread with a knife.**

PINEAPPLE UPSIDE-DOWN CAKE

CARAMEL TOPPING
1 cup brown sugar
½ cup unsalted butter,
    room temperature
1 can (20 oz.) pineapple slices

CAKE
1½ cups all-purpose flour
6 tablespoons cake flour

6 tablespoons ground almonds
    (from about 2 oz. almonds)
¾ teaspoon baking powder
½ teaspoon salt
1 cup unsalted butter, room temperature
1¾ cups sugar
4 large eggs
¾ teaspoon vanilla
¾ cup sour cream

1. Preheat oven to 325°F.

2. To make caramel topping: Combine brown sugar and butter in a small saucepan over medium heat. Cook until sugar dissolves and mixture is bubbly, 2 to 3 minutes. Pour mixture into a nonstick cake pan with 2-inch high sides. Arrange pineapple slices in a single layer on bottom of pan.

3.To make cake: Whisk together flour, cake flour, ground almonds, baking powder, and salt.

4. In a large mixing bowl, cream butter and sugar until light and fluffy. Add eggs one at a time, beating after each addition. Beat in vanilla. Add flour mixture alternately with sour cream to creamed mixture in two batches each, beating well after each addition.

5. Pour batter over caramel and pineapple slices in pan. Bake for 1 hour 15 minutes, or until a toothpick inserted in center comes out clean. Cool in pan on a wire rack for 10 minutes. Turn out cake onto a serving plate. Serve warm or at room temperature. Makes 12 to 14 servings.

✄ **SUMMER JUPIN,** Hawthorne, Florida
First Place, Youth Division, Florida State Fair, Tampa, Florida, 2005

APPLESAUCE CAKE

1 cup cake flour, plus more for pan

½ teaspoon baking powder

1 teaspoon baking soda

½ teaspoon salt

½ teaspoon ground cloves

1 teaspoon cinnamon

1 teaspoon ground allspice

½ cup shortening

1 cup sugar

1 egg

1 cup applesauce

1 cup raisins

¼ cup nuts

1. Preheat oven to 350°F. Grease and lightly flour a 9 x 5 x 3-inch loaf pan.

2. Sift together cake flour, baking powder, baking soda, salt, cloves, cinnamon, and allspice.

3. Cream shortening in a large mixing bowl. Add sugar and beat until light. Add egg and beat until fluffy. Stir in applesauce. Add flour mixture in batches, stirring well after each addition. Fold in raisins and nuts. Spoon batter into pan. Bake for 40 to 45 minutes. Cool on a wire rack. Makes 1 loaf cake.

✕ **LINDA WELCH,** Shoreham, Vermont
Rosette, Cakes, Addison County Fair & Field Days, New Haven, Vermont, 2004

LEMON AND BLUEBERRY SHORTCAKES

LEMON CURD

7 tablespoons fresh lemon juice

6 tablespoons sugar

4 large egg yolks

BISCUITS

1 lemon

5 tablespoons sugar, divided

1¼ cups all-purpose flour, plus more
for patting out dough

¼ cup yellow cornmeal

1½ teaspoons baking powder

¼ teaspoon baking soda

½ teaspoon salt

6 tablespoons chilled unsalted butter, diced

8 tablespoons chilled heavy cream, divided

SAUCE

3½ cups blueberries, divided

6 tablespoons water

3 tablespoons all-fruit blueberry spread

1 tablespoon sugar

⅔ cup heavy cream

GARNISH

Lemon slices

Fresh mint sprigs (optional)

1. Preheat oven to 400°F. Set aside a large, heavy baking sheet; do not grease.

2. To make lemon curd: Combine lemon juice, sugar, and egg yolks in a medium heavy-bottomed saucepan. Whisk over medium heat until mixture thickens and just comes to a boil, 6 minutes. Transfer curd to a medium bowl. Cool.

3. Using a vegetable peeler, remove peel from lemon in strips. Squeeze 2 tablespoons juice from lemon and set aside. Place peel and 3 tablespoons of the sugar in the bowl of a food processor. Blend until peel is finely ground.

4. Add flour, cornmeal, baking powder, baking soda, and salt to food processor; pulse to combine. Add butter and pulse until mixture resembles coarse meal. Add 6 tablespoons of the cream and 2 tablespoons reserved lemon juice. Pulse just until dough begins to clump.

5. Turn out dough, gather into a ball, and flatten into a disk. Pat out dough on a lightly floured surface to a ¾-inch thick round. Cut 6 rounds from dough with a floured 2¼-inch round biscuit cutter; gather up and use scraps if needed to cut the last few rounds. Place rounds on baking sheet. Brush tops with remaining 2 tablespoons cream. Sprinkle with remaining 2 tablespoons sugar. Bake for 15 minutes, or until cooked through and golden. Transfer to a plate. Cool to room temperature.

6. To make sauce: Combine 1½ cups of the blueberries, water, blueberry spread, and sugar in small heavy saucepan. Cook over medium-high heat, stirring gently, until mixture comes to boil and berries begin to release their juices, about 2 minutes. Remove from heat. Mix in 1½ cups of the blueberries. Cool.

7. In a medium mixing bowl, beat cream until stiff peaks form. Fold half of whipped cream into curd; fold in remaining whipped cream.

8. Cut biscuits horizontally in half. Place bottoms on 6 plates. Spoon sauce over each. Top with lemon curd mixture. Add biscuit tops. Garnish with remaining ½ cup blueberries and fresh mint sprigs and lemon slices. Makes 6 servings.

✕ **CHRISSY THIBODEAU,** Woodbridge, Virginia
Overall Winner, Wild Blueberry Festival Cooking Competition, Machias, Maine, 2002

WINNER'S CIRCLE TIP | Curd can be prepared 1 day ahead; be sure to cover and refrigerate. Biscuits can be made 3 hours ahead. Let stand at room temperature until ready to serve.

PEAR UPSIDE-DOWN CAKE

7 tablespoons unsalted butter, divided
¾ cup brown sugar, divided
1 large can (29 oz.) pear halves, drained
¼ cup molasses
1 cup boiling water
2 cups all-purpose flour
1 teaspoon baking soda

¼ teaspoon ground ginger
¼ teaspoon cinnamon
¼ teaspoon ground cloves
2 eggs
½ cup chopped walnuts
Maraschinos

1. Preheat oven to 350°F. Melt 3 tablespoons of the butter in the bottom of a 1½-quart shallow glass baking dish. Sprinkle ¼ cup of the brown sugar over butter. Arrange pears in dish cut side down.

2. In a medium mixing bowl, cream remaining 4 tablespoons butter and remaining ½ cup brown sugar. Add molasses and boiling water; mix well.

3. In a large mixing bowl, whisk together flour, baking soda, ginger, cinnamon, and cloves. Add molasses mixture and beat until well combined. Beat in eggs one at a time. Stir in walnuts.

4. Pour batter over pears. Bake for 40 minutes. Let stand 5 minutes. Turn out onto a serving plate so pears are on top. Place a Maraschino in each pear. Serve warm with whipped cream if desired. Makes 10 servings.

✕ **ULDENE WEIDLICK,** Belvidere, New Jersey
First Place, Warren County Farmers' Fair, Belvidere, New Jersey, 2005

Lemon-Lime Soda Cake

3 sticks unsalted butter, room temperature

3 cups sugar

5 eggs

1 teaspoon vanilla

1 tablespoon lemon juice

3 cups all-purpose flour

¾ cup lemon-lime soda

Confectioners' sugar

1. Preheat oven to 325°F. Lightly grease a 10 x 4-inch tube pan.

2. In a large mixing bowl, cream butter and sugar until well blended. Add eggs one at a time, beating well after each addition. Mix in vanilla and lemon juice. Add flour ½ cup at a time, mixing after each addition. Fold in lemon-lime soda.

3. Pour batter into pan. Bake for 60 to 70 minutes, or until a tester inserted in center comes out clean. Cool in pan for 15 to 20 minutes. Loosen sides and center of pan, invert onto a cake plate, and cool completely. Dust with confectioners' sugar. Makes 1 cake.

✕ **ERIC DODSON,** age 11, Hampstead, Maryland

Grand Champion, Cake of the Year, Carroll County 4-H & FFA Fair, Westminster, Maryland, 2005

WINNER'S CIRCLE TIP | **Use a round cardboard cake disk to support a cake while you invert it onto a cooling rack. These inexpensive disks are sold in the baking supply aisle at craft stores.**

Orange Chiffon Cake

2 cups all-purpose flour

1½ cups sugar

4 teaspoons baking powder

1 teaspoon salt

6 eggs, separated

¾ cup fresh orange juice

2 teaspoons grated orange zest

½ cup vegetable oil

½ teaspoon cream of tartar

GLAZE

½ cup unsalted butter, room temperature

2 cups confectioners' sugar

½ teaspoon grated orange zest

1. Preheat oven to 350°F. Set aside a 10 x 4-inch tube pan; do not grease.

2. In a large mixing bowl, combine flour, sugar, baking powder, and salt. Beat in egg yolks, orange juice, zest, and oil until smooth, about 5 minutes.

3. In a small mixing bowl, beat egg whites and cream of tartar until stiff but not dry. Fold into orange mixture.

4. Spoon batter into pan. Bake for 45 to 50 minutes, or until a toothpick inserted near center comes out clean. Immediately invert pan onto a wire rack; remove cake from pan when cool.

5. To make glaze: Melt butter in a small saucepan over low heat. Stir in confectioners' sugar and zest until smooth. Set cake on a plate. Pour glaze over top of cake, allowing it to drizzle down sides. Makes 1 cake.

✕ **RACHEL PENCE,** Hope, Indiana

Grand Champion, Open Class, Bartholomew County 4-H Fair, Columbus, Indiana, 2005

PUMPKIN-PECAN LAYER CAKE

CAKE

2 cups crushed vanilla wafers

1 cup chopped pecans

1 cup unsalted butter, room temperature, divided

1 package (8 oz.) spice cake mix

1 can (16 oz.) pumpkin

4 eggs

FILLING

3 cups confectioners' sugar

⅔ cup unsalted butter, room temperature

4 oz. cream cheese

2 teaspoons vanilla

¼ cup caramel topping

1. Preheat oven to 350°F. Grease and flour three 9 x 2-inch round cake pans.

2. To make cake: In a large mixing bowl, combine vanilla wafer crumbs, pecans, and ¾ cup of the butter. Beat at medium speed, scraping bowl often, until crumbly. Press mixture evenly in bottom of pans.

3. In the same mixing bowl, combine spice cake mix, pumpkin, remaining ¼ cup butter, and eggs. Beat at medium speed, scraping bowl often, until well mixed. Spread batter evenly over crumbs in each pan. Bake for 20 to 25 minutes, or until wooden pick inserted in center comes out clean. Cool in pans for 5 minutes and turn out onto wire racks. Cool completely.

4. To make filling: In a small mixer bowl, combine confectioners' sugar, butter, cream cheese, and vanilla. Beat at medium speed, scraping bowl often, until light and fluffy.

5. To assemble cake: Place one cake layer on a serving plate, cake side up. Spread ½ cup of filling over top. Add second cake layer and spread with ½ cup filling. Add third cake layer. Frost sides of cake with remaining filling. Spread caramel topping over top of cake, letting some drizzle down the sides. Garnish with pecan halves, if desired. Refrigerate until ready to serve. Makes 1 two-layer cake.

✕ **ELIZABETH SLOAN,** St. Ignatious, Montana
First Place, Cake Mix Combinations; Best of Show, Holiday Desserts Cook-Off, Western Montana Fair, Missoula, Montana, 2004

MIMI'S FIVE-FLAVOR POUND CAKE

2 cups unsalted butter, room temperature

3 cups sugar

6 eggs

4 cups all-purpose flour

1 cup milk

1 teaspoon lemon extract

1 teaspoon vanilla

1 teaspoon coconut extract

1 teaspoon rum extract

1 teaspoon butter extract

1. Preheat oven to 300°F. Grease and flour a 10 x 4-inch tube pan.

2. In a large mixing bowl, cream butter and sugar until light. Add eggs one at a time, beating well after each addition. Add flour alternately with milk, beating until well combined. Stir in lemon extract, vanilla, coconut extract, rum extract, and butter extract.

3. Pour batter into tube pan. Bake for 1 hour. Invert to cool. Turn out onto a wire rack. Makes 1 cake.

✕ **SHIRLEY GORDON,** King, North Carolina
First Place, Midstate Mills Un-iced Pound Cake Contest, Dixie Classic Fair, Winston-Salem, North Carolina, 2005

Pinto Bean Pound Cake

2 cups all-purpose flour, divided,
    plus more for pans

½ cup unsalted butter, room temperature

2 cups sugar

4 eggs

4 cups cooked pinto beans, drained and
    mashed (reserve juice for frosting)

2 teaspoons baking soda

½ teaspoon salt

2 teaspoons cinnamon

1 teaspoon ground allspice

1 teaspoon ground cloves

⅛ teaspoon nutmeg

1 tablespoon plus 1 teaspoon vanilla

4 cups peeled, cored, and diced cooking apples
    (such as McIntosh)

1½ cups chopped black walnuts, toasted

1½ cups golden raisins, plumped in hot water
    and drained

PINTO BEAN FROSTING

1 box (16 oz.) confectioners' sugar

1 tablespoon pinto bean juice

½ cup unsalted butter, room temperature

1 tablespoon vanilla

1 tablespoon milk

½ cup chopped black walnuts

1. Preheat oven to 350°F. Grease and flour a 10 x 4-inch tube pan.

2. In a large mixing bowl, cream butter. Gradually add sugar and beat well. Add eggs one at a time, beating well after each addition. Add pinto beans, beating at low speed until well combined.

3. Whisk together 1½ cups of the flour, baking soda, salt, cinnamon, allspice, cloves, and nutmeg. Add flour mixture gradually to bean mixture, beating until well combined. Stir in vanilla.

4. In a large bowl, combine apples, black walnuts, golden raisins, and remaining ½ cup flour. Toss to coat. Fold gently into batter. Spoon batter into tube pan. Bake for 1 hour and 15 minutes, or until a tester inserted near center comes out clean. Cool in pan for 10 minutes before turning out onto a wire rack. Cool completely.

5. To make pinto bean frosting: In a medium mixing bowl, combine confectioners' sugar, pinto bean juice, butter, vanilla, and milk. Beat until smooth and creamy. Spread frosting on sides and top of cake. Garnish with black walnuts. Makes 1 cake.

✕ **MATTIE FOWLER,** Winston-Salem, North Carolina
First Place, Winston-Salem Journal's Pinto Bean Contest, Dixie Classic Fair, Winston-Salem, North Carolina, 2005

COCONUT-CREAM CHEESE POUND CAKE

3 cups all-purpose flour, plus more for pan

½ cup unsalted butter, room temperature

½ cup shortening

1 package (8 oz.) cream cheese,
    room temperature

3 cups sugar

6 eggs

¼ teaspoon baking soda

¼ teaspoon salt

¾ cup shredded coconut

1 teaspoon coconut flavoring

1 teaspoon vanilla

1. Preheat oven to 325°F. Grease and flour a 12-cup Bundt pan.

2. Cream butter, shortening, and cream cheese in a mixing bowl. Gradually add sugar, beating at medium speed until well combined. Add eggs one at a time, beating after each addition.

3. Combine flour, baking soda, and salt. Add flour mixture to egg batter and stir just until blended. Fold in shredded coconut, coconut flavoring, and vanilla. Pour batter into pan. Bake for 1 hour 30 minutes, or until a toothpick inserted in center comes out clean. Cool in pan for 10 to 15 minutes before turning out onto a wire rack. Makes 1 Bundt cake.

※ **ANNE MURRAY,** Poughkeepsie, New York
Best of Culinary, Dutchess County Fair, Rhinebeck, New York, 2005

KEY LIME CAKE

Flour

1 box (18.2 oz.) lemon cake mix

1 package (3 oz.) lime gelatin

5 eggs

¾ cup orange juice

¾ cup oil

GLAZE

5 tablespoons confectioners' sugar

¼ cup lime juice

FROSTING

1 package (8 oz.) cream cheese

4 tablespoons unsalted butter or
    margarine, room temperature

2 tablespoons key lime juice

1 teaspoon vanilla

1 box (1 lb.) confectioners' sugar

1. Preheat oven to 325°F. Grease and flour two 9 x 9 x 2-inch baking pans.

2. In a mixing bowl, combine lemon cake mix, lime gelatin, eggs, orange juice, and oil; beat until smooth. Pour batter into pans. Bake for 20 to 30 minutes, or until a tester inserted in center comes out clean; do not overbake. Prick tops with a fork all over.

3. To make glaze: Stir confectioners' sugar and lime juice together until smooth. Drizzle over cakes.

4. To make frosting: In a large mixing bowl, beat cream cheese and butter until thoroughly combined and smooth. Beat in lime juice and vanilla. Add confectioners' sugar, beating until consistency is creamy. Assemble cake, spreading frosting between layers and on sides and top of cake. Makes 1 two-layer square cake.

※ **CARYLON MILLER,** Abilene, Texas
First Place, West Texas Fair & Rodeo, Abilene, Texas, 2005

Pumpkin Cake with Orange Glaze

2½ cups cake flour, plus more for pan

¾ butter-flavored shortening

2 cups brown sugar

4 eggs

1 can (29 oz.) pumpkin

¼ cup water

1 tablespoon plus 1 teaspoon
   baking powder

1½ teaspoons baking soda

1 tablespoon pumpkin pie spice

1 teaspoon salt

½ cup chopped walnuts

½ cup raisins

ORANGE GLAZE

1 cup confectioners' sugar

1 tablespoon plus 1 teaspoon orange juice

¾ teaspoon grated orange zest

Chopped walnuts

1. Preheat oven to 350°F. Lightly grease and flour a 10-cup Bundt pan.

2. In a large mixing bowl, beat shortening and brown sugar at low speed until well combined. Add eggs one at a time, beating well after each addition. Stir in pumpkin and water.

3. Whisk together cake flour, baking powder, baking soda, pumpkin pie spice, and salt. Slowly add to pumpkin mixture. Beat at medium speed until well blended, about 2 minutes. Fold in walnuts and raisins.

4. Pour batter into pan. Bake for 55 to 60 minutes. Cool. Invert cake onto a plate.

5. To make orange glaze: In a small bowl, combine confectioners' sugar, orange juice, and zest; stir until smooth. Spread glaze over cake. Sprinkle walnuts on top. Makes 1 Bundt cake.

✕ **Linda Gass,** Mango, Florida
First Place, Adult Division, Florida State Fair, Tampa, Florida, 2005

Peanut-Butter Cup Cake

1 cup all-purpose flour, plus more for pan

⅔ cup sugar

⅓ cup cocoa

¾ teaspoon baking powder

¾ teaspoon baking soda

¼ teaspoon salt

½ cup milk

½ cup water

¼ cup vegetable oil

1 large egg

1 teaspoon vanilla

⅓ cup peanut butter morsels

PEANUT BUTTER LAYER

1 cup creamy peanut butter

¼ cup unsalted butter, room temperature

1 small package (3 oz.) cream cheese,
   room temperature

⅓ cup peanut butter morsels, melted

½ teaspoon vanilla

1½ cups confectioners' sugar

GANACHE

1 cup heavy cream

2 cups semisweet chocolate chips

DECORATION

¼ cup milk chocolate chips, melted

¼ cup peanut butter chips, melted

Chocolate curls

1. Preheat oven to 350°F. Grease and flour one 9-inch round cake pan.

2. In a large mixing bowl, combine flour, sugar, cocoa, baking powder, baking soda and salt. Blend in milk, water, vegetable oil, egg and vanilla until moistened. Beat for 2 minutes.

3. Pour batter into pan. Sprinkle peanut butter morsels over top. Bake for 25 minutes, or until wooden pick inserted into the center comes out clean. Cool in pan for 10 minutes. Turn out onto wire rack and cool completely.

4. To make peanut butter layer: In a medium mixing bowl, combine peanut butter, butter, cream cheese, melted peanut butter morsels, and vanilla until well blended. Sift in confectioners' sugar; mix until smooth. Place cake on a serving platter. Spread peanut butter mixture on top of cake. Refrigerate for 30 minutes.

5. To make ganache: Heat cream in a small saucepan over medium-high heat until boiling. Remove from heat, add chocolate chips, and let stand for 5 minutes. Stir to combine. Refrigerate for 30 minutes, or until mixture is spreadable. Spread ganache on top and sides of cake.

6. To add decoration: Place milk chocolate and peanut butter chips in two separate zip-close plastic bags. Microwave on high for 45 seconds. Knead chips through bag to make sure they are melted; microwave another 10 to 15 seconds if needed. Snip off a lower corner of each bag. Squeeze the melted chocolate on top of the cake in a lattice pattern. Arrange chocolate curls around cake. Makes 10 to 12 servings.

※ **LISA ROBERTSON,** King, North Carolina
First Place, Village Tavern's Favorite Dessert Contest, Dixie Classic Fair, Winston-Salem, North Carolina, 2005

EVERYDAY CAKE

3 cups all-purpose flour, plus more for pans
½ cup unsalted butter, room temperature
1½ cups sugar
3 eggs, separated
1 teaspoon vanilla
3 teaspoons baking powder
½ teaspoon salt
1 cup milk

COCOA FROSTING
½ cup unsalted butter, room temperature
⅓ cup cocoa
1 box (1 lb.) confectioners' sugar
1 teaspoon vanilla
3 tablespoons cream or milk,
   plus more if needed

1. Preheat oven to 350°F. Grease and flour three 8 x 2-inch round cake pans.

2. In a large mixing bowl, cream butter and sugar. Beat in egg yolks and vanilla.

3. Whisk together flour, baking powder, and salt. With mixer running on low speed, add flour mixture and milk alternately to creamed mixture until well blended.

4. In a small mixing bowl, beat egg whites until stiff. Fold into batter. Pour batter into pans. Bake for 25 to 30 minutes, or until a toothpick inserted in center comes out clean. Cool on wire racks.

5. To make cocoa frosting: In a small mixing bowl, combine butter, cocoa, confectioners' sugar, vanilla, and cream or milk. Beat until smooth; add more cream or milk if needed for a more spreadable consistency.

6. Assemble the cake, spreading frosting between the layers. Spread remaining frosting on sides and top of cake. Makes 1 three-layer cake.

※ **DIANE TITE,** Chesterfield, Michigan
First Place, Grandma's Recipe, Michigan State Fair, Detroit, Michigan, 2002

Pecan Pie Cake

½ cup unsalted butter, room temperature,
    plus more for pans
2 cups all-purpose flour, plus more for pans
3 cups pecans, toasted and finely
    chopped, divided
½ cup shortening
2 cups sugar
5 eggs, separated
1 tablespoon vanilla
1 teaspoon baking soda
1 cup buttermilk
1 cup dark corn syrup

FILLING
⅓ cup cornstarch
⅛ teaspoon salt
4 egg yolks
½ cup brown sugar
1½ cups half-and-half
¾ cup dark corn syrup
3 tablespoons unsalted butter, room temperature
1 teaspoon vanilla

CREAM CHEESE FROSTING
1 package (8 oz.) cream cheese
½ cup unsalted butter, room temperature
½ teaspoon vanilla
½ teaspoon maple flavoring
6 cups confectioners' sugar

PASTRY GARNISH
¾ cup all-purpose flour, plus more
    for rolling out dough
2 tablespoons shortening
2 tablespoons unsalted butter, room temperature
⅛ cup milk
¼ teaspoon salt
1 egg
1 tablespoon water

1. Preheat oven to 350°F. Generously butter three 8 x 2-inch round cake pans; dust lightly with flour, shaking to coat bottoms and sides of pans. Layer 2 cups of the pecans into bottoms of pans.

2. In a large mixing bowl, cream butter and shortening until fluffy. Gradually add sugar. Add egg yolks one at a time, beating well after each addition. Stir in vanilla. Combine flour and baking soda; add to creamed mixture alternately with buttermilk, beating at low speed until well blended. Stir in remaining 1 cup pecans.

3. In a separate mixing bowl, beat egg whites until stiff. Fold one-third of egg whites into batter. Gently fold in remaining egg whites.

4. Pour batter into pans. Bake for 25 minutes, or until a toothpick inserted in center comes out clean. Cool in pans on wire rack for 10 minutes. Invert cakes onto wire racks lined with waxed paper. Brush tops and side with corn syrup. Cool completely.

5. To make filling: Combine cornstarch, salt, egg yolks, brown sugar, half-and-half, and corn syrup in a heavy pan; stir until smooth. Bring to a boil over medium heat, stirring continuously; boil for 1 minute. Remove from heat. Stir in butter and vanilla. Cover with waxed paper, setting it directly on surface of custard. Chill for 4 hours.

6. To make cream cheese frosting: In a large mixing bowl, beat cream cheese, butter, vanilla, and maple flavoring until fluffy. Gradually add confectioners' sugar, beating until fluffy.

7. To make pastry garnish: Preheat oven to 425°F. Place flour in a small mixing bowl. Cut in shortening and butter. Add milk and salt. Mix until dough forms into a ball. Roll out dough on a lightly floured surface. Cut out 8 to 12 leaves, using a cookie cutter or a knife; score leaf veins using the tip of a

knife. Place leaves on a baking sheet. For rounded leaves, roll pieces of aluminum foil into ½-inch balls and drape pastry over them for baking. Mix egg and water to make a wash; brush mixture onto each leaf. Bake for 6 minutes. Cool on a wire rack for 10 minutes.

8. To assemble cake: Place one cake layer on plate pecan side up. Spread half of filling over top. Add second layer, pecan side up, and spread with remaining filling. Top with third layer. Frost sides and top of cake with cream cheese frosting; frosting may also be piped onto cake. Garnish with pastry leaves. Makes 1 three-layer cake.

※ **ALLISON CONDRY,** Abilene, Texas
First Place & Best of Show, West Texas Fair & Rodeo, Abilene, Texas, 2003

CHOCOLATE CAKE

⅔ **cup unsalted butter,**
    room temperature
1¾ **cups sugar**
2 **eggs**
½ **cup cold water**
3 **teaspoons vanilla**
2½ **cups sifted cake flour**
1½ **teaspoons baking soda**
1 **teaspoon baking powder**

½ **teaspoon salt**
½ **cup cocoa**
1 **cup buttermilk**

CHOCOLATE FROSTING
1 **package (6 oz.) semisweet chocolate chips**
½ **cup half-and-half**
1 **cup unsalted butter, room temperature**
2½ **cups sifted confectioners' sugar**

1. Preheat oven to 350°F. Grease the bottoms of two 8 x 2-inch or 9 x 2-inch round cake pans. Cut circles to fit pans from waxed paper and insert in pans. Grease the waxed paper.

2. In a large bowl, cream butter until soft and fluffy. Gradually add sugar and beat on medium speed for 1 minute. Add eggs one at a time, beating for 1 minute after each addition. Add cold water and vanilla and beat for 1 minute.

3. Triple-sift flour, baking soda, baking powder, salt, and cocoa. Add flour mixture and buttermilk alternately to creamed mixture, beginning and ending with flour. Blend on low speed just until batter is smooth.

4. Pour batter into pans. Bake for 28 to 30 minutes, or until a toothpick inserted in the center comes out clean. Do not overbake. Let cool in pans on wire racks for 10 minutes. Turn out onto wire racks. Cool completely.

5. To make chocolate frosting: Combine chocolate chips, half-and-half, and butter in a medium saucepan. Cook over medium heat, stirring constantly, until chocolate is melted and butter is smooth. Remove from heat. Whisk in confectioners' sugar until smooth. Set saucepan over a bowl of ice and beat by hand until mixture is of spreading consistency.

6. Assemble cake layers, using about ½ cup of frosting as a filling. Then frost sides and top of cake. Makes 1 two-layer cake.

※ **FLORENCE NEAVOLL,** Salem, Oregon
Blue Ribbon, 1998; Winner of Gerry Frank Chocolate Cake Contest, 1979, Oregon State Fair, Salem, Oregon

PINEAPPLE-PEACH STAR UPSIDE-DOWN CAKE

FRUIT LAYER

1 can (20 oz.) pineapple rings, drained

1 star fruit or golden kiwi, sliced
   (peel kiwi, if using)

3 peaches, peeled and sliced

2 tablespoons unsalted butter,
   room temperature

⅓ cup brown sugar

1 tablespoon water

CAKE

2½ cups all-purpose flour

2½ teaspoons baking powder

½ teaspoon salt

⅔ cup unsalted butter, room temperature

1½ teaspoons vanilla

1¾ cups sugar

2 eggs

1½ cups milk

1. To make fruit layer: Line a Dutch oven with parchment paper. Arrange pineapple rings, star fruit or kiwi, and peaches on bottom of oven.

2. In a small saucepan, heat butter, brown sugar, and water until syrupy. Pour over fruit.

3. To make cake: Whisk together flour, baking powder, and salt.

4. In a large bowl, cream butter, vanilla, and sugar. Beat in eggs one at a time. Add flour mixture alternately with milk, mixing after each addition. Pour batter over fruit.

5. Set up oven for low propane on bottom and 18 coals on top. Cook for 30 to 35 minutes. Cool in oven. Invert onto a serving plate. Serve with caramel sauce, cherries, and whipped cream, if desired.

✂ **DANA HANCOCK AND DAVID JONES,** Ogden, Utah
First Place, Camp Chef Ultimate Dutch Oven Cook-off, Utah State Fair, Salt Lake City, Utah, 2005

JEWISH SPONGE CAKE

3 cups all-purpose flour

2 teaspoons baking powder

1½ teaspoons baking soda

Pinch of salt

½ cup unsalted butter, room temperature

2 cups sugar

4 eggs, separated

1 pint sour cream

2 teaspoons vanilla

1 teaspoon cinnamon

¼ cup brown sugar

1 cup chopped walnuts

1. Preheat oven to 350°F. Grease a 10 x 4-inch tube pan.

2. Whisk together flour, baking powder, baking soda, and salt.

3. Cream butter and sugar in a mixing bowl. Beat in egg yolks until light and fluffy. Add flour mixture and stir until well combined. Blend in sour cream.

4. Beat egg whites until foamy, add vanilla, and continue beating until stiff peaks form. Fold into batter.

5. Spoon half of batter into tube pan. Combine cinnamon, brown sugar, and walnuts in a small bowl. Sprinkle half of walnut mixture over batter in pan. Add remaining batter to pan and top with remaining walnut mixture. Bake for 1 hour. Makes 1 cake.

✂ **BEVERLY STEFKO,** Fort Pierce, Florida
Best of Show, St. Lucie County Fair, Fort Pierce, Florida, 2003

Italian Cream Cake

½ cup margarine, room temperature
½ cup shortening
2 cups sugar
5 eggs, separated
2 cups all-purpose flour
1 cup buttermilk

1 teaspoon baking soda
1½ cups coconut
½ cup pecans, chopped
½ teaspoon vanilla
Cream Cheese Frosting (recipe follows)

1. Preheat oven to 350°F. Grease and flour three 9-inch round cake pans.

2. In a large mixing bowl, cream margarine, shortening, and sugar. Add egg yolks one at a time, beating well after each addition. With mixer running on low speed, add flour and buttermilk alternately until well combined. Blend in baking soda, coconut, pecans and vanilla.

3. In a separate mixing bowl, beat egg whites until foamy. Fold into batter. Pour batter into pans. Bake for 25 minutes. Turn out onto wire racks. Cool completely.

4. Assemble layers, using cream cheese frosting for filling. Frost sides and top of cake. Makes 1 three-layer cake.

CREAM CHEESE FROSTING

½ cup margarine, room temperature
1 package (8 oz.) cream cheese, soft
1 box (1 lb.) confectioners' sugar

1 teaspoon vanilla
1 cup pecans, chopped (optional)
1 cup coconut (optional)

In a mixing bowl, cream margarine and cream cheese until light and fluffy. With mixer running on low speed, gradually add confectioners' sugar until well blended. Stir in vanilla and pecans and/or coconut. Makes 3½ to 4 cups.

※ **LINDSEY FRY,** Tuscola, Texas
First Place, West Texas Fair & Rodeo,
Abilene, Texas, 2004

THE CHOCOLATE DECADENCE CAKE

Flour

1 package (18.2 oz.) 2-layer chocolate
   cake mix

4 eggs

¾ cup water

½ cup sour cream

¼ cup vegetable oil

3 squares (1 oz. each) semisweet chocolate,
   chopped into small chunks

¾ cup unsalted butter, room temperature

3 cups confectioner's sugar

5 tablespoons milk, divided

⅓ cup raisins, plus more for garnish

⅓ cup dates, plus more for garnish

⅓ cup almonds, plus more for garnish

5 squares (1 oz. each) unsweetened chocolate,
   melted and cooled

1. Preheat oven to 350°F. Grease and flour two 9 x 2-inch round cake pans.

2. In a large mixing bowl, combine cake mix, eggs, water, sour cream, and oil until blended. Beat at medium speed for 4 minutes. Fold in chopped chocolate.

3. Pour batter into pans. Bake for 35 minutes, or until a tester inserted in center comes out clean. Cook in pans on wire racks for 10 minutes. Turn out onto wire racks. Cool completely.

4. In a mixing bowl, cream butter until soft. Blend in confectioners' sugar alternately with 3 tablespoons of the milk until mixture reaches spreading consistency. Place 1 cup of the mixture in a small bowl; stir in ⅓ cup each of raisins, dates, and almonds for the filling.

5. To the remaining mixture (in the mixing bowl), add melted chocolate and stir to blend. Stir in remaining 2 tablespoons milk for a smooth, creamy consistency for the frosting.

6. Assemble the cake layers, spreading filling in between. Frost sides and top of cake. Garnish with additional dates, raisins and almonds. Makes 1 two-layer cake.

✄ **BARBARA BAUMAN,** Drummond, Montana
Best of Show, It's Going To Be a Chocolate Sunday, Western Montana Fair, Missoula, Montana, 1996

TRIPLE CHOCOLATE CAKE

2 cups all-purpose flour, plus more for pans

¾ cup unsalted butter, room temperature

1½ cups sugar

1 egg

1 teaspoon vanilla

⅔ cup cocoa powder

2 teaspoons baking soda

¼ teaspoon salt

1 cup buttermilk

¾ cup sour cream

CHOCOLATE GANACHE

1½ cups semisweet chocolate chips

¾ cup heavy cream

1 tablespoon unsalted butter, room temperature

1 tablespoon sugar

EASY CHOCOLATE FROSTING

½ cup unsalted butter, room temperature

4 cups confectioners' sugar

¼ cup cocoa

½ cup milk

1½ teaspoons vanilla

1. Preheat oven to 350°F. Grease and flour two 9 x 2-inch round cake pans.

2. In a large mixing bowl, beat butter and sugar until light and fluffy. Beat in egg and vanilla until blended.

3. Combine flour, cocoa, baking soda, and salt. Stir buttermilk into sour cream. Add flour and buttermilk mixtures alternately to creamed mixture, beginning and ending with flour mixture, until well blended.

4. Pour batter into prepared pans. Bake for 30 to 35 minutes, or until a toothpick inserted in center comes out clean. Cool in pans on wire racks for 10 minutes. Turn out onto wire racks. Cool completely.

5. To make chocolate ganache: Place chocolate chips in a heat-resistant bowl. Combine heavy cream, butter, and sugar in a small saucepan over medium-high heat. Bring to a boil, mix well to combine, and pour over chocolate chips. Let stand for 5 minutes. Stir until smooth. Let stand until filling cools and reaches desired consistency, about 15 minutes.

6. To make frosting: In a large bowl, beat butter until creamy. Stir together confectioners' sugar and cocoa and add to butter alternately with milk, beating after each addition until smooth. Stir in vanilla.

7. Cut each cake layer in half horizontally. Place one layer of cake on serving plate, cut side up, and spread with ⅓ of ganache. Repeat layers two more times. Top with remaining cake layer. Spread frosting on sides and top of cake. Makes 1 two-layer cake.

※ **SUSAN HUSK,** Ferrisburg, Vermont
Rosette, Cakes, Addison County Fair & Field Days, New Haven, Vermont, 2004

SOUR CREAM NUT CAKE

2 cups all-purpose flour, plus more for pans
½ cup unsalted butter, room temperature
1 cup sugar
2 eggs
1 teaspoon baking powder
1 teaspoon baking soda
½ teaspoon salt
1 cup sour cream
1 teaspoon vanilla

TOPPING MIX
⅓ cup brown sugar
¼ cup sugar
1 teaspoon cinnamon
1 cup pecans, chopped

Bake and decorate this cake for Christmas or Valentine's Day.

1. Preheat oven to 325°F. Grease and flour an 8 x 8 x 2-inch baking pan.

2. In a large mixing bowl, cream butter and sugar. Add eggs one at a time, beating well after each addition.

3. Whisk together flour, baking powder, baking soda, and salt. Add flour mixture and sour cream alternately to butter mixture, beginning and ending with flour mixture. Mix until well blended. Stir in vanilla.

4. To make topping mix: Combine brown sugar, sugar, cinnamon, and pecans.

5. Pour half of batter into pan. Add half of topping mix and cut into batter with a knife. Pour in remaining batter, followed by remaining topping mix. Bake for 35 to 40 minutes. Cool in pan on a wire rack. Makes 1 cake.

※ **JARETTA CAMPBELL,** Abilene, Texas
First Place, West Texas Fair & Rodeo, Abilene, Texas, 2001

Sinfully Chocolate Cake

2¾ cups all-purpose flour, plus more for pans

1 cup cocoa

2 cups boiling water

1 cup unsalted butter or margarine,
   room temperature

2½ cups sugar

4 eggs

½ teaspoon baking powder

2 teaspoons baking soda

½ teaspoon salt

1½ teaspoons vanilla

ICING

12 tablespoons unsalted butter or margarine,
   room temperature

5⅓ cups confectioners' sugar

1 cup cocoa

⅔ cup milk

2 teaspoons vanilla

1. Preheat oven to 350°F. Grease and flour three 9 x 2-inch round cake pans.

2. Combine cocoa and boiling water, stirring until smooth. Cool.

3. In a large mixing bowl, cream butter or margarine until light and fluffy. Gradually add sugar, beating well. Add eggs one at a time, beating well after each addition.

4. Whisk together flour, baking powder, baking soda, and salt. With mixer running on low speed, add flour mixture and cocoa mixture alternately to creamed mixture, beginning and ending with flour mixture. Stir in vanilla. Do not overbeat.

5. Pour batter into pans. Bake for 20 to 25 minutes. Cool in pans for 10 minutes. Turn out cakes onto wire racks and cool completely.

6. To make icing: In a medium mixing bowl, cream butter or margarine until softened. With mixer running on low speed, slowly add confectioners' sugar and cocoa alternately with milk. Beat to spreading consistency, adding more milk if needed. Stir in vanilla. Makes 4 cups.

7. Assemble the cake layers, spreading frosting between the layers and on sides and top of cake. Makes 1 three-layer cake.

⌧ **LINDA CHILDERS,** Abingdon, Virginia
Specialty Cake Winner, Washington County Fair, Abingdon, Virginia, 2004

Siren's Chocolate Layer Cake

4 squares (1 oz. each) unsweetened
   chocolate

½ cup unsalted butter, room temperature

2 eggs

2 cups buttermilk

2 teaspoons vanilla

3 drops maple flavoring

2½ cups all-purpose flour

2 cups sugar

2 teaspoons baking soda

½ teaspoon salt

FROSTING

4 squares (1 oz. each) unsweetened chocolate

½ cup unsalted butter, room temperature

1 lb. confectioner's sugar, sifted

2 teaspoons vanilla

2 drops maple flavoring

⅓ cup evaporated milk, plus more if needed

1. Preheat oven to 350°F. Grease two 9 x 2-inch or three 8 x 2-inch round cake pans. Line with waxed paper.

2. Melt chocolate and butter in the top half of a double boiler over simmering water. Stir to combine. Cool.

3. In a large mixing bowl, beat eggs and buttermilk until frothy. Mix in vanilla and maple flavoring.

4. Sift together flour, sugar, baking soda, and salt. Stir flour mixture into egg mixture. Add chocolate and blend thoroughly.

5. Pour batter into baking pans. Bake for 30 minutes, or until a toothpick inserted in center comes out clean. Cool in pans on wire racks for 10 minutes. Turn out onto wire racks and cool completely.

6. To make frosting: Melt chocolate and butter in the top half of a double boiler over simmering water. Stir to combine. Cool. In a medium mixing bowl, combine chocolate mixture, confectioners' sugar, vanilla, maple flavoring, and evaporated milk. Beat until well blended. If icing is too thick, gradually beat in additional evaporated milk in small increments until proper consistency is achieved. Makes 3 cups.

7. Assemble the cake layers, spreading frosting between the layers and on sides and top of cake. Makes 1 two-layer or three-layer cake.

✁ **CHARLES BALDWIN,** High Point, North Carolina
First Place, WBFJ Heavenly Layered Cake Contest, Dixie Classic Fair, Winston-Salem, North Carolina, 2005

QUEEN MUM TORTE

¼ **cup all-purpose flour, plus more for pans**
1½ **cups unsalted butter, room temperature**
¾ **cup cocoa**
2 **cups sugar, divided**
1½ **cups almonds, finely ground**
6 **eggs, separated**
¼ **cup water**

CHOCOLATE GLAZE

¼ **cup unsalted butter, room temperature**
¼ **cup cocoa**
¼ **cup water**
1 **teaspoon vanilla**
2 **cups confectioners' sugar**

Chocolate leaves
Cocoa-flavored whipped cream

1. Preheat oven to 350°F. Grease and flour a 10 x 2½-inch springform pan.

2. Melt butter in medium saucepan over low heat. Stir in cocoa and 1½ cups of the sugar, blending until smooth. Remove from heat. Cool for 15 minutes. Blend in ground almonds and flour. Beat in egg yolks one at a time. Stir in water.

3. In large mixing bowl, beat egg whites until foamy. Gradually add remaining ½ cup sugar. Beat until soft peaks form. Gradually fold chocolate mixture into egg whites, blending thoroughly.

4. Pour batter into pan. Bake for 30 minutes, or until a tester inserted in center comes out clean. Cool for 15 minutes (cake will settle slightly in the middle), remove pan rim, and invert onto a serving plate.

5. To make chocolate glaze: Melt butter in a small saucepan over low heat. Add cocoa and water and continue cooking, stirring continuously, until mixture thickens. Do not boil. Remove from heat and stir in vanilla. Gradually whisk in confectioners' sugar until smooth. Spread glaze over sides and top of cake. Garnish with chocolate leaves and cocoa-flavored whipped cream. Makes 1 cake.

✁ **CAROLYNN RICHARDSON,** Huson, Montana
Best of Show, It's Going To Be a Chocolate Sunday, Western Montana Fair, Missoula, Montana, 2001

CHOCOLATE SYRUP SWIRL CAKE

2¾ cups all-purpose flour,
  plus more for pan

1 cup unsalted butter, room temperature

2 cups sugar

2 teaspoons vanilla

3 eggs

1 teaspoon baking soda

½ teaspoon salt

1 cup buttermilk

1 cup Hershey's chocolate syrup

¼ teaspoon baking soda

ROYAL GLAZE

⅔ cup semisweet chocolate chips

¼ cup heavy cream

¼ teaspoon vanilla

1. Preheat oven to 350°F. Grease and flour a 12-cup Bundt pan.

2. In a large mixing bowl, cream butter, sugar, and vanilla until light and fluffy. Add eggs and beat well.

3. Combine flour, baking soda, and salt. Add flour mixture and buttermilk alternately to creamed mixture, blending until well combined. Measure 2 cups of batter into a bowl. Combine chocolate syrup and baking soda; stir into 2 cups batter.

4. Pour vanilla batter into pan. Pour chocolate batter over vanilla batter in pan. Do not mix. Bake for 70 minutes. Cool in pan 15 minutes before turning out onto a wire rack. Cool completely.

5. To make royal glaze: Combine chocolate chips and heavy cream in a saucepan over medium heat. Cook until chocolate is melted. Remove from heat. Stir in vanilla. Cool 10 to 15 minutes, or until mixture thickens. Drizzle over cake. Makes 1 Bundt cake.

✖ **BETTY FINK,** Abilene, Texas
First Place, West Texas Fair & Rodeo, Abilene, Texas, 2003

WHITE CHOCOLATE CHRISTMAS CAKE

2½ cups sifted cake flour, plus
  more for pans

2 cups sugar

1 teaspoon baking powder

½ teaspoon salt

1 cup unsalted butter, room temperature

4 eggs, separated

¼ lb. white chocolate, melted and
  slightly cooled

2 teaspoons vanilla

1 cup buttermilk

1 cup chopped pecans

½ cup finely chopped candied cherries

½ cup finely chopped pitted dates

Fruit jam

CREAM CHEESE FROSTING

½ cup unsalted butter, room temperature

1 package (8 oz.) cream cheese, room temperature

4 cups confectioners' sugar

Dash of salt

1 teaspoon vanilla

Cream, if needed

1. Preheat oven to 350°F. Grease and flour three 9 x 2-inch round cake pans.

2. Sift and measure sugar. Add baking powder and salt and sift again.

3. In a large mixing bowl, cream butter and sugar mixture until light and fluffy. Add egg yolks and beat well. Beat in melted white chocolate and vanilla. Add flour and buttermilk alternately, beating after each addition.

4. Beat egg whites until stiff peaks form. Fold into batter. Stir in pecans, cherries, and dates. Turn batter into pans. Bake for 35 minutes, or until a wooden pick comes out clean. Cool on wire racks.

5. To make cream cheese frosting: Cream butter and cream cheese until fluffy. Slowly add confectioners' sugar, beating until smooth. Mix in salt and vanilla. If frosting is too thick, thin with 1 or 2 tablespoons of cream.

6. Spread fruit preserves between cake layers. Spread cream cheese frosting over top and sides. Makes 1 three-layer cake.

Use any red fruit jam, such as sweet cherry jam or seedless black raspberry jam, as the filling for this cake.

※ **CAROLYNN RICHARDSON,** Huson, Montana
Best of Show, Holiday Desserts, Western Montana Fair, Missoula, Montana, 1998

CHILI-CHOCOLATE CAKE OLÉ

3 squares (1 oz. each) semisweet
    chocolate, finely chopped
1 cup milk, divided
3 eggs, divided
1⅔ cups sugar, divided
½ cup shortening
1 teaspoon vanilla
¼ cup cinnamon liqueur
2 cups cake flour
1 teaspoon baking soda
½ teaspoon salt
6 to 10 small red dried chile peppers,
    finely ground (1 teaspoon)

1 teaspoon cinnamon
½ teaspoon nutmeg

GLAZE
1 cup heavy cream
8 squares (1 oz. each) semisweet chocolate,
    finely chopped
2 tablespoons cinnamon liqueur

Whipped cream

1. Preheat oven to 350°F. Set aside an 8 x 8 x 2-inch baking pan.

2. Combine chocolate, ½ cup of the milk, one egg, and ⅔ cup of the sugar in a saucepan. Cook over medium heat, stirring constantly, until thickened. Cool.

3. In a large mixing bowl, cream shortening, remaining cup of sugar, vanilla, and ¼ cup cinnamon liqueur. Add remaining two eggs and beat well.

4. Sift together cake flour, baking soda, salt, ground chiles, cinnamon, and nutmeg. Add flour mixture and remaining ½ cup milk alternately to creamed mixture, beating until smooth. Blend in chocolate mixture.

5. Pour batter into pan. Bake for 25 to 35 minutes, or until a toothpick inserted in center comes out clean. Cool on a wire rack.

6. To make glaze: Place heavy cream in a saucepan over medium-high heat. Bring to a boil and stir in chocolate. Remove from heat. Cool to between 85° and 95°F; stir in cinnamon liqueur.

7. Set cake on a wire rack. Slip a sheet of waxed paper underneath to catch drips. Pour glaze over top of cake, allowing it to dribble down the sides. Serve with whipped cream. Makes 6 to 8 servings.

※ **KIMBERLY STIPE,** Bethany, Oklahoma
First Place, Mexican Contest, Oklahoma State Fair, Oklahoma City, Oklahoma, 2005

CHOCOLATE-CHERRY FUDGE CAKE

2 cups all-purpose flour, plus more for pans

¾ cup sugar

1 teaspoon cinnamon

⅛ teaspoon salt

½ cup cocoa

¾ cup vegetable oil

2 eggs

2 teaspoons vanilla

1 teaspoon baking soda

1 can (21 oz.) cherry pie filling

6 oz. chocolate or swirled chocolate chips

WHITE CHOCOLATE CREAM CHEESE ICING

½ cup salted butter, room temperature

1 package (8 oz.) cream cheese,
   room temperature

2 oz. white chocolate, melted

4 cups confectioners' sugar

1 teaspoon vanilla

2 tablespoons heavy cream

Chocolate-covered cherries

1. Preheat oven to 350°F. Grease and flour two 9 x 2-inch round cake pans.

2. In a large mixing bowl, combine flour, sugar, cinnamon, and salt. With mixer running on low, add cocoa, oil, eggs, vanilla, and baking soda. Mix well. Stir in cherry pie filling and chocolate chips.

3. Pour batter into pans. Bake for 35 to 40 minutes, or until a cake tester inserted in center comes out clean. Cool in pan on rack for 10 minutes. Turn out onto wire racks and cool completely.

4. To make white chocolate cream cheese icing: In a mixing bowl, cream butter and cream cheese. Add white chocolate and blend well. With mixer running on low, gradually add confectioners' sugar, vanilla, and heavy cream until icing is of spreading consistency.

5. Assemble cake layers, spreading icing in between. Ice sides and top of cake. Decorate with chocolate-covered cherries. Makes 1 two-layer cake.

※ **KELLY EVERHART,** Seffner, Florida
First Place, Adult Division, Florida State Fair, Tampa, Florida, 2005

DELTA MOCHA CHIFFON CAKE

1¾ cups cake flour, plus more for pan

¾ cup boiling water

½ cup cocoa

1 teaspoon instant coffee granules

1¾ cups sugar

1½ teaspoons baking soda

½ teaspoon salt

8 large eggs, separated

½ cup vegetable oil

2 teaspoons vanilla

½ teaspoon cream of tartar

Chocolate-Coffee Buttercream Filling (recipe follows)

Chocolate Fudge Frosting (recipe follows)

1. Preheat oven to 325°F. Grease and flour four 9 x 2-inch round cake pans.

2. Combine boiling water, cocoa, and instant coffee granules, stirring until smooth.

3. In a large mixing bowl, combine sugar, baking soda, salt, and flour. With mixer running on low, add cocoa mixture, egg yolks, oil, and vanilla. Beat at medium speed until smooth.

4. In a separate mixing bowl, beat egg whites and cream of tartar at high speed until foamy. Fold into batter. Pour batter into pans. Bake 2 layers at a time on same rack of oven for 17 to 20 minutes, or until a wooden pick inserted in center comes out clean. Cool in pans on wire racks for 10 minutes. Turn out onto wire racks lined with waxed paper to prevent sticking. Cool completely.

5. Assemble cake layers with Chocolate-Coffee Buttercream Filling. Frost sides and top with Chocolate Fudge Frosting. Garnish with chocolate-covered coffee beans, if desired. Makes 1 four-layer cake.

CHOCOLATE-COFFEE BUTTERCREAM FILLING

⅔ cup unsalted butter, room temperature
2½ cups confectioners' sugar
1 tablespoon cocoa

½ cup heavy cream
2 teaspoons instant coffee granules
2 teaspoons coffee liqueur or 1 teaspoon vanilla

1. In a mixing bowl, cream butter, confectioners' sugar, and cocoa until fluffy.
2. Place cream in a microwave-safe container. Microwave on medium until warm; do not boil. Add instant coffee granules and stir until dissolved. Cool.
3. Add cream mixture and liqueur to butter mixture, beating until smooth. Makes 1½ cups.

CHOCOLATE FUDGE FROSTING

1 cup unsalted butter, room temperature
½ cup cocoa

6 cups confectioners' sugar
½ cup milk

In a mixing bowl, cream butter until light and fluffy. With mixer running, slowly add cocoa, confectioners' sugar, and milk. Beat until smooth. Makes 3½ cups.

※ **KATHY FRIERSON,** DeLand, Florida
First Place, Baked Goods, Senior Adult, Volusia County Fair, DeLand, Florida, 2004

CHOCOLATE CHIFFON CAKE

½ cup cocoa
¾ cup boiling water
1¾ cups all-purpose flour
1½ teaspoons baking soda
1¾ cups sugar

1 teaspoon salt
½ cup vegetable oil
8 eggs, separated
2 teaspoons vanilla
½ teaspoon cream of tartar

1. Preheat oven to 325°F. Set aside an ungreased 10 x 4-inch tube pan.
2. Combine cocoa and boiling water, mixing to dissolve. Allow to cool.
3. In a large mixing bowl, sift together flour, baking soda, sugar, and salt. Make a well in the center and add oil, egg yolks, and cocoa mixture. Beat well. Stir in vanilla.
4. Beat egg whites with cream of tartar until stiff peaks form. Fold into batter.
5. Pour batter into pan. Bake for 55 minutes. Increase oven temperature to 350°F and bake 10 minutes more. Immediately invert pan onto wire rack to cool completely. Remove from pan when cool. Makes 1 tube cake.

※ **LINDA BROWN,** Easton, Maryland
First Place and Best in Class, Cakes, Delaware State Fair, Harrington, Delaware, 2005

Easy Eggless Chocolate Layer Cake

3 cups all-purpose flour, plus more for pans
8 squares (1 oz. each) semisweet baking
    chocolate, broken into pieces
1½ cups sugar
2 teaspoons baking soda

1 teaspoon salt
2 cups water
⅔ cup vegetable oil
2 tablespoons white vinegar
2 teaspoons vanilla

1. Preheat oven to 350°F. Grease and flour two 9 x 2-inch round cake pans. Line bottoms with waxed paper.

2. Place chocolate in a small microwave-safe bowl. Microwave at high for 1½ to 2 minutes, or until chocolate is melted. Cool slightly.

3. In a large mixing bowl, stir together flour, sugar, baking soda, and salt. Add melted chocolate, water, oil, vinegar, and vanilla. Beat until thoroughly blended.

4. Pour batter into pans. Bake for 30 to 35 minutes, or until a toothpick inserted in center comes out clean. Cool in pans on wire racks for 10 minutes. Turn out onto wire racks, remove waxed paper, and cool completely. Assemble and frost layers as desired. Makes 1 two-layer cake.

✄ **CAROLYN DOOLEY,** Lake Odessa, Michigan
First Place, Chocolate Cake, Ionia Free Fair, Ionia, Michigan, 2003, 2004

Chocolate-Banana-Peanut Butter Delight

Flour

CHOCOLATE LAYERS
½ cup unsalted butter or margarine,
    room temperature
1¼ cups sugar
2 eggs
3 envelopes (1 oz. each) premelted
    unsweetened baking chocolate
¾ cup milk
1 teaspoon vanilla
2 cups all-purpose flour or
    2¼ cups cake flour
1 teaspoon baking soda
½ teaspoon salt
½ cup sour cream

BANANA LAYER
½ cup unsalted butter or margarine,
    room temperature
½ cup sugar
1 egg

¾ cup mashed ripe bananas (1½ medium)
¼ cup sour cream
½ teaspoon vanilla
½ teaspoon banana extract
1 cup all-purpose or 1 cup plus
    2 tablespoons cake flour
½ teaspoon baking soda
½ teaspoon baking powder
¼ teaspoon salt

PEANUT BUTTER FROSTING
1 cup unsalted butter or margarine,
    room temperature
1 cup creamy peanut butter
4 cups confectioners' sugar
¼ cup milk
½ teaspoon vanilla

Chocolate-covered peanuts or peanuts,
    chopped, for garnish
Chocolate chips, for garnish

1. Preheat oven to 350°F. Grease and lightly flour bottom and sides of three 8 x 2-inch or 9 x 2-inch round cake pans.

2. To make chocolate layers: Cream butter or margarine in a medium mixing bowl at medium speed. Add sugar and continue mixing, scraping bowl occasionally, until well blended. Beat in eggs one at a time. Beat in chocolate, milk, and vanilla. With mixer running on low speed, add flour, baking soda, and salt, scraping down sides of bowl constantly. Divide batter evenly between two pans. Bake 25 to 30 minutes, or until a toothpick inserted in center comes out clean. Cool 10 minutes in pans and then invert onto wire racks. Cool completely.

3. To make banana layer: Cream butter or margarine in a medium mixing bowl at medium speed. Add sugar and continue mixing, scraping bowl occasionally, until well blended. Beat in egg. Beat in banana, sour cream, vanilla, and banana extract. With mixer running on low speed, add flour, baking soda, baking powder, and salt, scraping down sides of bowl constantly. Pour batter into remaining pan. Bake 23 to 25 minutes, or until a toothpick inserted in center comes out clean. Cool 10 minutes in pan and then invert onto a wire rack. Cool completely.

4. To make peanut butter frosting: Cream butter or margarine in a mixing bowl until fluffy. Beat in peanut butter, ½ cup of the confectioners' sugar, milk, and vanilla. With mixer running, gradually add remaining 3½ cups confectioners' sugar and beat until smooth.

5. To assemble cake: Place a chocolate layer on plate. Spread one quarter of peanut butter frosting over top. Add banana layer and spread with another one quarter cup of frosting. Top with second chocolate layer. Cover top and sides of cake with remaining frosting. Garnish with peanuts and chocolate chips. Chill until ready to serve. Makes 1 three-layer cake.

※ **KAYLA DINKEL,** Buckeye Jr. Farmers 4-H Club, Hays, Kansas
Champion Senior Foods, Ellis County Fair, Hays, Kansas, 2005

CHOCOLATE ANGEL FOOD CAKE

¾ cup sifted cake flour

¼ cup cocoa

1½ cups sifted confectioners' sugar

1½ cups egg whites (approximately 12)

1½ teaspoons cream of tartar

⅓ teaspoon salt

1½ teaspoons vanilla

½ teaspoon almond extract

1 cup super-fine sugar

1. Preheat oven to 375°F. Set aside a 10 x 4-inch tube cake pan; do not grease.

2. Triple-sift cake flour, cocoa, and confectioners' sugar.

3. In a large mixing bowl, combine egg whites, cream of tartar, salt, vanilla, and almond extract. Beat until foamy. Gradually add super-fine sugar, 2 tablespoons at a time, beating until meringue holds stiff peaks.

4. Gradually sift flour-sugar mixture over the meringue and fold in gently just until the flour-sugar mixture disappears.

5. Place batter into tube pan. Gently cut through batter with a knife to break up any air pockets. Bake for 30 to 35 minutes, or until a toothpick inserted near center comes out clean. Invert until cool. Makes 1 cake.

※ **PAUL B. McDADE,** Middletown, Ohio
First Place, Ohio State Fair, Columbus, Ohio, 1999; First Place, Butler County Fair, Hamilton, Ohio, 2004; First Place, Warren County Fair, Lebanon, Ohio, 1999, 2000, 2004

Mexican Chocolate Cake

2¼ cups cake flour, plus more for pans

¾ cup cocoa

2 teaspoons baking soda

½ teaspoon baking powder

½ teaspoon salt

1¼ teaspoons cinnamon

1 cup unsalted butter, room temperature

2 cups sugar

2 teaspoons vanilla

2 eggs

1 cup buttermilk

¾ cup sour cream

MOCHA SILK FROSTING

½ cup cream

6 oz. semisweet chocolate, chopped

1 teaspoon instant coffee powder

1¼ cups unsalted butter, room temperature

3 cups confectioners' sugar

1 to 2 tablespoons coffee liqueur

1. Preheat oven to 350°F. Grease and flour three 8 x 2-inch round cake pans.

2. Whisk together flour, cocoa, baking soda, baking powder, salt, and cinnamon.

3. In a large mixing bowl, beat butter, sugar, and vanilla on medium speed, scraping bowl occasionally, until light and fluffy. Beat in eggs one at a time. Add flour mixture alternately with buttermilk and sour cream, beating after each addition until smooth.

4. Pour batter into pans. Bake for 25 to 30 minutes, or until cake springs back when pressed gently. Turn out onto wire racks. Cool completely.

5. To make mocha silk frosting: Combine cream and chocolate in a microwave-safe bowl. Microwave on high for 1 minute, repeating at 15-second intervals, until chocolate is melted and mixture is smooth. Stir in instant coffee powder. Chill 20 to 30 minutes. In a small mixing bowl, cream butter and sugar. Add chocolate mixture and liqueur and beat until light and fluffy.

6. Assemble cake layers, spreading frosting in between. Frost sides and top of cake. Makes 1 three-layer cake.

✕ **Mary Beth Pederson,** Morton, Illinois
Grand Champion, Illinois State Fair, Springfield, Illinois, 2004

Pecan-Fudge Sheet Cake

2 cups all-purpose flour, plus more for pan

2 cups sugar

½ teaspoon salt

½ cup sour cream

1 teaspoon vanilla

1 cup unsalted butter, room temperature

4 tablespoons cocoa

½ cup water

½ cup buttermilk

1 cup pecans, crushed

2 eggs, beaten

1 teaspoon baking soda

FROSTING

½ cup unsalted butter, soft

⅓ cup buttermilk

4 tablespoons cocoa

1 box (1 lb.) confectioners' sugar

1 teaspoon vanilla

1 cup pecans, chopped

1. Preheat oven to 350°F. Grease and flour a 12½ x 17 x 1-inch sheet pan.

2. In a large mixing bowl, combine flour, sugar, and salt.

3. Combine sour cream, vanilla, butter, cocoa, water, buttermilk, and pecans in a saucepan over medium-high heat. Bring to a boil. Pour over flour mixture, add eggs and baking soda, and mix well. Pour batter into pan. Bake for 20 to 25 minutes. Cool in pan on a wire rack.

4. To make frosting: In a mixing bowl, combine butter, buttermilk, cocoa, confectioners' sugar, and vanilla. Beat until creamy. Stir in pecans. Spread on cake while still warm. Makes 16 to 20 servings.

※ **CARYLON MILLER,** Abilene, Texas
First Place, West Texas Fair & Rodeo, Abilene, Texas, 2005

WHITE- AND-DARK CHOCOLATE-RASPBERRY CAKE

1¾ cups all-purpose flour, plus more for pans

2 teaspoons baking powder

1 teaspoon salt

3 oz. white chocolate

¾ cup cream, divided

3 oz. dark chocolate

4 eggs, separated

1 cup sugar

1 teaspoon vanilla

⅓ cup unsalted butter, room temperature

⅓ cup seedless raspberry jam

WHITE CHOCOLATE FROSTING

3 oz. white chocolate, melted

½ cup unsalted butter, room temperature

1 package (8 oz.) cream cheese, room temperature

1 box (1 lb.) confectioners' sugar

1 teaspoon vanilla

1 oz. dark chocolate, melted

1. Preheat oven to 350°F. Grease and flour three 9-inch round cake pans.

2. Whisk together flour, baking powder, and salt.

3. Combine white chocolate and ¼ cup of the cream in a small bowl. Set over hot water, stirring until chocolate melts. Melt dark chocolate and ¼ cup of the cream in the same way.

4. In a large bowl, beat egg yolks until fluffy. Add sugar, vanilla, butter, and remaining ¼ cup of cream; beat well. Fold in flour mixture.

5. Beat egg whites until stiff peaks form. Fold into batter. Pour one-third of batter into another bowl, add dark chocolate, and mix until well blended. Pour dark chocolate batter into one baking pan. Add white chocolate to remaining two-thirds batter. Divide between two baking pans. Bake for 25 minutes. Cool on wire racks.

6. To make white chocolate frosting: Cream white chocolate, butter, and cream cheese until smooth. Gradually beat in confectioners' sugar until spreading consistency. Beat in vanilla.

7. Place a white layer on a serving plate. Spread half of raspberry jam over top. Add chocolate layer and spread with remaining jam. Add remaining white layer. Frost sides and top of cake. Drizzle dark chocolate across the top. Makes 1 three-layer cake.

※ **KATHY CYPERT,** Buffalo Gap, Texas
First Place & Best of Show, West Texas Fair & Rodeo, Abilene, Texas, 2005

Sinsational Chocolate Cake

Flour

CHOCOLATE LAYERS
1 cup shortening
2 cups sugar
3 eggs
½ cup cocoa
2 teaspoons baking soda
½ teaspoon salt
1 cup milk
1 tablespoon vinegar
1 teaspoon vanilla
2½ cups all-purpose flour
1 cup hot water

MACAROON LAYERS
¾ cup sugar
½ teaspoon baking powder
3 egg whites
¾ cup coconut
½ cup pecans, chopped
1 cup vanilla cookie crumbs

WHITE CHOCOLATE FILLING
1 cup white chocolate chips
2 tablespoons brandy
1 cup half-and-half cream
1 package (8 oz.) cream cheese
1 cup heavy cream, whipped

CHOCOLATE FROSTING
1 package (8 oz.) cream cheese
6 tablespoons unsalted butter,
   room temperature
2¾ cups confectioners' sugar
¾ cup cocoa
5 tablespoons milk
1 teaspoon vanilla

1. Preheat oven to 350°F. Grease and flour five 9 x 2-inch round cake pans.

2. To make chocolate layers: In a large mixing bowl, cream shortening and sugar on high speed. Add eggs and mix well. Whisk together cocoa, baking soda, and salt; beat into creamed mixture. Combine milk, vinegar, and vanilla; add to batter alternately with flour. Blend in hot water. Pour batter into three baking pans. Bake for 30 to 35 minutes. Cool in pans for 10 minutes and turn out onto wire racks.

3. To make macaroon layers: Whisk together sugar and baking powder. In a large mixing bowl, beat egg whites until soft peaks form. Gradually beat in sugar mixture, 1 tablespoon at a time. Combine coconut, pecans, and cookie crumbs; gently fold into egg whites. Divide mixture evenly between two baking pans. Bake 15 to 20 minutes. Cool in pans for 10 minutes and turn out onto wire racks.

4. To make white chocolate filling: Combine white chocolate chips, brandy, and half-and-half in the top half of double boiler set over simmering water. Stir until smooth and melted. Cool completely. In a small mixing bowl, beat cream cheese until fluffy. Add chocolate mixture and beat until smooth. Fold in whipped cream.

5. To make chocolate frosting: In a small mixing bowl, beat cream cheese and butter until well blended. Add confectioners' sugar and cocoa alternately with milk and vanilla, beating until smooth.

6. To assemble layers: Place a chocolate layer on a serving plate and spread with one-fourth of the filling. Add a macaroon layer and spread with one-fourth of the filling. Add remaining three layers, alternating between chocolate and macaroon, in the same way. Frost sides and top of cake. Chill for 1 hour before serving. Makes 1 five-layer cake.

✕ **LINDA FRY,** Tuscola, Texas
First Place & Best of Show, West Texas Fair & Rodeo, Abilene, Texas, 1998

Mother Superior's Sour Cream Devil's Food Cake

2½ cups cake flour, plus more for pans

¾ cup shortening

1¾ cups sugar

1 teaspoon vanilla

3 eggs, separated

½ cup cocoa

½ cup plus 2 tablespoons brewed coffee, mixed well and cooled

2 teaspoons baking soda

½ teaspoon salt

1 cup sour cream

7-MINUTE ICING

2 cups brown sugar

5 tablespoons strong brewed coffee

2 egg whites

⅛ teaspoon cream of tartar

¼ teaspoon salt

¼ teaspoon vanilla

2 squares unsweetened chocolate

1 tablespoon unsalted butter, room temperature

1. Preheat oven to 345°F. Grease and flour two 9 x 2-inch round cake pans (cake will come to very top when baking) or three 8 x 1½-inch round cake pans.

2. Cream shortening and sugar in a large mixing bowl. Beat in vanilla and egg yolks until well combined. Whisk together cocoa and coffee, add to mixture, and beat until well combined.

3. Combine flour, baking soda, and salt. Add flour mixture and sour cream alternately to batter, mixing just until combined. Beat egg whites and fold into batter. Pour batter into pans. Bake for 45 minutes, or until a tester inserted in center comes out clean. Remove from pans and cool on wire racks.

4. To make 7-minute icing: Combine brown sugar, coffee, egg whites, cream of tartar, and salt in the top half of a double boiler set over boiling water. Cook, beating continuously with a hand-held mixer or immersion blender until stiff peaks form. Remove from heat and fold in vanilla.

5. Assemble and frost cake layers. Microwave chocolate and butter in a small dish until melted and stir to combine. Drip chocolate down sides of cake all around. Makes 1 two-layer or three-layer cake.

✖ **HELEN GETZ,** Missoula, Montana
Best of Show, It's Going To Be a Chocolate Sunday, Western Montana Fair, Missoula, Montana, 1988

Wild Mountain Huckleberry Cheesecake

CRUST

1 cup graham cracker crumbs

¼ cup sugar

4 tablespoons unsalted butter, melted

FILLING

5 packages (8 oz. each) cream cheese,
    room temperature

1½ cups sugar

3 tablespoons flour

1 tablespoon vanilla

Juice of 1 lemon (about 2 tablespoons)

3 eggs

1 cup sour cream

TOPPING

2 tablespoons potato starch

¼ cup water

2 cups wild mountain huckleberries

¾ cup sugar

FROSTING

4 oz. cream cheese

1 tablespoon unsalted butter,
    room temperature

2 cups confectioners' sugar

1. Preheat oven to 350°F. Set aside a 9 x 3-inch springform pan; do not grease.

2. To make crust: Combine graham cracker crumbs, sugar, and melted butter. Press mixture into bottom of pan. Bake for 8 minutes. Cool.

3. To make filling: In a large mixing bowl, beat cream cheese until creamy and smooth. Add sugar, flour, vanilla, and lemon juice; beat until well blended. Add eggs one at a time, beating well after each addition. Blend in sour cream. Pour filling over crust. Bake for 1 hour. Cool in pan on a wire rack.

4. To make topping: Combine potato starch and water; set aside. Combine huckleberries and sugar in a saucepan over medium-high heat. When mixture begins to boil, add potato starch liquid. Continue cooking, stirring continuously, until thickened. Cool slightly. Pour topping over cheesecake.

5. To make frosting: In a small mixing bowl, beat cream cheese until smooth and creamy. Add butter and mix until smooth. Gradually add confectioners' sugar, beating until smooth. Pipe or spread frosting around edge of cheesecake as desired. Chill for at least 4 hours. Makes 1 cheesecake.

✕ IMOGENE WOODSIDE, La Center, Washington
Winner, Dairy Women Cheesecake Contest, Clark County Fair, Ridgefield, Washington, 2005

Rich Golden Cupcakes

2⅛ cups all-purpose flour

1½ cups sugar

3 teaspoons baking powder

1 teaspoon salt

⅔ cup shortening, softened

1 cup milk

1½ teaspoons vanilla

3 eggs

CHOCOLATE FROSTING

1 cup sugar

5 tablespoons unsalted butter or
    margarine, room temperature

⅓ cup milk

1 cup chocolate chips

1. Preheat oven to 400°F. Insert paper liners in the cups of a 12-cup muffin pan.

2. Sift flour, sugar, baking powder, and salt into a large mixing bowl.

3. Add shortening, milk, and vanilla. Beat 2 minutes until smooth. Add eggs and beat another 2 minutes.

4. Pour batter into paper liners two-thirds full. Bake for 15 to 20 minutes, or until tops are lightly browned and spring back when lightly pressed with a spatula. Cool.

5. To make chocolate frosting: Combine sugar, butter or margarine, and milk in a saucepan over medium-high heat. Bring to a boil and cook for 1 minute. Remove from heat. Stir in chocolate chips. Continue stirring until chocolate is melted and mixture is smooth. Cool, stirring occasionally, until frosting reaches spreading consistency. Spread on top of cupcakes. Makes 12 cupcakes.

✂ **JOAN BINGHAM,** Cornwall, Vermont
Best Frosted Cakes or Cupcakes, Addison County Fair & Field Days, New Haven, Vermont, 2005

WHITE CHOCOLATE-BLACKBERRY CHEESECAKE

CRUST
1 cup slivered unsalted almonds
2 cups graham cracker crumbs
6 tablespoons unsalted butter, melted

FILLING
8 oz. white chocolate
4 packages (8 oz. each) cream cheese,
    room temperature

½ cup plus 2 tablespoons sugar
4 large eggs
2 large egg yolks
2 tablespoons all-purpose flour
1 teaspoon vanilla
2 cups fresh blackberries or 21 oz.
    frozen blackberries, thawed

1. Preheat the oven to 350°F. Set aside a 10 x 2½-inch springform pan; do not grease.

2. To make crust: Grind almonds in a food processor until fine. Combine ground almonds, graham cracker crumbs, and melted butter. Press mixture into bottom and two-thirds of the way up sides of pan.

3. To make filling: Melt white chocolate in the top half of a double boiler, stirring until smooth. Turn off heat. Rewarm chocolate if it starts to set up before you can use it.

4. In a large mixing bowl, beat cream cheese at a medium speed until fluffy. Beat in sugar. Add eggs and egg yolks one at a time, beating at low speed and scraping down sides of bowl after each addition. Beat in flour and vanilla until just combined. With mixer running on low, pour white melted chocolate in a slow stream; continue beating until well combined.

5. Arrange blackberries in a single layer over the crust. Pour filling over blackberries. Bake in the middle of the oven for 45 to 55 minutes, or until the filling 3 inches from the edge of the pan is set and center is still wobbly when the pan is gently shaken. Remove pan from oven and run a thin knife around edge of pan to loosen the crust. Cool in pan on a wire rack. The cheesecake will continue to set as it cools. Serve at room temperature or chilled. Makes 1 cheesecake.

Reserve a few whole blackberries to garnish the cheesecake slices.

SANDRA SCOTT, Pfafftown, North Carolina
First Place, Footsie Wootsie Cheesecake Bake-Off, Dixie Classic Fair,
Winston-Salem, North Carolina, 2005

Chocolate Cheesecake

Flour

QUICK CHOCOLATE CRUMB CRUST

1 cup crushed chocolate wafers

¼ cup unsalted butter or margarine,
  room temperature

CAKE

3 packages (8 oz. each) cream cheese,
  room temperature

1¼ cups sugar

1 container (8 oz. each) sour cream

2 teaspoons vanilla

½ cup cocoa

2 tablespoons all-purpose flour

3 eggs

QUICK CHOCOLATE DRIZZLE

½ cup semisweet chocolate chips

2 teaspoons shortening (do not use butter,
  margarine, spread, or oil)

1. Preheat oven to 450°F. Grease and lightly flour a 9 x 3-inch springform pan.

2. To make quick chocolate crumb crust: Combine crushed chocolate wafers and butter in a small bowl. Press mixture onto bottom of pan.

3. To make cake: Combine cream cheese and sugar in a mixing bowl. Beat until well blended. Add sour cream and vanilla; beat well to combine. With mixer running, slowly add cocoa and flour. Add eggs one at a time, beating after each addition.

4. Pour batter into pan. Bake for 10 minutes. Reduce oven temperature to 250°F and continue baking for 40 minutes. Set pan on a wire rack and run a knife around edge of pan to loosen cake. Cool completely before removing side of pan.

5. To make quick chocolate drizzle: Place chocolate chips and shortening in a small microwave-safe bowl. Microwave at high for 30 seconds. Remove from microwave and stir. If chips are not completely melted, heat another 15 seconds and stir again. Repeat if needed. Drizzle sauce over top of cake. Makes 1 cake.

✄ **CODY RUSSELL,** Valrico, Florida
First Place, Youth Division, Florida State Fair, Tampa, Florida, 2005

BLACK-BOTTOM CUPCAKES

CHEESE MIXTURE

1 package (8 oz.) cream cheese

⅓ cup sugar

1 egg

⅛ teaspoon salt

1 cup chocolate chips

CHOCOLATE CUPCAKE MIXTURE

2¼ cups all-purpose flour

1½ cups sugar

¼ cup plus 2 tablespoons cocoa powder

1½ teaspoons baking soda

¾ teaspoon salt

⅓ cup plus 3 tablespoons water

1½ tablespoons vinegar

1½ teaspoons vanilla

1. Preheat oven to 350°F. Insert paper liners into the cups of a 12-cup muffin pan.

2. To make cheese mixture: Combine cream cheese, sugar, egg, and salt in a small mixing bowl. Beat until creamy. Stir in chocolate chips.

3. To make cupcake mixture: Combine flour, sugar, cocoa powder, baking soda, salt, water, vinegar, and vanilla in a large mixing bowl. Beat well.

4. Fill each cupcake liner halfway with cupcake mixture. Top with a generous teaspoon of cheese mixture. Bake for 30 minutes, or until cheese mixture has run down the sides of the cupcake. Makes 12 cupcakes.

✁ **MICHELLE FERREIRAE,** age 12
First Place, San Diego County Fair, Del Mar, California, 2004

CHOCOLATE CHIP CHEESECAKE

1½ cups finely crushed creme-filled
    chocolate sandwich cookies

¼ cup melted margarine, room temperature

1 package (8 oz.) softened cream cheese

1 can (14 oz.) sweetened condensed milk

3 eggs

2 teaspoons vanilla

1 cup mini chocolate chips, divided

1 teaspoon flour

1. Preheat oven to 300°F.

2. Combine crushed cookies and margarine in a bowl. Press mixture firmly into bottom of a 9 x 3-inch springform pan.

3. Beat cream cheese in a large mixing bowl until fluffy. Add condensed milk and beat until smooth. Add eggs and vanilla. Mix well.

4. Toss ½ cup of the chocolate chips and flour in a small bowl to coat. Stir into cream cheese mixture. Pour batter into prepared pan. Sprinkle remaining ½ cup chocolate chips over the top. Bake 1 hour or until cake springs back when lightly touched. Turn off oven. Wait 1 hour before removing pan from oven. Cool to room temperature, remove sides of pan, and serve. Makes 1 cheesecake.

✁ **ERIN BARTELSON,** Waukesha, Wisconsin
Grand Champion, Waukesha County Fair, Pewaukee, Wisconsin, 1999

CARAMEL-MOCHACCINO-CHIP CHEESECAKE

1 cup chocolate wafer crumbs
¼ cup unsalted butter, melted
3 packages (8 oz. each) cream cheese,
    room temperature
1 cup sugar
¼ cup all-purpose flour
3 eggs

1½ cups sour cream
¼ cup strong brewed coffee
1 teaspoon vanilla
¼ cup semisweet chocolate chips
¼ cup butterscotch chips
¼ cup caramel topping

1. Preheat oven to 350°F. Grease one 9 x 3-inch springform pan or four 4 x 2-inch springform pans.

2. Combine chocolate wafer crumbs and melted butter. Press mixture onto bottom on pan. Bake for 8 minutes. Cool.

3. In a large mixing bowl, beat cream cheese and sugar until smooth. Add flour; beat until smooth. Add eggs one at a time, beating well after each addition. Add sour cream, coffee, and vanilla; mix until just combined.

4. Pour mixture into pan(s). Sprinkle chocolate chips and butterscotch chips over the top. Bake for 35 minutes (4-inch pans) or for 60 minutes (9-inch pan). Cool in pan(s). When completely cooled, place in refrigerator and chill overnight. Serve drizzled with caramel topping. Makes 1 large or 4 small cheesecakes.

✕ **STACEY RICKER,** Douglas, Wyoming
Second Place, Coffee Contest, Wyoming State Fair, Douglas, Wyoming, 2005

NEW ORLEANS PRALINE CHEESECAKE

CRUST
¾ cup chopped pecans
½ cup light brown sugar
¼ cup sugar
¾ cup quick-cooking rolled oats
¼ cup unsalted butter, melted

FILLING
3 packages (8 oz. each) lowfat cream cheese,
    room temperature
¾ cup sugar
⅓ cup dark corn syrup
5 teaspoons cornstarch
¼ teaspoon salt
1 egg yolk
3 whole eggs
2½ teaspoons vanilla
2 tablespoons bourbon or dark rum
⅔ cup chopped toasted pecans

TOPPINGS
1 tablespoon plus 1 teaspoon unsalted butter,
    room temperature
⅓ cup dark brown sugar
4½ teaspoons cream or milk
1¼ teaspoons cream of tartar
½ teaspoon vanilla
½ teaspoon bourbon or dark rum
¾ cup confectioners' sugar
Toasted pecan halves (about 20)

1. Preheat oven to 350°F. Grease a 9 x 3-inch springform pan.

2. To make crust: Combine chopped pecans, light brown sugar, sugar, oats, and melted butter. Press mixture into bottom of pan. Bake for 18 minutes, or until light golden. Cool completely.

3. To make filling: In a large mixing bowl, combine cream cheese, sugar, dark corn syrup, cornstarch, and salt. Beat on medium speed until smooth. Add egg yolk and eggs one at a time, beating well after each addition. Beat in vanilla and bourbon or rum. Stir in pecans.

4. Pour filling over crust. Bake for 15 minutes at 350°F. Reduce heat to 225°F and bake for 1 hour and 15 minutes, or until center is no longer looks wet. Remove from oven. Run and knife around edge to loosen. Cool completely in pan. Chill at least 8 hours.

5. To make topping: Melt butter in a small saucepan over medium heat. Stir in brown sugar, cream or milk, and cream of tartar; bring to a boil. Remove from heat and cool to lukewarm. Using a hand-held electric mixer, beat in vanilla, bourbon or dark rum, and confectioners' sugar until smooth. Add more cream or milk if necessary for spreading consistency. Spread warm topping over cheese-cake. Garnish with pecan halves. Chill. Makes 1 cheesecake.

�֍ **PAT NELSON,** Vermont, Illinois
Second Place, Baked Desserts Using Dairy Products, Illinois State Fair, Springfield, Illinois, 2005

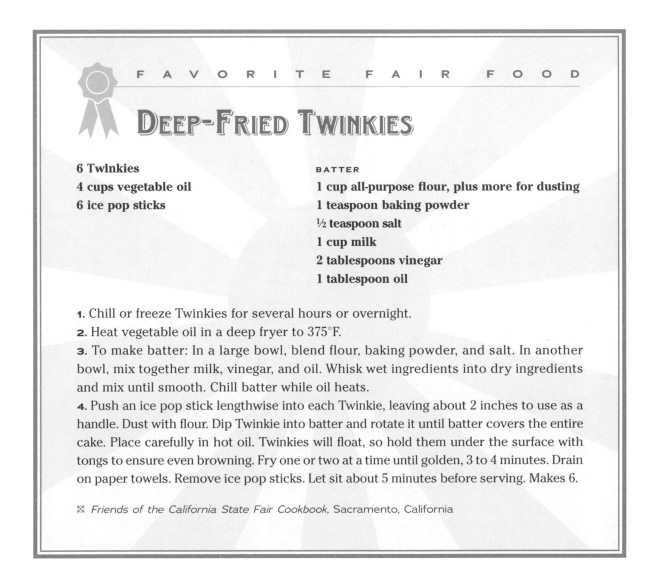

FAVORITE FAIR FOOD

DEEP-FRIED TWINKIES

6 Twinkies
4 cups vegetable oil
6 ice pop sticks

BATTER

1 cup all-purpose flour, plus more for dusting
1 teaspoon baking powder
½ teaspoon salt
1 cup milk
2 tablespoons vinegar
1 tablespoon oil

1. Chill or freeze Twinkies for several hours or overnight.

2. Heat vegetable oil in a deep fryer to 375°F.

3. To make batter: In a large bowl, blend flour, baking powder, and salt. In another bowl, mix together milk, vinegar, and oil. Whisk wet ingredients into dry ingredients and mix until smooth. Chill batter while oil heats.

4. Push an ice pop stick lengthwise into each Twinkie, leaving about 2 inches to use as a handle. Dust with flour. Dip Twinkie into batter and rotate it until batter covers the entire cake. Place carefully in hot oil. Twinkies will float, so hold them under the surface with tongs to ensure even browning. Fry one or two at a time until golden, 3 to 4 minutes. Drain on paper towels. Remove ice pop sticks. Let sit about 5 minutes before serving. Makes 6.

�֍ *Friends of the California State Fair Cookbook,* Sacramento, California

Praline Pecan Date Cheesecake

1 graham cracker crust for an 8- inch
   springform pan (see recipe page 308)
3 packages (8 oz. each) cream cheese
1¼ cups brown sugar
¼ cup heavy cream
3 eggs

1½ teaspoons vanilla
3 tablespoons flour, divided
2 cups chopped dates
¾ cup sugar
¾ cup water
1 cup chopped pecans

1. Preheat oven to 325°F. Press graham cracker crust into bottom of an 8 x 3-inch springform pan. Bake for 8 minutes. Cool.

2. Place cream cheese, brown sugar, heavy cream, eggs, vanilla, and flour in a blender. Mix on medium speed until creamy. Blend on a high speed for 1½ minutes. Pour filling into crust. Bake for 55 minutes. Cool.

3. Combine dates, sugar, water, and flour in a small saucepan over medium heat. Cook slowly until thickened, at least 10 minutes. Stir in pecans. Pour on top of cheesecake. Chill for at least 2 hours before serving. Makes 1 cheesecake.

✄ **Pamela Clute,** Palm Desert, California
First Place, Desserts, Riverside County Fair and National Date Festival, Indio, California, 2003–2004

> Store Praline Pecan Date Cheesecake up to 3 months in the freezer. It's a good keeper.

Chocolate Turtle Cheesecake

CRUST
1½ cups ground chocolate cookie crumbs
¾ pecan meal
⅓ cup light brown sugar
½ cup unsalted butter, melted

FILLING
3 packages (8 oz. each) cream cheese
1¼ cups sugar
½ teaspoon salt
1 tablespoon vanilla
4 eggs
1 cup sour cream
1 cup semisweet chocolate chips, melted

CARAMEL SAUCE AND TOPPING
¾ cup unsalted butter, divided
1 cup light brown sugar
¼ teaspoon salt
½ cup heavy cream
1 tablespoon vanilla
1 cup semisweet chocolate chips
1 cup chopped pecans

1. Preheat oven to 325°F. Lightly grease a 9 x 3-inch springform pan.

2. To make crust: Combine chocolate cookie crumbs, pecan meal, light brown sugar, and melted butter. Press mixture into bottom and 1 inch up the sides of pan. Bake for 10 minutes. Remove from oven.

3. To make filling: Beat cream cheese in a large mixing bowl until creamy. With mixer running, gradually add sugar, salt, and vanilla and beat well. Add eggs one at a time, mixing just until blended. Stir in sour cream.

4. Set springform pan on a double layer of wide heavy-duty foil. Pour two-thirds of batter into pan over crust. Mix half of melted chocolate into remaining batter. Pour half of chocolate batter over pan. Run a spatula through batter in pan to create a marbled effect. Stir remaining chocolate into remaining chocolate batter, pour into pan, and swirl. Bring foil up around sides of springform pan, set it into a larger pan, and place on middle rack of oven. Add hot water to outside pan to a depth of 1 inch. (Foil will prevent water from leaking into springform pan.) Bake for 1 hour 30 minutes. Turn off oven, crack the door open, and let cake sit undisturbed for 1 hour. Chill at least 8 hours, but preferably overnight, before removing pan rim.

5. To make caramel sauce: Combine ½ cup of the butter, light brown sugar, and salt in a saucepan over medium heat, stirring until sugar dissolves. Stir in cream. Remove from heat and stir in vanilla. Cool.

6. To assemble topping: Melt remaining ¼ cup butter in a saucepan over low heat. Add chocolate chips, remove from heat, and stir until melted. Spread chocolate mixture over cake. Chill for 15 minutes to set. Combine caramel sauce and pecans in a saucepan over medium-high heat. Bring to a boil and cook, stirring constantly, for 2 minutes. Cool for 10 minutes. Spread over chocolate on cake and chill to set. Remove cake from refrigerator 2 hours before serving. Cut into slices 1 hour before serving. Makes 1 cheesecake.

✳ **SHIRLEY J. MYRSIADES,** Pinellas Park, Florida
Best of Show—Adult Division, Florida State Fair, Tampa, Florida, 2005

CHOCOLATE-MALT CHEESECAKE

⅓ cup unsalted butter or margarine,
   room temperature
¼ cup sugar
1 cup graham cracker crumbs
3 packages (8 oz. each) cream cheese,
   room temperature

1 can (14 oz.) sweetened condensed milk
¾ cup chocolate malt powder
4 eggs
1 teaspoon vanilla
1 cup semisweet chocolate chips

1. Preheat oven to 300°F.

2. Combine butter or margarine, sugar, and graham cracker crumbs in a bowl. Press mixture firmly into bottom of a 9 x 3-inch springform pan.

3. Beat cream cheese in a large mixing bowl until fluffy. Add condensed milk and beat until well blended. Add malt powder, eggs, and vanilla and beat thoroughly. Fold in chocolate chips. Pour filling into crust. Bake for 65 minutes, or until cake springs back when lightly touched. Cool to room temperature and then chill in refrigerator. Makes 1 cheesecake.

✳ **KEVIN BERES,** Waukesha, Wisconsin
Grand Champion, Waukesha County Fair, Pewaukee, Wisconsin, 2001

WINNER'S CIRCLE TIP | Place a paper lace doily on top of a cool cake. Sprinkle with confectioners' sugar. Carefully remove doily to reveal the lacy design.

Maple-Pumpkin Cheesecake

CRUST

1¾ cups graham cracker crumbs

¼ cup brown sugar

¼ cup unsalted butter, melted

FILLING

3 packages (8 oz. each) cream cheese

1 can (14 oz.) sweetened condensed milk

1 can (15 oz.) pumpkin

3 eggs

¼ cup maple syrup

1½ teaspoons cinnamon

¼ teaspoon nutmeg

TOPPING

4 teaspoons cornstarch

2 tablespoons water

2 tablespoons unsalted butter, room temperature

½ cup maple syrup

½ cup raisins

1 cup coarsely chopped walnuts

1. Preheat oven to 325°F. Grease the bottom of a 9 x 3-inch springform pan.

2. To make crust: In a small bowl, whisk together graham cracker crumbs and sugar. Stir in melted butter. Press mixture into bottom of pan.

3. To make filling: In a large mixing bowl, combine cream cheese and sweetened condensed milk; beat until smooth. Beat in pumpkin. Add eggs, beating on low speed just until combined. Stir in maple syrup, cinnamon, and nutmeg.

4. Pour filling over crust. Set pan on a baking sheet. Bake for 90 minutes, or until center is almost set. Cool in pan on a wire rack for 10 minutes. Run a knife around edge of the pan to loosen cheesecake. Cool for 1 hour longer.

5. To make topping: Mix cornstarch in water until smooth. Melt butter in a small saucepan over medium heat. Add maple syrup and cornstarch mixture. Bring to a boil and cook over medium-high heat, stirring constantly, until thickened, 1 to 2 minutes. Remove from heat; stir in raisins and walnuts. Cool to lukewarm. Spoon topping over cheesecake. Refrigerate overnight before removing sides of pan. Makes 1 cheesecake.

✕ **STEPHANIE PIROT,** Anchorage, Alaska
First Place, Alaska State Fair, Palmer, Alaska, 2005

⊹ THE GREAT PUMPKIN ⊹

The Alaska State Fair holds an annual giant vegetable contest. In 2005, J.D. Megchelsen of Nikiski, Alaska, became a fair record-holder with his entry, a 942-pound pumpkin.

PUMPKIN CHEESECAKE

GINGER-MOLASSES COOKIE CRUST

¾ cup unsalted butter, melted,
    slightly cooled

1¼ cups sugar

¼ cup molasses

1 large egg

2 cups all-purpose flour

2 teaspoons baking soda

½ teaspoon salt

½ teaspoon ground cloves

½ teaspoon ground ginger

1 teaspoon cinnamon

FILLING

3 packages (8 oz. each) cream cheese, room temperature

1½ cups sugar

1 tablespoon plus 1 teaspoon cake flour

1½ teaspoons cinnamon

½ teaspoon ground cloves

½ teaspoon ground ginger

1 teaspoon vanilla

½ cup heavy cream

4 large eggs, slightly beaten

1¼ cups canned pumpkin

PUMPKIN CHEESECAKE FROSTING

2 cups heavy cream

2 tablespoons sugar

2 teaspoons brandy

1½ cups toasted and chopped almonds

1. To make ginger-molasses cookie crust: In a medium mixing bowl, combine melted butter, sugar, molasses and egg. Sift together flour, baking soda, salt, cloves, ginger, and cinnamon; add to creamed mixture, beating until well blended. Gather up dough, wrap in plastic wrap, and chill for 2 hours.

2. Heat oven to 350°F. Press cookie crust dough into bottom and two-thirds up the sides of a 10 x 2½-inch springform pan.

3. To make filling: In a large mixing bowl, beat cream cheese until light and fluffy. Beat in sugar. Sift together flour, cinnamon, cloves, and ginger; add to cream cheese mixture, beating on low to combine. Beat in vanilla and heavy cream. Whisk eggs into pumpkin and add to batter. Mix on low speed, scraping down sides of bowl, until well combined.

4. Pour filling into cookie crust in pan. Bake for 45 minutes. Turn oven off, leave oven door slightly ajar, and let rest for 15 minutes. Open door completely and let cake rest inside for 1 hour. Remove pan from oven and cool completely. Refrigerate overnight.

5. To make pumpkin cheesecake frosting: In a small mixing bowl, whip together cream, sugar, and brandy until stiff. Remove cake from pan and set on a plate. Spread frosting onto sides and top of cake. Garnish sides of cake with almonds. Makes 8 servings.

✕ **JUDITH BURROS,** Middleton, Massachusetts
First Place, Cheesecake, Topsfield Fair, Topsfield, Massachusetts, 2002

Cappuccino Cheesecake

CRUST

1½ cups finely chopped almonds

2 tablespoons sugar

3 tablespoons melted margarine,
    room temperature

FILLING

1½ tablespoons instant coffee granules

¼ teaspoon cinnamon

¼ cup boiling water

4 packages (8 oz. each) cream cheese,
    room temperature

1 cup sugar

3 tablespoons unbleached all-purpose flour

4 large eggs

1 cup sour cream

1. Preheat oven to 325°F.

2. To make crust: Combine almonds, sugar, and margarine. Press mixture into bottom of a 9 x 3-inch springform pan. Bake for 10 minutes. Remove pan from oven. Turn up oven to 450°F.

3. To make filling: Dissolve coffee granules and cinnamon in boiling water. Let cool.

4. Combine cream cheese, sugar, and flour in a large mixing bowl. Beat at medium speed until well blended. Add eggs one at a time, mixing well after each addition. Blend in sour cream. With mixer running, gradually add coffee mixture. Mix until well blended.

5. Pour batter into pan over crust. Bake for 10 minutes. Reduce oven temperature to 250°F and continue baking for 1 hour. Remove from oven. Run a narrow spatula around edge of pan to loosen cake. Cool completely before removing pan rim. Serve chilled. Makes 1 cheesecake.

✳ **CHRIS MEATS,** Rock Springs, Wyoming
First Place, Cheesecake Contest, and Third Place, Coffee Contest, Sweetwater County Fair, Rock Springs, Wyoming, 2003

WINNER'S CIRCLE TIP | **For a gourmet touch, serve slices of Cappucino Cheesecake garnished with whipped cream and whole coffee beans.**

Diabetic Cheesecake

Cooking spray

16 sugar-free shortbread cookies,
    finely crushed

1 tablespoon light butter–canola oil
    spread, melted

1 cup part skim-milk ricotta

2 packages (8 oz. each) "⅓-less fat"
    Neufchâtel cheese

1 cup sugar substitute

2 tablespoons flour

1 tablespoon sugar-free vanilla syrup

¼ teaspoon vanilla

3 eggs

Sugar-free hot fudge topping,
    warmed slightly

1. Preheat oven to 300°F. Coat the bottom of a 9 x 3-inch springform pan with cooking spray.

2. Combine cookie crumbs and melted butter spread. Shake loosely into bottom of pan.

3. In a large mixing bowl, cream ricotta and Neufchâtel cheese until smooth. Add sugar substitute, flour, vanilla syrup, and vanilla; mix until well blended. Add eggs one at a time, mixing just to incorporate.

4. Pour batter into the pan. Bake for 40 to 45 minutes. Run a knife around the edges to loosen cake from rim. Cool to room temperature. Chill until firm. Remove the rim. Drizzle sugar-free hot fudge topping over cake. Makes 1 cheesecake.

※ **RHONDA HITCH,** Kathleen, Georgia
First Place, Cooking Lite the ADA Way, Georgia National Fair, Perry, Georgia, 2005

WHITE CHOCOLATE CHEESECAKE

CRUST

1¼ cups graham cracker crumbs

¼ cup unsalted butter, room temperature

½ teaspoon cinnamon

FILLING

12 oz. fine-quality white chocolate, chopped

½ cup heavy cream

3 packages (8 oz. each) cream cheese

⅓ cup sugar

4 eggs

1 tablespoon vanilla

SOUR CREAM TOPPING

2 cups sour cream

¼ cup sugar

1 teaspoon vanilla

Cocoa powder for dusting

Chocolate curls

1. To make crust: Preheat oven to 350°F. Combine graham cracker crumbs, butter, and cinnamon. Press mixture into bottom of a 9 x 3-inch springform pan. Bake for 5 minutes. Remove pan from oven. Reduce temperature to 300°F.

2. To make filling: Combine white chocolate and cream in top of a double boiler set to simmer over medium heat. Cook, stirring, until chocolate is melted. Cool.

3. Beat cream cheese and sugar in a mixing bowl until smooth. Add eggs one at a time, beating well after each addition. Slowly beat in white chocolate mixture and vanilla.

4. Pour filling mixture into pan over crust. Set pan on baking sheet in middle of oven. Put a small pan of water on lowest rack of oven to create moisture during baking. Bake at 300°F for 45 to 50 minutes, or until edge of cake is firm but center is still slightly soft. Remove cake from oven. Increase oven temperature to 400°F.

5. To add topping: Combine sour cream, sugar, and vanilla until well blended. Spread topping over cake. Return to 400°F oven and bake 5 minutes. Cool completely. Refrigerate overnight. Just before serving, dust with cocoa and garnish with chocolate curls. Makes 1 cheesecake.

※ **JANIEL SANCHELLI,** Florence, Montana
First Place, Cheesecake, Western Montana Fair, Missoula, Montana, 1997

FROZEN PINEAPPLE CHEESECAKE

1 cup crushed graham crackers
1 cup sugar, divided
¼ cup unsalted butter, melted
1 package (8 oz.) cream cheese,
   room temperature
3 eggs, separated
1¼ cups heavy cream
1 cup crushed pineapple

PINEAPPLE GLAZE
⅓ cup sugar
1 tablespoon cornstarch
¼ cup pineapple juice

1. Combine graham cracker crumbs, ¼ cup of the sugar, and melted butter. Press mixture into bottom of a 10 x 2½-inch springform pan.

2. In a large mixing bowl, beat cream cheese, egg yolks, and remaining ¾ cup sugar.

3. In a separate bowl, beat egg whites until stiff.

4. In a separate bowl, beat heavy cream until stiff peaks form.

5. Fold egg whites into cream cheese mixture. Fold in whipped cream and crushed pineapple. Pour filling over crust in pan. Freeze until set, 4 to 5 hours.

6. To make pineapple glaze: Combine sugar and cornstarch in a small saucepan over medium heat. Add pineapple juice and bring to a slow boil, stirring continuously, until mixture thickens. Cool slightly. Drizzle over cheesecake. Makes 1 cheesecake.

✕ **KRISTINE SNYDER,** Kihei, Hawaii
First Prize, Maui Pineapple Festival, Maui, Hawaii, 2000

✦ THE MAUI PINEAPPLE FESTIVAL, ✦ MAUI, HAWAII

The pineapple—"the fruit of kings"—is both a celebrated food and a symbol of Hawaiian hospitality. For centuries the pineapple was a rare delicacy from South America; historians believe a Spanish shipwreck first brought the pineapple to Hawaii in the 1500s. It wasn't until the early 1900s when a New Englander named James Dole followed his dream to Hawaii that the pineapple was made available worldwide.

Today the island of Maui is the second largest producer of pineapple in the United States. For ten years, the Maui Pineapple Festival honored this most celebrated icon with the Pineapple Olympics, pineapple-carving demonstrations, and pineapple-eating contests, where contestants gorged on some of the island's sweetest and juiciest pineapple slices.

CHAPTER 12

BROWNIES,
BARS, SQUARES,
AND LOGS

REVEL BARS

1 cup unsalted butter, room temperature

2 cups brown sugar

2 eggs

3 tablespoons milk

2 teaspoons vanilla

2½ cups all-purpose flour

1 teaspoon baking powder

1 teaspoon salt

3 cups rolled oats

CHOCOLATE FILLING

1 cup chocolate chips

1 can (14 oz.) sweetened condensed milk

¼ cup unsalted butter, room temperature

½ teaspoon salt

1 cup chopped nuts

2 teaspoons vanilla

1. Preheat oven to 350°F. Grease one 15 x 10 x 1-inch baking pan or two 13 x 9 x 1-inch baking pans.

2. Cream butter and brown sugar. Add eggs, milk, and vanilla; beat until light and fluffy. Whisk together flour, baking powder, salt, and oats. Stir into batter.

3. To make chocolate filling: Combine chocolate, condensed milk, butter, and salt in a saucepan over medium heat. Cook, stirring continuously, until chocolate and butter are melted. Stir in nuts and vanilla.

4. Spread two-thirds of batter in baking pan. Cover with chocolate filling. Dot remaining batter on top. Bake for 25 to 30 minutes. Cool in pan. Cut into bars. Makes 30 bars.

✄ **ELAINE VILLENEUVE,** Menomonie, Wisconsin
Second Prize, Bars, Dunn County HCE, Dunn County Fair, Menomonie, Wisconsin, 2005

CHOCOLATE CHIP–PEANUT BUTTER BARS

Cooking spray

CRUST

2¼ cups quick-cooking rolled oats

1¼ cups brown sugar

1 cup all-purpose flour

½ teaspoon baking soda

1 cup unsalted butter, room temperature

FILLING

1 can (14 oz.) sweetened condensed milk

¼ cup peanut butter

½ teaspoon vanilla

1 cup semisweet chocolate chips

½ cup coarsely chopped salted peanuts

1. Preheat oven to 350°F. Coat a 13 x 9 x 2-inch pan with cooking spray.

2. In a large mixing bowl, combine rolled oats, brown sugar, flour, baking soda, and butter. Mix at low speed until crumbly. Set aside 2 cups of crumb mixture for topping. Press remaining crumb mixture in bottom of pan.

3. In a small bowl, combine condensed milk, peanut butter, and vanilla until well blended. Pour mixture evenly over base. Sprinkle with chocolate chips and peanuts. Sprinkle reserved crumb mixture over top; press down gently. Bake for 25 to 30 minutes, or until golden brown. Center will not be set. Cool in pan. Cut into bars. Makes 24 bars.

✄ **LISA FINDLAY,** Chubbuck, Idaho
First Place, North Bannock County Fair, Pocatello, Idaho, 2005

FUDGY MINT SQUARES

3 squares (1 oz. each) unsweetened
    chocolate, chopped
10 tablespoons unsalted butter, divided
3 eggs, divided
1½ cups sugar
2 teaspoons vanilla
1 cup all-purpose flour
1 package (8 oz.) cream cheese,
    room temperature

1 tablespoon cornstarch
1 can (14 oz.) sweetened condensed milk
1 teaspoon peppermint extract
4 drops green food coloring
1 cup semisweet chocolate chips
½ cup heavy cream

1. Preheat oven to 350°F. Grease a 13 x 9 x 2-inch baking pan.

2. Microwave chocolate and 8 tablespoons of the butter in a small bowl until melted. Stir to combine.

3. In a large bowl, beat 2 of the eggs, sugar, and vanilla. Add chocolate mixture and mix until well blended. Gradually beat in flour. Spread batter into pan. Bake 15 to 20 minutes, or until top is set.

4. Beat cream cheese and remaining 2 tablespoons butter until soft and creamy. Add cornstarch and beat until smooth. Gradually beat in condensed milk and remaining egg. Stir in peppermint extract and food coloring. Pour mixture over crust. Bake 15 to 20 minutes, until center is almost set. Cool.

5. Combine chocolate chips and heavy cream in a small saucepan over medium heat. Cook, stirring, until chips are melted. Cool until lukewarm, stirring occasionally, 30 minutes. Pour over cream cheese layer. Chill 2 hours. Cut into small squares. Makes 48 squares.

✖ **JONATHAN TWINING,** Land O'Lakes, Florida
First Place, Youth Division, Florida State Fair, Tampa, Florida, 2005

CARAMEL BARS

1 bag (10 oz.) caramels, unwrapped
5 tablespoons cream
½ cup unsalted butter, soft
½ cup milk

1 box (18.2 oz.) German chocolate cake mix
1 cup chopped pecans
1 package (6 oz.) chocolate chips

1. Preheat oven to 350°F. Grease a 13 x 9 x 2-inch baking pan.

2. Combine caramels and cream in a saucepan over medium heat. Cook until caramels are melted. Set aside.

3. Combine butter, milk, cake mix, and pecans in a mixing bowl until well blended.

4. Spread half of batter in baking pan. Bake for 6 minutes. Remove from oven. Sprinkle chocolate chips evenly over partially baked crust. Drizzle with caramel sauce. Spoon remaining cake batter over top and spread evenly. Bake for 15 to 18 minutes more. Cool in pan on a wire rack. Cut into bars. Makes 16 bars.

✖ **DONNA WIRT,** Lewiston, Minnesota
Blue Ribbon, Winona County Agricultural & Industrial Fair, Saint Charles, Minnesota, 1999

Apple Pie Bars

2½ cups all-purpose flour, plus
   more for rolling out dough
2 tablespoons sugar
1 teaspoon salt
1 cup lard
2 eggs, separated

Milk
1½ cups crushed cornflakes
8 large apples, peeled, cored, and sliced
1 cup sugar
2 teaspoons cinnamon

1. Preheat oven to 350°F.

2. Combine flour, sugar, and salt in a mixing bowl. Cut in lard until crumbly.

3. Place egg yolks in a measuring cup, add milk to make ½ cup, and pour over flour mixture. Stir until dough comes together.

4. Divide dough in half. Roll out one half on a lightly floured surface and place on a large baking sheet. Sprinkle crushed cornflakes over surface. Layer apples over cornflakes. Mix sugar and cinnamon in a small bowl and sprinkle over the apples. Roll out remaining dough and layer over apples. Beat egg whites and brush over the top crust. Bake for 1 hour. Cool in pan. Cut into bars. Makes 10 to 12 servings.

✄ **CAROLYN HARTMANN,** Dakota City, Iowa,
Blue Ribbon, Clay County Fair, Spencer, Iowa, 2004, 2005; Red Ribbon, Iowa
State Fair, Des Moines, Iowa, 2004

Almond-Crusted Mocha Log

⅔ cup all-purpose flour
⅓ cup cocoa
½ teaspoon baking soda
¼ teaspoon salt
3 eggs, separated
1 cup sugar, divided
⅓ cup water
1 teaspoon vanilla
⅛ teaspoon almond extract
Confectioners' sugar

COFFEE BUTTERCREAM FILLING AND FROSTING
⅔ cup sugar
¾ teaspoon cornstarch
2 tablespoons instant coffee crystals
5 large egg yolks
⅓ cup milk, scalded
½ teaspoon vanilla
1½ cups unsalted butter, room temperature
Sugared almonds
Meringue mushrooms

1. Preheat oven to 375°F. Line a jelly roll pan with aluminum foil. Grease lightly.

2. Whisk together flour, cocoa, baking soda, and salt.

3. In a large mixing bowl, beat 3 egg yolks until fluffy. Gradually add ½ cup of the sugar and beat until well mixed, 2 minutes. With mixer running on low, blend in water, vanilla, and almond extract. Gradually add flour mixture and beat until smooth.

4. In a separate large mixing bowl, beat egg whites until foamy. Gradually add remaining ½ cup sugar. Beat until stiff peaks form. Fold chocolate batter into meringue. Pour batter into pan and spread evenly into corners. Bake for 20 to 25 minutes, or until top springs back when lightly touched.

5. Sprinkle a piece of waxed paper with confectioners' sugar. Loosen cake around the edges, invert onto waxed paper, and remove the foil. Roll up cake in the waxed paper, starting at a narrow end. Cool on a wire rack, about 10 minutes. Chill.

6. To make coffee buttercream filling and frosting: In a 1-quart saucepan, combine sugar, cornstarch and instant coffee until well blended. Whisk in egg yolks, milk, and vanilla over medium heat. Cook until thickened, 2 minutes. Pour custard into a mixing bowl and beat until thickened. Cool 5 minutes. In a separate mixing bowl, beat butter until light and fluffy. Gradually beat in custard until well blended and light.

7. To assemble cake: Gently unroll cake and spread with ¾ cup buttercream filling. Roll up cake, place on a platter, and frost sides and top. Decorate with sugared almonds and meringue mushrooms. Makes 10 to 12 servings.

✄ **KATHLEEN LUCIDO,** Harper Woods, Michigan
Second Place, Fancy Chocolate Dessert Contest, Michigan State Fair, Detroit, Michigan, 2000

APRICOT CRUMBLE BARS

Cooking spray
1 cup all-purpose flour, plus more for pan
¾ cup coarsely chopped walnuts, divided
⅓ cup brown sugar

½ cup margarine, room temperature
¾ cup all-fruit apricot preserves
½ cup diced dried California apricots

1. Preheat oven to 350°F. Line bottom and edges of a 8 x 8-inch square baking pan with a single strip of foil, cut to extend beyond edges. Coat with cooking spray. Dust lightly with flour.

2. Combine ½ cup of the walnuts, flour, and brown sugar in a bowl. Cut in margarine with pastry blender until a soft dough forms. Set aside ½ cup of the dough. Press the remaining dough into pan.

3. Mix preserves and apricots and spread over dough in pan. Work remaining ¼ cup walnuts into reserved dough. Sprinkle over preserves. Bake for 35 to 40 minutes, or until golden brown. Cool in pan on a wire rack, 20 minutes. Lift foil at edges to remove from pan. Cool complete before cutting into bars. Store in an airtight container for up to 3 weeks or in refrigerator. Makes 8 bars.

✄ **JENNIFER HELMING,** Bristol, Connecticut
Blue Ribbon, Terryville Country Fair, Terryville, Connecticut, 2005

Snowcapped Blueberry-Lemon Roll

CAKE

4 eggs, separated
⅔ cup sugar, divided
1 tablespoon lemon juice
½ teaspoon grated lemon zest
⅔ cup cake flour
¼ teaspoon salt
Confectioners' sugar

LEMON FILLING

½ cup sugar
2 tablespoons cornstarch
Dash of salt
¾ cup cold water
2 egg yolks, lightly beaten
3 tablespoons lemon juice
1 teaspoon grated lemon zest
1 tablespoon unsalted butter or margarine,
    room temperature
1 cup fresh blueberries

MERINGUE

1 egg white
¼ cup sugar

1. Preheat oven to 350°F.

2. To make cake: In a large mixing bowl, beat egg whites until soft peaks form. Gradually add ⅓ cup of the sugar and beat until stiff peaks form.

3. In a small mixing bowl, beat egg yolks at high speed until thick and lemon-colored, 5 minutes. With mixer running, gradually add remaining ⅓ cup sugar. Stir in lemon juice and zest. Gently fold yolks into whites.

4. Sift together flour and salt. Fold half of flour mixture into batter, just until blended. Fold in remaining flour mixture. Spread batter evenly in 15 x 10-inch jelly-roll pan. Bake for 15 minutes. Loosen sides of cake and immediately turn out onto a towel generously sprinkled with confectioners' sugar. Starting at narrow end, roll cake and towel together into a log. Cool.

⚜ The Wild Blueberry Festival ⚜

The blueberry, one of the few native American fruits, is celebrated at the annual Machias Wild Blueberry Festival in Machias, Maine. Of course, blueberry treats are the featured favorite. With several main events, a dessert bar, two food courts, and many street vendors, there's something for everyone to enjoy. The banner contest, the cooking contest, the pie eating contest, and the blueberry run include children's categories, but the cooking contest is a highlight of the Wild Blueberry Festival tradition. People of all ages enter their favorite blueberry creations, with categories for: appetizers, breads, rolls and muffins, coffee cakes, dessert cakes, cookies, bars and squares, doughnuts, desserts and puddings, jams and jellies, pancakes and waffles, one-crust pies, two-crust pies, salads, punch and wines, relishes, entrees, and sugar-free.

5. To make lemon filling: In a saucepan, combine sugar, cornstarch, and salt. Gradually add water. Stir in egg yolks and lemon juice and zest. Cook over medium heat, stirring continuously, until bubbly. Cook 1 minute more. Remove from heat, add butter or margarine, and stir until melted. Cool.

6. To make meringue: In a small mixing bowl, beat egg white until soft peaks form. Gradually add sugar and beat until stiff peaks form.

7. Carefully unroll cake. Spread lemon filling over cake. Sprinkle blueberries over filling. Roll up cake (without towel) and place on an ungreased baking sheet. Spread meringue over top and sides. Bake for 12 to 15 minutes, or until golden brown. Makes 10 servings.

⊠ **RUTH THURSTON,** Machias, Maine
First Prize, Wild Blueberry Festival Cooking Competition, Machias, Maine, 2001

BRANDIED CHERRY-APRICOT BARS

FILLING

⅓ **cup golden raisins**

⅓ **cup dark raisins**

⅓ **cup dried cherries**

⅓ **cup snipped dried apricots**

½ **cup brandy**

2 **eggs**

1 **cup light brown sugar**

½ **cup all-purpose flour**

½ **teaspoon salt**

1 **teaspoon vanilla**

⅓ **cup chopped pecans**

CRUST

1 **cup all-purpose flour**

½ **cup pecan meal**

½ **cup light brown sugar**

⅔ **cup unsalted butter, room temperature**

Confectioners' sugar

1. To make filling: The day before, combine golden raisins, dark raisins, cherries, and apricots in a glass bowl. Pour brandy over the top. Cover with plastic wrap. Microwave on high 2 to 3 minutes. Cool. Chill overnight.

2. In a large mixing bowl, beat eggs at low speed for 4 minutes. Add light brown sugar, flour, salt, and vanilla. Mix until well combined. Stir in brandied fruits and pecans.

3. To make crust: Preheat oven to 350°F. Whisk together flour, pecan meal, and sugar. Cut in butter until the mixture resembles coarse crumbs. Press mixture into bottom of an 8 x 8 x 2-inch baking pan. Bake for 20 minutes, or until golden.

4. Spread filling over crust. Bake 40 minutes more. Cool in pan. Sprinkle with confectioners' sugar. Cut into 2 x 4-inch bars. Makes 8 bars.

⊠ **SHIRLEY J. MYRSIADES,** Pinellas Park, Florida
First Place, Adult Division, Florida State Fair, Tampa, Florida, 2005

WINNER'S CIRCLE TIP | Change the filling! To make raspberry apricot bars, mix ½ cup seedless raspberry preserves and ¼ cup apricot preserves.

Chocolate Ribbon Bars

1 package (10 to 11 oz.) butterscotch chips
1 cup peanut butter
8 cups crispy rice cereal
2 cups semisweet chocolate chips

¼ cup unsalted butter, cubed
2 tablespoons water
¾ cup confectioners' sugar

1. Grease a 9 x 9 x 3-inch baking pan.

2. In a large bowl, microwave butterscotch chips and peanut butter until melted and softened. Stir together until smooth. Gradually stir in cereal until well coated. Press half of mixture into bottom of pan. Set remaining mixture aside.

3. In another large bowl, microwave chocolate chips and butter until melted. Add water and stir until well blended. Gradually add confectioners' sugar, stirring until smooth.

4. Spread chocolate mixture over cereal layer. Cover with plastic wrap and chill for 10 minutes, or until chocolate layer is set. Spread remaining cereal mixture over the top. Chill. Cut into bars. Makes 12 bars.

※ **Juliette Iffland,** age 10, Whiting, Vermont
Rosette, Cookies, Addison County Fair & Field Days, New Haven, Vermont, 2004

Texas Pecan Fudge Bars

½ cup unsalted butter or margarine,
    room temperature
2 tablespoons cocoa
2 eggs
1 cup sugar
¾ cup all-purpose flour
¼ teaspoon salt
1 teaspoon vanilla
1 cup pecans, chopped
Mini marshmallows

QUICK FUDGE FROSTING
3 tablespoons confectioners' sugar
¼ cup cocoa
⅛ teaspoon salt
¼ cup evaporated milk
2 tablespoons unsalted butter,
    room temperature
1 teaspoon vanilla
¾ cup pecans, crushed

1. Preheat oven to 350°F. Grease an 8 x 8-inch baking pan.

2. Heat butter in a small saucepan over low heat until melted. Stir in cocoa until well blended.

3. In a large mixing bowl, beat eggs until light and fluffy. Gradually beat in sugar. Add cocoa mixture and stir until well blended. Sift together flour and salt and mix into batter. Stir in vanilla and pecans. Pour batter into pan. Bake for 20 to 25 minutes. Remove from oven. While still hot, press mini marshmallows on top.

4. To make quick fudge frosting: Sift together confectioners' sugar, cocoa, and salt. Combine milk and butter in a small saucepan over low heat, stirring until butter is melted. Add to cocoa mixture and beat well. Add vanilla and beat until smooth. Stir in pecans. Spread frosting on marshmallows to cover completely. Cool completely. Cut into 2-inch squares. Makes 16 squares.

※ **Carylon Miller,** Abilene, Texas
First Place, West Texas Fair & Rodeo, Abilene, Texas, 2005

Chocolate Chip Bars

1½ cups all-purpose flour
½ teaspoon baking soda
½ teaspoon salt
⅓ cup shortening
⅓ cup unsalted butter or margarine, room temperature
½ cup sugar
½ cup brown sugar
1 egg
1 teaspoon vanilla
½ cup chopped nuts
1 package (6 oz.) chocolate chips

1. Preheat oven to 375°F.
2. Whisk together flour, baking soda, and salt.
3. In a large mixing bowl, cream shortening, butter, sugar, and brown sugar. Beat in egg and vanilla. Add flour mixture and stir to combine. Fold in nuts and chocolate chips.
4. Spread batter in 13 x 9 x 2-inch baking pan. Bake for 20 to 25 minutes. Cool in pan. Cut into bars. Makes 16 bars.

※ **Pam Zeal,** Pocatello, Idaho
First Place, North Bannock County Fair, Pocatello, Idaho, 2005

Cherry-Cocoa Shortbread Squares

SHORTBREAD

½ cup unsalted butter, room temperature
¼ cup sugar
1 cup all-purpose flour
2 tablespoons cocoa

GLAZE

1 square (1 oz.) unsweetened chocolate
1½ teaspoons unsalted butter, room temperature

FROSTING

2 tablespoons unsalted butter, room temperature
2 cups confectioners' sugar
2 tablespoons milk
½ teaspoon vanilla
18 Maraschinos, drained, patted dry, and halved

1. Preheat oven to 350°F. Grease a 9 x 9 x 2-inch baking pan.
2. To make shortbread: Cream butter and sugar. Beat in flour and cocoa powder until smooth. Spread batter in pan. Bake for 15 minutes. Cool in pan.
3. To make frosting: Cream butter and confectioner's sugar. Beat in milk and vanilla until smooth. Spread frosting over baked crust. Arrange cherries on frosting layer and press down gently.
4. To make glaze: Melt chocolate and butter in microwave; stir until smooth. Drizzle over cherries. Refrigerate until glaze hardens. Cut into squares. Makes 25 squares.

※ **Jeremy Twining,** Land O'Lakes, Florida
First Place, Youth Division, Florida, State Fair, Tampa, Florida, 2005

WHITE CHOCOLATE–STRAWBERRY BARS

1 cup unsalted butter, room temperature
2 cups white chocolate chips, divided
4 large eggs
1 cup sugar
2 cups all-purpose flour

1 teaspoon salt
1 teaspoon almond extract
1 cup strawberry jam
½ cup toasted sliced almonds

1. Preheat oven to 325°F. Grease and sugar a 13 x 9 x 2-inch baking pan.

2. Melt butter in a medium bowl in microwave. Add 1 cup of the white chocolate chips. Do not stir.

3. Beat eggs in large mixing bowl until foamy. Add sugar and beat until light lemon-colored, about 5 minutes. Stir in white chocolate mixture. Add flour, salt, and almond extract. Mix at low speed until combined.

4. Spread two-thirds of batter into pan. Bake for 15 to 17 minutes, or until light golden brown around edges.

5. Heat jam in small saucepan over low heat. Spread jam over warm crust. Stir remaining cup of white chocolate chips into remaining batter. Drop by spoonfuls over jam. Sprinkle with almonds. Bake an additional 25 to 30 minutes, or until edges are browned. Cool in pan. Cut into bars. Makes 36 bars.

✂ **GEORGIA BISHOP,** Upper Arlington, Ohio
Blue Ribbon, Ohio State Fair, Columbus, Ohio, 2004

FUDGE MINT BROWNIES

Flour

FILLING
1 package (8 oz.) cream cheese,
    room temperature
¼ cup sugar
1 egg
1 teaspoon mint extract
4 drops green food coloring

BROWNIES
1 cup margarine or unsalted butter,
    room temperature
4 squares (1 oz. each) unsweetened
    chocolate, cut into pieces
2 cups sugar
2 teaspoons vanilla
4 eggs
1 cup all-purpose flour

FROSTING
2 teaspoons margarine or unsalted butter,
    room temperature
2 tablespoons corn syrup
1 teaspoon water
2 squares (1 oz. each) unsweetened chocolate,
    cut into pieces
1 teaspoon vanilla
1 cup confectioners' sugar

1. Preheat oven to 350°F. Grease and flour a 13 x 9 x 2-inch baking pan.

2. To make filling: Combine cream cheese and sugar in a small mixing bowl. Beat until smooth. Add egg, mint extract, and food coloring. Mix until well blended.

3. To make brownies: Melt margarine or butter and unsweetened chocolate in a large saucepan over very low heat, stirring constantly. Remove from heat. Cool 15 minutes.

4. Add sugar and vanilla to chocolate mixture and stir until smooth. Add eggs one at a time, beating well after each addition (use a wire whisk or hand-held mixer). Add flour and stir until well blended.

5. Spread batter in pan. Spoon filling over brownie batter. Swirl a knife or spatula through both layers. Bake for 45 to 50 minutes, or until set. Cool in pan on a wire rack for 1 hour.

6. To make frosting: Combine margarine, corn syrup, and water in a medium saucepan over medium heat. Bring to a rolling boil. Remove from heat, add chocolate, and stir until melted. Stir in vanilla and confectioners' sugar. Beat until smooth. Spread frosting over brownies in pan. Cut into bars. Store in refrigerator. Makes 24 brownies.

✄ **SAMUEL A. VILLA CORTA,** Interlachen, Florida
First Place, Youth Division, Florida State Fair, Tampa, Florida, 2005

PEANUT BUTTER BROWNIES

1½ cups all-purpose flour,
   plus more for pan
¼ cup unsalted butter, room temperature
¼ cup chunky peanut butter
1 cup light brown sugar
½ cup sugar
2 eggs
1 teaspoon vanilla
1 teaspoon baking powder

CHOCOLATE SWIRL
1½ oz. semisweet chocolate
2 teaspoons unsalted butter, room temperature

TOPPING
½ cup chunky peanut butter
½ teaspoon vanilla
2 tablespoons unsalted butter, melted
1½ oz. semisweet chocolate

1. Set oven rack in middle position. Preheat oven to 350°F. Grease and flour an 8 x 8 x 2-inch baking pan.

2. In a mixing bowl, cream butter until soft. Beat in peanut butter until well combined. Gradually add light brown sugar and sugar, beating until well combined. Beat in eggs one at a time and vanilla.

3. Sift together flour and baking powder. Stir flour mixture into peanut butter mixture until thoroughly combined. Spread batter evenly in pan.

4. To make chocolate swirl: Melt chocolate and butter in a small, heavy saucepan over very low heat, stirring continuously until smooth. Drizzle chocolate over the batter; then draw the tip of a knife or spatula through the chocolate and batter a few times lengthwise and clockwise to swirl them together slightly. Bake for 30 to 35 minutes, or until the top is crusty and the center is barely firm when touched lightly. Set pan on a wire rack to cool.

5. To make topping: Combine peanut butter, vanilla, and melted butter. Spread mixture over top of warm brownies. Melt chocolate and drizzle over top. Sprinkle with chocolate chips, if desired. Cut into squares. Makes 12 brownies.

✄ **TIM OLDMIXON,** age 10, New Paltz, New York
Best of Juniors, Dutchess County Fair, Rhinebeck, New York, 2001

German Chocolate Bars (A Cake Mix Fix-up)

1 package (18.2 oz.) German chocolate
    cake mix
⅔ cup margarine, room temperature

1 cup semisweet chocolate chips
1 container (16 oz.) creamy coconut pecan frosting
¼ cup milk

1. Preheat oven to 350°F. Grease a 13 x 9 x 2-inch baking pan.

2. Place cake mix in a medium bowl. Cut in margarine with a pastry blender or fork. Press ½ of cake mixture into bottom of pan. Bake for 10 minutes.

3. Sprinkle chocolate chips evenly over baked layer. Drop coconut pecan frosting by tablespoonful over chips.

4. Add milk to remaining cake mixture. Stir to combine. Drop by teaspoonfuls onto frosting layer. Bake 25 to 30 minutes, or until cake is slightly dry to touch. Cool in pan. Cut into bars. Makes 24 bars.

※ **Carolyn Hartmann,** Dakota City, Iowa
Blue Ribbon, Clay Country Fair, Spencer, Iowa, 2003, 2004

Best Brownies

1 cup unsalted butter or margarine,
    room temperature
6 tablespoons cocoa
2½ cups sugar
5 eggs

2 teaspoons vanilla
2 cups all-purpose flour
1 teaspoon salt
Nuts (optional)

1. Preheat oven to 350°F. Grease a 13 x 9 x 2-inch baking pan.

2. Cream butter and cocoa in a large mixing bowl. Add sugar and beat until well blended. Beat in eggs, one at a time. Add vanilla, flour, and salt and beat until well combined. Stir in nuts, if using.

3. Pour batter into pan. Bake for 35 to 40 minutes. Cool. Cut into squares or bars. Makes 20 to 30 brownies.

※ **Emily Sturman,** age 6, Pocatello, Idaho
First Place, North Bannock County Fair, Pocatello, Idaho, 2005

⊰ THE STRANGEST CONTESTS ⊱

The 2005 North Bannock County Fair, in Pocatello, Idaho offered some unique events. Among them was a worm-eating contest. The worms weren't real; they were of the gummy variety, but the event was a big hit with the children. The other was the tallest weed competition, which provided some incentive for the less-than-enthusiastic gardeners in attendance.

CHOCOLATE PECAN BROWNIES

¾ cup all-purpose flour
¼ teaspoon baking soda
¾ cup sugar
⅓ cup unsalted butter or margarine,
    room temperature

2 tablespoons water
1 teaspoon vanilla
1 package (12 oz.) semisweet chocolate chips, divided
2 large eggs
½ cup chopped pecans

1. Preheat oven to 325°F. Grease a 9 x 9 x 2-inch baking pan.
2. Whisk together flour and baking soda.
3. Combine sugar, butter, and water in a small saucepan over medium heat. Bring to a boil and then immediately remove from heat. Stir in vanilla and 1 cup of the chocolate chips. Continue stirring until chocolate is melted and mixture is smooth. Transfer to a medium mixing bowl. Let cool.
4. Add eggs to chocolate batter, beating well after each addition. Gradually stir in flour mixture until smooth. Stir in remaining chocolate chips and nuts.
5. Pour batter into pan. Bake for 30 to 35 minutes, or until a toothpick inserted in center comes out clean. Cool in pan on a wire rack. Cut into squares. Makes 16 brownies.

⁕ **LACEY LOCKWOOD,** Tulsa, Oklahoma
Sweepstakes, Tusla State Fair, Junior Division, Tulsa, Oklahoma, 2003

BROWNIES FOR A CROWD

1¼ cups all-purpose flour
1 teaspoon baking powder
1 teaspoon salt
¾ cup cocoa
½ cup unsalted butter, room temperature
¼ cup shortening
1 cup sugar
1 cup brown sugar
4 eggs

1 teaspoon vanilla
½ cup chopped nuts (optional)

CHOCOLATE FROSTING
3 tablespoons unsalted butter,
    room temperature
¼ cup cocoa
3 tablespoons milk
2½ cups confectioners' sugar.

1. Preheat oven to 350°F. Grease a 13 x 9 x 2-inch baking pan.
2. Whisk together flour, baking powder, salt, and cocoa.
3. In a large mixing bowl, cream butter, shortening, sugar, and brown sugar. With mixer running, add eggs, vanilla, and flour mixture. Beat at medium speed for 1 minute. Stir in nuts, if using.
4. Spread batter in pan. Bake for 25 to 30 minutes; for a denser brownie, bake 5 minutes longer. Cool in pan.
5. To make chocolate frosting: In a large mixing bowl, combine butter, cocoa, and milk. Add confectioners' sugar and beat until smooth. Spread frosting over brownie pan. Cut into squares or bars. Makes 24 brownies.

⁕ **SARIAH GAUNT,** age 7, Pocatello, Idaho
First Place, North Bannock County Fair, Pocatello, Idaho, 2005

CHIPPEDY BLONDE BROWNIES

6 tablespoons unsalted butter,
   room temperature
1 cup brown sugar
2 eggs
1 teaspoon vanilla

1¼ cups all-purpose flour
1 teaspoon baking powder
½ teaspoon salt
1 cup semisweet chocolate chips

1. Preheat oven to 350°F. Grease an 11 x 7 x 2-inch baking pan.

2. In a large mixing bowl, cream butter and brown sugar. Add eggs one at a time , beating well after each addition. Beat in vanilla.

3. Whisk together flour, baking powder, and salt. Gradually add to batter, mixing until well combined. Stir in chocolate chips.

4. Spread batter into baking pan. Bake for 25 to 30 minutes, or until a toothpick inserted near center comes out clean. Cool in pan on a wire rack. Cut into squares. Makes 20 blondies.

※ **RACHEL MONROE,** age 10, Forest Hills, Maryland
Rosette, Cookies, Addison County Fair & Field Days, New Haven, Vermont, 2005

BROWNIE DECADENCE

½ cup all-purpose flour, plus more for pan
5 squares (1 oz. each) semisweet chocolate
½ cup unsalted butter, room temperature
⅔ cup brown sugar
¼ cup water
2 eggs, separated
2 teaspoons vanilla
⅛ teaspoon salt

TOPPING

1 cup sugar
¾ cup plus 2 tablespoons heavy cream
⅔ cup unsalted butter, room temperature
1 cup chopped walnuts

1 package (6 oz.) chocolate chips
1 tablespoon shortening

1. Preheat oven to 350°F. Grease and flour an 8 x 8 x 2-inch baking pan.

2. Melt chocolate and butter in microwave. Cool.

3. In a mixing bowl, combine brown sugar, water, egg yolks, and vanilla. Beat until well blended. Fold in flour and salt.

4. Beat egg whites until stiff peaks form. Fold into batter. Pour batter into pan. Bake for 35 to 50 minutes. Cool in pan.

5. To make topping: Heat sugar without stirring in a skillet over medium-high heat until it melts and turns to a caramel-colored syrup. Stir in heavy cream. (Stand back; sugar will bubble up.) Add butter, stirring continuously until melted and well blended. Stir in walnuts. Remove from heat and pour over brownie pan. Chill until set.

6. Melt chocolate chips and shortening in microwave or on stovetop. Drizzle over topping. Cut into squares. Makes 16 brownies.

※ **CAROL BROMMERICH,** Winona, Minnesota
Blue Ribbon, Winona County Agricultural and Industrial Fair, Saint Charles, Minnesota, 1999

Lemon Bars

CRUST

1½ cups all-purpose flour
½ cup unsalted butter, room temperature
½ cup brown sugar

FILLING

2 eggs
1 cup brown sugar
½ teaspoon vanilla
1 cup chopped pecans
1½ cups coconut
2 tablespoons flour
½ teaspoon baking powder

FROSTING

1 cup confectioners' sugar
1 tablespoon unsalted butter, melted
Juice of 1 lemon (about 2 tablespoons)

1. Preheat oven to 275°F.
2. To make crust: Combine flour, butter, and brown sugar until crumbly. Pat mixture into bottom of a 13 x 9 x 2-inch baking pan. Bake for 10 minutes. Remove from oven. Increase oven temperature to 350°F.
3. To make filling: In a large mixing bowl, combine eggs, brown sugar, and vanilla. Beat until light and fluffy. Add pecans, coconut, flour, and baking powder and blend well. Pour filling mixture over hot crust and bake for 20 minutes.
4. To make frosting: Stir together confectioners' sugar, melted butter, and lemon juice. Spread frosting over warm filling. Cool in pan. Cut into bars. Makes 16 bars.

Doris Laska, Winona, Minnestota
Blue Ribbon, Winona County Agricultural & Industrial Fair, Saint Charles, Minnesota, 2000

Passover Brownies

1 cup unsalted butter, room temperature
2 cups sugar
4 eggs
½ cup milk
½ cup Passover cake meal
½ teaspoon salt
8 tablespoons cocoa
1 cup nuts

1. Preheat oven to 300°F. Set aside a 13 x 9 x 2-inch baking pan.
2. In a mixing bowl, cream together butter and sugar. Beat in eggs, one at a time.
3. Stir in milk, cake meal, salt, cocoa, and nuts until well combined. Spread batter into pan. Bake for 10 minutes. Increase oven temperature to 325°F and bake 30 minutes more. Cool in pan on a wire rack. Cut into squares. Makes 24 brownies.

Ruth Canty and Phoebe Gold, Butte, Montana
First Place Public Favorite, Jewish Holiday, Western Montana Fair, Missoula, Montana, 2004

ZUCCHINI BROWNIES

Vegetable oil spray
2 cups all-purpose flour
1½ cups sugar
1½ teaspoons baking soda
1 teaspoon salt
2 teaspoons cinnamon

¼ cup chopped nuts
1 egg
¼ cup oil
2 teaspoons vanilla
3 cups grated zucchini
1 package (12 oz.) chocolate chips

1. Heat oven to 350°F. Coat a 13 x 9 x 2-inch baking pan with vegetable oil spray.

2. Place flour, sugar, baking soda, salt, cinnamon, nuts, egg, oil, vanilla, zucchini, and chocolate chips in baking pan. Stir until all ingredients are evenly distributed. Bake for 45 minutes. Cool in pan on a wire rack. Cut into squares. Makes 24 brownies.

✂ **DESIREE WALLACE,** Chubbuck, Idaho
First Place, North Bannock County Fair, Pocatello, Idaho, 2005

PUMPKIN ROLL

¾ cup all-purpose flour, plus more for pan
1 teaspoon baking powder
1 teaspoon salt
2 teaspoons cinnamon
1 teaspoon ground ginger
½ teaspoon nutmeg
3 eggs
1 cup sugar
1 cup canned pumpkin

1 teaspoon lemon juice
1 cup chopped nuts
Confectioners' sugar

CREAM CHEESE FILLING
1 package (8 oz.) cream cheese
¼ cup soft unsalted butter, room temperature
1 teaspoon vanilla-butternut flavoring
2 cups confectioners' sugar

1. Preheat oven to 375°F. Generously grease a 17 x 12 x 1-inch jelly roll pan. Line bottom of pan with waxed paper and dust with flour.

2. Sift together flour, baking powder, salt, cinnamon, ginger, and nutmeg.

3. In a large mixing bowl, beat eggs for 5 minutes, gradually adding sugar. Add pumpkin and lemon juice; beat for 1 minute. Add sifted dry ingredients and mix well.

4. Pour batter into pan. Top with chopped nuts. Bake for 15 minutes, or until a toothpick inserted in center comes out clean. Cool 15 minutes and then turn out cake onto a dish towel sprinkled with confectioners' sugar. Peel off waxed paper. Roll towel and cake together jelly-roll style. Cool.

5. To make cream cheese filling: In a medium mixing bowl, combine cream cheese, butter, vanilla-butternut flavoring, and confectioners' sugar. Beat until smooth.

6. Unroll cake and remove towel. Spread cream cheese filling over cake. Reroll carefully and chill. To serve, cut into slices. Makes 10 to 12 servings.

✂ **ALITA HAFFNER,** Frenchtown, Montana
First Place, Public Favorite, Holiday Desserts, Western Montana Fair, Missoula, Montana, 2003

Praline-Caramel-Divine Brownies

CRUST

¾ cup all-purpose flour

½ cup brown sugar

¼ cup unsalted butter or margarine, melted

¾ cup finely chopped pecans

BROWNIES

3 squares (1 oz. each) unsweetened chocolate, chopped

¾ cup unsalted butter or margarine, room temperature

1½ teaspoons vanilla

3 eggs

¾ cup sugar

½ cup brown sugar

1¼ cups all-purpose flour

¾ cup chopped pecans

FILLING

1 can (16 oz.) caramel pecan frosting

TOPPING

1 square (1 oz.) unsweetened chocolate

¼ cup unsalted butter or margarine, room temperature

¼ cup milk

2¼ cups confectioners' sugar

1 tablespoon vanilla

1. Preheat oven to 350°F. Grease a 13 x 9 x 2-inch baking pan.

2. To make crust: Combine flour, brown sugar, butter or margarine, and pecans until crumbly. Press mixture evenly into bottom of pan.

3. To make brownies: Melt chocolate and butter in a medium saucepan over very low heat, stirring continuously until smooth. Remove from heat. Add vanilla, eggs, sugar, and brown sugar; blend well. Stir in flour and pecans until well combined. Spread mixture over crust. Bake for 22 to 30 minutes, or until set. Cool in pan on a wire rack.

4. To add filling: Spread caramel pecan frosting over cooled brownies.

5. To make topping: Heat chocolate, butter, and milk in a small saucepan over medium heat, stirring constantly until smooth. Remove from heat. Stir in confectioners' sugar and vanilla until smooth. Pour topping over filling and spread evenly. Chill for 30 minutes before cutting into squares. Store in refrigerator. Makes 24 brownies.

※ **Deborah Mulvey,** Waterbury Center, Vermont
Sweepstakes Winning Recipe, Champlain Valley Exposition, Essex Junction, Vermont, 2004

⊹ Pumpkins ⊹

Pumpkins originated in Central America, but the Connecticut-field variety is what we think of as the traditional American pumpkin. The pumpkin is a fruit from the squash family. Pumpkins range in size from less than a pound to over 1,000 pounds. They are 90 percent water. As we know now, pumpkins are best used as an ingredient in pies and other baked treats, but pumpkins were once recommended for removing freckles and curing snakebites.

Honey Pecan Pie Bars

CRUST

⅓ cup confectioners' sugar

⅓ cup brown sugar

2 cups all-purpose flour

1 cup unsalted butter, room temperature

TOPPING

⅔ cup unsalted butter, room temperature

½ cup honey

3 tablespoons heavy cream

1 teaspoon vanilla

½ cup brown sugar

3½ cups pecans, lightly toasted and chopped

1. Preheat oven to 350°F. Grease a 13 x 9 x 2-inch baking pan.

2. To make crust: In a large bowl, combine confectioners' sugar and brown sugar. Blend in flour. Cut in butter with a pastry blender until mixture resembles coarse meal. Pat mixture evenly into bottom of baking pan. Bake for 20 minutes.

3. To make topping: Warm butter and honey in large saucepan over low heat until butter is melted; stir to combine. Remove from heat. Stir in heavy cream, vanilla, brown sugar, and pecans. Spread topping evenly over crust and bake for 25 minutes longer. Cool in pan on a wire rack. Cut into bars. Makes 24 bars.

※ **HANNAH FARRELL,** Addison, Vermont
Best Honey Baked Goods, Addison County Fair & Field Days, New Haven, Vermont, 2004

Caramel Fudge Brownies

1 jar (12 oz.) caramel ice cream topping

1¼ cups all-purpose flour, divided

¼ teaspoon baking powder

Dash of salt

4 squares (1 oz. each) unsweetened
　chocolate

¾ cup unsalted butter, room temperature

2 cups sugar

3 eggs

2 teaspoons vanilla

¾ cup pecans, chopped

¾ cup semisweet chocolate chips

1. Preheat oven to 375°F. Grease a 13 x 9 x 2-inch baking pan.

2. Mix together caramel topping and ¼ cup of the flour. Set aside.

3. Whisk together remaining 1 cup all-purpose flour, baking powder, and salt.

4. In a large bowl, microwave unsweetened chocolate and butter until melted. Add sugar and stir to dissolve. Add eggs and vanilla and blend well. Slowly add flour mixture, stirring until well blended.

5. Spread batter into pan. Bake for 25 minutes. Spread caramel mixture over hot brownies. Sprinkle with pecans and chocolate chips. Cool in pan. Cut into 3-inch squares. Makes 12 brownies.

※ **LINDA GASS,** Mango, Florida
Best of Show, Adult Division, Florida State Fair, Tampa, Florida, 2005

FUDGY BROWIES

½ cup unsalted butter, room temperature
3 squares (1 oz. each) unsweetened
 chocolate, coarsely chopped
1 cup sugar
2 eggs

1 teaspoon vanilla
⅔ cup all-purpose flour
¼ teaspoon baking soda
⅔ cup chopped nuts (optional)

1. Preheat oven to 350°F. Grease an 8 x 8 x 2-inch baking pan.

2. In a medium saucepan, melt butter and chocolate over low heat, stirring constantly. Remove from heat. Cool.

3. Stir sugar into cooled chocolate mixture. Add eggs, one at a time, beating with a wooden spoon after each addition just until combined. Stir in vanilla.

4. Whisk together flour and baking soda. Add flour mixture to chocolate mixture; stir just until combined. Stir in nuts, if using.

5. Spread the batter in pan. Bake 30 minutes. Turn out onto a wire rack and cool. Cut into squares or bars. Makes 16 brownies.

✳ **HAYLEY BATTAGLIA,** Thontosassa, Florida
First Place, Youth Division, Florida, State Fair, Tampa, Florida, 2005

RASPBERRY BROWNIES

½ cup unsalted butter, room temperature
4 oz. unsweetened chocolate
2 cups sugar
1 teaspoon vanilla

4 eggs
1 cup all-purpose flour
2 cups walnut pieces
⅞ cup raspberry preserves

1. Preheat oven to 375°F Grease 13 x 9 x 2-inch baking pan.

2. Melt butter and chocolate in microwave or on stovetop. Transfer to a large mixing bowl. Add sugar and vanilla and mix until well blended. Beat in eggs one at a time. Add flour and beat until smooth. Stir in walnuts.

3. Pour half of batter into pan. Smooth the surface with a flat spatula. Freeze for 30 minutes. Refrigerate remaining batter.

4. Spread preserves in a thin, even layer on top of frozen batter. Pour the remaining batter over preserves and smooth with a spatula. Bake for 40 to 45 minutes, or until a tester inserted in center comes out clean. Cool in pan on a wire rack for 10 minutes. Cut into 1-inch squares, as these brownies are very rich. Makes 24 brownies.

✳ **ANNE MISEK,** Addison, Vermont
Rosette, Cookies, Addison County Fair & Field Days, New Haven, Vermont, 2005

SOUR CREAM RAISIN BARS

1½ cups raisins

1 cup unsalted butter, room temperature

1 cup brown sugar

1¾ cups rolled oats

1¾ cups all-purpose flour

1 teaspoon baking soda

2 cups sugar

½ teaspoon salt

6 tablespoons cornstarch

6 egg yolks, beaten

2 cups sour cream

1 teaspoon vanilla

1. Preheat oven to 350°F. Set aside a 13 x 9 x 2-inch baking pan.

2. Place raisins in a saucepan, add water to cover, and boil over medium-high heat until plump, 5 minutes. Drain well.

3. In a large mixing bowl, cream butter and brown sugar. Stir in oats, flour, and baking soda. Press half of oat mixture into pan. Bake for 10 minutes.

4. In a large saucepan, combine sugar, salt, cornstarch, egg yolks, and sour cream. Bring to a boil, stirring continuously to prevent scorching. Remove from heat. Stir in raisins and vanilla. Pour custard over crust. Sprinkle remaining oat mixture over filling. Bake for 30 minutes. Cool in pan on a wire rack. Cut into bars. Makes 24 bars.

✕ **KIMBERLY HITZ,** Wheeler, Wisconsin
First Prize, Youth Division—Bars, Dunn County HCE, Dunn County Fair, Menomonie, Wisconsin, 2005

PECAN SWIRLS

2 cups unsalted butter, room temperature

2 packages (8 oz. each) cream cheese,
    room temperature

2 teaspoons vanilla

4 cups all-purpose flour

½ teaspoon salt

2¼ cups finely chopped pecans

1⅓ cups sugar

1. In a large mixing bowl, cream butter and cream cheese until smooth. Beat in vanilla. Combine flour and salt; gradually add to creamed mixture. Divide dough in thirds, form into balls, and flatten slightly into disks. Wrap each disk in plastic wrap. Chill until easy to handle, 2 hours.

2. Combine pecans and sugar. Roll out each dough disk on a lightly floured surface to make a 16 x 9-inch rectangle. Sprinkle one-third of pecan mixture over top to within ½ inch of edges. Roll up tightly jelly-roll style, starting with a long side. Wrap in plastic wrap. Chill for 2 hours.

3. Unwrap dough logs and cut into ⅜-inch slices. Place slices 2 inches apart on lightly greased baking sheets. Bake in a preheated 400°F oven for 12 to 14 minutes, or until lightly browned. Cool on wire racks. Makes 8 dozen pecan swirls.

✕ **OLIVIA COOK,** Clearwater, Florida
First Place, Youth Division, Florida State Fair, Tampa, Florida, 2005

CHAPTER 13

✣

ICE CREAM, COOKIES, AND CANDY

BLUEBERRY-GINGER SORBET

1 cup plus 2 tablespoons sugar

1 cup plus 2 tablespoons water

3 tablespoons grated fresh ginger

3 pint fresh blueberries

¼ cup fresh lemon juice

1. Combine sugar, water, and ginger in a saucepan. Bring to a boil, reduce heat, and simmer 5 minutes. Cool.

2. Puree blueberries and lemon juice in a blender until smooth. Strain through a fine mesh sieve into a bowl.

3. Add ginger syrup to purée. Stir to combine. Refrigerate until cold. Freeze in an ice cream maker, following manufacturer's instructions. Makes 4 to 6 servings.

✕ **HOPE PRATT,** Rogue Bluffs, Maine
Overall Winner, Wild Blueberry Festival Cooking Competition, Machias, Maine, 2000

TROPICAL SNOWBALLS

1 can (13.5 oz.) coconut milk, unsweetened

1 can (20 oz.) crushed pineapple,
    well drained

1 can (11 oz.) mandarin oranges,
    well drained

1 very ripe banana, mashed

½ very ripe peach, peeled and cut in
    ½-inch cubes

¼ cup sugar substitute

1½ cups unsweetened shredded coconut

1. Combine coconut milk, pineapple, oranges, banana, peach, and sugar substitute in a blender. Blend briefly, so that mixture still retains some small pieces of fruit. Freeze mixture into an ice cream maker, following manufacturer's instructions.

2. Use a melon baller to scoop out and shape 1-inch balls of ice cream. Place balls on a baking sheet and place in freezer for 30 minutes. (Don't worry about perfect shapes as you will reshape them a bit in the next step.)

3. Remove balls from freezer. Gently roll and reshape each ball in your hands and then roll quickly in coconut to coat. The warmth of your hands will melt the surface slightly, allowing the coconut to adhere. Place completed snowballs on a clean baking sheet and return to freezer.

4. Remove ice cream balls from freezer 20 minutes before serving and allow to soften. Makes 1 quart, about 55 snowballs.

✕ **DEBBIE GARRETT,** Salem, Oregon
Winner, The Order of Amaranth & The American Diabetes Association—Make Your Best Sugar-Free Dessert Contest, Oregon State Fair, Salem, Oregon, 2005

WINNER'S CIRCLE TIP Churn-frozen ice cream will be soft. Always place freshly churned ice cream in the freezer to "harden off" for an hour. If it is left too long and becomes overly hard, microwave on low for a few minutes to soften.

Pumpkin-Ginger Ice Cream

1½ cups light cream
¾ cup sugar
¼ teaspoon salt
2 teaspoons pumpkin pie spice
4 egg yolks, slightly beaten

¾ cup canned pumpkin, pureed
½ cup ginger brandy
2 teaspoons vanilla
2 cups heavy cream
Gingersnaps

1. Scald light cream in top of double boiler until a thin skin forms. Add sugar, salt, and pumpkin pie spice; stir to dissolve.
2. Gradually stir about half of the hot cream mixture into egg yolks. Return tempered yolks to cream mixture in double boiler. Cook over boiling water, stirring gently, until custard reaches 175°F and coats a spoon. Strain immediately into a cool bowl to stop the cooking. Cool completely, 20 to 30 minutes.
3. Stir in pumpkin, brandy, and vanilla.
4. Whip heavy cream until it holds a soft shape. Gently fold into custard. Pour mixture into a freezer tray. Freeze without stirring until firm, 8 to 10 hours. Serve in a dessert dish with a gingersnap on the side. Sprinkle crushed gingersnaps on top. Makes 12 servings.

✄ **KAREN JACKSON,** Detroit, Michigan
First Place, Pumpkin Dessert Contest, Michigan State Fair, Detroit, Michigan, 2000

Italian Almond-Anise Biscotti

2½ cups all-purpose flour
2 teaspoons anise seeds
1½ teaspoons baking powder
½ teaspoon salt
½ cup unsalted butter, room temperature
1 cup sugar

1 tablespoon grated orange zest
2 eggs
½ teaspoon vanilla
¼ teaspoon anise extract
1½ cups coarsely chopped almonds

1. Preheat oven to 325° F. Set aside a baking sheet; do not grease.
2. Combine flour, anise seeds, baking powder, and salt.
3. In a large mixing bowl, cream butter, sugar, and orange zest until light and fluffy. Beat in eggs one at a time. Add vanilla and anise extract. Gradually beat in flour mixture. Stir in almonds.
4. Divide dough in half. Place both pieces of dough on an ungreased baking sheet and form into two flattened 14 x 3-inch logs, spaced 3 inches apart. Bake for 40 minutes, or until a light golden color.
5. Reduce oven temperature to 250°F. Transfer logs to a cutting board. Using a large serrated knife, cut logs crosswise and slightly on the diagonal into ¾-inch slices. Arrange biscotti cut side down on baking sheet. Return to oven and bake for 20 minutes, turning once to brown both sides. Cool on a wire rack. Store in an airtight container. Makes 3 dozen.

✄ **THOMAS PINA,** Land O'Lakes, Florida
First Place, Youth Division, Florida State Fair, Tampa, Florida, 2005

ICEBOX COOKIES

3½ cups all-purpose flour
1 teaspoon baking soda
¼ teaspoon salt
1 cup nuts, chopped
1 cup unsalted butter and lard, mixed

2 cups brown sugar
2 eggs, beaten
1 teaspoon cream of tartar
1 teaspoon vanilla

1. Combine flour, baking soda, salt, and nuts.

2. In a large mixing bowl, cream butter and lard. Add brown sugar and mix well. Beat in eggs, cream of tartar, and vanilla.

3. Form dough into 2 or 3 logs. Wrap in plastic wrap or waxed paper and refrigerate overnight.

4. Preheat oven to 350°F. Cut thin slices from log and place on baking sheets. Bake for 10 minutes. Cool on wire racks. Makes 6 dozen.

✕ **JANET PISTULKA,** Aberdeen, South Dakota
Best of Class, Brown County Fair and 4-H Show, Aberdeen, South Dakota, 1999, 2000

CHERRY-CHEESE PINWHEELS

⅓ cup shortening
⅓ cup margarine or unsalted butter,
    room temperature
2 cups all-purpose flour, divided
1 cup sugar, divided
1 egg
1 tablespoon milk
1½ teaspoons baking powder

1 teaspoon vanilla
¼ teaspoon salt
1 small package (3 oz.) cream cheese,
    room temperature
¼ teaspoon almond extract
½ cup Maraschinos, chopped
¼ cup toasted almonds, finely chopped

1. In a mixing bowl, cream shortening and margarine or butter on medium to high speed, 30 seconds. Add 1 cup of the flour, ¾ cup of the sugar, egg, milk, baking powder, vanilla, and salt. Beat until thoroughly combined, occasionally scraping down sides of bowl. Stir in remaining cup flour.

2. Divide dough in half. Wrap each portion in plastic wrap. Chill until dough is easy to handle, 3 hours.

3. In a small mixing bowl, combine cream cheese, remaining ¼ cup sugar, and almond extract. Stir in cherries.

4. Roll out each dough portion on a lightly floured surface to make a 10 x 10-inch square. Use a pastry wheel or sharp knife to cut each square into 16 pieces, each 2½ x 2½ inches square.

5. Place the dough squares ½ inch apart on ungreased baking sheets. Use a knife to cut 1-inch slits from each corner to center. Drop a level teaspoon of cream cheese mixture in the center of each square. Fold every other tip to the center to form a pinwheel. Sprinkle almonds in center and press firmly to seal. Bake in a preheated 350°F oven for 8 to 10 minutes, or until edges are firm and cookies are slightly puffed. Cool on baking sheets for 1 minute and transfer to wire racks. Makes 32.

✕ **SANDY FULLERTON,** Abilene, Texas
First Place, West Texas Fair & Rodeo, Abilene, Texas, 2004

Krazy Krunchy Kookies

1 cup all-purpose flour
½ teaspoon baking soda
¼ teaspoon salt
½ cup unsalted butter, room temperature
½ cup sugar
½ cup brown sugar

1 egg, beaten
½ teaspoon vanilla
1 cup crispy rice cereal
1 cup quick-cooking rolled oats
½ cup shredded coconut
½ cup raisins

1. Preheat oven to 350°F.

2. Whisk together flour, baking soda, and salt.

3. In a large mixing bowl, cream butter, sugar, and brown sugar. Beat in egg and vanilla. Stir in flour mixture, crispy rice cereal, and rolled oats. Fold in coconut and raisins.

4. Drop by teaspoonfuls onto ungreased baking sheets. Bake 10 minutes. Cool on wire racks. Makes 5 dozen.

✳ **JARED A. BLOODWORTH,** Plant City, Florida
First Place, Youth Division, Florida State Fair, Tampa, Florida, 2005

Chocolate Mallow Drops

½ cup unsalted butter, room temperature
1 cup sugar
1 egg
½ cup milk
1 teaspoon vanilla
1¾ cups all-purpose flour
½ cup cocoa
½ teaspoon baking soda
½ teaspoon salt

½ cup chopped pecans
Marshmallows, cut in half

FROSTING
¼ cup butter
2 squares (1 oz. each) unsweetened chocolate
1 square (1 oz). semisweet chocolate
2 cups confectioners' sugar
3 to 6 tablespoons brewed coffee

1. Preheat oven to 375°F.

2. In a large mixing bowl, cream butter and sugar. Beat in egg, milk, and vanilla.

3. Whisk together flour, cocoa, baking soda, and salt. Gradually add to butter mixture, mixing until well combined. Stir in pecans.

4. Drop by rounded tablespoonfuls onto ungreased baking sheets, spaced 2 inches apart. Bake for 6 minutes. Press a marshmallow half, cut side down, on top of each cookie. Bake 1 to 2 minutes longer. Cool on wire racks.

5. To make frosting: In a microwave-safe bowl, heat butter, unsweetened chocolate, and semisweet chocolate until melted. Beat in confectioners' sugar. Stir in 3 tablespoons of the coffee, adding more coffee if needed to make a spreading consistency. Put frosting in small zip-close plastic bag. Snip off a lower corner of the bag. Pipe frosting over cookies. Makes 2 dozen.

✳ **PAT KING,** Valparaiso, Indiana
Blue Ribbon, Dropped Cookies, Porter County Fair, Valparaiso, Indiana, 2005

PIZZELLES

3 eggs

¾ cup sugar

½ cup melted margarine, cooled

1 tablespoon vanilla

1¾ cups all-purpose flour

2 teaspoons baking powder

1. Heat electric pizzelle maker following manufacturer's instructions.

2. In a mixing bowl, beat eggs until light and fluffy. Gradually add sugar and beat until smooth. Stir in melted margarine and vanilla.

3. Sift together flour and baking powder; add to egg mixture and stir. Dough will be sticky enough to be dropped by spoon.

4. For each pizzelle, place a heaping teaspoonful of batter in the center of bottom grid. Close lid, squeezing handles together to compress and spread batter. Clip handles during baking. Bake until golden brown, 60 seconds per batch. Remove pizzelles from grid with a spatula. Lay flat to cool. Makes 3 dozen.

※ **DONNA McDADE,** Middletown, Ohio
First Place, Ohio State Fair, Columbus, Ohio, 2003, 2004

ORANGE-PINEAPPLE DELIGHT ICE CREAM

1 can (15½ oz.) crushed pineapple
   in heavy syrup

1 can (6 oz.) frozen orange juice concentrate

1 quart half-and-half

1 pint heavy cream

2 cans (14 oz. each) sweetened condensed milk

1 cup sugar

1 teaspoon vanilla

1. The day before, combine pineapple and orange juice concentrate in a food processor and purée to make a thick liquid. Chill overnight.

2. In a large bowl, combine pineapple mixture, half-and-half, heavy cream, condensed milk, sugar, and vanilla. Stir until well blended.

3. Freeze in a 1-gallon ice cream maker, following manufacturer's instructions. Makes 10 servings.

※ **THOMAS CARROLL,** Pfafftown, North Carolina
First Place, Ronnie and Darlene Turner's Homemade
Ice Cream Contest, Dixie Classic Fair, Winston-Salem,
North Carolina, 2005

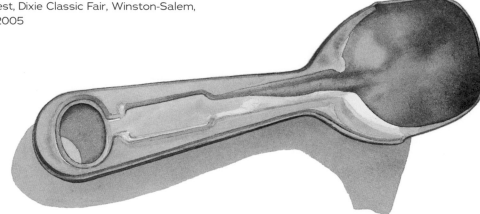

CHOCOLATE DROP COOKIES

1 box (18.2 oz.) chocolate cake mix
2 eggs

⅓ cup vegetable oil
1 cup white chocolate chips

1. Preheat oven to 350°F. Grease baking sheets.

2. In a mixing bowl, combine cake mix, eggs, and oil until well blended and smooth. Stir in white chocolate chips.

3. Drop by teaspoonfuls onto baking sheets. Bake for 9 to 12 minutes. Cool on wire racks. Makes 2 dozen.

✕ **ASHLIN CHEVALIER,** age 8, Chubbuck, Idaho
First Place, North Bannock County Fair, Pocatello, Idaho, 2005

JACK-O-LANTERN CHOCOLATE PUMPKIN COOKIES

1 pumpkin to carve
1 yam
2 cups plus 2 tablespoons flour
1 teaspoon baking powder
1 teaspoon pumpkin pie spice
½ teaspoon baking soda
¼ teaspoon salt

½ cup unsalted butter, room temperature
1 cup brown sugar
1 egg
2 teaspoons vanilla
Chocolate truffle candies (such as Lindt)
Chocolate bars to melt

Bake these Halloween cookies the same spooky night you carve your jack-o-lantern.

1. Preheat oven to 350°F.

2. Carve eyes, a nose, and a mouth in the pumpkin as desired to make a jack-o-lantern.

3. Place the scrap pumpkin pieces and yam in a baking dish. Cover with foil. Bake for 1 hour. Cool. Scrape pumpkin flesh into the bowl of a food processor. Cut yam in half, scoop out flesh, and add to food processor. Blend until smooth. Measure 2 cups of the pumpkin-yam purée.

4. Increase oven temperature to 375°F. Grease baking sheets.

5. Stir together flour, baking powder, pumpkin pie spice, baking soda, and salt.

6. In a large mixing bowl, cream butter and brown sugar until fluffy. Add egg, pumpkin-yam purée, and vanilla; beat until well combined. Stir in flour mixture just until moistened and combined.

7. Drop by heaping tablespoonfuls onto baking sheet. Bake for 8 to 10 minutes. Press a chocolate truffle onto each cookie. Cool on wire racks.

8. Break up chocolate bars and place pieces in a plastic zip-close bag. Microwave to melt the chocolate. Snip off a lower corner of the bag to make a small opening. Drizzle the chocolate over each cookie, making a design. Makes 2 to 3 dozen.

✕ **MARCI RODERER AND KEZIAH RODERER,** age 5, Wellsville, Utah
First Place C & H Cookie Contest, Utah State Fair, Salt Lake City, Utah, 2005

Sesame Cookies (Birdseed Cookies)

⅔ cup sesame seeds

½ cup unsalted butter or margarine, room temperature

½ cup sugar

½ cup brown sugar

1 egg

1 teaspoon vanilla

1¼ cups all-purpose flour

½ teaspoon baking powder

¼ teaspoon cinnamon

¼ teaspoon salt

1. Preheat oven to 350°F. Lightly grease two baking sheets.

2. Spread sesame seeds on a baking sheet. Toast in oven, stirring occasionally to prevent burning, 10 minutes. Cool.

3. In a mixing bowl, cream butter, sugar, and brown sugar. Beat in egg and vanilla. Whisk together flour, baking powder, cinnamon, and salt; add to dough and beat until well mixed. Fold in half of sesame seeds.

4. Shape dough into 1-inch balls. Roll balls in remaining sesame seeds to coat. Place on baking sheet and flatten with the palm of your hand. Bake for 10 minutes, or until golden brown. Makes 2 dozen.

✕ **KAREN TUCKER,** Chubbuck, Idaho
First Place, North Bannock County Fair, Pocatello, Idaho, 2005

Gingersnaps

2¼ cups all-purpose flour

1 cup brown sugar

¾ cup shortening

¼ cup molasses

1 egg

1 teaspoon baking soda

1 teaspoon ground ginger

1 teaspoon ground cinnamon

½ teaspoon cloves

½ cup sugar

1. Preheat oven to 375°F.

2. In a mixing bowl, combine about half of the flour, brown sugar, shortening, molasses, egg, baking soda, ginger, cinnamon, and cloves. Beat with an electric mixer on medium to high speed until thoroughly combined. Beat in the remaining flour.

3. Shape dough into 1-inch balls. Roll in sugar until evenly coated. Set 2 inches apart on ungreased baking sheets. Bake for 7 to 10 minutes, or until set and tops are crackled. Cool on wire racks. Makes 4 dozen.

✕ **KIM SHAKELTON,** Guilford, Connecticut
Blue Ribbon, Any Other Cookie Class; Rosette, Best Cookie; Best in Show, Guilford Fair, Guilford, Connecticut, 1999

WINNER'S CIRCLE TIP | Be careful not to underbake or overbake these cookies. Underbaking causes cookies to sink. Overbaking creates wide crackles that cause the cookies to split. The perfect crackle depends on exactness in following the recipe directions and close observation during the final minutes of baking.

LEMON GINGER CREAMS

½ cup sugar

¼ cup shortening

½ cup molasses

½ cup hot water

¼ cup frozen egg product

2 cups all-purpose flour

1 teaspoon baking soda

½ teaspoon salt

½ teaspoon ground ginger

1 teaspoon cinnamon

½ teaspoon ground cloves

¼ cup crystallized ginger, finely minced

GLAZE

2 cups confectioners' sugar

1 teaspoon grated lemon zest

2 tablespoons lemon juice

2 tablespoons unsalted butter,
  room temperature

1 to 2 tablespoons milk

1. Preheat oven to 375°F. Lightly grease baking sheets or line with parchment paper.

2. In a large mixing bowl, combine sugar, shortening, molasses, hot water, and egg product. Beat until well combined.

3. Whisk together flour, baking soda, salt, ginger, cinnamon, cloves, and crystallized ginger. Add to creamed mixture, stirring just until blended. Let stand 5 to 10 minutes. Drop batter by teaspoonfuls 2 inches apart onto baking sheets. Bake for 8 to 12 minutes, or until edges are lightly golden brown. Cool completely on wire racks before glazing.

4. To make glaze: In a small mixing bowl, combine confectioners' sugar, lemon zest and juice, and butter. Beat in milk to make a smooth, thick consistency. Spread glaze on cookies. Makes 4 dozen.

✄ **SUE SCHWABER,** San Diego, California
First Place, San Diego County Fair, Del Mar, California, 2004

SNICKERDOODLES

1½ cups plus 3 tablespoons sugar, divided

½ cup margarine or unsalted butter,
  room temperature

½ cup shortening

2 eggs

2¾ cups unbleached flour

2 teaspoons cream of tartar

1 teaspoon baking soda

¼ teaspoon salt

3 tablespoons sugar

3 teaspoons cinnamon

1. Preheat oven to 400°F.

2. In a large bowl, mix 1½ cups of the sugar, margarine, shortening, and eggs until well combined. Stir in flour, cream of tartar, baking soda, and salt.

3. In a small bowl, combine 3 tablespoons remaining sugar and cinnamon. Shape dough by rounded teaspoonfuls into balls. Roll balls in cinnamon sugar.

4. Place balls 2 inches apart on baking sheets. Bake for 8 to 10 minutes, or until set. Transfer immediately to a wire rack to cool. Makes 6 dozen cookies.

✄ **NICHOLE REECE,** age 11, Moncks Corner, South Carolina
First Place Cloverleaf Division, 4-H Kooky Cookie Cook-off, Coastal Carolina Fair, Ladson, South Carolina, 2005

SPRITZ COOKIES

1½ cups unsalted butter, room temperature
1 cup sugar
1 egg
1 teaspoon vanilla
2 tablespoons milk

½ teaspoon almond extract
4 cups sifted all-purpose flour
1 teaspoon baking powder
Colored sugar (optional)

1. Preheat oven to 400°F.

2. In a large mixing bowl, cream butter and sugar until light and fluffy. Beat in egg, vanilla, milk, and almond extract until well combined.

3. Sift together flour and baking powder. Add to butter mixture, blending to form a smooth dough.

4. Force room temperature dough through a cookie press onto ungreased baking sheets. Sprinkle with colored sugar, if desired. Bake 7 to 8 minutes. Cool on wire racks. Makes 5 dozen.

※ **CHRISTOPHER KRAVITZ,** Trinity, Florida
First Place, Youth Division, Florida State Fair, Tampa, Florida, 2005

CHINESE ALMOND COOKIES

1 cup unsalted butter, room temperature
½ cup brown sugar
¾ cup confectioners' sugar, plus
    more for rolling out dough
¼ teaspoon vanilla
¼ teaspoon almond extract
2¼ cups all-purpose flour

½ teaspoon salt
1 cup finely chopped almonds

GLAZE
1 egg, slightly beaten
1 tablespoon water
1 cup sliced almonds

1. Preheat oven to 350°F.

2. In a large mixing bowl, cream butter, brown sugar, and confectioners' sugar until light and fluffy. Beat in vanilla and almond extract. With mixer running on low speed, gradually add flour and salt; mix until well blended. Fold in almonds.

3. Divide dough in half. On a surface lightly dusted with confectioners' sugar, roll out one portion of dough to a ⅛-inch thickness. Cut dough with 2-inch round cookie cutter. Place ¾ inch apart on ungreased baking sheets. Gather up scraps, reroll, and cut more cookies. Repeat with second half of dough.

4. To add glaze: Whisk together egg and water. Using a pastry brush, lightly brush glaze over each cookie. Arrange 4 almond slices on top of each cookie in a flower pattern. Reglaze to set the almonds.

5. Bake for 8 to 10 minutes, or until golden brown. Cool on baking sheet 1 to 2 minutes and transfer to a wire rack. Cool completely. Makes 4 dozen.

If the dough is sticky, wrap it in plastic wrap and refrigerate for 1 hour before rolling.

※ **FRAN NEAVOLL,** Salem, Oregon
Blue Ribbon and Judges' Choice Award, Best Foreign Cookie, Oregon State Fair, Salem, Oregon, 2004

RANGER COOKIES

1 cup margarine, room temperature
1 cup sugar
1 cup brown sugar
2 eggs
1 teaspoon vanilla
2 cups all-purpose flour

1 teaspoon baking soda
½ teaspoon baking powder
2 cups quick-cooking rolled oats
2 cups crispy rice cereal
1 cup coconut

1. Preheat oven to 350°F.

2. Cream margarine, sugar, and brown sugar in a large mixing bowl. Beat in eggs and vanilla until well blended. Sift together flour, baking soda, and baking powder; stir into dough. Stir in rolled oats, cereal, and coconut until well combined.

3. Drop by teaspoonfuls onto baking sheets. Bake 11 to 12 minutes. Makes 5 dozen.

✂ **CAROLYN HARTMANN,** Dakota City, Iowa
Blue Ribbon, Clay County Fair, Spencer, Iowa, 2004

PEANUT BUTTER–CHOCOLATE CHIP COOKIES

⅓ cup unsalted butter or margarine,
  room temperature
2 eggs

½ cup chunky peanut butter
1 box (18.2 oz.) yellow cake mix
1 cup chocolate chips

1. Preheat oven to 350°F. Lightly grease baking sheets.

2. In a large mixing bowl, cream butter, eggs, and peanut butter. Stir in cake mix. Fold in chocolate chips.

3. Drop by teaspoonfuls onto baking sheet. Bake for 9 to 12 minutes, or until golden brown around the edges. Cool on a wire rack. Makes 3 to 4 dozen.

✂ **JADEN CHEVALIER,** age 11, Chubbuck, Idaho
First Place, North Bannock County Fair, Pocatello, Idaho, 2005

Hermits

2½ cups all-purpose flour

1½ teaspoons baking soda

½ teaspoon salt

1 teaspoon cinnamon

¾ teaspoon ground ginger

¾ teaspoon ground cloves

¾ cup shortening

1 cup sugar

1 egg

¼ cup light molasses

½ cup chopped walnuts (optional)

½ cup raisins

1. Preheat oven to 375°F. Set aside 2 baking sheets; do not grease.

2. Whisk together flour, baking soda, salt, cinnamon, ginger, and cloves.

3. In a large mixing bowl, cream shortening and sugar. Beat in egg and molasses until well blended. Add flour mixture and stir to combine. Stir in walnuts, if using, and raisins.

4. Gather up dough into a ball and divide in fourths. Roll each piece into a 12-inch log. Place 2 logs on each baking sheet. Flatten each log into a bar, 1½ inches wide and ¾ inch high. Bake for 10 minutes. Cool on baking sheet 5 minutes. Cut into pieces and cool on wire rack. Makes 4 dozen.

✕ **DEBBY PAYNE,** Wappingers Falls, New York
Blue Ribbon, Dutchess County Fair, Rhinebeck, New York, 1998

Oatmeal Sandwich Cookies

1½ cups shortening

2⅔ cups brown sugar

4 eggs

2 teaspoons vanilla

2¼ cups all-purpose flour

1½ teaspoons baking soda

1 teaspoon salt

2 teaspoons cinnamon

½ teaspoon nutmeg

4 cups rolled oats

FILLING

¾ shortening

3 cups confectioners' sugar

1 jar (7 oz.) marshmallow crème

1 to 3 tablespoons milk

1. Preheat oven to 350°F. Lightly grease baking sheets.

2. In a large mixing bowl, cream shortening and brown sugar. Add eggs one at a time, beating well after each addition. Beat in vanilla.

3. Whisk together flour, baking soda, salt, cinnamon, and nutmeg; add to creamed mixture and mix until well combined. Stir in oats. Drop by rounded teaspoonfuls 2 inches apart onto baking sheets. Bake for 10 to 12 minutes, or until golden brown. Cool completely on wire racks before adding filling.

4. To make filling: In a mixing bowl, cream shortening, confectioners' sugar, and marshmallow crème. Stir in milk, a tablespoon at a time, adding just enough to achieve spreading consistency. Spread filling on the flat bottom of half of the cookies. Press the flat side of the remaining cookies on top, sandwiching the filling in between. Makes 4½ dozen.

✕ **MARGIE RAINWATER,** Abilene, Texas
First Place, West Texas Fair & Rodeo, Abilene, Texas, 2005

Snowcapped Date Delight

¾ cup unsalted butter, melted
1¼ cups brown sugar
2 tablespoons heavy cream
1 tablespoon vanilla
1 egg
1¾ cups all-purpose flour
1 teaspoon salt
¾ teaspoon baking soda
1 cup chopped dates

1 cup mini semisweet chocolate chips
1 tablespoon grated orange zest

TOPPING

1 lb. white chocolate
1 cup chopped dates
1 cup mini semisweet chocolate chips
   or chopped pecans
½ cup grated orange zest

1. Preheat oven to 375°F.

2. In a large mixing bowl, combine melted butter, brown sugar, heavy cream, and vanilla; stir until blended. Beat in egg. Add flour, salt, and baking soda; mix well. Stir in dates, chocolate chips, and orange zest.

3. Drop dough by heaping tablespoonful onto ungreased baking sheets. Bake for 8 to 10 minutes. Cool on wire racks.

4. To make topping: Melt white chocolate in the microwave at 50% power, stirring at 1-minute intervals, until creamy. In a separate bowl, combine dates, chocolate chips or pecans, and orange zest. Dip each cookie halfway into melted white chocolate and then into date mixture to coat. Cool until white chocolate is solid. Makes 4 dozen.

✖ **PAMELA CLUTE,** Palm Desert, California
First Place, Cookies, Riverside County Fair and National Date Festival, Indio, California, 2003–2004

Lisa's Chocolate Chip Cookies

½ cup unsalted butter, room temperature,
   plus more for baking sheets
½ cup shortening
¾ cup sugar
¾ cup brown sugar
2 large eggs
1 package (3.4 oz.) instant vanilla pudding mix
1 tablespoon vanilla

1 teaspoon baking soda
1 teaspoon water
1 teaspoon cinnamon
1 teaspoon nutmeg
½ teaspoon salt
1 cup rolled oats
2¼ cups all-purpose flour
1 package (12 oz.) chocolate chips

1. Preheat oven to 375°F. Butter baking sheets.

2. In a large mixing bowl, cream shortening and butter. Beat in sugar and brown sugar until fluffy. Blend in eggs, pudding mix, vanilla, baking soda, water, cinnamon, nutmeg, and salt. Mix in oats, then flour. Stir in chocolate chips.

3. Drop by tablespoonfuls onto baking sheets. Bake for 12 minutes. Cool for 5 minutes on baking sheets and transfer to wire racks. Makes 6 dozen.

✖ **LISA DAVEY,** San Diego, California
First Place, San Diego County Fair, Del Mar, California, 2004

Chocolate-Peanut Butter Oatmeal Rounds

¾ cup unsalted butter, room temperature
½ cup peanut butter
1¼ cups all-purpose flour
1 cup sugar
½ cup brown sugar
2 eggs

1 teaspoon baking powder
1 teaspoon vanilla
½ teaspoon baking soda
2 cups rolled oats
½ cup semisweet chocolate chips
½ cup milk chocolate chips

1. Preheat oven to 375°F.

2. In a large mixing bowl, beat butter and peanut butter on medium speed until combined, 30 seconds. Add half of the flour. Add sugar, brown sugar, eggs, baking powder, vanilla, and baking soda. Beat until combined.

3. Stir in remaining flour. Stir in oats, semisweet chocolate pieces, and milk chocolate pieces.

4. Drop by rounded teaspoonful onto ungreased baking sheets, spaced 2 inches apart. Bake for 10 minutes, or until edges are lightly browned. Cool on a wire rack. Makes 5 dozen.

※ **Sherri L. Hamlin,** Cape Coral, Florida
First Place, Adult Division, Florida State Fair, Tampa, Florida, 2005

Chocolate-Raspberry Macadamia Nut Cookies

1 package (12 oz.) semisweet chocolate chips
2⅔ cups plus 2 tablespoons all-purpose flour
1 teaspoon baking soda
1 teaspoon salt
1 cup unsalted butter, room temperature
1 cup light brown sugar

½ cup sugar
1 teaspoon vanilla
3 large eggs
4 cups raspberry-flavored chocolate, chopped
2 cups macadamia nuts, chopped

1. Preheat oven to 375°F. Line baking sheets with parchment paper.

2. Melt semisweet chocolate chips in a saucepan over low heat. Set aside.

3. Combine flour, baking soda, and salt.

4. In a large mixing bowl, beat butter, light brown sugar, sugar, and vanilla until well blended. Add eggs one at a time, beating well after each addition. Beat in the melted chocolate. Gradually add flour mixture, beating until combined. Stir in chopped chocolate and nuts.

5. Drop by teaspoonfuls onto baking sheets. Bake approximately 10 minutes. Cool completely on wire racks. Makes 5 dozen.

※ **Darlene Shaub,** San Diego, California
First Place, San Diego County Fair, Del Mar, California, 2004

CHOCOLATE CHIP SNOWBALLS

¾ cup unsalted butter or margarine,
   room temperature
½ cup sugar
¼ teaspoon baking powder
1 egg yolk

¾ teaspoon vanilla
1¾ cups all-purpose flour
½ cup mini semisweet chocolate chips
Confectioners' sugar, sifted

1. Preheat oven to 325°F. Set aside baking sheets; do not grease.

2. In a large mixing bowl, cream butter or margarine on medium to high speed for 30 seconds. Add sugar and baking powder; beat until well combined. Beat in egg yolk and vanilla. Beat in flour. Stir in chocolate chips.

3. Shape dough into 1-inch balls. Place balls 1 inch apart on ungreased baking sheets. Bake for 15 to 17 minutes, or until edges are firm and bottoms are very lightly browned. Cool on wire racks.

4. Sift confectioners' sugar into a zip-close plastic bag. Add a few warm cookies at a time and shake gently to coat. Return cookies to wire rack. When completely cool, sift more confectioners' sugar over the top. Makes 40.

✄ **AMY EICHELBERGER,** Odessa, Florida
First Place, Adult Division, Florida State Fair, Tampa, Florida, 2005

CHOCOLATE-ALMOND BISCOTTI

½ cup unsalted butter or margarine,
   room temperature
1¼ cups sugar
2 eggs
1 teaspoon almond extract
2¼ cups all-purpose flour

¼ cup Dutch-processed cocoa
1 teaspoon baking powder
¼ teaspoon salt
1 cup sliced almonds
Melted chocolate, for dipping

1. Preheat oven to 350°F.

2. In a large mixing bowl, beat butter or margarine and sugar until blended. Add eggs and almond extract. Beat well.

3. Stir together flour, cocoa, baking powder, and salt; add gradually to butter mixture, beating until smooth. (Dough will be thick.) Stir in almonds using a wooden spoon.

4. Divide dough in half. Shape into two 11-inch long rolls. Place rolls 3 to 4 inches apart on an ungreased baking sheet. Bake for 30 minutes, or until rolls are set.

5. Remove baking sheet from oven. Cool rolls on baking sheet for 15 minutes. Using a serrated knife, cut rolls diagonally with a sawing motion into ½-inch-thick slices. Arrange slices, cut sides down, on baking sheet. Bake for 8 to 9 minutes. Turn slices over; bake an additional 8 to 9 minutes. Remove from oven; set baking sheet on a wire rack to cool. Dip one end of biscotti in chocolate. Makes 2½ dozen.

✄ **MARJORIE WIMSATT,** Valrico, Florida
First Place, Adult Division, Florida State Fair, Tampa, Florida, 2005

CHOCOLATE DROP COOKIES

½ cup sugar

½ cup cocoa

½ cup brown sugar

1 cup all-purpose flour

1 teaspoon salt

1 teaspoon baking soda

½ cup mint chocolate baking chips

1 cup unsalted butter, melted

1 egg

1 teaspoon vanilla

1. Preheat oven to 375°F.

2. In a large mixing bowl, combine sugar, cocoa, brown sugar, flour, salt, and baking soda. Stir in baking chips.

3. Add melted butter, egg, and vanilla. Mix until completely blended.

4. Roll dough into 1-inch balls. Set on ungreased baking sheets and flatten slightly. Bake for 7 to 8 minutes. Cool on wire racks. Makes 3 dozen.

✄ **HEATHER CLEAVER,** age 18, Inkom, Idaho
First Place, North Bannock County Fair, Pocatello, Idaho, 2005

PEANUT BUTTER-AND-CHOCOLATE CHUNK-FILLED COOKIES

½ cup shortening

1 cup peanut butter

⅓ cup sugar

⅓ cup brown sugar

1 egg

2 tablespoons soy milk

1 teaspoon vanilla

1½ cups rice flour

1 teaspoon baking soda

½ teaspoon salt

¾ cup white chocolate chunks

¾ cup milk or dark chocolate chunks

½ cup peanuts

FILLING

1 cup peanut butter

1 cup confectioners' sugar

1 teaspoon oil

1. Preheat oven to 350°F. Lightly grease baking sheets.

2. In a large mixing bowl, cream shortening, peanut butter, sugar, and brown sugar. Beat in egg, soy milk, and vanilla. Add rice flour, baking soda, and salt; mix well. Fold in white chocolate chunks, milk or dark chocolate chunks, and peanuts.

3. Drop by tablespoonfuls onto baking sheets. Press down to flatten slightly. Bake for 10 to 15 minutes. Cool completely on a wire rack before filling.

4. To make filling: In a small mixing bowl, combine peanut butter, confectioners' sugar, and oil until smooth. Spread filling on the smooth side of half of the cookies. Press the smooth side of the remaining cookies on top, sandwiching the filling in between. Makes 17 medium sandwich cookies.

✄ **ALAN REID,** Detroit, Michigan
Second Place, Wheat- & Dairy-Free Dessert, Michigan State Fair, Detroit, Michigan, 2001

MICHELLE'S OLD-FASHIONED OATMEAL COOKIES

3 eggs, well beaten

1 cup raisins

1 teaspoon vanilla

1 cup butter-flavored shortening

1 cup brown sugar

1 cup sugar, plus more for coating

2½ cups all-purpose flour

1 teaspoon salt

2 teaspoons baking soda

1 teaspoon cinnamon

2 cups rolled oats

1 cup nuts (optional)

1. Combine eggs, raisins, and vanilla in a bowl. Let stand for 1 hour.

2. In a large mixing bowl, cream shortening, brown sugar, and sugar.

3. Whisk together flour, salt, baking soda, and cinnamon; add gradually to creamed mixture until well combined. Add egg mixture and stir to blend. Fold in oats and nuts, if using, to make a stiff dough.

4. Roll dough into 1-inch to 1½-inch balls; roll in sugar to coat. Place 2 inches apart on lightly greased baking sheets. Bake in a preheated 350°F oven for 10 to 12 minutes. Cool on wire racks. Makes 7 dozen.

✖ **MICHELLE MUSE,** Pocatello, Idaho
First Place, North Bannock County Fair, Pocatello, Idaho, 2005

PECAN SHORTBREAD
BLACK RASPBERRY COOKIES

1 cup unsalted butter, room temperature

⅔ cup sugar

1 teaspoon vanilla

½ teaspoon almond extract

2 cups all-purpose flour, plus
    more for rolling out dough

1 cup pecans, ground

¼ cup seedless raspberry preserves

Confectioners' sugar

1. In a large mixing bowl, cream butter, sugar, vanilla, and almond extract at medium speed, scraping bowl often, 1 to 2 minutes. Reduce speed to low, add flour and pecans, and beat until well mixed, 1 minute.

2. Divide dough in half. Wrap each half in plastic wrap and refrigerate until firm, 1 to 2 hours. Keep dough chilled until ready to use.

3. Roll out dough on a lightly floured surface to a ⅛-inch thickness. Cut with a 2-inch or 3-inch scalloped round cookie cutter. Place 1 inch apart on ungreased baking sheets. Use a 1-inch round cutter to cut a hole in half of the cookies. Roll out and cut remaining dough in same way. Bake in a preheated 350°F oven for 9 to 12 minutes, or until lightly browned. Cool completely on wire racks before filling.

4. Spread cookies without holes with ½ teaspoon preserves. Layer cookies with holes on top, sandwiching preserves in between. Sprinkle with confectioners' sugar. Makes 2 dozen.

✖ **SANDY FULLERTON,** Abilene, Texas
First Place and Best of Show, West Texas Fair & Rodeo, Abilene, Texas, 2002

HONEY GINGERSNAPS

½ cup shortening

¼ cup unsalted butter, room temperature

1½ cups sugar, divided

¼ cup honey

1 egg

1 teaspoon vanilla

2 cups all-purpose flour

2 teaspoons baking soda

⅛ teaspoon salt

1 tablespoon ground ginger

⅛ teaspoon ground cloves

1. Preheat oven to 350°F. Lightly grease baking sheets.

2. In a large mixing bowl, cream shortening and butter until smooth. Gradually beat in 1 cup of the sugar until blended. Beat in honey, egg, and vanilla until fluffy.

3. Whisk together flour, baking soda, salt, ginger, and cloves. Gradually stir into creamed mixture until well combined.

4. Shape dough into 1-inch balls. Place remaining ½ cup sugar in a shallow bowl; roll balls in sugar to coat. Place balls 2 inches apart on baking sheets. Bake for 10 minutes, or until golden brown. Makes 4 to 5 dozen.

✖ **JANET PISTULKA,** Aberdeen, South Dakota
Best of Class, Brown County Fair and 4-H Show, Aberdeen, South Dakota, 1997, 2000, 2001

GIANT PEANUT BUTTER-CHOCOLATE CHIP OAT COOKIES

1¼ cups all-purpose flour

1 teaspoon baking powder

1 teaspoon baking soda

¼ teaspoon salt

2½ cups plain or quick-cooking rolled oats

1 cup unsalted butter, room temperature

1 cup peanut butter

1 cup sugar, plus more for coating

1 cup brown sugar

2 eggs

1 teaspoon vanilla

1 cup chocolate chips

1. Preheat oven to 350°F.

2. Whisk together flour, baking powder, baking soda, salt, and oats.

3. In a large mixing bowl, cream butter and peanut butter. Add sugar and brown sugar and mix well. Beat in eggs and vanilla. Stir in chocolate chips. Gradually add flour mixture until well combined.

4. Drop by heaping tablespoonfuls onto ungreased baking sheets (6 cookies per sheet). Dip the bottom of a glass in sugar and press down on dough to flatten slightly. Bake for 15 minutes, or until golden. Cool on a wire rack. Makes 2 dozen.

✖ **KELLEY MURPHY,** North Ferrisburg, Vermont
Rosette, Addison County Fair & Field Days, New Haven, Vermont, 2005

PEACHY KEEN COOKIE BITES

1 box (12 oz.) vanilla wafers, crushed
½ cup pecans, chopped
1 box (16 oz.) confectioners' sugar,
    plus more for coating

1 cup dried peaches, diced
½ cup unsalted butter, melted
1 container (6 oz.) frozen orange juice
    concentrate, thawed

1. In a large bowl, combine vanilla wafers, pecans, confectioners' sugar, and peaches. Stir in orange juice concentrate and melted butter. Mix until well combined. Chill for 20 minutes.
2. Roll mixture into bite-size balls. Roll in confectioners' sugar to coat. Makes 6 dozen.

✕ **RHONDA HITCH,** Kathleen, Georgia
Second Place, Just Peachy Contest, Georgia National Fair, Perry, Georgia, 2005

PFEFFERNUESSE (GERMAN SPICE COOKIES)

3½ cups all-purpose flour
2 teaspoons baking powder
½ teaspoon baking soda
½ teaspoon salt
1½ teaspoons cinnamon
1 teaspoon ground ginger
½ teaspoon ground cloves

½ teaspoon ground cardamom
¼ teaspoon white pepper
1 cup unsalted butter, room temperature
1 cup sugar
¼ cup dark molasses
1 egg
Confectioners' sugar

1. Preheat oven to 350°F. Grease baking sheets.
2. Whisk together flour, baking powder, baking soda, salt, cinnamon, ginger, cloves, cardamom, and white pepper.
3. In a large mixing bowl, cream butter and sugar until light and fluffy. Beat in molasses and egg. Gradually add flour mixture, beating on low speed until dough forms. Shape dough into a disk, wrap in plastic wrap, and chill 30 minutes.
4. Roll dough into 1-inch balls. Place on baking sheets. Bake for 11 to 14 minutes, or until golden brown. Set on wire racks to cool, dusting lightly with confectioners' sugar while still warm. Makes 5 to 6 dozen.

✕ **DARLENE SHAUB,** San Diego, California
First Place, San Diego County Fair, Del Mar, California, 2004

WINNER'S CIRCLE TIP | These spicy drop cookies are called *Pfeffernüsse* in Germany, *Pebernodder* in Denmark, and *Peppernøtter* (see page 378) in Sweden. They are found throughout Northern Europe at Christmas time.

Swedish Tea Cakes

1 cup butter
½ cup confectioners' sugar,
   plus more for coating
2 teaspoons vanilla

2 cups all-purpose flour
1 cup finely chopped or ground pecans
½ teaspoon salt

1. Preheat oven to 325°F.

2. In a large mixing bowl, cream butter, confectioners' sugar, and vanilla until soft and fluffy. Stir in flour, pecans, and salt until dough holds together.

3. Shape dough into 1-inch balls. Place 1 inch apart on ungreased baking sheets. Bake for 15 to 20 minutes, or until set but not brown. Cool slightly, then roll in confectioners' sugar. Set on waxed paper and cool completely. Roll again in confectioners' sugar. Makes 5 dozen.

✂ **Sandee Budzinski,** Brookfield, Wisconsin
Grand Champion, Waukesha County Fair, Pewaukee, Wisconsin, 2001

Coconut-Macadamia Cookies

1 cup unsalted butter, room temperature
¾ cup sugar
1 cup brown sugar
1½ teaspoons vanilla
2 eggs

3 cups all-purpose flour
1 teaspoon baking soda
¼ teaspoon salt
1 cup flaked coconut
3½ oz. chopped macadamia nuts

1. Preheat oven to 350°F.

2. In a large mixing bowl, cream butter, sugar, and brown sugar until fluffy. Add vanilla and eggs; blend well. Stir in flour, baking soda, and salt and mix well. Stir in coconut and nuts.

3. Drop by teaspoonfuls unto ungreased baking sheets. Bake for 10 to 12 minutes. Cool in pan 1 minute before removing to a wire rack. Makes 4 dozen.

✂ **Angela Flesland,** age 15, Poughkeepsie, New York
Blue Ribbon, Dutchess County Fair, Rhinebeck, New York, 2004

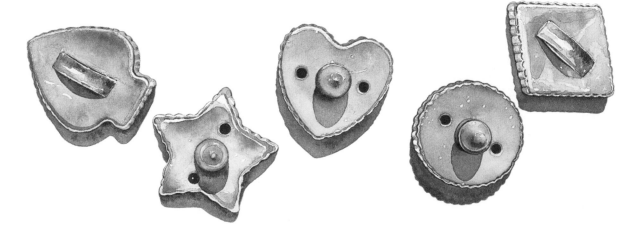

Chocolate Cutout Cookies

1 cup unsalted butter, room temperature

1 cup sugar

2 eggs

1½ teaspoons vanilla

3 squares (1 oz. each) baking chocolate, melted

3 cups all-purpose flour

2 teaspoons baking powder

½ teaspoon salt

Confectioners' sugar

1. Preheat oven to 350°F.

2. In a large mixing bowl, cream butter and sugar. Beat in eggs and vanilla. Stir in melted chocolate until well blended.

3. Whisk together flour, baking powder, and salt; stir into chocolate mixture. Chill until firm.

4. Roll out dough onto a surface sprinkled with confectioners' sugar. Cut out using cookie cutters. Place on ungreased baking sheets. Bake for 8 to 10 minutes. Cool on wire racks. Add frosting, if desired. Makes 4 to 5 dozen.

※ **Carol Laska,** Winona, Minnesota
Blue Ribbon, Winona County Fair, Saint Charles, Minnesota, 1998

Jumbo Strawberry-Orange Vanilla Crisps

2 tablespoons strawberry preserves

1 tablespoon orange juice

½ cup unsalted butter, room temperature

½ cup sugar

2 eggs

2 teaspoons vanilla

1⅓ cups all-purpose flour

1 teaspoon baking powder

1 teaspoon salt

ICING

1 box (16 oz.) confectioners' sugar

¼ cup orange juice

1 tablespoon grated orange zest

½ cup unsalted butter, room temperature

2 strawberries, mashed, plus more for garnish

1 teaspoon vanilla

Dipping chocolate

Chopped nuts

1. Preheat oven to 400°F.

2. Combine preserves and orange juice in a small bowl.

3. In a large mixing bowl, cream butter and sugar. Beat in eggs and vanilla. Whisk together flour, baking powder, and salt. With mixer running, add flour and strawberry mixtures alternately to creamed mixture, blending until well combined.

4. Drop by heaping tablespoonfuls onto ungreased baking sheets. Bake 8 to 12 minutes. Cool.

5. To make icing: In a mixing bowl, combine confectioners' sugar, orange juice and zest, butter, mashed strawberries, and vanilla until well blended. Spread the flat side of a cookie with icing and top with a second cookie to make a sandwich. Drizzle with dipping chocolate, sprinkle with chopped nuts, and top each cookie with half a strawberry. Makes 1 dozen.

※ **Rick Wilks,** Ruskin, Florida
First Place, Sweepstakes Division, Florida State Fair, Tampa, Florida, 2005

POTATO CHIP COOKIES

1 cup unsalted butter, room temperature
½ cup sugar, plus more for pressing
1 teaspoon vanilla
½ cup crushed potato chips

½ cup chopped pecans
2 cups all-purpose flour
Whole pecan halves

1. Preheat oven to 350° to 375°F. Grease two baking sheets.
2. Cream together butter and sugar. Stir in vanilla, crushed potato chips, pecans, and flour.
3. Shape dough into small balls and place on baking sheets (or drop by teaspoonfuls). Flatten each ball with a glass dipped in sugar. Top each cookie with a pecan half. Bake for 8 to 10 minutes, or until golden brown. Cool on wire racks. Makes 2 dozen.

※ **LOUISE PIPER,** Garner, Iowa
First Place, Drop Cookies, Iowa State Fair, Des Moines, Iowa, 2005

TRIPLE GOLD COOKIES

1½ to 1¾ cups all-purpose flour, divided
1 cup chopped fresh peeled and
    seeded orange slices
½ teaspoon baking powder
½ teaspoon baking soda
½ teaspoon salt
⅔ cup unsalted butter or margarine,
    room temperature

⅔ cup sugar
⅔ cup brown sugar
1 egg
2 teaspoons water
1 teaspoon vanilla
1½ cups oatmeal
1 cup shredded coconut

1. Preheat oven to 350°F. Lightly grease baking sheets.
2. Combine ½ cup of the flour and orange slices, stirring to coat.
3. Sift together remaining 1 to 1¼ cups all-purpose flour, baking powder, baking soda, and salt.
4. In a large mixing bowl, cream butter, sugar, and brown sugar. Beat in egg, water, and vanilla. Add flour mixture and blend well. Stir in oatmeal, coconut, and orange slices. Roll dough into balls, place on baking sheets, and press to flatten. Bake for 8 to 10 minutes. Cool on wire racks. Makes 4 to 5 dozen.

※ **ROBIN WHEELER,** El Cajon, California; Kalie and Tyler Murphy, Cambria Wood, California
First Place, San Diego County Fair, Del Mar, California, 2004

HONEY SAND BALLS

1 cup unsalted butter, room temperature
½ cup sifted confectioners' sugar,
    plus more for coating
2 tablespoons honey

2 cups all-purpose flour
¾ cup chopped walnuts
1 teaspoon vanilla
¼ teaspoon salt

1. Preheat oven to 325°F. Lightly grease baking sheets.

2. In a large mixing bowl, cream butter, confectioners' sugar, and honey on medium speed until well combined. Beat or stir in flour, walnuts, vanilla, and salt. Mix thoroughly, using your hands if necessary.

3. Shape dough into 1-inch balls. Place balls 1½ inches apart on baking sheets. Bake for 14 to 16 minutes, or until very lightly browned. Cool slightly on wire racks. Roll cookies in confectioners' sugar while still warm. Cool completely on wire racks. Roll in confectioners' sugar once again. Makes 5 dozen.

※ **KATHY FRIERSON,** DeLand, Florida
First Place, Baked Goods—Senior Adult, Volusia County Fair, DeLand, Florida, 2004

WHITE CHOCOLATE–CITRUS MACAROONS

6 tablespoons all-purpose flour, plus
    more for baking sheets
1 package (5⅓ cups) coconut
5 or 6 squares (1 oz. each) white
    baking chocolate, chopped
⅔ cup sugar

¼ teaspoon salt
4 large egg whites
2 teaspoons grated orange zest
1 teaspoon almond extract

1. Preheat oven to 325°F. Lightly grease and flour baking sheets.

2. In a large bowl, combine coconut, white baking chocolate, sugar, flour, and salt.

3. Stir in egg whites, orange zest, and almond extract until well blended.

4. Press small portions of batter between your fingers to form 1½-inch balls. Place on baking sheets. Bake 15 to 17 minutes, or until lightly browned on bottom. Remove immediately and cool on wire racks. Makes 3 dozen.

※ **DARLENE SHAUB,** San Diego, California
First Place, San Diego County Fair, Del Mar, California, 2004

EM'S ELDERBERRY COOKIES

1 cup unsalted butter, room temperature
⅔ cup sugar
2 large egg yolks

2 teaspoons vanilla
2 cups all-purpose flour, sifted
½ cup elderberry jelly

1. Preheat oven to 375°F. Lightly grease baking sheets.

2. In a mixing bowl, cream butter and sugar until very light in color. Beat in egg yolks until fluffy. Stir in vanilla. Gradually add flour until well combined.

3. Gently pat dough into 1-inch balls. Set balls on baking sheets. Press the top of each ball with your fingertip to make an indentation. Spoon elderberry jelly into each indentation. Bake for 8 minutes, or until edges are light golden brown. Makes 4 dozen.

※ **EMILY TRAPP,** Red Hook, New York
Blue Ribbon, Dutchess County Fair, Rhinebeck, New York, 2002

WORLD'S BEST CHOCOLATE CHIP COOKIES

1 cup unsalted butter, room temperature

¾ cup sugar

1 cup brown sugar

2 eggs

1 tablespoon vanilla

3 cups all-purpose flour

¾ teaspoon baking soda

¾ teaspoon salt

3 cups semisweet chocolate chips

1. Preheat oven to 350°F.

2. In a large mixing bowl, cream butter, sugar, and brown sugar. Beat in eggs and vanilla.

3. Whisk together flour, baking soda, and salt; add to creamed mixture until well blended. Stir in chocolate chips.

4. Drop by teaspoonfuls onto ungreased baking sheets. Bake for 10 to 12 minutes. Cool on wire racks. Makes 5 dozen.

✄ **CAROLYN HARTMANN,** Dakota City, Iowa
Blue Ribbon, Clay County Fair, Spencer, Iowa, 2004

CRACKED SUGAR COOKIES

1 cup unsalted butter or margarine,
    room temperature

1 cup sugar, plus more for coating

½ cup brown sugar

1 egg

1 teaspoon vanilla

2 cups all-purpose flour

2 teaspoons cream of tartar

2 teaspoons baking soda

½ teaspoon salt

1. Preheat oven to 375°F. Grease baking sheets.

2. In a large mixing bowl, cream butter or margarine, sugar and brown sugar. Beat in egg and vanilla.

3. Whisk together flour, cream of tartar, baking soda, and salt. Add to egg mixture; stir until well blended. Roll dough into balls. Roll in sugar and place on baking sheet. Bake for 10 to 12 minutes. Cool on wire racks. Makes 3 dozen cookies.

✄ **JEANETTE D. CHUCKER,** Owasso, Oklahoma
Sweepstakes, Tulsa State Fair, Tulsa, Oklahoma, 2003

CAROLYN'S SUGAR COOKIES

1 cup margarine, room temperature

1 cup shortening

1 cup sugar, plus more for pressing

1 cup confectioners' sugar

2 eggs

½ teaspoon almond flavoring

1 teaspoon vanilla

4 cups all-purpose flour

1 teaspoon baking soda

1 teaspoon cream of tartar

½ teaspoon salt

1. In a large mixing bowl, cream margarine and shortening. Add sugar and confectioners' sugar and cream until well blended. Beat in eggs, almond flavoring, and vanilla.

2. Whisk together flour, baking soda, cream of tartar, and salt. Blend into creamed mixture to form a dough. Chill 1 to 2 hours.

3. Roll dough into balls. Place 2 inches apart on ungreased baking sheets. Flatten with a glass that has been dipped in sugar. Bake in a preheated 350°F oven for 8 to 10 minutes. Cool on wire racks. Makes 6 dozen cookies.

※ **CAROLYN HARTMANN,** Dakota City, Iowa
Blue Ribbon, Clay County Fair, Spencer, Iowa, 2004; Blue Ribbon, Iowa State Fair, Des Moines, Iowa, 2005

ORANGE SUGAR COOKIES

½ **cup unsalted butter, room temperature**
1½ **cups sugar, divided**
½ **teaspoon salt**
1½ **teaspoons grated orange zest**
1 **egg**
1 **tablespoon milk**

1 **tablespoon orange juice concentrate**
2 **cups all-purpose flour**
1 **teaspoon baking powder**
½ **teaspoon baking soda**
¾ **teaspoon nutmeg**

1. In a large mixing bowl, cream butter, 1 cup of the sugar, salt, and orange zest. Beat in egg, milk, and orange juice concentrate.

2. Sift together flour, baking powder, and baking soda; blend into creamed mixture until well combined. Chill for 1 hour.

3. Combine remaining ½ cup sugar and nutmeg in a shallow bowl. Form dough into walnut-sized balls; roll in sugar mixture to coat. Place 2 inches apart on ungreased baking sheets. Bake in a preheated 375°F oven for 8 to 10 minutes. Cool on wire racks. Makes 4 dozen.

※ **KENNA-MARIE MCCULLEY,** Pierson, Florida
First Place, Baked Goods—Youth Junior, Volusia County Fair, DeLand, Florida, 2004

HONEY-PEANUT BITES

1 **box (12 oz.) vanilla wafers, crushed**
1 **cup honey roasted peanuts, finely ground**
1 **box (16 oz.) confectioners' sugar,**
   plus more for coating

1 **container (8 oz.) frozen orange juice**
   concentrate, thawed
½ **cup unsalted butter, melted**

1. In a large mixing bowl, combine vanilla wafers, peanuts, and confectioners' sugar. Add orange juice concentrate and melted butter; mix until well combined. Chill for 20 minutes.

2. Roll mixture into bite-size balls. Roll in confectioners' sugar to coat. Makes 6 dozen.

※ **RHONDA HITCH,** Kathleen, Georgia
Second Place, Georgia Peanut Recipe—Sweet, Georgia National Fair, Perry, Georgia, 2005

MERINGUES

3 egg whites
¼ teaspoon cream of tartar
⅛ teaspoon salt
¾ cup sugar

GLAZE
½ cup semisweet chocolate chips
2 tablespoons unsalted butter, room temperature
Candy dots

1. Preheat oven to 275°F. Lightly grease baking sheets.

2. In a large mixing bowl, beat egg whites, cream of tartar, and salt until foamy. With mixer running, beat in sugar 1 tablespoon at a time; continue beating until stiff and glossy.

3. Spoon meringue into a pastry bag fitted with a medium size star tip. Pipe 1 inch apart onto baking sheets. Bake 45 minutes or just until edges are lightly browned. Cool on baking sheets.

4. To make glaze: Melt chocolate chips and butter in a small saucepan over very low heat, stirring continuously until smooth. Dip tops of meringues into melted chocolate and sprinkle with candy dots. Makes 2 dozen.

✖ **TULIE TREJO,** Chula Vista, California
First Place, San Diego County Fair, Del Mar, California, 2004

HANNAH'S CHOCOLATE CHIP COOKIES

½ cup unsalted butter or margarine,
   room temperature
½ cup shortening
¾ cup sugar
¾ cup brown sugar
2 eggs

1 teaspoon vanilla
1 teaspoon salt
1 teaspoon baking soda
3⅓ cups all-purpose flour
2 cups chocolate chips

1. Preheat oven to 350°F.

2. In a large mixing bowl, cream butter or margarine, shortening, sugar, and brown sugar until fluffy. Beat in eggs and vanilla. Add salt, baking soda, and flour, mixing well after each addition. Fold in chocolate chips.

3. Drop by teaspoonfuls onto ungreased baking sheets. Bake 10 minutes for a soft cookie, 12 minutes for a firmer cookie. Cool on wire racks. Makes 4 dozen.

✖ **HANNAH BARNES,** age 9, Chubbuck, Idaho
First Place, North Bannock County Fair, Pocatello, Idaho, 2005

MEXICAN WEDDING CAKES

1¼ cups confectioners' sugar, divided
1 cup unsalted butter, room temperature
2 teaspoons vanilla or almond flavoring

2 cups all-purpose flour
1 cup chopped or ground almonds or pecans
¼ teaspoon salt

1. Preheat oven to 325°F.

2. In a large mixing bowl, combine ½ cup of the confectioners' sugar, butter, and vanilla or almond flavoring. Beat until light and fluffy. Add flour, almonds or pecans, and salt. Mix to form a dough.

3. Shape dough into 1-inch balls. Place on ungreased baking sheet. Bake for 13 to 17 minutes, or until set but not brown. Remove immediately from baking sheet and cool on wire racks for 10 minutes. Roll cookies in remaining ¾ cup confectioners' sugar. Cool completely. Reroll in confectioners' sugar to coat. Makes 4½ dozen.

For a colorful variation, divide the dough in half and color with red and green food coloring.

❉ **ALVEENA MOIR,** Phoenix, Arizona
First Place, Cookie Recipes, Arizona State Fair, Phoenix, Arizona, 2005

PEANUT BUTTER OATMEAL COOKIES

1½ cups shortening	3½ cups sifted all-purpose flour
1 cup sugar	2 teaspoons baking soda
1½ cups brown sugar	¾ teaspoon salt
3 eggs	2 cups oats
1½ cups peanut butter	

1. Preheat oven to 350°F.

2. In a large mixing bowl, cream shortening, sugar, and brown sugar. Add eggs one at a time, beating well after each addition. Mix in peanut butter.

3. Whisk together flour, baking soda, salt, and oats. Add to creamed mixture and blend thoroughly.

4. Drop by teaspoonfuls onto baking sheets. Bake for 12 to 15 minutes. Cool on wire racks. Makes 9 dozen.

❉ **HEATHER CLEAVER,** age 18, Inkom, Idaho
First Place, North Bannock Country Fair, Pocatello, Idaho, 2005

ALMOND BARK CLUSTERS

2½ lbs. white almond bark	2½ cups mini marshmallows
2½ cups crunchy peanut butter cereal	2 cups salted cashews
2½ cups crispy rice cereal	1 cup chow mein noodles

1. Melt white almond bark in a microwave at 50% power, stirring at 1-minute intervals.

2. In a large bowl, combine peanut butter cereal, rice cereal, mini marshmallows, cashews, and chow mein noodles. Pour melted almond bark over top. Toss until well coated.

3. Drop by teaspoonfuls onto waxed paper. Let stand until firm. Store in an airtight container. Makes 7 dozen.

❉ **MARILYN BLOCK,** Winona, Minnesota
Grand Champion, Winona County Agricultural & Industrial Fair, Saint Charles, Minnesota, 1987

Rocky Road Surprise

1 bag (12 oz.) chocolate chips
1 bag (12 oz.) butterscotch chips
1 cup peanut butter

1 cup chopped dates
2½ cups mini marshmallows

1. Combine chocolate chips and butterscotch chips in a large microwave-safe bowl. Microwave at 50% power, stirring at 1-minute intervals, until melted.
2. Add peanut butter, dates, and marshmallows. Mix to combine.
3. Pour mixture into a 13 x 9 x 2-inch pan. Cool and cut into bars. Makes 54 bars.

✕ **DAVID AND KARLENE PONTE,** San Jacinto, California
Second Place, Desserts, Riverside County Fair and National Date Festival, Indio, California, 2003–2004

Peppermint Bark

12 peppermint candy canes
2 lbs. white chocolate chips

½ teaspoon peppermint extract

1. Line a baking sheet with waxed paper.
2. Unwrap candy canes, layer between sheets of waxed paper, and break into bite-size pieces. Place in a bowl.
3. Heat white chocolate chips in a microwave on high, stirring at 30-second intervals, until melted, about 5 minutes. Add to bowl with crushed candy canes; stir to combine. Stir in peppermint extract.
4. Turn out mixture onto baking sheet and spread evenly. Allow to cool and harden. Break into pieces. Makes 2¼ lbs.

✕ **LISA FINDLAY,** Chubbuck, Idaho
First Place, North Bannock County Fair, Pocatello, Idaho, 2005

Korbel Candies

1 cup crispy rice cereal
1 cup grapenuts
1 cup crunchy peanut butter

1 jar (7 oz.) marshmallow crème
5 oz. chocolate almond bark

1. In a bowl, combine rice cereal, grape-nuts, peanut butter, and marshmallow crème. Mix well. Chill for 2 hours.
2. Melt chocolate almond bark over medium heat. Roll cereal mixture into 1-inch balls and dip in melted almond bark. Set on waxed paper to cool. Makes 4 dozen.

✕ **JANET PISTULKA,** Aberdeen, South Dakota
Best of Class, Brown County Fair and 4-H Show, Aberdeen, South Dakota, 2001

Milk Chocolate Fudge

4½ cups sugar

1 can (12 oz.) evaporated milk

½ cup margarine, room temperature

3 packages (6 oz.) milk chocolate chips

1 package (10 oz.) miniature marshmallows

1 teaspoon vanilla

2 cups pecans, chopped

1. In a heavy saucepan, combine sugar and evaporated milk over medium heat. Slowly bring to a boil, stirring often. Boil 7 to 8 minutes, stirring constantly.

2. Remove from heat. Stir in margarine, chocolate chips, and marshmallows until all ingredients are melted and mixture is smooth. Mix in vanilla and pecans.

3. Spread mixture into an ungreased 9 x 9 x 2-inch pan. Cool and cut into squares. Makes 7 to 8 dozen.

※ **Billie Ivy,** Eula, Texas
First Place, West Texas Fair & Rodeo, Abilene, Texas, 2004

Raspberry Hamentaschen

1 to 1½ cups unsalted butter,
   room temperature

3 cups all-purpose flour

Grated orange or lemon zest

1 cup confectioners' sugar, plus
   more for rolling out dough

2 tablespoons orange or lemon juice

1 jar (24 oz.) raspberry jam

1 egg, beaten

1. Preheat oven to 350°F.

2. In a mixing bowl, lightly combine butter, flour, zest, and confectioners' sugar. Do not overmix. Add juice and mix just until dough comes together.

3. Turn out dough onto work surface. Roll out dough on a surface lightly sprinkled with confectioners' sugar to a ¼-inch thickness. Using a 3½- to 4-inch round cookie cutter, cut out circles of dough.

4. Place 1 tablespoon jam in center of each dough circle. Brush edges of circle with egg wash. Bring up edges with your fingers to form a triangular-shaped cup around the jam filling. Press edges together to seal. Set on an ungreased baking sheet. Bake 12 to 15 minutes, or until edges are lightly browned. Makes 4 dozen.

※ **Linda J. Abrams,**
Carlsbad, California
First Place, San Diego County Fair,
Del Mar, California, 2004

Caramels

½ cup unsalted butter, room temperature
2 cups sugar
2 cups light corn syrup

1 cup heavy cream
Dash of salt
1 teaspoon vanilla

1. In a large, heavy saucepan, cream butter and sugar with an electric hand-held mixer. Blend in corn syrup. Stir in cream and salt.
2. Cook over medium-high heat, stirring continuously, until temperature on a candy thermometer reaches the soft-ball stage (234°F–240°F). Remove from heat; stir in vanilla.
3. Pour mixture into a buttered 8 x 8 x 2-inch square pan. Allow to cool. Cut into 1-inch squares. Makes 64.

✕ **Donna McDade,** Middletown, Ohio
First Place, Butler County Fair, Hamilton, Ohio, 1993, 1994, 1997, 2000, 2001, 2003, 2004; First Place, Montgomery County Fair, Dayton, Ohio, 1998

Beth's Peanut Butter Cookies

½ cup unsalted butter, room temperature
½ cup peanut butter
½ cup sugar, plus more for coating
½ cup brown sugar
1 egg

½ teaspoon vanilla
1¼ cups all-purpose flour
¾ teaspoon soda
¼ teaspoon salt

1. Preheat oven to 350°F.
2. In a large mixing bowl, cream together butter, peanut butter, sugar, and brown sugar until thoroughly blended. Beat in egg and vanilla.
3. Sift together flour, baking soda, and salt; blend into creamed mixture.
4. Shape dough into 1-inch balls. Roll in sugar to coat. Place 2 inches apart on ungreased baking sheets. Flatten by pressing with fork tines in a crisscross pattern. Bake for 10 to 12 minutes. Cool on wire racks. Makes 4 dozen.

✕ **Beth Halverson,** age 10, Spencer, Iowa
Blue Ribbon, 2004; Red Ribbon, 2005; Clay County Fair, Spencer, Iowa

Linzer Tort Cookies

2½ cups all-purpose flour
1 teaspoon cocoa
Dash of cinnamon
Dash of ground cloves
10 oz. ground almonds
1½ cups unsalted butter, room temperature

1½ cups sugar
1 egg
1 to 2 tablespoons whiskey
Confectioners' sugar
5 tablespoons raspberry jam
1 egg yolk, beaten

1. Whisk together flour, cocoa, cinnamon, cloves, and almonds.

2. In a mixing bowl, cream butter and sugar. Beat in egg and whiskey. Gradually add flour mixture until well blended. Chill dough at least 1 hour.

3. Roll out dough on a surface sprinkled lightly with confectioners' sugar to a ¼-inch thickness. Using a 2-inch doughnut cookie cutter with a removable center, cut out an equal number of solid circles (for the bottoms) and circles with a hole (for the tops).

4. Transfer bottom dough circles to a baking sheet. Spread with raspberry jam. Place top circles on jam top and press gently, sandwiching jam between the layers. Jam will show through opening. Brush tops with egg yolk for shine. Bake in a preheated 350°F oven for 20 to 25 minutes. Makes 2 dozen cookies.

⌘ **REBECCA McCULLEY,** Pierson, Florida
First Place, Baked Goods—Adult, Volusia County Fair, DeLand, Florida, 2004

ROCKY ROAD FUDGE

2 packages (6 oz. each) chocolate chips
2 tablespoons margarine, room temperature
1 can (14 oz.) sweetened condensed milk

2 cups dry, roasted peanuts
1 package (10.5 oz.) mini marshmallows

1. Line a 13 x 9 x 2-inch baking pan with waxed paper.

2. In a saucepan, heat chocolate chips, margarine, and condensed milk over medium heat until chocolate is melted.

3. In a large bowl, combine peanuts and marshmallows. Pour chocolate mixture over nut mixture and toss to combine. Spread evenly in pan. Chill 2 hours. Cut into squares. Makes 8 to 9 dozen.

⌘ **BETSY BRUGMAN,** Royal, Iowa
Red Ribbon, Open Class, Clay County Fair, Spencer, Iowa, 2004

CANDIED FRUIT DROPS

1 cup unsalted butter, room temperature
¾ cup brown sugar
1 egg
1¾ cups all-purpose flour
½ teaspoon baking soda

½ teaspoon salt
1 package (8 oz.) chopped dates
1 cup chopped red candied cherries
1 cup chopped candied pineapple
1½ cups chopped nuts

1. Preheat oven to 350°F.

2. In a large mixing bowl, beat butter and brown sugar until light and fluffy. Beat in egg. Mix in flour, baking soda, and salt until well blended. Stir in dates, cherries, pineapple, and nuts.

3. Drop by teaspoonfuls onto ungreased baking sheets. Bake for 10 to 12 minutes. Cool 1 minute and transfer to wire racks. Makes 7 dozen.

⌘ **JESSICA SQUITIERI,** Brandon, Florida
First Place, Youth Division, Florida State Fair, Tampa, Florida, 2005

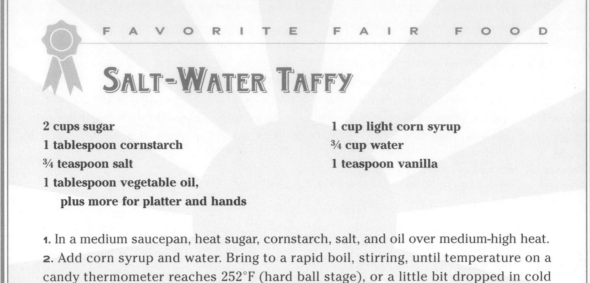

SALT-WATER TAFFY

2 cups sugar

1 tablespoon cornstarch

¾ teaspoon salt

1 tablespoon vegetable oil,
   plus more for platter and hands

1 cup light corn syrup

¾ cup water

1 teaspoon vanilla

1. In a medium saucepan, heat sugar, cornstarch, salt, and oil over medium-high heat.

2. Add corn syrup and water. Bring to a rapid boil, stirring, until temperature on a candy thermometer reaches 252°F (hard ball stage), or a little bit dropped in cold water forms a fairly hard ball. Remove from heat. Stir in vanilla.

3. Pour mixture onto a lightly oiled large platter. Oil your hands. When taffy is cool enough to handle, pull into a rope and cut in 1-inch lengths. Makes 3 dozen.

※ *Friends of the California State Fair Cookbook*, Sacramento, California

CHOCOLATE CARAMEL CANDY

Butter

CHOCOLATE BASE

1 cup (6 oz.) milk chocolate chips

¼ cup creamy peanut butter

¼ cup butterscotch chips

FILLING

¼ cup unsalted butter or margarine,
   room temperature

1 cup sugar

¼ cup evaporated milk

1½ cups marshmallow crème

¼ cup creamy peanut butter

1 teaspoon vanilla

CARAMEL LAYER

1 package (14 oz.) caramels

¼ cup heavy cream

ICING

1 cup (6 oz.) milk chocolate chips

¼ cup creamy peanut butter

¼ cup butterscotch chips

1. Line a 13 x 9 x 2-inch pan with foil; butter the foil.

2. To make chocolate base: In a small saucepan, combine milk chocolate chips, peanut butter, and butterscotch chips. Warm over low heat, stirring, until melted and smooth. Spread mixture evenly in pan. Chill until set.

3. To make filling: In a heavy saucepan, melt butter over medium heat. Add sugar and milk; bring to a gentle boil. Reduce heat to medium-low and boil, stirring, for 5 minutes. Remove from the heat. Stir in marshmallow crème, peanut butter, and vanilla. Spread filling over chocolate base. Chill until set.

4. To make caramel layer: In a saucepan, combine caramels and cream. Cook over low heat, stirring until melted and smooth. Cook, stirring, for 4 minutes longer. Spread over filling. Chill until set.

5. To make icing: In a saucepan, combine milk chocolate chips, peanut butter, and butterscotch chips. Cook over low heat, stirring until melted and smooth. Pour over caramel layer. Chill for at least 4 hours. Let stand at room temperature for 20 minutes, remove from pan, and cut into 1-inch squares. Makes 8 dozen.

✕ **ROBIN SPIRES,** Tampa, Florida
Best of Show, Adult Division, Florida State Fair, Tampa, Florida, 2005

EASY CHOCOLATE FUDGE

1 package (8 oz.) semisweet chocolate chips
1 can (14 oz.) sweetened condensed milk
Dash of salt

1½ teaspoons vanilla
½ cup chopped nuts (optional)

1. Line 9 x 9 x 2-inch pan with waxed paper.

2. In a heavy saucepan, combine chocolate chips, condensed milk, and salt over medium heat. Cook, stirring, until chocolate is melted.

3. Remove pan from heat. Add vanilla and nuts, if using; mix well. Spread mixture into pan. Chill for 2 hours.

4. Turn out fudge onto a cutting board. Peel off waxed paper. Cut into squares. Store loosely covered at room temperature. Makes 7 to 8 dozen.

✕ **MARY WICHERT,** Oconomowoc, Wisconsin
Reserve Grand Champion, Waukesha County Fair, Pewaukee, Wisconsin, 2001

CHOCOLATE BUFFALO HAYSTACKS

2 cups sugar
½ cup milk
3½ cups quick-cooking rolled oats
½ cup chopped walnuts
Dash of salt

⅓ cup cocoa
½ cup unsalted butter or margarine,
    room temperature
1 cup flaked coconut
½ teaspoon vanilla

1. In a saucepan, combine sugar, milk, oats, and walnuts over medium-high heat. Bring to a full boil.

2. Remove pan from heat. Stir in salt, cocoa, butter or margarine, coconut, and vanilla. Drop quickly from teaspoon onto waxed paper. Allow to cool. Makes 4 dozen.

✕ **THOMAS PINA,** Land O'Lakes, Florida
First Place, Youth Division, Florida State Fair, Tampa, Florida, 2005

Oatmeal/Date/Coconut Cookies

1 cup unsalted butter, room temperature

1 cup brown sugar

½ cup sugar

2 eggs

1 teaspoon vanilla

1½ cups all-purpose flour

1 teaspoon baking soda

1 teaspoon cinnamon

½ teaspoon salt

3 cups quick-cooking rolled oats

1 cup pitted, chopped dates

½ cup coconut

1 cup chopped walnuts

1. Preheat oven to 350°F.

2. In a large mixing bowl, beat butter, brown sugar, sugar, eggs, and vanilla until light and fluffy.

3. Sift together flour, baking soda, cinnamon, and salt; gradually beat into creamed mixture. Stir in oats, dates, coconut, and walnuts. Drop by teaspoonfuls onto ungreased baking sheets. Bake for 10 minutes. Makes 7 dozen.

✳ **MARILYN BLOCK,** Winona, Minnesota
Blue Ribbon, Winona County Agricultural & Industrial Fair, Saint Charles, Minnesota, 1987

Pumpkin Cookies

1 cup shortening

3 cups sugar

2 eggs

2 teaspoons vanilla

1 can (15 oz.) pumpkin

5 cups all-purpose flour

2 teaspoons baking powder

2 teaspoons baking soda

1 teaspoon salt

2 teaspoons cinnamon

2 teaspoons nutmeg

1 package chocolate chips

1. Preheat oven to 350°F.

2. In a large mixing bowl, cream shortening and sugar. Beat in eggs and vanilla. Add pumpkin and mix well.

3. Whisk together flour, baking powder, salt, cinnamon, and nutmeg. With mixer running, gradually add dry ingredients to creamed mixture until well blended. Stir in chocolate chips. Drop by tea-spoonfuls onto ungreased baking sheets. Bake for 10 to 12 minutes. Makes 6 dozen.

✳ **JENNY STURMAN,** age 14, Pocatello, Idaho
First Place, North Bannock County Fair, Pocatello, Idaho, 2005

Jessica's Peanut Butter Fudge

¾ cup margarine, room temperature

3 cups sugar

1 can (12 oz.) evaporated milk

1 package (10 oz.) peanut butter chips

1 teaspoon vanilla

1 jar (12 oz.) marshmallow crème

1. Lightly grease a 13 x 9 x 2-inch baking pan.

2. In a large saucepan, combine margarine, sugar, and evaporated milk over medium heat. Bring to a full rolling boil and cook, stirring continuously, for 5 minutes.

3. Remove from heat. Add peanut butter chips, stirring until melted. Add vanilla and marshmallow; mix. Pour mixture into pan. Cool to room temperature. Cut into squares. Makes 48.

※ **JESSICA SQUITIERI,** Brandon, Florida
Best of Show, Youth Division, Florida State Fair, Tampa, Florida, 2005

DOUBLE WHITE-CHOCOLATE DECADENCE

½ cup unsalted butter (no substitute)

4 cups confectioners' sugar

⅔ cup sweetened condensed milk

1 teaspoon vanilla

2 cups finely chopped pecans

1 cup finely chopped white chocolate

1 lb. white chocolate candy coating, melted

1. In a large saucepan, melt butter over medium heat. Add confectioner's sugar, condensed milk, and vanilla, stirring until smooth. Stir in nuts and white chocolate. Transfer mixture to a bowl. Cover and refrigerate overnight.

2. Drop mixture by tablespoonfuls onto waxed paper. Roll into small balls. Cover and refrigerate.

3. Dip balls into white candy coating. Set on waxed paper to harden. Makes 50.

※ **GEORGIA BISHOP,** Upper Arlington, Ohio
Blue Ribbon—Best of Show in Candies and Confections, Ohio State Fair, Columbus, Ohio, 2005

BETH'S SUGAR COOKIES

⅔ cup shortening

¾ cup sugar

1 teaspoon vanilla

1 egg

2 cups all-purpose flour, plus
    more for rolling out dough

1½ teaspoons baking powder

¼ teaspoon salt

4 teaspoons milk

1. In a large mixing bowl, cream shortening, sugar, and vanilla until thoroughly blended. Add egg; beat until light and fluffy.

2. Sift together flour, baking powder, and salt. Add flour mixture and milk alternately to creamed ingredients until well blended. Chill 1 hour.

3. Grease a baking sheet. Roll out dough on a lightly floured surface to a ⅛-inch thickness. Cut shapes from dough using cooking cutters. Transfer to greased baking sheet. Bake in a preheated 375°F oven for 6 to 8 minutes. Cool slightly and transfer to wire racks. Makes 2 dozen.

※ **BETH HALVERSON,** age 10, Spencer, Iowa
Blue Ribbon, Clay County Fair, Spencer, Iowa, 2004, 2005

MOLASSES SUGAR COOKIES

¾ cup margarine, room temperature

1 cup light brown sugar

¼ cup molasses

1 egg

2 cups all-purpose flour

2 teaspoons baking soda

½ teaspoon salt

½ teaspoon ground cloves

1 teaspoon ground ginger

1 teaspoon cinnamon

Sugar

1. Preheat oven to 375°F. Lightly grease baking sheets.

2. In a large mixing bowl, cream margarine and light brown sugar. Beat in molasses and egg.

3. Whisk together flour, baking soda, salt, cloves, ginger, and cinnamon. Gradually add flour mixture to creamed mixture until well combined. Roll dough into 1-inch balls. Roll balls in sugar to coat. Place 2 inches apart on baking sheets. Bake for 8 to 10 minutes. Makes 4 dozen.

⌘ **DONNA McDADE,** Middletown, Ohio
First Place, Warren County Fair, Lebanon, Ohio, 2004

BLUEBERRY-CREAM BONBONS

3 cups blueberries

1½ cups water

1 cup unsalted butter, room temperature

6 cups confectioners' sugar

24 oz. semisweet chocolate chips

4 squares (1 oz. each) unsweetened chocolate

¾ squares paraffin wax

1. In a saucepan, combine blueberries and water over medium-high heat. Bring to a boil, reduce heat, and simmer until reduced by half, 20 minutes. Strain off blueberries, reserving liquid.

2. In a mixing bowl, combine butter, confectioner's sugar, and 6 tablespoons blueberry liquid until well blended. Refrigerate overnight.

3. Roll mixture into bite-size balls, place on baking sheet, and freeze.

4. Melt chocolate chips, unsweetened chocolate, and paraffin in the top of a double boiler. Dip balls into melted chocolate. Set on waxed paper to harden. Makes 8 dozen.

⌘ **ROBERT PLAISTED,** Jonesboro, Maine
First Prize, Wild Blueberry Festival Cooking Competition, Machias, Maine, 2001

XARVELL'S M&M DELIGHTS

1 cup all-purpose flour

1 teaspoon baking powder

¼ teaspoon baking soda

Pinch of salt

⅓ cup unsalted butter, room temperature

1 cup brown sugar

1 teaspoon vanilla

1 egg, well beaten

½ cup M&M's candies

1 cup vanilla chips

1. Preheat oven to 350°F. Grease a baking sheet.

2. Triple-sift flour, baking powder, baking soda, and salt.

3. Melt butter in a saucepan over low heat, stirring constantly with a wire whisk. Remove from heat and let butter sit for one minute. With a spoon, remove the whey that floats to the surface.

4. Add brown sugar to butter; whisk until well blended. Stir in vanilla and egg. Beat with a hand-held electric mixer on medium speed. Fold in flour mixture with a rubber spatula. Add M&M's and vanilla chips.

5. Drop by tablespoonfuls 2 inches apart on baking sheet. Bake for 20 to 25 minutes. Cool on a wire rack. Makes 4 dozen.

※ **XARVELL BARKLEY,** DeLand, Florida
First Place, Baked Goods—Exceptional, Volusia County Fair, DeLand, Florida, 2004

BUTTER-PECAN FUDGE

Cooking spray
½ cup unsalted butter, room temperature
½ cup heavy cream
½ cup sugar
½ cup light brown sugar

⅛ teaspoon salt
1 cup pecan halves or chopped pecans
1 teaspoon vanilla
2 cups confectioners' sugar

1. Coat an 8 x 8 x 2-inch baking dish with cooking spray.

2. In a large saucepan, bring butter, cream, sugar, light brown sugar, and salt to a boil over medium heat, stirring frequently. Boil, stirring constantly, for 5 minutes.

3. Remove from heat. Stir in pecans and vanilla. Add confectioners' sugar and stir until smooth and well blended. Spread mixture into dish. Cool to room temperature. cut into 1-inch squares. Makes 64 pieces.

※ **SHARON OWENS,** Clyde, Texas
First Place, West Texas Fair & Rodeo, Abilene, Texas, 2004

PINEAPPLE FUDGE

3 cups sugar
1 small can (8 to 10 oz.) crushed pineapple
1 cup evaporated milk
¼ cup light corn syrup

¼ teaspoon cream of tartar
¼ cup unsalted butter, room temperature
1 cup macadamia nuts or pecans

1. Lightly butter an 8 x 8 x 2-inch baking pan.

2. In a 3-quart saucepan, combine sugar, pineapple, evaporated milk, corn syrup, and cream of tartar. Cook over medium heat, stirring, until a candy thermometer registers the soft-ball stage (234°F–240°F).

3. Remove from heat, add butter and nuts, and let stand for 5 minutes.

4. Beat for 2 minutes with an electric hand-held mixer until smooth. Pour evenly into pan and chill. When firm, cut into squares. Makes 64 pieces.

※ **KIM ONDOV,** Missoula, Montana
First Place, Candy—Holiday Desserts, Western Montana Fair, Missoula, Montana, 1998

PEPPERNØTTER (PEPPER COOKIES)

2 cups unsalted butter, room temperature

2 cups sugar

2 teaspoons baking soda

1 cup heavy cream, divided

3 teaspoons ground ginger

2 teaspoons cinnamon

2 teaspoons pepper

1 teaspoon ground cardamom

8 cups all-purpose flour

1 teaspoon baking powder

1. Preheat oven to 350°F. Lightly grease baking sheets.

2. In a large mixing bowl, cream butter and sugar. Dissolve baking soda in a few tablespoons of the cream. Add soda mixture, remaining cream, ginger, cinnamon, pepper, and cardamom to butter mixture.

3. Whisk together flour and baking powder. Add flour mixture to butter mixture, mixing until well combined. Roll into walnut-sized balls and set on baking sheet. Bake for 12 minutes, or until light golden brown. Cool on wire racks. Store in an airtight container for 1 week to mellow the flavors. Makes 8 dozen.

✄ **MARGE DODGE,** Missoula, Montana
First Place, Foreign Cookies, Western Montana Fair, Missoula, Montana, 1998

SUE'S PEANUT BUTTER COOKIES

2½ cups all-purpose flour

½ teaspoon baking powder

½ teaspoon baking soda

½ teaspoon salt

1 cup unsalted butter, room temperature

1 cup sugar

1 cup brown sugar

1 cup crunchy peanut butter

2 eggs

2 teaspoons vanilla

1 cup salted roast peanuts,
chopped in food processor

1. Preheat oven to 350°F.

2. Sift together flour, baking powder, baking soda, and salt.

3. In a large mixing bowl, cream butter until light and fluffy. Add sugar and brown sugar; beat for 3 minutes. Beat in peanut butter, eggs, and vanilla. Gently stir in flour mixture until well combined. Stir in peanuts.

4. Roll dough into small balls. Place balls on ungreased baking sheets and press with a fork from two directions to make a crisscross design. Bake for 10 to 12 minutes. Makes 6 dozen.

✄ **SUE SHUDDE,** Abilene, Texas
First Place, West Texas Fair & Rodeo, Abilene, Texas, 2005

CHOCOLATE-COVERED CHERRIES

⅔ cup sweetened condensed milk

1 tablespoon light corn syrup

4½ to 5 cups confectioners' sugar

2 jars (16 oz. each) Maraschinos

2½ lbs. dark chocolate candy coating

1. In a mixing bowl, combine condensed milk and corn syrup. Gradually beat in 4½ cups of the confectioners' sugar to make a stiff fondant.

2. Drain cherries, reserving 6 tablespoons of juice. Set cherries aside. Beat cherry juice into fondant. Add additional confectioners' sugar if necessary to keep consistency stiff.

3. Roll fondant into 1-inch balls. Flatten balls into 2-inch circles. Wrap each circle around a cherry and carefully shape into a ball. Place on waxed paper; cover loosely.

4. Melt candy coating in a heavy saucepan or in microwave. Dip cherries in melted chocolate and set on waxed paper to harden. Place in an airtight container and refrigerate until candy ripens and centers soften, 1 to 2 weeks. Makes 8 dozen.

✂ **BARBARA MEFFERD,** Apollo Beach, Florida
First Place, Adult Division, Florida State Fair, Tampa, Florida, 2005

PEANUT PATTIES

2½ cups sugar
⅔ cup light corn syrup
¾ cup evaporated milk
3 cups raw peanuts

2 tablespoons margarine,
   room temperature
1 teaspoon vanilla
Red food coloring

1. In a large, heavy saucepan, combine sugar, light corn syrup, and evaporated milk. Bring to a boil, add peanuts, and cook, stirring constantly, until a candy thermometer registers the soft ball stage.

2. Remove from heat. Add margarine, vanilla, and a few drops of red food coloring. Beat until mixture cools and becomes thick and creamy. Drop by spoonful onto waxed paper. Allow to cool. Store in an airtight container. Makes 7 dozen.

✂ **BILLIE IVY,** Eula, Texas
First Place, West Texas Fair & Rodeo, Abilene, Texas, 2004

1930S TOFFEE SUPREME

1 lb. sugar
1 oz. white chocolate
1 lb. unsalted butter, room temperature

12 oz. chocolate
¼ cup almonds, toasted and finely chopped

1. In a 2-quart saucepan, combine sugar, white chocolate, and butter over medium-high heat. Bring to a boil; continue boiling until a candy thermometer registers 305°F, or the hard-crack stage. Pour out toffee onto a hard, nonstick surface. Allow to cool.

2. Melt chocolate in the top half of a double boiler.

3. Break up toffee. Dip broken pieces into melted chocolate and sprinkle with toasted almonds. Place on waxed paper. Drizzle with more chocolate. Allow to cool and harden. Makes 2¾ lbs.

✂ **RICK WILKS,** Ruskin, Florida
First Place, Adult Division, Florida State Fair, Tampa, Florida, 2005

DATE-RICE KRISPIES DELIGHT

1 cup brown sugar

½ cup margarine, room temperature

1 cup chopped dates

1 egg

1 cup chopped nuts

1 teaspoon vanilla

2 cups crispy rice cereal

Sweetened flaked coconut

1. In a large saucepan, combine brown sugar, margarine, dates, and egg. Cook, stirring, over medium heat until butter and sugar are melted and well blended. Allow to cool.

2. Stir in nuts, vanilla, and rice cereal. Roll the mixture into 1-inch balls. Roll the balls in coconut to coat. Makes 4 dozen.

✄ **R. G. WILSON,** Indio, California
Second Place, Confections, Riverside County Fair and National Date Festival, Indio, California, 2003–2004

DIET DEMOLITION

1 package (8 oz.) sweet baking chocolate

2 tablespoons unsalted butter,
    room temperature

4 oz. semisweet baking chocolate

4 oz. white chocolate

1½ cups heavy cream, divided

2 tablespoons hazelnut extract or hazelnut liquor

½ cup hazelnuts, chopped

1. Grease a 9-inch round cake pan or a 12 x 4-inch rectangular tart pan.

2. Place sweet baking chocolate and butter in a microwave-safe bowl. Microwave on high, stirring every 30 seconds, until melted. Brush melted chocolate onto the sides and bottom of pan. Let cool.

3. In a food processor, chop semisweet baking chocolate. Add hazelnut extract or liquor.

4. Microwave ½ cup of the heavy cream until boiling. With motor running, pour cream into food-processor bowl in a steady stream. Chill in refrigerator. Spread mixture evenly over chocolate in tart pan. Sprinkle with chopped hazelnuts.

5. In a food processor, chop white chocolate. Microwave another ½ cup of the heavy cream until boiling. With motor running, pour cream into food processor bowl in a steady stream. Let cool.

6. Beat remaining ½ cup heavy cream. Fold into white chocolate mixture. Spread evenly over hazelnuts. Chill until set. Garnish with chocolate or chopped hazelnuts. Cut thin slices. Makes 8 to 10 servings.

✄ **SALLY SIBTHORPE,** Rochester Hills, Michigan
First Place, Fancy Chocolate Desserts, Michigan State Fair, Detroit, Michigan, 2000

OLD-FASHIONED CHOCOLATE CARAMELS

1 cup unsalted butter, plus more for pan

2¼ cups brown sugar

½ cup light corn syrup

½ cup dark corn syrup

1 can (14 oz.) sweetened condensed milk

2 oz. milk chocolate, coarsely chopped

1½ teaspoons vanilla

1. Line a 9 x 9 x 2-inch pan with foil and butter lightly.

2. In a heavy 3-quart saucepan, melt butter over medium heat. Add brown sugar and mix well. Stir in light corn syrup and dark corn syrup. Cook until sugar dissolves and mixture is well blended.

3. Remove pan from heat. Stir in condensed milk. Return pan to medium heat and cook, stirring constantly, until mixture reaches the soft-thread stage (230°F on a candy thermometer), 20 to 30 minutes. Stir in chocolate and continue cooking until mixture reaches the soft-ball stage (240°F), about 15 minutes.

4. Remove from heat. Stir in vanilla. Pour hot mixture into pan. Cool to room temperature. When candy has completely set, carefully remove from pan. Using a thin-bladed knife, cut with a sawing motion into bite-size pieces. Wrap pieces individually in small pieces of waxed paper. Store in refrigerator. Makes 2¾ pounds.

✕ **SANDEE BUDZINSKI,** Brookfield, Wisconsin
Grand Champion, Waukesha County Fair, Pewaukee, Wisconsin, 2001

CRISPY CHOCOLATE-PEANUT BUTTER BARS

½ cup light corn syrup
¼ cup brown sugar
Dash of salt
1 cup peanut butter

2 cups crispy rice cereal
1 cup cornflakes, slightly crushed
1 cup semisweet chocolate chips
1 teaspoon vanilla

1. In a 2-quart saucepan, combine corn syrup, brown sugar, and salt. Cook over medium-high heat, stirring, until mixture comes to a full boil. Stir in peanut butter. Remove from heat.

2. Stir in rice cereal, cornflakes, chocolate chips, and vanilla. Press mixture into an ungreased 8 x 8 x 2-inch glass pan. Chill for 1 hour. Cut into bars. Makes 32 bars.

✕ **DANIELLE TUCKER,** Interlachen, Florida
First Place, Youth Division, Florida State Fair, Tampa, Florida, 2005

DIVINITY

2½ cups sugar
½ cup light corn syrup
½ cup water

2 egg whites
1 teaspoon vanilla
1 cup pecans, chopped

1. In a saucepan, combine sugar, corn syrup, and water. Cook on medium-high heat without stirring until a candy thermometer registers 260°F. Remove from heat.

2. In a mixing bowl, beat egg whites until stiff peaks form. With mixer running on high speed, gradually add hot sugar mixture, pouring it in a slow, steady stream.

3. Add vanilla; beat until candy loses its gloss. Stir in pecans. Drop by teaspoonfuls onto waxed paper. Makes 3 to 4 dozen.

✕ **SANDY FULLERTON,** Abilene, Texas
First Place & Best of Show, West Texas Fair & Rodeo, Abilene, Texas, 2000

Coconut Date Candies

1 box (16 oz.) confectioners' sugar
2 cups flaked coconut
1 can (14 oz.) sweetened condensed milk
¾ cup unsalted butter, room temperature

1 cup dates
3 teaspoons coconut flavoring
Dipping chocolate

1. In a mixing bowl, combine confectioners' sugar, coconut, condensed milk, butter, dates, and coconut flavoring. Chill for 1 hour.
2. Shape mixture into 1-inch balls.
3. Melt dipping chocolate, following package directions. Dip balls in chocolate to coat. Set on waxed paper to cool. Makes 4 dozen.

⁋ **David and Karlene Ponte,** San Jacinto, California
First Place, Confections, Riverside County Fair and National Date Festival, Indio, California, 2003–2004

Cella Roba Chocolates

1 cup figs
1 cup sweetened dried cranberries
1 cup dates
1 cup almonds

1 cup walnuts or pecans
3 tablespoons lemon juice
1 package (12 oz.) semisweet
   chocolate chips, melted

1. Grind figs, dried cranberries, dates, almonds, and walnuts or pecans in a meat grinder or food processor. Add lemon juice and mix thoroughly.
2. Shape mixture into a ball. Wrap tightly in plastic wrap. Store in a cool place until mellow, 1 week.
3. Break off teaspoon-size pieces and roll into balls. Dip each ball into melted chocolate to coat. Set on waxed paper to cool and harden. Makes 8 to 9 dozen.

⁋ **Marcella Ruhle Ransom,** Ronan, Montana
Best of Show, Candy—Holiday Dessert, Western Montana Fair, Missoula, Montana, 2003

Orange Chocolate Meltaways

1 package (11.5 oz.) milk chocolate chips
¾ cup heavy cream
1 teaspoon grated orange zest
2½ teaspoons orange extract
1 cup semisweet chocolate chips
1½ cups finely chopped pecans

COATING
1 cup milk chocolate chips
2 tablespoons shortening

1. Place milk chocolate chips in a mixing bowl.

2. In a saucepan, combine cream and orange zest over medium-high heat. Bring to a gentle boil. Pour immediately over chocolate chips. Let stand for 1 minute. Whisk until smooth. Whisk in orange extract. Cover and chill for 30 minutes.

3. Beat until mixture lightens in color, 10 to 15 seconds; do not overbeat. Spoon by rounded teaspoonful onto waxed paper–lined baking sheets. Cover and chill for 5 minutes.

4. Gently shape into balls. Roll in semisweet chocolate chips and pecan pieces.

5. To make coating: Melt milk chocolate chips and shortening in microwave at 50% power, stirring at 1-minute intervals. Dip balls into melted chocolate and set on waxed paper. Allow to cool and harden. Makes 5 dozen.

※ **ROBIN SPIRES,** Tampa, Florida
First Place, Adult Division, Florida State Fair, Tampa, Florida, 2005

English Toffee

1 lb. unsalted butter (must not have
    been frozen), plus more for pan
Cooking spray
2⅔ cups sugar

6 tablespoons water
2 tablespoons light corn syrup
2 cups chopped pecans, divided
10 oz. chocolate, chopped

1. Line 2 large jelly roll pans with foil; grease lightly with butter. Coat the bottom of a 2-quart copper saucepan with cooking spray. Coat a silver serving spoon with cooking spray.

2. Combine butter, sugar, water and corn syrup in copper saucepan. Cook over low to medium heat, stirring often with a wooden spoon, until mixture turns a caramel color and a candy thermometer reaches 295°F, the hard-crack stage, about 45 minutes. Remove from heat.

3. Stir in 1½ cups of the pecans. Pour mixture into pans and spread evenly with silver serving spoon. Sprinkle chopped chocolate over top. After chocolate melts, spread gently with spoon. Sprinkle with remaining ½ cup pecans. Cool completely. Break into pieces. Store in tightly covered tins. Makes about 2 lbs.

For a thicker toffee, pour the entire batch into one jelly roll pan.

※ **SUE FLYNN,** Tulsa, Oklahoma
Sweepstakes Winner, Tulsa State Fair, Tulsa, Oklahoma, 2001

Chocolate-Sweet Potato Cups

6 oz. dark chocolate
2 medium sweet potatoes,
   cooked and peeled
1½ oz. cream cheese
3 tablespoons unsalted butter,
   room temperature
¼ cup milk

¼ cup sugar
1 teaspoon ground allspice
Dash of coriander
½ teaspoon honey
½ cup flaked coconut
½ cup chopped nuts

1. Melt chocolate in microwave for 2 minutes on 50%, stirring halfway through. Spoon chocolate into paper cupcake cups. Spread with a pastry brush to coat sides. Put in freezer for 3 minutes to harden.
2. Mash sweet potatoes in a large saucepan. Add cream cheese, butter, milk, sugar, allspice, coriander, and honey. Cook over low heat, stirring until warm and well combined, 10 minutes.
3. Puree sweet potato mixture in a blender. Spoon into chocolate cups. Top with flaked coconut and nuts. Serve immediately. Makes 12.

✕ **ALBERTA ALLISON,** Kathleen, Georgia
Second Place, Yammy Good Sweet Potatoes—Sweet Class, Georgia National Fair, Perry, Georgia, 2005

Chocolate-Peanut Butter Fudge

3 cups sugar
¾ cup milk
1 teaspoon vanilla
1 tablespoon unsalted butter,
   room temperature

2 teaspoons cocoa
1½ cups semisweet chocolate chips
1 jar (12 oz.) peanut butter
1 jar (7 oz.) marshmallow crème

1. Grease a 9 x 11 x 2-inch glass pan.
2. In a large saucepan, combine sugar, milk, vanilla, butter, cocoa, and chocolate chips over medium-high heat. Bring to a boil; boil for 3 minutes.
3. Remove pan from heat. Add peanut butter and marshmallow crème. Mix with a hand-held electric mixer until well combined. Pour mixture into pan. Let cool. Cut into squares. Makes 8 to 9 dozen.

✕ **CODY CASHMAN,** age 13, New Windsor, Maryland
First Place, Maryland State Fair, Timonium, Maryland, 2005

Coconut Bars

1 cup all-purpose flour
1 cup sugar
2 teaspoons baking powder
1 cup milk

3 egg whites
Confectioners' sugar frosting
Toasted coconut or finely ground peanuts

1. Preheat oven to 350°F.

2. Triple-sift flour, sugar, and baking powder. Sift once more into a large mixing bowl.

3. Heat milk almost to boiling. Pour over flour mixture. Stir to combine. Let stand until cool.

4. Beat egg whites to form stiff peaks. Gently fold into flour-milk mixture. Spread mixture into a 13 x 9 x 1-inch pan or a large jelly roll pan (for a thinner bar). Bake for 15 minutes or just until lightly browned. Drizzle with confectioners' sugar frosting and sprinkle with coconut or peanuts. Let cool. Cut into bars. Makes 2 to 3 dozen.

※ **MARILYN BLOCK,** Winona, Minnesota
Blue Ribbon, Winona County Agricultural & Industrial Fair, Saint Charles, Minnesota, 2005

PEANUT BUTTER SPECIALS

½ **cup sugar**
14 **oz. peanut butter**
½ **cup light corn syrup**
2½ **cups Special K cereal**

CHOCOLATE FROSTING
1 **square (1 oz.) baking chocolate**
2 **tablespoons margarine, room temperature**
2 **cups confectioners' sugar, divided**
⅛ **to** ¼ **cup milk**
¾ **teaspoon vanilla**

1. Combine sugar, peanut butter, light corn syrup, and cereal until well blended. Press mixture into an 8 x 8 x 2-inch pan.

2. To make chocolate frosting: In a large saucepan, melt chocolate and margarine over low heat. Blend in 1 cup of the confectioners' sugar. Add ⅛ cup of the milk and vanilla, stirring until well blended. Add more milk if needed to make a spreading consistency.

3. Spread frosting over cereal mixture and sprinkle with remaining confectioners' sugar. When frosting is set, cut into squares. Makes 64 squares.

※ **JARROD CHAPMAN,** Sarasota, Florida
First Place, Youth Division, Florida State Fair, Tampa, Florida, 2005

SURPRISE BUCKEYE BALLS

½ **cup unsalted butter, melted**
1 **lb. confectioners' sugar**
1½ **cups homemade peanut butter**

1 **teaspoon vanilla**
Roasted and skinned peanuts
2 **cups semisweet chocolate chips**

1. Combine melted butter, confectioners' sugar, peanut butter, and vanilla; mix well. Chill until firm, 1 hour.

2. Roll mixture into 1-inch balls, hiding a peanut inside each ball. Set on waxed paper.

3. Melt chocolate chips in microwave on 50% power, stirring at 1-minute intervals. Use a toothpick to pick up and dip balls into melted chocolate, leaving a small uncovered area so balls resemble buckeyes. Set on waxed paper. Use fingers to blend in toothpick holes. Refrigerate until chocolate is firm. Makes 5 dozen.

※ **KENNA-MARIE McCULLEY,** Pierson, Florida
First Place, Baked Goods—Youth Junior, Volusia County Fair, DeLand, Florida, 2004

FAST AND EASY PEANUT BRITTLE

1 cup dry-roasted salted peanuts

1 cup sugar

½ cup light corn syrup

1 tablespoon margarine,
    room temperature

1 teaspoon vanilla

1 teaspoon baking soda

1. Grease a rimmed baking sheet.

2. In a large microwave-safe glass bowl (do not use plastic), combine peanuts, sugar, and light corn syrup. Microwave on high for 8 minutes, stirring at 4 minutes.

3. Add margarine and vanilla; microwave for 2 minutes.

4. Add baking soda and stir until foamy. Pour mixture onto baking sheet. Allow to cool. Break up brittle. Makes 1 lb.

✄ **PHYLLIS CANIPE,** Lawndale, North Carolina
Blue Ribbon, Cleveland County Fair, Shelby, North Carolina, 2005

AMY'S PEANUT BUTTER FUDGE

2 tablespoons unsalted butter,
    room temperature, plus more for pan

⅔ cup whole milk

2 tablespoons light corn syrup

Pinch of baking soda

1 cup sugar

1 cup light brown sugar

½ cup creamy peanut butter

1. Line an 8 x 8 x 2-inch baking pan with foil, extending foil up sides of pan. Butter lightly. Fill kitchen sink with 1 inch of cold water for the water bath.

2. In a heavy 3-quart saucepan, combine milk, light corn syrup, butter, baking soda, sugar, and light brown sugar. Cook over medium heat, stirring occasionally, until mixture comes to a boil. Cover and boil 2 minutes. Uncover and continue cooking, stirring occasionally, until a candy thermometer reaches the soft-ball stage (234°F). Be careful not to scrape the sides of the pan while you are stirring.

3. Remove pan from heat and set in cold water bath. Cool for 1 minute.

4. Remove pan from water. Add peanut butter and vanilla. Beat with an electric hand-held mixer until mixture holds its shape and begins to lose its sheen. Pour fudge into pan and smooth surface. Cool at room temperature until firm, 1 to 2 hours. Lift foil out of pan and cut into squares. Store in a tightly covered container in the refrigerator up to 3 weeks. Makes 64 pieces.

✄ **AMY EICHELBERGER,** Odessa, Florida
First Place, Adult Division, Florida State Fair, Tampa, Florida, 2005

THREE-CHOCOLATE TRUFFLES

2 tablespoons chocolate syrup

4 oz. white chocolate chips

6 tablespoons heavy cream, divided

19 caramels

8 oz. milk chocolate

1 lb. semisweet dipping chocolate

1. Line a baking sheet with waxed paper.

2. Drizzle chocolate syrup on a small plate and freeze until firm.

3. Combine white chocolate chips and 2 tablespoons of the heavy cream. Melt in microwave at 50% power, stirring at 1-minute intervals, or on stovetop. Chill until stiff enough to hold a shape. Using a ½ teaspoon measuring spoon, scoop up bits of white chocolate and form into small balls. Flatten slightly into a disk. Chill.

4. Break off less than ⅛ teaspoon of frozen chocolate syrup. Place in center of white chocolate disk. Shape white chocolate into a ball, surrounding the dark center. Chill.

5. Cut caramels into 4 pieces each and flatten. Form 6 pieces around each white chocolate ball. Chill.

6. Melt milk chocolate with remaining 4 tablespoons heavy cream. Cover and chill. Using a ½ teaspoon measuring spoon, form the milk chocolate around the caramel-coated core. Chill.

7. Melt and temper semisweet chocolate. Dip truffles in chocolate to coat. Set on baking sheet. Decorate as desired. Store in refrigerator. Makes 12.

✖ **PAULA BECK,** San Marcos, California
First Place, San Diego County Fair, Del Mar, California, 2004

WHITE CRANBERRY-MACADAMIA FUDGE

Cooking spray

4½ cups sugar

1 cup unsalted butter, room temperature

1 can (12 oz.) evaporated milk

2 packages (12 oz. each) white chocolate chips

1 jar (7½ oz.) marshmallow crème

2 teaspoons vanilla

12 oz. sweetened dried cranberries

1 cup chopped macadamia nuts

1. Line a 13 x 9 x 2-inch baking pan with foil. Coat foil lightly with cooking spray.

2. In a 2-quart saucepan, cook sugar, butter, and evaporated milk over medium heat, stirring constantly, until mixture comes to a boil. Boil for 5 minutes.

3. Remove from heat. Add white chocolate chips and marshmallow crème, stirring until melted. Stir in vanilla. Add cranberries and nuts; mix well.

4. Immediately pour mixture into pan. Chill for 1½ hours. Cut into squares. Return pan to refrigerator and chill to set squares, about 1 hour. Store in a covered container in the refrigerator for up to 2 weeks or in the freezer for up to 3 months. Makes 4 lbs.

✖ **DEBBIE THELEN,** Tomah, Wisconsin
Second Place, Process Cranberry, Warrens Cranberry Festival, Warrens, Wisconsin, 2005

PAULA'S PEANUT BUTTER FUDGE

2 tablespoons unsalted butter,
    room temperature, plus more for pan
1 cup sugar
1 cup brown sugar
Pinch of salt

½ cup evaporated milk
1 cup miniature marshmallows
1 cup peanut butter
1 teaspoon vanilla

1. Butter an 8 x 8 x 2-inch baking pan.

2. In a large, heavy saucepan, combine sugar, brown sugar, butter, salt, and evaporated milk. Cook over medium heat to soft ball stage.

3. Add miniature marshmallows, peanut butter, and vanilla. Stir until smooth. Pour into pan. Let set until cool. Cut into squares. Makes 36 pieces.

✕ **PAULA HORN,** Mason, Michigan
First Place, Ingham County Fair, Mason, Michigan, 1990–2005

OLDE-FASHIONED DOUBLE-DECKER TOFFEE WITH LITTLE DEVIL PEANUT BUTTER FILLING

1 lb. unsalted butter, room temperature
1 lb. sugar
½ lb. dipping chocolate
2 oz. almonds, crushed

LITTLE DEVIL PEANUT BUTTER FILLING
1 cup confectioners' sugar
1 teaspoon vanilla
1 cup peanut unsalted butter, room temperature
¼ cup unsalted butter, room temperature

1. In a 3-quart saucepan, combine butter and sugar over high heat. Cook until a candy thermometer registers 305°F (the hard-crack stage). Pour mixture onto a nonstick surface. Allow to cool.

2. To make little devil peanut butter filling: Combine confectioners' sugar, vanilla, butter, and peanut butter until well blended. Roll into balls or logs.

3. Break up toffee. Place a ball or log of filling between two pieces of toffee and squeeze gently to make a sandwich. Makes 24 sandwiches.

✕ **RICK WILKS,** Ruskin, Florida
First Place, Sweepstakes Division, Florida State Fair, Tampa, Florida, 2005

SOUR CREAM PECAN PRALINES

2 tablespoons unsalted butter, room
    temperature, plus more for baking sheet
1½ cups sugar
½ cup brown sugar

1 cup (8 oz.) sour cream
2 tablespoons corn syrup
½ teaspoon vanilla
1 cup pecans

1. Butter a baking sheet.
2. In a saucepan, combine sugar, brown sugar, sour cream, and corn syrup over medium heat. Bring to a boil, stirring constantly; continue cooking until mixture reaches the soft-ball stage (234°F on a candy thermometer).
3. Remove from heat. Add butter and vanilla; beat until candy loses most of its gloss. Stir in pecans. Drop by teaspoonful onto baking sheet. Allow to cool. Makes 4 to 5 dozen pralines.

✖ **GERTRUDE FILIPOVICH,** Abilene, Texas
First Place, West Texas Fair & Rodeo, Abilene, Texas, 2004

MICROWAVE PEANUT BRITTLE

1 tablespoon unsalted butter, room temperature, plus more for pan	½ cup light corn syrup
1 cup raw peanuts	⅛ teaspoon salt
1 cup sugar	1 teaspoon vanilla
	1 teaspoon baking soda

1. Line a rimmed baking sheet with foil and butter generously.
2. In a rectangular glass dish, combine peanuts, sugar, light corn syrup, and salt. Microwave on high 3 minutes; stir. Microwave on high 2 more minutes.
3. Add butter and stir until melted. Microwave 4 to 5 minutes, checking at 2-minute intervals. Stop cooking when you can smell the peanuts and color shows a spot of light brown.
4. Stir in vanilla and baking soda. Pour mixture over foil. Allow to cool and set. Break into pieces. Makes 1 lb.

✖ **LISA FINDLAY,** Chubbuck, Idaho
First Place, North Bannock County Fair, Pocatello, Idaho, 2005

BECKY'S FAMOUS PEANUT BUTTER FUDGE

3 cups sugar	2 teaspoons cocoa
¾ cup milk	1 jar (12 oz.) peanut butter
1 teaspoon vanilla	1 jar (7 oz.) marshmallow crème
1 tablespoon unsalted butter, room temperature	

1. Grease a 9 x 11 x 2-inch glass baking dish.
2. In a large, heavy saucepan, combine sugar, milk, vanilla, butter, and cocoa over medium-high heat. Bring to a boil and cook for 3 minutes.
3. Remove from heat. Add peanut butter and marshmallow crème. Blend using a hand-held electric mixer. Pour into baking dish. Allow to cool. Cut into squares. Makes 7 to 8 dozen.

✖ **CODY CASHMAN,** age 13, New Windsor, Maryland
Special Award and First Place, Maryland State Fair, Timonium, Maryland, 2005

MEXICAN PRALINES

1 cup brown sugar
½ cup light corn syrup
2 tablespoons unsalted butter,
   room temperature

1 cup cream
½ teaspoon vanilla
2 cups chopped pecans

1. Lightly grease a sheet of waxed paper.

2. In a large saucepan, combine brown sugar, light corn syrup, butter, and cream over medium-high heat. Bring to a rolling boil. Continue boil, stirring continuously, until mixture reaches the soft-ball stage (234°F on a candy thermometer).

3. Remove from heat. Add vanilla. Beat 350 strokes. Stir in pecans. Drop by spoonfuls onto greased waxed paper. Makes about 6 dozen pralines.

✕ **JOY CARROLLO,** Abilene, Texas
First Place, West Texas Fair & Rodeo, Abilene, Texas, 2000

SOUTHERN PRALINES

2 tablespoons unsalted butter or margarine,
   room temperature, plus more for foil
1 cup sugar
1 cup brown sugar

½ cup light cream
¼ teaspoon salt
1 teaspoon vanilla
1 cup pecan halves

1. Lightly butter a sheet of aluminum foil.

2. In a large saucepan, combine sugar, brown sugar, light cream, and salt. Cook over medium heat, stirring continuously, until a candy thermometer registers 228°F (mixture spins a thread about 2 inches long when dropped from a spoon).

3. Stir in butter, vanilla, and pecans. Continue cooking, stirring constantly, until thermometer registers 236°F (a small amount of mixture dropped into very cold water will form a small ball which flattens when removed from water).

4. Remove from heat; cool 5 minutes. Beat with wooden spoon until slightly thickened but still glossy; candy should coat nuts. Drop by tablespoonfuls onto foil. Makes about 18 pralines.

✕ **MARGE RAINWATER,** Abilene, Texas
First Place, West Texas Fair & Rodeo, Abilene, Texas, 2005

TURTLES

½ cup unsalted butter, room temperature,
   plus more for waxed paper
2 cups sugar
2 cups cream
¾ cup light corn syrup

3 cups pecans, whole
1 package (12 oz.) milk chocolate chips
½ cup semisweet chocolate chips
⅓ cake paraffin wax

1. Lightly butter a sheet of waxed paper.
2. In a large saucepan, combine sugar, butter, cream, and light corn syrup over medium heat. Cook, stirring frequently, until candy thermometer registers 245°F (the firm-ball stage).
3. Stir in pecans. Drop by tablespoonfuls onto waxed paper. Cool completely.
4. Melt milk chocolate chips, semisweet chocolate chips, and paraffin in microwave at 50% power, stirring at 1-minute intervals, or on stovetop over low heat, stirring until well blended. Dip turtles into chocolate to coat. Set on waxed paper to cool. Makes 8 to 9 dozen.

※ **LINDA FRY,** Tuscola, Texas
First Place, West Texas Fair & Rodeo, Abilene, Texas, 2000

RASPBERRY TRUFFLES

4 cups confectioners' sugar,
    plus more for coating
1 package (8 oz.) cream cheese
8 oz. raspberry-flavored chocolate chips,
    melted and cooled to room temperature

1 teaspoon vanilla
Ground almonds

1. In a mixing bowl, cream confectioners' sugar and cream cheese. Blend in melted chocolate chips and vanilla. Cover. Refrigerate at least 2 hours or overnight.
2. Shape mixture into small balls. Roll in confectioner's sugar or ground almonds to coat. Store in refrigerator. Makes 36 to 40 truffles.

※ **GEORGIA BISHOP,** Upper Arlington, Ohio
Blue Ribbon, Ohio State Fair, Columbus, Ohio, 2005

EASY CHOCOLATE TRUFFLES

2 squares (1 oz. each) unsweetened
    baking chocolate, coarsely chopped
1 package (12 oz.) semisweet chocolate chips
1 container (8 oz.) frozen whipped topping,
    thawed, divided

¼ teaspoon vanilla
Assorted coatings such as toasted coconut,
    chopped nuts, and colored sprinkles

1. In a microwave-safe bowl, combine unsweetened chocolate, chocolate chips, and half of the whipped topping. Microwave on high, stirring every 20 seconds, until chocolate is melted and smooth, 1½ to 2 minutes. Cool slightly. Fold in remaining whipped topping and vanilla.
2. Spread mixture on a cutting board. Chill just until firm enough to scoop, about 30 minutes. If chocolate hardens, coatings will not adhere. If chocolate gets too hard, let soften slightly at room temperature.
3. Using a melon scoop, form mixture into balls. Roll each ball in toasted coconut, chopped nuts, or colored sprinkles to coat. Set on waxed paper to harden. Makes about 40 truffles.

※ **BRITTANY WINSLOW,** Center Barnstead, New Hampshire
First Place, Senior Division, Belknap County 4-H Food Festival, Belmont, New Hampshire, 2006

CONTRIBUTING FAIRS

Alabama National Fair, Montgomery, Alabama

Alaska State Fair, Palmer, Alaska

Tanana Valley State Fair, Fairbanks, Alaska

Arizona State Fair, Phoenix, Arizona

Arkansas State Fair, Little Rock, Arkansas

Alameda County Fair, Pleasanton, California

California State Fair, Sacramento, California

Los Angeles County Fair, Pomona, California

Riverside County Fair and National Date Festival,
    Indio, California

San Diego County Fair, Del Mar, California

Arkansas Valley Fair & Expo, Rocky Ford,
    Colorado

Guilford Fair, Guilford, Connecticut

Terryville Country Fair, Terryville, Connecticut

Delaware State Fair, Harrington, Delaware

Central Florida Fair, Orlando, Florida

Florida State Fair, Tampa, Florida

St. Lucie County Fair, Fort Pierce, Florida

Volusia County Fair and Youth Show, DeLand,
    Florida

Georgia National Fair, Perry, Georgia

Maui Pineapple Festival, Maui Onion Festival, and
    Local Grinds Festival, Maui, Hawaii

Bonner County Fair, Sandpoint, Idaho

North Bannock County Fair, Pocatello, Idaho

Heart of Illinois Fair, Peoria, Illinois

Illinois State Fair, Springfield, Illinois

Bartholomew County 4-H Fair, Columbus, Indiana

Elkhart County 4-H Fair, Goshen, Indiana

Porter County Fair, Valparaiso, Indiana

Clay County Fair, Spencer, Iowa

Iowa State Fair, Des Moines, Iowa

Central Kansas Free Fair, Abilene, Kansas

Ellis County Fair, Hayes, Kansas

Boyd County Fair, Ashland, Kentucky

State Fair of Louisiana, Shreveport, Louisiana

Wild Blueberry Festival, Machias, Maine

Carroll County 4-H FFA Fair, Westminster,
    Maryland

Maryland State Fair, Timonium, Maryland

Topsfield Fair, Topsfield, Massachusetts

Ingham County Fair, Mason, Michigan

Ionia Free Fair, Ionia, Michigan

Michigan State Fair, Detroit, Michigan

Dakota County Fair, Farmington, Minnesota

Winona County Agricultural & Industrial Fair,
    Saint Charles, Minnesota

Copiah County Fair, Gallman, Mississippi

Southeast Missouri District Fair, Cape Girardeau,
    Missouri

Western Montana Fair, Missoula, Montana

River City Roundup Rodeo, Omaha, Nebraska

Nevada State Fair, Reno, Nevada

Belknap County 4-H Fair, Belmont, New Hampshire

Warren County Farmers' Fair, Belvidere,
    New Jersey

New Mexico State Fair, Albuquerque, New Mexico

Dutchess County Fair, Rhinebeck, New York

Cleveland County Fair, Shelby, North Carolina

Dixie Classic Fair, Winston-Salem, North Carolina

North Carolina Mountain State Fair, Fletcher,
    North Carolina

North Carolina State Fair, Raleigh, North Carolina

Red River Valley Fair, West Fargo, North Dakota

Ohio State Fair, Columbus, Ohio

Fulton County Fair, Wauseon, Ohio

Oklahoma State Fair, Oklahoma City, Oklahoma

Tulsa State Fair, Tulsa, Oklahoma

Oregon State Fair, Salem, Oregon

Bloomsburg Fair, Bloomsburg, Pennsylvania

Favorite Foods Fair, West Greenwich,
    Rhode Island

Southern Rhode Island 4-H Fair, Richmond,
    Rhode Island

Coastal Carolina Fair, Ladson, South Carolina

Brown County Fair and 4-H Show, Aberdeen,
    South Dakota

Wilson County Fair, Lebanon, Tennessee

West Texas Fair and Rodeo, Abilene, Texas

Utah State Fair, Salt Lake City, Utah

Addison County Fair and Field Days, New Haven,
    Vermont

Champlain Valley Fair, Essex Junction, Vermont

Washington County Fair, Abingdon, Virginia

Clark County Fair, Ridgefield, Washington

Spokane County Interstate Fair, Spokane,
    Washington

State Fair of West Virginia, Lewisburg, West
    Virginia

Dunn County Fair, Menomonie, Wisconsin

Walworth County Fair, Elkhorn, Wisconsin

Warrens Cranberry Festival, Inc., Warrens,
    Wisconsin

Waukesha County Fair, Pewaukee, Wisconsin

Sweetwater County Fair, Rock Springs, Wyoming

Teton County Fair, Jackson, Wyoming

Wyoming State Fair & Rodeo, Douglas, Wyoming

INDEX